# Language
# Development

# BPS Textbooks in Psychology

BPS Blackwell presents a comprehensive and authoritative series covering everything a student needs in order to complete an undergraduate degree in psychology. Refreshingly written to consider more than North American research, this series is the first to give a truly international perspective. Written by the very best names in the field, the series offers an extensive range of titles from introductory level through to final year optional modules, and every text fully complies with the BPS syllabus in the topic. No other series bears the BPS seal of approval!

Each book is supported by a companion website, featuring additional resource materials for both instructors and students designed to encourage critical thinking, providing for all your course lecturing and testing needs.

For other titles in this series, please go to www.bpsblackwell.co.uk.

*"This is an outstanding book, based on an incredibly impressive range of detailed and thorough scholarship... The book will be invaluable to students encountering the field of child language for the first time, and it will also be a vital resource for anyone wishing to update their knowledge about the latest findings and current understandings in the field. The authors are to be congratulated on their remarkable achievement."*

**Professor Martyn Barrett**, University of Surrey, UK

*"Language Development by Patricia Brooks and Vera Kempe is an outstanding up-to-date introduction to this field, covering current scientific literature on all standard topics, plus more specialized topics such as language and the brain. The text is accessible to novices in the field through the extensive use of summary sidebars, glossary and supplementary boxed materials. At the same time it goes deeply enough, with extensive references, to serve as a guide to the current state of the field for established professionals. Its focus on the social conditions of language learning and development is especially valuable, and the inclusion of material on second and multi-language use, language disabilities, deaf language learning, and literacy broadens its applicability to interdisciplinary use."*

**Professor Katherine Nelson,** City University of New York, USA

*"Patricia Brooks and Vera Kempe did an outstanding job.* Language Development *is the optimal textbook: it stirs up interest and excitement in the reader, it is encyclopedic in its coverage, and it is a model of clear writing. There are several important extensions beyond the usual topics, among them a thorough discussion of atypical acquisition; coverage of phenomena concerning older children such as the role of literacy in language development; and a description of recent neuroimaging work examining the effect of language processing on the brain. The listing of key terms for every chapter at its start and a glossary explaining them at the end of the book is a wonderful touch. I expect this book to be a winner with teachers and students."*

**Professor Anat Ninio**, The Hebrew University of Jerusalem, Israel

# Language Development

**PATRICIA J. BROOKS**

**VERA KEMPE**

DEVELOPMENTAL PSYCHOLOGY
SERIES EDITOR

MARTYN BARRETT

The British Psychological Society | **BPS BLACKWELL**

This edition first published 2012 by the British Psychological Society
and John Wiley & Sons Ltd

BPS Blackwell is an imprint of John Wiley & Sons Ltd

All effort has been made to trace and acknowledge ownership of copyright. The publisher would be glad to hear from any copyright holders whom it has not been possible to contact.

*Registered office*
John Wiley & Sons Ltd, The Atrium, Southern Gate, Chichester, West Sussex, PO19 8SQ, United Kingdom

For details of our global editorial offices, for customer services and for information about how to apply for permission to reuse the copyright material in this book, please see our website at www.wiley.com.

The rights of Patricia J. Brooks and Vera Kempe to be identified as the authors of this work have been asserted in accordance with the UK Copyright, Designs and Patents Act 1988.

Wiley publishes in a variety of print and electronic formats and by print-on-demand. Some material included with standard print versions of this book may not be included in e-books or in print-on-demand. If this book refers to media such as a CD or DVD that is not included in the version you purchased, you may download this material at http://booksupport.wiley.com. For more information about Wiley products, visit www.wiley.com.

Designations used by companies to distinguish their products are often claimed as trademarks. All brand names and product names used in this book are trade names, service marks, trademarks or registered trademarks of their respective owners. The publisher is not associated with any product or vendor mentioned in this book. This publication is designed to provide accurate and authoritative information in regard to the subject matter covered. It is sold on the understanding that the publisher is not engaged in rendering professional services. If professional advice or other expert assistance is required, the services of a competent professional should be sought.

*Library of Congress Cataloging-in-Publication Data*

Brooks, Patricia (Patricia J.)
    Language development / Patricia Brooks, Vera Kempe.
        p   cm
    Includes bibliographical references and index.
    ISBN 978-1-4443-3146-2 (pbk.)
        1. Language acquisition.   I. Kempe, Vera.   II. Title.
    P118.B687   2012
    401'.93—dc23                                          2012000093

A catalogue record for this book is available from the British Library

Set in 11/12.5pt Dante MT by MPS Limited, Chennai, India
Printed in Great Britain by TJ International, Padstow, Cornwall

The British Psychological Society's free Research Digest e-mail service rounds up the latest research and relates it to your syllabus in a user-friendly way. To subscribe, go to www.researchdigest.org.uk or send a blank e-mail to subscribe-rd@lists.bps.org.uk.

| | |
|---|---|
| Senior Commissioning Editor: | Andrew McAleer |
| Assistant Editor: | Katharine Earwaker |
| Marketing Managers: | Fran Hunt and Jo Underwood |
| Project Editor: | Juliet Booker |

To our mentors Tatyana V. Akhutina, Martin D. S. Braine,
Brian MacWhinney and Michael Tomasello.

# Brief Contents

# Contents

# Acknowledgements

This book would not have been possible without Martyn Barrett, who encouraged us to embark on this adventure in the first place, read multiple drafts of the entire book, and provided extremely helpful and constructive suggestions for improvements in structure and content. We would like to thank Michael Almodovar for creating clear figures to our multiple (and sometime conflicting) specifications, and Naomi Aldrich for her dedicated help with the glossary. A number of colleagues generously read portions of the book, contributed advice, and/or shared materials: Julia Carroll, Morten Christiansen, Ewa Dąbrowska, Virginia Gathercole, Trevor Harley, Carmel Houston-Price, Neil Kirk, David LaRooy, Danielle Matthews, Anat Ninio, Sonia Ragir, Harriet Tenenbaum, Robin Thompson, Gabriella Vigliocco, Dave Vinson, as well as several anonymous reviewers. Mid-way through the writing it was immensely helpful to receive detailed feedback on drafts of the first six chapters from the 2011 Advanced Cognitive Psychology class at the University of Abertay, and from the undergraduates taking Language Development at the College of Staten Island, CUNY. We are also grateful for the continuous encouragement provided by our editor, Andrew McAleer. It goes without saying that all remaining errors and inconsistencies are entirely our own.

A big warm special Thank You goes to our children Erica, Ike, Max and Marius for the countless moments of inspiration found in their developing language, for many often hilarious linguistic examples, for their interest and curiosity about our work, and for growing up wonderfully despite their mothers' preoccupations with academic pursuits.

Last but not least, our husbands David Lobel and Ian Veltman had to bear the brunt of responsibility for keeping domestic affairs from sliding into chaos over the past two years. Without their continuous encouragement and support, delicious home-cooked meals, and vacation time, we simply would not have been able to muster the resources and persistence a project like this requires. It takes considerably more than our own language proficiency to adequately express how grateful we are to them.

*Patty Brooks*
*Vera Kempe*

# 1 What Enables Infants to Acquire Language?

## KEY TERMS

- alloparents • artificial language • babbling • collective breeders • communicative intentions • conspecifics • constructions • coordinated interpersonal timing • discourse • Duchenne smiles • dyadic interaction • encephalisation • executive functioning • fundamental frequency • hominin • intersubjectivity • joint attention • Less-Is-More • natural pedagogy • scaffolding • social shaping • still-face effect • terrestrial bipedalism

## CHAPTER OUTLINE

Language is a universal human ability. Children at a young age learn to speak and to understand others' speech; they learn to use language to share ideas, negotiate activities, and cooperate with others. They do this in spite of the fact that there is extraordinary complexity and diversity in the sound patterns, word meanings, and grammatical structures of the approximately 7000 human languages that have been catalogued throughout the world (Gordon & Grimes, 2005; Lewis, 2009). All human languages have a degree of complexity that surpasses by far the communication system of any other species. Yet the process of language development seems to be easy, effortless, and does not require specific instruction. So how do children do it?

In this book we will try to understand what language development entails and what lies behind this extraordinary human achievement. Humans have evolved to learn language over an extended period of childhood. Children grow up as members of communities in which language constitutes the primary mechanism by which social activities are coordinated and ideas are exchanged. In this chapter, we will examine the sociocultural context in which language development takes place and begin to explore the social and cognitive abilities that allow human infants to learn language so readily. Among other things, infants show precocious sensitivity to the sound patterns of languages, and in Chapter 2 we will discuss what abilities enable infants to crack the sound code of their native language very early in life. Infants are also able to communicate through gesture at a stage when their ability to use spoken language is still very rudimentary. In Chapter 3 we will show how shared attention and non-verbal communication provide the basis for the development of spoken language. Building on this ability, infants are able to figure out what others mean when they produce specific speech patterns, and in Chapter 4 we will trace how the meanings of words are negotiated in the context of shared activities with others. Once the first words are acquired, infants and toddlers start combining and modifying them. In Chapter 5, we will describe how infants discover the myriad ways in which speakers of their language combine and modify words to create new meanings. Even though language development is a universal aspect of human development, there is variation in the learning trajectories of individual children. In Chapter 6 we will examine the nature of children's language input and what consequences, if any, variability in the quality and quantity of language input has for language development.

Obviously, using language encompasses more than just knowing the meanings of words and how to put them together to create sentences. Children learn to use language in socially appropriate ways, to tease others and make them laugh, to argue, lie and deceive, to tell stories, retrace the past and plan for the future, as well as for many other purposes. These abilities take time to develop, and Chapter 7 traces the acquisition of pragmatic and conversational skills. Chapter 8 returns to the phenomenon of linguistic diversity and explores how specific features of languages and bilingualism influence cognitive development. In many cultures, like our own, language develops further as children learn to read and write. Chapter 9 provides an overview of literacy acquisition and its role in language development.

Despite the fact that most children acquire language with apparent speed and ease, language development is not always a smooth path. Some children have impairments in language learning and processing, and Chapter 10 summarises what is known about the possible causes of their difficulties. Chapter 11 explores sign language development in deaf children who are not able to perceive the sound patterns of a spoken language. Studying deaf children provides a unique opportunity to observe what happens when exposure to a language (spoken or signed) is delayed during development. To what extent does the brain remain plastic enough to accommodate language learning at ages beyond early childhood? This question is explored further in Chapter 12, which looks at the neural basis of language development.

In describing the trajectory of human language development, this book will try to incorporate evidence from children acquiring different languages in different cultures. As the bulk of research on language development has been carried out with children who are acquiring a few languages spoken in industrialised Western societies, we acknowledge that much is still not known about language development elsewhere. We urge readers to be cautious in their conclusions about what is culturally and linguistically universal in language development.

# 1.1 WHAT IS THE EVOLUTIONARY CONTEXT OF LANGUAGE DEVELOPMENT?

Over the past two decades there has been growing interest in how humans evolved to have language. Much research in this area has asked what is unique about human language and communication. At some point in human evolutionary history, there emerged a precursor to a symbolic communication system; that is, some sort of a rudimentary proto-language which may have been gesture-based, sound-based, or both. There is considerable debate as to whether humans subsequently evolved special adaptations that are unique to language (Pinker & Bloom, 1990), or whether the features of human languages were shaped by more general social and cognitive abilities, which enabled humans to adapt to a wide variety of different environments through cultural learning (Kirby, Christiansen & Chater, 2009; Tomasello, 2008). In other words, did changes in our genetic make-up provide humans with an innate capacity to acquire and process language, or alternatively, did human languages evolve under selective pressure to fit our ancestors' social and cognitive capabilities and ecological niche (Chater & Christiansen, 2010; Christiansen & Chater, 2008; Levinson & Evans, 2010; Lupyan & Dale, 2010; Nettle, 2007)? Models of gene–culture co-evolution suggest that increased complexity in communication may have pushed genetic evolution in a direction that enhanced the social and cognitive skills needed for language acquisition and processing (Deacon, 1997; Richerson & Boyd, 2010). This debate to some extent informs our understanding of how language development is ultimately tied to children's social and cognitive development.

In this chapter, we set the stage by briefly sketching the evolution of the conditions under which language development takes place. These conditions pertain to (a) the time course of language development – that is, how long it takes for a person to master a language; (b) the nature of social and communicative engagement between children and others; and (c) the wider social environment that supports language development over the lifespan. We will then take a brief look at the social and cognitive abilities of human infants that support their entry into communities defined by their sociocultural and linguistic practices.

## 1.1.1   *Extended period of immaturity*

Many authors emphasise the speed and ease with which human children acquire the basic principles of language (e.g. O'Grady, 1997). By four years of age most sentences uttered by most children will be meaningful and more or less grammatically correct. In comparison to adult language learners, who often attain only limited proficiency in a new language after years of study, the linguistic achievements of children seem quite remarkable indeed. However, it is important to bear in mind that the time course of language development in humans is much more extended in comparison to the relative rapidity with which other species acquire their respective communication systems. Humans acquire language over a relatively long period of social and cognitive immaturity (Konner, 2010), and human language learning extends over the lifespan. How did this extended period of childhood, which is unusual in comparison with other apes (Bruner, 1972; Gould, 1977; Locke & Bogin, 2006), come about, and what might be its consequences for the process of language development?

**hominin** refers to humans and their ancestors, and includes all the Homo species, all the Australopithecines, and others such as Ardipithecus; this term is more specific and replaces the previous term 'hominid'.

**terrestrial bipedalism** two-footed walking on the ground.

One idea is that adaptations to bipedalism initiated a series of changes that extended the life history of humans, relative to other apes. At least four million years ago, our hominin ancestors shifted from quadramanus (four-handed) climbing to terrestrial bipedalism (two-footed walking). This shift in posture most likely came about as an adaptation to changes in habitat and diet (Coppens, 1994; Wrangham, Cheney, Seyfarth, & Sarmiento, 2010). Regardless of the specific causes of bipedalism, an undisputed consequence is that it altered the shape of the hominin pelvis through horizontal realignment, and thereby effectively narrowed the birth canal (Abitbol, 1987; Rosenberg, & Trevarthan, 2002). Pelvic realignment would have generated considerable selective pressure to delay skeletal maturation (Ragir, 2001; Ruff, 1995); that is, to allow a neonate with a softer, less mature skeleton to pass through the constricted birth canal. Over the subsequent course of human evolution, additional adjustments in growth parameters may have occurred as dietary advances (e.g. hunting, cooking, and food preservation) improved year-round access to nutrients and increased the weight of females and the weight and size of their offspring. Increased foetal size would become problematic if the skeleton became too big to successfully deliver through the birth canal (Rosenberg & Trevarthan, 1996). Consequently, each dietary advance may have triggered further maturational delays to ensure successful birth of hominin infants. Altering the rate of skeletal maturation through adjustments to growth parameters would also have lengthened the time course of neural development. Such adjustments would have increased brain size, because brain size increases proportionally as neural development is prolonged (Finlay, Darlington, & Nicastro, 2001), which would have contributed to the encephalisation (increased cranial volume relative to body size) characteristic of modern humans. Crucially, a more slowly maturing brain has greater neural plasticity and behavioural flexibility, thus leaving increased room for learning about the physical and social environment in a rapidly changing world (Chrysikou, Novick, Trueswell, & Thompson-Schill, 2011; Ragir, 1985; Thompson-Schill, Ramscar, & Chrysikou, 2009).

> **encephalisation** increased cranial volume relative to body size (i.e. the amount of brain mass that exceeds what is expected given the animal's body mass).

There is debate about the extent to which neurobiological development after birth obeys a genetically predetermined maturational schedule and whether this controls language acquisition. Although the infant brain appears to be uniquely adapted to learn and process language, humans nevertheless retain considerable neural plasticity throughout childhood and into adulthood to cope with newly encountered languages and to reorganise the brain in response to injury (see Chapter 12). While some aspects of language are acquired in the first year of life (e.g. a language's rhythmic structure and its inventory of speech sounds; see Chapter 2), other aspects are acquired much later in childhood (e.g. story-telling, sarcasm, humour, literacy; see Chapters 7 and 9). In many respects, language learning is a life-long endeavour with vocabulary, grammar, and discourse skills continue to grow throughout adolescence and even adulthood.

> **discourse** conversational aspects of language use, which may be applicable to specific social contexts.

The prolonged human childhood is a period of intense learning during which children acquire language as well as many other complex skills, such as mathematical reasoning, cooking, and chess. Irrespective of factors such as bipedalism and diet that may have triggered the uniquely human life history (as described above), it is also possible to view prolonged immaturity as an adaptation to the need to acquire complex skills. Note, however, that slow maturation also occurs in other species, for example, tortoises and elephants; it therefore seems unlikely that prolonged immaturity is an adaptation to the need for complex skill acquisition. But note also that elephants, like humans, are collective breeders that pool the resources of group members to care for their offspring (Hrdy, 2009). Collective breeding reinforces early immaturity, and in humans it provides a stable sociocultural context over which there is sufficient time for complex skills like language to develop.

> **collective breeders** certain species of animals (including humans) that pool the resources of group members to care for their offspring.

In the next section, we turn to the role of childcare in language development.

### 1.1.2   Alloparental care

Prolonged immaturity and nutritional dependency of infants requires prolonged and costly childcare. Human parents have to invest considerable resources into their immature offspring. As if this was not difficult enough, dietary improvements such as the domestication of fire, which helped to preserve food and to reduce parasite load, resulted in increased fertility of hominin females and a reduction of the spacing

**Figure 1.1** *Parents recruit the assistance of alloparents (grandparents, friends, teachers, professional caregivers, older siblings, and other kin) to care for their dependent children.*

*Source:* © Muellek Josef. Used under licence from Shutterstock.

**alloparents** individuals besides the parents who engage in the care and provisioning of offspring.

between births (Bogin, 1998). This created situations in which mothers had to juggle the needs of a young infant while caring for other semi-dependent children. Because the cost of childcare exceeds what individual mothers are able to provide, hominins have evolved to be cooperative breeders: to ensure child survival, mothers recruit **alloparents** to assist in the care of their children (Hrdy, 1999); see Figure 1.1. Alloparental support is especially important after weaning, when young children have to rely on other members of the community for provisioning.

In humans, the role of alloparents is often taken on by kin – grandmothers, older siblings, aunts, great aunts, and, to a varying degree, fathers. For a range of cultures as diverse as hunter-gatherers, horticulturalists, and peasants, shorter birth intervals and increased child survival are linked to the availability of matrilineal kin, especially maternal grandmothers (Voland, Chasiotis, & Schiefenhoevel, 2004). Similarly, the availability of older sisters has also been linked to child survival rates (Sear, Steel, McGregor, & Mace, 2002). In addition, in many cultures, alloparental care is also provided by non-kin alloparents such as younger women or fellow mothers or, more recently, hired childcare providers such as wet nurses, child-minders, au pairs, or nannies. What compels non-kin helpers to engage in caring for other people's children without any direct benefit to their own reproductive success? One suggestion is that young non-kin females benefit from providing childcare because they can hone their own mothering skills (Konner, 2010). Furthermore, many human childcare arrangements may be based on direct reciprocity, such that non-kin take care of each other's children or receive direct remuneration for their services. Human mothers weigh a number of factors, such as the degree of available alloparental support, in deciding whether a particular infant is worth their investment (Hrdy, 1999). Perhaps for this reason, human infants have to play their part in ensuring their own survival by soliciting care from their mothers and other potential caregivers. It is imperative for young infants to use whatever communicative means they have at their disposal to solicit care. Infants who are able to engage their mothers and other caregivers from birth have a better chance of survival than those who do not.

### 1.1.3 Reciprocal interaction between young infants and caregivers

To solicit care, human infants need to engage in social interactions and to monitor the behaviours of others for signs of commitment. When interacting with their caregivers, infants produce various types of vocalisation, such as grunting, crying, laughter, cooing, and babbling. These vocalisations are not intentionally communicative in the earliest stages of development; neonates obviously cannot voluntarily control their bouts of crying. Nevertheless, even the earliest vocalisations of infants provide information about their physical states (health, distress) and needs (food, comfort, sleep). More mature individuals, in turn, are predisposed to respond to infant signs of immaturity and need. This predisposition is not only evident in mothers, but in other adults or even juveniles, who all potentially may serve as alloparents. Indeed, it may have co-evolved with infant immaturity to ease the burden of costly childcare.

> **babbling** obligatory vocalisations of pre-verbal infants; includes canonical and vari-egated babbling stages.

In early infancy, vocalisation functions primarily as a means to initiate and maintain rapport with others. Dyadic vocal interactions (see Figure 1.2) between young infants and their caregivers are, for the most part, emotional in nature (Locke, 2001), and only later become referential as caregivers use language to draw their infant's attention to things in the world. The sharing of positive affect through dyadic interaction fosters a continuous sense of bonding and connectedness, which plays a crucial role in the establishment of attachment to the caregiver (Bowlby, 1982). Reciprocal face-to-face exchanges between infant and caregiver create mutual awareness

> **dyadic interaction** a communicative inter-action between two individuals; here mainly used to describe the face-to-face commu-nicative interactions of infants and their caregivers.

**Figure 1.2** *In face-to-face dyadic interaction, caregivers and infants use facial expressions, eye gaze, volcalisation, and touch to convey interest and emotion, and to modulate arousal.*
*Source:* © Lucian Coman. Used under licence from Shutterstock.

of internal states such as pleasure, through the alignment of vocalisation, eye contact, and facial expression. These interactions have a rhythmic structure that approximates the turn-taking and give-and-take of conversation, and in many cultures, caregivers treat infants as worthy conversational partners almost from birth. Early on, infants are capable of coordinating their behaviour with a caregiver in face-to-face interaction by modulating eye contact – establishing eye contact to signal readiness to communicate, and withdrawing eye contact when the social stimulation becomes too intense (Lavelli & Fogel, 2005). In a pioneering study, Haith, Bergman and Moore (1977) reported developmental increases in the amount of time infants fixated on their mother's face from 3 to 11 weeks of age: while infants at 3–5 weeks fixated on faces only 22 per cent of the time, this amount increased to 87.5 per cent of the time for infants at 7 weeks of age. Importantly, child-directed speech increased the amount of face scanning in children at 7 weeks of age and older. Coordinated interpersonal timing is evident from at least 6 weeks of age, as infants initiate and maintain eye contact in response to their mothers' vocalisations, and mothers time their vocalisation in response to their infants' gaze behaviour (Crown, Feldstein, Jasnow, Beebe, & Jaffe, 2002). The coordination of infant–caregiver behaviour in dyadic interaction is even more robust at 4 months of age, as infants at this age coordinate their vocalisations with those of strangers as well as their mothers (Jaffe, Beebe, Feldstein, Crown, & Jasnow, 2001).

**coordinated interpersonal timing** changes in the temporal patterning of one person's behaviour in response to another person's behaviour.

Infants vocalise to engage and maintain closeness with their caregivers, who vocalise in return to reassure, soothe, elicit attention, or make infants smile. Infants produce different qualities of vocalisation depending on whether they are alone or engaged with others, which suggests that they can vary their prelinguistic vocalisations for purposeful communication (Papaeliou & Trevarthan, 2006). Adults, in turn, are highly sensitive to differences in the quality of infants' vocalisation (Bloom & Lo, 1990). The intuitive appeal of certain types of infant vocalisations (e.g. cooing and babbling) in contrast to the negative valence of others (e.g. crying) leads adults to selectively reinforce specific qualities of infant vocalisation over others. For example, when 2- to 4-month-old infants make cooing sounds, adults intuitively perceive them as playful and friendly, and respond favourably towards them (Locke, 2006; Snow, 1977; Watson, 1972). In contrast, excessive crying elicits caregiver stress, frustration, and aggression. The process whereby caregivers respond contingently and positively to their infants' communicative bids is called social shaping, and has been shown to increase both the quality and the quantity of babbling in infants (Goldstein, King, & West, 2003; Goldstein & Schwade, 2008). Because cooing and babbling are effective in eliciting adult attention, positive affect, social stimulation, and caretaking, infants readily learn to use vocalisation as a means to establish and maintain positive rapport with others (Goldstein, Schwade, & Bornstein, 2009). Recent neuro-imaging work suggests that close social interaction between individuals leads to the coupling of neural responses, which further reinforces the execution of coordinated, joint behaviours (Hasson, Ghazanfar, Galantucci, Garrod, & Keysers, 2012). Thus, the interplay between infants who are primed to engage their caregivers and caregivers who

**social shaping** the process whereby a caregiver responds contingently and positively to an infant's communicative bids, and thereby increases the quantity and quality of the infant's speech and gesture.

are primed to respond to their infants' needs drives the development of language and other social and cognitive skills.

### 1.1.4 Complex social environments

Coincidental with the fossil record indicating changes in growth parameters and encephalisation, there is evidence for changes in the structure of hominin societies. Based on assemblages of stone tools collected at butchering sites, one can be fairly certain that hominins engaged in cooperative hunting of large game from about 1.5 million years ago (Haidle, 2010; but see McPherron et al. [2010] for dating of stone tool use to 3.4 million years ago), and used fires for cooking starting at least about 400,000 years ago (James, 1989; Rolland, 2004; but see Wrangham, Jones, Laden, Pilbeam, & Conklin-Brittain [1999] for dating of control of fire to 2 million years ago). The variety of tool types in the archaeological record (e.g. hammers, choppers, and scrapers) suggests that tools were used for hunting, fishing, and butchering, as well as to manufacture and shape other tools. The existence of these tools implies division of labour, specialised knowledge, fine-motor control, and hierarchical planning of activities – in effect, the presence of the socio-cognitive abilities necessary for language (Ragir, 2000).

Technological advances in cooperative hunting and cooking would have supported directly the growth of larger communities, and the emergence of specialised trades. Domestication of fire for cooking, in particular, probably increased the differentiation of the labour force, as some members of the group stayed at home bases to tend the fire while others engaged in hunting and foraging activities. Moreover, the establishment of home bases around fires might have provided a context for various members of the community to congregate with their young dependents. Larger social groups, engaged in more sophisticated activities, would increase the need for more efficient communication. Furthermore, the increased group size and improved nutrition most likely increased the proportion of infants and semi-dependent children in the groups (McBrearty & Brooks, 2000), thus leaving room for peer interaction and play. In this context, language would have been an important medium for organising joint activities, and for cultural transmission of knowledge.

As tool use and cooking techniques became more sophisticated, the ways in which objects were manufactured and used became more opaque and less self-explanatory. Humans may have adapted to this situation by evolving what Csibra and Gergely (2009, 2011) have termed natural pedagogy; see Figure 1.3. Although such ostensive signals may be non-linguistic (e.g. pointing or the use of eye gaze to indicate referential intent), the process of knowledge transmission is greatly enhanced by language, and language learning itself may benefit from the availability of such ostensive signalling. There is controversy about the extent to which human adults engage in direct teaching, as opposed to expecting children to learn from observation, imitation, and overhearing: in many contemporary non-industrial societies there is much less direct teaching and verbal instruction of children in comparison to Western industrialised societies (Lancy, 2009; Rogoff, 1990). Still, natural pedagogy seems to be largely absent in other species, which suggests that there is an important place for language in the transmission of generalisable cultural knowledge.

> **natural pedagogy** the use of ostensive signals to indicate that cultural knowledge is being taught within a communicative interaction.

**Figure 1.3**  *Humans devote considerable time and effort to teaching their young culturally significant practices. Such natural pedagogy requires the teacher and student to achieve a mutual understanding of what they are doing together and for what reason. Here a grandmother is teaching her grandson how to prepare meat dumplings.*

*Source:* © shalunishka. Used under licence from Shutterstock.

**intersubjectivity**
mutual awareness between two or more people that they are experiencing something together and have a shared understanding of the situation.

Language not only accompanies and facilitates joint activity and information exchange, but is also used to cement social alliances and to share states of mind (Carpendale & Lewis, 2004). In fact, it has been suggested that the need for language arose when human groups became too large to engage in direct mutual grooming (Dunbar, 1993, 1996). Mutual grooming, being both pleasurable and a hygienic necessity, serves to cement social alliances because it implies reciprocity – as in 'You scratch my back and I'll scratch yours'. As group sizes increased, language may have taken over the social function of mutual grooming by allowing individuals to share internal states and important social information through gossip.

Human communication, at a fundamental level, requires cooperation. Recently, it has been suggested that the emergence of language in human evolution is a reflection of our seemingly innate proclivity to engage cooperatively with others (Tomasello, 2008). Coordination of point of view is necessary for any communicative act to be mutually understood. The creation of shared meanings between members of a group requires a mechanism for achieving **intersubjectivity**. Intersubjectivity emerges early in infancy as caregivers and infants share positive rapport through dyadic face-to-face interaction (Stern, 1985; Trevarthen, 2001). If one views human language as a system of arbitrary relationships between linguistic forms and their associated meanings (Bates, Benigni, Bretherton, Camaioni, Volterra, et al. 1979), each pairing of form and meaning had to have emerged through negotiations among community members to achieve mutual understanding (see Chapter 11 for further discussion of the social factors that support language emergence). Every human language reflects the consensus of a community of speakers regarding what is to be understood in the context of language use and community practice. All human languages comprise complex systems of social conventions predicated upon communities of cooperatively interacting speakers (Clark, 1996; Tomasello, 2008; Wittgenstein, 1953). For two individuals to use a human language to communicate with one another, they must adopt the conventional ways of speaking the language, and they must mutually appreciate when communication has been successful. If one fails to cooperate in using the socially agreed upon constructions of the language, communication breaks down, and shared understanding has to be re-negotiated. For a child to break into such a system, the child must share a willingness to engage with others in jointly constructed activities, whereby the communicative intentions of others are made transparent and mutual understanding is achieved. Under this view, language develops as the child grasps the myriad ways that community members use linguistic utterances to coordinate their perspectives in order to achieve shared goals.

> **constructions** also called syntactic structures; the structural configurations of words in a sentence.

> **communicative intentions** a speaker's goals that motivate an act of communication in a specific context.

## 1.2 WHAT ARE THE ABILITIES OF LANGUAGE-READY NEWBORNS?

Just why humans evolved widespread tendencies towards cooperation is a hot topic in evolutionary psychology. One explanation is that increased cooperation in hominins was driven by inter-group competition: culture, which requires cooperation, made groups more successful in adapting to changing environments, and thus allowed them to outcompete neighbouring groups (Richerson & Boyd, 2004). Another view is that the necessity of alloparental support for child rearing required a considerable level of trust, cooperation, and mutual understanding between mothers and other group members (Hrdy, 2009): for their infants to survive, mothers must have been able to identify trustworthy others (i.e., extended kin) to care for their young, and infants must have been able to solicit care and provisioning from these trustworthy others. Regardless of the evolutionary scenario, modern human infants come equipped with social and cognitive skills that enable them to coordinate their behaviour with others. In this section we explore the earliest abilities of human infants that provide the basis for their subsequent language development.

### 1.2.1 *Attending to others*

Human infants have very limited information-processing capacity, which makes it advantageous for them to be selective in sampling information from the environment. Reid and Striano (2007, 2009) have suggested that the social abilities of human infants allow them to use interactions with other humans to hone in on what is relevant in the environment. From birth, neonates exhibit preferences and proclivities that focus their interests and attention on the social world around them. Infants' abilities encompass a range of components necessary for successful social interactions: infants need to be able to detect and recognise potential social partners, they need to be able to identify the focus of attention of these partners in relation to themselves and to the environment, and, finally, they need to be able to discern a social partner's goals and intentions. There is evidence that most of these components are in place very early in development, as we will discuss below and in Chapter 3.

One important cue for identifying potential social partners is the detection of biological motion: animals and humans move in self-propelled ways that preserve biomechanical integrity and are different from the movement patterns of non-biological entities. This capacity is already apparent in 3-month-olds, who can distinguish moving point-light displays that preserve the biomechanical integrity of the moving parts, from displays that do not (Bertenthal, Profitt, & Kramer, 1987). But of course identifying an animate entity is not sufficient for social interaction; infants must also be able to recognise who is a potential communicative partner and what constitutes a potential social sig-

**conspecifics** members of one's own species.

nal. Indeed, infants are very good at identifying their conspecifics. From birth, human infants demonstrate a discernible preference for human faces and voices (Farroni, Johnson, Menon, Zulian, Faraguna, & Csibra, 2005; Vouloumanos & Werker, 2007). Not only can infants identify others as human, they also have a preference for familiar partners: shortly after birth infants already show a preference for their mother's face over the faces of female strangers (Bushnell, Sai, & Mullin, 1989).

**fundamental frequency** the lowest of the formants, abbreviated F0; what is perceived as the voice pitch of different speakers.

Human infants also appear to have specific preferences for human speech. For example, Vouloumanous and Werker (2004) created speech and non-speech sounds that were carefully matched on a range of physical features (fundamental frequency, duration, and timing), and found that neonates preferred the speech sounds to the non-speech sounds. There is evidence that some neural circuits are already specialised for speech processing from very early on: Peña and colleagues (2003) played speech forwards and backwards to neonates and found that only forward speech elicited greater activation in specific areas of the left hemisphere involved in language processing. Krentz and Corina (2008) obtained further confirmation that it is the linguistic aspects of the signal that capture infants' attention: they investigated speech signals in another modality – the visual gestures of American Sign Language (ASL) – and demonstrated that 6-month-old hearing infants who had never been exposed to ASL preferred signs that are part of ASL over matched non-linguistic gestures akin to pantomime. It appears, then, that human neonates are predisposed to identify familiar individuals, which is crucial for the establishment of social interactions, and to attend specifically to those stimuli in the environment that are important for language acquisition.

However, it is not sufficient for infants to be able to identify potential communicative partners; they also must be able to monitor where their partner's attention is focused. The relevant cues for an individual's focus of attention are the orientation of the eyes, the orientation of the face, and the orientation of the whole body. Some of these cues are processed from birth: neonates are able to discriminate faces with the eyes oriented towards them from faces with the eyes oriented away from them (Farroni, Csibra, Simeon, & Johnson, 2002). By the time infants reach 4 months of age, detecting whether someone's gaze is directed towards them or away from them takes only 250ms. At this age infants appreciate whether an adult is providing relevant feedback in a socially contingent or non-contingent way (Striano, Henning, & Stahl, 2005) – that is, they expect adult behaviour in face-to-face interaction to be responsive to their own behaviour (see Section 1.1.3 for a description of the coordinated interpersonal timing of infant–caretaker interactions). Infants from birth are highly sensitive to the cessation of a social interaction: when an adult's face suddenly freezes, 0- to 4-day-old newborns decrease eye contact and show signs of distress (Nagy, 2008), a phenomenon known as the **still-face effect** (Tronick, Als, Adamson, Wise, & Brazelton, 1978; see Methodology Box 1.1). From early infancy, eye contact plays an important role in calming infants (Zeifman, Delaney, & Blass, 1996). When an adult partner freezes her face and looks away, infants at 6 weeks of age reduce their smiling and gazing and try to re-engage their partner (Bertin & Striano, 2006). Interestingly, infants respond more negatively in the still-face paradigm when the still face is administered by their mother, as opposed

**still-face effect** infants exhibit distress when an adult suddenly freezes movement of her face in dyadic interaction; an indicator that young infants have social expectations that people will engage responsively and provide contingent feedback during face-to-face interaction.

## METHODOLOGY BOX 1.1    THE STILL-FACE PARADIGM

How can we probe infants' early competencies in social interaction? What kind of behaviours do infants expect from their caregivers in interactive situations? In 1978, Tronick and collaborators (Tronick, Als, Adamson, Wise, & Brazelton, 1978) presented observations of infants' reactions towards an unusual and unexpected type of caregiver behaviour: the still face, that is, a sudden unnatural freeze of the caregiver's face, resulting in a flat emotionless expression for a period of up to three minutes. When confronted with this behaviour, infants typically display a complex range of behaviours that indicate distress, such as reducing their smiling, averting their gaze from the caregiver and even crying. They also try to re-engage their communication partner through smiling and cooing. These reactions of distress and social initiative have been observed from birth (Nagy, 2008) and persist until about 9 months, at which age infants become more sophisticated in self-regulation and are able to redirect their attention towards other objects in the environment. The infant behaviours observed in the still-face paradigm are testimony to the amazing early social sophistication of human

infants, which is evidenced by the distress experienced from a withdrawal of social interaction, as well as by the wide repertoire of behaviours that infants use to initiate social exchange and to re-engage their communication partners.

To study the still-face effect in the laboratory, mothers or other caregivers are first videotaped while engaging in normal reciprocal communicative exchange with the infant. Caregivers are then instructed to suddenly withdraw communicative interaction by freezing their facial expression. Interestingly, while the still-face effect itself is considered to be quite robust and dramatic (Adamson & Frick, 2003), procedures vary widely across studies from differences in the duration and presentation of the still face (front, profile, etc.) to differences in the coding of infant behaviour. Nonetheless, the still-face paradigm is widely used to probe the developmental trajectory of infant social behaviour; for example, to study gender and ethnic differences in early social competencies as well as the social competencies, of infants with developmental disorders such as Down syndrome or autism spectrum disorder.

to a stranger; this indicates that infants develop strong social expectations early on about how their mother ought to behave in face-to-face interaction (Melinder, Forbes, Tronick, Fikke, & Gredebäck, 2010). Over time, infants develop the ability to sustain attention towards non-social as well as social aspects of the environment, the latter indicated by infants' more prolonged and stable gaze patterns towards their mothers (Messinger, Ekas, Ruvolo, & Fogel, 2012). The abilities of young infants to create rapport and sustain social interaction with their caregivers through reciprocity, shared affect, and imitation provides the foundation for later developments in understanding the intentions of others (Rochat, 2007); see Chapter 3.

For an infant to discover the meanings of words, he or she must be able to discern what others are talking about – in effect, to read their communicative intentions as relevant to the present situation. This fundamentally involves an ability to grasp another person's focus of attention, and in the special case of learning the names of things (e.g. objects, actions, colours), to determine what aspect of the environment the speaker is referring to when producing a particular linguistic expression. The development of the ability to identify the referents of linguistic forms is the topic of Chapter 4, and relies on the infant's ability to engage in episodes of **joint attention**, whereby the infant coordinates their own attention with that of another person (Carpenter, Nagell, & Tomasello, 1998; Eilan, Hoerl, McCormack, & Roessler, 2005; Moore & Dunham, 1995); see Figure 1.4. Infants' developing ability to engage in joint attention with others, and the role of caregivers in **scaffolding** joint attention, will be described at length in Chapter 3. Chapter 3 also describes the role of gaze cues and communicative gestures, such as pointing, in facilitating joint attention between infants and their caregivers. The human ability to engage cooperatively and infer the communicative intentions of others enables individuals to grasp the potentially infinite number of ways that sound patterns of language can link to meaning. The innate biases of infants allow them to overcome their limited attention span by predisposing them to focus on those aspects of the environment that are socially relevant.

> **joint attention** the coordination of the infant's attention with that of another person to some aspect of the world.

> **scaffolding** caregiver behaviour that supports a child's joint activity with others, by taking into consideration the child's developmental status.

## 1.2.2  Engaging others

From birth, infants are emotionally expressive. At about 1 month of age smiling and laughter appear. As with crying, both the facial expression of smiling and the vocal behaviour of laughter start out as a reflexive response to some internal or external stimulus, such as tickling (Oller, 2000). However, infants gradually come to produce smiles to elicit attention and maintain rapport with their caregivers. In adults, smiles that express genuine enjoyment, called Duchenne smiles, can be identified not just by a raising of the corners of the lips but also by a characteristic cheek raise. In contrast, purely social non-Duchenne smiles lack the cheek raise (Ekman & Friesen, 1978) and are qualitatively different from Duchenne smiles. In infants, however, Duchenne and non-Duchenne smiles often appear together such

> **Duchenne smiles** smiles that express genuine enjoyment; can be identified by a raising of the corners of the lips, accompanied by a cheek raise that creates crow's feet around the eyes.

**Figure 1.4**  *Infants follow their caregivers' direction of eye gaze and pointing gestures to identify objects of interest to others. During periods of joint attention, infants and caregivers are aware of sharing attention to an object of mutual interest. Here a grandfather directs the attention of his grandson.*

*Source:* © StockLite. Used under licence from Shutterstock.

that Duchenne smiles tend to develop out of non-Duchenne smiles within the same interactive episode (Messinger, Fogel, & Dickson, 1999). This suggests that early on, social signalling and expression of internal emotional states may be tightly linked; this fits well with the view that early social interactions between infants and caregivers are primarily emotional in nature, and that infant emotion expressions can serve as important triggers for these interactions.

While engaging with their social partners, infants try to approximate the communicative behaviours of others. One important way of learning culturally important behaviours is through imitation. Meltzoff and Moore (1977), in a seminal study, showed that 12- to 21-day-old neonates were able to imitate facial expressions (tongue or lip protrusions and mouth openings) as well as sequential finger movements (opening a hand one finger at a time). This suggests that neonates already have the ability to map their perceptions of other people's actions onto their own actions. Most importantly, these imitative abilities of infants extend to the vocal domain: 18- to 20-week-old infants can imitate sounds like /a/, /i/, and /u/ (Kuhl & Meltzoff, 1982). (Note that by convention meaning-bearing sounds of a language are placed between forward slashes.)

Amazingly, such vocal imitation can already be detected in neonates. Chen, Striano, and Rakoczy (2004) showed that 1- to 7-day-old infants imitated sounds like /a/ as well as sounds like /m/ by either opening or clutching their mouth, and that they did so even when their eyes were closed. This means that neonates are capable of auditory–oral matching – in effect, they are able to produce the appropriate articulatory gestures based solely on what they hear. While neonates are capable of immediate imitation, older infants are able to defer imitation – to imitate an observed behaviour at a later point in time. How the infant's growing skills in observing and imitating others helps them in learning language and sociocultural skills will be described in Chapter 3.

### 1.2.3  Neurological and cognitive immaturity

One manifestation of the extended period of childhood in human life history is that the neocortex takes a very long time to mature, resulting in the restricted information-processing abilities of infants and small children. Paradoxically, having restricted

**Less-Is-More** a proposal that the limited working memory capacity of infants aids language learning by restricting the size of the units they can process.

processing capacity may be of benefit for language learning: Newport (1990) proposed a Less-Is-More account which links children's language-learning success to their limited information-processing capacity. According to this account, limited working memory capacity restricts infants to processing only small chunks of input, which, in turn, might help them to notice more fine-grained linguistic details, for example the subtle changes in word endings that mark grammatical functions. The Less-Is-More account, however, still needs to be reconciled with the observation that in, school-aged children and adults, larger processing capacity correlates with better language learning abilities. For example, in many studies with children as young as two years of age, phonological short-term memory (typically measured using a non-word repetition task) has been shown to predict individual differences in vocabulary size (Adams & Gathercole, 1996; Gathercole & Baddeley, 1989, 1990; Gathercole, Hitch, Service, & Martin, 1997; Stokes & Klee, 2009). Furthermore, as will be described in Chapter 10, children with language impairments often show marked deficits in verbal working memory capacity that are predictive of their error rates in sentence comprehension (Marton & Schwartz, 2003; Montgomery, 2000; Montgomery & Evans, 2009; see Montgomery, Magimairaj, & Finney [2010] for a review). In studies of foreign language acquisition, adult learners with larger working memory capacities show greater success in learning the grammatical features of a new language, and better performance on measures of sentence processing and comprehension (Ellis & Sinclair, 1996; Harrington & Sawyer, 1992; Kempe & Brooks, 2008; Miyake & Friedman, 1998; Williams & Lovatt, 2005). To accommodate these findings, the Less-Is-More account must posit that the restricted processing capacity that provides an advantage during infancy becomes a liability with age.

Another perspective on how prolonged cognitive and neurological immaturity might be beneficial for language learning has to do with the development of the prefrontal cortex. Mapping studies of grey matter density have indicated

**executive functioning** a control system, mainly situated in the **frontal lobe** of the neocortex, that manages other cognitive functions; involved in the deliberate control of attention, amongst other functions.

that the cortical areas responsible for executive functioning and control of attention mature only around puberty (Gogtay et al., 2004). Consequently, when it comes to solving complex tasks, children exhibit immature executive functioning, which is manifest in problems in which the child must consider several competing response alternatives. In such tasks young children will tend to over-select the most frequent or prepotent response. Adults, in contrast, tend to weigh the different response alternatives according to their probabilities of being correct, and provide responses that reflect those probabilities. So how might the young child's tendency to over-generalise highly frequent responses benefit the process of language learning? As described earlier, language learning is, in essence, the learning of social conventions. Ramscar and colleagues (Ramscar & Gitcho, 2007; Thompson-Schill, Ramscar, & Chrysikou, 2009) have argued that when it comes to learning conventions, cognitive flexibility may actually be a disadvantage. In situations with competing choices, children's lack of flexibility in weighing response alternatives supports learning of just the one alternative that occurs most frequently and is most supported by the context. In essence, immaturity of the prefrontal cortex leaves children at the mercy of the winning cue, whereas adults are able to override such maximising behaviour to consider the probabilities of the other cues as well. Indeed, comparing artificial language learning between children and adults has confirmed that adults tend to reproduce faithfully whatever inconsistencies and irregularities are present in the input, whereas children are more likely to over-regularise irregular patterns (Hudson Kam & Newport, 2005). Given that language learners generally are only ever exposed to a subset of the language they are learning, which leaves them with countless indeterminacies about how linguistic forms may relate to underlying meanings, rampant over-generalising can aid the young language learner in discovering regularity and structure.

**artificial language** experimental methodology which teaches participants aspects of an artificially created miniature language to control for prior knowledge and to reduce the complexity associated with natural languages.

In sum, prolonged immaturity in humans, in the context of social communities reliant on cooperative practices provides conditions that facilitate learning and make the development of complex social and cognitive skills such as language possible. Language learning benefits from the neural and behavioural plasticity associated with prolonged immaturity. At the same time, language learning builds upon a set of social and cognitive abilities that are linked to the human propensity for cooperation. The social environment that human infants find themselves in promotes the need for communication on the part of the child and the desire to facilitate this process on the part of adults. Language learning is fundamentally a social affair.

## SUMMARY

- **Evolutionary constraints associated with bipedalism and dietary improvements due to advanced hunting techniques and domestication of fire resulted in the evolution of delayed maturation, larger brains, and a period of prolonged postnatal immaturity in our hominin ancestors.**

- **Lengthy childhoods provide a substantial period of neural and behavioural flexibility conducive to learning.**

- **Lengthy periods of immaturity necessitate alloparenting by other members of the community. This exerted pressure on human infants to develop communicative behaviours that are effective in soliciting care from others.**

- **Increasing cultural sophistication may have precipitated the emergence of 'natural pedagogy', that is, the use of communicative interaction to teach opaque cultural knowledge. Language development can capitalise on these available channels of information transmission.**

- **Language is based on cooperative abilities because it involves sharing of information and internal states. As a system of social conventions it also constitutes a cooperative endeavour in itself. Thus, social and cognitive abilities for cooperation must be in place for language learning to occur.**

- Infants possess a range of cognitive and social abilities that constitute prerequisites for language development:
  - From birth, infants show preferences for social partners and for social signals.
  - Infants learn quickly to attend to others and to determine the focus of joint attention.
  - During the first year of life, infants also learn to read others' intentions.
  - Infants use emotional signals such as laughter and crying to engage potential communication partners.
  - Infants are able to imitate behaviours of their communication partners and to map auditory signals onto simple motor programmes.
  - Late maturation of the prefrontal cortex prevents children from considering multiple response alternatives in complex tasks. This results in over-regularisation, which may facilitate the learning of conventions such as language.

# FURTHER READING

## *Key studies*

To better understand the specifics of how language may have evolved to fit the social and cognitive capacities of the human brain, read Kirby, S., Cornish, H. & Smith, K. (2008). Cumulative cultural evolution in the laboratory: An experimental approach to the origins of structure in human language. *Proceedings of the National Academy of Sciences of the USA*, *105*, 10681–10686.

## *Overview articles*

For an accessible treatment of how immaturity of the prefrontal cortex may be beneficial for language learning, read Thompson-Schill, S., Ramscar, M. & Chrysikou, E. (2009). Cognition without control: When a little frontal lobe goes a long way. *Current Directions in Psychological Science*, *18*, 259–263.

## *Books*

For an account of how language development builds on pre-existing cooperative abilities, read Tomasello, M. (2008). *Origins of Human Communication*. Cambridge, MA: MIT Press.

## KEY TERMS

• allophones • babbling • babbling drift • canonical babbling • closed syllables • co-articulation • consonants • cooing • diminutives • formants • fundamental frequency • glottis • high-amplitude sucking procedure • iambic • International Phonetic Alphabet (IPA) • intonation • low-pass filtered • MacArthur–Bates Communicative Development Inventory (CDI) • magnetoencephalography (MEG) • manner of articulation • metrical stress • mismatch negativity • mora • mora-timed • oddball detection paradigm • open syllables • phonemes • phones • phonetics • phonology • phonotactic constraints • place of articulation • pro-sodic boundaries • prosody • quasi-vowel • reduplicative babbling • rime • sign languages • statistical learning • stress-timed languages • syllable coda • syllable nucleus • syllable onset • syllable-timed languages • syllables • trochaic • vari-egated babbling • Voice Onset Time (VOT) • voicing • vowels

# CHAPTER OUTLINE

Most children produce their first words at around one year of age. For this reason, the first year of life has often been viewed as a pre-verbal or prelinguistic phase of development. It is now clear, however, that infants acquire some remarkable linguistic skills well before they speak their first words. In the first year of life infants learn to recognise and, to some extent, reproduce the sound patterns of their native language. They also begin to isolate and recognise individual words amidst the fluent speech around them, and they start to relate these words to features of the surrounding environment. The timeline of major milestones of speech perception and production reached during the first year of life and the underlying learning mechanisms are outlined in Figure 2.1.

To most adults, the question of what constitutes a sound or a word of a language seems trivial. To get a sense of the task facing the infant, imagine yourself listening to a conversation in a language that you have never heard before. You would encounter many difficult-to-pronounce speech sounds, and often you would fail to notice meaningful differences in how similar-sounding words are said. It would be hard to figure out where a word ends and the next one begins. Trying to discern what the conversation was about would pose yet another challenge. In this chapter, we will begin to explore how infants solve these problems by focusing on how infants discover the sound structure of their language, and how they come to identify words in fluent speech. Chapter 4 will continue our exploration of word learning by focusing on how children discover the meanings of words.

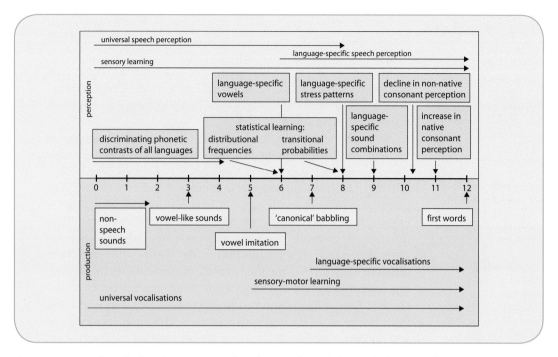

**Figure 2.1** *Timeline of infants' perception and production of speech during the first year of life.*

*Source:* Adapted from Kuhl et al. (2008). Phonetic learning as a pathway to language: new data and native language magnet theory expanded (NLM-e). *Philosophical Transactions of the Royal Society B, 363,* 979–1000. Reprinted with permission of the Royal Society.

# 2.1 WHAT IS THERE TO LEARN?

## 2.1.1 Speech sounds

The various speech sounds that humans are able to produce are called phones; phones that carry distinctions in meaning are called phonemes, and the scientific discipline that studies how sounds encode meaning is called phonology. Overall, there are about 800 phones in the world's languages (Ladefoged, 2001), but each language uses only a small number of these. As a result, languages differ in the specific inventory of phones they use for building words. For example, English has both a phoneme /l/ and a phoneme /r/ (linguistic convention puts phonemes between slashes and phones between brackets), whereas Japanese only has /r/ but no /l/. Some languages (e.g., Rotokas, a language spoken in Papua New Guinea) use as few as eleven phonemes, while others (like Taa, a language spoken in parts of Botswana and Namibia) use over 100 phonemes, some of

**phones** the various speech sounds that humans are able to produce.

**phonemes** phones that carry distinctions in meaning.

**phonology** the subfield of linguistics concerned with the sound patterns of languages (i.e., how speech sounds encode meaning).

them rather unusual ones like clicks. (If you want to know what these clicks sound like, go to YouTube and find the great Miriam Makeba singing *The Click Song*.) Thus, all languages differ in their phonemic inventories, with English using between 42 and 47 phonemes depending on the variety (Anglo-English, Scottish, American, Australian, etc.).

**allophones** pronunciation variants of individual speech sounds that do not mark distinctions in meaning.

**vowels** phonemes like /a/, /i/, or /u/ that are produced with an open vocal tract (i.e., the airflow above the glottis is not constricted); vowel articulation differs in tongue position and lip rounding; acoustically, vowels differ in first and second **formant**.

**consonants** phonemes like /p/, /t/, or /s/ that are produced by constricting the airflow in different parts of the oral cavity in different ways.

**glottis** the part of the vocal tract that contains the vocal folds.

**place of articulation** specifies where in the oral cavity the airflow is constricted during speech sound production.

**manner of articulation** how the airflow during speech production is manipulated by the movements of articulators, such as the tongue, lips, and jaws.

**voicing** refers to an aspect of articulation (i.e. whether the vocal folds are vibrating or not while the airflow is manipulated during speech sound production).

Phonemes are pronounced in different ways depending on their surrounding context and their position in a word. For example, in English, /p/ is pronounced with an aspiration, that is, with a little burst of air, as [pʰ] at the beginning of a word, but without aspiration as [p] in the middle or at the end of a word. These pronunciation variants are called allophones, and allophones do not mark distinctions in meaning.

Some phones are allophones in one language but phonemes in another. For example, in English, the allophonic difference between the unaspirated [t] and the aspirated [tʰ] is not associated with a difference in meaning, whereas in Hindi /t/ and /tʰ/ are different phonemes. In other words, aspiration is a feature indicating a meaningful contrast in Hindi but not in English, where it simply creates different allophones of the same phoneme. Not only do phonemes differ depending on their position in the word (which results in different allophones), but they can also sound differently depending on the dialect, mood, or specific voice characteristics of the speaker. One of the most fundamental tasks in language learning is therefore to acquire phonemic categories. This entails figuring out which characteristics of the sound are relevant for membership in a given category and which are not.

One important phonemic distinction to master is that between vowels and consonants. Vowels are phonemes like /a/, /i/, or /u/, in which the airflow above the glottis, the part of the vocal tract that contains the vocal folds, is not constricted. In terms of articulation, vowels differ in tongue position and lip rounding. These articulatory movements change the resonance characteristics of the oral cavity and result in differences in the acoustic properties of the sound. For example, when producing a high back vowel like /i/ the tongue has to be raised to the palate and positioned in the back of the mouth. Vowels like /u/ additionally require a rounding of the lips.

Consonants, that is, phonemes like /p/, /t/, or /s/, are produced by constricting the airflow in different parts of the oral cavity and in different ways. Place of articulation specifies where in the oral cavity the airflow is constricted, while manner of articulation specifies the way in which the airflow is manipulated, that is, whether it is fully, partially or not constricted. The term voicing refers to whether the vocal folds are vibrating or not while the airflow is manipulated. For example, a bilabial consonant like /b/ is created by briefly constricting the airflow using both lips while allowing the vocal folds to vibrate. To create the consonants /d/ and /z/ the tongue is positioned just behind the front teeth, at the alveolar ridge, and the vocal folds are vibrating. However, in the case of /d/, the airflow is fully blocked for a brief moment, whereas in /z/ the flow of air is constricted only enough to create turbulence.

Phonemes can also be described in terms of physical characteristics like amplitude (loudness) and frequency. In general, speech sounds are complex sounds consisting of a spectrum of frequencies. The frequencies that are most prominent in the spectrum in terms of amplitude are called formants. What we perceive as the voice pitch of different speakers is the lowest of the formants – called fundamental frequency and abbreviated as $F_0$. In addition, voiced speech sounds differ in their first (F1) and second (F2) formants. For example, for the vowel /a/, American male speakers typically produce formant frequencies of 730 Hz for F1 and 1090 Hz for F2. For the vowel /i/, these values are 270 Hz for F1 and 2290 Hz for F2 (Peterson & Barney, 1952). The scientific discipline that studies the articulatory and acoustic properties of speech sounds is called phonetics. While phonemes can be described in terms of their acoustic characteristics, it is important to understand that these characteristics are by no means invariant, but vary depending on the speaker and on the phonetic context. Because our articulatory apparatus accommodates the context of sounds due to co-articulation, the acoustic signature of every phoneme will be somewhat different depending on which phonemes are produced before or afterwards. This can easily be appreciated by observing your lip position when you produce the /t/ in *tip* and the /t/ in *top*: as a result of the different lip positions, the two variants of /t/ will have slightly different acoustic characteristics.

Because phonemes are the building blocks of words, infants have to learn how their language arranges them into meaningful sequences. In each language, certain phoneme sequences occur while others do not – restrictions on possible sequences of phonemes are called phonotactic constraints. For example, in English, the consonant sequence /sl/ may occur at the beginning or middle of a word (e.g. *sled, misled*), whereas the sequence /sr/ occurs only in the middle (e.g. *misread*). The combination /lp/ is a 'legal' sequence at the end of a syllable (e.g. as in *helper*), but not at the beginning. Tacit knowledge of phonotactic constraints allows English speakers to appreciate that *slirk* could possibly be an English word (even if it is not) whereas *srilk* could not.

## 2.1.2   Rhythm and intonation

Within words, sequences of phonemes are organised into syllables. It has been suggested that the structure of syllables is based on cycles of jaw openings and closings (MacNeilage & Davis, 2000). Most syllables start with one or several consonants, called the syllable onset, followed by a vowel called the syllable nucleus. There can also be one or several consonants at the end of a syllable, called the syllable coda. Nucleus and coda make up the rime – the part that is invariant in words like *cat, mat, hat,* and *bat*. Languages differ in syllable structure. For example, Japanese and Hawaiian allow only open syllables – that is, syllables with no coda, like the English words *me* or *pie*. Languages that permit codas have so-called closed syllables, like the words *meat* or *pipe*.

---

**formants**  the most prominent frequencies, in terms of amplitude, in the sound spectrum of the voice.

**phonetics**  the subfield of linguistics concerned with the articulatory and acoustic properties of speech.

**co-articulation**  how the pronunciation of a speech sound is influenced by the articulation of the preceding and following speech sounds.

**phonotactic constraints**  language-specific restrictions on what sequences of phonemes are permissible.

**syllables**  units of organisation of sequences of phonemes within words; contains a syllable nucleus and an optional syllable onset and/or syllable coda.

**syllable onset**  refers to one or several consonants at the beginning of a syllable.

**syllable nucleus**  the syllable peak, usually the vowel, but occasionally a syllabic consonant, as in the final syllable of *button* or *butter*.

**syllable coda**  refers to one or several consonants at the end of a syllable.

**rime**  part of a syllable, consisting of the syllable nucleus and optional syllable coda (e.g. the *at* in words like *cat, mat, hat,* and *bat*).

**open syllables**  type of syllable structure in which syllables lack a syllable coda, for example as in the words *eye, pay, spy*.

**closed syllables**  type of syllable ending in a consonant, as in *mop* or *pad*.

**metrical stress**  phenomenon where one syllable tends to be more prominent than the others when multiple syllables are combined to form words.

**stress-timed languages**  type of stress pattern in languages where the metrical stress tends to occur at regular intervals.

**trochaic**  a strong–weak stress pattern, as in *daddy* or *candle*.

**iambic**  a weak–strong stress pattern, as in *guitar* or *surprise*.

**syllable-timed languages**  type of stress pattern in languages where the metrical stress tends to be placed on a certain syllable in the word (e.g. the next-to-last syllable) and syllables are otherwise of roughly equivalent length.

**mora-timed**  a type of stress pattern in languages where the rhythmical structure is based on a unit smaller than the syllable (i.e. the mora).

**mora**  a unit of syllable weight; consonant–vowel syllables with short vowels, (e.g. *the*) have one mora, whereas consonant–vowel syllables with long vowels (e.g. *pie*) have two morae.

In some languages, syllable onsets and codas may comprise clusters of consonants, as in *spy*, *east*, or *blink*. It is customary to describe the structure of syllables in terms of vowel (V) and consonant (C) templates, as in CV for syllables like *me*, CVC for syllables like *meat*, and CCVCC for syllables like *blink*.

When multiple syllables are combined into words, one syllable tends to be more prominent than the others. This phenomenon is called metrical stress. The vowels of stressed syllables are characterised by a combination of features including longer duration, slightly higher pitch, and increased amplitude (loudness). Languages differ with respect to their predominant stress patterns. In stress-timed languages, like English or Dutch, stress tends to occur at regular intervals. Content words (nouns, verbs, adjectives) are stressed, whereas function words, such as determiners (*the*, *an*), auxiliaries (*is*, *can*), and prepositions (*in*, *of*) tend to be unstressed. Placement of stress varies across words, and must be learned as part of the word's sound structure. In English, the majority of bisyllabic content words have a trochaic (strong–weak) stress pattern, as in *daddy* or *candle*, but iambic (weak–strong) stress patterns, as in *guitar* or *surprise*, are also permitted. In syllable-timed languages, such as French and Spanish, metrical stress tends to be placed on a certain syllable in the word (e.g. the next-to-the-last syllable) and syllables are otherwise of roughly equivalent length. A third type of language, called mora-timed, has a rhythmic structure based on a unit smaller than the syllable called a mora. For example, a word like *bee* consists of two morae due to its long vowel. Japanese is an example of a mora-timed language.

Although caregivers occasionally produce words in isolation (e.g. when labelling an object, or saying *No* or *Hello*), most of the time infants hear words in a connected stream of speech. At the level of the entire utterance, speech has a sound structure called prosody, which encompasses changes in voice quality, rhythm, speech rate, and intonation. Intonational patterns vary considerably across languages; for example, speakers of French tend to raise the pitch towards the end of an utterance, whereas English speakers tend to lower the pitch. Intonation is also used to distinguish types of utterances, such as questions versus affirmative statements; for example, *Jim likes apples* (with pitch falling off towards the end) versus *Jim likes apples?* (with pitch rising towards the end). Prosody encompasses contrastive stress, as in *Jim likes APPLES, not pears*, whereby stress – increased vowel length, loudness, and higher pitch on the first syllable of *apples* – helps to convey the speaker's focus. In some cases, changes in prosody also help to disambiguate the syntactic structure of a sentence. For example, to distinguish the phrase *chocolate, cake, and ice cream* from *chocolate cake and ice cream*, speakers are likely to increase the length of the pause between *chocolate* and *cake*. Prosody also conveys information about the speaker, such as his or her health and mood. For example, when happy or ecstatic, speakers tend to talk faster and show an exaggerated pitch contour, whereas when sad, speakers tend to talk slowly with a flat pitch contour. Prosody also varies depending on whether the speaker is conversing with a child, a pet, an elderly adult, or a non-native speaker of the language. As will be described in more detail in Chapter 6, speech directed at small children tends to show exaggerated pitch contours and lengthened vowels.

> **prosody** the sound structure of speech at the level of the entire utterance; encompasses changes in voice quality, rhythm, speech rate, and intonation.

While this description of the structure of speech sounds necessarily has to remain brief and very general, it is important to appreciate that each language has its own phonemic inventory, and that for any given language, there is a certain degree of systematicity and regularity in how phonemes combine into larger units, and how stress and other prosodic features are distributed across the speech stream. In the next section, we will examine what abilities newborns possess that would enable them to acquire the sound structure of their language.

> **intonation** variation in pitch while speaking; used for emphasis as well as for other communicative purposes, such as asking a question, stating a point of fact or conveying sarcasm; can also convey emotion.

## 2.2   WHAT ARE THE LINGUISTIC ABILITIES OF NEWBORNS?

At first glance, this question does not seem to make much sense. Everybody knows that newborns cannot talk; they cannot even understand language, so obviously their linguistic abilities must be non-existent. In this section, we want to scrutinise this initial impression to understand what capabilities newborns come equipped with that might help them to get their foot in the door when it comes to learning language.

### 2.2.1   Recognising language

The first thing to note is that the human auditory system is fairly well developed even before birth, although it does not yet exhibit full adult capacity. A foetus is able to process sounds roughly from 28 weeks of gestation onwards (Fernald, 2001; Saffran, Werker, & Werner, 2006). However, the processing of ambient sounds is severely limited by the filtering properties of the womb: speech is 'muffled', which prevents identification of individual phonemes, but allows for the perception of rhythm and intonation. Newborns thus gain considerable prenatal experience with certain aspects of sounds emitted by their mothers and other humans in close proximity. Evidence for a preference for auditory stimuli that have become highly familiar during the prenatal period comes from findings that newborns prefer their mother's voice to the voice of another woman (DeCasper & Fifer, 1980), and they prefer passages of text their mothers read to them before birth to unfamiliar passages (DeCasper & Spence, 1986). This evidence was obtained using a methodology called the high-amplitude sucking procedure (see Methodology Box 2.1). Even more impressively, newborns appear to be able to process rhythm and intonation of speech in

> **high-amplitude sucking procedure** a habituation procedure that allows researchers to study how neonates and very young infants (up to 5 or 6 months of age) discriminate stimuli by measuring their rate of sucking on a pacifier.

# METHODOLOGY BOX 2.1    METHODS FOR ASSESSING INFANTS' SPEECH PERCEPTION

Many auditory perception studies use operant conditioning. In these methods, infants are presented with two sounds that differ in some way that is of interest to the researcher. Infants are then rewarded for some behaviour associated with attention to the sounds. There are three major subgroups of methods: habituation procedures, auditory preference procedures, and visually reinforced headturn procedures (Fernald, 2001).

## A. THE HIGH-AMPLITUDE SUCKING PROCEDURE

The high-amplitude sucking procedure is a habituation procedure that allows researchers to study the ability to discriminate sounds from two categories in neonates and very young infants up to 5 to 6 months of age. Auditory stimuli are played to the infant for as long as she sucks on a non-nutritive pacifier at a certain rate. The pacifier is connected to a computer so that the sucking frequency can be recorded. Over time, the infant will habituate and suck less frequently. When the sucking rate drops to a certain criterion, the sound is switched to a sound from another category. If the infant detects a change between the sounds, the sucking rate is expected to increase again as the infant is motivated to hear the new sound. If the infant cannot detect the change from one sound category to the other, dishabituation does not occur, that is, the rate of sucking remains unchanged. In this procedure, the auditory stimulus acts as a conjugate reinforcer, that is, it serves as a reward for spontaneous sucking behaviour, which indicates attention.

## B. THE HEADTURN PREFERENCE PROCEDURE

This procedure is a form of auditory preference procedure in which presentation of sound is made contingent upon a learned behaviour such as sustained looking at a visual stimulus; see Figure 2.2 for an illustration of the experimental set up. Infants typically sit on a caregiver's lap while the caregiver is listening to masking music over headphones to prevent them from inadvertently influencing the infants' behaviour. The infant first sees a visual stimulus, for example, a blinking blue light, in front of them. Once this light stops blinking, another visual stimulus, for example, a blinking red light, is presented to the left or to the right of the infant. As soon as the infant looks at the light on the left or the right, a sound from one category is presented from a loudspeaker situated next to the light. The sound will disappear if the infant looks away for a certain period of time and the blinking blue light in front of the infant will reappear again. Once this visual stimulus has attracted the infant's attention, the next trial starts with another visual stimulus presented to one side of the infant and accompanied by a sound as long as the infant looks at this visual stimulus. The infant hears multiple examples from the two sound categories interspersed over a number of trials. Longer average looking/listening time for one sound category indicates the infant's preference.

Sometimes infants are pre-trained to sounds from one category to see how familiarity influences listening preferences. Depending on age and familiarity with the sound, infants sometimes look longer at familiar stimuli and sometimes at novel stimuli. This procedure is most suitable for infants older than 6 months of age.

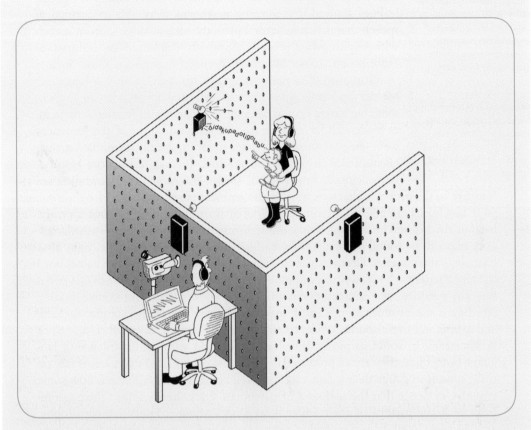

**Figure 2.2**  *Setup for the headturn preference procedure.*
*Source:* Image by Michael Almodovar.

## C. THE CONDITIONED HEADTURN PROCEDURE

In this procedure, infants are conditioned to make headturns in response to sounds by receiving a visual reward, such as viewing an attractive moving toy after a correct headturn in the direction of the sound. Infants again sit on a caregiver's lap while the caregiver is listening to masking music over headphones. Infants are first trained on one sound, for example, /ba/, which they hear over and over again. When the sound switches, for example, to /pa/, they are rewarded for moving their head in the direction of the moving toy. In the test phase, infants often are presented with sound category changes that are more subtle than the ones used for the conditioning phase. Half of the trials contain no category change, and the other half contain the change of interest. Infants are only rewarded for correct headturns, which indicate their ability to discriminate between sounds belonging to different categories.

**magnetoencephalogra-phy (MEG)** a brain-imaging technique that records the magnetic fields generated by the brain's electrical activity.

their sleep: using magnetoencephalography (MEG), Sambeth and colleagues showed that sleeping newborns were able to distinguish speech that is rich in natural prosody, such as singing, from speech with impoverished prosody (Sambeth, Ruohio, Alku, Fellman, & Huotilainen, 2008). Moreover, prenatal experience allows infants to distinguish their native language from an unfamiliar language: Mehler and colleagues showed that newborns born to French-speaking parents could distinguish French from Russian sentences, as evidenced by an increased sucking rate, even if the sentences were low-pass filtered to render them similar to the muffled speech

**low-pass filtered** natural speech that has passed through a filter to block sound wave frequencies above a specific cut-off point.

encountered in the womb (Mehler, Jusczyk, Lambertz, Halsted, Bertoncini, & Amiel-Tison, 1988). This shows that newborns are sensitive to the prosodic characteristics of the ambient language.

If newborns are able to discriminate familiar from unfamiliar languages on the basis of rhythm and intonation, then it is interesting to know whether a similar familiarity bias can be found in infants' very early vocalisations. For example, right after birth, do babies born to German parents sound in any way different from babies born to French parents? To answer this question we need to look at what sounds newborns typically produce. The most frequent and salient vocalisation is, of course, crying. Newborns also produce a number of vegetative sounds like burps, coughs, sneezes, and grunts. All these sounds reflect bodily states like hunger, discomfort, illness, or bodily strain. It would seem that they have little to do with the emergence of language except that they are all produced by the vocal system, and that parents rely on these sounds to gauge their infant's state of well being. However, there is now some tentative evidence that the melodies of newborns' cries already reflect the predominant prosodic pattern of their ambient language. Mampe, Friederici, Christophe, and Wemke (2009) studied individual crying bouts and found that French newborns tended to produce pitch and intensity peaks later in the crying bout than German newborns. This difference in the relative timing of pitch and intensity peaks reflects the typical intonation contour of the two languages, which is rising in French and falling in German. It appears then that newborns' familiarity with the rhythm and intonation of their native language might affect not only their perception, but some aspects of their early vocalisation as well.

## 2.2.2   Discriminating between languages

We have just described how newborns are sensitive to the rhythm and intonation of the speech they have encountered in the womb. In this section we ask whether their perceptual abilities allow them to go beyond their prenatal experience. If newborns rely only on familiarity they may be able to distinguish their ambient language from an unfamiliar language, but would they also be able to distinguish two unfamiliar languages? The answer, it turns out, is quite counterintuitive: it would seem reasonable to expect newborns to recognise only their native language at first, and only later to learn to differentiate other languages as well. When Mehler and colleagues (1988) tested French newborns on French and Russian, they also exposed them to two unfamiliar languages, English and Italian. Although their first analysis of the data suggested that the newborns did not discriminate between the two unfamiliar languages, this conclusion was reconsidered after a more careful analysis of the data (Mehler & Christophe, 1995). Subsequently, Nazzi and colleagues presented French newborns with low-pass filtered English and Japanese sentences, and confirmed that they could distinguish the two unfamiliar languages (Nazzi, Bertoncini, & Mehler, 1998). However, as newborns gain experience with the rhythm and intonation of what will become their native language, they seem to lose their ability to distinguish unfamiliar languages. American infants at 2 months of age, when presented with two unfamiliar languages, Russian and French, were unable to discriminate between them (Mehler *et al.*, 1988). Similarly, 2-month-old English infants could discriminate between English and Japanese, but not between French and Japanese (Christophe & Morton, 1998). We shall return to this apparent loss of sensitivity when we discuss infants' acquisition of phonemes.

Interestingly, some of the English infants in Christophe and Morton's (1998) study failed to discriminate English from Dutch, a language that although foreign, shares many rhythmic features with English (i.e., both are stress-timed languages, whereas Japanese is a mora-timed language). At 2 months of age, infants discriminate their native language based on its rhythm and intonation, in particular the relationship between the lengths of its vowels and consonants (Ramus & Mehler, 1999). Discrimination of languages based on individual speech sounds, which would help to distinguish, for example, English from Dutch or British English from American English, emerges only at around 5 months of age (Nazzi, Jusczyk, & Johnson, 2000).

# 2.3  HOW DO INFANTS DISCOVER THE SOUNDS OF LANGUAGE?

## 2.3.1  Phonemic categories

We described earlier that individual phonemes differ acoustically depending on their word position and adjacent phonemes, as well as the speech rate and voice characteristics of the speaker. Nevertheless, adults readily disregard these 'unimportant' differences to form categories of phonemes: the sound [p] spoken by a male speaker and by a female speaker, the aspirated [pʰ] at the beginning of a word and the [p] in the middle of a word are all perceived as different instances of the phoneme /p/. When and how do infants acquire the ability to form such categories?

In a classic study, 1- and 4-month-old infants were presented with sounds spanning the continuum from /ba/ to /pa/, which varied in small steps (Eimas, Siqueland, Jusczyk, & Vigorito, 1971). The acoustic feature that distinguishes /ba/ from /pa/ is the time that elapses between the release of air and the onset of vocal fold

**voice onset time (VOT)** the amount of time that elapses between the release of air and the onset of vocal fold vibration in consonant production.

vibration – called Voice Onset Time (VOT). If voicing starts earlier than 25ms after the release burst, adult native English speakers tend to perceive the consonant as /b/; conversely, if voicing starts later than 25ms after the release burst, they perceive the consonant as /p/. Using the high-amplitude sucking procedure, Eimas and colleagues habituated infants to one sound from this continuum and then presented another sound that differed by 20ms of VOT. The crucial manipulation was that the second sound lay either within the same category (e.g. a VOT of 80ms following a VOT of 60ms with both sounds corresponding to adult /p/, or a VOT of 0ms following a VOT of −20ms with both sounds corresponding to adult /b/) or across the category boundary (e.g. a VOT of 40ms following a VOT of 20ms corresponding to adult /p/ and /b/, respectively). In the control group, the same sound was presented throughout the entire duration of the experiment. Naturally, infants in the control group showed a continuous decrease in sucking rate, as would be expected in a habituation procedure. The same was found for infants who heard a second sound that originated from within the same category as the first sound. Crucially, infants sucked more frequently when the second sound originated from across the category boundary, which indicated that they perceived the second sound as different from the first. Note that in both conditions the second sound differed from the first sound by the same VOT. Subsequent research demonstrated infant categorical perception for other consonants (e.g. Eimas, 1975) as well as for vowels (e.g. Trehub, 1973). Not only are infants at 1 month of age or younger able to perceive rather subtle differences between speech sounds (Bertoncini, Bijeljac-Babic, Blumstein, & Mehler, 1987; Cheour-Luhtanen et al., 1995), but they seem to do so in a manner approximating adult categorical perception. For example, electrical brain responses of sleeping Finnish newborns showed that they were able to discriminate between the Finnish vowels /i/ and /y/, which differ only in the second formant (Cheour-Luhtanen et al., 1995). In this study, a set of identical phonemes (e.g. /y/) was occasionally interspersed with a different phoneme (e.g. /i/). This is called an oddball detection paradigm and is based on the established finding that if the brain detects an oddball in a series of auditory stimuli it elicits a specific electrical signature called the mismatch negativity (see Näätänen et al., 1997). Two-month-old infants are also able to distinguish between allophones, such as the /t/ in *night rate* and in *nitrate* (Hohne & Jusczyk, 1994), an ability that will become useful for word segmentation, as will be discussed in the next section.

**oddball detection paradigm** an event-related potential (ERP) paradigm used to measure a specific electrophysical response to a novel auditory stimulus (i.e. a mismatch negativity).

**mismatch negativity** a specific electrical signature (event-related potential) elicited by the brain's detection of an oddball in a series of auditory stimuli.

From these early studies of early categorical perception of phonemes several conclusions were drawn: the first was that categorical perception of sounds must be unique to language. This conclusion was subsequently challenged by the demonstration of categorical perception for non-speech sounds. By varying the time it takes an artificially generated sound wave to reach a certain amplitude in small increments, Jusczyk and colleagues were able to show that even 2-month-old infants perceived such stimuli categorically as either 'plucked' or 'bowed' sounds, just as adults do (Jusczyk, Rosner, Cutting, Foard, & Smith, 1977). The second conclusion was that categorical perception of speech sounds must be unique to humans. This conclusion was challenged by animal studies demonstrating categorical perception of phonemes, for example, in chinchillas (Kuhl & Miller, 1975). Thus, a more accurate conclusion is that newborns' biases in processing sound are not specifically tied to language processing; rather, human languages seem to have evolved to capitalise on the processing biases of the auditory system.

Recall that by 2 months of age infants have lost their ability to distinguish two unfamiliar languages on the basis of prosody. A similar loss of sensitivity has been observed with respect to phoneme perception, albeit somewhat later in development. It is well established that adults have great difficulties in discriminating certain phonemes that do not appear in their native language (e.g. Lisker & Abramson, 1971). For example, Japanese adults have difficulty distinguishing English /l/ from /r/, although some sensitivity can be acquired over time (Flege, Takagi, & Mann, 1996). For other contrasts, for example, between the dental and the retroflex /t/ of Hindi, discrimination may remain impossible even after prolonged training (Bowers, Mattys, & Gage, 2009), although some adults are more successful than others (Golestani & Zatorre, 2008). At what age does this transition from universal to language-specific perception of phonemes occur and why? Werker and Tees (1984) showed that 6- to 8-month-old infants from English-speaking homes were able to distinguish non-native contrasts such as the difference between the Hindi dental and the retroflex /t/, but 10- to 12-month-old infants were not. Similarly, Japanese infants lose their ability to discriminate between the English /l/ and /r/ between 6 and 12 months of age (Kuhl, Stevens, Hayashi, Deguchi, Kiritani & Iverson, 2006). Thus, in the second half of the first year of life, infants lose sensitivity to contrasts that are not marked in their native language, while at the same time showing increased sensitivity to features of their native language, as will be described in more detail below.

## 2.3.2 Early vocalisations

Before we return to the issue of changing perceptual sensitivity to native and non-native speech sounds, let us examine whether a similar transition from universal to language-specific abilities is mirrored in infants' vocalisations. The development of infant vocalisation is to some extent shaped by changes the infant vocal tract undergoes during the first year of life. Not only is the infant vocal tract initially smaller than that of an adult but it is also of different shape with a proportionally larger tongue mass (Kent, 1992). The anatomical restructuring that takes place during the first year of life constrains the range of sounds infants can produce at different stages of their development.

Starting at around 2 months of age, infants produce cooing (or gooing) sounds, followed by a quasi-vowel. Unlike crying, laughing, and other infant vocalisations that are indicators of bodily and affective states, quasi-vowels are considered to be infants' first

**cooing** 'gooing' sounds that begin around 2 months of age, involving tongue articulations at the back of the mouth.

**Figure 2.3**  *Young infants produce cooing sounds and other vocalisations, such as grunts, that convey their interest and arousal during physical activity.*

© Franck Boston. Used under licence from Shutterstock.

**quasi-vowel**  a sound that infants begin to make at around 2 months of age; involves a short uninterrupted vowel-like sound.

**canonical babbling**  pre-verbal vocalisations consisting of repetition of syllables such as *dadada* or *bababa*.

**reduplicative babbling**  the first stage of babbling, consisting of repetitions of consonant–vowel syllables such as *dadada* or *bababa*.

**variegated babbling**  the second stage of babbling that incorporates different combinations of syllables, such as in the sequence *badabu*.

truly voluntary vocalisations (Oller, 2000); see Figure 2.3. Cooing is gradually augmented by clearer vowels and more syllable-like sound patterns containing CV combinations, which ultimately lead to the emergence of babbling at around 6 months of age. Canonical babbling first consists of repetition of syllables such as *dadada* or *bababa*, a phase that is known as reduplicative babbling. Gradually, babbling incorporates more complex combinations of varied syllables. This second stage, known as variegated babbling, coincides with and extends beyond the onset of first word production.

Are cooing sounds universal or are they shaped by the ambient language? Do 4-month-old infants sound the same the world over or can differences attributable to the ambient language already be observed at this young age? Although no existing research, to our knowledge, answers these questions, there is some evidence of a relationship between infant vocalisation and the ambient language in neonates, and in older infants. As described previously, newborns' crying patterns may already reflect the prosody of the ambient language (Mampe et al., 2009). Infant babbling has been shown to incorporate language-specific stress patterns at 8 months of age (de Boysson-Bardies, Sagard, & Durand, 1984) and phonetic features at 8 to 10 months of age (de Boysson-Bardies, Hallé, Sagart, &

Durant, 1989; de Boysson-Bardies & Vihman, 1991; Lee, Davis & MacNeilage, 2010). How might infant vocalisations come to resemble the ambient language? Neonatal imitation of speech sounds suggests bimodal perception of speech from birth: newborns show more mouth clutching when an adult articulates an /m/ in front of them and more mouth opening when the adult articulates an /a/, even if they do not look at the speaker (Chen, Striano, & Rakoszy, 2004; see Chapter 1). Somewhat later, at around 4 months of age, infants are able to match their vocalisations to target vowels presented by adults (Kuhl & Meltzoff, 1982, 1996). These findings provide evidence for an auditory–articulatory map, which would enable infants to adjust their articulatory movements to match perceived target sounds. There is also evidence that at around 12 weeks of age, infants have rudimentary templates of different vowels in memory, which may serve as auditory targets for infants to match with their own vocalisations (Kuhl & Meltzoff, 1996). Cooing and babbling would provide infants with information about the acoustic consequences of their articulatory movements, which could then be compared with the stored representations (Kuhl & Meltzoff, 1996). As language-specific information about phonemes in memory gradually increases, infants produce more accurate approximations of ambient speech sounds – a notion that has been termed babbling drift (Brown, 1959).

> **babbling drift** infants' production of more accurate approximations of ambient speech sounds as language-specific information about phonemes in memory gradually consolidates.

However, babbling often also contains sounds that are not part of the ambient language. Indeed, some researchers have gone so far as to claim that babbling infants can produce all the sounds of human languages, even extremely rare ones (Jakobson, 1941). This disagreement between views of early infant vocalisations as approximating versus being distinct from the ambient language may in part be due to the difficulties associated with identifying and classifying very early infant vocalisations. Historically, the first systematic attempts at describing infant sounds came from diary studies which used alphabetical and later phonetic transcriptions to render the infants' vocalisations (e.g. Leopold, 1947). This seemed like an accurate method because the system used for phonetic transcription, the International Phonetic Alphabet (IPA), contains a carefully developed inventory of signs that can be used to describe the phonemes of all the world's languages. In fact, it has been developed to describe previously uncharted languages, and if it is suitable for transcribing the sounds of languages of remote tribes in Papua New Guinea or the Amazon rainforest, should it not also be suitable for describing

> **International Phonetic Alphabet (IPA)** a standardised system of phonetic transcription that uses an inventory of signs (letters and diacritics) to represent the sounds used in spoken languages.

the vocalisations of a human infant? The problem is that describing infant sounds in terms of adult phonemes obscures the ways in which infant sounds *deviate* from adult phonemes. If one transcribes the sounds produced by a 3-month-old infant using the IPA and then asks a trained phonetician to reproduce those sounds based on the transcription, the result will be unlikely to resemble the original infant vocalisations. As Oller (2000) put it, the IPA is no more adequate for describing the sounds produced by an infant than the onomatopoeic *cockadoodledoo* is for describing the sounds produced by roosters.

Modern studies use acoustical analyses, for example, of vowel formant frequencies (de Boysson-Bardies et al., 1989; Kuhl & Meltzoff, 1996), to analyse whether infant vocalisations approximate the ambient language. These studies confirm that infant vocalisations do resemble the ambient language to some extent. However, the process by which these vocalisations come to approximate adult targets is a very long and complex one, which seems to involve a lot of articulatory experimentation during the babbling phase. As a result, production clearly trails behind perception in terms of phonetic accuracy. To appreciate the problem, imagine how long it would take you to learn to make subtle melodic, harmonic, and rhythmic distinctions when listening to violin music. It would probably take a while. Now imagine how much longer it would take you to learn to play the violin to such a degree of proficiency that would enable you to re-create these subtle differences, especially when learning from memory and without formal instruction. It would probably take much, much longer. Indeed, some speech sounds are produced correctly only by 8 years of age, while accuracy in perception is achieved much earlier. This lag of speech production behind perception and representation has endearingly been termed the 'fis'- phenomenon, referring to an anecdote first published by Berko and Brown (1960): 'One of us … spoke to a child who called his inflated plastic fish a *fis*. In imitation of the child's pronunciation, the observer said "This is your *fis*?" "No," said the child, "my *fis*."' He continued to reject the adult's pronunciation until he was told, 'This is your *fish*.' 'Yes,' he said, 'my *fis*' (Berko & Brown, 1960: 531). Indeed, learning to coordinate the over 70 muscles and 10 body parts involved in articulation and phonation (Thelen, 1991) is no mean feat!

The idea that babbling is a form of practise designed to bring immature vocalisations closer to well-formed adult targets is supported by the existence of juvenile vocalisations akin to babbling in animal species that use vocal communication systems, such as song birds or primates. In humans, babbling is also independent of the modality of the communication system. As we will explain in greater detail in Chapter 11, hearing infants exposed to sign languages spoken by their deaf parents are able to extract the rhythmic patterns of that visual/gestural communication system, and to engage in a form of silent manual babble (Petitto, Holowka, Sergio, & Ostry, 2001; Petitto, Holowka, Sergio, Levy, & Ostry, 2004). Thus, infants appear to be sensitive to the rhythmic structure of whatever communication system they are exposed to and have a propensity to imitate and practise sounds or movements that will ultimately result in well-formed communication signals. Babbling may also serve the function of eliciting parental care (see Chapter 1); responsive caretaking, in turn, may support the production of more well-formed and mature vocalisation in young infants (Locke, 2006).

> **sign languages** types of language used by communities of deaf individuals that rely on manual gestures and facial expressions.

## 2.3.3   Tuning into the native language

We can conclude from the findings on infant babbling that the gradual development of speech production mirrors the gradual development of speech perception, albeit on a much longer timescale. So how then do infants come to improve their native-language abilities while gradually losing their non-native abilities? One explanation suggests that the increase in cognitive control that brings about the ability to inhibit irrelevant information is what leads to the consolidation and refinement of native-language speech discrimination abilities and the gradual loss of non-native abilities (Werker & Pegg, 1992). However, some non-native speech sounds, for example certain click contrasts present in several African languages, can still be perceived by older infants and adults. Other contrasts, for example, the difference between the English interdental fricative [ð] as in *there* and the alveolar stop [d] as in *dare*, appear to be very difficult to learn and are mastered fairly late even if they are in the infant's native language. To account for this, other researchers have linked decline in non-native sensitivity to similarity in articulatory gestures (Best & McRoberts, 2003). Phonetic contrasts that require different gestures made by the same organ (e.g. the lips) are more difficult to distinguish than contrasts that require gestures of different organs (e.g. the lips and the larynx). Thus, as infants grow more attuned to the articulatory gestures of their native language, their perception of contrasts requiring different gestures in organs that are used for native contrasts will decline, because such contrasts will be assimilated by sound categories based on the familiar, native articulatory gestures. At the same time, infants may retain the ability to distinguish phonemes based on gestures involving different articulatory organs (such as the African clicks for English-learning infants). Finally, Kuhl and colleagues argue that learning of phonemic categories is related to experience: phonemes of the ambient language will 'warp' perceptual space and act like perceptual magnets. As an example, consider the continuum of possible voice onset times (VOTs) discussed earlier (Kuhl et al., 2008). In a language like English, the VOTs an infant is exposed to in bilabial plosives (the phonemes /b/ and /p/) will cluster around 0ms (for /b/) or 50ms (for /p/), even though there will be variability around these values associated with different allophones and different speaker characteristics. Over time, sounds with VOTs between those two values will be 'attracted' by the prototypes, gradually strengthening infants' representations of the phonemes /b/, and /p/ and resulting in improvement of native discrimination abilities. As their perception of the English contrast is fine-tuned, infants lose their ability to perceive contrasts that involve other ranges of the continuum, such as between negative VOTs and VOTs around 0ms, as in Spanish. For a 10-month-old infant attuned to English, both of the Spanish bilabials, /p/ as in *peso* and /b/ as in *beso,* would be attracted by the perceptual magnet /b/, leading to a decline in their discrimination of the non-native Spanish contrast.

Kuhl and her colleagues asked whether measures of infants' sensitivity to native and non-native contrasts at 6 to 12 months of age were predictive of language-learning outcomes at 2 to 3 years of age (Kuhl et al., 2008). Native and non-native phonetic discrimination ability was tested either with a headturn conditioning paradigm (see Methodology Box 2.1) or an oddball detection paradigm used to elicit a mismatch negativity (Näätänen et al., 1997). Language development at 2 and 3 years of age was assessed with the MacArthur–Bates Communicative Development Inventory (CDI), an established measure of early vocabulary size (described in greater detail in Methodology Box 4.1). Kuhl et al.'s (2008) crucial finding was that sensitivity to native contrasts as measured by the conditioned headturn procedure

**MacArthur–Bates Communicative Development Inventory (CDI)** a parental checklist that measures vocabulary development in infants and toddlers.

and by the amplitude of the mismatch negativity was positively correlated with future language abilities at age 2 to 3 years. In contrast, the same measures obtained for non-native contrasts were negatively correlated with future language abilities. A plausible interpretation of this finding is that the extent to which an infant can discriminate native contrasts reflects the degree of neural commitment to native language patterns. Conversely, the extent to which an infant can still discriminate non-native contrasts reflects the degree to which the brain has remained uncommitted to native language patterns. It is assumed that for neural commitment to take place a mapping between the sensory templates of speech sounds and the motor programmes by which these sounds are created needs to be forged; such mappings would emerge as infants explore the auditory consequences of their vocalisations. Interestingly, infants normally engage in extended bouts of vocal play during which they produce speech sounds in non-communicative contexts seemingly for their own pleasure (Locke, 1993); these bouts of vocal play may serve the purpose of consolidating links between speech perception and production routines.

A body of research has attempted to specify what kinds of experiences help infants to tune into their native language. In Chapter 1 we described the importance of social interaction for language learning. In the context of phoneme acquisition, the question arises as to whether infants simply absorb the phonological and phonemic properties of their ambient language from overhearing, or whether social interaction is required for this learning to occur. It appears that infants do not easily learn language from overhearing speech on television or in audio recordings. When native speakers of Mandarin Chinese read to and played with 9-month-old infants from English-speaking homes for twelve 25-minute sessions, the infants readily learned to distinguish phonetic contrasts that were unique to Mandarin. However, when other groups of infants were exposed to Mandarin through videotapes or audiotapes of the same twelve sessions, they did not learn the phonetic contrasts (Kuhl, Tsao, & Liu, 2003). These findings led Kuhl et al. (2003) to suggest that language learning in infancy depends crucially on social interaction. There are several important reasons why this might be so. First, human faces provide salient cues that aid in speech recognition. Facial gestures, such as lip and tongue movements, are coordinated in time with speech production. Such synchronised movements capture infants' attention and enhance learning (Gogate & Hollich, 2010). Infants from 2 months of age are able to recognise the facial gestures that co-occur with the production of specific speech sounds (Patterson & Werker, 2003; see also Kuhl & Meltzoff, 1982, 1984, with 3- to 4-month-olds). By 7.5 months of age, infants can use synchonised timing of faces and voices to aid speech perception in contexts where more than one speaker is talking at the same time (Hollich, Newman, & Jusczyk, 2005). Second, face-to-face interactions serve to modulate infant attention and arousal, and provide a context for vocal learning (see Chapter 1). In social interactions, parents respond contingently to their infants' communicative bids, which improves the quality of infant vocalisation (Goldstein & Schwade, 2008). Thirdly, social interaction provides the context for infants to make sense of words (Nelson, 1985; Tomasello, 2003; see Chapters 3 and 4 for further discussions of this topic). As infants come to recognise words, such as their own names (Bortfeld, Morgan, Golinkoff, & Rathbun, 2005), they can begin the task of parsing connected stretches of speech into meaningful units.

# 2.4  HOW DO INFANTS DISCOVER WORDS?

Speech sounds are rarely, if ever, produced in isolation: phonemes are embedded in words, and words are embedded in a continuous stream of speech. Figure 2.4 shows the sound wave of a recording of the sentence *These are speech sounds*. Although the sentence consists of four words, there are no periods of silence visible in the wave. How do infants learn to carve up the speech stream into discrete units if there are no reliable acoustic cues to word boundaries? To illustrate the problem of word segmentation, consider a toddler's utterance *Mummy, take my socks-on off!* This child's error reflects her history of hearing sentences such as *Shall we put your socks on?*, where frequent co-occurrence of *socks* with *on* has prevented correct word segmentation. Despite such occasional mishaps, current evidence suggests that infants are able to integrate many different sources of information that provide reliable cues to word boundaries. In this section, we will review findings that show how and when different types of cues to word boundaries are learned.

## 2.4.1  Distributional information

As described previously, newborns are sensitive to the rhythmic structure of different languages. Sensitivity to rhythm involves sensitivity to the relative durations of vowels and consonants, and duration can also serve as an informative cue to word boundaries. Christophe and colleagues used French words like *mathématicien* and phrases like *format ticket* to see if newborns could distinguish whether the spliced-out part /mati/ came from within a word or from across a word boundary (Christophe, Dupoux,

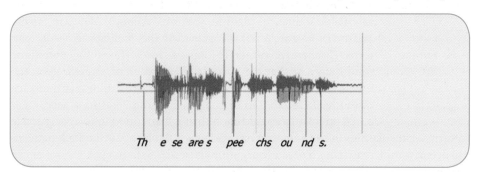

**Figure 2.4**  *Sound wave of the sentence* These are speech sounds.

Bertoncini, & Mehler, 1994). Acoustic measurements revealed that the vowel /a/ and the consonant /t/ tended to be slightly longer at a word boundary compared to within a word. Using the high-amplitude sucking paradigm, Christophe and colleagues showed that 3- to 4-day-old newborns were sensitive to this difference. This suggests that infants are likely to notice the subtle durational differences associated with articulation at word boundaries.

Another factor that aids the process of word segmentation early on is related to the fact that some words in the infants' language input do occur in isolation, most notably infants' own names, which are already recognised at about 5 months of age (Mandel, Juczyk, & Pisoni, 1995). Knowing the boundaries of a familiar word, like one's name, helps to segment adjacent words, and infants show evidence for this already at 6 months of age (Bortfeld et al., 2005).

At around 8 months of age, infants start using distributional information, more specifically, information about sequences of syllables, to aid them in word segmentation. Specific syllable combinations will occur often in speech to children because those sequences comprise frequently used words. Consider the following example given by Saffran, Aslin, and Newport (2006). If a child repeatedly hears the word *pretty* in phrases such as *pretty baby*, *pretty dress*, *pretty doll*, and so on, the probability that the syllable *pre* is followed by the syllable *ty* will be quite high. In contrast, the probability that the syllable *ty* is followed by the syllable *ba*, as in *pretty baby* is fairly low, as many different syllables follow a word-final syllable like *ty*. In other words, syllables within words and across word boundaries differ in their transitional probabilities. In a famous study, Saffran et al. (1996) demonstrated that 8-month-olds were able to keep track of transitional probabilities and use them for word segmentation: after listening for 2 minutes to a continuous sequence of syllables like *golabupabikututibu-babupugolabu* in which pseudowords (such as *golabu* or *pabiku*) were repeatedly spoken, infants listened longer to strings like *bupabi* and *kutuki* which straddled a 'word' boundary than to pseudowords like *golabu*. Given that there were no breaks between words in the speech stream, for infants to have registered sequences like *bupabi* as 'unfamiliar' relative to *golabu*, they must have relied on the differences in transitional probabilities between versus within pseudowords.

Further studies by Saffran and her colleagues demonstrated that statistical learning of transitional probabilities extends to tone sequences as well as syllable sequences (Saffran, Johnson, Aslin, & Newport, 1999), and other researchers have extended the findings to visual patterns (Kirkham, Slemmer, & Johnson, 2002). Taken together, these results suggest that the ability to keep track of sequences of elements relies on a general learning mechanism rather than a mechanism specifically tied to language acquisition. Statistical learning is based on invariance detection through attention to relatively stable patterns or regularities in the environment (Gogate & Hollich, 2010). Such patterns can occur within a modality, as in auditory stimuli used by Saffran et al. (2006), or can occur across modalities, as in the synchronised faces and voices used by Hollich et al. (2005). Statistical learning of sequences impacts various aspects of language acquisition, such as learning of morphology and syntax (as will be discussed in Chapter 5),

**statistical learning**
implicit, procedural learning of probabilistic co-occurrence patterns (e.g. between adjacent and non-adjacent morphemes, speech sounds, letter combinations).

and continues to play a role in language processing throughout the lifespan (Conway, Bauernschmidt, Huang, & Pisoni, 2010); see Methodology Box 11.1 for a description of tasks used to study statistical learning of sequential patterns.

## 2.4.2 Prosodic and phonological cues

Statistical learning of syllable sequences, albeit a powerful cue to word boundaries, is more reliable for certain languages than others. For example, differences in transitional probabilities of syllables within and between words are not a useful cue if words are predominantly monosyllabic. However, languages provide other cues that can facilitate the detection of word boundaries, even if each of these cues is less than 100 per cent reliable. From early on, infants are sensitive to the rhythmic properties of their native language. Cutler (1994) has suggested that infants might use a metrical segmentation strategy to locate word boundaries – that is, use the predominant stress pattern of their language as a cue to word onsets. In English, the majority of bisyllabic content words exemplify a trochaic (strong–weak) stress pattern. Infants exposed to English will hear trochaic words in isolation, such as nicknames like *Patty* or *Sammy*, or diminutives like *teddy* or *bunny*, and may generalise the pattern to new words. Jusczyk, Houston, and Newcombe (1999) have shown that by 7 to 8 months of age, infants exposed to English use metrical stress as a word onset cue. This leads them to correctly isolate new words like *KINGdom* from the speech stream, but temporarily results in mis-segmentation of words like *surPRISE*, such that *PRISE* is treated as a word. A metrical segmentation strategy would be even more helpful for learning languages with more regular stress patterns than English, such as Hungarian, which always places stress on the first syllable.

> **diminutives** derivational affixes used to modify word forms to express smallness, intimacy, and endearment; diminutives are frequent in the child-directed speech registers of many languages.

Other studies have shown that infants at 9 to 10 months of age can utilise allophonic variation and phonotactic restrictions as cues to word boundaries (Jusczyk, Hohne, & Bauman, 1999; Mattys, Jusczyk, Luce, & Morgan, 1999; Mattys & Jusczyk, 2001). Allophony refers to the different ways in which phonemes are pronounced depending on their position in the word, for example, as in *night rate* versus *nitrate* (Hohne & Jusczyk, 1994). In English, certain consonants such as /p/ or /t/ are aspirated (produced with a puff of air) at the beginning of a word, but not at the end; this feature of English renders an aspirated [pʰ] or [tʰ] a highly informative indicator of a word onset. Phonotactics concerns the possible ways that phonemes can be sequenced in a language. Phonotactic restrictions are language-specific and tend not to reflect ease of pronunciation. For example, English words never begin with the sequence /nt/, but often end with /nt/, which renders the phoneme combination /nt/ a reliable indicator of an upcoming word boundary. Other sequences, such as /mk/, almost always occur between words (and never as word onsets or offsets), providing further indicators of word boundaries.

Although none of these cues is sufficiently reliable to solve the word segmentation problem on its own, infants can successfully use them in combination. The way the cues are weighted in combination changes over time, reflecting the increasingly sophisticated perceptual capabilities of infants. For example, around 6 months of age, infants prioritise transitional probabilities over metrical stress, whereas stress becomes dominant over transitional probabilities at around 9 months. This suggests that infants' earliest word segmentation efforts are made possible by a domain-general statistical learning mechanism. Once infants have accumulated enough word forms to be able to detect their predominant stress patterns, statistical learning is supplemented by the use of metrical stress information. These cues are then further supplemented by information about language-specific phonotactic and allophonic variation.

Of course, many of the recurrent sequences that children may come to recognise in speech will not be words in the adult sense. The challenge for the child is to map the segmented units onto entities in the outside world. It appears that prosodic information may facilitate this process. Shukla, White, and Aslin (2011) showed that 6-month-old infants were more likely to map non-words consisting of two syllables with high transitional probability onto an object if these non-words were aligned with prosodic information pertaining to larger units like utterances or phrases. These larger units are separated by prosodic boundaries, which are characterised by a lowering of pitch and a lengthening of the preceding speech sounds. If a non-word was initially presented embedded in a stream of syllables but followed by a prosodic boundary, infants looked at the object more often when encountering that non-word again in isolation than if the non-word originally had straddled a prosodic boundary. Apparently, infants may find it easier to segment and learn words when they occur under natural prosodic conditions. The transition – from simply noticing recurrent units in the speech stream to recognising words as conveying meanings and referring to entities in the outside world – occurs in the context of the infant's interactions with others, a topic that will be covered in detail in Chapters 3 and 4.

**prosodic boundaries**
end of a prosodic unit (i.e. a stretch of speech with a distinct prosodic contour); boundaries are often marked by a lowering of pitch and a lengthening of the preceding speech sounds.

## SUMMARY

- **Languages differ in phonemic inventories, phonotactic constraints, and prosody. Infants have to learn these language-specific sound patterns.**

- **Neonates are sensitive to the rhythm of language. They can differentiate familiar languages from unfamiliar ones based on prenatal experience.**

- **Neonates are also able to distinguish unfamiliar languages that are sufficiently different in rhythm.**

- Around 6 months of age, infants are able to distinguish phonetic contrasts from many languages other than their ambient language. This ability is lost around 9 months of age as native phonemes become more entrenched.

- Around 6 months of age, infants also start to produce strings of syllables, which at first are reduplicative but then become more variegated.

- Although infants' repertoire of vocalisations may include sounds not found in the ambient language, their babbling gradually starts to approximate the ambient language. Babbling allows infants to practise articulatory movements required to produce target sounds.

- Greater sensitivity to native phonemes is linked to faster language development, indicating greater neural commitment to the native language. Greater sensitivity to non-native phonemes is linked to slower language development.

- The acquisition of phonetic contrasts is facilitated by face-to-face interaction in which caregiver responses are contingent upon infant vocalisations.

- At around 8 months of age, infants learn to track transitional probabilities between syllables, which are informative with respect to word boundaries.

- Sensitivity to transitional probabilities between syllables is subsequently supplemented by sensitivity to metrical stress, allophonic variation, and phonotactic constraints, all of which can be used in combination thereby providing heuristic cues for solving the word segmentation problem.

# FURTHER READING

## *Key studies*

For changes in phoneme perception abilities over the first year of life, read Werker, J. F. & Tees, R. C. (1984). Cross-language speech perception: Evidence for perceptual reorganisation during the first year of life. *Infant Behavior and Development, 7,* 49–63.

Republished in 2002 with three commentaries for their special 25th anniversary issue: *Infant Behavior and Development, 25* (1), 121–133.

For effects of the ambient language on babbling, read Lee, S. A. S., Davis, B. & MacNeilage, P. (2010). Universal production patterns and ambient language in babbling: A cross-linguistic study of Korean- and English-learning infants. *Journal of Child Language, 37,* 293–318.

For a very influential study on word segmentation abilities in infants, read Saffran, J. R., Aslin, R. N. & Newport, E. L. (1996). Statistical learning by 8-month-old infants. *Science, 274* (5294), 1926–1928.

## Overview articles

If you want to know more about the neuroscience of infant speech perception, read Kuhl, P. K. & Rivera-Gaxiola, M. (2008). Neural substrates of early language acquisition. *Annual Review of Neuroscience, 31*, 511–534.

For a concise overview of statistical learning in word segmentation, read Saffran, J. R. (2003). Statistical language learning: Mechanisms and constraints. *Current Directions in Psychological Science, 12*, 110–114.

## Books

For a detailed coverage of studies of infant phoneme perception and word segmentation using the preferential headturn procedure that have been conducted in the 1980s and 1990s, read Jusczyk, P. (1997). *The discovery of spoken language.* Boston, MA: MIT Press.

# Support Language Development?

## KEY TERMS

- autism spectrum disorder (ASD) • autobiographical memory • babbling • baby sign programmes • communicative intentions • conventional gestures • declarative memory • deferred imitation • deictic gestures • Down syndrome • emotive gestures • emphatic gestures • epistemic triangle • gaze following • generalised imitation • iconic gestures • joint attention • over-imitation • predicate–argument structure • pretend play • recognitory gestures • ritualisation • role-reversal imitation • sign languages • social referencing • statistical learning • symbolic gestures • symbolic reference • triadic interactions • word-to-world mapping

# CHAPTER OUTLINE

Learning to relate the sounds of language to entities in the outside world is a process that is embedded in a rich network of social interactions, aided by cognitive advances that take place during the first two years of life. In this chapter, we discuss how infants' social and cognitive development interacts with their growing ability to communicate with other people about the world around them.

# 3.1   WHAT DO INFANTS LEARN FROM INTERACTING WITH OTHERS?

## 3.1.1   Incorporating the environment into the interaction

In Chapter 1, we described how infants use vocalisation, mutual gaze, and facial expressions to engage with others in reciprocal social interaction during the first months of life. By 2 months of age, infants exhibit responsiveness, contingency, timing, and turn-taking in their dyadic interactions with caregivers. By 9 to 10 months of age, infants no longer spend the majority of their waking hours in face-to-face interactions with others. At this point in time, interactions with others serve to draw the infant's attention to interesting objects and events in the environment. That is, infants move

**Figure 3.1**   *During the first year of life, caregivers and infants begin to engage in triadic forms of interaction that incorporate objects of mutual interest.*

*Source:* © Khamidulin Sergey. Used under licence from Shutterstock.

from primarily dyadic forms of interaction devoted to establishing emotional rapport with their caregivers to triadic interactions that include entities in the environment (see Figure 3.1). These triadic interactions involve communication between the child and another person about the child's experience with a referent in the outside world, as well as the other person's experience with the same referent. This constellation, which involves the child, her interlocutor, and a referent, can be viewed as a form of epistemic triangle (Carpendale & Lewis, 2004; Chapman, 1991). The establishment of such a triangle (see Figure 3.2) marks an important milestone in the development of a child's social understanding, and constitutes the essential setting for referential communication to occur. This transition from dyadic to triadic forms of interaction has also been described as a move from primary intersubjectivity of the sort described in Chapter 1 to secondary intersubjectivity, that is, communication with others about something in the world (Trevarthen & Hubley, 1978). As mentioned in Chapter 1, there is much discussion in the evolutionary psychology literature about how and why the ability for referential communication as a form of cooperative behaviour has come about – the interested reader is referred to Richerson and Boyd (2004) and Hrdy (2009). Here, we will focus on describing the social and cognitive abilities that support the emergence of referential communication at the end of the infant's first year of life.

**triadic interactions** communicative interactions between two individuals involving joint attention to entities (object, events) in the world.

**epistemic triangle** refers to the social context of referential communication (i.e. word learning); for shared meanings to be established, both the child and another person must be mutually attentive to some aspect of the external world.

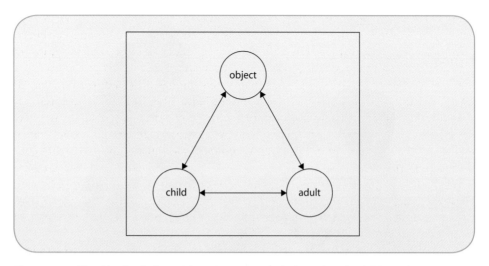

**Figure 3.2** *The triangle of referential communication, which involves the child, another person, an outside referent, and their communication about their experiences with the referent. Note that this triangle does not necessarily imply that the referent has to be present in the here and now.*

## 3.1.2   Understanding social signals

The beginnings of referential communication emerge when infants start perceiving the direction of an adult's gaze as a cue that draws their attention to an object. It has been argued that the white sclera of the human eye, which is camouflaged in the eyes of other primates, allows humans to more clearly signal to others the object that is their current focus of visual attention (Kobayashi & Koshima, 2001); such social signalling is thought to have evolved for the purpose of informing others about one's intentions in the context of cooperative activities. Thus, gaze following is an important human social skill that allows infants to discern the focus of another person's attention. Over time, children gradually come to understand that the eyes provide a looker with an internal representation of the looked-at object.

**gaze following** the ability to visually track where another individual is looking.

Some studies suggest that infants already start following gaze around 4 months of age (Reid, Striano, Kaufman, & Johnson, 2004). Others pinpoint 10 months as the age at which infants first grasp that eye movements, and not just head movements, indicate the direction of gaze. Brooks and Meltzoff (2005) have shown that 10-month-old infants, but not 9-month-olds, are more likely to follow the head movements of a person with open eyes as opposed to a person with closed eyes. This reflects their developing understanding of the importance of the eyes as perceptual organs.

**social referencing** the tendency to look at a significant other (e.g. a caregiver) when faced with an ambiguous situation or stimulus to gain information from the caregiver's reaction about that situation or stimulus.

At around 9 months of age, infants also start to engage in social referencing – that is, they take into account the reactions and facial expressions of their caregiver or another trusted person when trying to establish whether to approach or avoid an unfamiliar object or person (Campos & Sternberg, 1981). At this age, the interpretation of a situation provided by another person factors into the infant's own appraisal of the situation; for example, 10-month-olds are more like to be friendly towards a stranger when their mother has provided positive non-verbal cues than when she has provided neutral cues, or no cues at all (Feinman & Lewis, 1983). Interestingly, 10-month-old infants, but not 7-month-olds, are more likely to seek information from a stranger about a potentially scary object if the stranger is attending to them, as opposed to looking away (Striano & Rochat, 2000). This indicates that by 10 months of age, infants appreciate that gaze is an important cue to the **communicative intentions** of others – that a stranger who is looking at them in the context of a scary object is potentially trying to tell them something about it. Infants' ability to use non-verbal social information about entities in the outside world through gaze following and social referencing is clearly an important building block of referential communication.

Tracking social signals such as eye gaze, facial expression, and vocal affect allows infants to identify which entities are socially as well as culturally relevant. For referential communication to take place, it is important that these entities remain the focus of the infant's attention as he or she engages with others in meaningful activities (Racine & Carpendale, 2007). By 9 months of age, infants show enhanced patterns of attention to objects that are the focus of **joint attention** in comparison to those that are not (Striano, Reid, & Hoehl, 2006). At first, episodes of joint attention tend to be other-led, with adult caregivers either drawing their infant's attention to something of interest, or shifting their own attention to focus on whatever has captured their infant's interest and attention. In doing so, adults transform infant interactions with objects into social interactions. Over time, infants increasingly learn to direct the attention of others (Bakeman & Adamson, 1984), often using gestures as a way of indicating the focus of their interest, as will be described below.

Establishing joint attention is necessary for linking the linguistic utterances that infants hear with entities in the world. Infants who are better at establishing joint attention have more information that can help them to discern the communicative intentions of others, an ability that is crucial for word learning. Indeed, infants' ability to establish joint attention by following adult gaze at 10 months of age has been shown to predict their language abilities at 14 and 18 months of age (Brooks & Meltzoff, 2005). Likewise, in an earlier longitudinal study (Carpenter, Nagell, & Tomasello, 1998), the amount of time infants spent in joint engagement with their mothers, and the mother's use of language to comment on her infant's focus of attention, were strong predictors of infants' communicative development (gesture use and first words). For children with developmental disabilities, such as **autism spectrum disorder (ASD)** or **Down syndrome**, the amount of joint engagement with others is an especially strong predictor of language-learning outcomes (Adamson, Bakeman, Deckner, & Romski, 2009; Bono, Daley & Sigman, 2004; Charman, Baron-Cohen, Swettenham, Baird, Drew, & Cox, 2003). Importantly, it is most advantageous for early word

**autism spectrum disorder (ASD)** developmental disability characterised by social and communicative deficits, restriction of interests, repetitive behaviour.

**Down syndrome** a developmental disability caused by all or part of an extra 21st chromosome; Down syndrome is associated with abnormalities in physical growth and facial characteristics, and with mental retardation.

learning for caregivers to shift their own attention to match their infant's focus of attention, rather than the other way around – presumably because shifts of attention tax infants' limited cognitive capacities. Adults who follow their infant's lead allow infants to devote their cognitive resources to processing the linguistic and perceptual information at hand (Akhtar, Dunham, & Dunham, 1991; Dunham, Dunham, & Curwin, 1993); see also Chapter 4. For children with autism, a disorder characterised by impaired social interaction and communicative development, language outcomes up to age 16 years have been linked to the extent to which caregivers synchronise their own behaviours to match their child's focus of attention and activity (Siller & Sigman, 2002, 2008).

### 3.1.3   Understanding intentions

Even if an adult and an infant are looking at the same object, it may be unclear to the infant what the sounds or gestures emitted by the adult have to do with the object. To understand referential acts of communication, the infant must grasp an intention on the part of the adult to provide relevant information about the object (Sperber & Wilson, 2004). Not all communicative signals require an understanding of intentions – facial expression and vocal affect, for example, can serve as social signals even if they are not intended as such, simply by 'leaking' information about emotional states of others. Reference, in contrast, requires the infant to hone in on what is relevant to communicate in a given context. Pointing gestures, for example, are highly ambiguous communicative acts that can only be understood in a context from which their meaning can be inferred. To understand a pointing gesture one has to understand *why* the person is pointing at something. If a child enters the room and her mother points to a cup on the table this can mean a myriad of things, such as *I poured some milk for you to drink* or *Could you bring me that cup so I can put it in the sink?* But if the child had previously been asking for something to drink, then the gesture can be interpreted as pointing towards the desired drink. At around 14 months of age, infants are able to use shared experience and common knowledge to interpret ambiguous communicative signals like pointing. For example, when 14-month-olds were playing a tidy-up game with an adult and the adult then pointed at a toy, the infants would tidy up the toy, acknowledging the shared experience of the game. If, however, another adult, who was not involved in the tidy-up game, pointed at the same toy, the infants were much less likely to tidy it up (Liebal, Behne, Carpenter, & Tomasello, 2009). This indicates that infants at 14 months are able to take into account knowledge shared with their interlocutors and interpret pointing gestures accordingly.

Some aspects of the ability to read others' intentions seem to emerge even earlier: in one study, 9-month-olds, but not 6-month-olds, were able to distinguish whether an expected transaction failed because the adult was unwilling or unable to hand over the object (Behne, Carpenter, Call, & Tomasello, 2005); infants reacted with less frustration when failure to hand over the desired object was due to inability rather than unwillingness, for example if the object was dropped accidentally or the adult was distracted. Moreover, at 9 months infants start to recognise when another person is intentionally imitating their own actions (Agnetta & Rochat, 2004). The ability to infer intended actions develops more fully by 18 months: when infants at this age observed an adult trying to perform an unfamiliar action, but failing to complete it, they completed the action themselves when given the objects to manipulate – thus displaying clear evidence of having understood the adult's intentions (Meltzoff, 1995).

The evidence discussed so far suggests that there is a period at around 9 to 10 months of age when important social and cognitive abilities like gaze following, social referencing, and grasp of communicative intentions all come together. These abilities set the stage for the child to produce his or her first referential acts of communication. It is therefore not surprising that the first words a child utters follow shortly thereafter, at around 12 months of age.

### 3.1.4   Learning to imitate

In Chapter 1 we summarised research findings that neonates can imitate facial expressions (Meltzoff & Moore, 1977) and speech sounds (Chen, Striano, & Rakoczy, 2004). Building on this ability, many infants and caregivers engage in considerable bouts of reciprocal vocal imitation over the first months of life. These vocal imitation games serve primarily to consolidate emotional rapport, social affiliation, and

**Figure 3.3**   *Young infants readily imitate the vocalisations, facial expressions, and gestures of others.*

*Source:* © Kletr.  Used under licence from Shutterstock.

intersubjectivity. At the same time, mothers tend to selectively imitate the more complex aspects of their infants' vocalisations as they appear in their repertoires; maternal imitations contain more accurate pronunciations of the speech sounds of the ambient language, and provide infants with appropriately challenging vocal templates to match in their subsequent vocalisations (Papoušek & Papoušek, 1989). By acting as if their infants are able to match these templates, mothers first and foremost teach them to imitate, as if acknowledging the importance of vocal imitation for language development. Indeed, infants' ability for vocal imitation of vowels early in life serves as the foundation for their later acquisition of other speech sounds (Kuhl & Meltzoff, 1996).

Imitation, of course, is not confined to the speech modality; see Figure 3.3. Infants increasingly imitate the gestures and actions of others (see Chapter 6 for a description of the special qualities of gestures produced by caregivers). Over the course of the first year, as infants acquire an understanding of others as intentional and goal-directed agents, they start imitating others' actions to learn about objects and events in the world (Užgiris, 1981). At the end of the first year, infants will even copy quite silly actions if these actions appear to be intended by the adult (Schwier, van Maanen, Carpenter, & Tomasello, 2006). At the same time, 1 year-olds are able to focus on accomplishing the goal of an action rather than faithfully copying the means by which this goal was achieved (Nielsen, 2006). This suggests that at the end of the first year, infants have developed a flexible understanding of the environmental constraints that may necessitate certain actions, as well as of the internal motives of agents that may lead them to choose certain actions over others.

However, over the second year of life infants gradually become more faithful in their imitations. Unlike 12-month-olds, 18-month-olds (and especially 24-month-olds) do not just emulate the goal of an action, but tend to copy all the specific action components modelled by an adult (Nielsen, 2006). By 3 years of age and beyond, children demonstrate a behaviour termed *over-imitation* – the tendency to copy even those action components that are quite obviously irrelevant to the attainment of a goal, such as tapping the side of a jar with a feather before unscrewing the lid (Lyons, Young, & Keil, 2007). Over-imitation does not occur in chimpanzees and, thus, seems to be a uniquely human behaviour (Horner & Whiten, 2005). Several explanations have been suggested for why human children over-imitate. Over-imitation may reflect children's tendency to encode all actions performed by an adult as causally necessary for goal attainment, a strategy that may be beneficial for learning about how things work but which can lead to erroneous assumptions in the case of irrelevant actions (Lyons et al., 2007). However, when children over-imitate in situations in which the causality of all actions is made transparent, this is more likely a manifestation of prescriptive norm learning (Kenward, Karlsson, & Persson, 2011). Thus, a better explanation is that over-imitation occurs because children perceive others as intentional agents and assume that there must be a reason for performing seemingly unnecessary actions. Indeed, at 18 months of age, infants were more likely to over-imitate a demonstrator's idiosyncratic action style if they had been shown the outcome of the action previously. Already knowing the outcome seemingly made the action style more socially relevant (Southgate, Chevallier, & Csibra, 2009).

> **over-imitation** faithful reproduction of a modelled action, to include wasteful or unnecessary details that are irrelevant to the goal of the action.

Over-imitation, it has been argued, serves the purpose of promoting social learning, as it allows children, and even adults, to acquire social norms and conventions (McGuigan, Makinson, & Whiten, 2011). It is this latter aspect of over-imitation that may play a role in language learning. After all, language is a system of arbitrary signs that are linked to meanings by social convention (see Chapter 11 for further discussion of how systems of linguistic conventions, such as new languages, might emerge). By being unquestioning imitators of adult behaviours, young children may be well equipped to acquire all sorts of cultural conventions, including the languages used in their communities.

# 3.2 WHAT DO INFANTS LEARN ABOUT THE WORLD?

A fundamental property of language is that in the majority of instances words do not label individual objects or entities, but refer to categories of things (i.e. concepts). A cup is a *cup* regardless of its colour, material, or size. Even proper nouns, which refer to specific people or places, refer to these individuals over time and space (i.e. including various representations of the individual as in drawings or photographs). In Chapter 4 we will chart the trajectory along which infants learn the words of their language, and in Chapter 8 we will discuss how learning a specific language can shape one's conceptual representations. In this section, we briefly discuss what conceptual knowledge infants bring to the table at the outset of word learning. What do infants know about the world at the time when they start engaging in acts of reference?

## 3.2.1 Knowledge about objects

In episodes of joint engagement with toys, infants and caregivers have access to the various objects present in the here and now. When a caregiver says *Give me the ball* in a situation where a ball is physically present, the child merely has to work out which toy to hand over. However, much of conversation refers to objects or activities that are not present, for example when a mother asks *Where is your teddy bear?* or *Shall we take a bath?* In these situations, a link needs to be made between an utterance and an internal representation of an object (the teddy bear), or an event (taking a bath). For these links to develop, infants need to be able to store conceptual representations of objects and activities in memory. Do prelinguistic infants have such conceptual representations of the world?

The answer to this question comes from several lines of research that exploit infants' ability to imitate actions, as described above. One technique uses **deferred imitation**: infants watch an adult perform an action and later are given an opportunity to imitate the

> **deferred imitation**
> imitation of another person's behaviour without cueing; requires a delay between the child observing the action-to-be-imitated and the child's imitation of it.

**declarative memory**
one of two types of long-term memory (the other being procedural memory); comprises memory for facts and knowledge that can be consciously recalled.

**generalised imitation**
the ability to imitate a modelled action using a new set of objects.

action. If they are able to do so after a delay then they must have retained some representation of the event in memory. Because the infants are not given the opportunity to practise the actions, the representations they rely on for deferred imitation must be stored in their declarative memory, the memory system that contains various facts and knowledge about the world that can be consciously recalled. Deferred imitation studies show that by 9 months of age, infants can imitate simple actions, like pushing a hidden button on a box to elicit a sound, after a 24-hour delay (Meltzoff, 1988a). By 14 months, infants can imitate even after one week (Meltzoff, 1988b), and they can do so even if the action is novel and would never occur in their normal environment.

Another technique uses generalised imitation to study the conceptual representations of prelinguistic infants. In this technique, an action is demonstrated using a specific object, for example, a toy replica of a dog is given a drink from a little cup. The infant is then given the opportunity to imitate the action with a new object; for example, the infant is given the little cup along with two other toys, a bird and an airplane. Will the infant attempt to give the bird a drink from the cup? Will he or she also give the airplane a drink? The generalised imitation technique sheds light on infants' conceptual understanding about the properties of different entities – do infants know that animals drink but vehicles do not? If infants imitate the drinking action more often with the bird than with the airplane then this suggests that they distinguish the properties of animals and vehicles conceptually (Mandler & McDonough, 1998). Indeed, at around 14 months of age, infants readily generalise the action of drinking from a cup to various other animals, but not to vehicles or items of furniture; they likewise generalise another action (starting an engine with a key) to other vehicles but not to animals.

Finally, infants' conceptual understanding can be studied by observing the ways in which they manipulate objects. When given several toy replicas from one category (e.g. small plastic animals) to play with, followed by a toy replica from another category (e.g. a vehicle), 7-month-olds will inspect and manipulate the vehicle for longer, which indicates that they have distinguished it from the animals. It is unlikely that such differentiation between animals and vehicles is based solely on perceptual features: at 9 months of age, infants differentiate birds and airplanes, which are perceptually similar, but fail to differentiate dogs and fish, which are perceptually quite distinct (Mandler, 2004). That is, at this age, infants do not yet conceptually distinguish different basic-level categories of animals such as dogs, cats, and birds (Mandler & McDonough, 1993), despite the fact that they can perceptually distinguish them from at least 3 months of age (Quinn & Eimas, 1996; Quinn, Eimas, & Rosenkrantz, 1993; Quinn, Eimas, & Tarr, 2001).

### 3.2.2  Knowledge about actions and events

From birth, infants participate in the activities of daily life, such as bathing, napping, getting dressed, and being fed; these activities have a predictable script-like structure which forms the basis for infants' earliest memories of the days of their lives (Nelson, 1986; Nelson & Gruendel, 1986). Although preverbal infants cannot yet recall specific details of individually experienced events (see Chapter 8 for a discussion of the emergence of autobiographical memory), their schematic representations of recurring events allow them to make sense of what people are doing (i.e. to infer their goals) and to anticipate future actions (Bauer, 2006; Nelson, 2007).

**autobiographical memory** assemblage of memories of personally experienced events.

As mentioned above, infants at 18 months of age tend to represent people's actions in terms of goals; they will imitate the goal of an action even if the demonstrator was unable to achieve the goal (Meltzoff, 1995). When do goals become such a prominent aspect of infants' representations of actions? Even at around 12 months of age, infants tend to preferentially represent the goal rather than the source of an action. For example, when first shown a duck moving out of a bowl and onto a block, infants tended to look longer at the duck moving towards a new goal in the same location than at the duck moving to the same goal in a new location (Lakusta, Wagner, O'Hearn, & Landau, 2007). This suggests that infants find the goal of an action to be more salient than its location. This goal bias can even be observed with self-propelled inanimate objects (Luo & Baillargeon, 2005). At 12 months of age, infants also recognise when actions have similar goals, even when there are salient dissimilarities among the actions, such as in the manner of motion of an entity towards its goal (Olofson & Baldwin, 2011). It has been suggested that infants parse continuous actions by imposing boundaries that correlate with the initiation and completion of intentions (Baldwin, Baird, Saylor, & Clark, 2001); this bias leads infants to look longer at events that are disrupted in the midst of an actor's pursuit of a goal, in comparison to events that are disrupted after the goal has been reached.

Thus, infants at around their first birthday seem to have considerable conceptual knowledge of global object categories (e.g. animals, plants, vehicles, and furniture) and differentiate the components of basic actions (e.g. sources and goals). This conceptual knowledge is evident at a much earlier age than was proposed in classical theories of cognitive development (Piaget, 1952). Some scholars have theorised that the ability to form these basic conceptual representations is part of innate core systems for representing objects and actions. These core systems are assumed to belong to the universal cognitive endowment of humans, but may also be present in non-human primates and possibly other animals as well (Spelke & Kinzler, 2007). Others have cautioned that many of the conceptual generalisations that infants make in experiments can be explained through statistical learning of the perceptual features of various category exemplars (Mareschal & Quinn, 2001). The debate as to whether cognitive development during infancy involves the re-description of perceptual information to arrive at conceptual representations (Karmiloff-Smith, 1992), or whether category learning in the absence of language just constitutes gradual enrichment of perceptual similarity information (Sloutsky, 2003), is still very much ongoing.

Leaving aside questions about the mechanisms underlying early category formation, we can ask whether these fairly global distinctions are useful when it comes to word learning. After all, caregivers rarely use words like *animal* or *vehicle*; instead, they tend to label objects at a more basic level using words like *cat, dog, car,* or *truck*. Indeed, for the mapping of concepts to words to succeed, infants must have categories available at varying levels of abstractness. Mandler (2004) suggests that infants make conceptual distinctions among the various vehicles (e.g. ones that are on the ground versus ones that are in the air) only at 20 months of age, and for animals only at 24 months. However, as we will see in Chapter 4, children acquire the names of basic-level categories (e.g. *dog, cat, car, truck*) well before they reach their second birthday, which suggests that rich conceptual knowledge is not necessary for successful word learning, and that perceptual categories are sufficient for word-to-world mapping. Thus, while early conceptual representations may set the stage for language learning, exposure to language may subsequently facilitate and shape the development of conceptual representations (see also Chapter 8).

> **word-to-world mapping** the process of associating words with their referents in the world.

## 3.3   WHAT IS THE ROLE OF GESTURES IN LANGUAGE DEVELOPMENT?

The development of spoken language is accompanied and supplemented by non-linguistic forms of communication. In this section, we explore how facial and gestural communication develop in tandem with speech and how they foster interactive exchanges that provide the basis for understanding the essence of communication and meaning.

Gestures play a crucial role in the onset of intentional communication as they precede and accompany spoken language. Over the first two years of life infants learn to produce a wide variety of manual and full-body gestures to communicate with others (Blake, Vitale, Osborne, & Olshansky, 2005). Some gestures are emotive gestures (e.g. clapping hands, jumping, or bouncing up and down), others are used for protest or refusal (e.g. using hands to push things away, shaking one's head from side-to-side), others are used to request help (e.g. pointing at an out-of-reach object, handing an object to someone to open or fix), and others are used to comment on states of the world (e.g. pointing at pictures in a book, holding up an object for others to see). Some gestures are symbolic gestures, in the sense that the gesture has a specific meaning (e.g. finger to lips = 'be quiet'), others are emphatic gestures and are used to stress a particular word or idea one is saying (e.g. putting one's fist in

> **emotive gestures** hand and body movements that express emotion, such as jumping up and down, or stamping one's feet.

> **symbolic gestures** communicative hand and body movements associated with specific meanings; encompasses iconic, conventional, and deictic gestures.

> **emphatic gestures** hand and body movements that punctuate a speaker's message (i.e., are used to emphasise a point).

one's hand while making a point) or to express uncertainty (e.g. shrugging one's shoulders).

### 3.3.1   Development of gestures

One of the first gestures to appear in infancy is pointing (see Figure 3.4). Even very young infants (3-month-olds) may extend an index finger with the other fingers curled up (Fogel & Hannan, 1985; Hannan & Fogel, 1987). These early 'points' appear to be non-social orienting behaviours, that is, akin to reaching to touch objects of interest (Carpendale & Carpendale, 2010). Later, at around 8 to 11 months of age, infants begin to use pointing to reference or 'pick out' interesting objects to show others. In such situations, the infant actively seeks to establish joint attention with their communicative partner, and will alternate looks to their partner with pointing, as if to check whether their partner is noticing the object of interest. It is important to note here that the conventional form of pointing, like other gestures, varies considerably across cultures, with some communities pointing with their lips (Enfield, 2001; Sherzer, 1972), and others using other hand shapes besides index-finger pointing (Kita, 2003). Just as they learn to follow the linguistic conventions of their communities, children also learn how to gesture in culturally appropriate ways.

Infants not only point to communicate their interests to others, but they also point to seek help, to request objects out of reach, and to inform or help others achieve their goals (e.g. pointing to where things go when putting away toys or groceries) (Tomasello, Carpenter, & Liszkowski, 2007). Throughout infancy, infants continue to point both non-socially (e.g. pointing while alone) as well as socially. Importantly, infants almost always vocalise while pointing to communicate with others (Franco & Butterworth, 1996; Locke, 2007). That is, prior to producing their first words, infants use vocalisation, such as grunts, as accompaniments to their communicative gestures and actions (McCune, Vihman, Roug-Hillichius, Delery, & Gogate, 1996). These vocalisations reveal the infant's emotional state, for example, their focused attention

**Figure 3.4**   *Pointing, using a variety of hand shapes, is one of the first gestures to appear in infancy.*

*Source:* © Sergiy Bykhunenko. Used under licence from Shutterstock.

**ritualisation** a learning mechanism by which an abbreviated portion of an action sequence comes to elicit a specific response; for example, the infant may use an extended arm gesture to request an out-of-reach object.

**iconic gestures** hand and body movements that physically resemble their referents.

**conventional gestures** culture-specific hand and body movements used to convey specific meanings (e.g. nodding one's head indicates 'yes', shaking one's head indicates 'no' in Western Europe, but not in Greece, Turkey or Bulgaria).

**deictic gestures** hand and body movements, such as pointing, that can only be interpreted in context, because their meaning varies depending on their circumstances of use.

**recognitory gestures** also called nominal gestures, gestural labels or gesture names; realistic play actions on objects, such as holding an empty cup to one's lips or using a spoon to pretend eat.

and urgency when pointing towards an out-of-reach object, and no doubt help the caregiver to grasp their infant's intentions.

From about 8 months of age infants use a variety of gestures that elicit specific responses from their caregivers – for example, an infant might use the 'arms-over-head' gesture as a request to be picked up, or may point with their arm outstretched to request an object. Many of these early gestures are learned through a process of ritualisation (Lock, 1978; Tomasello, 1999), whereby part of an action sequence comes to elicit the target response. For example, an infant who wants to be picked up might attempt to climb up the body of their caregiver; once the caregiver recognises the infant's intentions, he or she may anticipate the infant's goal even before the infant begins to climb. Similarly, an infant may learn to point to request an out-of-reach object – that is, the infant leans forward with an outstretched hand while grunting, and the caregiver responds by retrieving the desired object. Over time the action sequence becomes increasingly abbreviated to create the arms-over-head gesture or the imperative pointing gesture. Ritualised gestures emerge through repeated social interactions whereby the behaviour of one individual shapes the partner's behaviour. Ritualisation does not require the infant to observe another person use the same gesture, nor attempt to imitate their behaviour. (And, needless to say, it would be rather odd for an adult to direct the arms-over-head gesture towards their infant!) As a consequence, an infant might use a ritualised gesture, but might not understand the gesture when others use it (Franco & Butterworth, 1996).

Some of the symbolic gestures infants learn are iconic gestures and physically resemble what they represent (e.g. closing one's eyes and putting one's hands to the side of one's face as a gesture for 'sleeping', flapping one's arms as a gesture for 'bird'), and others are conventional gestures (e.g. nodding one's head for 'yes', shaking one's head for 'no'). Infants learn to use gestures as greetings and as parts of other social routines (e.g. waving goodbye, bowing, giving a 'high-five', clapping), and they use so-called deictic gestures, such as pointing, showing, and offering, to pick out specific referents from the immediate environment. From about 12 months of age, toddlers produce recognitory gestures (also called 'nominal gestures' or 'gestural labels') in which they reproduce a brief action that is associated with a specific object (e.g. holding one's fist next to one's ear as a gesture for 'telephone'; touching an empty cup up to one's lips as a gesture for 'drink') (Bates & Dick, 2002). Toddlers pick up such gestures from their caregivers who produce them alongside words as names for things (Namy, Acredolo, & Goodwyn, 2000). When parents model such gestures, for example blowing on hot food and waving their hand over it to indicate that the food is hot, the gesture is embedded in a rich context that supports the child's interpretation of it. Recognitory gestures are taken up by the child through a process of role-reversal imitation (Tomasello, 1999): by observing their caregiver's gesture, and by grasping their focus of attention and communicative goals, the infant learns to use the same gesture for similar purposes on future occasions, and over time to extend it appropriately to novel circumstances. Toddlers' recognitory gestures become more abstract over time. Initially, such gestures are produced while holding the relevant object (e.g. holding a cup to one's lips for 'drink'); empty-handed gestures appear soon thereafter, first with the child using their hand as a substitute object (e.g. holding one's hand as if it were the cup), and later incorporating an imaginary object (e.g. holding one's hand as if it were grasping the handle of an imaginary cup) (Boyatzis & Watson, 1993).

> **role-reversal imitation** an act of imitation in which the infant assumes the role of the caregiver; for example, the mother performs an action on her son (e.g., touches his nose) and the child subsequently performs the same action back on his mother.

## 3.3.2 The relationship between gesture and speech

From infancy and throughout adulthood, speech and gesture form an integrated system of communication (Bates & Dick, 2002; Iverson & Thelen, 1999; Kendon, 2004; McNeill, 1992). Speakers use their voices, eyes, facial expressions, hands, and body postures all together to communicate, with each modality providing complementary information. Neurological studies confirm that the coordination of the hands and the mouth involves the same motor control system (Gentilucci & Dalla Volta, 2008). Similarly, behavioural studies confirm the role of manual activity in the development of speech (Iverson, 2010). Young infants show increased amounts of vocalisation during bouts of intense limb movements, and their vocalisations vary in quality as they orally and manually explore objects (Bernardis, Bello, Pettenati, Stefanini, & Gentilucci, 2008; Fagan & Iverson, 2007). At 6 to 9 months of age, when infants begin to produce syllable-like consonant–vowel sequences, such as *dada* or *ata* (i.e. babbling, see Chapter 2), they also produce increased amounts of rhythmic hand and arm movements, as well as sound-producing hand banging (Ejiri, 1998; Iverson, Hall, Nickel, & Wosniak, 2007). Infant vocalisations accompanied by body movements are more speech-like, with respect to their acoustic features (e.g. 'syllable' length), than vocalisations without accompanying body movement (Ejiri & Masataka, 2001). As bouts of rhythmic limb movement coincide with vocalisation during infancy, Iverson and Fagan (2004) have suggested that the periodicity of hand and arm movements entrains vocalisation, in effect, synchronising the rhythmic and temporal patterns of speech and gesture. During bouts of hand banging, infants gain practice in producing rhythmically timed actions; they feel and see themselves move and hear the resultant sounds produced. Iverson (2010) has proposed that such experiences in coordinating sensory and motor information (i.e. one's actions and their effects) create perception–action feedback loops that might later help infants to monitor and adjust their articulatory movements in response to hearing their own voice.

### 3.3.3 Gesture as a possible facilitator of language development

In most instances, gestures are used as an accompaniment to vocalisation, both in child speech and in child-directed speech. Caregivers tend to manipulate objects or use deictic gestures, for example pointing at or offering objects, or tracing objects in picture books, at the same time as they label them. These experiences may play a formative role in children's grasp of symbolic reference. Indeed, it has been shown that the onset of pointing to share attention to objects is highly correlated with the age at which infants first comprehend object names (Harris, Barlow-Brown, & Chasin, 1995).

> **symbolic reference** the notion that words and gestures are used to refer to things (i.e., to point out something about the world).

The high degree of iconicity between a recognitory gesture (e.g. putting an empty cup to one's lips) and its referent (*drink*) may help infants to grasp the idea of reference in a situation where the relationship between the symbol and what it stands for is maximally transparent. Grasping the idea that gestures and vocalisations can pick out things in the world paves the way for children to acquire the arbitrary mappings between words and their meanings (Werner & Kaplan, 1963). Toddlers produce recognitory gestures at the same age as they are initially learning names for things, and at the earliest stages of word learning, gestures and words may be used interchangeably to name objects (Iverson, Capirci, & Caselli, 1994). Children who produce greater numbers of recognitory gestures as names for things tend to have larger vocabularies than children who produce fewer such gestures (Acredolo & Goodwyn, 1988); furthermore, the concepts expressed through such gestures tend to enter children's productive vocabularies as words soon thereafter (Iverson & Goldin-Meadow, 2005). Not surprisingly, recognitory gestures tend to drop out of conversational use as toddlers grow their vocabularies. Still, these gestures form the basis for elaborative sequences of pretend play, whereby toddlers use combinations of gestures to support their make-believe games (Figure 3.5). It has been shown that toddlers' ability to engage in pretend play (e.g. using a featureless block as a prop) at 24 months of age predicts their language comprehension at 36 months (O'Reilly, Painter, & Bornstein, 1997); likewise, their comprehension of adult-produced recognitory gestures at 24 months predicts their language comprehension a year later. Other studies with even younger toddlers have similarly shown that better pretend play skills are associated with larger vocabularies (Bates, Bretherton, Snyder, Shore, & Volterra, 1980; Lyytinen, Laakso, Poikkeus, & Rita, 1999; McCune-Nicolich, 1981). These findings suggest that use of recognitory gestures and word learning have similar cognitive requirements – an ability to understand that symbols may stand for objects and actions.

> **pretend play** in an act of pretence, the child creates an imaginary scenario in which an object or person (or an imaginary object or person) takes on the properties and/or roles of another object or person.

Infants seem to first grasp the combinatorial potential of language by combining gestures with words (e.g. pointing at a carton of milk while saying *drink*), and by sequencing gestures to produce gesture combinations (e.g. pointing at a carton of milk followed by the hand-to-mouth drinking gesture). That is, through gesture sequences and gesture + word combinations, children express different aspects of an event, such as the desired object (e.g. milk) and the desired activity (e.g. drink). Such partitioning of complex meanings into component parts forms the basis for the **predicate–argument structure** of language, whereby some words refer to properties and relationships, while other words are used to indicate the entities that have those properties and relationships. Several studies have shown that children's production of gesture + word combinations is a strong predictor of later development in combinatorial speech (Capirci, Iverson, Pizzuto, & Volterra, 1996; Morford & Goldin-Meadow, 1992; Özçalişkan & Goldin-Meadow, 2005, 2009). In particular, toddlers who express different components of

**Figure 3.5** *Toddlers use symbolic gestures in bouts of pretend play, often with a toy replica used in place of a real object.*
*Source:* © emin kuliyev. Used under licence from Shutterstock.

meaning in gesture + word combinations (e.g. pointing at a hat while saying *Mummy*) tend to produce two-word combinations earlier (e.g. *Mummy hat*) than children who express only redundant information in their gesture + word combinations (e.g. pointing at a hat while saying *hat*) (Iverson & Goldin-Meadow, 2005; Morford & Goldin-Meadow, 1992). Furthermore, when one examines different relational meanings, such as possessor + object or action + object, each relational meaning tends to be expressed first in a gesture + word combination (e.g. point at hat + *Mummy*; point at cookie + *eat*) prior to its expression in a two-word combination (e.g. *Mummy hat*; *eat cookie*) (Özçalişkan & Goldin-Meadow, 2005, 2009).

> **predicate–argument structure** the propositional content of an utterance, comprising a set of entities (i.e. arguments) and their relationships and/or properties (i.e. predicates).

Given findings that children use communicative gestures prior to the production of their first words, a parenting movement has emerged in the United States, the United Kingdom and elsewhere that encourages parents to teach their children symbolic gestures as a way of enhancing their communicative skills. In the *Baby Signs* programme (Acredolo & Goodwyn, 1996), parents are encouraged to use an augmentative system of symbolic gestures to communicate with their infants, and in the *Sign with Your Baby* programme (Garcia, 1999), parents teach their infants signs borrowed from American Sign Language or British Sign Language (see Chapter 11 for a description of the **sign languages** of deaf communities). It is important to emphasise that in both programmes, infants are not exposed to a sign language (i.e. a visual/gestural language with a large vocabulary and complex grammar). Instead, infants learn a limited number of symbolic gestures that they can substitute for the spoken words they cannot yet produce. These programmes provide a way for parents to offset their infant's immature speech production – parents can interpret their infant's symbolic gestures even if they cannot make sense of their words. Users of such programmes typically see a peak in the production of baby signs during the second year of life, with a steep drop off at around age two as toddlers start producing more intelligible speech and stop producing their signs (Pizer, Walters, & Meier, 2007).

Although the commercial baby sign programmes were designed to facilitate parent–infant communication and to reduce infant frustration at not being understood, they have been promoted as a means to 'forge bonds of attachment and satisfaction that will last a life time', enabling babies to 'develop skills that actually enrich their comprehension of language' (quotes taken from the back cover of Acredolo & Goodwyn, 1996). It seems that many parents are drawn to these programmes with hopes of accelerating their child's social and language development in preparation for formal schooling. For such parents, it is important to know whether the expected gains from the use of a baby sign programme are worth the considerable investment of time and effort, as well as the expense of attending local baby sign classes.

> **baby sign programmes** parenting movement that advocates the teaching of symbolic gestures to pre-verbal infants.

To date, there is considerable anecdotal evidence that baby sign programmes increase infants' use of communicative gestures (Doherty-Sneddon, 2008): parents are generally enthusiastic to report how their infants use signs to express their needs, desires, and thoughts. In contrast to the positive reviews from families, there is a dearth of scientific evidence that these programmes produce any long-term benefits for language development; for example, a review of 17 training studies found mostly null effects (Johnston, Durieux-Smith, & Bloom, 2005). Indeed, even the research of Goodwyn and Acredolo (1993) reports only modest gains (i.e. less than one month) in the age of first symbol use for infants exposed to an augmentative set of symbolic gestures relative to a control group (see also Goodwyn, Acredolo, & Brown, 2000). These findings are consistent with the work of Folven and Bonvillian (1991), who examined the onset of referential language in children exposed to American Sign Language from birth: although the infants exposed to ASL tended to produce their first signs at very young ages (5 to 6 months of age), their first signs tended to be imitations of adult usage, parts of interactive routines or requests, rather than referential expressions. Infants' first referential signs appeared at about the same age as hearing children begin to name things (at around age 12 to 13 months), which suggests that conceptual understanding of the principle of reference is not advanced through exposure to sign (see also Chapter 11). Furthermore, case studies of three infants in baby sign programmes (Pizer et al., 2007) found that only one infant used the majority of his signs in the context of labelling things. In another family, baby signs were used primarily as a way to encourage politeness; even after the child had learned the words *please* and *thank you*, family members continued to use the PLEASE and THANK YOU signs as a way of discretely prompting the child to use her words. The popularity of baby sign programmes probably reflects contemporary views of the importance of creating a home environment that is conducive to child well being and proper socialisation. Many parents are drawn to baby sign programmes because they are eager to know what their infant is thinking, and they want their infant to participate more actively in family life. How these various child-rearing practices and trends impact language and other aspects of social and cognitive development is an important topic for further study; we will revisit it in Chapter 6.

## SUMMARY

- Towards the end of their first year of life, infants find themselves increasingly in interactions with their caregivers in which they share attention to entities in the outside world. These episodes of joint attention rely on a number of social and cognitive abilities.

  - Infants increasingly excel at reading social signals that are important for the development of referential communication.

  - Infants also learn to understand others as intentional agents. This is an important prerequisite for the interpretation of communicative acts as meaningful.

  - In this context, imitation constitutes an important learning mechanism, not just for honing perceptual and motor skills associated with speech but also, as indicated by the phenomenon of over-imitation, for the faithful copying of social conventions including those inherent in languages.

- Before infants learn their first words they display conceptual knowledge about global object and action categories such as *animal* or *goal*. A gradual refinement of conceptual representations accompanies early word learning.

- Before infants start to speak they use gestures, first to attract their caregivers' attention, but later also in a referential manner. Use of gestures often accompanies early speech and has proven to be of predictive value for future language development, perhaps because gestures tap into the same abilities of referential communication as words.

- Because gesture and speech are similar in establishing symbolic reference, their development goes hand in hand. However, there is no clear evidence that teaching children specific symbolic gestures before the onset of speech, as advocated by the baby sign movement, has facilitating effects on language development.

# FURTHER READING

## *Key studies*

One of the seminal studies on infant imitation is Meltzoff, A. N. (1995). Understanding the intentions of others: Re-enactment of intended acts by 18-month-old children. *Developmental Psychology*, *31*, 838–850.

To better understand research on infant pointing, read Tomasello, M., Carpenter, M. & Liszkowski, U. (2007). A new look at infant pointing. *Child Development*, *78*, 705–722.

## *Overview articles*

For different views on early category formation, read Sloutsky, V. M. (2003). The role of similarity in the development of categorization. *Trends in Cognitive Sciences*, *7*, 246–251 and Mandler, J. M. (2004). Thought before language. *Trends in Cognitive Sciences*, *8*, 508–513.

To understand how prelinguistic categories interact with language, read Clark, E. V. (2004). How language acquisition builds on cognitive development. *Trends in Cognitive Sciences*, *8*, 472–478.

## *Books*

For an overview of how humans learn through imitation, read Meltzoff, A. N. & Prinz, W. (eds) (2002). *The imitative mind: Development, evolution and brain bases*. Cambridge: Cambridge University Press.

# 4 How do Children Learn Words?

# CHAPTER OUTLINE

Once infants start segmenting invariant chunks out of the speech stream, they have to figure out what these chunks of language mean. Over the first two years of life, infants learn that many of these chunks are words that refer to specific entities in the world: they learn that some words pick out individuals, whereas others refer to categories of things; that some refer to objects, and others to actions, events or locations; and that some refer to features or properties of things, whereas others indicate relationships. How do infants identify the specific referents of words given the staggering complexity of the world and the infinite number of possible word meanings? To accomplish the task of word learning, children rely on abilities that emerge during the first year of life: first is the infant's ability to engage with others and to partake in the sociocultural activities of family and community. To determine how patterns of sounds relate to the world around them, infants need to grasp the **communicative** intentions of others – to figure out what meaning is relevant in the context of a particular utterance and situation. Word learning succeeds because infants are motivated to communicate with others and are able to hone in on the communicative goals of others to make sense of their words. Infants are eager to participate in the give-and-take of conversation, and despite their immaturity, they have the social know-how to engage in jointly constructed, collaborative activities that provide the context for early word learning.

Second is the infant's ability to form associations between words and entities in the world. This process of associating words with their referents is referred to as word-to-world mapping. Infants use their conceptual understanding of objects and activities to constrain their hypotheses about the meanings of new words. After an initial slow start, most children, by 18 months of age, show rapid word learning – so-called fast mapping – and become increasingly efficient in identifying the referents of new words. We will explore how expertise in word-to-world mapping is achieved. As infants begin to accumulate words in their vocabularies, they use their skills of statistical learning to find patterns of word structure and co-occurrence; generalisation of these patterns aids vocabulary growth. Many word forms in a language are complex in that they comprise more than one morpheme or unit of meaning. From early on, children learn to segment words into roots and affixes, and to track morphological patterns across words. As they develop their vocabularies, children also register co-occurrence patterns across words to learn the idiosyncratic meanings of word combinations (e.g. *give up* 'quit') and idioms (e.g. *throw in the towel* 'quit'). Co-occurrence patterns play a crucial role in constraining hypotheses about verb meanings, which tend to be underspecified by context. More generally, co-occurrence patterns help children to discern the grammatical status of new words, for example, by helping them to identify a novel word as a noun, verb, or adjective.

> **fast mapping** a process supporting rapid word learning in toddlers; an ability to link a new word to a concept after only a few exposures to the word in an informative context.

> **morpheme** the basic building block of word meaning; the smallest linguistic unit with distinct conceptual meaning.

> **word combinations** sequences of words; some word combinations are idioms (e.g. *give up* 'quit').

> **idioms** types of non-literal expression, in which a word or phrase has a conventional meaning that differs from its literal meaning.

# 4.1 HOW DOES SOCIAL INTERACTION SUPPORT WORD LEARNING?

## 4.1.1 Inferring word meanings from social cues

During infancy, most words are acquired in the context of the infant's joint engagement with others (L. Bloom, 1993; P. Bloom, 2002; Tomasello, 2003). Infants learn words that are associated with the objects, activities, and events that they have interest in. They learn all sorts of words such as *bye, uh-oh, ouch, yum, no, all-gone,* and *up,* in addition to learning the names of important people, pets, and objects such as *Mummy, doggie, bottle,* and *milk* (Tardif, Fletcher, Liang, Zhang, Kaciroti, & Marchman, 2008).

**Figure 4.1** *Toddlers exposed to picture books frequently point at objects of interest, which encourages caregivers to label and describe them.*

*Source:* © Monkey Business Images. Used under licence from Shutterstock.

Caregivers tend to talk about the objects, activities, and events that have captured their infant's interest and attention, at times providing a running commentary on what their infant is doing. In such moments of joint attention (see Chapter 3), the language spoken to the infant matches up with what he or she already has in mind, so that categories and words can be linked together (Mayor & Plunkett, 2010). This match between what is said and what the infant understands is crucial for the child to grasp the meanings of words (Macnamara, 1972). That is, to work out the relationship between a word and its referent requires that the child have a grasp of the speaker's intended meaning.

Bruner and Ninio (Bruner, 1983; Ninio & Bruner, 1978) identified recurrent activities, such as picture book reading, and games, such as *peek-a-boo*, as ritualised contexts for language learning. Turn-taking games like *peek-a-boo* simulate features of conversation, such as role reversal and the use of a conventional vocabulary, in an activity that is highly predictable and enjoyable for the infant. Infants at around 4 months of age begin to grasp the timing and structure of such games (Rochat, Querido, & Striano, 1999), and gradually learn to use the words and gestures of the game to initiate new rounds of play and to keep the game going (Bruner, 1983). In literate societies, picture book reading constitutes another activity for learning the names of things (Ninio & Bruner, 1978; Ninio, 1980); see Figure 4.1. Infants readily learn to point at pictures in books while uttering, for example, *What's that?* or *Dat?*, to elicit from their caregiver the names of the depicted objects. Such routines are advantageous for word learning because the caregiver's choice of words tends to match up with their infant's focus of attention.

Tomasello and his colleagues have conducted numerous experiments demonstrating that children as young as 18 months of age can use an adult's goals, as well as their emotional reactions, to make inferences about the meanings of novel words (see Tomasello [2003] for a comprehensive review of these studies). For example, in one study (Akhtar & Tomasello, 1996, Experiment 1), the adult set out to find a *toma*. Before using the novel word as a label for an unfamiliar object, the adult opened up a set of containers to show the child that an unusual object was in each one. On the crucial trial, the adult announced their intention to get the *toma* and approached a specific container. Although the container was 'locked' and would not open, the toddlers nevertheless associated the word *toma* with the object previously seen in that container. In another study, toddlers used emotional cues to ascertain whether the adult had found the object they desired. The adult announced their search for a *toma*, and then proceeded to open a set of containers, each containing an unusual object (Tomasello, Strosberg, & Akhtar, 1996). As the adult opened each container, she would retrieve the object in it and express disappointment, until she opened a container with an enthusiastic *Ah!* In a subsequent test, toddlers showed learning of *toma* as the name of the desired object. In another study (Tomasello & Akhtar, 1995, Experiment 1), toddlers heard a novel word used in the context of an unfamiliar object involved in an unfamiliar action. If the action had already been performed with a different object, and the unfamiliar object was new to the situation, then children treated the novel word as the name of the object, but if the object had already been played with, and the action was new, then children treated the novel word as the name of the action. This suggests that **discourse novelty** is used as a cue to the referents of novel words.

> **discourse novelty** any aspect of an event (e.g. a novel object or action) that is new information within the context of an ongoing conversation.

Infants initially learn words very slowly (Clark, 1993; Dromi, 1987). The words children learn in the first year of life are the ones they have heard on numerous occasions in the context of daily routines. However, over the second year of life, infants become increasingly skilful at using a variety of cues to infer word meaning. Toddlers use social cues, such as the direction of a speaker's gaze, their gestures, facial expressions, and tone of voice, as well as situational cues, such as the ongoing activity, and the people and objects present in the extra-linguistic context. By 19 months of age, toddlers can use the caregiver's focus of attention to infer what they are talking about; when the caregiver is focused on something different from their own activity, they will use the caregiver's focus of attention to make sense of what has been said (Baldwin, 1993). Toddlers not only pay attention to speech directed to them, but also to speech directed to others (Akhtar, 2005; Akhtar, Jipson, & Callanan, 2001; Oshima-Takane, Goodz & Deverensky, 1996), and overheard speech may be especially helpful for the child to figure out the role reversal underlying usage of personal pronouns such as *you* and *I* (Oshima-Takane, 1988; Oshima-Takane et al., 1996). Even speech directed to a pet potentially supports word learning, as the toddler easily understands when the dog is commanded to *Move, Sit,* or *Stay* (Tomasello, 1992).

## 4.1.2 Inferring word meanings from activities and routines

As infants and their caregivers engage in ordinary activities throughout the day, language serves as an accompaniment to each activity, much as the *Happy Birthday* song accompanies the presentation of a birthday cake and the blowing out of the birthday candles. The language that coincides with the everyday activities of infants tends to be highly repetitive. Moreover, it is strongly focused on the here and the now, in effect helping the infant to anticipate what will happen next (Nelson, 1985, 1986). Infants are motivated to grasp meaning at the utterance level – that is, they try to make sense of the entire utterance, rather than isolate the meanings of individual words (Tomasello, 1999, 2003). As they make sense of utterances as communicative

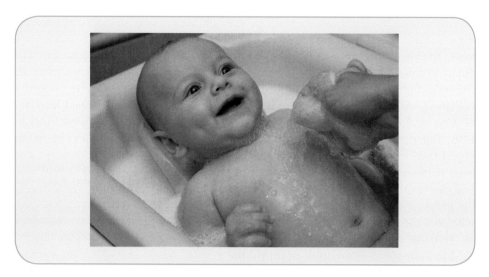

**Figure 4.2** *Children are exposed to words accompanying daily routines such as taking a bath. During such routines, they learn the different contrasts of words belonging to a semantic field.*
*Source:* © Rafal Olechowski. Used under licence from Shutterstock.

acts, they gradually hone in on the meanings of the individual words and the objects, properties, states, and activities to which they refer. Infants' first words are invariably extracted from the activities in which they participate – these words eventually come to stand for or 'represent' all or part of the activity (Barrett, 1983). Words such as *bath* or *beddy-bye* that name important activities are learned as readily as words such as *bottle* or *blanket* that name important objects.

One of the most important features of words is that they apply across situations and are not specifically tied to a particular entity at a particular moment in time. Infants come to appreciate that words apply across situations through their experiences of everyday activities, where the accompanying language is repeated with each recurrence of the activity. For example, the infant may hear their Mummy and Daddy say *bye-bye* each time they leave home, and *night-night* each time they head off to bed. This pairing of words with contexts of use effectively teaches the child that there are conventional ways of talking when engaged in different sorts of activities, and that specific words apply each time the context occurs. As infants grasp more of the language that coincides with familiar and predictable activities, they create semantic fields in which words are related thematically to one another and contrast in meaning; see Figure 4.2. For example, they learn words such as *soap, shampoo, bubbles, wet, water, wash, scrub, hair, face, toes, towel* that designate important components of the bath routine. Learning the meaningful contrasts between words within a semantic field aids the child in learning how words convey distinct entities and their properties and relationships. This partitioning of real-world events into entities, properties, and relationships is fundamental to grasping the predicate–argument structure of language (Braine, 1992; Tomasello, 1999).

> **semantic fields** sets of words that are related in meaning, which are used in reference to particular domains of experience.

### 4.1.3 How caregivers can support word learning

Caregivers are often motivated to communicate with their infants, and can support word learning in a variety of ways. Chapter 6 will describe how variation in the language of caregivers impacts language development; here we take only a cursory look at the myriad ways in which caregivers provide a 'language acquisition support system' that encourages word learning during infancy (Bruner, 1983). Many researchers, following Vygotsky (1978, 1986) and Bronfenbrenner (1986), view caretaking as contributing directly to children's social-cognitive development and emotional well being (Bornstein, 1989; Bornstein, Tamis-LeMonda, Hahn & Hayes, 2008; Bradley et al., 1989): parental responsiveness, emotional warmth, and the provision of stimulating materials and activities correlate with positive learning outcomes for children. Responsive caretaking provides scaffolding that structures social interactions by taking into consideration the changing capabilities of the child (Adamson & Bakeman, 1984; Adamson, 1995). Caregivers often look for stimulating toys and activities to engage their infants. They might bring an interesting object into their young infant's line of sight and move it about to capture his or her attention (Gogate, Bahrick, & Watson, 2000). They might allow the infant to manipulate and mouth the object, and talk about it while their infant is engaged. Responsive caregivers pay attention to what interests their infant and they join in without redirecting their infant's focus of attention. Infants learn more words when caregivers adopt such an attention-following strategy – in effect, following the infant's lead to achieve joint attention – as opposed to an attention-shifting strategy whereby the caregiver attempts to draw their infant's attention to something new – thus requiring the infant to follow their lead (Akhtar, Dunham, & Dunham, 1991; Dunham, Dunham, & Curwin, 1993). As the infant's behavioural repertoire expands, caregivers make adjustments to allow the infant to face challenges and gain mastery in new situations. The expansion in the range of shared experiences provides new opportunities for word learning, as there are new topics and ideas to be explored through conversation.

Throughout infancy and childhood, caregivers support word learning by responding promptly, continently, and appropriately to children's communicative bids (Tamis-LeMonda, Bornstein, & Baumwell, 2001), providing encouragement through speech, physical contact, eye contact, and positive affect. Caregiver responses provide the feedback necessary for infants to gauge the success of their communicative attempts. By repeating what the child has said, by asking questions for clarification, by reformulating utterances, and by elaborating on the topics that interest their child, caregivers provide feedback on the structure and content of their child's speech (Bohannon & Stanowicz, 1988; Moerk, 1991, 1994; Saxton, 2000; Saxton, Houston-Price, & Dawson, 2005). Reformulations, in which the caregiver repeats the child's utterance with minor changes to correct its form, may be especially helpful in teaching children the conventional ways of speaking (Chouinard & Clark, 2003).

Using an unusually dense corpus comprising over 4000 hours of audio/video recordings of an infant's language development from 9 to 24 months of age (i.e. averaging 9.6 hours per day for over 400 days), Roy and colleagues examined how caregivers might scaffold word learning on a word-by-word basis (Roy, Frank, & Roy, 2009). During the recorded period, the researchers traced the 'births' of over 500 words, as measured by the infant's first usage of each word. Then they tracked changes in the mean length of caregiver utterances containing each target word leading up to the day of its birth. Interestingly, caregiver utterances containing a target word decreased in length over the weeks preceding its appearance in the infant's vocabulary, and subsequently increased in length as the infant mastered its usage in the weeks and months to follow. Although these findings need to be confirmed in other families, the results suggest that caregivers are remarkably sensitive to whether an infant understands a given word prior to his or her first use of it. By simplifying the input – for example, by using a target word more often in single-word utterances – caregivers might help infants to isolate a word's form just at the time when the word's meaning has come within reach.

## 4.2 WHEN DO CHILDREN LEARN THEIR FIRST WORDS?

### 4.2.1 Word comprehension

As detailed in Chapter 2, infants begin to extract words from continuous speech well before they have spoken their first words. Starting at around 5 months of age, infants begin to show recognition of a few words, such as their own name and the words *mummy* and *daddy* (Mandel, Jusczyk, & Pisoni, 1995; Tincoff & Jusczyk, 1999); at a slightly older age of 8 months they show long-term (2-week) retention of words heard repeatedly in stories (Jusczyk & Hohne, 1997). At roughly the same age, infants start to form associations between words and their referents. Gogate and her colleagues (Gogate, Bolzani, & Betancourt, 2006; Gogate, 2010) have demonstrated that 6- to 8-month-olds can readily learn pairings of novel words (e.g. *tah* and *gih*) with novel objects if the labelling of each object is synchronised with attention-capturing movement of that object. However, without synchronised movement, infants at 8 months fail to learn the word-to-object mapping, but are successful at 14 months (Werker, Cohen, Lloyd, Casasola, & Stager, 1998). Over the second year of life, infants become increasingly efficient at recognising words and matching them with their referents (Fernald, Perfors, & Marchman, 2006). By 18 months of age they are already able to use partial acoustic information to recognise familiar words. When shown pictures of two objects, such as a dog and a baby, infants will move their eyes to look at the baby even if they have heard only half of the word (*bei*) (Fernald, Swingley, & Pinto, 2001). Thus, like adults, infants seem to process speech incrementally, and use the initial sounds of the words to narrow down their search for possible referents.

## *4.2.2 Word production*

At around 12 months of age, infants begin producing their first words in so-called 'holophrases' with discourse-appropriate intonation and emotional tone of voice (Barrett, 1982; Ninio, 1992). Infants use their holophrases (single-word utterances) to convey the same sorts of communicative intentions for which they use their gestures (Bates, Benigni, Bretherton, Camaioni, & Volterra, et al., 1979; Tomasello, 2008): to make requests (e.g. saying *More* in the context of cookies, or *Up!* to be picked up), to share interest (e.g. saying *Doggie* when seeing a nice fluffy dog), and to inform or help others (e.g. saying *Here!* when their mother is carrying a heavy package and needs to put it down). As their communicative intentions become more elaborate, infants are compelled to find new words that fit their needs (Bloom & Tinker, 2001); they are motivated to learn new words because a larger repertoire of words is helpful for getting one's point across. Vocabulary grows as children seek new means of expression for what they have in mind: as children learn more about the world, they have increasing numbers of things to talk about, and this discrepancy between what they have in mind and their means of expression drives word learning forward (L. Bloom, 1993; Bloom & Tinker, 2001).

Of course, it is necessary to point out that more is required for intelligible speech production than merely having something to say. First, infants must have representations of word forms stored in memory that can serve as templates for word production, and they must have sufficient retrieval skills to access these representations. Evidence suggests that infants have detailed phonological representations of familiar words from a young age; for example, at 11 months of age, infants treat correct pronunciations of familiar words differently from those with mispronounced onsets or offsets (Swingley, 2005). Other studies have shown that toddlers prefer the conventional forms of words (e.g. *fish*) to their immature forms (e.g. *'fis'*) (Berko & Brown, 1960), and show more accurate recognition of words taken from adult speech as opposed to their own immature speech (Dodd, 1975).

Second, as discussed in Chapter 2, infants must develop considerable speech motor skills to achieve adult-like pronunciations of words. Infants have to figure out how to control their articulation and phonation to yield sound sequences that match the input they receive (Stoel-Gammon, 2011). From infancy through early childhood, children engage in vocal play in which they produce speech in non-communicative contexts (e.g. when alone in their crib), seemingly for their own entertainment (Locke, 1993; Nelson, 1989). As discussed in the context of babbling, infants benefit from hearing their own attempts at production; by comparing their speech production with representations stored in memory, and by relating auditory feedback to the kinaesthetic sensations associated with speech production, infants create an auditory–articulatory feedback loop (Stoel-Gammon, 2011). This feedback loop, in turn, may direct their attention to speech sounds in the ambient language that match their own productions. The process of fine-tuning articulation to improve the accuracy of production extends over a period of several years. Initially, many of the infant's attempts at word production result in unintelligible or simplified forms involving, for example, reduced consonant clusters (saying 'poon' for spoon), reduplicated segments ('fifished' for fin-ished), omitted unstressed syllables ('ba' for bottle, 'puter' for computer) or codas ('daw' for dog), and replacements of fricatives with more easy-to-produce obstruents ('dat' for that) (Kehoe & Stoel-Gammon, 1997; Stoel-Gammon & Cooper, 1984). It takes chil-dren years to master the production of all the various consonants and consonant clus-ters of English. Indeed, young infants may begin producing words with only a handful of consonants and syllable structures in their productive repertoires (Vihman, 1996).

Throughout infancy there are strong and consistent relationships between prelin-guistic vocalisation and early word production, such that individual differences in the amount and diversity of prelinguistic vocalisation are predictive of individual differ-ences in the rate of expressive vocabulary development. Infants who vocalise more and have a greater variety of consonants and vowels in their babble have more building blocks at their disposal for word production (Vihman, 1996; Stoel-Gammon, 2011). Although infants differ in their phonological repertoires at the onset of word produc-tion, infants utilise the same speech sounds and syllable structures they use in babble in producing their first words (Ferguson & Farwell, 1975; McCune & Vihman, 2001; Vihman, Ferguson, & Elbert, 1986; Vihman, Macken, Miller, Simmons, & Miller, 1985). Thus, the first words of English-speaking infants tend to be monosyllabic, with simple word shapes (e.g. CV, CVC, CVCV), and with easy-to-pronounce onsets such as [b], [m], and [d] (Ferguson & Farwell, 1975; Oller, Wieman, Doyle, & Ross, 1976; Stoel-Gammon, 2011). There is even evidence that infants choose words to produce based on their sound patterns: in a series of word-learning experiments with non-word stim-uli (Schwartz & Leonard, 1982; Schwartz, Leonard, Frome Loeb, & Swanson, 1987), infants showed a bias in word production (but not in comprehension) favouring non-words made up of speech sounds that were already in their repertoires. Toddlers are more accurate in producing new word forms if they contain highly frequent articula-tory sequences (Edwards, Beckman, & Munson, 2004; Munson, 2001; Munson, Kurtz, & Windsor, 2005b), which suggests that articulatory practice benefits fluent speech production. Words-sharing similarities in form, for example, so-called phonological neighbours such as cat, cab, can, cut, kit, kite, cot, caught, mat, hat, fat, sat, and scat, have overlapping sets of articulatory requirements and reinforce each other with respect to fluency in their production (Storkel, 2004, 2009). Phonological development and lexical development therefore appear to be mutu-ally interdependent. At the earliest stages, phonological development impacts lexical development by influencing which word forms are likely to be used by children. Later, as children grow their vocabularies, they discover similarities across phonological word forms and recognise sublexical patterns among words that might influence the struc-ture of phonological representations, as well as the rate of vocabulary growth.

> **phonological neigh-bours** words that differ in pronunciation only with respect to a single phoneme (e.g. bet has the neighbours set, bat, beg).

## 4.2.3   Word production errors

In Section 4.1.2 we showed that words are tightly coupled with specific situations and contexts of use. This may lead the child to under-extend word usage initially (Barrett, Harris, & Chasin, 1991; Dromi, 1987). For example, an infant might use a particular word such as *truck* when the refuse truck collects the rubbish, but may fail to use the word in the context of toy trucks, fire trucks, pick-up trucks, and so on (L. Bloom, 1973). Such under-extension seems to occur only at the earliest stages of word learning, and is likely to be eliminated through cross-situational learning whereby the child hears the word used in a wider range of contexts and comes to use the word in similar ways (Smith & Chen, 2008). In addition to under-extension errors, toddlers make numerous speech errors that appear to involve over-extension of a word to items outside its category. For example, the child might produce a word whose referent shares semantic features with the target (e.g. calling a kangaroo *mouse*), or even a word whose referent bears only percep- tual similarities to the target (e.g. calling the moon *ball*). It is difficult to know the exact source of a naming error when it occurs, but at the earliest stages one can safely assume that there are numer- ous gaps in a toddler's vocabulary; in their quest to get their point across, they are willing to substitute a related word, or to coin one of their own, such as calling a gardener a *garden-man* (Becker, 1994b; Clark, 1982, 1993; Swan, 2000). Some lexical innovations suggest an awareness of a pattern of derivational morphology, such as using a noun as a verb, as in *to broom*. Such innovations may be generated by analogy with other noun–verb pairs such as *a hammer, to ham- mer*, and so on. Other lexical innovations appear to reflect blends of other words (e.g. *yarden* 'garden'). As children learn the conven- tional ways of talking about things, their innovative forms seem to be discarded.

Although children make more errors than adults when speaking (Brooks & MacWhinney, 2000; Jaeger, 1992, 2005; Vousden & Maylor, 2006), even adults quite often mispronounce words, or retrieve the wrong word. Among so-called lexical errors (i.e. errors that are real words), some are semantic in nature (e.g. calling someone by the wrong name, such as calling a child by the name of one's other child), some are phonological (e.g. saying *world* when the target was *word*), and some appear to be both (e.g. calling a lobster an *oyster*, or calling a girl named *Caroline* by the name *Catherine*) (Dell & Reich, 1981; Harley, 1984; MacKay, 1970). Most models of lexical access assume that words with overlapping semantic features compete with each other for selection during speech production, and at times the wrong word is selected (Levelt, Roelofs, & Meyer, 1999; Abdel Rahman & Melinger, 2009). Phonological errors, on the other hand, probably reflect mistakes in sequencing operations; for a word to be spoken, the sounds that make up the word must be retrieved and the articulatory commands must be arranged in proper order (Dell, 1986). The fact that children make more speech errors than adults may be a consequence of a number of factors, including sparser semantic representations (i.e. the child's representations lack sufficient detail to distinguish between related concepts), greater susceptibility to retrieval failure (i.e. the word is known but is not accessed in time for production), and fragile representations of word forms (Gershkoff-Stowe, 2002; Gershkoff-Stowe, Connell, & Smith, 2006; McGregor, Friedman, Reilly, & Newman, 2002).

**under-extension** word-learning errors that occur when a child uses a word in one context yet fails to use the same word in other appropriate contexts.

**over-extension** word-learning errors that occur when a child uses a word to refer to items outside its category.

**semantic features** the specific components of meaning associated with a linguistic unit.

**derivational morph- ology** the subfield of linguistics concerned with the processes by which word-form modifications create new words with distinct meanings; relies on changes in derivational affixes.

**semantic representa- tions** mental representa- tions of the meanings of linguistic units.

# 4.3   HOW IS THE CHILD'S VOCABULARY ORGANISED?

**lexicon** a person's vocabulary knowledge, which includes word meanings, pronunciations, spellings, and grammatical information.

The lexicon of a language comprises a system of words defined in terms of their relationships to other words. From the outset of word learning, children acquire a system in which words contrast with each other with respect to their forms, meanings, and patterns of usage.

## 4.3.1   Organisation by meaning

Words may be related to each other in a variety of ways, both thematically and taxonomically. Clusters of words related thematically are acquired through association with different activities and through co-occurrence in the accompanying speech. Associated words may be antonyms (*boy–girl*, *up–down*), part–whole pairs (*car–bumper*, *tree–branch*), or components of idiomatic expressions (*needle–haystack*, *kick–bucket*), and may instantiate a wide variety of thematic, attributive, functional or taxonomic relationships (*squirrel–acorn*, *cup–saucer*, *lion–roar*, *green–grass*, *cow–milk*, *boat–dock*, *broom–floor*, *collie–dog*, *appliance–stove*). Associative links between words play an important, facilitative role in word retrieval (Meyer & Schvaneveldt, 1971). Words that have just been heard, spoken, or read spread activation to their associates, which increases the likelihood that an associated word will come to mind. Measuring these associations between words using event-related potentials (ERPs) (see Methodology Box 12.1) shows that 2-year-old children already have established meaning-based associations, for example, between two members of the same category, such as *dog* and *horse* (Torkildsen, Syversen, Simonsen, Moen, & Lindgren, 2007). The priming effect of semantic associations can also be found in spoken-word production (Brooks, Seiger-Gardner, & Sailor, under review).

**event-related potentials (ERPs)** electrophysiological response to an external stimulus; ERPs are measured using electroencephalography (EEG) by averaging the multiple electrical responses that are time-locked to a specific event.

**semantic associations** links between words that are based on meaning and co-occurrence of use within a semantic field, such as *salt* and *pepper*.

## 4.3.2   Organisation by form

Words in the child's growing lexicon are related not only with respect to meaning, but also with respect to form. Although the word-to-world mapping of a language is largely arbitrary, there are nevertheless formal cues to word meaning. Onomatopoeia is the most obvious example, where word forms bear similarities to what they represent (such as *tick-tock*, *hiccup*, *splash*, *moo*, *bang*, *ouch*). Learning of onomatopoetic words is no doubt aided by the transparency of the mapping of form to meaning (Gogate & Hollich, 2010); it is not surprising that these words are among the first that children learn (Nelson, 1978; Tardif et al., 2008). However, even at the level of individual sounds, there exist formal regularities that provide reliable cues to the meanings of words (as well as to their grammatical status, see Chapter 5). Languages contain clusters of words, such as *slick, slime, sleet, sleek, slug, slip, slither, slink, slouch,* and *slobber* for which specific segments, such as the word-initial [sl], provide reliable cues to word meaning (Nuckolls, 1999). Recent research indicates that the sound patterns of novel words influence naming preferences (Imai, Kita, Nagumo, & Okada, 2008; Maurer, Pathman & Mondloch, 2006; Nygaard, Cook, & Namy, 2009). Given a choice between a pointy object and a blob-like object, and two novel words *kiki* and *bouba*, toddlers, as well as adults, tend to associate *kiki* with the pointy object and *bouba* with the blob-like object (Maurer et al., 2006). Although the source of the *bouba–kiki* effect in toddlers is presently unknown, an intriguing possibility is that sound–shape correspondences arise as infants mouth objects of various shapes, and attempt to vocalise while mouthing the objects (Bernardis, Bello, Pettenati, Stefanini, & Gentilucci, 2008). Mouthing a pointy object would not require the mouth to be fully open – perhaps similar to the mouth shape required to say *kiki* – whereas mouthing a bulbous object would require a fully opened mouth – more similar to the mouth shape required to say *bouba*.

### 4.3.3   *Organisation by morphological relatedness*

One salient case of form overlap within the lexicon involves morphologically related words, such as *roll, rolls, rolled, unroll, roller,* and so on. Morphological patterns involve a variety of inflectional affixes and derivational affixes that change the meaning of words to fit new semantic and grammatical contexts. Inflections mark features such as subject–verb agreement (e.g. *-s* in *He runs*), verb tense (e.g. *-ed* in *She walked*), aspect (e.g. *-ing* in *They are running*), and number (e.g. *-s* in *cats*). Derivations change the meaning of the stem, and often its part of speech (e.g. adding *-ment* to the verb *govern* creates the noun *government*). In richly inflected languages, such as Lithuanian, Russian, or Turkish, virtually every content word is inflected for one or more features (tense, aspect, number, etc.). Children adapt to the morphological complexity of their language, and produce the majority of their words with appropriate inflections (e.g. Aksu-Koç, 1998; Bar Shalom, 2002; Caprin & Guasti, 2009). They come to learn that morphological changes (e.g. case-marking inflections on nouns) do not signal a change in reference (i.e. the entity to which the word refers), but indicate the grammatical role of the word in the sentence (i.e. who did what to whom). As children learn about the morphological patterns of their language, they are increasingly able to infer the meanings of inflected words (Anglin, 1993) and are able to productively create new words as well. Both of these processes contribute to the learning of new words.

**inflectional affixes** word-form modifications that change the meaning of a word to fit its grammatical context; for example, adding the suffix *-s* to indicate plural number, as in *bottle → bottles*.

**derivational affixes** word-form modifications that change the meaning of a word to fit a new semantic context and/or to change its part of speech.

**agreement** grammatical phenomenon in which a grammatical feature of one word is aligned with a grammatical feature of another word (e.g. a noun might agree with a verb, adjective or pronoun in person, number or gender).

## 4.3.4   Organisation by phonological similarity

Often, words are similar in their sound patterns regardless of semantic and morphological relatedness. Priming studies in adults have shown that hearing a word like *cup* affects subsequent recognition of a word like *plate*, which is related in meaning, but also a word like *car*, which starts with the same phoneme /k/. Is the lexicon of small children also organised by phonological similarity? Mani and Plunkett (2010) found that when 18-month-old children were first presented with the picture of a familiar word and then with pictures of two other familiar words, one of which was labelled aloud, they looked more often to the labelled image if its name started with the same consonant as the name of the preceding picture (e.g. *cup* followed by *car*). Thus, the first word may have pre-activated the phoneme /k/, making it easier to process the name of the picture starting with /k/.

However, this does not mean that the lexical representations of 18-month-olds are phonologically organised. If words are organised in phonological neighbourhoods, then activation of one word can spread to other words in the same phonological neighbourhood; these other activated words create competition that can interfere with the recognition of other phonologically related words. For example, the word *cup* might activate the words *cub, cut, cuff, keep, cop, cap*, which, in turn, might compete with the target *car*. Such interference effects require a lexicon large enough for neighbourhoods of phonologically similar words to form. Indeed, when Mani and Plunkett (2011) tested 24-month-old children, they found that phonologically related words inhibited the recognition of subsequent target nouns, which manifested itself in fewer looks to the labelled image if its name started with the same consonant as the name of the preceding picture – a finding exactly opposite to what was found with 18-month-olds. This effect was more pronounced for words from larger phonological neighbourhoods. Thus, during the period between 18 and 24 months, which is associated with rapid growth in vocabulary size, the lexical representations of children show organisation by phonological similarity.

## 4.3.5   Learning combinations of words

The lexicon of a language does not just contain individual words, but also contains numerous word combinations and idiomatic expressions; a word combination will be stored in the lexicon if its conventional meaning is not fully predictable from the meanings of its parts (Di Sciullo & Williams, 1987). The English language contains literally thousands of compound words, such as *dishwasher, maybe*, and *overflow*, verb–preposition combinations, such as *give up* (quit) and *put down* (insult), as well as idioms, such as *drag one's feet* (procrastinate) and *make up one's mind* (decide), with idiosyncratic meanings and contexts of use. To learn such word combinations as lexical items, the child must utilise their statistical learning skills to detect invariant sequences in the input. Once the sequence has been noticed, it can be associated, as a whole, with a particular meaning and context of use. When children learn sequences of words, they do not necessarily break them down

> **compound words** a word consisting of more than one stem; the result of a word-formation process by which a new word is created by combining other words.

into their component parts; that is, it may take some time for the child to discover the individual words that make up the sequence. For example, a child might learn to produce phrases such as *piece-a-bread*, *piece-a-cake* or *piece-a-ice* and only later come to recognise that *piece* and *of* are distinct words (Peters, 1983; Peters & Menn, 1993).

# 4.4 HOW DO CHILDREN LEARN SO MANY WORDS IN SUCH SHORT TIME?

Most children begin to use words at about 12 months of age, and initially word learning is slow. The average child produces only 40 words at 16 months – this works out to their learning one new word about every three days between the ages of 12 and 16 months. In contrast, at 24 months of age, the average child will know 300 words – which works out to their learning a new word every day at ages 17–24 months (Fenson, Dale, Reznick, Bates, & Thal, 1994). This threefold increase in the rate of word learning in the second year of life has been described as a **vocabulary spurt**, although it is much more accurate to describe it as part of an accelerating growth curve, indicative of the accelerating effect of practice (Ganger & Brent, 2004; Heathcote, Brown, & Mewhort, 2000; McMurray, 2007; Ninio, 2006; Regier, 2005; see Figure 4.3).

> **vocabulary spurt** an increase in the rate of word learning occurring in the second year of life.

Simply put, as the number of words in the child's vocabulary increases, it takes less time for the child to accrue their next word. The rate of word learning continues to increase over childhood. If one estimates the average 6-year-old to have at least 6000 words in their vocabulary (Stoel-Gammon, 2011), then he or she will have learned roughly 120 words per month, or four per day, between the ages of 2 and 6 years.

To understand how children become such expert word-learners, researchers have looked for changes in their word-learning strategies. In the second year of life, toddlers appear to undergo a qualitative shift from simply associating words with events (such as *uh-oh* when spilling juice) to treating words referentially, as names for things (DeLoache, 2004; Mayor & Plunkett, 2010). In other words, infants, throughout much of the first year of life, seem to merely associate words with activities (Bates, et al. 1979) while toddlers learn that words are symbols that refer to things in the world. Below we describe the processes that bring about this transition.

## 4.4.1 Mapping words to meanings

An important change during the second year of life is the emergence of a phenomenon referred to as fast mapping, first described by Carey (Carey, 1978; Carey & Bartlett, 1978). Fast mapping has been demonstrated in infants as young as 13 months,

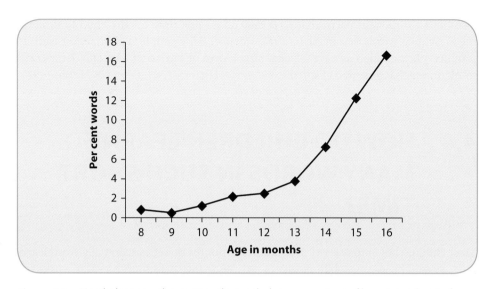

**Figure 4.3**  *Vocabulary growth over time: the graph shows percentage of known words out of 385 words from the infant form of the MacArthur-Bates Communicative Development Inventory (see Methodology Box 4.1) for children at various ages. There is controversy about whether such curves exemplify a sudden transition (the 'vocabulary spurt') that is indicative of a qualitative change in the underlying learning mechanism, or whether they are better explained as exponential growth curves arising from accelerating incremental accumulation of vocabulary knowledge.*

## METHODOLOGY BOX 4.1    ESTIMATING TODDLERS' VOCABULARIES WITH THE MACARTHUR–BATES COMMUNICATIVE DEVELOPMENT INVENTORY

In early childhood, an efficient way to estimate a toddler's production and comprehension vocabularies is to administer parental questionnaires. A set of standardised questionnaires, known as the MacArthur–Bates Communicative Developmental Inventory (CDI), has been developed for English and has been adapted to over 40 other languages. The questionnaires consist of checklists containing several hundred words. For each word, the primary caregiver has to decide whether the child is able to comprehend and to produce it. There is an infant form for children aged 8 to 16 months and a toddler form for children aged 16 to 30 months.

It is not easy to assess the validity of parental reports as parents may be prone to overestimating the children's language development, and may be trying to be consistent in this across different questionnaires. However, the CDI has been cross-validated with estimates of children's vocabularies obtained from naturalistic conversation and with a laboratory-based test, the Expressive One Word Picture Vocabulary Test (Gardner, 1990), in which children are presented with pictures and prompted to supply the words. The correlations between these measures and the CDI are generally high, ranging from .73 to .85 (Fenson et al., 1994), suggesting that the CDI captures important components of a child's vocabulary. Information about the MacArthur-Bates CDI can be found on the San Diego State University College of Sciences website. Information about how to estimate true vocabulary size from the MacArthur–Bates CDI score can be found in Mayor and Plunkett (2011).

in the context of their learning the names of objects (Gershkoff-Stowe & Hahn, 2007; Houston-Price, Plunkett & Harris, 2005; Schafer & Plunkett, 1998; Werker et al., 1998; Woodward, Markman, & Fitzsimmons, 1994). In a typical study (Schafer & Plunkett, 1998), infants are exposed to two novel words (e.g. *bard* and *sarl*), each paired with a unique novel object. During the exposure phase, each object is shown, one at a time, and labelled several times. In the test phase, the two objects are shown side by side, and one of them is named. Test trials are repeated to test the names of both novel objects, and to vary their left–right positions. If infants have learned the name of an object they will look at it longer than at the distractor.

Fast mapping simply means rapid word learning – the toddler is able to establish a new lexical entry based on only a few exposures to the new word. Rovee-Collier and Giles (2010) have suggested that the emergence of selective attention in the second year of life underlies the fast mapping phenomenon – as children come to recognise more and more words, they become increasingly biased in what they encode when hearing a new word. However, the new lexical entry created via fast mapping is fragile and may easily be forgotten (as in the many experiments in which novel words like *toma* are introduced as names of unusual objects). Only if the word is repeatedly encountered will its lexical entry become more stable, and more of its semantic and grammatical properties will be discovered (Carey, 2010).

> **lexical entry** the listing of an individual word in one's mental vocabulary; contains information about the word's meaning, pronunciation, part of speech, grammatical features, spelling.

As toddlers expand their vocabularies, words come to be special in their capacity to direct children's attention to aspects of their world. Languages differ in how they organise experience for the purpose of talking about it (Choi & Bowerman, 1991; Evans & Levinson, 2009; Haspelmath, 2007); see Chapter 8. As the child's language grows and their memory improves, talk moves away from the here and now to the past and the future (Nelson, 2007). As children talk about their experiences with others, they learn all sorts of words that are not names of things, such as words for time (*yesterday*, *July*), mental states (*need*, *think*), feelings (*hurt*, *angry*), abstract concepts (*fair*, *wrong*), and grammatical function words (e.g. determiners, prepositions, pronouns, auxiliary verbs). Very few, if any, of these words are learned through fast mapping, but are learned gradually through exposure to their varied contexts of use – a process called slow mapping. Initially, toddlers may know enough about a word to use it correctly in a limited number of contexts, but may lack full understanding of its meaning. For example, they might use the verb *know* in the phrase *I dunno*, but may fail to grasp how *know* contrasts with

> **slow mapping** a process of gradual learning whereby a word's lexical entry becomes more detailed as the child is exposed to its varied contexts of use.

other verbs such as *think*, *guess*, and *understand*. Children may learn some words in a seemingly piecemeal fashion. For example, they might hear the verb *go* in phrases such as *Let go* (meaning 'give up'), *It's gone* ('no longer here'), *I'm gonna do it* ('future intent'), *What's going on?* ('What is happening?'), and *He went home* ('movement towards a goal'), and only gradually figure out how the various forms of *go* are morphologically and semantically related (Theakston, Lieven, Pine, & Rowland, 2002).

In many instances, children rely on non-overlapping contexts of use to distinguish words with similar meanings. For example, the quantifiers *all* and *each* are nearly synonymous in some contexts (*All of the boys are riding their bikes* vs. *Each of the boys is riding his bike*). Their distinctiveness comes out in sentences such as *She walked all the way home*, *The cookies are all gone*, and *They all went to the movies*, which emphasise 'completion' and 'togetherness', in contrast to sentences like *You may each pick out a toy*, *They played nicely with each other*, which emphasise 'individuality', 'one-to-one correspondence', and 'reciprocity'. By learning non-overlapping contexts of use, children come to treat the quantifiers differently in ambiguous sentences, for example, interpreting *All of the alligators are in a bathtub* 'collectively' with all the alligators in one bathtub, but *Each alligator is in a bathtub* 'distributively' with each alligator in its own bathtub (Brooks & Braine, 1996).

### 4.4.2   Eliminating unlikely meanings of novel words

An important property of the lexicon of a language is that it contains very few, if any, true synonyms. Even words that appear to be nearly synonymous in meaning, such as *bunny* and *rabbit*, have differing degrees of formality and patterns of usage. Although one might argue that languages contain numerous slang terms for topics of disgust or taboo, even here the various slang terms are likely to differ in their contexts of use (Clark, 1993). This property of language – that changes in the forms of words reliably signal changes in meaning or usage – seems to aid the child in the task of word learning. Each time a child hears a novel word form, he or she can safely assume that the new word has a meaning that differs from that of other (familiar) words. This shortcut to figuring out the meaning of a new word has been variously described as the mutual exclusivity bias (Markman, 1989; Merriman & Bowman, 1989), the novel name, nameless category (N3C) principle (Golinkoff, Hirsh-Pasek, Bailey, & Wenger, 1992; Mervis & Bertrand, 1994), and the principle of contrast (Clark, 1993). Mutual exclusivity implies that children assume that the meanings of words are distinct from one another without any overlap in the range of their referents. Under mutual exclusivity a child should resist learning a category label (e.g. a superordinate term like *animal* or *clothing*) when it is applied to a familiar object the child can readily label (e.g. a dog or a shirt). Children, however, do tolerate multiple terms for the same referent (Mervis, Golinkoff, & Bertrand, 1994). To accommodate this finding, the N3C principle states that children will search for a yet-to-be-named category whenever they hear a novel word, but may map the novel word to aspects of familiar objects in the absence of a novel category. The N3C principle is a learned strategy that increases the efficiency of word learning by allowing the child to entertain smart initial hypotheses about the possible referents of new words. The principle of contrast is the least elaborate of the claims; it simply asserts that children resist synonyms. Each of these characterisations of the constraint blocking synonyms implies that children use a process of elimination to narrow down the possible meanings of novel words. If a new word is used in a context in which a familiar word could have been used,

**mutual exclusivity bias**
a word-learning heuristic whereby children assume that the meanings of different words are distinct from one another without any overlap in the range of their referents.

**novel name, nameless category (N3C) principle**
a word-learning heuristic whereby children will search for a yet-to-be-named category whenever they hear a novel word.

**principle of contrast**  a word-learning heuristic whereby children resist synonyms; the notion that all the words in one's vocabulary have different meanings and contexts of use.

the child seems to assume that the speaker had something else in mind. From around age 16 months, infants first start to apply this principle of exclusion to narrow their search for a referent of a new word (Markman, Wasow, & Hansen, 2003). Toddlers' use of this strategy increases as their vocabularies grow throughout the preschool period (Merriman & Bowman, 1989; Mervis & Bertrand, 1994).

There is some disagreement about the origins of the constraints that block synonyms. Some have suggested that mutual exclusivity is a built-in constraint that helps to get word learning off the ground (Markman, 1989). Others have viewed mutual exclusivity as emerging from general-purpose learning mechanisms: as the associative links between objects and their labels get strengthened over multiple encounters, the links with alternative labels gradually weaken (Regier, 2003). As children learn language, they come to appreciate the non-overlapping meanings of words. The application of the process of elimination to word learning does not appear to be unique to humans – even some dogs apply the strategy in learning the names of objects to fetch (Kaminski, Call & Fischer, 2004; Pilley & Reid, 2011).

The words of a language contrast with respect to their meanings and patterns of usage, but not necessarily with respect to their referents. Speakers often use multiple terms to refer to the same referents, using different terms to mark contrasts in their attitude and perspective. Listeners, in turn, attempt to grasp the communicative intentions of the speaker, and use words as clues to what the speaker has in mind. Caregivers use a variety of terms when referring to their children, such as *William*, *Billy*, *you*, *he*, *him*, *munchkin*, *sweetie*, *kiddo*, *child*, *boy*, *son*, *grandson*, *brother*, *swimmer*, *fifth-grader*, and *student*. Children seem to take it for granted that multiple labels refer to the same individuals under differing circumstances, and they appear to use multiple referring expressions flexibly in their own speech from a young age (Clark, 1997; Deák & Maratsos, 1998).

### 4.4.3   Making assumptions about word meanings

In learning the names of things, toddlers follow a principle of extendibility, which means that they generalise usage of a label to objects of like kind (Golinkoff, Mervis, & Hirsh-Pasek, 1994; Markman, 1989). This word-learning principle, also called the taxonomic bias, reflects a very important fact about words – namely, that words label categories of things as opposed to a specific thing at a specific moment in time. Even proper names refer to individuals across situations (over their lifespan and beyond), and can be used in the context of photographs or other objects that are 'like the person', as in the sentence *That dress is so Patty*. Toddlers embrace the principle of extendibility to such an extent that researchers have suggested that words invite toddlers to form categories (Waxman & Markow, 1995; Waxman & Braun, 2005). Word learning thus supports inductive generalisation (Gelman & Markman, 1986, 1987). So, when asked which of two objects shares the internal properties (e.g. means of breathing) of an exemplar (e.g. a black *bird*),

> **taxonomic bias** a word-learning heuristic whereby children follow a principle of extendibility, and assume that words label categories of things as opposed to specific individuals.

> **inductive generalisation** process by which children generalise properties of an exemplar to other members of the category.

children are more likely to extend the properties to an object labelled the same as the exemplar (e.g. a penguin labelled as a *bird*) than to a perceptually similar object (e.g. a *bat*). Numerous studies have shown that labels alter task performance by reorienting attention. The use of labels helps infants to isolate objects from complex scenes (Xu, 2002) and improves learning of categories (Ferry, Hespos, & Waxman, 2010; Fulkerson & Waxman, 2007; Lupyan, Rakison, & McClelland, 2007), while worsening recognition of the individual items that make up the categories (Fisher & Sloutsky, 2005; Lupyan, 2008).

**shape bias** a word-learning heuristic marked by toddlers' selective attention to the shapes of objects as the main feature that distinguishes object names (e.g. the important feature that distinguishes *cup* from *plate* is shape and not colour or material).

Toddlers also begin to selectively attend to the shapes of objects when learning their names. Toddlers' shape bias is evident in word-extension tasks, wherein the child is taught the name of a novel object (e.g. a *dax*) and is asked to pick out other ones from a set of objects, each sharing only a single feature (shape, size, texture/material, or colour) with the original exemplar (see Figure 4.4). Under such conditions, toddlers readily generalise the new word to other objects of similar shape (Landau, Smith, & Jones, 1988), but not to objects of similar size, texture/material, or colour. Children's reliance on the shape bias is specifically tied to their acquisition of count nouns; children do not adopt a shape bias in learning other types of words, such as adjectives or mass nouns (Landau, Smith, & Jones, 1992; Smith, Jones, & Landau, 1992) – for example, if a novel substance is introduced as 'some *dax*', children tend to generalise on the basis of material rather than shape (Soja, 1992). Training infants to attend to shape in the laboratory results in a dramatic increase in their rate of learning count nouns at home, but does not affect their rate of learning other sorts of words (Smith, Jones, Landau, Gershkoff-Stowe, & Samuelson, 2002). Under natural conditions, the shape bias emerges only after children have considerable numbers of count nouns in their vocabulary (Gershkoff-Stowe & Smith, 2004), which suggests that it is a generalisation over prior instances of word-to-world mapping.

**whole-object bias** word-learning bias marked by toddlers' tendency to assume that words label whole objects as opposed to salient parts.

Another word-learning bias, called the whole-object bias, is toddlers' tendency to assume that words label whole objects as opposed to salient parts (Hollich, Golinkoff & Hirsh-Pasek, 2007; Markman, 1989). Gogate and Hollich (2010) have suggested that this bias emerges out of infants' sensorimotor experiences with objects moving as wholes. In conjunction with the shape bias, the whole-object bias also makes it easier for children to learn count nouns, as opposed to other types of words. Although toddlers learn all sorts of words, count nouns tend to comprise a disproportionate share of their growing vocabularies. Interestingly, the strength of the noun bias differs considerably across languages, with learners of some languages (e.g. Ngas [Nigerian], Korean, and Mandarin Chinese) showing much less of a bias towards learning names of things than children learning English (Childers, Vaughan, & Burquest, 2007; Choi & Gopnik, 1995; Tardif, 1996). The noun bias may be weaker in languages in which it is grammatical to omit subject and object nouns from sentences, and in which the verb often occurs at the end of the sentence, making it more perceptually salient. However,

**noun bias** a word-learning bias marked by a disproportionate number of count nouns in toddlers' early vocabularies.

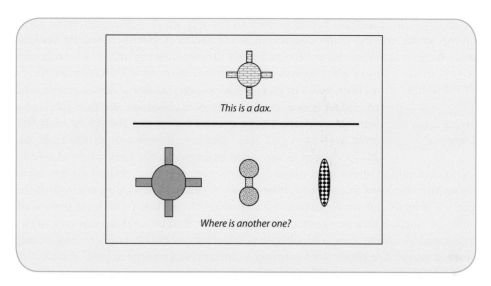

**Figure 4.4** *Illustration of stimuli used in word-extension tasks that demonstrate the shape bias, indicated by children selecting the left-most object in the bottom row. Typically, the stimuli are three-dimensional object made of wood, clay, styrofoam, cloth or plastic.*
*Source:* Based on material reported in Landau et al. (1988) and Samuelson and Smith (2005).

structural differences between languages are only part of the story. When Chinese and American adults viewed silent videos of Chinese and American mothers playing with their 18- to 24-month-old children, and were asked to guess from the situational context what the mothers were saying, both groups of viewers correctly identified more nouns than verbs from the videos of the American mothers, but equal numbers of nouns and verbs from the videos of the Chinese mothers (Snedeker, Li, & Yuan, 2003). This suggests that the activities of American mothers and their toddlers tend to promote labelling to a greater extent than Chinese mother–toddler interactions. Certain activities common in Western cultures, such as pointing at objects in picture books, strongly promote the learning of names for things (Ninio & Bruner, 1978; Ninio, 1980; Weizman & Snow, 2001), and toddlers who regularly partake in such activities will tend to show a larger noun bias than other children (Choi, 2000; Tardif, Gelman, & Xu, 1999).

There has been considerable controversy with respect to the origins of such biases. Because a child could entertain a seemingly unlimited number of different hypotheses about a word's meaning (Does *dog* refer to the head, tail, legs, fur, smell of the creature, or the entire creature as a whole?), some researchers have proposed that the biases described above must be innate – that is, children must come equipped with some domain-specific assumptions that constrain the process of word learning from the outset (Markman, 1990). However, as empirical work on the emergence and disappearance of the shape bias has demonstrated, biases can arise from the structure of early vocabularies: as children construct hypotheses about the meanings of individual words, they also construct hypotheses about the way words in general tend to carve up the world, and the count nouns typically found in children's very early vocabularies happen to name object categories best differentiated by shape. Recently, this insight has been formalised more rigorously within the mathematical framework of hierarchical Bayesian modelling, which can be used to explain how inductive inferences about specific data can lead a learner to construct more general hypotheses about how such data must have been generated (Perfors, Tenenbaum, Griffiths, & Xu, 2011). To give a simplified example, at the same time as a child learns that certain animals are called *dog*, others are called *cat*, and others are called *bunny*, the child also learns about how words in general are used to distinguish the various animals and which features of animals are important to warrant the use of different labels. This more abstract knowledge can then be used to constrain subsequent word learning. Crucially, without postulating any innate word-learning biases, abstract knowledge about word-learning constraints can emerge in parallel with concrete knowledge about the referents of specific words.

> **hierarchical Bayesian modelling** a mathematical framework used to model hierarchical Bayesian inference.

An alternative explanation of the emergence of word-learning biases comes from neuro-computational modelling. In such models, which implement simple associative learning mechanisms, word-learning biases emerge once sufficient phonological and conceptual development has taken place. For example, a bias like the shape bias or the taxonomic bias emerges once perceptually or functionally based object categories are sufficiently developed. When a member of a category (e.g. a cup) is labelled with a word (e.g. *cup*) during an episode of joint attention, the word is mapped onto an already understood category (e.g. 'object of a particular size/shape used for drinking') and can be linked to all other exemplars of that category without further explicit labelling (Mayor & Plunkett, 2010). Although neuro-computational accounts based on associative learning mechanisms do not invoke abstract knowledge, they also view early word-learning biases as emergent from the way learning in various domains unfolds.

> **syntax** the subfield of linguistics concerned with how words are arranged to form sentences.

### 4.4.4  Using syntax to infer meanings of novel words

> **morphology** the subfield of linguistics concerned with the processes by which word forms are modified, using derivational and inflectional affixes to create new words.

> **lexical bootstrapping** hypothesis proposing that knowledge of grammar is the product of accumulated item-specific knowledge of how individual words are used.

Bates and Goodman (1997) proposed that grammar (syntax and morphology) emerges from the lexicon – in effect, from an accumulation of item-based learning, as children learn specific words and their contexts of use. They called this process lexical bootstrapping, whereby the child learns the combinatorial properties of their language by keeping track of the co-occurrence patterns of individual words. Once the child has learned some of the grammatical constructions of their language, he or she can run the process in reverse, using the linguistic context in which a new word occurs to make inferences about its meaning. The idea that children can use syntax to infer properties of a novel word, such as its part of speech, is called syntactic bootstrapping (Gleitman, 1990). For example, many studies have demonstrated that toddlers can use syntactic information (i.e. sentence structure) to distinguish count nouns (*This is a dax*) from mass nouns (*This is made of dax*), and from adjectives (*This is a daxy one*) (Brown, 1957; Landau et al., 1992; Prasada, 1993; Smith et al., 1992; Soja, 1992).

> **syntactic bootstrapping**
> a proposal that children can use syntactic information to infer properties of a novel word, such as its part of speech.

Gleitman (1990) has argued that syntactic information is especially important for learning the meanings of relational words, such as verbs. Verb learning may lag behind noun learning precisely because children need to acquire some of the grammar of their language in order to work out a verb's meaning (Gleitman, Cassidy, Nappa, Papafragou, & Trueswell, 2005). Whereas count nouns, such as *ball*, tend to be used in situations in which the designated object is present, verbs are less strongly tied to specific actions or situations (Gentner, 1982). Any action can be described from multiple perspectives (e.g. *chasing*, *fleeing*, *running*, *escaping*, *going*), and it is difficult to guess the meaning of the verb with only the extra-linguistic context as a cue (Gillette, Gleitman, Gleitman, & Lederer, 1999; Piccin & Waxman, 2007). However, if the child can identify the referents of the nouns in the sentence, and has some understanding of sentence structure, he or she can begin to make reasonable guesses about the meaning of a verb. In other words, linguistic context supplements extra-linguistic context to provide sufficient information for children to learn verbs: if the child were to hear *The girl is chasing the boy*, the child could infer that *chasing* refers to whatever the girl is presently doing to the boy. In contrast, hearing *The boy is running away from the girl* would lead the child to focus on what the boy is doing. Naigles (1990) conducted the first study to provide evidence of syntactic bootstrapping in toddlers' acquisition of verbs. She presented 2-year-olds with sentences containing unfamiliar, made-up verbs in sentences like *The duck is gorping the bunny* or *The duck and the bunny are gorping*. Simultaneously, the children saw two videos next to each other, 'a duck forcing a rabbit into a bending position' versus 'a duck and a rabbit making arm gestures in parallel'. The children looked longer at the video matching the sentence content. For example, when hearing the sentence *The duck is gorping the bunny*, they looked longer at the video in which the duck was doing something to the rabbit. Thus, the children inferred aspects of verb meaning from the sentence structure.

### 4.4.5   Using morphology to infer meanings of novel words

Children also use morphological cues to infer word meanings and to grow their vocabularies (Jolly & Plunkett, 2008). Morphological patterns, that is, patterns of inflection and derivation, tend to be quasi-regular and vary with respect to their frequency, transparency, and productivity. Frequency refers to how often an affix occurs in the language input, which depends on how essential it is to the construction of well-formed utterances. The high frequency of certain affixes, such as verb inflections like *-ed*, or noun inflections like *-s*, is due in large part to the obligatory

> **frequency** how often a morpheme occurs in the language; for affixes, frequency is largely determined by how essential they are to the generation of well-formed utterances.

**transparency** the extent to which a word stem is recognisable when it occurs in the context of an affix.

**productivity** the extent to which a prefix or suffix may be applied to a variety of different word types.

marking of features such as tense and number in English. Affixes that are high in frequency are learned first, and are the first to be generalised to new vocabulary. The extent to which a word stem is recognisable when it occurs in the context of an affix is referred to as transparency. Some stems undergo seemingly idiosyncratic changes during affixation (*solve–solution, electric–electricity, chaos–chaotic*), which decreases the transparency of the morphological pattern. In English, most stems are freestanding words that the child might already know, for example, the word *act* is easy to recognise in the derived form *actor*. Other morphologically complex words contain stems that never occur without affix, for example, *struct* in *structure, construct, construction, instruct, instructor, instruction, destruction*. To infer the meaning of the stem, children must learn enough affixed word forms to allow them to partition words into their component morphemes. Finally, productivity refers to the extent to which an affix can be applied to any word of a particular word class. For example, aspect-marking inflections such as the progressive *-ing* and tense-marking affixes like *-ed* are applied productively to the majority of English verbs, whereas most derivational affixes like *-er* or *-tion* show more limited productivity.

**over-generalisation errors** speech production errors that occur when a child uses an affix or a grammatical **construction** with a word for which the affix or construction does not normally apply; this results in the production of unconventional forms such as *goed* (went) or *broom it* (sweep it).

The quasi-regular patterns of word formation lead children to make numerous over-generalisation errors, in which they apply affixes to words that are not conventionally used with that affix. As will be described in more detail in Chapter 5, the most commonly reported errors are over-generalisations of noun and verb inflections such as plural *-s* (*mouses* for *mice*) and past tense *-ed* (*swimmed* for *swam*); however, any morphological pattern that is sufficiently frequent, transparent, and productive will support lexical innovations, such as *debalance* (to make unbalanced) *physicalise* (make something imaginary physical) or *mayhemic* (wild, out-of-control, like mayhem) (all examples from our children). These forms appear to be generated when the child has something in mind but is unable to access a word with just the right meaning. Children produce novel forms when they fail to retrieve the correct form, for example, producing *gooder* for *better*, or when a morphological pattern has a limited domain of application, for example, producing *successfullest* for 'most successful'. Crucially, for the child to produce such forms, he or she must have acquired sets of related words (called morphological paradigms), such as *highest, softest, tallest*, and so on, or *dethrone, deflate, deforest*, and so on, which instantiate the morphological pattern and provide the basis for the child to infer the meaning of the affix so that it can be applied productively. In Chapter 5, we will elaborate on one such example, the use of diminutive affixes, such as the English *-y* in *doggy, buggy*, and *bootie*. Diminutives tend to be pervasive in child-directed speech, and are often the first derivational affixes to be used productively, as in *blanky* 'blanket' and *botty* 'bottom' (Savickienė & Dressler, 2007).

**morphological paradigm** a set of words with the same stem but with different inflections (e.g. *high, higher, highest* or *strong, stronger, strongest*).

As the size and diversity of the inventory of morphologically complex words grows in the child's vocabulary, so does the efficiency of word learning (Anglin, 1993). The child's ability to parse words into stems and affixes, and their grasp of the meaning of different affixes, greatly enhances the child's ability to infer the meanings of new words. At the same time as they learn new words and their combinatorial properties, they grow their knowledge of the morphological and syntactic properties of the language. Children's growing knowledge of syntax and morphology makes them more efficient word learners because they can exploit structural cues to the meanings of unfamiliar words. The combined effect of lexical bootstrapping and syntactic bootstrapping is that the rate of vocabulary growth increases as a function of how much of the language the child already knows. This cyclical process is the engine behind the massive increase in vocabulary size that occurs during the school years as children encounter morphologically complex words in printed text and their vocabulary continues to grow to an estimated 40,000 to 100,000 words by the time they graduate from high school (P. Bloom, 2002; Nagy & Anderson, 1984). This means that during the course of their school years, children learn an astonishing 12 to 18 new words per day. Just how exactly children accomplish this feat will be discussed in more detail in the context of literacy development in Chapter 9.

## SUMMARY

- **Early word learning involves mapping words onto references in the world around them.**

- **Children infer word meaning through social interactions with others, relying on joint attention and the ability to read others' intentions.**

- **Children also infer word meaning from speech accompanying activities and routines.**

- **Caregivers can aid word learning through enhanced responsiveness that is contingent upon the infant's actions and speech.**

- **Children's early word productions are constrained by their immature phonological representations and articulatory abilities as well as by the phonological structure of their early vocabularies.**

- **As early word learning is embedded in specific situations and activities, children produce over-extension and under-extension errors before learning that words are symbols for concepts that have situational constancy.**

- **Gradually, organisation of early vocabularies by semantic, morphological, and phonological features emerges.**

- As children become capable of selective attention they are able to 'fast map', that is, to rapidly associate labels with objects. Abstract and relational words are acquired more gradually by tracking the contexts of their usage.

- During the second year of life, increased vocabulary size leads to the emergence of word-learning strategies such as assuming that different labels refer to different concepts, that labels refer to whole objects and to categories rather than specific exemplars or parts of things, and that members of categories to be labelled tend to be organised by shape.

- Children also use their emergent knowledge of grammar to infer meanings of novel words. Increases in vocabulary size, in turn, then support the acquisition of grammar.

# FURTHER READING

## Key studies

Gogate, L. J. (2010). Learning of syllable–object relations by preverbal infants: The role of temporal synchrony and syllable distinctiveness. *Journal of Experimental Child Psychology, 103*, 178–197.

Samuelson, L. K. & Smith, L. B. (2005). They call it like they see it: Spontaneous naming and attention to shape. *Developmental Science, 8*, 182–198.

## Overview articles

For a detailed review for syntactic bootstrapping, read Gleitman, L. R., Cassidy, K., Nappa, R., Papafragou, A. & Trueswell, J. C. (2005). Hard words. *Language Learning and Development, 1*, 23–64.

For a history of the research on fast mapping and slow mapping, read Carey, S. (2010). Beyond fast mapping. *Language Learning and Development, 6*, 184–205.

For an accessible description of computational accounts of the emergence of word-learning biases, read Regier, T. (2003). Emergent constraints on word-learning: A computational review. *Trends in Cognitive Science, 7*, 263–268.

## Books

Bloom, P. (2002). *How children learn the meaning of words. (Learning, development and conceptual change).* Cambridge, MA: MIT Press.

# 5 How do Children Learn to Combine and Modify Words?

## KEY TERMS

agreement • argument structure • arguments • artificial grammar • artificial language • case markers • Construction Grammar • constructions • content words • diminutives • ditransitive verbs • function words • Generative Grammar • generativity • hierarchical Bayesian inference • inflectional morphology • intransitive verbs • item-based • lexicon • logical problem of language acquisition • merge • morphemes • morphology • negative evidence • noun phrase • object • over-generalisation errors • parameters • parsing • parts of speech • phonological bootstrapping • poverty of the stimulus • predicates • pre-emption • principles • quantifier spreading errors • recursion • schemas • semantic • semantic role • speech act • statistical learning • structural alignment • subject • syntactic priming • syntax • token frequency • transitive verbs • type frequency • Universal Grammar • valence • verb phrase • visual world paradigm • word classes • word-specific formulae • wug test

# CHAPTER OUTLINE

**speech act** the functional aspect of an utterance, for example whether the utterance asks a question, makes a promise or affirms someone's point of view.

From their first utterances, children use language to do all sorts of things, for example, to make or refuse requests, express interest, ask questions, share experiences, offer help or greet family members. The functional aspect of an utterance is called a **speech act**. (Austin, 1962; Searle, 1969). Starting with single-word utterances such as *more, all-gone, bye-bye,* or *no,* toddlers attempt various speech acts with whatever linguistic means are at their disposal. Towards the end of their second year of life, toddlers begin to combine words into longer utterances, marking the transition to grammar. Over time, utterances become considerably more complex as two-word utterances (e.g. *more milky*) give way to longer (e.g. *I want more milk*) and longer utterances (e.g. *Would you hand me the milk that's on the kitchen counter, please?*). In only a few years, children's utterances come to exemplify the stunning complexity of a proficient language user; to do so, children will have learned that words are not put together in arbitrary ways, but in compliance with conventions that are shared by members of their community. In this chapter we will describe how children acquire the conventions that underlie their ability to combine and modify words in meaningful ways.

In describing children's acquisition of grammar, we will not treat the development of the two parts of grammar, syntax and morphology, as separate topics, as is common in many introductory texts. In linguistics, syntax refers to how words are arranged to form sentences and morphology refers to how the grammatical status of words is changed by adding affixes, as in *work-s*, *work-ing*, *work-er-s* or *re-work-ed*. From a descriptive point of view, it is perfectly legitimate to make a distinction between syntax and morphology; however, from a developmental point of view, the distinction is less appropriate because general learning mechanisms, such as the statistical learning of sequences, play an important role in the acquisition of both syntax and morphology. Treating the acquisition of syntax and morphology separately also potentially obscures important commonalities in their functions. One reason for the separation of syntax and morphology is that the study of language development has historically focused on the development of English. English has a more rigid word order and fewer inflectional morphemes than many other languages. To learn English, children have to discover that word order conveys information about who did what to whom, such that in sentences like *The boy chased the girl* and *The girl chased the boy*, the first noun indicates the one doing the chasing, and the second noun indicates the one who is chased. To learn a language like Hungarian, on the other hand, children must discover that case markers rather than word order, marks the various roles of nouns in sentences. For example, the Hungarian sentence *A fiú kergetik a lányt* [The boy chased the girl] has the same meaning as *A lányt kergetik a fiú*, and the sentence *A lány kergetik a fiút* [The girl chased the boy] has the same meaning as *A fiút kergetik a lány*. To acquire the grammar of any language, children have to learn how to arrange words and how to modify words, with the specific functions of these two aspects of grammar dependent on the language.

> **case markers** inflections that mark the thematic roles of nouns (i.e., who did what to whom).

# 5.1 WHERE DOES GRAMMATICAL KNOWLEDGE COME FROM?

Below we will briefly review, in the most general of terms, the two main approaches to the nature of grammatical knowledge and the question of where this knowledge comes from.

> **poverty of the stimulus** assertion put forth by Noam Chomsky that the grammars of human languages are too complex to be learned, given the limited amount of language input that children receive; that language acquisition must be supported by innate knowledge of grammar.

## 5.1.1 Nativist approaches to grammar

The nativist approach draws on arguments by Noam Chomsky (1965) that the rich knowledge of grammar that children attain cannot be extracted from the rather limited linguistic input that children receive. This poverty of the stimulus claim led Chomsky

**Universal Grammar** a component of the theoretical framework proposed by Noam Chomsky; the innate language faculty that constrains children's hypotheses about the grammar of their language.

**negative evidence** evidence in the input provided to children that potentially tells them what forms are incorrect; for example, caregivers might correct children's pronunciation, vocabulary or grammar each time they produce an incorrect form.

**object (direct object, indirect object)** grammatical roles that occur with transitive and ditransitive verbs; for example, in the sentence *Mary baked John a cake*, the direct object is a *cake* and the indirect object is *John*.

**logical problem of language acquisition** the view that languages are too complicated to be learned from the input; that children must have innate knowledge of language because the input is too impoverished to provide sufficient information regarding the structure of the ambient language.

**principles** within the Generative Grammar framework, all languages are thought to have the same underlying abstract rules (principles) and to vary only with respect to specific parameters.

to propose that children come equipped with an innate language faculty in the form of a Universal Grammar that constrains their hypotheses about the grammar of their language. Chomsky (1965) argued that general learning mechanisms such as trial and error are not sufficient for language learning: for trial and error to succeed, children need negative evidence, that is, explicit hints about which word combinations and modifications are ungrammatical. This is like telling an English-learning child that she cannot say *three mouses* or *I swimmed in the pool* or *Giggle me!* Yet parents and other caregivers almost never provide grammar lessons of this sort, and on those rare occasions when they do, children are considered to be impervious to this kind of feedback. This whole conundrum is called the logical problem of language acquisition, and Chomsky's solution was to propose that children come equipped with innate knowledge about the rules that constrain their potentially unlimited hypotheses about grammatical structure.

Chomsky's theory of Universal Grammar proposed that all human languages share the same underlying syntactic principles of grammar, and differ from each other only with respect to a finite set of parameters, that is, often conceived as switches that can be turned on or off (Roeper & Williams, 1987; Roeper, 2007). For example, some languages, like English, require sentences to have overt subjects (subject and object are grammatical roles of nouns in a sentence), which results in sentences like *It is raining* in which the subject *it* is a dummy element that fulfils the grammatical function of subject but does not have semantic content; other languages, like Chinese or Spanish, freely allow subjects to be dropped, as in the Spanish equivalent *Está lloviendo*. Another parameter is assumed to pertain to whether a dependent element (such as the direct object of a verb) occurs before or after its 'head': in a head-initial language, like English, verbs precede direct objects (e.g. *Eat your vegetables!*), determiners precede nouns (e.g. *the carrots*), nouns precede relative clauses (e.g. *vegetables that are grown in the garden*), and prepositions (as opposed to postpositions) are used to mark other dependent relationships, such as spatial location (*on your plate*), instrument (*with your fork*), or possession (*of mine*). In head-final languages, like Japanese or Turkish, verbs tend to follow the nouns they modify, and postpositions, rather than prepositions, are used to mark other dependent relationships. According to this approach, the setting of parameters (e.g. head-initial vs. head-final) for any language is triggered by exposure to relevant sentences in the input, and does not require the child to receive any corrective feedback on the grammaticality of their utterances.

One of the hallmarks of language is its unlimited productivity, or generativity – each of us can create an infinite number of new sentences that have never been said before and yet are perfectly sensible and understandable to others. The generativity of language led Chomsky to conclude that language cannot be learned through imitation, because one cannot have learned through imitation what one has never encountered before. For language to be used productively, users must share tacit knowledge about the conventions that underlie the use of words in their language. Chomsky (1957) famously pointed out that even though sentences like *Colourless green ideas sleep furiously* and *Furiously sleep ideas green colourless* are completely novel and nonsensical, speakers of English agree that the first one is grammatically correct while the second one is not. Because it is possible for any speaker of a language to generate an unlimited number of grammatically correct, yet novel, sentences, Chomsky proposed that speakers must have an internal system of rules called a **Generative Grammar**. The Generative Grammar of a particular language is acquired though the setting of the parameters of Universal Grammar to match the language input.

The reason an English sentence like *Colourless green ideas sleep furiously* is grammatically correct is because the words in the sentence are placed into appropriate slots, defined with respect to **word classes**, such as nouns, verbs, adjectives, adverbs, pronouns, prepositions, determiners, and so on. *Colourless* and *green* are both adjectives and precede the noun *ideas*, thereby complying with the head-initial parameter of English which specifies that adjectives precede nouns. *Sleep* is the verb denoting what the ideas are doing and *furiously* is an adverb modifying the action of sleeping. To productively use grammar, children have to know which words in their vocabulary fall into which word classes, because the generative rules operate over word classes rather than individual words.

However, generative rules are not linear rules of the type: *to form a sentence, string together adjective (+ optional adjective) + noun + verb + adverb*, or any other sequence of word classes, for that matter. Instead, the underlying structure is hierarchical. Take the sentence *Daddy likes beer.* This sentence is construed, not as a linear sequence containing a noun, a verb, and a noun, but as a **noun phrase**, *Daddy*, merged with a **verb phrase**, *likes beer*. Noun and verb phrases may incorporate various dependencies between words; for example, noun phrases may contain determiners, adjectives, prepositional phrases, and relatives clauses that modify the noun. Despite differences in complexity, there is a functional equivalence across noun phrases. Any noun phrase – such as *Daddy*, or *the tall man with the cup of coffee who is sitting at the kitchen table*, or even *a colourless green idea* – can combine with the verb phrase *likes beer*, as long as the grammatical features of the noun phrase (singular, third-person) are in agreement with those of the verb phrase. Thus, one

**parameters** within the Generative Grammar framework, all languages are thought to have the same underlying principles and to vary only with respect to specific features (parameters).

**subject** the most prominent grammatical role in a sentence; what the *predicate* is about.

**generativity** the unlimited productivity of human languages (i.e. the property of a self-contained system that generates an infinite number of possible sentences).

**Generative Grammar** a theoretical framework for the study of syntax, first proposed by Noam Chomsky, that involves a set of abstract rules to generate all possible sentences of a language; contrasts with Construction Grammar.

**word classes** also called **parts of speech**; grammatical categories of words (e.g. noun, verb, adjective, etc.), determined by the range of syntactic contexts in which the word appears, and its morphological forms.

**noun phrase** a grammatical phrase based on a noun or a pronoun.

**verb phrase** a grammatical phrase based on a verb.

**merge** a single combinatory operation that combines words into syntactic units, whereby the merged unit retains the grammatical features of one of its constituents.

**recursion** feature of Generative Grammar whereby syntactic rules (e.g. *merge*) can be applied to their own output to build increasingly complex syntactic units.

might conceive of grammar as a set of instructions of the type: *to build a sentence, combine a noun phrase and a verb phrase; to build a noun phrase, combine an optional determiner with an optional adjective and a noun.* In more contemporary linguistic theory (Chomsky, 1995), a single combinatory operation known as merge combines words into syntactic units, where the merged unit retains the grammatical features of one of its constituents, for example, an adjective–noun combination like *lukewarm beer* retains the grammatical features of the noun *beer*. An important feature of Generative Grammar is recursion, which means that merge can be applied to its own output to build increasingly complex syntactic units. For example, the verb phrase *likes lukewarm beer* is the product of merging the verb *likes* with the noun phrase *lukewarm beer*, which is the product of a previous merge operation. At its most extreme, recursion can result in unwieldy structures like *This is the cow with the crumpled horn, that tossed the dog, that worried the cat, that killed the rat, that lay in the house that Jack built*. While it is generally assumed that recursion is a property of Universal Grammar (Hauser, Chomsky, & Fitch, 2002; but see Everett [2005] for arguments that an Amazonian language, Pirahã, may lack recursion), there are language-specific constraints on its application; for example, not all languages allow recursive combinations of possessives, as in *John's cousin's friend's sister's hat* (Roeper, 2007). In any language, limitations in working memory will tend to put a cap on how far speakers take recursion.

One of the basic assumptions of the Generative Grammar framework is that children have innate knowledge about the hierarchical structure of human grammars, in the form of a Universal Grammar. It is worth noting, however, that it is possible to explain, in principle, how abstract representations of hierarchical grammars can emerge through a process of rational inference, based on the language input avail-

**hierarchical Bayesian inference** a process of inference that allows a rational learner to evaluate a hypothesis (e.g. a set of grammatical rules) about how certain data (e.g. the specific language input encountered) may have been generated; can operate on multiple levels.

able to the child. Hierarchical Bayesian inference, mentioned already in Chapter 4, is a process that allows a rational learner to maximise the trade-off between the simplicity of the grammatical rules used to generate sentences, and the fit of the grammatical rules to the specific language data encountered. Computational modelling has shown that, of the various ways in which sentences can potentially be generated, hierarchical phrase-structure rules tend to show the best trade-off between parsimony and fit. Of course this does not mean that children are rational learners trying to infer the underlying grammar of their language through systematic hypothesis testing. The point is that even if one adopts the Generative Grammar assumption that all human grammars have hierarchical structure, one does not need to assume that knowledge of grammatical structure has to be innate (Perfors, Tenenbaum, & Regier, 2011).

In any case, it is important to note that the abstract phrase-structure rules of Generative Grammar are not sufficient to determine which sentences are well formed – for example, that *Daddy likes cookies* and *Daddy bakes me cookies* are well-formed sentences, but *Daddy likes me cookies* is not. Similarly, phrase-structure rules do not specify that the indefinite article *a* combines with count nouns (e.g. *a banana*) but not mass nouns (e.g. *a grain of rice* but not *a rice*). Information about the highly idiosyncratic combinatorial properties of individual words is stored in the lexicon (Di Sciullo & Williams, 1987). Generative Grammar maintains a strict division of labour between the lexicon, which stores word forms, their parts of speech, and their meanings in an associative memory, and grammar which exists in the form of abstract rules or procedures for combining and modifying words (Pinker, 1999; Ullman, 2001).

Verbs, in particular, are notoriously choosy in how they combine with other words (Levin, 1993; Pinker, 1989). A verb's lexical entry contains its expectations about the number of noun phrases, sentential complements or prepositional phrases required, for example, that the verb *sleep* does not take a direct object. One can think of these verb-specific expectations as slots that need to be filled. This property of verbs is called their argument structure or valence. Intransitive verbs, such as *sleep*, require only one argument (e.g. the one doing the sleeping); transitive verbs, such as *throw*, have two arguments (e.g. the one throwing the object and the object thrown); and ditransitive verbs, such as *give*, have three arguments (e.g. the giver, the recipient, and the gift). English verbs have a variety of other argument structures, for example *think* takes a sentential complement as in *I think Bob will join us for dinner*, and *put* requires a prepositional phrase, as well as a noun phrase, as in *She put the milk in the refrigerator*.

Most verbs have multiple argument structures, for example, *break* in the intransitive *The glass broke* versus the transitive *Jane broke the glass*. Thus, even if the verb is inherently transitive – as, for example, *eat*, which requires an eater and something to be eaten – the verb may have a number of different argument structures which allow a semantic role to be omitted – as in *Sarah is eating in the kitchen* or *The lasagne was eaten last night*. In other words, there may be more semantic roles in a verb's lexical entry than slots in its argument structure. A verb's range of argument structures allows for flexible assignments of semantic roles to sentence structures, as in *The soup is cooking in the kitchen* versus *The woman is cooking in the kitchen*. Every language handles these possibilities differently, using word order and morphology to indicate who did what to whom. For example, in Croatian, the sentence *Juha kuha* ('Soup cooking') is distinct from its counterpart *Žena je za kuhanje* ('Woman cooking'), which has more elaborate morphological marking. At the same time, different verbs can combine with the same sets of words and yield contrasting interpretations. For example, *Jill promised Mark to wash the dishes* versus *Jill persuaded Mark to wash the dishes*, where the omitted subject of *wash* is co-referential with Jill in the *promise* sentence, but co-referential with *Mark* in the *persuade* sentence. In the Generative Grammar framework, all this complexity is part of a verb's lexical entry, keeping the grammatical rules simple.

**parts of speech** also called word classes; grammatical categories of words (e.g. noun, verb, adjective, etc.) determined by the range of syntactic contexts in which the word appears, and its morphological forms.

**argument structure** also called **valence;** verb-specific expectations regarding the number and placement of noun phrases and other obligatory grammatical constituents.

**intransitive verbs** verbs that require only one argument (the subject), for example the verb *sleep* in the sentence *The baby is sleeping*.

**transitive verbs** verbs that require two arguments (subject, direct object), for example the verb *carry* in the sentence *Jill is carrying the baby*.

**ditransitive verbs** verbs that require three arguments (subject, direct object, indirect object), for example the verb *give* in the sentence *John gave Mary a book*.

**semantic role** the relationship of a participant in an event (i.e. an argument) to the main verb (i.e. a predicate); also called a thematic role.

## 5.1.2 Usage-based approaches to grammar

Over the years, an increasing number of child language researchers (e.g. Bates & MacWhinney, 1979; Bloom, 1991; Goldberg, 2006; MacWhinney, 2004; Nelson, 2007; Tomasello, 2003) has challenged Chomsky's 'poverty of the stimulus' claim that the language input to children is too impoverished to support grammar acquisition. These researchers emphasise that languages are learned through participation in richly structured, culturally and linguistically mediated social activities in which children attempt to reproduce the linguistic conventions of their community. Children are exposed to the myriad complexities of language use, and extract grammatical patterns through general learning mechanisms, such as statistical learning, in combination with a strong propensity to imitate and act like others. Usage-based researchers counter Chomsky's position that language learning occurs without feedback by showing how caregivers respond to the grammaticality of their children's utterances, by repeating what their child has said, by asking questions when they fail to understand their child, and by recasting their children's utterances when they are ill-formed (Chouinard & Clark, 2003; Moerk, 1991, 1994; Saxton, 2000; Saxton, Houston-Price, & Dawson, 2005). Ambridge and Lieven (2011) provide a detailed description of how usage-based approaches tend to differ from the nativist, Generative Grammar approach; here, we briefly summarise some of the main theoretical differences.

Usage-based approaches tend to focus on the diversity of grammatical forms that children encounter across languages, and even suggest that there may not exist any universal principles of grammar (Evans & Levinson, 2009; Everett, 2005; Haspelmath, 2007) – that is, Chomsky's main premise of a Universal Grammar is questioned. In contrast to the Generative Grammar assertion that grammatical rules apply to word classes (e.g. nouns and verbs) innately available through Universal Grammar, usage-based accounts have proposed that rules operating over word classes emerge only after considerable item-based learning of individual word combinations has taken place (Bannard, Lieven, & Tomasello, 2009). Taking more seriously the diversity of formal categories observed across the world's languages, some usage-based theorists explicitly argue against the view that word classes are basic linguistic units: Croft (2001, pp. 83) states that '... the systematic application of distributional analysis does not yield a small number of parts of speech with sharp boundaries (leaving aside fixes such as subclasses and multiple class membership, which must be motivated by other means). This latter fact suggests that the categories which distributional analysis defines are not only not the traditional parts of speech, but that they are not the sort of atomic primitives that we would like to use as the building blocks of our models of syntactic representation for particular languages.'

**Construction Grammar**
a theoretical framework for the study of syntax that views linguistic constructions as the basic building blocks of grammar; contrasts with Generative Grammar.

Usage-based approaches tend to dispense with the separation of lexicon and grammar, and view knowledge about how to combine and modify words as emerging from item-specific learning of lexical co-occurrence patterns (Bates & Goodman, 1997); see the discussion of lexical bootstrapping in Chapter 4. One such framework, **Construction Grammar** (Croft, 2001; Goldberg, 1995, 2006), proposes that in addition to the words themselves, the **constructions** in which words occur also contribute meaning to sentences, and are stored alongside words in the lexicon. For example, a multitude of occurrences of noun–verb–noun combinations will eventually lead to the emergence of the transitive construction. This construction can then be used to generate novel sentences (e.g. *I'll broom the floor*). In addition to creating meaning, constructions can also provide a starting point or perspective for interpreting the situation (MacWhinney, 1977) as in the contrast between active transitives, like *Ike hit the ball*, and passives, like *The ball was hit by Ike*. These abstract constructions are defined as linguistic patterns for which some aspect of either their form or meaning is not fully predictable from the component parts (Goldberg, 2006). Given sufficient frequency of use, any combination of words (e.g. *the ace of spades*) becomes a construction, stored in the lexicon as a pre-compiled unit paired with a specific meaning and context of use.

In Chapter 4 we described the lexicon as a system of words defined with respect to their relationships to other words. If we expand the definition to encompass constructions, the lexicon is a system in which constructions contrast with each other in their forms, meanings, and patterns of usage, although these differences may be very subtle in some instances. Compare the sentences *The garden is swarming with bees* with *Bees are swarming in the garden* (Fillmore, 1968). Although the words in the two sentences are almost identical, the constructions, and the resulting meanings of the sentences, are different: whereas the first sentence suggests that the garden is full of bees, this need not be the case in the second sentence (Goldberg, 1995). Other pairs of constructions, such as *He loaded hay onto the wagon* versus *He loaded the wagon with hay* similarly convey subtle differences in meaning (Pinker, 1989).

Some constructions, such as the transitive, are used with an enormously wide range of verbs, as in *Ike hit the ball, Ike chipped his tooth, Ike liked the story, Ike received his allowance*, or *Ike weighs 30 kilos*. Other argument structure constructions, such as the *ditransitive*, tend to be used with fairly restricted sets of verbs, as in *Ike told his dad a story, Ike baked his dad a cake, Ike gave his dad a kiss*, or *Ike's broken arm cost him a month of swimming*. Some constructions appear to be organised around specific words, such as the *way*-construction or the *let alone*-construction, as in *Chris slept his way through class* and *Sam won't comb his hair, let alone wash it*. Others are not built around specific words; for example, in the resultative construction, as in *The door creaked open* or *Jane cried herself to sleep*, the meaning 'as a result of' appears to be associated with the construction as a whole (Goldberg & Jackendoff, 2004). By positing constructions as meaning-bearing forms that exist in the lexicon alongside individual words, Construction Grammar readily accounts for sentences in which verbs are used in constructions that seem to 'violate' their inherent transitivity, for example, using an intransitive verb in a transitive construction as in *Kay sneezed the foam off her cappuccino* (Goldberg, 1995), as well as the American habit of treating nouns like verbs, as in *Should I cream-cheese your bagel?*

Not surprisingly, not all researchers agree with the view that abstract constructions, such as the transitive or the ditransitive, are necessary or sufficient to explain young children's syntactic development. Ninio (2006, 2011) has proposed a radically item-based view of grammatical development, in which children generalise

**item-based** the view that children learn the combinatorial properties of each word they encounter on an item-by-item basis.

word combinations to create new sentences based on analogy. However, Ninio, as well as O'Grady (2005), maintain that an operation like merge is necessary to account for children's ability to combine words and word combinations into increasingly complex syntactic units. Take, for example, a sentence from a children's story (DiCamillo, 2006: 7): *The china rabbit was in possession of an extraordinary wardrobe composed of hand-made silk suits, custom shoes fashioned from the finest leather and designed specifically for his rabbit feet, and a wide array of hats equipped with holes so that they could easily fit over Edward's large and expressive ears.* This sentence contains numerous predicates (verbs, adjectives, and prepositions), which, together with their arguments (nouns), are arranged in a complex syntactic configuration that allows the listener to ascertain which predicative terms are modifiers of which nouns, and to determine co-reference relationships between nouns and pronouns. Starting with the subject *The china rabbit*, the listener builds a structure in which syntactic dependencies are resolved by linking arguments with predicates, in such a way as to ensure that the syntactic requirements of the verbs are fulfilled. All human languages have ways of packaging information into complex structures that reduce redundancy, and allow previously mentioned information to be omitted. To unpack the aforementioned sentence into its individual propositions (*The rabbit was made of china, The rabbit possessed a wardrobe, The wardrobe was extraordinary, The wardrobe was composed of suits, The suits were hand-made*, etc.) would exhaust both the speaker and the listener, and would impede communication. To package information, a basic combinatorial operation like merge is needed for structure building.

> **predicates** linguistic expressions that describe a property or relationship of their argument(s); predicates are typically verb phrases.

> **arguments** linguistic expressions that indicate what a predicate is about; usually a noun phrase, but other grammatical constituents are possible arguments (e.g. 'how to drive his tractor' in *John taught me how to drive his tractor*).

## 5.2   CAN INFANTS LEARN ABOUT GRAMMAR BEFORE THEY EVEN START TO SPEAK?

Regardless of one's theory of grammar, it is undeniable that there are patterns of regularity in language. Children need to discover these patterns and to generalise them to other instances (other words, other sentences). But children also must learn to limit their generalisations to instances where the pattern is appropriate, and refrain from generalising to instances where the pattern does not hold. For example, having learned that the past tense of many English verbs is expressed by adding the suffix *-ed* as in *He walked home*, children must learn to avoid forms like *He goed home* – acknowledging that the 'add *-ed*' rule does not apply uniformly. In Chapter 2, we introduced statistical learning as a powerful learning mechanism that aids infants in word segmentation. We will now explore whether statistical learning also plays a role in the acquisition of grammar.

## 5.2.1 Extracting grammar from sound

The ability to use phonological and prosodic cues to identify grammatical structure has been termed phonological bootstrapping (Morgan & Demuth, 1996). There are three prosodic features that tend to coincide with syntactic clauses and phrases. First, speakers often place pauses between phrases and clauses. Second, phonemes tend to be longer right before a syntactic boundary than in the middle. Third, changes in pitch tend to coincide with boundaries between constituents. Typically, pitch declines steadily over the course of an utterance, but at major clause or phrase boundaries speakers tend to reset their pitch to a higher value. Infants are sensitive to combinations of these three cues by six months of age, which allows them to distinguish word sequences that contain a clause boundary – as in *John doesn't know what rabbits eat. Leafy vegetables taste so good*, from those that do not – as in the statement *Rabbits eat leafy vegetables* (Hirsh-Pasek, Kemler Nelson, Jusczyk, Cassidy, Druss, & Kennedy, 1987; Seidl, 2007). Children also learn to use prosodic cues to locate phrase boundaries, for example, to distinguish the meaning of *Can you touch (the cat with the spoon)?* from *Can you touch the cat (with the spoon)?* (Snedeker & Yuan, 2008).

> **phonological bootstrapping** a proposal that children use phonological and prosodic cues to identify grammatical structures.

In Chapter 2 we described how infants use phonological and prosodic information for word segmentation. This information can also help children to discover word classes and grammatical structure. Phonological features of words are often correlated with word classes. For example, an analysis of over 5 million words from speech directed to small children revealed that English content words (e.g. nouns and verbs) tend to contain more phonemes, more syllables, and more complex consonant clusters than grammatical function words (e.g. determiners like *the* and prepositions like *on*) (Monaghan, Chater, & Christiansen, 2005; St. Clair, Monaghan, & Christiansen, 2010). Furthermore, function words are more likely than content words to have phonologically reduced vowels (e.g. the so-called 'schwa' in *the* or *a*). These cues provide sufficient information to allow even newborns to distinguish content words from function words (Shi, Werker, & Morgan, 1999). Phonological features also provide useful cues for distinguishing between different types of content words, like nouns and verbs. English nouns, for example, have on average more syllables than verbs, a cue that has been shown to help children to distinguish them from verbs (Kelly, 1992; Cassidy & Kelly, 2001; Monaghan et al. 2005). There is also a tendency for English nouns and verbs to differ in their pattern of metrical stress (Kelly & Bock, 1988), which becomes apparent when comparing words like *record* or *permit* when used as verbs (e.g. *recOrd*) or nouns (e.g. *rEcord*), where the capital letters indicate the

> **content words** nouns, verbs, adjectives, and adverbs (i.e. the words that convey content or meaning); content words contrast with function words, which have grammatical functions.

> **function words** determiners, pronouns, auxiliary verbs, conjunctions, prepositions, and particles (i.e. words that indicate the grammatical relationships between other words in the sentence); contrast with content words.

primary lexical stress. Of course, the specific information that co-occurs with different word classes will vary from language to language, but there is increasing evidence that children become sensitive to these patterns of co-occurrence in their ambient language from a very early age.

### 5.2.2   Extracting grammar from distributional information

In addition to the phonological and prosodic cues discussed in the previous section, distributional information is another source that is helpful in categorising words according to word classes. For example, in English, determiners such as *a*, *one*, and *the* co-occur with nouns, while auxiliaries such as *is*, *can*, and *do* and inflections such as *-ed* and *-ing* occur with verbs (Maratsos, 1990; Mintz, Newport, & Bever, 2002). Saffran (2002) found that both school-aged children and adults learned an artificial language containing such predictive dependencies (i.e. with words of type A always preceding words of type B) faster and more reliably than an artificial language lacking such predictive dependencies. There is now evidence that even infants as young as 1 year of age are able to categorise words based on such distributional information (Gómez & Lakusta, 2004).

As described in Chapter 2, infants can use transitional probabilities between syllables to discover word boundaries (Saffran, Aslin, & Newport, 1996). It is doubtful that this type of statistical learning would operate in a selective manner such that infants first fully segment the input into words before trying to identify regularities in the sequencing of the words. More likely, the two steps are linked in a cascading fashion – as soon as infants have identified some words in the speech stream, they are ready to track patterns in the sequences of these words. Indeed, Saffran and Wilson (2003) found that 12-month-olds were able to segment words from continuous speech, and, subsequently, use this knowledge to learn a rudimentary artificial grammar.

**artificial grammar** experimental methodology which examines implicit learning of grammatical patterns; participants are tested on their ability to distinguish sequences that follow the rules from those that do not.

Grammatical patterns often involve elements (words, morphemes) that are not adjacent to each other. This is often the case in a grammatical phenomenon called agreement, that is, when a grammatical feature of one word is aligned with a grammatical feature of another word. For example, in English, subject and verb agree in the grammatical feature of number, as in *The man likes beer* versus *The men like beer* and in person, as in *I like beer* versus *He likes beer*. In Russian, subjects and past-tense verbs agree not just in number and person but also in gender, as in *ona upala* [she fell-feminine], *on upal* [he fell-masculine], and *ono upalo* [it fell-neuter]. Agreement between sentence constituents provides cross-reference and adds redundancy by highlighting certain grammatical relations. This is especially useful for keeping track of grammatical relations when agreement encompasses long distances of multiple intervening words as in *The man in the red shirt at the kitchen table likes beer* versus *The men in the red shirts at the kitchen table like beer*.

Can infants track such long-distance patterns of agreement? Using the preferential headturn procedure, Santelmann and Jusczyk (1998) presented 15- and 18-month-olds with passages containing sentences with natural dependencies, such as *Everybody is baking bread*, and contrasted them with passages containing ungrammatical dependencies, such as *Everybody can baking bread*. They found that 18-month-olds, but not 15-month-olds, listened longer to passages with natural dependencies, even if there were up to three intervening syllables, as in *Everybody is of₁ten₂ ba₃king bread* (the three intervening syllables are numbered by indices). One could argue that perhaps prosodic or co-articulatory differences rendered the ungrammatical sequence *Everybody can baking bread* less natural sounding than its grammatical counterpart, thus allowing infants to distinguish the two sentences on that basis. This problem can be overcome by using the artificial language methodology to control other sources of information (see Methodology Box 11.1). Using this methodology, Gómez (2002) examined whether 18-month-old infants could track long-distance patterns of agreement between first and last syllables in four-syllable nonsense sequences like *pel-wadim-rud*. She found that infants only discovered the long-distance agreement patterns if the training sequences contained many different intervening middle segments (24, to be exact), as in *pel-wadim-rud, pel-kicey-rud, pel-puser-rud*, and so on, but not when fewer (3 or 12) different intervening segments occurred over the course of training. Apparently, variability in the intervening segments helps infants to discover the invariant part of the sequence. If we conceptualise the intervening segments as word stems and the external syllables as inflectional morphemes or grammatical function words, the relevance of these findings to grammar learning becomes clearer. Consider, for example, the patterns of inflections in the Russian case-marking system

**Table 5.1**   *Patterns of long-distance agreement between Russian prepositions and case markers (shown for three masculine nouns). These patterns of agreement provide a direct natural language analogy to the artificial stimuli tested in Gómez (2002).*

| case | | | |
|---|---|---|---|
| **Genitive** | **ot** *stola* [from the table] | **ot** *doma* [from the house] | **ot** *barabana* [from the drum] |
| **Dative** | **k** *stolu* [to the table] | **k** *domu* [to the house] | **k** *barabanu* [to the drum] |
| **Accusative** | **na** *stol* [onto the table] | **na** *dom* [onto the house] | **na** *baraban* [onto the drum] |
| **Instrumental** | **pod** *stolom* [under the table] | **pod** *domom* [under the house] | **pod** *barabanom* [under the drum] |
| **Locative** | **v** *stole* [in the table] | **v** *dome* [in the house] | **v** *barabane* [in the drum] |

(see Table 5.1), where specific prepositions co-occur with specific case-marking suffixes on nouns. Subsequent studies have shown that not just children, but also adult learners of a foreign language benefit from hearing more different words instantiate such long-distance patterns of agreement (Brooks, Kempe, & Sionov, 2006).

### 5.2.3   Generalising to novel words

Productive language use requires generalisation. A crucial question, therefore, is whether infants can generalise extracted patterns to novel words, and if so, at what age. To answer this question, Marcus, Vijayan, Bandi Rao, and Vishton (1999) had 7-month-old infants listen to sequences of nonsense syllables such as *ga-ti-ti* or *li-na-na*, which instantiated a specific pattern (e.g. ABB). If infants had extracted a pattern from these sequences they should differentiate the familiar sequences from novel ones like *ga-ti-ga* or *li-na-li*. However, this discrimination could be made purely on the basis of transitional probabilities if infants learn, for example, that *ga* never follows *ti* and *li* never follows *na*. To find out whether infants were able to generalise beyond individual items, the researchers played sequences containing novel syllables that either were consistent (e.g. *wo-fe-fe*) or not consistent (e.g. *wo-fe-wo*) with the pattern presented before. Quite impressively, 7-month-old infants distinguished sequences that were consistent with the learned pattern from inconsistent ones. Marcus and his colleagues (1999) interpreted their result to mean that the infants acquired an abstract symbolic rule. We will evaluate this argument at the end of the chapter. For now we shall just note that infants have the ability to generalise sequential patterns extracted from language input. By the end of the first year, infants can detect and generalise patterns of even greater complexity involving longer sequences of up to six syllables (Gómez & Gerken, 1999).

In sum, there is now a compelling body of empirical evidence demonstrating that infants use statistical learning to exploit distributional information and co-variation between grammar and sound to detect aspects of grammatical structure. Thus, owing to general-purpose learning mechanisms enabling sequence learning and invariance detection, the foundations of grammatical knowledge are laid long before the first word is even spoken.

## 5.3   HOW DO CHILDREN LEARN TO COMBINE AND MODIFY WORDS?

In this section we will describe children's emerging productivity in combining and modifying words. As mentioned above, syntax and morphology acquisition have traditionally been studied separately. It seems, however, that the challenges involved in learning both domains are similar, and the underlying learning mechanisms may be the same as well. In both domains, children must learn to generalise a grammatical pattern to new words, while at the same time limiting its use in compliance with the conventions of their language community.

### 5.3.1   Item-based learning of grammatical structures

Toddlers' first discernible word combinations appear to be imitations of simple patterns encountered in parent–child interaction. These patterns typically consist of a verb, a preposition, or some other relational term (e.g. *all-gone*) preceded or followed by a noun or a pronoun (e.g. *all-gone juice*). Braine (1976) proposed that children develop simple word-specific formulae consisting of a relational term and a slot (e.g. *all-gone* _____); these simple combinatory formulae are sufficient to support generalisation of the pattern to new words, for example, saying *all-gone sticky* following a hand washing (Braine, 1971).

**word-specific formulae** the child's first syntactic templates or schemas used to produce word combinations; these consist of a relational term and a slot (e.g. *all gone* ____ used to produce utterances such as *all gone milk* or *all gone cookies*).

Because verbs have specific combinatory requirements (see discussion of verb argument structure in Section 5.1.1), and thus serve as the key determinants of sentence structure, much attention has been paid to children's first word combinations involving verbs (Tomasello, 1992; Pinker, 1989; Ninio, 2006, 2011). Tomasello (1992) kept a detailed diary of his daughter's early use of verbs, and reported that she used each of her verbs in a seemingly idiosyncratic way. For example, she only ever produced the verb *cut* in verb–object combinations like *cut paper*, but produced the verb *draw* in a variety of constructions like *draw kitty*, *draw on paper*, *draw kitty on paper*, *draw kitty for Mummy* (Tomasello, 1992, 2000). Tomasello argued that the best predictor of how his daughter would use a particular verb on a particular day was her prior history of usage of that verb; that is, what the child was discovering about grammatical structure was tied to her learning of the combinatorial properties of individual verbs.

Item-based productions have also been observed in the acquisition of morphology: children start out by using inflected forms of nouns selectively and idiosyncratically. For example, Gvozdev (1961), in his detailed record of his Russian-speaking son's early speech, noted that certain case markers would only appear with certain nouns; for example, the instrumental case marker -*om* would only be used with nouns denoting instruments, even though the instrumental case expresses a variety of other relationships in the language. Early use of function words is also very much item-based: in a corpus of 12 English-speaking children, Pine and Lieven (1997) observed that early use of the determiners *the* and *a* was at first confined to completely different sets of nouns.

Given that early patterns of word usage are item-based, how do children come to expand these patterns to produce more complex utterances? One view is that children tend to re-use familiar patterns in slightly different ways rather than create novel patterns from scratch. Children start by inserting different words into the slots of word-specific formulae, which allows them to creatively construct novel utterances (e.g. *all-gone Daddy*). Essentially, children 'cut' pieces of language they have already used before and 'paste' them into slots opened up by other familiar words. Tomasello (2000) illustrates this process with the following example: a child may have used the pattern *See ball* or *See this* and the pattern *Daddy's car* and *Daddy's pen*. She may then combine them into *See Daddy's car* simply by inserting one pattern into the slot of the other one. Thus, multi-word utterances may arise from children gradually concatenating words onto the beginnings or ends of word-specific formulae (Lieven, Behrens, Speares, & Tomasello, 2003).

## 5.3.2   Discovering schemas

**schemas** patterns or representations that are an abstraction over learned exemplars and support generalisation.

Over time, children may notice that groups of words exhibit similar patterns of usage. In studies of morphology acquisition, such groups of words are often referred to as schemas (Dąbrowska, 2006). For example, having encountered a sufficient number of inflected forms like *walked, talked, cooked* or *stung, strung, clung* or *slept, wept, crept*, children will notice the recurrent patterns and form the appropriate schema. Similarly, Slobin and Bever (1982) referred to recurrent syntactic patterns such as subject–verb–object as sentence schemas.

Schemas are built up as children notice relational similarities in the usage of words, for example, that the verbs *walked* and *talked* share a similar ending and that they both express past tense, or that the verbs *walk* and *run* occur in similar constructions that express similar meanings. Such comparison processes have been termed structural alignment (Gentner & Namy, 2006). With respect to morphology, similarities in the sound patterns of words facilitate the productive use of a schema (Rumelhart & McClelland, 1986; Dąbrowska, 2006). For example, in some morphologically rich languages like Polish, Russian, and Lithuanian, diminutives – morphological derivations that express smallness and endearment like *doggy* or *Patty* – share salient suffixes that render them more similar to each other than simplex nouns; for example, the Russian simplex nouns *stol* [table], *dom* [house], and *baraban* [drum] are less similar to each other than their corresponding diminutive forms *stolik, domik,* and *barabanchik*. Diminutives are often very frequent in child-directed speech (Kempe, Brooks, & Pirott, 2001). As a result, children learning languages like Polish, Russian or Lithuanian acquire aspects of inflectional morphology such as gender agreement or case marking earlier with diminutives than with simplex forms of nouns (Kempe, Ševa, Brooks, Mironova, Pershukova, & Fedorova, 2009; Dąbrowska, 2006). For example, Russian 3-year-olds are more likely to provide correct adjective–noun gender agreement for diminutive nouns (e.g. *krasnaya vazochka* [red-feminine vase-feminine diminutive]) than for simplex nouns (e.g. *krasnaya vaza* [red-feminine vase-feminine]). The advantage for similar-sounding words like diminutives holds not only for familiar words, but also generalises to novel, made-up

**structural alignment** the detection of an invariant relational pattern over different lexical items; a mechanism that underlies the use of analogy to support generalisation or metaphor comprehension.

**inflectional morphology** the subfield of linguistics concerned with the processes by which word-form modifications mark changes in grammatical features, such as number, gender, and tense; relies on inflectional affixes.

words (Kempe, Brooks, Mironova, & Fedorova, 2003). Dąbrowska (2006) has suggested that diminutives constitute a low-level schema that co-exists with other higher-level schemas to support productive use of morphology; thus, different degrees of abstraction may co-exist in the child's as well as in the adult's grammatical system (Albright & Hayes, 2003; Dąbrowska, 2008).

For a schema to be noticed, a pattern needs to have a sufficiently high type frequency, that is, it needs to be used sufficiently frequently with different words (as opposed to being used mainly with the same words, which would result in a high token frequency). We discussed this already in the context of learning long-distance dependencies (Gómez, 2002). Patterns with high type frequency are more likely to be generalised (Marchman & Bates, 1994). For example, the more different verbs ending in *-ed* children hear, the more likely they will be to use the *-ed* ending to form the past tense of a new verb (Bybee, 1985, 1995). Similarly, if a relational term (e.g. *all-gone*) has appeared often with a variety of slot fillers (e.g. *all-gone cookie, all-gone milk, all-gone juice*), children will be more likely to use it with other nouns (Bannard & Matthews, 2008; Matthews & Bannard, 2010). Ninio (1999, 2006) traced children's first productions of verb–object (e.g. *Want cookie*) and subject–verb–object combinations (e.g. *Daddy made that*) and found that each grammatical pattern showed exponential growth indicative of the effects of practice. The more verbs a child already knew how to use in a particular combinatory pattern, the faster they learned to use other verbs with that pattern. There was relatively little overlap in the verbs that occurred in verb–object and subject–verb–object combinations, which suggests that children used the two sentence schemas for different communicative functions (e.g. making requests vs. sharing experiences).

**type frequency** how often a given construction or schema is used with different words.

**token frequency** how often a given construction or schema is used in general, regardless of how many different words it occurs with.

There are conflicting views on the role of semantic similarity in children's acquisition of grammar. Ninio (2005) and others (e.g. Howe, 1976; Tomasello, 1992) have shown that toddlers' word combinations are not readily describable in terms of broad semantic categories, such as agent and patient (i.e. with 'agent' referring to an individual performing an action on an object, and 'patient' referring to the object acted on). Rather, children's first verbs (e.g. *want, see, make, get,* and *eat*) express different relationships with their arguments; this suggests that the semantic role assigned to a particular noun in a grammatical construction (e.g. subject–verb–object) is dependent on the particular verb involved. Others (Gleitman, 1990; Goldberg, 2006; Pinker, 1989) have argued that verbs with similar meanings strongly tend to have similar argument structures; children pick up on these co-occurrence patterns, and they influence how children generalise usage of verbs.

### 5.3.3 Understanding and producing verbs

As discussed in Section 5.1.1, each verb has its own range of possible argument structures. With the verb *cook*, one can say *Sam is cooking the soup* or *The soup is cooking*; in contrast, with the verb *stir*, one can say *Sam is stirring the soup* but not

*The soup is stirring.* Even verbs with a high degree of semantic overlap may have different argument structures; compare *She dropped the box* with the ungrammatical *She falled the box.* How do children learn which argument struc-

tures go with which verbs? To answer this question, researchers have adapted the elicited production task, pioneered in the famous **wug test** of children's productivity with morphology (Berko, 1958), to probe children's use of argument structure constructions (see Methodology Box 5.1). First a made-up verb like *tam, meek* or *gorp* is paired with a novel action (e.g. jiggling objects suspended from a pendulum and is introduced in a particular sentence structure, such as *The lion is tamming the orange* or, alternatively, *The orange is tamming all around* (Braine, Brody, Fisch, Weisberger, & Blum, 1990). The child is prompted to use the novel verb through questions carefully devised to encourage their production of sentences with either *the lion* or *the orange* as subject. Using this technique, a number of studies (e.g. Akhtar & Tomasello, 1997; Brooks & Tomasello, 1999b; Olguin & Tomasello, 1993; Tomasello, Akhtar, Dodson, & Rekau, 1997; Tomasello & Brooks, 1998) have shown that 2-year-olds overwhelmingly tend to use a novel verb in the same construction as they have heard it used by others, albeit with pronouns substituted for nouns, and with some of the arguments omitted. For example, having heard sentences like *The lion is tamming the orange*, 2-year-olds are likely to answer the question *What is the lion doing?* by saying *Tamming it*, and they are likely to answer the question *What's happening with the orange?* by saying *He's tamming it.*

Yet despite their strong preference for matching an adult's usage of novel verbs, toddlers occasionally use verbs in ways that go beyond the input (Braine et al., 1990; Tomasello & Brooks, 1998). Tomasello and Brooks (1998) introduced 2-year-olds to one verb in a transitive construction (e.g. *The rabbit is meeking the ball*) and a second verb in an intransitive construction (e.g. *The orange is tamming all around*), and probed for the opposite construction with elicitation questions (as described above). Not surprisingly, the toddlers mostly used the transitive-introduced verb in the transitive construction and the intransitive-introduced verb in the intransitive construction – that is, they produced 10 times as many utterances 'matching' the construction as 'mismatching' it. Nevertheless, over half of the toddlers at age 2 years, 6 months used the 'intransitive' novel verb at least once with a direct object – for example, after hearing *The orange is tamming all around*, they answered the question *What is the lion doing?* by saying *Tamming it.* Similarly, for the 'transitive' novel verb, over half of the toddlers produced intransitive utterances – for example, after hearing *The rabbit is meeking the ball*, they answered the question *What is happening with the ball?* by saying *It's meeking.* (However, at 2 years 0 months, fewer than 1 out of 5 toddlers showed such productivity.) Brooks and Tomasello (1999b) similarly reported that the majority of children at 2 years, 10 months who heard one verb modelled in an active-voice construction (e.g. *The lion is tamming the orange*) and a second verb in the passive-voice construction (e.g. *The ball is getting meeked by the rabbit*) used one of the verbs in the opposite construction at least once, for example, answering the question *What happened to the orange?* by saying

# METHODOLOGY BOX 5.1    ELICITED PRODUCTION STUDIES WITH NOVEL WORDS

The advantage of using novel words is that the effects of prior learning can be controlled and grammatical knowledge can be studied separately from the influence of word meaning. Jean Berko Gleason pioneered the use of made-up words for the study of children's linguistic knowledge. In her seminal 1958 study, preschoolers and first-graders were presented with a drawing of an unfamiliar creature called a *wug* (Figure 5.1). After having demonstrated that they were able to repeat the word, children were then shown a picture of two creatures and told *Now there are two of them. There are two ____?* Production of the correct form *wugs* was taken as an indicator that children had learnt the abstract rule of plural formation. The children were also tested on other morphological forms, for example, on nonce verbs, to elicit past-tense formation. Children were shown a picture and told *This is a man who knows how to rick. He is ricking. He did the same thing yesterday. What did he do yesterday? Yesterday, he ____.* The children readily produced forms like *wugs* and *ricked,* but performed poorly with forms like *nizzes* and *bodded,* indicating that morphological processes are affected by a word's phonological features. All of Berko's original stimuli have been made publically available for download through the CHILDES online database.

Another application of the elicited production task, as explained in the text, involves the use of novel verbs to study children's generalisation of constructions. For example, when shown the action of a lion swinging an orange suspended from a pendulum, accompanied by a sentence like *The lion is tamming the orange,* (Figure 5.2) children will tend to respond to the subsequent question *What's happening to the orange?* with *He is tamming it,* but will occasionally say *It is tamming* or *It's getting tammed* (Brooks & Tomasello, 1999a, 1999b).

*This is a wug.*

*Now there are two of them. There are two ____ .*

**Figure 5.1**    *Example of the stimuli used for the wug test*

*Source:* Based on Berko, 1958.

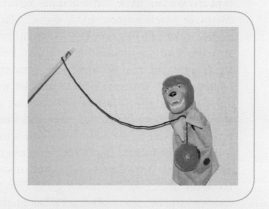

**Figure 5.2**    *Apparatus used in the elicited production experiments of Brooks and Tomasello (1999a, 1999b).*

*Source:* Photograph courtesy of Patricia Brooks and Vera Kempe.

**syntactic priming** the tendency to use the same grammatical construction over successive utterances.

*It got tammed.* These studies, and others (e.g. Bencini & Valian, 2008), demonstrate that modelling verbs in a particular argument structure primes toddlers to use the same argument structure with other verbs. This phenomenon is called syntactic priming, and is well documented in studies with older children (e.g. Huttenlocher, Vasilyeva, & Shimpi, 2004; Savage, Lieven, Theakston, & Tomasello, 2006) as well as adults (e.g. Bock, 1986; Pickering & Branigan, 1998).

In contrast to elicited production studies, which document toddlers' strong tendency to use novel verbs in the same syntactic constructions in which they are modelled, studies of children's early comprehension paint a somewhat different picture of children's grammatical development. Gertner, Fisher, and Eisengart (2006) showed children around 2 years of age two pictures with different actions performed by the same actors: in one picture, a bunny was performing some action on a rabbit, and in the other picture, the rabbit was performing a different action on the bunny. Children then heard a sentence containing a nonce verb like *The rabbit is gorping the bunny*, and were prompted by requests like *Find gorping!* to look at the picture corresponding to the sentence. Note that since children do not know what *gorping* means, the only way to figure out which picture corresponds to the sentence is to rely on word order. The results showed that children reliably looked longer to the picture matching the action, thus showing evidence for knowledge of word-order rules in English. Slightly older children were even able to map intransitive sentences containing nonce verbs (e.g. *Bunny is gorping*) to the correct pictures (Fernandes, Marcus, DiNubila, & Vouloumanos, 2006). The authors' interpretation of these findings is that the children must have acquired abstract knowledge of word-order rules for identifying who did what to whom, since verb meaning could not have helped in differentiating the depicted actions.

However, an alternative interpretation of these findings is that, as children are exposed to language, they acquire many probabilistic cues to sentence meaning (Bates & MacWhinney, 1979; Bates, MacWhinney, Caselli, Devescovi, Natale, & Venza, 1984). For example, the first noun of a sentence with two protagonists is very likely to denote the one who is 'doing' the action, because this is the case in the majority of English sentences. This noun is more likely than not to refer to an animate entity, and may have overt case marking (e.g. pronouns such as *he* and *him* distinguish English subjects and objects). Consequently, in the Gertner et al. (2006) study, the finding that children looked longer at the matching sentence may simply reflect their use of the 'The first noun is the agent' cue in English. These conflicting interpretations show that the issue of whether children acquire abstract grammatical knowledge is at the heart of theoretical debates in language development research. Does the ability to detect and generalise patterns of regularity mean that children uncover and represent abstract rules of the type posited by Generative Grammars, or are children relying on mechanisms of statistical learning, imitation, and analogy to transfer the detected regularities from one instance to the next without recourse to abstract rules?

# 5.4 WHY DO CHILDREN MAKE GRAMMATICAL ERRORS AND HOW DO THEY STOP?

## 5.4.1 Errors in production

Once children combine words productively, they start producing over-generalisation errors such as *I goed, two mouses, Don't giggle me* or *Stay it there*. Over-generalisation errors appear in syntax and in morphology. Syntactic over-generalisation errors involve the child's use of a verb in a construction that is not conventional in their language community (Bowerman, 1988; Pinker, 1989). In many cases, children use transitive subject–verb–object or verb–object constructions with intransitive verbs (Bowerman & Croft, 2007; Loeb, Pye, Richardson, & Redmond, 1998), but errors with other syntactic patterns are also common, as in *Explain me your answer* or *I spilled it of orange juice*. Children at this age also creatively devise 'lexical innovations' (Clark, 1993; Swan, 2000), such as *Let me broom the floor* (meaning 'sweep'), *I'm softing you right here* (meaning 'stroke softly'), or *I'm gonna higher you up* (meaning 'lift you higher'), in which the child uses a noun or an adjective as if it were a verb. Morphological over-generalisation errors involve regularising irregular forms that are considered exceptions to a general pattern (e.g. *goed, mouses*). In morphologically rich languages, where the variety of morphological patterns makes it difficult to distinguish regular and irregular forms, over-generalisation errors involve application of an inflection that applies to one group of words to another group of words. In Russian, for example, children may use masculine gender agreement or case markers with feminine nouns (Gvozdev, 1961). Over-generalisation errors are especially common in 3- to 6-year-olds, although estimates of their frequency vary widely (Marcus et al., 1992; Clark, 2003). Proponents of rule-based approaches to grammatical knowledge interpret over-generalisations as the misapplication of an abstract rule (e.g. 'add *-ed*' to form the past tense of English verbs). Proponents of usage-based approaches interpret them as manifestations of on-the-spot pressures to produce fluent speech, and not as systematic deviations in the child's grammatical representations (Braine & Brooks, 1995; MacWhinney, 2004; Ramscar & Yarlett, 2007). Even adults occasionally produce such errors, which may be a consequence of fatigue or distraction.

Over time, over-generalisation errors become less frequent. A central, and not entirely resolved, question in language acquisition research is what makes these errors disappear. One answer, which has been developed based mainly on studies of English past-tense formation, assumes that children start out producing correct irregular forms like *went* and *came* while their repertoire of verbs is still small. Once they acquire more verbs they discover the 'add *-ed*' rule, and start applying it productively.

In adults, the application of this rule to irregular verbs like *go* and *come* is blocked by retrieval of the irregular past-tense form from the lexicon. However, in children this blocking mechanism is hampered by insufficient memory capacity, so that irregular forms are in some cases not immediately accessible. As memory capacity increases, over-generalisation errors will gradually disappear (Marcus et al., 1992).

There are several problems with this explanation. First, if children discover a rule, then its application should mark a sudden increase in the use of regular past-tense forms. The developmental data do not support this prediction. Careful analyses of speech corpora from a number of children suggest that the increase in the use of regular past-tense forms in the third year of life is continuous and gradual (Brown, 1973; McClelland & Patterson, 2002). Secondly, if children form regular inflections using a rule, then there should be no effects of similarity in sound or meaning. However, wug test-like studies with adults, which examined past-tense formation for nonce verbs that vary in phonological and semantic similarity to real regular verbs, did show effects of similarity, at least for adults (Albright & Hayes, 2003; Ramscar, 2002). Such similarity effects have also been attested for the over-generalisation of verb constructions. For example, English-speaking children are more willing to over-generalise the transitive subject–verb–object construction with an intransitive verb denoting a manner of motion (e.g. verbs such as *roll, swing, bounce, jiggle*) than with an intransitive verb referring to a motion in a specific direction (e.g. verbs such as *fall, come, descend, rise*) (Brooks & Tomasello, 1999a) or an intransitive verb referring to an internally caused action (e.g. verbs such as *cough, laugh, blush, squeal*) (Ambridge, Pine, Rowland, & Young, 2008). Similarity effects constitute evidence against the idea that use of inflections and constructions is based on the application of abstract rules.

A more plausible explanation for the gradual decline of over-generalisation errors is that erroneous forms (generated in analogy with existing correct forms) and correct forms (encountered in the language input) may co-exist in associative memory. During childhood these two forms compete, so that retrieval of each form is possible. This is in line with developmental data showing that children tend to oscillate between correct and over-generalised forms. Recovery from over-generalisation takes place as a by-product of learning and practice during which the representation of the correct form (e.g. *mice*) is gradually strengthened, so that it eventually out-competes the alternative (e.g. *mouses*) (Ramscar & Yarlett, 2007). As children hear and produce the correct form more and more often, this form gradually becomes entrenched (Braine & Brooks, 1995); words with more entrenched patterns of usage become more resilient to error. As a result, children are more likely to make errors with newly introduced (or low-frequency) words for which they lack the relevant experience (Brooks, Tomasello, Dodson, & Lewis, 1999; Theakston, 2004). It is likely that improved cognitive control, which comes with maturation of the prefrontal cortex (Gogtay et al., 2004), may also explain why older children can resolve competition between alternative forms in a more efficient way.

**pre-emption** when a linguistic expression blocks production of another form; for example the irregular past-tense form *went* blocks production of *goed*.

Another factor that helps children to avoid producing ungrammatical forms is pre-emption. When children encounter sentences like *She went to the store, Don't make me giggle* or *The child that was afraid ran home*, these alternative constructions may pre-empt (i.e. block) the production of ungrammatical forms like *She goed to the store, Don't giggle me* or *The afraid child ran home* (Boyd & Goldberg, 2011; Braine & Brooks, 1995; Goldberg, 1995, 2006). Brooks and Zizak (2002) taught children the novel verbs *tam* and *dack*, with one verb introduced in transitive sentences and the other in intransitive sentences. Some of the children also heard alternative constructions; for example, if *tam* was introduced as a transitive verb (*The bird is tamming the house*), the children also heard passive sentences like *The house is getting tammed*. Likewise, if *dack* was introduced as an intransitive verb (*The car is dacking all around*), the children also heard periphrastic causative sentences like *The rabbit made the car dack*. If pre-emption blocks over-generalisation, then children who hear *The rabbit made the car dack* should avoid saying *The rabbit dacked the car* when asked *What did the rabbit do?* That is, use of a periphrastic construction (and non-use of the transitive) should signal to the child that the simple transitive is not grammatical. However, when alternative constructions were presented, only older children (6- to 7-year-olds), but not younger children (4-year-olds), produced fewer over-generalisation errors compared to a control group who did not hear the pre-empting constructions (see also Brooks & Tomasello, 1999a). This suggests that pre-emption plays a role in the recovery from argument structure over-generalisation only fairly late in development.

In addition to over-generalisation errors, children make occasional errors in executing syntactic operations throughout childhood. A great deal of research has explored the difficulties English-speaking children experience in mastering the subject–auxiliary inversion operation crucial for question formation (e.g. *Sam likes milk. What does Sam like?*). Children make errors in producing questions by omitting auxiliaries (*What he doing?*), failing to invert the subject and auxiliary (*Who she is hitting?*), and generating double auxiliaries (*What does she does like?*) or double tensing (*What does he likes?*) (Ambridge, Rowland, Theakston, & Tomasello, 2006; Rowland, 2007; Santelmann, Berk, Austin, Somashekar, & Lust, 2002). The distribution of these errors can also be explained by entrenchment: the frequency of errors varies as a function of the specific *wh*-word + auxiliary combination, with highly entrenched combinations (i.e. those most frequent in caregiver speech) seemingly protected from error in children's language (Ambridge et al., 2006; Rowland, 2007).

## 5.4.2 Errors in comprehension

Children often have difficulties interpreting sentences that are complex in structure – this ability to analyse and interpret the syntactic structure of a sentence is called parsing. Numerous studies (Donaldson & McGarrigle, 1974; Freeman, 1985; Inhelder & Piaget,

> **parsing** the ability to analyse and interpret the syntactic structure of a sentence.

1958, 1964) have demonstrated that children make errors in parsing sentences containing universal quantifiers (*all, each, every*). In a picture-choice task (Brooks & Braine, 1996; Brooks & Sekerina, 2005 / 2006), children are shown two sets of objects in partial one-to-one correspondence (see Figure 5.3) and are asked to select the picture where

**Figure 5.3**    *Pictures used to test children's understanding of the scope of universal quantifiers like* every.

*every cat is on a chair* or, alternatively, to select the picture where *every chair has a cat on it*. Children younger than 9 years of age make numerous errors, seemingly unsure as to which set (cats or chairs) is modified by the quantifier *every* (Brooks & Braine, 1996; Brooks & Sekerina, 2005 / 2006); similar errors have also been documented in adults with low educational attainment (Street & Dąbrowska, 2010). In a sentence–picture verification task, children are shown just one picture or scene – for example, the one with three cats and two extra chairs – and are asked *Is every cat on a chair?* Young children usually say *no*, and frequently point out the extra chairs as needing cats. Such errors, termed quantifier spreading errors, suggest that children interpret *every cat is on a chair* as entailing its converse, that *every chair has a cat on it* (Geurts, 2003; Kang, 2001; Roeper, 2007).

A particularly interesting example of children's parsing errors involves sentences containing structural ambiguities, as studied using the visual world paradigm (see Figure 5.4). Children are shown an array of objects – for example, two dogs, two napkins, and a box, with one of the dogs sitting on a napkin – and are given an instruction to follow, for example, *Put the dog on the napkin in the box* (Trueswell, Sekerina, Hill, & Logrip, 1999). This instruction is difficult to parse because it contains a reduced relative clause (*the dog on the napkin*) that is temporarily ambiguous – the prepositional phrase *on the napkin* could denote either the location of the dog or the destination of the action (unlike the unreduced relative clause *the dog that's on the napkin*). When asked to follow such instructions, 5-year-olds typically interpret the prepositional phrase as a destination, rather than a modifier – they place one of the dogs on the empty napkin, and sometimes move it into the box. Adults, in contrast, tend to make few errors – they correctly select the dog that is sitting on the napkin and put it in the box. Nevertheless, by monitoring their eye movements to the objects in the visual world (using a special head-mounted camera), we can see the consequences of the temporary ambiguity

**quantifier spreading errors** comprehension errors involving sentences containing a universal quantifier, such as *every* or *each*; the child incorrectly infers that a sentence like *Every car is in a garage* entails its converse – that every garage has a car in it.

**visual world paradigm** an experimental task used with an eye-tracking device; monitors a participant's attention to objects in a visual array as they process a set of spoken instructions to manipulate specific objects.

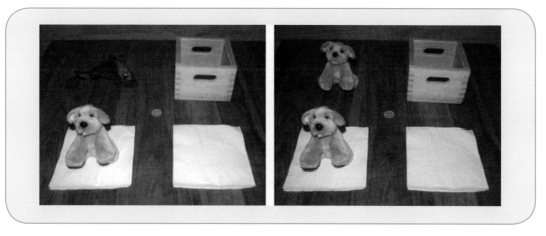

**Figure 5.4** *One-referent (left panel) and two-referent (right panel) context for the sentence* Put the dog on the napkin in the box *used in a visual world paradigm.*

*Source:* Photograph courtesy of Patricia Brooks and Vera Kempe.

on sentence processing. Adults typically look first to the incorrect dog (i.e. the one that is *not* on a napkin), but as they hear more of the sentence, they revise their initial interpretation and correctly select the other dog and put it into the box. Children seem to have difficulty taking into account contextual cues – the presence of two identical dogs that need to be distinguished – and they fail to revise their initially incorrect interpretations, even when the remaining words in the sentence do not fit (Trueswell et al., 1999; see also Snedeker & Trueswell, 2004; Snedeker & Yuan, 2008; Kidd, Stewart, & Serratrice, 2011). However, when asked to describe the two dogs, 5-year-olds are perfectly capable of producing well-formed responses containing reduced relative clauses, for example, *Which dog visited Mrs. Bear's house? The one on the napkin!* (Hurewitz, Brown-Schmidt, Thorpe, Gleitman, & Trueswell, 2000).

When it comes to learning sounds and words, children's comprehension is usually ahead of production, as described in Chapters 3 and 4. Here, the situation seems to be reversed. So what then accounts for this peculiar discrepancy between production and comprehension? Firstly, children seem to respond strongly to lexical cues, that is, their knowledge of how words are typically used in sentences. Overwhelmingly, in the sentences children encounter, the verb *put* is accompanied by a prepositional phrase that refers to an object's destination (as in *Put the groceries in the refrigerator*). Thus, the argument structure of *put* biases the listener to interpret a prepositional phrase as a destination as opposed to a modifier. Secondly, comprehension requires taking into account a multitude of probabilistic cues, and such cues require time to acquire. We have seen that in infants' use of probabilistic cues when discovering word boundaries, word classes, and simple grammatical units. But it is a great leap from there to the sophisticated integration of multiple cues involved in sentence parsing. Thirdly, when listeners encounter linguistic ambiguities, considerable processing capacity is required to keep in mind the possible interpretations of an ambiguous word or structure (Clahsen & Felser, 2006); at 5 years of age, working memory capacity is still rather limited (Cowan & Alloway, 2009). In production, on the other hand, speakers usually pursue just one intended interpretation, so less processing capacity is required. Finally, to be able to revise an initial interpretation later on, if need be, requires cognitive flexibility (Novick, Trueswell, & Thompson-Schill, 2005): executive control of attention and the ability to shift between mental sets depend on the functioning of the prefrontal cortex. Given the slow maturation of this cortical region (Gogtay et al., 2004), the lack of control of attention in children might limit their ability to reanalyse sentences after an initial interpretation has been assigned, and might bias them to select the most frequent interpretation of an ambiguous structure (Thompson-Schill, Ramscar, & Chrysikou, 2010).

In this chapter, we have discussed the remarkable abilities of infants and toddlers to squeeze regularity out of noisy language input. The same factors that lead young children to extract and generalise frequent patterns might also explain some of their comprehension errors. Only with time are children's syntactic abilities fine-tuned to deal adequately with all the various complexities and uncertainties of human verbal communication.

## SUMMARY

- **Children have to learn the conventions of their language communities that determine how to combine and modify words to produce meaningful utterances.**

- **Research on how children learn grammar has been inspired by linguistic theories. Some theories postulate the existence of abstract rules that govern how to combine words according to word class, whereas other theories describe grammar as patterns of usage that are specific to individual words.**

- **During their first year of life, children use statistical learning to extract patterns of regularity in language. Infants are able to capitalise on the fact that phonological and prosodic cues tend to co-occur with word classes and with boundaries between syntactic constituents. They are also sensitive to distributional regularities in word sequences and can transfer learnt patterns to novel items.**

- **Children's early word combinations and modifications are word-specific and conservative. Patterns that are encountered more often are likely to be used more often and are also more likely to be transferred to novel words.**

- **Patterns of usage that are encountered with many different words and in many different contexts can aggregate into schemas which may form the** basis for more abstract representations. This is why grammatical development is tightly linked to vocabulary development.

- Between 3 and 6 years of age children tend to produce over-generalisation errors which gradually disappear. One explanation is that, with time, the correct but weaker form gains in associative strength due to practice, and eventually out-competes the incorrect form.

- Children also show some deficits in comprehension which may be associated with limited cognitive control impairing the ability to consider several interpretations in parallel.

# FURTHER READING

## Key studies

For an experimental study eliciting over-generalisation errors, read Brooks, P. J., Tomasello, M., Dodson, K. & Lewis, L. (1999). Young children's overgeneralizations with fixed transitivity verbs. *Child Development*, *70*, 1325–1337.

## Overview articles

These articles describe the various mechanisms underlying grammar learning:

Gentner, D. & Namy, L. L. (2006). Analogical processes in language learning. *Current Directions in Psychological Science*, *15*, 297–301.

Saffran, J. R. (2003). Statistical language learning: Mechanisms and constraints. *Current Directions in Psychological Science*, *12*, 110–111.

Tomasello, M. (2000). The item-based nature of children's early syntactic development. *Trends in Cognitive Sciences*, *4*, 156–163.

## Books

For a better theoretical understanding of grammatical development, read Goldberg, A. (2006). *Constructions at work: The nature of generalization in language*. Oxford: Oxford University Press and Ninio, A. (2006). *Language and the learning curve: A new theory of syntactic development*. Oxford: Oxford University Press.

# 6 What Kind of Language do Children Encounter?

## KEY TERMS

• alloparents • analytic strategy • child-directed speech • Child Language Data Exchange System (CHILDES) • Codes for the Human Analysis of Transcripts (CHAT) • Computerised Language Analysis (CLAN) • discourse • holistic strategy • hyper-articulation • indirect negative evidence • infant-directed speech • inflectional morphology • joint attention • longitudinal studies • mean length of utterances (MLU) • motionese • polyadic interactions • prosody • sign languages • speech register • tonal languages • schemas

# CHAPTER OUTLINE

Nativist accounts of language acquisition regard language input as a mere trigger for the maturation of language competence. Consequently, its specific features are not deemed to be of much theoretical importance. Usage-based accounts, on the other hand, assign great importance to the input children hear. The previous chapters discussed how infants extract important information about the structure of language from the input. Given this theoretical tension, it is important to take a closer look at what language input children actually receive. Obviously, children born into English-speaking environments grow up speaking English, and children born into Japanese-speaking environments end up speaking Japanese. Still, within each linguistic community, what exactly is the nature of input children learn from and how does it shape language learning? Can differences in the input be linked to differences in learning outcomes? Is language actually being taught to children in some way, or do they just pick it up from whatever snippets of speech they may encounter? These questions are of considerable theoretical importance, as they may help us to understand how universal the process of language acquisition is. Do all children proceed at the same speed and pass important milestones of language learning at around the same time regardless of input? Does the richness of the input determine how quickly children acquire language and perhaps even what their ultimate level of attainment will be? Such variability in outcomes would suggest that language learning relies on general learning mechanisms which operate over whatever input is available. What is special about human language then is that it may have evolved to be exquisitely compatible with such general human learning mechanisms (see Chapter 1).

In the first two sections of this chapter, we will examine the nature of children's language input, its features, and how it shapes language acquisition. In this context, we will discuss language addressed to children and language overheard by children. In the final section, we will examine the effect of variability in language input on language-learning outcomes.

# 6.1 HOW DO WE ADDRESS CHILDREN?

In our society, interaction with a baby or toddler tends to elicit a very special way of speaking which in other social situations could be perceived as inadequate or even embarrassing (see Figure 6.1). Early research into this way of speaking focused on mothers and used the term 'motherese' to describe the **speech register** used to speak to infants and small children (Snow &

> **speech register** a speech style used in a specific social situation and/or with specific people; it may involve variation in the prosodic, phonological, grammatical, and lexical characteristics of speech.

**Figure 6.1**  *In some cultures, caregivers have conversations with pre-verbal infants, which may encourage infants to vocalise.*

*Source:* © leolintang. Used under licence from Shutterstock.

Ferguson, 1977). The term 'speech register' refers to a specific way of speaking used in certain social situations and with certain people, and may involve variation in the prosodic, phonological, grammatical, and lexical characteristics of speech. Because the special way of addressing children is not unique to mothers, but is in some form used by other speakers such as fathers, siblings, grandparents, and other caregivers, it is more appropriately called infant-directed speech or child-directed speech, depending on the age of the child. For simplicity, we will use the term child-directed speech (CDS), but we will discuss how speech addressed to children changes over developmental time. The most common way to study CDS is to record children in natural interactions with their caregivers. Of course, it is very time-consuming to record, transcribe, and code conversational data, especially if one is interested in longitudinal studies that follow individual children as they develop language over a period of months or years. Fortunately, many researchers have collected such datasets from children learning a wide variety of languages, and they have donated their data for public access and use through the Child Language Data Exchange System (CHILDES), see Methodology Box 6.1.

**child-directed speech** also called **infant-directed speech**; the typical speech register used when talking to infants and small children.

**longitudinal studies** a research design whereby individual development is tracked over a period of time.

**Child Language Data Exchange System (CHILDES)** an online, publicly available archive of child language data with transcripts, audio, and video of children acquiring their first language(s).

## 6.1.1   Child-directed speech prosody

The most salient feature of CDS is that it simply sounds very different from adult-directed speech (ADS). Comparisons of audio-recordings of adult–child conversations with adult–adult conversations have revealed that when addressing infants and small children, adults raise the pitch of their voice and produce intonation contours with more exaggerated highs and lows covering a wider pitch range (see Figure 6.2).

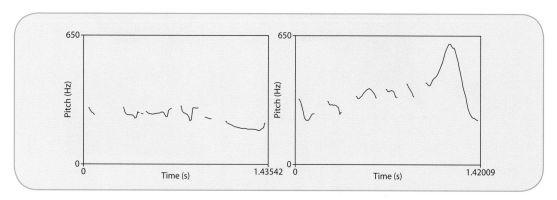

**Figure 6.2**    *Pitch contour for the sentence* Touch the dog with the flower *spoken by a mother addressing an adult (left panel) and her 2-year-old child (right panel).*

## METHODOLOGY BOX 6.1   THE CHILD LANGUAGE DATA EXCHANGE SYSTEM (CHILDES)

The CHILDES database (MacWhinney & Snow, 1985) was created to disseminate coded transcripts of speech obtained from audio- and video-recordings of adult–child interactions occurring in natural situations. Researchers use a common system for coding and transcribing speech called Codes for the Human Analysis of Transcripts (CHAT). CHAT format allows transcripts to be subjected to automated searches and analyses using specially developed software called Computerised Language Analysis (CLAN). The CLAN programs make it possible to perform searches of specific words or morphemes, conduct frequency counts, analyse co-occurrence patterns between words or morphemes, calculate the mean length of utterances (MLU), analyse the morpho-syntactic properties of utterances, and much more. The database is open access at the Cargenie Mellon University website, and contains over 44 million words from over 30 languages, including data from some clinical populations (e.g. children with autism spectrum disorder, Down syndrome or Specific Language Impairment). Data using the CHILDES system have so far resulted in over 3000 scientific publications. Below we provide a CHAT excerpt from a short conversation between a boy aged 3 years 6 months and his father from the MacWhinney corpus. The lines underneath each utterance, which start with '%mor' and '%gra' code the morphological and grammatical information for that utterance using conventional symbols devised in the CHAT transcription system. They have been included just to provide a flavour of the kind of information that can be coded and analysed in CHILDES.

**Codes for the Human Analysis of Transcripts (CHAT)** a system for transcribing and coding speech samples; this common format allows users to conduct searches and analyse transcripts using CLAN software (all transcripts in the CHILDES archive are in CHAT format).

**mean length of utterances (MLU)** a commonly used measure of grammatical development; a measure of the average number of **morphemes** per utterance.

**Computerised Language Analysis (CLAN)** a set of computerised analytical tools (software) that allow users to conduct searches and analyse CHAT-formatted transcripts; users may analyse any of the transcripts in the CHILDES archive using the CLAN programs.

| @Situation: | Ross has a little thing that he puts his Star Wars troopers in. |
|---|---|
| *CHI: | **mommy wanted to take it away** (.) **but I was stronger** .  ☐ 974649_994339 ☐ |
| %mor: | n\|mommy v\|want-PAST inf\|to v\|take pro\|it adv\|away conj:coo\|but pro\|I v:cop\|be&PAST&13S adj\|strong-CP . |
| %gra: | 1\|2\|SUBJ 2\|7\|COORD 3\|4\|INF 4\|2\|XCOMP 5\|4\|OBJ 6\|4\|JCT 7\|0\|ROOT 8\|9\|SUBJ 9\|7\|COORD 10\|9\|PRED 11\|7\|PUNCT |
| *FAT: | **what happened** (.) Ross ?  ☐ 994339_996549 ☐ |
| %mor: | pro:wh\|what v\|happen-PAST n:prop\|Ross ? |
| %gra: | 1\|2\|OBJ 2\|0\|ROOT 3\|2\|VOC 4\|2\|PUNCT |

*(Continued)*

| | |
|---|---|
| *CHI: | **I didn't let her** +... ☐ 996549_998154 ☐ |
| %mor: | pro\|I aux\|do&PAST~neg\|not v\|let&ZERO pro\|her +... |
| %gra: | 1\|4\|SUBJ 2\|4\|AUX 3\|2\|NEG 4\|0\|ROOT 5\|4\|OBJ 6\|4\|PUNCT |
| *CHI: | **take it away** . ☐ 998154_1005296 ☐ |
| %mor: | v\|take pro\|it adv\|away . |
| %gra: | 1\|0\|ROOT 2\|1\|OBJ 3\|1\|JCT 4\|1\|PUNCT |
| *FAT: | **what do you use it for ?** ☐ 1005296_1006497 ☐ |
| %mor: | pro:wh\|what aux\|do pro\|you v\|use pro\|it prep\|for ? |
| %gra: | 1\|4\|OBJ 2\|4\|AUX 3\|4\|SUBJ 4\|0\|ROOT 5\|4\|OBJ 6\|4\|JCT 7\|4\|PUNCT |
| *CHI: | **for Star trooper and Chewbacca to race off** . ☐ 1006497_1024330 ☐ |
| %mor: | prep\|for n:prop\|Star n\|trooper conj:coo\|and n:prop\|Chewbacca inf\|to v\|race adv\|off . |
| %gra: | 1\|4\|COORD 2\|1\|POBJ 3\|2\|MOD 4\|0\|ROOT 5\|4\|COORD 6\|7\|INF 7\|5\|XMOD 8\|7\|JCT 9\|4\|PUNCT |

In addition to coding the actual utterances, for some languages, CHAT also provides a standardised way of tagging parts of speech in the MOR-tier and syntactic relations in the GRA-tier. Corresponding analytical tools within the CLAN program allow researchers to perform analyses of morphological and syntactic properties of caregiver and child language.

They also tend to speak louder and lengthen phonemes and pauses, which results in an overall slower speech rate (Fernald, Taeschner, Dunn, Papousek, de Boysson-Bardies, & Fukui, 1989). CDS displays some very distinct intonation contours (Fernald, 1992). A soothing and comforting intonation predominates in speech addressed to neonates, while attention-eliciting intonation containing pitch rises and falls tends to be used with infants around 3 months of age and older (Kitamura, Thanavishuth, Burnham, & Luksaneeyanawin, 2002). The communicative intentions behind specific intonation patterns are easier to identify in CDS than in ADS, even in an unfamiliar language (Bryant & Barrett, 2007), and infants are able to distinguish them starting from 6 months of age (Spence & Moore, 2002).

Does the exaggerated prosody of CDS facilitate language acquisition? The evidence here is controversial: on the one hand, CDS is much richer in word segmentation cues than ADS due to its exaggerated stress patterns, shorter utterances, and longer and more frequent pauses (Redford, Davis, & Miikkulainen, 2004). Not surprisingly, computational word segmentation models have shown superior performance when run with input from CDS compared to ADS (Aslin, Woodward, LaMendola, & Bever, 1996; Brent & Cartwright, 1996; Christiansen, Allen, & Seidenberg, 1998;

Batchelder, 2002). In addition, increases in pitch and loudness serve to draw children's attention to the speech signal. Thus, when 7-month-old infants listened to a stream of nonsense syllables in which the only cue to word boundaries was the statistical structure of the speech (i.e. the transitional probabilities of certain syllables following other syllables), they were able to segment words out of the speech stream only when the sentences were spoken with typical child-directed prosody, but not when they were spoken with adult-directed prosody (Thiessen, Hill, & Saffran, 2005). This suggests that the exaggerated prosody of CDS can facilitate word segmentation at a very early age by providing an additional source of information and by directing the child's attention to the signal. In some cases, when exaggerated prosody is absent, learning may be impaired. For example, mothers who suffer from post-partum depression tend to produce very flat CDS that lacks the typical exaggerated pitch range (Bettes, 1988; Kaplan, Bachorowski, & Zarlengo-Strauss, 1999). When snippets of such flat speech were presented right before the appearance of a smiling face on a computer screen, 4-month-old infants failed to learn the association between the speech sound and the appearance of the face, but did so in a control condition with normal CDS (Kaplan et al., 1999). Thus, most likely the exaggerated prosody of CDS facilitates statistical and associative learning by capturing infants' attention.

On the other hand, not all features of child-directed prosody aid language learning. For example, while exaggerated pitch contours may facilitate vowel discrimination, the rise in pitch may actually hinder it, for a variety of acoustic reasons (Trainor & Desjardins, 2002). Similarly, while it is uncontroversial that prosodic cues like pauses and pitch peaks can potentially help learners to discover the grammatical structure of their language, for example by helping them to figure out that an adjective–noun combination such as *hot soup* constitutes a grammatical unit, adults tend to be inconsistent in providing such cues. Some studies have shown that CDS does contain helpful prosodic cues to phrase boundaries (Fisher & Tokura, 1996; Soderstrom, Blossom, Foygel, & Morgan, 2008), while other studies have shown that these cues are not always supplied consistently: in some cases, the longer pauses in maternal CDS can actually obscure the intended syntactic structure by being placed in the wrong locations (Kempe, Schaeffler, & Thoresen, 2010).

## 6.1.2   Child-directed speech phonology

In Chapter 2 we saw that phoneme discrimination starts during the first month of life. At one month of age, infants already show categorical perception of continuous features like voice onset time (VOT), which helps them to discriminate voiced from voiceless stop consonants like /b/ from /p/ (Eimas, Siqueland, Jusczyk, & Vigorito, 1971). Does CDS support this emerging skill? Again, the evidence here is mixed. Some studies have shown that mothers increased VOT for voiceless consonants, but only when the infants were around 16 months old – that is, at an age when this discrimination had already been fully mastered. Other studies observed a general increase in VOT, while yet other studies showed a general decrease in VOT (Soderstrom, 2007). The picture looks a bit brighter for vowels: even though high pitch in general may obscure differences between vowels (Trainor & Desjardins, 2002), there is clear evidence that mothers hyper-articulate vowels, leading to greater separation of the first and second formants, thereby rendering acoustic differences between vowels more salient (Kuhl, Andruski, Christovich, Christovich, Kozhevnikova, Ryskina et al., 1997). Such **hyper-articulation** (see Figure 6.3) has been demonstrated for

**hyper-articulation**
exaggerated articulation that maximises the acoustic differences between phonemes (e.g. between different vowels).

mothers speaking Russian, Swedish, American English, and Mandarin Chinese, and has been shown to facilitate language learning (Liu, Kuhl, & Tsao, 2003). Interestingly, it occurs only when adults address children, but not when they address their pets (Burnham, Kitamura, & Vollmer-Conna, 2002), which suggests that CDS may serve as a tool for teaching language. We will discuss the functions of CDS in Section 6.2. At this point, let us just note that a phenomenon similar to hyper-articulation has also been observed in child-directed signing, where hand movements become slower, more exaggerated, and more repetitive when directed at deaf children (Masataka, 1996, 1998).

On the other hand, some studies have shown that mothers actually use a more informal way of speaking to their children that is less clearly articulated, presumably

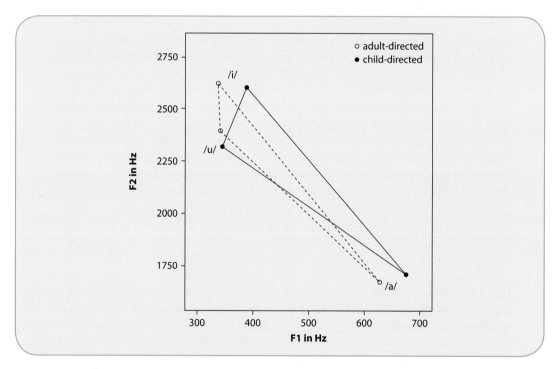

**Figure 6.3**   *Mean area in vowel space encompassed by the vowels in the words* sheep, shark *and* shoe *spoken by 50 female Scottish adolescents addressing an adult and a 5-month-old infant. The vowel area is larger in CDS than in ADS, which is evidence for hyper-articulation. Note that the vowels /i/ and /u/ are closer in Scottish English than in any other variety of English.*

to convey intimacy (Shockey & Bond, 1980) or due to its increased redundancy (Bard & Anderson, 1983). Still, the suggestion remains that clearly articulating one's speech when talking to children might help them to learn their native speech sounds. Indeed, for infants learning Chinese, researchers were able to demonstrate a link between how clearly mothers articulated vowels in CDS and how well their infants subsequently were able to distinguish the consonants in their language, which suggests an across-the-board benefit of hyper-articulation for speech-sound identification (Liu et al., 2003). However, it might also be the case that the mothers who had stronger verbal abilities also tended to have babies with strong verbal abilities. We will return to the issue of whether maternal speech is causally linked to language-learning outcomes in Section 6.3.

### 6.1.3 Grammar and content of child-directed speech

Utterances addressed to young children are shorter and grammatically simpler than ADS (Ferguson, 1977). Moreover, adult speakers tend to place novel words at the ends of utterances, where they are in a salient position that makes it easier for learners to notice and remember them (Fernald & Mazzie, 1991; Golinkoff & Alioto, 1995). CDS is characterised by repetitions and reduplications. Although there is a tendency for caregivers to produce more single-word utterances when speaking to children (Soderstrom et al., 2008), this is not a consistent feature of CDS (Aslin, 1993).

CDS also tends to be rich in emotional expressions, and uses special vocabulary such as diminutives – that is, words like *doggie* and *horsie*, to express endearment (Berko Gleason, Perlmann, Ely, & Evans, 1994). As morphological derivations, diminutives convey smallness, child-centredness, affection, tenderness, and intimacy. Unlike English, which has diminutive derivations for only a limited number of animal names and baby things (e.g. *bootie*, *nappy*, *doggie*), other languages allow speakers to change the forms of almost any concrete noun, as well as of some adjectives and adverbs. For example, in Russian, adjectives like *sinij* [blue] can be diminutivised as *sinen'kij* and in Spanish, the adverb *ahora* [now] can be diminutivised as *ahorita*. In some languages, like Lithuanian, Polish, Russian, or Latin American Spanish, diminutives are so pervasive in CDS as to encompass about half of all the nouns spoken to young children (Kempe, Brooks, & Pirott, 2001; Melzi & King, 2003; Savickienė & Dressler, 2007). Because diminutives end in very salient suffixes, they carry helpful cues for word segmentation (Kempe, Brooks, & Gillis, 2005). In addition, as described in Chapter 4, diminutives constitute clusters of words with similar patterns of usage (so-called schemas) that facilitate the acquisition of inflectional morphology. Interestingly, in languages in which diminutives are used heavily in CDS (e.g. Russian, Latin American Spanish), mothers often use a diminutive form interchangeably with the corresponding simplex form of the same word (e.g. the equivalents of *doggie* and *dog*) in the same conversational episode with their child (Kempe, Brooks, Mironova, Pershukova, & Fedorova, 2007; King & Melzi, 2004). In these situations, mothers do not seem to be marking a contrast in

**Figure 6.4**   *When gesturing to young children, caregivers often convey their enthusiasm through exaggerated hand movements and facial expressions.*

*Source:* © mangostock. Used under licence from Shutterstock.

the size of the objects they are talking about. Instead, their apparent word play with diminutives may serve to illustrate the morphological structure of the language for the child by emphasising that the first part of the word conveys referential meaning, whereas the suffix at the end has a purely grammatical function. Thus, caregivers' use of a grammatical form that is pragmatically motivated can provide their child with information about linguistic structure.

### 6.1.4   Child-directed gestures

Several studies have examined whether caregivers' gestures in child-directed interactions exhibit special qualities. One study found that when mothers demonstrated the properties of novel objects to their children, their gestures and movements occurred in closer proximity to the child, and were more enthusiastic, repetitive, larger in scale, and simpler (Brand, Baldwin, & Ashburn, 2002); see Figure 6.4. This mode of action has been dubbed motionese. It suggests that certain behavioural modifications that attract the child's attention and highlight important structural properties of novel information can be found not just in speech, but in other domains of interaction as well.

Motionese encompasses an exaggeration of gestures used for demonstrating object properties. However, in normal discourse, speakers routinely make a variety of gestures while speaking. These are concrete iconic gestures, abstract symbolic gestures, and pointing gestures, as well as gestures that can be called emphatic, punctuating, or rhythmic (see Chapter 3 for a description of gesture development in infants). While speech-accompanying gestures are a ubiquitous feature of human communication, their prevalence varies between cultures. They often supplement the information provided verbally, for example, when using the hand to draw the shape of an object, for example, the coastline of Great Britain, that otherwise would be difficult to describe (Goldin-Meadow, 1999). Given that CDS exaggerates prosody, it seems reasonable to assume that such gestures might also be exaggerated in child-directed communication. However, the few studies that have researched the gestures accompanying CDS have found no evidence of across-the-board exaggeration. For example, Italian mothers displayed much fewer and much more simplified gestures than would be expected from the large amount of gesturing common in Italian culture (Iverson, Capirci, Longobardi, & Caselli, 1999). Moreover, the gestures tended to reinforce rather than supplement the verbal content of the utterances, and most of the time temporally coincided with spoken utterances. This aspect, temporal synchrony, seems to be the crucial characteristic of gestures accompanying CDS. Several studies have shown that mothers spontaneously tend to move toys at the same time as they talk about them with their infants (e.g. Messer, 1978; Zukow-Goldring, 1997). When mothers were asked to teach their infants novel verbs for unfamiliar actions and novel nouns for unfamiliar objects, their accompanying gestures tended to be temporally aligned with the utterances containing the novel words (Gogate, Bahrick, & Watson, 2000). Thus, mothers named objects in synchrony with the movements of these objects, and they produced novel verbs in synchrony with demonstrations of the novel actions. This tendency to synchronise movement with labelling was strongest with 5- to 8-month-old infants and less pronounced with 21- to 30-month-olds.

What might be the benefit of temporal synchrony between gestures and speech, especially for younger infants? When people speak, their articulatory movements are temporally aligned with the sounds they produce, such that facial gestures and speech supply complementary information. At 4 months of age, infants already have a preference for such cross-modal temporal synchrony: they prefer vowels that match with the shape of a simultaneously presented mouth compared to vowels that do not match the shape of the mouth (Kuhl & Meltzoff, 1988), a disposition that is easily appreciated by recalling how irritating it can be when lip movements and speech are occasionally misaligned on television. From a young age, infants are also sensitive to temporal alignment between manual gestures and speech. As described in Chapter 4, 6-month-old infants readily learn arbitrary syllable–object relations only when the labelling of the novel object is synchronised with its movement (Gogate, 2010). Maternal gestures seem to exploit the infants' preference for temporal synchrony of gesture and

> **motionese** a mode of action displayed by mothers when demonstrating the properties of novel objects to their children; characterised by gestures and movements in close proximity to the child, which are enthusiastic, repetitive, and relatively large in scale.

sound to draw their attention to word–meaning relationships, especially at a time when infants cannot yet themselves detect those relationships. By highlighting the relationship between label and referent through temporal synchrony, child-directed gesturing may help infants cope with the arbitrariness of signs – that words do not resemble the referents they represent (Gogate & Hollich, 2010).


# 6.2   WHAT ARE THE FUNCTIONS OF CHILD-DIRECTED SPEECH?

From an evolutionary perspective, CDS can be viewed as belonging to a set of child-rearing behaviours that humans engage in to ensure survival of their progeny (Falk, 2004). However, in addition to their ultimate adaptive function, child-rearing behaviours can also be explained by a variety of internal or external proximate causes, such as social and environmental triggers or underlying emotional, cognitive, neurophysiological, or hormonal processes. We will consider three possible functions of CDS and how they might contribute to infant well being. But before discussing these functions, we need to examine how widespread CDS really is.

## 6.2.1   Relevance of child-directed speech

In addition to mothers, there is evidence that fathers, grandparents (Shute & Weldall, 2001), and, to some extent, older siblings (Hoff-Ginsberg & Krueger, 1991) also engage in CDS. In these groups, the similarities to maternal CDS generally outweigh minor differences. For example, increases in pitch and pitch range have been observed in fathers, but are a bit more restrained than in mothers (Fernald et al., 1989), possibly because, for men, extremely high pitch may be more difficult to produce and is less socially acceptable (Kempe, 2009). Fathers also tend to curtail their prosodic modifications at an earlier age of the child; that is, unlike mothers, fathers tend to address 5-year-olds and adults in similar ways (Warren-Leubecker & Bohannon, 1984). Research on how children adjust their speech when talking to younger children suggests that the typical modifications of CDS take some time to learn. Thus, 5-year-olds, when asked to address an infant, do not yet consistently produce increases in pitch and pitch range, but do slow down their speech (Weppelman, Bostow, Schiffer, Elbert-Perez, & Newman, 2003), perhaps because control over speech rate is easier to achieve than control over pitch modifications. Furthermore, CDS is not restricted to next-of-kin; adolescent and adult non-relatives also display many of its characteristic features, even in situations of pretence where no child is actually present (Jacobson, Boersma, Fields, & Olson, 1983; Penton-Voak, Cahill, Pound, Kempe, Schaeffler, & Schaeffler, 2007). The widespread use of CDS is a manifestation of the fact that various relatives and non-kin often assume the role of alloparents and contribute to childcare (Hrdy, 1999; see Chapter 1).

The features of CDS described in Section 6.1 have been documented for languages like American, Australian and British English, German, French, Spanish, Hebrew, Japanese, Chinese, Thai, Russian, Polish, Serbian, and Lithuanian. Converging observations from all these languages have led some researchers to propose that CDS is a human universal (Falk, 2004; Fernald, 1992). However, these languages constitute only a very small sample of the 7000 or so human languages; and most are spoken mainly in industrial societies. We know relatively little about the structure of the input to children in other societies, especially traditional non-industrial societies, so any generalisations are necessarily tentative. Anthropologists report that child-rearing practises differ widely (Lancy, 2009), and that in some societies the entire register of CDS or certain features of it are absent. For example, in Quiche Mayan, mothers do not increase their voice pitch or pitch range when speaking to their children (Pye, 1986). The Warlpiri in Australia do not regard infants as appropriate conversational partners (Bavin, 1992); pre-linguistic infants are carried, caressed, and played with, but are rarely spoken to. For the Kaluli of Papua New Guinea, parenting attitudes and practises limit the amount of talk directed to pre-linguistic infants (Schieffelin, 1985). Even in rural communities of the American South, strong beliefs exist that talking to infants is a futile activity due to their inability to understand (Heath, 1983). Although the cross-cultural evidence is scant, it is important not to view CDS in industrial societies as the norm and to dismiss these reports as anecdotal evidence of rare aberrations. To date, we simply do not have enough data to understand what accounts for the cross-cultural variability in child-directed interactions. Adaptive pressures can be different in different environments and for different societies, and human behaviour is flexible enough to accommodate this. It is possible that different functions of CDS dominate not just at different ages of the child, but also in different societies. Perhaps in those societies where CDS seems to be entirely absent, other child-rearing behaviours take over some of its functions. So what then are the functions of CDS that ultimately contribute to promoting infant survival?

### 6.2.2 Affective bonding

In cultures where people are generally encouraged to express emotions openly, as, for example, in North America, the prosodic features of CDS tend to be more exaggerated (Fernald et al., 1989). This suggests that CDS supports caregivers' expression of positive emotions towards their children. Brain imaging studies have shown that the sight of an infant is a very strong positive mood inducer for mothers, as indicated by activation of the orbitofrontal cortex, a brain region involved in emotion processing (Bartels & Zeki, 2004; Nitschke, Nelson, Rusch, Fox, Oakes, & Davidson, 2004), and activation is strongest when the mothers look at pictures of their own baby. For children, positive regard from caregivers fosters secure attachment (Locke, 2001). It is well attested that 1-month-old infants prefer to listen to CDS over ADS (Cooper & Aslin, 1990). However, when researchers have controlled for the amount of expressed positive affect by exposing 6-month-old infants to happy-sounding ADS and happy-sounding CDS, the preference for CDS disappears (Singh, Morgan, & Best, 2002). Indeed, acoustic measurements show that features like pitch height and pitch range of emotional ADS and CDS are virtually indistinguishable (Trainor, Austin, & Desjardins, 2000), which suggests that the unique prosody of CDS stems from caregivers' more open expression of emotion.

In addition to prosodic means, positive affect can also be expressed by lexical means, through words that connote endearment, intimacy, and affection. The diminutives mentioned earlier are just one example. Depending on the language, there may be a trade-off between prosodic and lexical means of expressing positive affect. **Tonal languages** present an interesting case in this respect. In languages such as Chinese and Thai, where changes in pitch distinguish words or their inflections, large pitch modifications might obscure the meaning-bearing properties of lexical tone, potentially making it harder for infants to learn words. Interestingly, mothers who speak Thai tend to vary the pitch of their voices to a lesser extent than a comparison group of Australian mothers, but use a greater number of emotional expressions (Kitamura, Thanavishuth, Burnham, & Lusaneeyanawin, 2002).

> **tonal languages**
> languages that use pitch to distinguish word meanings (e.g. Mandarin Chinese).

### 6.2.3 Regulating the child

Anybody who has ever tried to soothe a crying infant will confirm that expressing positive affect is not the only function of CDS. Another important, and presumably universal, impetus of CDS is to control children's arousal states and behaviours; this function may account for many of its typical features. When crying is at its peak in neonates and very young infants, soothing and comforting intonation patterns predominate in infant-directed speech. Attention-eliciting, approving, and prohibiting intonation patterns gain in frequency when infants are around 3 months old and show greater social responsiveness. From this age on, CDS serves increasingly to direct children's attention and to prohibit them from engaging in dangerous activities (Fernald, 1992). As the linguistic abilities of children increase, the controlling function shifts from prosody towards the content of verbal messages as adults use persuasive and directive messages to manage their children's behaviour.

### 6.2.4 Teaching language and other things

As language is crucial for full participation in human society, it would make sense for parents to use CDS to teach children this important skill. The phenomenon of cross-modal motherese (Gogate et al., 2000; Gogate, 2010), described in Section 6.1.4, provides a compelling example of how mothers teach their infants the names of things. To what extent is the explicit teaching of language widespread? Adults have a keen interest in helping children to learn all sorts of valuable skills – and this may hold true not only for humans. A recent study showed how macaques teach their offspring the technique of dental flossing: after having pulled strands of long hair from the heads of visiting women, macaque mothers exaggerated their flossing behaviour by incorporating longer pauses, more repetitions, and longer periods of flossing when their infants were in close proximity and facing them (Masataka, Koda, Urasopon, & Watanabe, 2009). Of course, no other species compares to humans in their expenditure of time and effort in educating their young.

In many societies it is appropriate use of language rather than its structure that may be taught very directly. For example, once their children start talking, the Kaluli often model utterances for their children and then request the children to repeat them (Schieffelin, 1985). In English-speaking families, children tend to be taught routines for politeness (e.g. saying *please*, *thank you*, and *sorry*). Caregivers model polite discourse, and often prompt their children to use polite words when they are omitted, for example by saying *What's the magic word?* (Becker, 1994a; Ely & Gleason, 2006; Gleason, Perlmann, & Greif, 1984; Greif & Gleason, 1980). Parents may be especially direct in communicating their disapproval when their child's speech is rude or otherwise inappropriate (Snow, Perlmann, Gleason, & Hooshyar, 1990). CDS teaches specific conventions for language use in different social situations. For example, cultures differ in the value placed on oral narration and the ways in which narratives are structured; in many cultures CDS is used to teach children how to tell a good story (Minami & McCabe, 1995). These observations support the view that, cultural variation notwithstanding, CDS can be a rich source of linguistic and social information that aids children in learning how to use language appropriately.

CDS can also teach children about societal values and social roles. This starts with exposing children to the relevant features of their dialect, which often varies as a function of the socio-economic status of the parents and the gender of the child. For example, working-class mothers from Newcastle (UK) were observed to produce a greater frequency of glottal variants of /t/ (a sound produced in the back of the mouth when /t/ occurs in the middle of a word as in *bottle*) when speaking with their sons than with their daughters (Foulkes, Docherty, & Watt, 2005). This particular speech sound is associated with the local dialect of this community, and its heavy usage with boys may encourage their identification with the community, whereas the more frequent use of the standard variant of /t/ with girls might reflect different expectations, for example, about their potentially greater social mobility. Thus, in their speech, caregivers not only model usage of conventional ways of speaking, but also provide children with information about social variants of language and the situations in which to use them. Other aspects of caregiver–child interaction may convey expectations of social and gender roles. For example, it has been observed that parents visiting a science museum were three times more likely to provide an explanation of the scientific principle behind a specific exhibit to their boys than to their girls, even though boys and girls engaged with the exhibits to the same degree (Crowley, Callanan, Tenenbaum, & Allen, 2001). Through conversation, parents seem to encourage somewhat different academic and career paths for their sons and daughters (Tenenbaum & Leaper, 2003; Tenenbaum, 2009).

While parents' attempts at teaching appropriate language use and associated social behaviours are well documented, there has been controversy about the extent to which parents provide feedback when their children make errors with respect to language structure, for example grammatical errors. In Chapters 4 and 5 we presented examples of morphological over-generalisation errors that children make, such as saying *swimmed* for *swam*, or *gooder* for *better*. Children also make many other sorts of errors (phonological, lexical, syntactic) as well. Do parents, like foreign language teachers, correct their children's errors? In what is perhaps the first study to address this question, Brown and Hanlon (1970) argued that parents do not disapprove of their children's grammatical errors, and are much more concerned with the truthfulness of their statements, as the following two examples from Brown and Hanlon (1970) suggest:

(a)  *Eve*: Mama isn't boy, he a girl.
     *Eve's mother*: That's right.

(b)  *Adam*: And Walt Disney comes on Tuesday.
     *Adam's mother*: No, he does not.

In addition, it has been suggested that even in those rare cases when overt correction occurs, it tends not to be taken into account by the child, as the following example demonstrates:

*Erica (4;0)*: Please I can have some cake?

*Erica's father (correcting her)*: Please can I have some cake?

*Erica*: Please can I can have some cake?

**indirect negative evidence** information available in the input that potentially indicates which child-produced forms are ungrammatical; for example when a caregiver repeats what their child has said, but recasts the utterance using the correct grammatical construction.

There are, however, other ways in which feedback about the child's grammatical mistakes can be signalled. Adults may ask for clarification if the error prevents them from understanding their child's utterance. Adults also often recast children's utterances in modified ways to maintain the flow of conversation. These are considered to be forms of indirect negative evidence. When recasts follow grammatical errors they tend to repair the error and present the utterance in correct form, as the following example demonstrates:

*Erica (3;6)*: I want fish fingers over my dinner.

*Erica's mother*: Yes, let's have fish fingers for dinner.

There is evidence that children recover more quickly from grammatical errors after such recasts (Saxton, 2000; Saxton, Houston-Price, & Dawson, 2005). Beyond English-speaking parents, however, it is not known how widespread recasts and other forms of indirect negative evidence are in CDS. Given the lack of cross-cultural data, we cannot at present be sure about the role of indirect negative feedback in child language development.

## 6.2.5   The multi-functional nature of child-directed speech

The different functions of CDS may sometimes be at odds with each other. Even in the CDS of attentive and child-oriented Western mothers, some features may not necessarily be aligned with the needs of children at each point in their language development. For example, in some situations mothers may emphasise affective bonding over the presentation of carefully enunciated speech. This can account for why high pitch is maintained even though it can hinder vowel discrimination (Trainor & Desjardins, 2002), and why pitch peaks and pauses may sometimes be ill placed with respect to grammatical structure (Kempe, et al., 2010), as discussed earlier. Another example of competition between affective and didactic functions comes from child-directed sign languages: deaf mothers signing to their toddlers tend to avoid producing facial expressions that are used to express wh-questions (i.e. questions starting with *who, what, where, when, why*) because these signs require a facial expression that might be interpreted as negative (Reilly & Bellugi, 1996). Thus, mothers who try to express positive affect tend to avoid these expressions despite the fact that they are an essential feature of the grammar of American Sign Language.

**Figure 6.5**   *The language input to second-born children differs considerably from that of first-born children; younger children often learn language by overhearing conversations between caregivers and older children.*
*Source:* © Losevsky Pavel. Used under licence from Shutterstock.

It is noteworthy that CDS shares some features with the way people talk to pets (Hirsh-Pasek & Treiman, 1982), foreigners (Knoll & Uther, 2004), lovers, and the elderly (Kemper, 1994). The similarities of CDS to pet-directed speech lie mainly in prosody. Features beneficial for language learning, such as hyper-articulation of speech sounds, are absent from pet-directed speech (Burnham, Kitamura, & Vollmer-Conna, 2002) but present in foreigner-directed speech (Knoll & Uther, 2004). This demonstrates that some but not all the functions of CDS may be important in other speech registers: pet-owners and lovers are likely to express positive affect, whereas speakers addressing foreigners and the elderly may focus on clarity to aid their conversation partner's comprehension.

Taken together, in certain environments, like Western industrial societies, part of the language input children encounter may constitute a rich source of information in which certain features are emphasised to aid language learning. As we have shown, however, this enriched input is not available in all cultures and at all times during early development. This suggests that CDS *per se* is not a necessary prerequisite for language learning. To put things in perspective, it may be helpful to consult quantitative estimates of how much of the language children hear is actually addressed to them. Sadly, only one such estimate is available to date (van de Weijer, 2002); in this study, CDS accounted for only 15 per cent of the total language input of a Dutch-learning infant, which amounted to just about 20 minutes per day. Given that so much of the language in an infant's environment is not directed to them, how then do they learn language? Akhtar (2005) demonstrated that 2-year-olds readily learn words through overhearing conversations between adults, even when they are engaged in a distracting activity like playing with a toy, and even when the new words occur in non-salient positions in the middle of utterances. This suggests that at least by 2 years of age, children closely monitor third-party interactions (see Figure 6.5). As we will discuss below, overheard speech may play more of a role in the language development of second-born children (Oshima-Takane, Goodz, & Deverensky, 1996), who continuously hear conversations between their parents and older siblings, and may be especially important in traditional societies where the young are cared for in groups and are expected to learn through observation (Rogoff, 2003).

# 6.3 DO DIFFERENCES IN LANGUAGE INPUT AFFECT LANGUAGE DEVELOPMENT?

Having described the features of the input to small children in some detail, we now examine what effects variability in CDS has on language-learning outcomes.

## 6.3.1 Cultural effects

Can the cross-cultural differences in the amount of CDS described above be linked to differences in the rate of language acquisition? This question is not easy to answer. Cross-cultural differences in rates of language acquisition are difficult to document due to structural differences between languages. In addition, there may be variability in other sources of input depending on how much children are included in communal activities. Finally, societies differ in how much children are expected to talk, so that the amount of talking children do themselves may be determined not just by their linguistic competence, but also by cultural expectations. Perhaps future cross-cultural comparisons of comprehension abilities in children of different ages can shed some light on whether language development is slower or faster in different societies (Hoff, 2006).

However, some effects of cross-cultural differences on learning outcomes have been suggested: in cultures where children are rarely addressed directly, they tend to be included in polyadic interactions (see Figure 6.6). We have mentioned previously that speech directly addressed to children tends to present words in isolation (e.g. in the context of labelling things) and contains many cues for word segmentation. As a result, children

**polyadic interactions**
communicative interactions involving more than two individuals.

**Figure 6.6**  *Infants often engage in polyadic interactions involving more than one communicative partner.*
*Source:* © Rob Marmion. Used under licence from Shutterstock.

**analytic strategy** style of early language production whereby children heavily use individual words and a high proportion of object names to convey meanings; compare with holistic strategy.

**holistic strategy** a style of early speech production whereby the infant uses a high proportion of unanalysed holistic phrases as single-word utterances (e.g. here-you-are or what's-dat?); compare with analytic strategy.

may start out producing many single-word utterances, which are gradually elaborated into more complex utterances (see Chapter 5). Heavy use of single-word utterances to convey meanings has been called an **analytic strategy** (Bretherton, McNew, Snyder, & Bates, 1983). In contrast, children from societies with a stronger emphasis on polyadic interaction, who learn language primarily from overhearing and observing conversations between others, may start out producing longer stretches of speech containing unanalysed phrases such as 'you-do-it' or 'gimme-dat'; this has been described as a **holistic strategy**. Such holistic stretches of speech are often produced with quite recognisable prosodic contours, and subsequently must be partitioned into their constituent words (Lieven, 1994). While differences in analytic versus holistic utterance production can be found even among English-speaking children (Bretherton et al., 1983; Peters, 1983; Pine, Lieven & Rowland, 1994), the predominance of one or the other path to language production is to a considerable extent also influenced by cultural factors. Culture also determines what caregivers choose to talk to children about; for example, whether they focus attention on objects or activities in their interactions with children. As described in Chapter 4, cultural differences in parent–child activities, labelling routines, and grammatical features of languages affect the strength of the noun-bias in children's early vocabularies (Childers, Vaughan, & Burquest, 2007; Choi, 2000; Choi & Gopnik, 1995; Tardif, 1996; Tardif, Gelman, & Xu, 1999).

### 6.3.2   Socio-economic and demographic effects

Within Western society, the amount of talk that children hear tends to increase with their socio-economic status (SES), as measured by maternal education and family income (Hoff, 2003, 2006; Huttenlocher, Vasilyeva, Waterfall, Vevea, & Hedges, 2007). Mothers with university degrees talk to their children roughly twice as much as working-class mothers, who, in turn, talk roughly twice as much as mothers on public assistance (Hart & Risley, 1995). Not only do mothers of higher SES talk more to their children, but they also produce a greater variety of words and more complex grammatical constructions. High SES mothers also tend to use language differently than their low SES peers: less of their talk is directive language used to prohibit and control their children's behaviour, and more of their talk is used to analyse, reflect, and reason about situations, and to encourage their children to do so as well. There is evidence that age affects mothers' CDS independently of SES: low SES teenage mothers tend to produce more directive speech (e.g. commands), but generally speak less to their children than low SES mothers in their twenties (Culp, Osofski, & O'Brien, 1996). A similar style of interaction – less talk overall, but more commands – has been observed in 8- to 12-year-old maids who work as baby nurses in rural Kenya (Nwokah, 1987).

It is important to keep in mind that quantitative estimates of the effect of socio-economic status on amount and complexity of CDS vary from sample to sample (Hoff, 2006). Still, differences in CDS are associated with differences in learning outcomes. The most consistently observed relationship is between the amount of maternal CDS and child vocabulary size (Hoff, 2003). Hart and Risley (1995) showed that 3-year-old children from high SES families knew about 1000 words, while 3-year-old children from low SES families knew only about 500 words. But it is not just quantity that matters. Another crucial factor that affects vocabulary size is how many low-frequency words mothers use (Weizman & Snow, 2001). Differences in maternal speech according to SES also affect grammatical development: children from high SES families tend to produce longer and grammatically more complex utterances (Huttenlocher, Vasilyeva, Cymerman, & Levine, 2002) than their low SES peers. Indeed, very high rates of language delay have been reported for American children growing up in poverty, with approximately 2 out of 3 children from very low-income families showing clinically significant language impairments in areas of expressive vocabulary, grammar, and sentence imitation (Nelson, Welsh, Vance Trup, & Greenberg, 2011). Of the children with language delays in the Nelson et al. study, 50 per cent tested in the normal range for non-verbal intelligence, which suggests that their impairments were specific to language. Nevertheless, poor verbal skills were strongly predictive of emergent academic and socio-emotional skills, including basic mathematics, print knowledge, and emotion recognition.

The relationship between parental speech and children's language ability could exist for a number of reasons: (1) children may simply just repeat the more complex utterances produced by their parents; (2) they may inherit from their parents an aptitude for language; or (3) rich and complex input has a facilitative effect on the learning process itself. Huttenlocher and her colleagues (2002) provide evidence that the first two explanations cannot fully account for why the amount and complexity of parental speech are linked to gains in language development: in their study, complexity of parental speech was shown to be positively correlated with the complexity of children's speech in school settings when parents were not present, as well as to their ability to comprehend complex sentences, which rules out repetition as an explanation. Moreover, growth of children's grammatical abilities over the course of the school year was related to the complexity of their teachers' language, which suggests that input has an independent effect in addition to any potential genetic explanations. This supports the conclusion that language input shapes learning.

In Section 6.1.3 we noted that CDS tends to be grammatically simpler than ADS. How can this be reconciled with findings that more rather than less grammatical complexity in CDS seems to facilitate language development? One answer is that grammatically complex CDS is still less complex than most ADS. The grammatical complexity in the child's input must be processable by the child, and input that is too complex will simply be tuned out. However, tuning out language that is too complex is probably easier than trying to make up for missing complexity.

## 6.3.3   Effects of parental communication styles

Even within a culture, and within a social group, children differ in their rate of language development. In Chapter 10 we will discuss to what extent individual differences in rate of language growth and adult language skills are heritable. But since heritability explains only one part of the variance in language development, the other part must be explained by effects of input. Parents differ in how much they engage with their children. We already discussed the importance of contingency of responses in Chapter 2, of joint attention in Chapter 3, and of clarity of maternal speech earlier in this chapter.

Maternal responsiveness predicts how quickly children achieve basic milestones of language development, with respect to lexical and grammatical development (Tamis-LeMonda, Bornstein, & Baumwell, 2001). Maternal responsiveness encompasses not just the extent to which mothers produce contingent responses to their children's verbalisations, but also how affectively attuned mothers are to their children in general (Nicely, Tamis-LeMonda, & Bornstein, 1999). Affective responsiveness can promote language learning because it illustrates for the child the most basic function of communication: the sharing of internal states.

Furthermore, the amount of time that caregivers and young children spend jointly engaged in activities is an important predictor of vocabulary development. As discussed in Chapter 3, toddlers most readily learn words that are relevant to what they already have in mind. When caregivers and their toddlers are jointly attending to the same thing, it is easier for toddlers to grasp what their caregiver is saying. Notably, the extent to which mothers follow the attentional focus of their child, as opposed to attempting to redirect it, has been shown to facilitate vocabulary growth (Akhtar, Dunham, & Dunham, 1991; Dunham, Dunham, & Curwin, 1993). In the previous section, we mentioned that teenage mothers tend to use a directive communication style, as opposed to an elaborative one. This may have negative effects on language development for several reasons: directives do precisely what we just identified as being unhelpful – they try to redirect the child's attention. Directives also tend to be rather simple and do not introduce new words or varied constructions. More generally, directives may be indicators of a communication style that does not engage the child in verbal interaction (Hoff-Ginsberg, 1991; Hoff, 2006).

Several studies have shown that the clarity of CDS affects children's ability to discriminate phonemes and words. For example, Liu et al. (2003) reported that if Chinese mothers hyper-articulated vowels in CDS, their infants showed better performance on consonant discrimination. This study, however, was correlational and can be interpreted as supporting a genetic hypothesis that mothers with better verbal skills tend to have babies who are more linguistically advanced. Pine, Lieven, and Rowland (1997), however, showed that very specific maternal communication styles – such as using words in isolation or repeating phrases with slight modifications – were linked to better word segmentation abilities in their infants. This finding provides more direct evidence that parental communication styles causally affect children's language development.

Even stronger evidence comes from studies of the effects of birth order on language development (Hoff-Ginsberg, 1998; Hoff, 2006). In many industrial societies, singletons and first-born children typically enjoy more individualised attention from their mothers and, as a result, hear more speech directed specifically to them. Later-born children, in contrast, often interact with their older siblings or, as mentioned in Section 6.2.5, witness interactions between older siblings and parents (Oshima-Takane et al., 1996). As a result, older siblings and first-borns tend to have larger vocabularies and younger siblings tend to have more sophisticated conversational skills, presumably because they have to work harder to enter into conversations and maintain the floor (Hoff, 2006). The more frequent participation of younger siblings in polyadic interactions favours holistic production of unanalysed chunks of speech (Lieven, 1994) and facilitates acquisition of personal pronouns (Oshima-Takane et al., 1996), perhaps because of more opportunities to observe that pronouns like *you* or *he* refer to different people in different situations. The differences in the trajectories of language development between siblings confirms that the ways in which parents talk to their children affects their language development, over and above any genetic influence.

Taken together, the evidence suggests that the quality and quantity of the input matter. This is not to say that the success of a child's language development is dependent only on parental input. We have seen that teachers, siblings, and other members of the family and community also provide important sources of input. Learning outcomes are affected by the total amount and complexity of the input. The greatest effects of variability in language input are probably found in how children use language, that is, how they construct narratives and talk in different social situations. But variability in input also has an effect on the development of vocabulary and grammar, although the quantitative estimates of the size of these effects vary (Hoff-Ginsberg, 1998). Children who hear more language learn more words and discover more of their language's morphological and syntactic patterns. Thus, language input influences the learning process in two ways, by showing children how communication works, and by providing a database from which children extract knowledge about the meaning of words and their use in utterances.

## SUMMARY

- **Most adults and older children use a special speech register, child-directed speech (CDS), when addressing infants and small children.**

- **CDS is characterised by prosodic, phonological, grammatical, and lexical modifications.**

  - **The prosodic modifications encompass higher pitch, exaggerated pitch range, and slower speech rate. These modifications can attract the child's attention and aid word segmentation and, in some situations, identification of grammatical constituents.**

- Speakers also tend to hyper-articulate vowels when addressing small children, which may aid identification of phonemes.

- CDS tends to present novel words in isolation or place them in salient positions at the end of utterances, which may aid vocabulary learning.

- Some forms, like diminutives, are used to express affection and smallness, but may – as a by-product – facilitate word segmentation and learning of morphology.

- Gestures that demonstrate use of new objects tend to be temporally aligned with CDS.

- CDS is used by kin and non-kin speakers alike, but can differ somewhat across cultures; CDS is not used in all cultures and societies to the same extent.

- CDS can serve to facilitate the emotional bond with the child, to control the child's arousal state and behaviour, and to teach appropriate use of language. These functions can occasionally compete with each other.

- CDS differs in amount and complexity due to maternal socio-economic status and age. These differences affect language development by modifying the source of information from which to extract patterns. Generally, the more caregivers talk, the more complex their speech, and the more responsive they are, the faster will their children reach the major milestones of language development.

- CDS only constitutes a fraction of the language input children encounter. Children also learn language from overhearing the conversations of others.

# FURTHER READING

## Key study

For evidence on the effects of language input on language development, read Huttenlocher, J., Vasilyeva, M., Cymerman, E. & Levine, S. (2002). Language input at home and at school: Relation to child syntax. *Cognitive Psychology*, *45*, 337–374.

## Overview articles

For an overview of the input to babies, read Soderstrom, M. (2007). Beyond baby-talk: Re-evaluating the nature and content of speech input to preverbal infants. *Developmental Review*, *27*, 501–532.

For an overview of the effects of socio-economic and demographic variables on language development, read Hoff, E. (2006). How social contexts support and shape language development. *Developmental Review*, *26*, 55–88.

# 7 How do Children Learn to Use Language?

Even though normally developing children attain a basic grasp of their language during the preschool years, it would be wrong to suggest that language development is completed when children have acquired a vocabulary of about 5000 words and produce well-formed sentences. To view language as a system for transmitting information, using one's knowledge of phonology, grammar, and vocabulary, does not do justice to the purpose and richness of human communicative skills. Communication is, fundamentally, about expressing and recognising intentions (Wilson & Sperber, 2004) within a specific social and situational context. Children need to learn to 'do things with language', such as persuading, requesting, sharing, teasing, and concealing information. They need to learn how to initiate and sustain conversations, to produce coherent narratives, to be polite, to use humour, sarcasm, irony, and other non-literal forms of language. Children need to learn how to use language appropriately in different social

**pragmatics** the subfield of linguistics concerned with the use of language in social context.

situations and with different addressees; this aspect of language development is called **pragmatics.**

To achieve pragmatic competence, children often need to acquire different registers and varieties such as dialects, non-standard vernaculars and, increasingly, other languages too. In many societies, children also learn to use language for religious and ceremonial purposes, for example in prayer. Children learn to use language in ways that reflect their age, social status, and gender. Learning to use language appropriately in social contexts is closely tied to children's social, emotional, and cognitive development, and we will discuss aspects involved in attaining communicative competence, such as children's ability to tell personal stories or narratives. In closing the chapter, we will explore whether communicative styles develop differently for boys and girls.

# 7.1  HOW DO CHILDREN DEVELOP COMMUNICATIVE COMPETENCE?

To communicate effectively with others, children have to learn to follow the conventions of turn taking, to provide appropriate amounts of relevant information, to adjust the content of their utterances to the state of knowledge of their conversational partner, to repair the dialogue when a breakdown occurs, and to provide a coherent narrative (Ninio & Snow, 1996). The foundations for these skills emerge during the first year of life, when children engage in sequences of alternating action and inaction patterns typical for mother–child interactions (Kaye, 1977; see also Chapter 3). By the end of the first year, children start to initiate conversational interactions by soliciting an adult's attention: they may alternate their gaze between an object and the adult, point at something, and persistently wait for the desired response from the adult (Carpenter, Nagell, & Tomasello, 1998; Pan & Snow, 1999; Tomasello, Carpenter, & Liszkowski, 2007). However, initiating joint engagement with others is only one of the required skills; sustaining the conversation in a way that is relevant to the topic at hand and informative for the conversational partner is another skill that takes years to acquire. When Sehley and Snow (1992) asked 7- to 12-year-old children to play talk show host by interviewing an adult who was responsive to the child, but not very forthcoming, some children were not able to maintain the conversation for the required 4 minutes. These children were not yet very adept at supplying topics of mutual interest and at sustaining the conversational flow, a skill that may take many more years to hone.

In cultures such as our own, where child-rearing practices encourage mothers to treat their infants as serious conversational partners, mothers tend to interpret grunts, burps, and smiles as intentional conversational turns which warrant response and elaboration (Snow, 1977). In general, caregivers scaffold turn-taking with children below the age of 2 years by prompting children to supply the information that is relevant at each point in the conversation (see Figure 7.1). At this age it is mainly the adult who has to be credited for the conversational success, as becomes apparent when observing attempted conversations of toddlers with peers and siblings (Ervin-Tripp, 1974), where 'conversations' often end up being monologues produced in the presence of others. Nevertheless, interacting with peers and siblings helps the child to acquire more sophisticated conversational skills, as children learn expressions such as *and then ...* to hold the floor (Jisa, 1985; Peterson & McCabe, 1988). As a result, as discussed in Chapter 6, younger siblings, who engage in more child–child interactions, tend to have better conversational skills (Hoff, 2006).

## 7.1.1   Perspective taking

Maintaining a conversation relies, among other things, on the speakers' ability to distinguish between given and new discourse entities, to take the other person's perspective into account, to identify conversational common ground, and to use their turn in the conversation to add to the common ground. These abilities call for the use of appropriate linguistic markers. For example, one way of marking the distinction between what is given and what is new in the conversation is to use indefinite determiners (*a, an*) with entities that are new and definite determiners (*the*) or pronouns (*his, her, its*) with entities that are given. Thus, in the statement *Yesterday I saw a famous actor checking into the Ritz but I forgot his/the actor's name*, a pronoun or a definite article is appropriate for the second mention of *actor*, as these forms indicate that *actor* is now a given entity. The statement *Yesterday I saw a famous actor checking into the Ritz but I forgot an actor's name* is infelicitous, as it fails to mark *actor* as given on the second mention. One-year-old infants have some understanding of what objects in their environment are familiar or new to their interlocutors (Tomasello & Haberl, 2003). The question is when and how this understanding manifests itself in appropriate use of linguistic markers. Although children start producing definite and indefinite determiners and pronouns around 2 years of age, it is not clear when they acquire the pragmatic conventions governing their use. For example, when are children able to identify whether some discourse entity is part of common ground, based on shared knowledge, general world knowledge or context, and therefore does not have to be marked as new?

Although children are able to use pronouns for referents that are given in the discourse by about 3 years of age (Campbell, Brooks, & Tomasello, 2000; Matthews,

**Figure 7.1** *Children depend on caregivers to teach them the give-and-take of conversation, how to take turns and provide relevant responses.*

*Source:* © Miramiska.  Used under licence from Shutterstock.

Lieven, Theakston, & Tomasello, 2006), they still often tend to overestimate a listener's state of knowledge and may use definite determiners or pronouns also for referents that are new to the discourse (Hickman, 2003). Moreover, 3-year-olds still have difficulties with the use of appropriate markers (e.g. definite determiners) for new discourse entities that are in the common ground (Rozendaal & Baker, 2010). Given that 3-year-olds are able to use these markers to indicate the given versus new distinction, an inability to mark the distinction between what is and what is not common ground suggests that perspective taking is not yet fully developed at this age. This is consistent with evidence that children at 3 years of age do not yet have a fully developed Theory of Mind (Wellman & Cross, 2001; Wimmer & Perner, 1983).

Another way of studying perspective taking in conversation involves the use of a referential communication task. In this task, two participants typically are seated in front of an array of objects they will be required to refer to in their communication. One participant, called the director, has to instruct the other participant to perform actions with the objects in the

> **Theory of Mind** awareness that people have mental states (such as knowledge, beliefs, desires, and intentions) which may differ from one's own.

> **referential communication task** a perspective-taking task involving two participants who must communicate with each other about a complex object display; the critical feature of the task is that the participants are seated on opposite sides of the display, with part of the display occluded from one side.

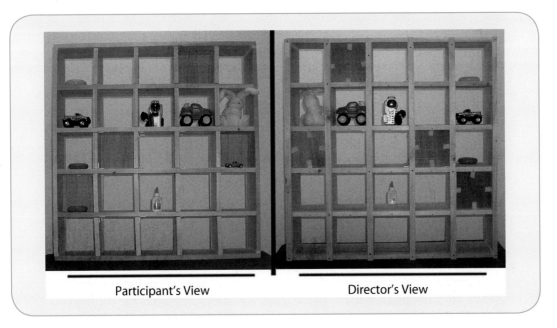

**Figure 7.2**   *Occluded and mutually visible objects from the director's (right array) and the other participant's (left array) perspective.*

*Source:* Reprinted from Epley, N., Morewedge, C. K., Keysar, B. (2004). Perspective taking in children and adults: equivalent egocentrism but differential correction. *Journal of Experimental Social Psychology,* 40, 760–768, figure 1, © 2004, with permission from Elsevier. Photographs courtesy of Epley, Morewedge and Keysar.

array. Crucially, to induce differences in perspective, some objects are occluded from the view of one of the participants (see Figure 7.2).

Consider the array depicted in Figure 7.2. When asked by the director to move the small truck, more than half of 4- to 12-year-old children reached for the smallest truck – that is, the one that was occluded from the director's view and, thus, could not possibly have been the referent of the director's request (Epley, Morewedge, & Keysar, 2004). Thus, the children displayed a strong egocentric bias (see also Glucksberg, Krauss, & Weisberger, 1966; Krauss & Glucksberg, 1969). This result seems to contrast with a study by Nadig and Sedivy (2002) in which 6-year-old children were presented with a similar, albeit much simpler, array and were asked to move the truck. In that study, children very quickly looked at and moved the mutually visible object, thus indicating an ability to take the other person's perspective. The difference between the two studies lies in the way the occluded object fits the request: when asked to move *the small truck*, it is more difficult to overcome the egocentric bias because the occluded truck, being the smallest, fits the request best. In contrast, when asked to move *the truck*, both objects fit the description equally well, which seemingly makes it easier to take the director's perspective into account. Still, sensitive online measurements show that egocentric biases are pervasive: when Epley et al. (2004) asked adults to move the small truck, they reached for the occluded tiny truck considerably less often than children (only 22 per cent of the time) but initially looked at it more than 80 per cent of the time (as did the children), indicating that at first they considered it as a potential referent – despite the fact that it was out of the director's view. The main developmental difference was that the majority of adults, but not children, suppressed this initial bias, and settled on an interpretation that fitted the discourse and situational context. The fact that most adults looked first to the tiny truck suggests that adults may never fully overcome their egocentric bias (Birch & Bloom, 2007), but they learn to correct for it. Thus, similar to the results of sentence-processing studies described in Chapter 5 (e.g. Trueswell, Sekerina, Hill, & Logrip, 1999; Kidd, Stewart, & Serratrice, 2011), adults often reanalyse their initial interpretations of sentences to take into account contextual factors. Children, on the other hand, generally stick with their initial interpretations, and thus remain egocentric in the referential communication task.

Another technique for assessing communication skills utilises cooperative games in which players must exchange information to play the game successfully (e.g. Garrod & Anderson, 1987). For example, in a cooperative maze game, two players are each given a maze to navigate, but for each player, the locations of obstacles (blocked paths) and switches (to open blocked paths) are visible only to their partner. At the same time, a player's position within his or her own maze is visible only to the player. Thus, to successfully reach their goal within the maze, each player has to communicate their position so that their partner can tell them the locations of nearby obstacles and switches. Garrod and Clark (1993) used this task to examine how school-aged children (7- to 12-year-olds) coordinate their use of vocabulary within dialogues. They found that children across ages converged on common vocabularies to communicate their positions within their respective mazes. For example, whereas some pairs of children referred to locations using line descriptions (e.g. *third row down*), other pairs used path descriptions (e.g. *two down from left top corner*), and others used matrix descriptions (e.g. *fourth box down, fourth box in*). Despite the diversity of descriptions across pairs, children tended to use the same terms as their partners. What differed across ages was the extent to which the children fine-tuned their descriptions of locations when communication broke down. When their partners expressed a lack of understanding, 9- to 12-year-olds (but not 7- to 8-year-olds) tended to provide additional information by elaborating their descriptions with new terms. This suggests that young children are primed to use the same words as others within a dialogue, but often fail to recognise when their choice of words fails to be adequately informative; thus they are less likely to modify their descriptions by introducing new terminology when needed.

## 7.1.2 Pragmatic principles of conversation

One of the reasons conversational skills take a long time to develop is that children need to acquire the pragmatic knowledge that underlies these skills. Conversations only work when both partners are cooperative. The philosopher Paul Grice (1975) formulated a set of maxims that govern cooperative verbal exchange. According to these **Gricean maxims**, conversation partners are expected to be truthful (Maxim of Quality), to be as informative as required (but not more) (Maxim of Quantity), to be relevant (Maxim of Relation), and to be clear (Maxim of Manner). For example, if a person were to launch into a detailed description of their state of health after the simple greeting *How are you?*, this would be in violation of the Gricean Maxim of Quantity. There is controversy about whether these maxims are prescriptive (how should one talk to be cooperative?) or descriptive (how does one talk when one is being cooperative?). Still, from the point of view of the acquisition of pragmatic competence, it is important to consider when and how children start to understand and use these conversational maxims.

> **Gricean maxims** a set of principles that govern cooperative verbal exchanges of information.

An early understanding of Gricean maxims emerges during the preschool years. Sensitivity to Gricean maxims can already be detected in 3-year-olds in situations where adhering to Gricean maxims implicitly guides children's behaviour. It is more difficult to detect it when children are being asked to evaluate utterances as silly or appropriate, which imposes metalinguistic demands. In one study (Eskritt, Whalen, & Lee, 2008), 3- to 5-year-old children were asked to choose between two puppet-advisors to give them advice in solving a task – one that always followed Gricean maxims and one that flouted them consistently. For example, when children were allowed to ask a puppet to help them find a sticker hidden under one of four coloured cups, 3-year-olds preferred the advice of the puppet who during practice would truthfully tell them that *The sticker is under the blue cup* and not the advice of the puppet who would say *These are pretty cups* (i.e. flouting the Maxim of Relation). On the other hand, if the second puppet would say *The sticker is under one of the cups* (i.e. flouting the Maxim of Quantity), 3-year-olds picked puppet advisors at chance and only 4- and 5-year-olds preferred the more informative puppet. This suggests that the Maxim of Relation is acquired earlier than the Maxim of Quantity, which suggests that relevance may be a more fundamental aspect to cooperative communication than informativeness (Wilson & Sperber, 2004). More generally, what this research shows is that a full understanding of the Gricean maxims that govern cooperative verbal exchange may not develop until the end of the preschool years.

## 7.1.3 Non-literal use of language

In some situations, speakers violate conversational maxims to make a specific communicative point – for example, a person might respond to the question *Shall I switch on the TV?* with the answer *The baby is sleeping*. Such intended violations are called **conversational implicatures**, and they work because communicative partners assume cooperation; they can easily recognise a discrepancy between the **semantic** domains of the question and the answer, and work out the intended communicative point. At face value, the response *The baby is sleeping*

> **conversational implicatures** utterances where a speaker intentionally violates one of the Gricean maxims to make a specific communicative point (i.e. to express a non-literal meaning).

> **semantic** pertaining to the meanings of linguistic units.

seems to violate the Maxim of Relation; however, the questioner is able to use shared knowledge about how the two semantic domains might be linked (*TVs are noisy; Noise wakes up babies; Wakeful babies need attention*) to infer the intended meaning (*No, do not turn on the TV*) from its literal meaning (a statement of fact that the baby is sleeping). Thus, understanding and producing conversational implicatures requires a considerable amount of cognitive and social inference (Hilton, 1995). Children begin to understand conversational implicatures that require detection of a semantic discrepancy at around 5 to 6 years of age (Bernicot, Laval, & Chaminaud, 2007).

**scalar implicature** a form of conversational implicature, involving a quantifier (e.g. *all*, *some*, *many*); when a weak term is used, the listener assumes that the speaker had a reason for not using a stronger term (e.g. *some* leads to the inference *not all*).

One widely researched form of conversational implicature is scalar implicature – as found in statements like *Some of the students did really well on the exam* – where listeners interpret *some* to mean *not all* and assume that the other students did not do that well on the exam. Note that the quantifier *some* is logically consistent with *all* because it denotes a proper subset of *all*. Thus, if some of the students did well, this does not logically exclude the possibility that all the students did well. The same holds for *Half of the students did really well on the exam* – where listeners take it to mean that the other half of the students did not do so well. Scalar implicatures are statements that are weak in terms of their informativeness, usually leading to the logically incorrect, but pragmatically correct, inference on the part of the listeners that the more informative statement does not hold. They work because they are contingent upon an understanding of the Gricean Maxim of Quantity, which requires speakers to be as informative as necessary. This leads listeners to assume that the speaker must have had a reason for not using the stronger statement *All of the students did really well on the exam*; therefore the stronger statement must not hold.

A considerable body of evidence suggests that children have difficulties with scalar implicature up until about 7 years of age (Barner, Brooks, & Bale, 2011), either because they do not yet fully understand the Maxim of Quantity or because they are unable to identify what the strong alternative for a given scale might be (e.g. *all* as an alternative to *some*). As a result, children are less likely to reject under-informative, but logically correct statements such as *Some elephants have trunks* (Katsos & Bishop, 2011; Noveck, 2001). There is also evidence that children are simply more tolerant of pragmatic infelicity and do not consider pragmatic violations severe enough to warrant outright rejection. In a recent study (Katsos & Bishop, 2011), 5- to 6-year-old children were shown animated scenarios and were given the opportunity to provide graded judgements on the felicity of descriptive statements. For example, one scenario showed an elephant alongside a set of trucks and buses; in real time the elephant was shown pushing each of the trucks, but none of the buses. When children were asked to judge under-informative statements like *The elephant pushed some of the trucks* they ranked them lower than true statements (*The elephant pushed all of the trucks*), thereby showing sensitivity to informativeness, but higher than false statements (*The elephant pushed some of the buses*), thereby showing tolerance of pragmatic violations. Nevertheless, to fully grasp scalar implicature, children not only need to determine that a statement is under-informative, but they also need to make the inference that the speaker intended the statement as a rejection of a stronger statement. Such inferences impose substantial cognitive demands and might therefore take considerable time to acquire.

In addition to conversational and scalar implicatures, there is a wide range of other non-literal expressions that create a gap between what is said and what is meant. All these non-literal expressions require complex cognitive and social inferences; their development is therefore dependent on general cognitive and social development. Hints, for example, require the listener to establish that an utterance is not meant as a simple statement (*It is quite drafty in here*), but as an indirect request (e.g. to close the window). Here, simply detecting a discrepancy in semantic domains, as occurs with conversational implicature, is not sufficient to recover the non-literal meaning; instead, the listener has to take into account the social context in which the statement is made and the potential intentions of the speaker in order to correctly interpret the hint. Research shows that 5-year-olds are capable of understanding hints (Bernicot et al., 2007) if the situational context supports the non-literal interpretation, but have more difficulties when less contextual support is provided.

> **hints** speech acts that require the listener to infer that an utterance was not meant as a statement, but as an indirect request.

Taking into account situational and social context is insufficient for the comprehension of another type of non-literal expressions, idioms, which often rely on linguistic convention. To understand that *pass the buck* and *pass the hat* mean very different things ('to avoid taking responsibility by blaming someone else' vs. 'to ask for money'), it is first necessary to identify that the literal meaning is not at issue. Knowing the meanings of the words *buck* and *hat* is only of limited help here – in effect, the less transparent the idiom, the less the listener can rely on inferences based on the meanings of individual words. As described in Chapter 4, idioms are part of the lexicon (Di Sciullo & Williams, 1987), and are acquired alongside individual words and word combinations (e.g. compound words such as *hairdresser*; verb–preposition combinations such as *dress up*) using general word-learning mechanisms. Learners acquire idioms as complex lexical units, based on their contexts of use. Highly frequent and transparent idioms are grasped more easily than less frequent and more opaque ones (Bernicot et al., 2007). Knowledge of idioms as well as other vocabulary expands rapidly during the school years as children acquire literacy (see Chapter 9), and continues well into adulthood.

During middle childhood, children also learn to grasp sarcasm and irony. While there is considerable debate regarding the differences between sarcasm and irony, what is important for our purposes is that they are expressions intended to mean the opposite of what the speaker says, as when a driver stuck in traffic says *Great way to start the day!* (Dews, Winner, Kaplan, Rosenblatt, Hunt, Lim, et al., 1996). Correctly interpreting an exchange like *A: Shall I switch on the heating? B: No, I love to freeze to death* requires one to notice the contradictory terms *love* and *freeze* and consider the unpleasant effects of freezing to death based on general world knowledge. These are inferences of considerable complexity, which tax children's cognitive abilities and take time to learn, especially when only sparsely accompanied by prosodic and other non-verbal cues which signal that a literal meaning is not intended (Bernicot et al., 2007). Early on, children are able to identify ironic and sarcastic statements

> **sarcasm** an expression intended to mean the opposite of what the speaker has said; a cutting remark produced with the intention of taunting or ridiculing another person.

> **irony** a non-literal expression intended to mean the exact opposite of what the speaker has said.

only when they are accompanied by salient prosodic cues that identify the statement as intended to be understood in a non-literal way. Even 8- to 9-year-old children are largely oblivious to sarcasm when it can be detected only on the basis of contextual cues, without the benefit of prosodic or non-verbal cues (Capelli, Nakagawa, & Madden, 1990). Gradually, children acquire the social function of sarcasm and irony: for example, they come to recognise that a sarcastic statement like *Your haircut looks great!* (when it really looks terrible) is a way of softening criticism. It takes considerably longer for children to realise that ironic comments are often intended to be humorous (Dews & Winner, 1995; Harris & Pexman, 2003; Pexman, Glenwright, Krol & James, 2005).

**metaphor** non-literal language use involving an implied comparison of two unlike things that happen to share one or more important characteristics.

**understatement** non-literal language which uses restraint when describing a situation, for example, by conveying a situation as less important or serious than it actually is.

**hyperbole** non-literal language use consisting of an exaggerated statement or claim.

Over the course of middle childhood, children come to learn to use other forms of non-literal language, such as metaphor, understatement, and hyperbole (Demorest, Silberman, Gardner, & Winner, 1983). The development of all these forms of non-literal language use is closely tied to children's social and cognitive development because children have to learn to read the situation, to take their interlocutor's perspective into account, to process social cues to their interlocutor's intentions, and to make inferences about the links between the literal and non-literal meaning of an expression. The more complex social and cognitive inferences non-literal expressions require, the later they are acquired.

**Figure 7.3**    *Caregivers teach their children to use language as an effective means of conflict resolution.*
*Source:* © Dubova. Used under licence from Shutterstock.

## 7.1.4 Humour and teasing

From infancy, children enjoy clowning around with their caregivers and siblings, and they do various things to provoke responses from others. Toddlers demonstrate their sense of humour by making funny faces, sounds and gestures, by performing all sorts of incongruous actions (e.g. using a sponge as a hat in pretend play), by engaging in intentionally 'naughty' behaviour (e.g. running away from a caregiver who is trying to catch them), and by repeating such behaviour to elicit additional laughter (Loizou, 2005; Reddy, 2001). By age 3 toddlers can differentiate other people's jokes from mistakes by using laughter as a cue to their intentions (Hoicka & Gattis, 2008). Parents support their children's grasp of humour by communicating disbelief; for example, in a recent study of parent–toddler storybook reading (Hoicka, Jutsum & Gattis, 2008), parents commented on humorous story events by pointing out violations of norms (e.g. *Ducks don't say moo. That's silly!*). Such extra-textual comments were more prevalent for humorous story events than for non-humorous ones. During the preschool years, children come to recognise incongruities between actions and objects, such as the humour of using a banana as a telephone. By kindergarten, children can look at a humorous picture – for example, of a man in a bathtub with his clothes on – and explain why the picture is funny (Loizou, 2006).

In many cultures, including North American and Western European, parents playfully tease their children in myriad ways (Eisenberg, 1986; Miller, 1986; Schieffelin, 1986). Teasing has two components: intentional provocation of a behavioural response, and non-verbal markers (facial expressions, laughter) that distinguish what is being communicated from the literal meaning of what is said (Keltner, Capps, Kring, Young, & Heerey, 2001). In teasing young children, parents create tension and conflict; such experiences might serve the purpose of helping children to discover indirect or playful means of conflict resolution, for example, using humour or laughter to dissipate a tense situation (see Figure 7.3). Participation in playful bouts of 'kidding around', followed by the resolution of the induced conflict and tension, may facilitate parent–child, sibling, and peer bonding. Of course, teasing also subsumes a variety of aggressive and competitive behaviours, such as the use of fighting words, taunts, and bullying (see Figure 7.4). Sibling rivalry increases during the second year of life, and toddlers engage with their older siblings in teasing, insulting, and play fighting (Dunn & Munn, 1985). Already by preschool age, children differ in how they use language in the context of sibling and peer interactions, reflecting differences in personality and social experience. During middle childhood, children further develop personal styles (e.g. self-enhancing, self-deprecating, affiliative-friendly, or aggressive) in their use of humour with family and peers (Klein & Kuiper, 2006). By 10 to 12 years of age, children readily distinguish when someone is 'joking around with someone' versus 'teasing to purposely hurt someone', and they rate boys as more likely to engage in aggressive forms of teasing than girls (Barnett, Burns, Sanborn, Bartel, & Wilds, 2004), an observation that we will discuss in greater detail in Section 7.2. Indeed, Führ (2002) surveyed boys and girls (aged 11–14 years) in their use of humour to cope with stress and found that boys more often reported using aggressive forms of humour (i.e. poking fun at others), whereas girls more often

**Figure 7.4**  *Children also learn to use language to harass or bully their peers.*
*Source:* © Mandy Godbehear. Used under licence from Shutterstock

reported using humour to get cheered up (i.e. saying something funny to put oneself in a better mood).

During the school years, children make major strides in their understanding of non-literal language; this allows them to grasp jokes and solve riddles involving various sorts of linguistic ambiguities (Shultz, 1974). For example, Shultz and Pilon (1973) presented children with jokes containing phonological (e.g. *Why did the cookie cry? Because its mother had been a wafer so long!*), lexical (e.g. *Why did the farmer name his hog Ink? Because he kept running out of the pen!*), or syntactic ambiguities (e.g. *What animals can jump as high as a tree? All animals – trees cannot jump!*), and found that phonological ambiguities were easiest, lexical ambiguities were intermediate, and syntactic ambiguities were most difficult to detect. Thus, increasing social competence and development of the ability to process non-literal language form the basis for children's development of humour.

## 7.1.5  Telling stories

There are two ways of maintaining a topic: to continue a dialogue or to launch into a monologue. Most conversational interactions that infants or toddlers have with adults are negotiations of ongoing activities or discussions of objects and people present in the immediate environment, that is, the here and now (Nelson & Gruendel, 1986;

Nelson, 2007). These conversations are usually characterised by short conversational turns and frequent turn taking. However, as children grow older, parents begin eliciting narrative accounts of events about the not-so-distant past. Thus, conversations lay the foundation for the development of narrative skills, which involve the ability to tell coherent stories and, in many societies, to write coherent stories as well.

Stories are accounts of causally organised, goal-directed events. The earliest stories that preschool children produce are autobiographical in nature – accounts of events that happened to them, often prompted by questions from adults like *What did you eat for lunch today?* These first-person accounts rely on autobiographical episodic memory as well as on scaffolding from adult caregivers through hints and open-ended prompts like *Did you eat fish-fingers?* or *Did you have pudding today?* The more adults use an elaborative style of prompting that encourages the child to supply information from their own perspective, the more elaborate children's early autobiographical memories tend to be (Nelson & Fivush, 2004). We will return to discuss such findings further in Chapter 8.

Gradually, children learn to relay third-person accounts, albeit with very limited success initially. To tell a story well requires maintaining a coherent plot line up to a climax, tracking sub-themes, and providing evaluations of the narrated content. Narrative development has been studied extensively in a cross-linguistic research project including languages like Spanish, Polish, Hebrew, Turkish, and English (Berman & Slobin, 1994). Children and adults were shown a wordless picture book called *Frog, where are you?* (Mayer, 1969) and were asked to narrate the story of a small boy searching for his missing pet frog, see Methodology Box 7.1. Several interesting findings of that project are of note: first, narration implies decontextualised use of language; that is, speaking about events that are outside the present moment. Narrative development thus requires a grasp of grammatical devices for marking tense, mood, and other aspects of events – real or imagined – to distinguish them from the ongoing present (Tomasello, 2008). For example, to talk about the past or the future requires children to gain control over how their language marks tense. Similarly, talking about fantasy worlds or hypothetical events requires children to mark appropriately when a shift from one perspective to another occurs, using linguistic markers such as the use of the conditional *if* or the subjunctive mood (Kuczaj & Daly, 1979). However, languages differ in what aspects or features of events they mark obligatorily. For example, in some languages, like Polish or Russian, verb inflections mark whether an event or action is beginning, ongoing or finished. In other languages, like German, this information can be omitted or optionally supplied through lexical means. Thus, children need to learn which aspects of the world their language requires them to encode through obligatory morphemes, a process that Slobin (1996) has termed thinking for speaking.

Second, narration requires the narrator to be coherent. Coherence can be achieved through temporal conjunctions or cohesive devices like pronouns and relative clauses. Compare the two story fragments produced by a 3-year-old and a 5-year-old as shown in Figures 7.5a and 7.5b; (adapted from CHILDES Archive - files 03b.cha and 05k.cha).

**thinking for speaking** the idea that each language requires its own language-specific modes of thinking; that speakers of a language must attend to aspects of the world that are obligatorily encoded in the grammar of their language.

# METHODOLOGY BOX 7.1    ELICITING NARRATIVES WITH THE FROG STORIES

Child language researchers of more than 50 languages have used Mercer Mayer's frog stories to study the development of narrative skills. These wordless picture books trace the adventures and developing relationship of a boy and his pet frog. To date, the overwhelming majority of research has used the second frog story *Frog, where are you?* to explore cross-linguistic differences in narrative structure and content – how children develop the ability to capture and convey events in their stories, and do so in ways that reflect the structure of their language (Berman & Slobin, 1994). More recently, researchers (Aldrich et al., 2011) have begun using the frog story *One frog too many* to elicit talk about the complex emotion of jealousy. A brief description of each frog story and its major theme is provided below. The typical procedure for eliciting frog narratives has been to instruct the child to look through the entire book while paying attention to each picture; the child is then asked to go through the book again while telling the story.

Examples of frog narratives (from eight languages) may be downloaded through the CHILDES database.

| | |
|---|---|
| A boy and his pet dog try to catch a frog at a pond. After an adventurous day of chasing the frog without catching him, the boy and his dog walk home. The frog follows the pair home and joins them as they take their bath. | Mayer, M. (1967). *A boy, a dog, and a frog*. New York: Dial Press. |
| After the boy's new pet frog escapes from his jar, the boy and his dog head off to the woods in search of their pet. The boy and his dog experience many adventures and mishaps along the way before being reunited with their frog. | Mayer, M. (1969). *Frog, where are you?* New York: Dial Press. |
| The boy, his dog, and his frog go on a fishing trip, and catch a turtle. After a scuffle with the dog, the turtle plays dead. The boy and frog are angry at the dog and prepare to bury the turtle. When the turtle wakes up, everyone becomes friends. | Mayer, M. & Mayer, M. (1971). *A boy, a dog, a frog and a friend*. New York: Dial Press. |
| The boy takes his dog and frog to the park, and accidently leaves his frog alone. The pet frog gets into all sorts of trouble and has many adventures before he is reunited with the boy. | Mayer, M. (1973). *Frog on his own*. New York: Dial Press. |
| The frog sneaks along with the boy and his family to a fancy restaurant, and wreaks havoc on all. Both the boy and his frog are severely scolded as the family is escorted from the restaurant. Once alone in their room, the boy and his frog share their laughter. | Mayer, M. (1974). *Frog goes to dinner*. New York: Dial Press. |
| The frog becomes very jealous when the boy receives a new pet frog. The older frog is terribly mean to the new frog until the new frog is lost. After much effort and an unsuccessful search, the new frog finds his way home and the family lives happily ever after. | Mayer, M. & Mayer, M. (1975). *One frog too many*. New York: Dial Press. |

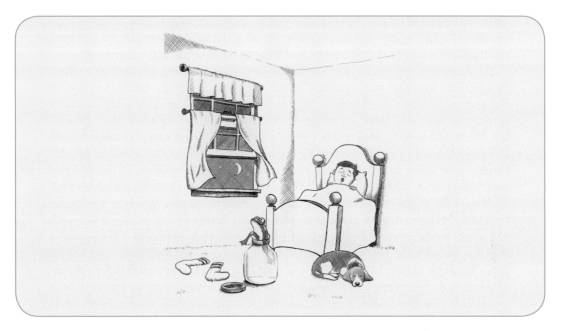

**Figure 7.5a**  *Child (5;11): When the boy and the dog were asleep, the frog jumped out of the jar. And then the boy and the dog woke up…*
*Source:* Original artwork by Robert Powers, based on Mayer (1969).

**Figure 7.5b**  *Child (3;4): They're looking at it and there's a frog. He's looking at the jar. Cause his frog is not there…*
*Source:* Original artwork by Robert Powers, based on Mayer (1969).

These examples illustrate how children move from merely commenting on local events to using the appropriate linguistic devices like subordinate clauses and temporal conjunctions (e.g. *cause, when, and then*) to build referential coherence.

Furthermore, coherence can be maintained by expressing the narrator's own perspective, feelings, and opinions about the story through evaluative devices like frames of mind (*he thought..., they were upset..., she wanted...*), story character speech (*the turtle said 'yikes'...*), hedges (*by the way..., you may not realise that...*), negative states and actions (*they couldn't find the little frog...*), and causal connectors (*the little frog fell into the water because the big frog kicked him*) (Aldrich, Tenenbaum, Brooks, Harrison, & Sines, 2011). Bamberg and Damrad-Frye (1991) looked at the distribution of evaluative comments across different story events to determine whether children were developing an overarching theme in their narratives. Whereas 5-year-olds tended to make evaluative comments about local details of the stories, 9-year-olds and adults made more globally evaluative statements that emphasised key points in the story as a whole. Similarly, in narrating a frog story about jealousy (*One frog too many*, Mayer & Mayer, 1975), Aldrich and colleagues (2011) reported that 7- to 8-year-olds more often expressed the emotional theme of the story in comparison to 5- to 6-year-olds. Taken together, these studies suggest that the skills needed to maintain coherence, relate character perspectives, develop plot lines, and express emotional themes through story-telling develop gradually during the school years.

## 7.2 DO BOYS AND GIRLS DIFFER IN HOW THEY LEARN AND USE LANGUAGE?

Many people have strong beliefs that men and women have different ways of communicating; such views have been expressed as popular metaphors that literally suggest gender differences of astronomical proportions (Gray, 1992; Tannen, 1990). Our account of the development of communicative competence would not be complete without addressing the question of how these alleged differences arise during language development.

### 7.2.1 Gender differences in general language development

It is a common impression that girls produce intelligible speech at a younger age, and begin accumulating words in their vocabularies at a faster pace than boys. During the toddler years (roughly ages 8 to 20 months), several studies have documented larger vocabularies and a faster rate of word learning in girls than boys, using assessments such as the MacArthur–Bates Child Development Inventory (e.g. Bauer, Goldfield, & Reznick, 2002; Bornstein & Haynes, 1998; Fenson, Dale, Reznick, Bates, Thal, & Pethick, 1994; Huttenlocher, Haight, Bryk, Seltzer, & Lyons, 1991). More recently, in four longitudinal studies, girls outperformed boys at ages 2 to 5 years on various measures of language development (expressive and receptive vocabulary size, mean length of utterances, expressive and receptive communication skills), yet failed to show advantages at younger or older ages (Bornstein, Hahn, & Haynes, 2004). Nevertheless, despite some inconsistencies in the findings across studies, the overwhelming majority of significant gender effects in early language development favour girls over boys. Additionally, as will be discussed in Chapter 10, boys are more likely to be characterised as late talkers during the toddler years and are more often diagnosed with Specific Language Impairment (SLI) (e.g. Broomfield & Dodd, 2004; Preston et al., 2010; Shriberg, Tomblin, & McSweeny, 1999).

**late talkers** toddlers at 24 months of age who have fewer than 50 words in their expressive vocabularies and do not yet produce any multi-word utterances.

**Specific Language Impairment (SLI)** a developmental disability characterised by clinically significant delays in language development in the absence of mental retardation, brain injury, or disease.

Due to the considerable interest in identifying gender-related differences in behaviour and/or ability, a large number of studies have compared the verbal skills and communicative styles of boys and girls, as well as men and women. Given the large numbers of available studies, researchers have used meta-analysis as a statistical technique to examine overall trends across studies and to identify possible moderators of effect sizes across studies. With respect to general language ability, an early meta-analysis examined gender differences in individuals of all ages (Hyde & Linn, 1988), and found a slight advantage for females across 165 studies measuring various aspects of verbal competence. Although the gender effects were of negligible size for reading comprehension, vocabulary size, essay writing, anagrams, and verbal analogies, a somewhat larger effect was observed for speech production. All effects favoured females, with the exception of verbal analogies, and there was little variation in effect sizes across age groups (5 years and younger, 6 to 10 years, 11 to 18 years, 19 to 25 years, 26 years and older). Interestingly, the effect sizes for studies published prior to 1973 were significantly larger than for studies published after 1973, which Hyde and Linn interpreted as possibly due to changing publication biases that over time may have encouraged publication of studies documenting null effects; that is, failures to find significant gender differences in abilities.

**meta-analysis** a statistical technique used to examine overall trends across studies and to identify possible moderators of effect sizes across studies.

## 7.2.2 Gender differences in the development of communicative styles

Even if gender differences in general measures of language ability are so small as to be deemed negligible, perhaps there are gender differences in specific ways of

**talkativeness** a general index of verbal ability, often measured as the amount of speech produced per unit of time.

**affiliative speech** use of language as a means of establishing and maintaining connectedness to others, through collaborative or obliging speech acts that support, elaborate or affirm the remarks of others.

**assertive speech** use of language to influence others and to assert one's independence.

using language that might be associated with different activities and ways of socialising. Indeed, boys and girls are thought to develop patterns of language use that differ with respect to three dimensions: talkativeness, affiliative speech, and assertive speech (Gleason & Ely, 2002; Leaper & Smith, 2004). Talkativeness is a general index of verbal ability, typically measured as the amount of speech produced. Affiliative speech refers to the use of language as a means of establishing and maintaining connectedness to others, through collaborative or obliging speech acts that support, elaborate, or affirm the remarks of others. Assertive speech is used to influence others and to assert one's independence; this category comprises controlling or negative speech acts such as directive statements, disagreements, interruptions, and speech used to achieve utilitarian goals.

Given Hyde and Linn's observation that gender differences in language competence were most robust for speech production, several meta-analytic studies have re-examined the literature for evidence of gender differences in child speech (Leaper & Smith, 2004), child-directed speech (Leaper, Anderson, & Sanders, 1998), and adult speech (Anderson & Leaper, 1998; Leaper & Ayers, 2007). With respect to talkativeness, the results of the meta-analyses have varied markedly by age. Among children, girls tend to talk more than boys, especially at younger ages: in a meta-analysis of 61 published studies with 73 independent samples, the gender effect was significantly larger for children at 12 to 35 months of age than for children over 36 months (Leaper & Smith, 2004). Furthermore, the child's conversational partner moderated the observed gender effect, such that there were larger gender differences in talkativeness in child–adult interactions than in peer interactions.

Perhaps some of the observed gender differences in vocabulary development and talkativeness among children are due in part to gender-related differences in the quantity and quality of child-directed speech? In studies of child-directed speech, mothers have been observed to be more talkative than fathers (18 studies), and more talkative with their daughters than with their sons (25 studies) (Leaper et al., 1998). It is important to note that the greater talkativeness of women observed in samples of child-directed speech does not generalise to adult-directed speech. Indeed, men have been observed to talk more than women (in 63 published studies with 70 independent samples), especially when conversing with their spouse/partner, in groups of people of mixed familiarity, and with strangers (Leaper & Ayers, 2007). Thus, for adults as well as children, the communicative situation strongly modulates the effect of gender on talkativeness.

It is a strongly held view that females are more polite than males, and place more emphasis on inclusiveness, cooperation, and positive rapport when interacting with others (Gleason & Ely, 2002). In their social interactions with peers, girls are more likely than boys to validate or expand on others' contributions; they are more likely to ask for help, and to compromise when there is a disagreement (e.g. Kyratzis, Ross, & Koymen, 2010; Leaper, 1991; Leman, Ahmed, & Ozarow, 2005; Miller, Danaher, & Forbes, 1986; Thompson, 1999). Evidence in support of a gender difference in affiliative speech has been found in meta-analyses of child speech, child-directed speech, and adult speech. Across 35 studies with 46 independent samples of children, girls were observed to produce significantly more affiliative speech than boys (Leaper & Smith, 2004); see Figure 7.6. The type of affiliative speech moderated the findings, with a larger gender effect for measures of responsive language (e.g. elaborating on others' comments) than for measures of praise, acknowledgement, or agreement. Furthermore, children tend to show larger gender differences in affiliative speech in the context of unstructured, as opposed to structured, activities.

In studies of child-directed speech, mothers have been observed to use more supportive speech (e.g. praise, approval, collaboration) than fathers (10 studies) and to be more supportive with their daughters than with their sons (11 studies) (Leaper et al., 1998). Likewise, across 47 studies with 54 independent samples of adult speech, women were observed to use more affiliative speech than men. The gender effect was especially robust for measures of active understanding (reflective comments and probing questions), socio-emotional speech (expressions of solidarity and affection), and supportive speech. The gender effects were larger when adults interacted with strangers than with spouses/partners, close friends or relations. Interestingly, as was found in Hyde and Linn's meta-analysis (1988), the publication year also significantly impacted the findings: studies published prior to 1985 tended to report larger

Figure 7.6   *Gender stereotypes suggest that girls are more likely than boys to use language to create bonds of affiliation.*
*Source:* © ARENA Creative. Used under licence from Shutterstock.

gender differences than studies published more recently. Again, whether this reflects changing norms for verbal behaviour or publication bias is difficult to ascertain.

A third stereotype is that boys have a more assertive and commanding communicative style than girls. Boys are thought to be more competitive or adversarial in their social interactions – thus, more likely to interrupt others, make insults or threats, brag, and use more controlling or directive language (e.g. Leaper, 1991; Leman, Ahmed, & Ozarow, 2005; McCloskey, 1996; Miller et al., 1986; Sheldon, 1990). In a meta-analysis of 59 studies with 75 independent samples, boys produced more assertive language than girls (Leaper & Smith, 2004), yet the overall effect was so small that it was deemed negligible. Nevertheless, for general measures of assertive language and for directive speech (imperatives and direct suggestions), the gender effects were considerably larger than the overall effect, and significantly larger than for measures of negative speech (criticism or disapproval) or provision of information (offering opinion, explanation, or descriptive information). Furthermore, the gender effect was stronger when children were engaged in same-gender interactions, as opposed to mixed-gender interactions. Thus, it appears that the more assertive communication style associated with boys is more evident in all-male groups.

In studies of child-directed speech (Leaper et al., 1998), fathers have been observed to use more directive speech (12 studies) and to offer more information (12 studies) than mothers. In contrast, mothers have been observed to use more negative speech (criticism, disapproval, or disagreement) than fathers (16 studies). Unfortunately, there is insufficient evidence to determine whether mothers and fathers use assertive language differentially with their sons and daughters. In a meta-analysis of assertive speech in adults (Leaper & Ayers, 2007), there was only a negligible overall effect of gender across 39 studies with 50 independent samples. However, there were some stronger effects favouring men for certain types of assertive language, such as general task-oriented speech (a combination of giving suggestions, opinions, and directions), and the offering of suggestions. The gender effect was also significantly stronger for interactions between strangers than for interactions involving friends or family. Similarly to the pattern observed for children, the gender effect was considerably larger for same-gender interactions than for mixed-gender interactions. Thus, men seem to be more likely to engage in assertive speech when interacting with unfamiliar men.

For each of these three aspects of language use – talkativeness, affiliative speech, and assertive speech – the overall effects of the meta-analyses have tended to be small to negligible. Given such small overall effects, the focus has shifted from the child to the activity as the source of individual differences in communicative style (e.g. Leaper, 2000). As noted by Gleason and Ely (2002, pp. 138), 'the language that accompanies high levels of active and competitive play (e.g. running and roughhousing) is likely to be very different from the language that accompanies quieter, more sociable play (e.g. dressing up, make believe).' Thus, to the extent that parents and their children choose different activities that vary in accordance with gender, and provide differential opportunities for role modelling, one might expect persistence of gender-related differences in communicative style.

## SUMMARY

- Acquiring communicative competence involves not just transmitting information but expressing and decoding intentions in different social situations. This requires skills like perspective taking, understanding of pragmatic conventions, decoding non-literal language use, and maintaining narrative coherence while illuminating internal states of story protagonists. These skills are closely tied to children's social and cognitive development.

  - Children need to learn to take into account the perspective of their interlocutor. Perspective taking is linked to the development of a Theory of Mind and requires cognitive effort. Although children may never fully overcome an egocentric bias in communication, they gradually learn to compensate for this bias.

  - Children also need to learn the pragmatic principles that underlie cooperative verbal exchange, which require speakers to be truthful, relevant, informative, and clear (Gricean maxims). Children show some sensitivity to those maxims from around 3 years of age, but it takes considerably longer to develop a full understanding.

  - The development of non-literal language is contingent upon an understanding of Gricean maxims and forms the basis for humour and teasing. It requires processing of situational and contextual cues and inferring links between literal and non-literal meanings. Children fully develop non-literal language use only during middle childhood and adolescence.

  - Narrative development interacts with further grammatical development as narratives facilitate decontextualised use of language. Narrative development also involves acquisition of linguistic devices that maintain coherence, relay inner states of protagonists and express the speaker's stance on the topic.

- Gender differences in general language abilities are much smaller than expected by popular beliefs and mainly pertain to specific differences in conversational styles, which are tied to the different activities that boys and girls typically are engaged in.

# FURTHER READING

## Key studies

For research on pragmatic knowledge and cognitive abilities required for non-literal language use, read Katsos, N. & Bishop, D. V. M. (2011). Pragmatic tolerance: Implications for the acquisition of informativeness and implicature. *Cognition, 120*, 67–81.

For a meta-analysis on gender differences in verbal abilities, read Hyde, J. S. & Linn, M. C. (1988). Gender differences in verbal ability: A meta-analysis. *Psychological Bulletin, 107*, 139–155.

## Overview articles

For an understanding of the pragmatics underlying human verbal exchange, read Wilson, D. & Sperber, D. (2004). Relevance theory. In G. Ward & L. Horn (eds), *Handbook of Pragmatics* (pp. 607–632). Oxford: Blackwell Publishing.

## Books

For an overview of the development of pragmatic skills, read Ninio, A. & Snow, E. C. (1996). *Pragmatic development*. Boulder, CO: Westview Press.

To understand how child development in general, and language development in particular, are embedded in social interaction, read Nelson, K. (2007). *Young minds in social worlds: Experience, meaning and memory*. Boston, MA: Harvard University Press.

# 8   How does Language Development Affect Cognition?

# CHAPTER OUTLINE

Previous chapters have examined the cognitive and social foundations of language development. We have explored how infants interact and engage socially with others, and how the mechanisms of imitation, sensorimotor and associative learning enable infants to extract regularities in language input which then can be brought in relation to referents in the environment. Here, we consider the effects of the child's developing language abilities on their cognition.

Language is not simply a skill that is 'added on' to human cognition. It shapes cognition in profound ways, so much so that some researchers have suggested that language constitutes the foundation for a variety of cognitive abilities including memory and thought (Vygotsky, 1934/1987; Nelson, 1996, 2007). First we will explore how the development of conversational and narrative skills affects the emergence and consolidation of autobiographical memory and Theory of Mind. Then we will examine how the acquisition of language shapes the development of abstract concepts, attention, perception, and cognitive control.

# 8.1   HOW DOES USING LANGUAGE SUPPORT COGNITIVE DEVELOPMENT?

As their narrative and conversational skills develop children become increasingly able to relay the past events of their lives. One interesting question is whether children's developing language abilities merely serve as a means for recalling past events, or whether they themselves contribute to the formation of memory for past events.

## 8.1.1   Encoding and retrieving memories

In an elegant study, Simcock and Hayne (2002) presented 2- and 3-year-olds with an unusual and memorable experience of watching a shrinking machine turn several big toys into smaller ones. Half of the toddlers were asked to recall the event 6 months later and the other half 12 months later. Children's receptive and expressive vocabularies were measured at both encounters – crucially, at the time of exposure to the shrinking machine, the toddlers did not know the names of all the toys, but at the time of testing they did. The researchers sought to find out whether children would later recall details of the event for which they lacked words at the time of exposure. Interestingly, the children's verbal recall of the event appeared to be frozen in time, reflecting their earlier vocabularies. That is, the children were only able to verbally recall information about the shrinking event for which they had had words in their productive vocabularies at the time of exposure. Although the children failed to verbally recall many of the details of the shrinking event, they were more accurate in recognising photographs of the toys and in behaviourally re-enacting the operation of the shrinking machine. Thus, conscious verbal recall, in contrast to recognition or re-enactment, seems to require that specific aspects of an event be verbally encoded at the time of the event.

These findings illuminate the role of language in the formation of autobiographical memory and the offset of childhood amnesia. Autobiographical memory refers to the assemblage of memories of personally experienced events – specific events or moments in one's life that can be brought to mind. Recalling an autobiographical memory invokes the quality of reliving a moment in the past (Tulving, 1985, 2002). Childhood amnesia refers to the inability of adults to recall personally experienced events from infancy and early childhood. The time period that is inaccessible to recall varies considerably across individuals: while some people can recall events that occurred around 3 years of age, others can recall events only from around 8 years of age (White & Pillemer, 1979). The observed inability of children to 'translate' memories from the pre-verbal period into language suggests that language contributes to the

**childhood amnesia**
inability of adults to recall personally experienced events from infancy and early childhood.

offset of childhood amnesia by providing a format for encoding of memories and for subsequent verbal recall.

Despite the demonstrated importance of language, the offset of childhood amnesia and the emergence of autobiographical memory are not associated with a sudden qualitative shift. In Simcock and Hayne's (2002) study children who witnessed the shrinking event at 27 months of age recalled significantly less, both verbally and non-verbally, than children who witnessed the event at 39 months of age. This suggests that, during the toddler years, children gain skill at encoding, storing, and retrieving information both verbally and non-verbally. They become more adept at incorporating visual, auditory, olfactory, gustatory, tactile, and proprioceptive information into their memories of events. Most likely, such general improvements in encoding, retention, and retrieval of sensorimotor information conspire to promote the emergence of stable autobiographical memories. Still, children's increasing ability to encode memories in a language-based format and to use language-based retrieval cues improves the quality and durability of autobiographical memory (Hayne, 2004), allowing children's personal memories to develop from fragments of scenes into more coherent episodes.

## 8.1.2 Development of a personal past, present, and future

Throughout infancy and early childhood, children's recall of personally experienced events is initiated and practised in the context of social interaction with caregivers. Young children depend on their caregivers to organise their memories for past events. Caregivers often introduce topics and forms of conversation that are valued in their family and community, and they prompt their children to recall past personal experiences in culturally appropriate ways (Nelson & Fivush, 2004); see Figure 8.1. Haden, Ornstein, Eckerman, and Didow (2001) have shown that toddlers tend not to recall memories of events without external scaffolding by a caregiver. That is, 30- to 42-month-old children tend to recall only those aspects of novel events that they have talked about with others.

Given the important role of caregiver engagement in toddlers' memory for past events, we can ask whether caregivers differ in how they reminisce about past events with their toddlers. Observations of mother–child interactions show that mothers differ considerably in their reminiscing style. So-called elaborative mothers tend to question their children about particular details of past events and supply those details gradually when their children are unable to retrieve them, by saying, for example, *Remember when we took a walk? Where did we walk? Remember, when we walked on the beach? And what did we pick up? We picked up sea…shells. Remember all the seashells?* In contrast, non-elaborative mothers tend to ask fewer, more general and more redundant questions, by saying, for example, *Tell me about that. How did you do that? Who was there? Who else was there?* (These examples were adapted from Nelson & Fivush, 2004.) Maternal reminiscing style is different from mere talkativeness (Haden & Fivush, 1996), and mothers tend to be remarkably consistent in how they reminisce with their children over time (Harley & Reese, 1999). Several longitudinal studies have shown that maternal reminiscing style early in development is predictive of children's

**Figure 8.1**    *Sharing memories with others supports the development of a child's autobiographical memory.*
*Source:* © Blend Images. Used under licence from Shutterstock.

later autobiographical memory skills, as measured by the amount of new information the child is able to contribute to the recall of an earlier event (Reese, Haden, &
Fivush, 1993; Harley & Reese, 1999).

How exactly does reminiscing style contribute to the formation of autobiographical memory? Firstly, an elaborate reminiscing style provides detailed verbal cues for
retrieval, which aids the child in using language to create more detailed and more
accessible memories. Secondly, elaborate reminiscing can facilitate children's sense of
time, by helping them to situate specific details of past events on a timeline. Through
conversation, children acquire specific terms for points in time, such as *yesterday,
tomorrow, Tuesday, July, midnight, soon, later, this afternoon,* and *many years ago.* Such
terms comprise conventional time patterns (e.g. hours of the day, days of the week,
months of the year) that help children to think about the past and make plans for the
future (Friedman, 2004, 2005). Explicit talk about moments in time provides a foundation for the human capacity to contemplate even the remote past and future (e.g. the
lives of our hominin ancestors, the eventual explosion and death of our Sun).

Thirdly, when engaging in joint reminiscing, there may be disagreements
about the details of past events that need to be negotiated. These negotiations
foster the child's understanding that different people may remember shared experiences in different ways, and that the details of one's memories of past events
may be inaccurate. This latter effect of joint reminiscing links the development of
autobiographical memory to the development of a Theory of Mind – to children's

emerging understanding of the mental lives of people (Carpendale & Lewis, 2004; Nelson, Plesa, & Henseler, 1998; Nelson, Plesa Skwerer, Goldman, Henseler, Presler, & Walkenfeld, 2003). Performance on various Theory of Mind tasks (e.g. false belief understanding, distinguishing appearance from reality, perspective taking, emotion comprehension) is correlated with various indices of language development such as children's vocabulary size, semantic development, and syntactic complexity (e.g. Cutting & Dunn, 1999; Slade & Ruffman, 2005), and may be related to the acquisition of mental state vocabulary, conversational and pragmatic skills, and the mastery of specific syntactic structures, such as the complement constructions used to express contents of mind, as in *Mary thought that Fred went to the movies* (Astington & Baird, 2005; Bartsch & Wellman, 1995; de Villiers, 2000). Much of what we know about the role of language development in facilitating development of a Theory of Mind comes from studies of children with very limited access to language during early childhood due to congenital deafness. These studies will be discussed in Chapter 11.

Maternal reminiscing style has also been implicated in gender differences with respect to autobiographical memory and the offset of childhood amnesia. Women tend to have earlier autobiographical memories than men and their memories tend to be more frequent and elaborate (Pillemer, 1998). This gender difference in the density and level of detail of autobiographical memories has been linked to a difference in how mothers reminisce with their daughters and sons. Several studies have reported greater maternal elaboration in interactions with daughters than with sons (Fivush, 1998), which might be due, in part, to girls' stronger interest in social interaction, which creates a more favourable context for parent–child reminiscing about the past (Connellan, Baron-Cohen, Wheelwright, Bataki, & Ahluwalia, 2000; Maccoby & Jacklin, 1989). These interactions, in turn, may reinforce parental expectations about girls' social inclinations, so that more elaborate reminiscing becomes a more entrenched communication style with girls.

Maternal reminiscing style may also contribute to cultural differences in autobiographical memory. Individuals from Western cultures tend to have earlier and more detailed personal memories than individuals from Asian cultures (Leichtman, Wang, & Pillemer, 2003). This difference has been linked to cultural differences in maternal reminiscing style, with Korean and Chinese mothers tending to be less elaborative than European American mothers (Mullen & Yi, 1995; Wang, Leichtman, & Davies, 2000). Different styles of reminiscing are likely to be a reflection of different cultural values: while Westerners tend to emphasise the roles of individuals in creating their own life experiences, Asians favour a more interdependent sense of self which de-emphasises the individual in favour of the communal past. Reminiscing style therefore serves as a mediator between cultural values regarding memories of the past and children's emerging autobiographical memories.

The link between maternal reminiscing style and the development of children's autobiographical memory supports the view that cognitive development emerges through social interaction with caregivers (Lock, 1991; Nelson, 2007; Racine & Carpendale, 2007). Engaged, elaborative caregivers scaffold the development of narrative skills in their children. Through their personal narratives, children create organisational structures that help them to make sense of their past experiences and keep track of important events in their lives. Over time, the child's own narratives take on the role previously fulfilled by the caregiver's external scaffold. Throughout childhood and into adulthood, improvements in narrative skills continue to support the construction of richer and more detailed personal memories (Kleinknecht & Beike, 2001). Furthermore, as children become more skilful users of language, they find more opportunities to enter into dialogues about past experiences; such recall of personally relevant events further aids in the consolidation of representations of past events. Parent–child conversational patterns, thus, not only provide a format for the encoding and retrieval of information, but also affect the organisation and durability of autobiographical memories. As children develop narrative skills through participation in verbally mediated social interaction, their ability to remember their personal past and to contemplate their future is established.

# 8.2 DOES IT MATTER WHICH LANGUAGE CHILDREN LEARN?

So far we have been considering language in its generic sense. But of course, individuals learn a specific language, and – as repeatedly illustrated in the previous chapters – languages differ in their inventory of phonemes, in prosody and rhythm, in syntax and morphology, and in how individual words label entities in the world, as well as their properties and relationships (Evans & Levinson, 2009). Quite often the words of a language may be difficult to translate into another language; for example, the German word *Schadenfreude* 'pleasure derived from another person's misfortune' does not have an English counterpart. We now turn to ask whether the way a language represents the world shapes a child's emergent ability to process information from the world. Early in the 20th century, the linguist Edward Sapir and his student Benjamin Lee Whorf conjectured that the diverse features of the world's languages might promote different ways of perceiving and thinking about the world – a proposal that became known as the Sapir–Whorf hypothesis or linguistic relativism (Sapir, 1921; Whorf, 1956). Although still controversial, this hypothesis has received renewed attention and some empirical support; the interested reader can find overview articles on this topic at the end of the chapter. Here we will examine how cognitive effects attributable to the specific language that a child acquires might arise during development. To illustrate this process we will restrict the discussion to domains of cognition for which there currently is sufficient developmental evidence.

> **Sapir–Whorf hypothesis** also called **linguistic relativism** a conjecture that the diverse features of the world's languages might promote different ways of perceiving and thinking about the world.

## 8.2.1 Language and colour cognition

Colour cognition is considered an ideal domain for exploring the effects of language on cognition. Humans have visual sensitivity in a restricted portion of the electromagnetic spectrum. Within the visible portion of the spectrum, the visual system perceives different combinations of frequencies (wavelengths) of visible light as different colours. Languages, however, vary enormously in how they refer to colour, both in the number of available colour terms and in the way these terms carve up the visible spectrum (Kay & Regier, 2006). Even for pure spectral colours, made up of light of a single frequency (wavelength), different languages impose different boundaries on colour categories. For example, many languages, such as Vietnamese and Zulu, do not have distinct colour words for *blue* and *green*, and most do not mark the *pink–red* contrast of English. Russian, on the other hand, has two basic colour terms that differentiate between light blue and dark blue. Berinmo, a language spoken in Papua-New Guinea, has only five basic colour terms, and these terms differ considerably from their English counterparts (Roberson, Davies, & Davidoff, 2000). Roberson and colleagues have demonstrated that Berinmo speakers show categorical perception effects corresponding to the colour boundaries of their language: stimuli that straddle a category boundary are perceived as more distinct than stimuli that originate from within the same category, even when all stimuli have been equated for physical distance in colour space. Specifically, Berinmo speakers have difficulty distinguishing between *green* and *blue*, a distinction that does not exist in their language, but show much better performance when distinguishing between colours corresponding to their native categories of *nol* (a category encompassing English yellow, orange, and brown) and *wor* (a category encompassing English green, blue, and purple).

Such effects of vocabulary on colour perception might come about through the spontaneous activation of lexical representations (i.e. category names) while performing a perceptual task. As will be described in Chapter 12, the neural networks responsible for language tend to be localised in the left hemisphere of the cerebral cortex. To test whether the effects of language on colour perception are due to neural activity in the left cerebral hemisphere, Gilbert, Regier, Kay, and Ivry (2005) asked English speakers to fixate a point in the middle of a screen and then flashed a pair of colour chips either to the left or right of the central fixation point (i.e., to the left vs. right visual field). Due to a convenient peculiarity of neural organisation, visual stimuli displayed to the right or left of centre initially project to the opposite cerebral hemisphere. When equidistant colour chips were presented for discrimination in the right visual field (which projects initially to the left cerebral hemisphere implicated in language processing) discrimination was faster when the colours originated from different categories (e.g. *blue* vs. *green*) than when they originated from the same colour category (different shades of *blue*). No such differences were found for presentations in the left visual field (which projects initially to the right cerebral hemisphere). Moreover, when participants had to perform a concurrent task to tax their verbal working memory (i.e. silently rehearsing an 8-digit number), the laterality effect disappeared, which suggests that categorical perception of colour in the left hemisphere is disrupted when linguistic resources are expended on another task.

Given these findings, we now ask at what point in development does language begin to shape a child's perception of colour? If language plays an important role in the partitioning of colour space, then one might expect pre-linguistic infants to fail to show categorical perception of colour, with categorical perception arising at the time that children learn colour names. However, a series of studies has demonstrated that 4-month-old infants already show categorical perception of colour (Franklin & Davies, 2004). Strikingly, in infants, categorical perception of colour appears to be localised in the right cerebral hemisphere (Franklin, Drivonikou, Bevis, Davies, Kay, & Regier, 2008), whereas in adults it appears to be localised in the left. This puzzling finding has been interpreted as evidence for a separate form of categorical colour perception that is not influenced by language.

If categorical perception of colour is initially localised in the right cerebral hemisphere, what causes it to be localised in the left hemisphere later in life? To explore this question, Franklin, Drivonikou, Clifford, Kay, Regier, and Davies (2008) identified a group of toddlers (mean age 32 months) who could not yet reliably identify and label the colours *blue* and *green*, and a group of slightly older children (mean age 46 months) who could. Both groups were given the task of identifying whether a colour chip differed from a series of background chips. As in the Gilbert et al. (2005) study with adults, the colour chips displayed equidistant colours – some of which straddled the boundary between *blue* and *green* and some of which did not – and were shown in the left versus the right visual field. As expected, both groups of children showed categorical perception of colour (which was measured as the time it took them to move their gaze from the fixation point towards the one colour chip that was different from the surrounding colour chips); however, the effect varied as a function of visual field in accordance with children's colour word vocabulary. For children who knew the terms *blue* and *green*, categorical perception was found only when the stimuli were presented in the right visual field. For these children, categorical perception of colours was localised in the left hemisphere, as it is in adults. In contrast, toddlers who were still learning the colour terms showed categorical perception for colour stimuli presented in the left visual field, thereby mirroring the pattern of right-hemispheric categorical perception found in pre-linguistic infants. These findings clearly demonstrate that language can shape the way we perceive the world: knowing colour terms changes the pattern of lateralisation of the associated perceptual categories, with neural reorganisation occurring as toddlers learn the relevant colour terms.

Given these findings, one might ask what determines the colour categories that govern pre-linguistic, right-hemispheric categorical perception of colour. Are these pre-linguistic colour categories universal? And if so, where does the variability in colour terms come from? Interestingly, although colour terms vary across languages, this cross-linguistic variability is not entirely arbitrary: across the world's languages, colour names tend to cluster at certain points along the colour spectrum in ways that suggest an optimal partitioning of colour space (Kay & Regier, 2003). Thus, cross-linguistic variability pertains more to the location of the boundaries between colour categories than to the location of the *focal colours* (the best exemplar of each colour category) (Regier, Kay, & Khetarpal, 2008; Regier & Kay, 2009). This suggests that universal principles underlie colour cognition to some extent; at the same time, there is room for cross-linguistic variability to influence how the cognitive system processes colour.

Language affects not just perception but also memory for colours. Roberson, Davidoff, Davies, and Shapiro (2004) compared Himba (a semi-nomadic tribe living in Northern Namibia) and English-speaking children in their memory for focal colours.

Himba and English differ considerably with respect to colour vocabulary, as Himba has only five basic colour terms (*serandu*: red/orange/pink, *dumbu*: beige/yellow/light green, *zoozu*: dark/black, *vapa*: light/white, and *burou*: green/blue/purple), whereas English has eleven (*red, blue, yellow, green, orange, brown, purple, pink, white, black, grey*), as well as a vast number of non-basic colour terms such as *magenta, beige, teal*, and *aquamarine*. The children were shown a colour chip for 5 seconds and then asked to identify it from a set of 22 other colour chips. English and Himba children who did not yet know any colour terms were more accurate in remembering focal colours than non-focal colours, irrespective of whether the chip was a focal colour in English or Himba. This suggests that memory of colour is initially perceptually driven. However, once children had acquired some of the colour terms of their language, recognition was better for the Himba focal colours in the Himba-speaking children, and for the English focal colours in the English-speaking children.

It is worth noting that the way colour terms in different languages divide up the colour space is reminiscent of how phonemes in different languages carve up acoustic space – recall the different Voice Onset Times which characterise the boundaries between /b/ and /p/ in Spanish and English, as discussed in Chapter 2. From the research on categorical perception of phonemes we know that native phonemic categories become entrenched through exposure to the ambient language during the second half of the first year of life. The effects of the native language on categorical perception of colour discussed here further support the idea that as language is acquired it starts shaping perception and memory.

## 8.2.2 Language and spatial cognition

Among other things, languages also differ in how they convey notions related to space and time (see Figure 8.2). To be able to describe the locations of objects in space, one needs a frame of reference. A person can use his or her own body as a frame of reference (e.g. *to my right, behind me*); alternatively, one can use the object itself (e.g. *in front of the house*), or an absolute system of fixed bearings (e.g. *North, South, East*, and *West*). Languages differ in which of these options they employ. English speakers tend to use what is known as a relative, egocentric frame of reference according to which the sink, for example, is located *to the right* of the stove – where *right* is determined from the point of view of the speaker facing the sink. It is also possible to use an intrinsic, object-centred frame of reference, as in *The car is in front of the house*, which requires determination of various distinctive parts of the object (e.g. the front, back, and sides of the house). English speakers tend to use an absolute frame of reference only when talking about geographical space (e.g. *The harbour is to the west of town*). However, other languages, like the Australian language Guugu Yimithir, use absolute frames of reference, even when referring to body parts, as in *You have an ant on your south leg*, and do not have words, such as *right* or *left*, that encode relative spatial positions (Majid, Bowerman, Kita, Haun, & Levinson, 2004).

Interestingly, even when performing non-linguistic spatial tasks, adults tend to use the frame of reference common to their language (Peterson, Danziger, Wilkins, Levinson, Kita, & Senft, 1998). In one study, adult speakers of Dutch (an Indo-European

**Figure 8.2**  *Like maps, languages provide a system for representing locations. Languages may differ considerably in how the system of spatial terms is organised.*

*Source:* © Wessel du Plooy.  Used under licence from Shutterstock.

language with a relative frame of reference) and Tzeltal (a Mayan language with an absolute frame of reference) were shown an array of objects and then were rotated in their chairs by 180 degrees. The two groups were later asked to choose which of four spatial configurations matched the array they had seen prior to their 180-degree rotation, with one configuration preserving the absolute configuration of the objects in space, another rotated to maintain the relative positions of the objects in relation to the participant's new position, and two distractor configurations oriented perpendicularly to the target configurations (see Figure 8.3). Whereas Dutch speakers predominantly chose the relative solution, Tzeltal speakers preferred the absolute solution, in accordance with the spatial reference system of their language (Levinson, 2003).

Linguistic differences in spatial reference systems also impact how people use gestures to express spatial and temporal meanings (Kita, 2009). One study compared speakers of two Mayan languages, Yucatec and Mopan, which vary in their spatial reference systems. Whereas Yucatec uses a relative frame of reference, Mopan uses an absolute frame of reference and lacks words for *left* and *right*. When asked to describe events, Yucatec speakers often use lateral hand movements (i.e. left to right, right to left), and they extend these gestures metaphorically when locating events in time. Mopan speakers, in contrast, rarely produce lateral hand movements, and instead use the sagittal (front–back) axis to gesture about object location or motion, or to sequence events in time (Kita, Danziger, & Stolz, 2001).

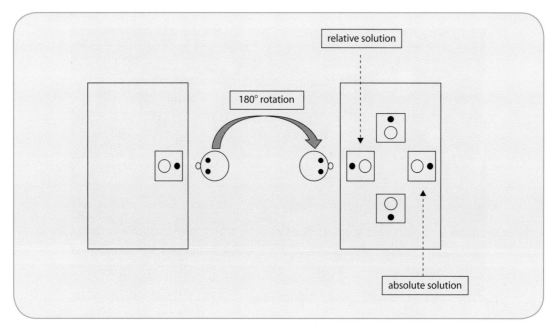

**Figure 8.3**   *Memory of spatial configurations: participants were placed in front of a table (left) and shown a card with a configuration of a circle and a dot. After 30 seconds, they were rotated 180° towards another table (right) with four cards, and asked to select the card identical to the one they had seen before. Almost all Dutch speakers chose the relative solution, while about two thirds of the Tzeltal speakers chose the absolute solution.*

*Source:* Adapted from Figure 2 p.110 in Majid, Bowerman, Kita, Haun, and Levinson (2004) with permission from Elsevier.

From a developmental perspective, an important question is whether one type of reference system is more natural and, therefore, easier to learn than another. For languages with relative frames of reference like English, Italian, or Turkish, children acquire the intrinsic, object-centred frame of reference (e.g. *the ball is in front of the house*) at around 4 years of age and the egocentric frame of reference (e.g. *the ball is in front of the box*) about a year later (Johnston, 1988). Similarly, for languages with absolute frames of reference like Tzeltal, Tzotzil, or Balinese, children also acquire the absolute spatial terms at around 4 years of age (Brown & Levinson, 2000; De Léon, 1994; Wassmann & Dasen, 1998). Thus, there appears to be no evidence for an innately privileged frame of reference; rather, language exposure would appear to determine what preferences guide spatial cognition.

In addition to differing with respect to spatial frames of reference, languages also differ in what kinds of spatial relationships are explicitly contrasted. As with basic colour terms, the cross-linguistic variability in spatial terms is not entirely arbitrary, but seems to reflect an optimal partitioning of the similarity space of spatial relations (Khetarpal, Majid, & Regier, 2009). Still, within this general constraint, there is considerable cross-linguistic variability. For example, the English prepositions *in* and *on* distinguish between the spatial relationships of containment and support. Thus, containment relations, such as putting an apple in a bowl or putting a piece in a puzzle, are markedly differently from support relations, such as putting a cup on a

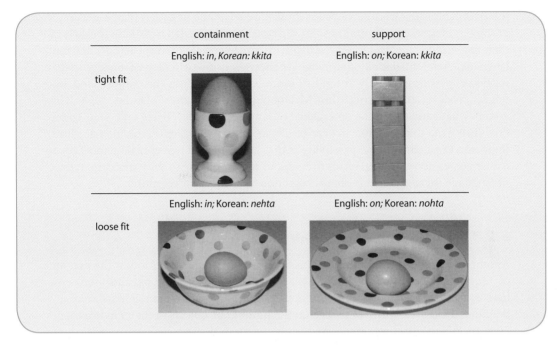

**Figure 8.4**   *Examples for different spatial terms in English and Korean.*

*Source:* Photographs courtesy of Patricia Brooks and Vera Kempe.

table or attaching a Lego block onto a stack of Lego blocks. Korean carves up spatial meanings in a different way, using verbs to distinguish between tight fit (*kkita*: putting an egg in an egg cup and snapping a Lego block onto a stack of Lego blocks) and various relations of loose fit (*nohta*: putting an egg on a plate; *nehta*: putting an egg in a bowl; see Figure 8.4). Does the way that their language marks spatial relations shape children's early spatial categorisation? To answer this question, McDonough, Choi, and Mandler (2003) presented videos of Korean *kkita* and *nohta* relationships to 9- to 14-month-old English-speaking infants. Using a preferential-looking task they determined that the infants were able to learn the contrast between tight fit and loose fit, even though it is not marked in English. However, English-speaking adults failed to

> **inattentional blindness**
> a failure to perceive something in plain sight.

learn the Korean contrast, in spite of the fact that English has the words *tight* and *loose* that distinguished the spatial relationships. It seems that the adults experienced inattentional blindness (Mack & Rock, 1998) as a consequence of their over-reliance on notions of containment (*in*) and support (*on*) in spatial categorisation. Similar to the loss of the ability to distinguish non-native phonemic contrasts discussed in Chapter 2, learning a language seems to lead to a loss of the ability to notice a wide variety of spatial relationships.

   When does the effect of language on spatial cognition emerge? To address this question, Bowerman and Choi (Bowerman, 1996; Choi, 1997) used an elicited production task to examine how English, Dutch, and Korean children would label different spatial configurations: if children were to describe two or more configurations in the same way (e.g. by using the same English preposition), this would suggest that these configurations were perceived as similar to each other. At 2 years of age, children's groupings of spatial configurations showed considerable overlap with adult speakers of their native language, and lesser overlap with same-aged children speaking a different language. Preferential-looking studies have shown sensitivity to native-language spatial relationships arising already around 18 months, when children can comprehend, but not yet produce, spatial terms (Choi, McDonough, Bowerman, & Mandler, 1999). This is somewhat earlier than the emergence of language-specific effects on colour cognition during the third and fourth year of life, as described earlier (Franklin et al., 2008; Roberson et al., 2004). One possibility is that linguistic and perceptual factors favour earlier acquisition of spatial terms over colour terms, leading to the earlier emergence of language-specific effects in spatial cognition than in colour cognition.

## 8.2.3   Language and numerical cognition

Another domain, in which cross-linguistic differences shape cognition, is the domain of numbers. Human infants, like other animals (e.g. rats, pigeons, and monkeys), have a primitive system of numerical approximation, which is limited in its accuracy, but nevertheless allows them to size up the number of objects in their environment. Human infants also have access to a second system that is sensitive to exact numbers but only for sets of up to three items (Feigenson, Dehaene, & Spelke, 2004). Neither of these systems can handle exact enumeration of larger sets, an ability that is acquired later in life and appears to rely on language. Indeed, at around 4 years of age, most children acquire natural number concepts that denote the cardinality of large sets. Children initially learn a counting routine that puts an ordered series of number words (*one*, *two*, *three*, *four*, etc.) in one-to-one correspondence with items to be counted; later they discover the cardinal word principle (Wynn, 1992). In effect, they learn that *five* refers to a set with 5 items in it, that *ten* refers to a set with 10 items in it, and that any set can be counted to determine its exact number. Children learn that the series of number words can be extended indefinitely, such that any set of things, no matter how large, can in principle be counted to determine its exact number.

**cardinal word principle**
the underlying principle of counting which implies that the last number reached as items are counted indicates the number of items in the whole set.

However, not all children grow up learning a counting routine for computing exact numbers. As discussed with respect to the cross-linguistic diversity of colour and spatial terms, languages also provide different vocabularies for children to talk about numbers. At one extreme are languages like the Amazonian language of Pirahã, which has only a few number words, roughly corresponding to *one*, *two*, *few*, and *many* (Gordon, 2004). Moreover, the Pirahã words tend to refer to approximate rather than exact numbers – for example, the Pirahã word for *two* is similar to the English word *couple*, as in *I watched the game last night with a couple of friends*. Another Amazonian language, Mundurukú, contains words for exact numbers up to three and words for approximate numbers up to five (Pica, Lemer, Izard, & Dehaene, 2004). Similarly, Warlpiri, spoken in the Northern Territories of Australia, contains only number words corresponding to *one*, *two*, and *greater than two*, and Anindilyakwa, also spoken in rural Australia, only expresses number categories corresponding to *one*, *two*, *three*, and *more than three* (Butterworth, Reeve, Reynolds, & Lloyd, 2008).

The diversity of number vocabularies across languages has led researchers to ask whether the development of exact number concepts for quantities larger than three is dependent on knowing the corresponding words. If this were the case then children acquiring languages with sparse number vocabularies would be expected to have difficulties in learning to exactly enumerate quantities exceeding the available number words in their language. This should manifest itself not just in an inability to count larger sets of items, but also to perform other cognitive operations that require exact number concepts. Unfortunately, evidence from children speaking such languages is sparse. Gordon (2004) found that adult speakers of Pirahã had difficulties putting sets of items greater than three in one-to-one correspondence. Similarly, Pica and colleagues (2004) found that adult and child speakers of Mundurukú performed similarly to French-speaking controls in tasks requiring numerical approximation, but considerably worse in tasks requiring exact enumeration of larger sets. On the other hand, Butterworth and colleagues (2008) compared 4- to 7-year-old speakers of Warlpiri, Anindilyakwa, or English on tasks requiring exact enumeration of sets of up to ten items. The children had to memorise quantities, match the number of a set of items to the number of times wooden blocks were tapped together, and determine the size of a set after an item had been added. In contrast to the studies of Pirahã and Mundurukú, some of the Warlpiri and Anindilyakwa speakers showed a high level of performance on the tasks requiring exact enumeration that was comparable to the English-speaking controls. Although it is possible that their superior performance in comparison to the Pirahã and Mundurukú was due to task differences, one might also speculate that the cultural practices of the Australian participants encourage greater use of number concepts than the cultural practices of the Amazonian participants.

To disentangle the effects of language and culture, Spaepen and colleagues tested deaf young adults in Nicaragua who had grown up in a numerate culture but had never acquired Nicaraguan Sign Language, and, thus, never acquired a vocabulary of number words and a counting routine (Spaepen, Coppola, Spelke, Carey, & Goldin-Meadow, 2010). Instead, these individuals relied on gestures called **home sign** to communicate with the people around them (see Chapter 11 for further description of home sign). They had experience handling money in everyday life and also understood that signs were used to communicate exact numbers. Still, they did not always correctly extend the number of fingers when communicating about set sizes greater than three and did not always correctly match set sizes. Unlike deaf individuals who grew up learning Nicaraguan Sign Language, the deaf home signers failed to use gestures corresponding to exact numbers correctly and reliably. These findings seem to suggest that the extent to which a language provides a vocabulary for a counting routine affects how well individuals can represent and use exact number concepts. However, in light of the similarity in performance between English-speaking versus Warlpiri- and Anindilyakwa-speaking children on enumeration tasks (Butterworth et al., 2008), it is also possible that other aspects of language use influence the development of number concepts; for example, how consistently

**home sign** the gestural communication systems created by isolated deaf children who are not exposed to a sign language.

**numerical cognition** the cognitive underpinnings of number concepts and mathematics.

and reliably speakers use the available numerical expressions to refer to exact quantities.

The role of language in numerical cognition has also been tested by comparing speakers of languages that differ in the transparency of the number terms for quantities greater than ten. The decimal numeral system is based on powers of ten, and languages differ in how transparently the base-ten number system is reflected in the names for numbers. For example, Chinese, Japanese, and Korean use a simple, predictable system in which numbers 11, 12, 13 are labelled 'ten-one', 'ten-two', 'ten-three'; 20, 30, 40 are labelled 'two-ten', 'three-ten', 'four-ten', and so forth, with children needing to learn special terms only for numbers 0 to 9, 100, 1000, and 10,000. English, in contrast, uses special terms for 0 to 12, a set of unusual compound words ending in *teen* for 13–19, proceeding to a fairly transparent system for numbers greater than 20, but still requiring children to learn special terms like *twenty*, *thirty*, and *fifty* (and not *two-ty*, *three-ty*, and *five-ty*). As a result of having to learn this more complicated system, English-speaking children exhibit more difficulties in counting beyond ten than Chinese-speaking children (Miller & Stigler, 1987). Similar difficulties have been observed in children speaking Italian, which has a system of number words like that of English (Agnoli & Zhu, 1989). The transparency of marking base ten has been implicated in the early emergence of mathematical concepts among speakers of Asian languages. For example, Japanese, Chinese, and Korean children show an earlier understanding of the place value concept than children learning English, Swedish, or French (Miura, Okamoto, Kim, Steere, & Fayol, 1993; Miura, Okamoto, Kim, Chang, Steere, & Fayol, 1994). It has even been suggested that the persistent advantages of Asian over American students in mathematics achievement might be attributable in part to cross-linguistic differences in number-naming systems (McKnight et al., 1987; Miller, Smith, Zhu, & Zhang, 1995).

**digit span** the length of the longest list of numbers that an individual can repeat back in the correct order immediately after presentation of the last number.

A range of other effects of language on numerical cognition has been documented. In an early study, Ellis and Hennelly (1980) observed that English–Welsh bilingual children had a smaller digit span when recalling lists of numbers in Welsh than in English. They reported that it takes slightly longer for speakers to articulate the Welsh number words in comparison to their English counterparts. Thus, if less material can be encoded in phonological short-term memory, the longer duration of Welsh numbers has the potential to adversely affect the efficiency of mental arithmetic performed in Welsh. Similarly, the shorter articulation times to name numbers in Mandarin relative to English may account for the advantage of Chinese over English speakers in measures of forward and backward digit span (Chen, Cowell, Varley, & Wang, 2009).

Another effect of language can be found in magnitude estimations for larger numbers: generally, it takes longer to identify the larger number of a pair of two-digit numbers (e.g. 47 vs. 62) if separate comparisons of tens (4 < 6) and units (7 > 2) are incompatible, relative to pairs (e.g. 42 vs. 57) where both tens and units are in a compatible relationship, with 4 < 5 and 2 < 7, even when absolute distance (e.g. 15) is equal. This has been taken as evidence that processing of numbers greater than 10 is decompositional (Pixner, Moeller, Hermanova, Nuerk, & Kaufmann, 2011).

However, the magnitude of this effect depends on the order in which the language encodes tens and units. Some languages order numerical information as tens and units, as in the English *twenty-one* or the Chinese *er-shi-yi* (*two-ten-one*); in such languages the compatibility effect is relatively small. Other languages, like German, reverse the order of tens and units, as in *einundzwanzig* (literally *one and twenty*); in such languages the compatibility effect is much more pronounced, presumably because fronting of the units makes the incompatibility with the magnitude of the tens more prominent and misleading. Interestingly, in speakers of languages like Czech that allow both principles of number word formation, for example, *dvadset jeden* (*twenty-one*) and *jeden a dvadset* (*one and twenty*), the compatibility effect is of intermediate size (Pixner et al., 2011). Finally, a recent study provides further evidence of how a language's number naming system impacts numerical cognition, by examining the speed of mental arithmetic in speakers of Basque, a language in which number words are based on multiples of 20 rather than 10 (Colomé, Laka, & Sebastián-Gallés, 2010). Across several experiments, Basque speakers were faster at solving addition problems that matched the structure of their language (e.g. 20 + 15) than problems that did not (e.g. 10 + 25), despite the fact that all the addition problems were presented as Arabic digits, and responses were typed. Thus, even in tasks that do not require overt naming, the number naming system has the potential to impact mathematical processing.

### 8.2.4 Mechanisms behind effects of language on cognition

Several mechanisms have been suggested as accounts of how language impacts cognitive processing (Majid et al., 2004). First, any given language may selectively direct attention to some features in the environment but not other features. Language learning thus creates habitual patterns of selective attention (e.g. to the tightness of fit between two objects or to the exact number of items in large sets). Over time, this results in perceptual tuning as the non-attended features that are not systematically marked in the language lose their perceptual salience and tend to be ignored.

Second, language use can lead to a re-description or recoding of initially acquired categories in the same way as novices recode representations once they gain more experience with a domain and develop expertise (Karmiloff-Smith, 1992). For example, children may perceptually distinguish different numbers of objects (such as 1 vs. 2 vs. 3), but will grasp the idea that any set of objects has exact numerocity only through exposure to a system of number words for counting. Thus, for categories that have been established non-linguistically, language can serve as a means of re-describing the categories based on which features receive verbal labels and which features do not.

Third, many cognitive operations require structural alignment, that is, the use of higher-order similarities to establish correspondences across different conceptual domains (Gentner & Namy, 2006). For example, the use of a metaphor like *Lawyers are sharks* requires one to find similarities (e.g. aggressive, thick-skinned)

**Figure 8.5**    *Comprehension of metaphors utilises a process of structural alignment whereby the features of one entity, such as a lawyer, are lined up with the features of another entity, such as a shark.*

*Source:* © HitToon.com.  Used under licence from Shutterstock.

between the concept of a lawyer and that of a shark (see Figure 8.5). In learning a language, children may notice how the same words are used in different situations. This may invite comparisons that promote extraction of higher-order relationships. For example, the use of the Korean word *kkita* to describe the fit of an egg in an egg cup and a Lego block onto a stack of Lego blocks may invite the detection of similarities in how objects fit together that would come to mind less readily for speakers of other languages.

Finally, it has been suggested that the way languages encode aspects of the world may result in different costs of computation for similar operations. For example, English speakers with a relative frame of reference may be perfectly capable of expressing absolute bearings, for example, when providing driving directions (e.g. drive north on the M1 for 10 km, then east for 6 km). However, to compute where north is when walking about London, English speakers may have to remember how many left or right turns they have taken (i.e. using their relative frame of reference to determine absolute coordinates), which may incur considerable processing costs due to demands on working memory. In contrast, Mopan speakers with an absolute frame of reference may rely on a different set of computations based on geographical features, which may be optimal for their everyday circumstances.

# 8.3  DOES IT MATTER HOW MANY LANGUAGES CHILDREN LEARN?

So far our explorations have discussed the effects of specific features of different languages on perception, memory, and categorisation. In this section, we will explore how the acquisition of multiple languages impacts cognitive development.

In many parts of the world, children grow up being exposed to more than one language. In fact, from a cross-cultural perspective, monolingualism is the exception rather than the norm (Tucker, 2003). Different situations can lead to the acquisition of multiple languages. Some children hear one language spoken by their father and another language spoken by their mother. Other children encounter one language at home and another language outside home. Yet other children grow up in bilingual communities or with bilingual parents and hear both languages spoken by the same speakers. All these situations, involving acquisition of two or more languages, are typically subsumed under the term bilingualism, although the age at first exposure to the second language and the amount of exposure to the two languages can vary considerably. The situation that presents the strongest contrast to monolingual language development is that of balanced or simultaneous bilingualism in which children receive input in two languages from birth and acquire, in essence, two first languages.

> **bilingualism** acquisition and use of two languages.

## 8.3.1  Rate of development in two languages

In situations where children are exposed to more than one language, the ability to distinguish between them is an important prerequisite for bilingual language development. How do infants in bilingual environments learn to distinguish between the two languages? In Chapter 2 we highlighted the abilities of newborns born into a monolingual environment to discriminate languages from different rhythmic classes, such as English and Japanese (Nazzi et al., 1998), but not languages from the same rhythmic class, such as English and Dutch (Christophe & Morton, 1998). The latter ability emerges a few months later, but is restricted to being able to distinguish between the ambient language and an unfamiliar language. Young infants are not able to distinguish between two unfamiliar languages from the same rhythmic class (Nazzi et al., 2000). So how dissimilar must the two familiar languages be for children in a bilingual environment to be able to discriminate between them? Bosch and Sebastián-Gallés (2001) studied whether 4-month-old bilingual infants could discriminate between Spanish and Catalan, two languages belonging to the same rhythmic group. They found that infants immersed in a bilingual environment were able to distinguish these two languages, thereby displaying sensitivity to the subtle metrical and phonological differences between them. Bilingual infants display such sensitivities not just for auditory information, but also for visual cues – that is, for the articulatory movements associated with different ambient languages. For example, 8-month-old bilingual infants were able to distinguish silent videos of English versus French speech when their monolingual peers had already lost this ability (Weikum, Vouloumanos, Navarro, Soto-Faraco, Sebastián-Gallés, & Werker, 2007). Thus, increased variability in the input facilitates the emergence of early discrimination abilities and longer retention of the acquired sensitivities.

What about bilingual infants' ability to discriminate phonemes? In Chapter 2 we noted that monolingual infants' ability to discriminate non-native phonemic contrasts declines during the second half of the first year of life (Werker & Tees, 1984). Do infants reared in bilingual environments retain sensitivity to a larger repertoire of phonemic contrasts? Recent findings using an Anticipatory Eye Movement paradigm suggest an affirmative answer. In this paradigm, infants look towards the anticipated location of a toy (left vs. right) that is contingent upon change in the speech stimuli. Just like monolingual Catalan infants, Catalan–Spanish bilingual infants maintained the ability to discriminate the uniquely Catalan phonemic contrast between /e/ and /ɛ/ at the age of 7–8 months, by which time monolingual Spanish infants had lost this ability (Albareda-Castellot, Pons, & Sebastián-Gallés, 2011). These early perceptual sensitivities are affected by language dominance: bilingual infants show better discrimination for whichever language dominates their environment (Sebastián-Gallés & Bosch, 2002). This suggests that early exposure to two or more phonological systems may attenuate language-specific phonological tuning, resulting in a more flexible system (Kaushanskaya & Marian, 2009).

While the described perceptual sensitivities allow bilingual children to discriminate sounds and to segment words in the bilingual language input, the most formidable challenge is to establish two mental lexicons containing different phonological, semantic, and grammatical information (Werker & Byers-Heinlein, 2008). For example, for a Russian–English bilingual the lexical entry for the Russian noun *kniga* has to contain, in addition to a phonological form different from the English noun *book*, different grammatical information to indicate that the noun is feminine. Not many studies have addressed how word learning differs between bilinguals and monolinguals, but there is some evidence that bilingual infants learn to associate minimally different nonce syllables (e.g. *bih* and *dih*) with different meanings at a somewhat older age than monolingual infants (i.e. at 20 months in comparison to 17 months for monolingual infants). This delay for bilinguals may be a consequence of the increased cognitive load associated with establishing two lexicons (Fennell, Byers-Heinlein, & Werker, 2007).

Given that infants exposed to two languages have an increased cognitive load due to greater exposure to a diversity of word forms and meanings, it is testimony to the remarkable plasticity of early learning that bilinguals' vocal development proceeds on the same timescale as that of monolinguals (Oller, Eilers, Urbano, & Cobo-Lewis, 1997). Bilingual children do not show delays in word learning if their joint vocabulary in both languages is compared with the vocabulary of age-matched monolinguals (Pearson, Fernandéz, & Oller, 1993). However, because bilinguals have to acquire twice the number of words, and because the amount of exposure to each of their languages tends to be reduced due to fewer hours of exposure to each language, bilingual children tend to have somewhat smaller receptive vocabularies in each of their languages compared to monolingual children (Mahon & Crutchley, 2006; Oller & Eilers, 2002).

In adult bilinguals, this disadvantage in lexical knowledge manifests itself in their performance on psycholinguistic measures of speech production. Bilingual adults show slower lexical retrieval – it takes them slightly longer to find the right word to say (Roberts, Garcia, Desrochers, & Hernandez, 2002; Gollan, Montoya, Fennema-Notestine, & Morris, 2005). In a verbal fluency task, when asked, for example, to produce as many words as possible, beginning with the letter *f*, in 1 minute, bilinguals produce fewer words than monolinguals, especially if they are tested in a language that was acquired after their first language (Gollan, Montoya, & Werner, 2002; Portocarrero, Burright, & Donovick, 2007). Bilinguals experience **tip-of-the-tongue** states more often than monolinguals (Gollan & Acenas, 2004). Taken together, these studies indicate that there are processing costs associated with being bilingual which are related to bilinguals experiencing slightly more difficulty in retrieving words in each of their languages.

> **tip-of-the-tongue** a phenomenon involving a failure to retrieve a word; it is accompanied by a strong feeling of imminent retrieval – the person knows the word but cannot bring it to mind.

## 8.3.2 Cognitive effects of learning two languages

Despite the subtle disadvantages that bilinguals may experience when accessing lexical knowledge in each of their languages, researchers have long wondered whether there may be advantages associated with bilingualism. At first, these advantages were assumed to lie in the linguistic domain. One such candidate for a beneficial effect of bilingualism is metalinguistic awareness. To test for a bilingual advantage, Bialystok (1986, 1988) asked children to perform grammaticality judgements by asking them to say whether a sentence was said 'the right way' or 'the wrong way'. A semantically plausible sentence like *Apples growed on trees* required children to ignore the meaningfulness of the sentence to identify the grammatical error (*growed* should be *grew*), whereas a semantically implausible sentence like *Apples grow on noses* required children to ignore the implausible meaning of the sentence to identify the sentence as grammatically correct. Bialystok's findings of better performance of bilingual children suggest that they were more able to suppress irrelevant semantic information when judging whether the sentences were well formed.

> **metalinguistic awareness** explicit awareness or knowledge about the structure and properties of a language.

The interesting question is whether the superior ability of bilingual children to control attention and to suppress irrelevant information generalises to non-linguistic tasks. One of the first studies to address this question examined monolingual and bilingual children's control over attention in a counting task: when given towers of Lego blocks and Duplo blocks and asked to count the number of segments, bilingual Spanish–English 4-year-olds showed greater accuracy when the Lego towers had more segments but were shorter than the Duplo towers – that is, when there was conflict between tower height and number of segments. Thus, bilingual children were better able to focus on counting the segments and were less distracted by conflicting height information (Bialystok & Codd, 1997).

**dimensional change card sorting (DCCS) task** a widely used measure of the executive control of attention in preschool-aged children; they must sort cards first by one dimension (e.g. shape) and then by a different dimension (e.g. colour).

The classical test to measure executive control of attention in preschool-aged children is the dimensional change card sorting (DCCS) task (Zelazo, Frye, & Rapus, 1996). In this executive functioning task, children are instructed to sort a set of picture cards (e.g. red boats, blue trucks) according to one dimension (e.g. colour) and then are instructed to switch to the other dimension (e.g. shape). Typically, preschool-aged children find it difficult to switch (e.g. to shape) and continue to sort the cards in accordance with the first set of rules (e.g. sort by colour). If participants successfully switch to the new dimension in the post-switch phase, this can be taken as evidence of good control over attention. Bialystok (1999) administered the DCCS task to 3- to 6-year-old English monolingual and English–Chinese bilingual children. Not surprisingly, the 5- to 6-year old children made fewer mistakes in the post-switch phase than the 3- to 4-year-old children, demonstrating that control of attention improves during the preschool years (Tipper, 1992). Crucially, the bilingual children significantly outperformed their monolingual peers, suggesting that bilingual children have superior control of attention and are better able to inhibit irrelevant information (e.g. the colour of the cards when sorting by shape). The bilingual advantage in card-sort tasks has been shown for rules involving perceptual dimensions (e.g. sort by colour, shape, contour) but not for semantic categories (sort the 'toys' vs. 'clothes', or the 'things used inside the house' vs. 'things used outside the house'). This suggests that bilingual children are not better at representing meaning, but are better at inhibiting attention to salient perceptual features of objects (Bialystok & Martin, 2004). Superior inhibitory control in bilingual children has been demonstrated in other tasks too: for example, 6-year-old bilingual children were better at identifying the alternative image hidden in an ambiguous figure (Bialystok & Shapero, 2005), and 3- to 6-year-old bilingual children were better at detecting violations of conversational rules (Siegal, Iozzi, & Surian, 2009).

Bilinguals and monolinguals not only differ with respect to their knowledge of language, but may also differ in other dimensions such as socio-economic status and cultural values. Is it possible that socio-economic and other cultural differences are responsible for the bilingual advantage? Morton and Harper (2007) failed to find any differences in inhibitory control between 6- to 7-year-old English-speaking monolingual and English–French bilingual children; instead, socio-economic status was positively related to inhibitory control. Similarly, cultural values can also affect executive functioning: when tested, monolingual Chinese preschoolers showed higher executive functioning than their American counterparts (Sabbagh, Xu, Carlson, Moses, & Lee, 2006). Still, when Chinese monolingual and Chinese–Korean fourth-graders were compared, the bilingual children showed superior selective attention (Choi, Won, & Lee, 2003).

Mounting evidence suggests that the bilingual advantage in inhibitory control is a real phenomenon that extends beyond childhood (Bialystok, Martin, & Viswanathan, 2005). Bialystok (2007) has proposed that the advantage is due to bilinguals' continuous practice in inhibiting interference from whatever language is not currently in use. When bilinguals communicate, neither language is ever completely 'turned off'.

This availability of both languages allows bilinguals rapidly to switch between languages as needed, with some bilinguals code-switching within a single sentence, as 'Give me a kiss *o te pego*' [translation: or I hit you] (Zentella, 1997: 112). As described in the previous section, bilinguals may experience processing costs in accessing words for speech production. Successful retrieval of words from one language requires bilinguals to suppress words from their other language. Over time, extensive practise in suppressing words from the language not currently in use leads to improvements in inhibitory control of attention, which transfers to other, non-linguistic tasks. This explanation of the bilingual advantage is supported by recent neuro-imaging findings showing that bilinguals recruit brain areas involved in language control for non-linguistic tasks (Garbin, Sanjuan, Forn, Bustamante, Rodriguez-Pujadas, Belloch, et al., 2010).

Early experiences with two languages affect cognitive control in quite specific ways: bilingual children show an advantage in tasks requiring the management of conflicting demands on attention, but not in tasks that require impulse control, for example, to forfeit a small immediate reward to obtain a larger reward at a later point in time (Carlson & Meltzoff, 2008). There is also evidence that the bilingual advantage extends to the ability to anticipate upcoming events: when Italian monolingual and bilingual 6- to 12-year-olds learned a sequence of colours and were asked to anticipate upcoming colours in the sequence, the bilinguals outperformed their monolingual peers (Bonifacci, Giombini, Bellocchi, & Contendo, 2010). Anticipation is part and parcel of normal language use – one constantly anticipates what words are going to come up next based on the context and what previously has been said. The advantage in anticipation is assumed to arise from bilinguals doing twice as much anticipatory work when using both of their languages.

Such findings lead one to wonder how much exposure to and use of two languages is necessary for a bilingual advantage to arise. To explore this question, Kovács and Mehler (2009) gave 7-month-old infants an executive function task that required a switch from one response to another response. In the pre-switch phase, infants were trained to associate a speech sound (e.g. *le-le-mo*) with a reward that consistently appeared on one side of a screen. As expected, infants from monolingual and bilingual homes learned to direct their gaze towards the rewarded side at an equal rate. In the post-switch phase, another speech sound (e.g. *le-mo-mo*) was associated with a reward appearing on the opposite side of the screen. Here infants had to learn to redirect their gaze to the new location. Interestingly, infants raised bilingually disengaged from the old side and learned to anticipate the reward at its new location. In contrast, infants raised monolingually showed no change in gaze direction. As with preschool-aged children tested using the DCCS card sort task, the bilingual advantage in infants also carried over to a non-linguistic task in which the stimuli were sequences of visual figures. These findings show that a bilingual advantage may arise even before children have produced their first words. Apparently, it is sufficient for young infants to process two languages to reap the benefits of enhanced executive functioning. It appears that exposure to two languages from birth enhances cognitive control of attention right from the start – a finding that is important for educators and reassuring for bilingual families.

# SUMMARY

- Communicative competence related to conversational and narrative skills facilitates the development of autobiographical memory and contributes to the offset of childhood amnesia by providing children with a format for encoding and retrieving memories. Joint reminiscing with caregivers serves as a scaffold for organising representations of the past.

- The specific language children grow up with shapes cognition in non-linguistic domains.

  - Languages differ in number and type of basic colour terms. Once children acquire their native colour terms they show categorical perception of colour in accordance with these terms. This effect is much stronger in the right visual field, indicating involvement of the language-processing areas of the left cortical hemisphere.

  - Languages also differ in frames of spatial reference and in spatial terms. Children acquire their native frame of reference at around 4 years and show sensitivity to some native spatial terms already at 18 months. The early ability to classify spatial configurations in accordance with native spatial terms leads to a loss of the ability to learn spatial configurations not marked in the native language.

  - Finally, languages differ in how they express numbers and the concept of place value. This affects how well children learn to count and to compare exact quantities greater than three as well as their understanding of place value.

- Learning more than one language is not detrimental for language development but has linguistic as well as general cognitive benefits.

  - Bilingual infants retain sensitivity to phonemic contrasts in both of their languages at a time when monolingual children already lose sensitivity to non-native contrasts.

  - Although the size of the vocabularies of bilingual children in each of their languages tends to be somewhat smaller than that of monolingual children, their general language development is not delayed when taking into account the combined knowledge of vocabulary in both languages.

  - Bilingual children show improved meta-linguistic awareness, allowing them to ignore one aspect of an utterance (e.g. meaning) while considering another (e.g. grammar).

  - Having to manage use of two languages is associated with improved cognitive control; specifically, the ability to inhibit irrelevant information and to anticipate upcoming events. These benefits can be detected in non-linguistic domains and manifest themselves already at around 7 months of age.

# FURTHER READING

## *Key studies*

For research on how language abilities affect memory, read Simcock, G. & Hayne, H. (2002). Breaking the barrier? Children fail to translate their preverbal memories into language. *Psychological Science, 13*, 225–231.

For evidence of effects of language on colour cognition, read Franklin, A., Drivonikou, G. V., Clifford, A., Kay, P., Regier, T. & Davies, I. R. L. (2008). Lateralization of categorical perception of color changes with color term acquisition. *Proceedings of the National Academy of Sciences USA, 105*, 18221–18225.

For evidence of effects of language on spatial cognition, read McDonough, L., Choi, S. & Mandler, J. (2003). Understanding spatial relations: Flexible infants, lexical adults. *Cognitive Psychology, 46*, 229–259.

For cognitive effects of bilingual upbringing in infants, read Kovács, A. M. & Mehler, J. (2009). Cognitive gains in 7-month-old bilingual infants. *Proceedings of the National Academy of Sciences, 106*, 6556–6560.

## *Overview articles*

For an up-to-date overview of research on Whorfian effects in colour cognition, read Regier, T. & Kay, P. (2009). Language, thought and color: Whorf was half right. *Trends in Cognitive Sciences, 13*, 439–446.

For an overview on Whorfian effects in spatial cognition, read Majid, A., Bowerman, M., Kita, S., Haun, D. & Levinson, S. (2004). Can language restructure cognition? The case for space. *Trends in Cognitive Sciences, 8*, 108–114.

For on overview of research on the bilingual advantage in executive control, read Bialystok, E. (2009). Bilingualism: The good, the bad, and the indifferent. *Bilingualism: Language and Cognition, 12*, 3–11.

## *Books*

To better understand the different ways that languages may structure spatial cognition, read Levinson, S. C. (2003). *Space in language and cognition: Explorations in cognitive diversity*. Cambridge: Cambridge University Press.

To learn more about the relationship between language development and autobiographical memory, read Nelson, K. (2007). *Young minds in social worlds: Experience, meaning and memory*. Boston, MA: Harvard University Press.

# 9 What is the Role of Literacy in Language Development?

## KEY TERMS

• abjads • alphabets • analytic phonics • constructions • deep orthography • developmental dyslexia • digraphs • doublets • etymology • genetic linkage • grapheme-to-phoneme conversion rules • graphemes • home literacy environment • homophones • latent semantic analysis (LSA) • lexical route • lexicon • logographic scripts • morae • morphemes • morphological awareness • orthography • phonemic awareness • phonics approach • phonological awareness • phonological decoding • phonological recoding • phonological route • semantic • shallow orthography • slow mapping • Specific Language Impairment (SLI) • statistical learning • syllabic script • synthetic phonics • whole-language approach • whole-word approach

# CHAPTER OUTLINE

In many societies, literacy is a highly valued skill that children have to master to fully participate in community life. Growing up in such a society, a toddler might encounter picture books on a daily basis and be encouraged to read along with others (see Figure 9.1). Well before the onset of formal literacy instruction – typically at 4 to 6 years of age – toddlers develop an interest in books through interactive routines in which they point to and label objects in picture books, and learn to listen attentively as others read to them (Fletcher & Reese, 2005; Ninio & Bruner, 1978). These pre-literacy skills – that is, an interest in books and an ability to sustain attention and engage responsively while others read aloud – are associated with positive literacy and language development outcomes in school (Deckner, Adamson & Bakeman, 2006; Saracho & Spodek, 2010; Sénéchal, & LeFevre, 2002; Snow & Ninio, 1985). Differences in the quality of the home literacy environment strongly impact literacy development (Burgess, Hecht, & Lonigan, 2002; Foy & Mann, 2003; Griffin & Morrison, 1997; Hood, Conlon, & Andrews, 2008; Sénéchal, 2006; Weigel, Martin, & Bennett, 2006), as well as other aspects of language development such as vocabulary size and narrative skills (Hart, Petrill, DeThorne, Deater-Deckard, Thompson, Schatschneider, et al., 2009; Payne, Whitehurst & Angell, 1994; Rodriguez, Tamis-LeMonda, Spellman, Pan, Raikes, Lugo-Gil, et al., 2009; Sénéchal, Pagan, Lever, & Ouellette, 2008). Thus, support for literacy is another dimension by which caregivers

**home literacy environment** the extent to which the home environment supports children's literacy development; this includes factors such as the number of books and other written materials in the home, as well as how often and for how long the child reads with caregivers.

**Figure 9.1**   *Literacy development benefits from a supportive home environment, where children have access to books and other printed media.*

*Source:* © William Ju. Used under licence from Shutterstock.

vary in how they provide input for their child's language development (see Chapter 6 for a discussion of how individual differences in child-directed speech impact language-learning outcomes).

Of course, not all children learn to read. There are still many societies in which literacy education is unavailable or takes place much later in life, often in a language other than the one spoken at home. According to UNESCO statistics, 1.25 billion people, or roughly 20 per cent of the world's population, speak so-called minority languages without a literary tradition. More than two-thirds of these people remain illiterate, either because writing systems for their languages are non-existent, or because resources for literacy acquisition are not available. It is therefore important to keep in mind that the process of literacy acquisition described in this chapter is by no means universal. Nevertheless, in societies where children do learn to read and write, literacy greatly expands their knowledge of vocabulary and grammar, increases meta-linguistic awareness, and provides new modes of thinking as children navigate the world of written media (Olson, 1994, 1996, 2002). In this chapter we examine the process by which children acquire literacy and its role in cognitive development.

# 9.1 HOW DO CHILDREN LEARN TO READ AND WRITE?

Children typically require several years of formal schooling and considerable numbers of hours of practice to become fluent and independent readers. Other aspects of literacy, such as accurate spelling and expository or creative writing skills, generally take even longer to master. Why is literacy difficult for many children to achieve, and what factors influence the time-course of acquisition of basic reading and spelling skills? To answer these questions, we start by examining how the writing systems of languages are organised, and how the relationship between written and oral language impacts literacy acquisition.

## 9.1.1 The structure of writing systems

**graphemes** visual symbols (e.g. letters) used in writing systems that encode aspects of sound or meaning.

**abjads** writing systems in which symbols (graphemes) encode consonants but not vowels.

Writing systems that encode language (as opposed to mathematical or musical notations) consist of graphemes. There are about 60 different writing systems in current use; several more (e.g. the runic alphabet) have fallen out of use over the course of history. Writing systems vary along two dimensions: the size of units coded by graphemes and the consistency or transparency with which graphemes map onto phonemes. The first writing systems that represented phonemes were abjads, still used in Hebrew and Arabic. This fits well with the morphological structure of Semitic languages, where roots consist of sets of consonants and vowels fit into the slots of the consonant grid to convey grammatical information. In these writing systems, letter-by-letter conversion of graphemes to phonemes is often insufficient to access a word's pronunciation (Frost, Katz, & Bentin, 1987), although the use of diacritic symbols to mark vowels, as is found in children's books and religious texts, can enhance phonological clarity.

**alphabets** writing systems that code both consonants and vowels.

**orthography** the writing system of a language.

Alphabets such as the Greek, Latin, or Cyrillic alphabet code both consonants and vowels, thereby allowing for greater spelling–sound consistency. Alphabetic writing systems differ in their orthography, that is, in the way different graphemes relate to phonemes. The consistency of grapheme-to-phoneme mappings varies widely amongst alphabets, depending on how each writing system deals with a mismatch between number of letters and number of phonemes in the language. These discrepancies arise because alphabets, most notably the Latin one, are often used to write languages for which they were not designed. Some orthographies such as Greek (using the Greek alphabet), Italian (using the Latin alphabet) or Serbian (using the Cyrillic or the Latin alphabet) are characterised by very consistent spelling–sound correspondences.

These languages have what is called a shallow orthography. For instance, Greek has five vowel sounds and seven vowel letters to convey the sounds; this contrasts markedly with British English, which has 21 different vowel sounds but only five vowel letters (a, e, i, o, u) to convey them (Nunes & Bryant, 2009; O'Connor, 1982). Readers of a language with a shallow, transparent orthography benefit from an almost optimal match between the phonemic repertoire of the language and the number of letters in the alphabet. This match allows readers to use a set of consistent grapheme-to-phoneme conversion rules to compute the pronunciation of any word, familiar or not.

**shallow orthography** a transparent writing system in which each letter corresponds to a single phoneme and each phoneme is usually expressed with a single letter, e.g. Finnish.

But not everybody is so lucky. English is notorious for its inconsistent spelling system in which different letters or letter combinations map onto different phonemes depending on context and position in the word. For example, the letter *c* is pronounced as /k/ in some words like *cat* or *immaculate* but as /s/ in other words like *cerebral* or *lace*. Or, as mentioned above, the phoneme /f/ is sometimes rendered by the letter *f* as in *face* and at other times by the letter combination *ff* as in *stiff* or *gaffe*, *gh* as in *laugh* or *rough*, or *ph* as in *phoneme* or *graph*, even though the letters *g*, *h*, and *p* in isolation map onto entirely different phonemes. Moreover, there is also inconsistency in the mapping from phoneme to grapheme: for example, the same phoneme /iː/ can be spelled in quite a few different ways, as in *me*, *sea*, *see*, *key*, *peace*, *piece*, *ceiling*, and *quay*. Thus, within the alphabetic languages, English is an extreme example of a deep orthography, which is mainly a consequence of the fact that the number of phonemes in English (42–47, depending on the variety) by far exceeds the 26 letters of the Latin alphabet. Historical changes in word pronunciation and the lack of spelling reforms have aggravated this inconsistency over time. Other alphabetical writing systems have adopted the use

**deep orthography** a writing system in which there is no simple one-to-one correspondence between the letters of the alphabet and the phonemes of the language (e.g. English).

of diacritic symbols to cope with a mismatch between the numbers of sounds and letters in the language. For example, German, which uses the Latin alphabet, uses the umlauts *ä*, *ö*, and *ü* to accommodate the extra vowels, thereby increasing spelling–sound transparency. Similarly, Serbian, when written with the Latin (rather than the Cyrillic) alphabet, uses diacritics, for example the hacek, to distinguish *s* and *c* from *š* and *č*, which also facilitates orthographic consistency. English uses letter combinations called digraphs as a way of coping with the insufficient numbers of letters for speech sounds. For vowels, this includes the use of split digraphs, *a_e*, *e_e*, *i_e*, *o_e*, *u_e*, (the underscore _ stands for any consonant), to distinguish the vowels in words like *pal*,

**digraphs** letter combinations such as *ng*, *th*, *sh* or *ch*, as in *thing*, *chair*, and *shingle*, used to represent phonemes.

*secret*, *kit*, *rot*, and *cut* from those in words like *pale*, *secrete*, *kite*, *rote*, and *cute*. Another English strategy for coping with the shortage of letters is to double the consonant to change the pronunciation of the preceding vowel, as in word pairs like *super–supper*, *biding–bidding*, *mate–matte*, and so on. The variety of English digraphs adds considerable complexity to the English spelling system, and consequently, it takes children considerable time to master these details (Ehri & Soffer, 1993; Nunes & Bryant, 2009; Treiman, 1993).

**syllabic script** a type of writing system whereby symbols (graphemes) encode syllables.

Graphemes can also represent units larger than phonemes, such as syllables or morphemes. The Japanese Kana syllabary is one example of a syllabic script where each grapheme stands for a syllable consisting of a consonant and a vowel. Logographic scripts, such as Chinese, code entire morphemes, thus resulting in several thousand graphemes that need to be memorised. The advantage of logographic systems is that meaning can be expressed without recourse to pronunciation, so that written script becomes readable by speakers of different dialects of the language and even different languages, as the use of Chinese characters for writing Japanese (Kanji) and Korean (Hanja) demonstrates.

**logographic scripts** writing systems whereby symbols (graphemes) encode entire morphemes.

The writing systems of language not only reflect the sound patterns of words, but also represent how words are related in meaning. As described in Chapter 4, many English words contain two or more morphemes. The spellings of words like *walked*, *magician*, *action*, and *partial* are more or less predictable if the child knows their underlying morphological structure (*walk* + *ed*, *magic* + *ian*, *act* + *ion*, *part* + *ial*), but are highly irregular if one attempts to spell them by mapping letters onto phonemes – for example, a strategy of sounding out the word *magician* might yield the spelling *majishen*. Morphology plays a very important role in reading, by allowing children familiar with root words and affixes to infer the meanings of polymorphemic words the first time they are encountered (Bower, Kirby, & Deacon, 2010). For the word *magician*, the child would still need to learn that the *c* in *magic* is pronounced differently from the *c* in *magician*, but nevertheless could grasp its meaning straight away.

**etymology** the historical origins of words.

How a word is written might also reflect its origin or etymology. English words that are borrowed from other languages, such as Italian (e.g. *gnocchi*, *broccoli*) or Japanese (e.g. *tsunami*, *karaoke*), retain spelling patterns that are typical for the language of origin, even if they are atypical for English. Other unusual spellings, such as *ght* for the phoneme /t/ in words like *light* and *daughter*, reveal their origins in Old English. Thus, to read and write English words accurately requires children to learn letter-to-sound correspondences involving individual letters as well as digraphs, inflectional and derivational morphemes, and atypical spelling patterns of borrowed words (Nunes & Bryant, 2009; Verhoeven & Perfetti, 2003; Ziegler & Goswami, 2005). Learning the correspondence rules between graphemes and phonemes is complicated, because most graphemes are pronounced in different ways across different words (e.g. compare the pronunciations of *ough* in the words *rough*, *through*, *dough*, and *cough*), and most phonemes have different spellings in different words, which might be more or less predictable given the position of the phoneme in the word and the adjacent phonemes (e.g. compare the spellings of the /k/ sound in *hectic*, *kick*, *cackle*, and *character*).

Once a sequence of graphemes has been processed, it can be linked to a word's pronunciation and meaning. Neuro-imaging studies (Marinkovic, Dhond, Dale, Glessner, Carr, & Halgren, 2003) have shown that the visual processing of letter sequences takes about 250 ms (in adults); after that the word-form information is processed along two major pathways which correspond to the two processing routes that operate during reading (see Figure 9.2). The phonological route accesses the meaning of words via sound: using grapheme-to-phoneme conversion rules, graphemes (i.e. letters or letter combinations) are recoded into the corresponding phonemes and the sound of the word is assembled. For example, the English graphemes *f, ff, ph* or *gh* (e.g. in *fuss, stuff, phone, laugh*) would be linked to the phoneme /f/, which would then be blended with the other phonemes of the word to yield the word's pronunciation. The lexical route goes directly from print to the lexicon by processing individual morphemes and accessing pronunciation commands stored with their lexical entries. This route is necessary for retrieving the pronunciations of words with unusual spelling patterns, such as *yacht, aisle,* or *quay* (Rayner, Foorman, Perfetti, Pesetsky, & Seidenberg, 2001), and is used whenever familiar words are recognised as whole units by sight (Ehri, 2005).

It would seem reasonable to assume that in writing systems with consistent grapheme-to-phoneme mappings, reading would proceed via the phonological route, whereas in inconsistent alphabetical systems or in logographic systems, reading would rely on the lexical route. This is, however, not the case. There is consensus that both routes are involved in the development of reading, but dissent about their relative importance for skilled reading. The interplay between sound mediation or direct access to meaning often depends on the language and the type of word being processed: the phonological route comes to the rescue whenever readers encounter words or letter strings they have never seen in print before. In general, even in words with unusual spellings such as *island, sword,* or *pint,* the majority of letters are likely to be linked to phonemes in a predictable way (e.g. the *p, n,* and *t* of *pint*); hence the phonological route is likely to be involved in decoding almost all words the first time they are encountered (Ehri & Rosenthal, 2007; Rack, Hulme, Snowling, & Wightman, 1994). Converting graphemes into speech sounds and assembling these sounds in succession is what allows us to read novel or made-up words, such as *moop* or *tavicate.* Even Chinese characters contain phonological markers that provide information about word pronunciation, and evidence suggests that adult readers of Chinese utilise the phonological route to some extent (Perfetti & Zhang, 1995). However, the more familiar the written form of a word becomes, regardless of whether its spelling is linked to sound in a consistent fashion or not, the more often the phonological route will be bypassed. Thus, the lexical route dominates processing whenever one reads words that are well practiced and highly familiar (Ehri, 2005): when reading for comprehension (as opposed to skimming), skilful adult readers of English process an average of 200 to 400 words per minute, and children often achieve a reading rate of 200 words per minute by age 12 (Carver, 1990). When reading relatively easy material, the overwhelming majority of words are accessed as whole units without the use of grapheme-to-phoneme correspondence

**phonological route** one of two processing routes involved in reading; the reader accesses the meaning of words by converting letters and letter combinations into speech sounds.

**grapheme-to-phoneme conversion rules** probabilistic rules that associate printed symbols (e.g. individual letters and letter combinations) with speech sounds, potentially allowing any newly encountered word to be pronounced irrespective of its meaning.

**lexical route** one of two processing routes involved in reading; the reader accesses a word's meaning and pronunciation directly from its spelling, using whole-word recognition as opposed to phonological decoding.

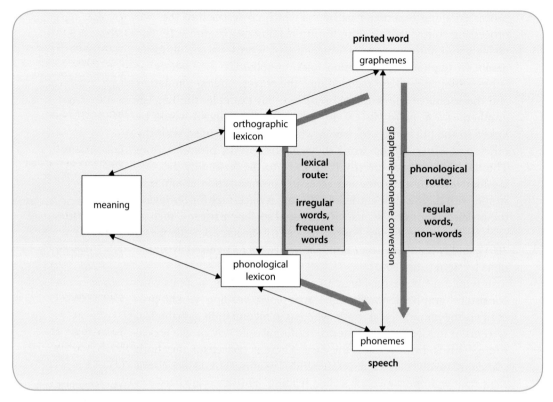

**Figure 9.2** *Dual-route model of reading and word recognition.*

*Source:* Adapted from figure 7, Coltheart, Rastle, Perry, Langdon, and Ziegler (2001). *Psychological Science, 108,* 204–256. Adapted with permission from APA.

rules. Such automaticity in accessing the meanings and pronunciations of highly familiar words may be achieved after only a year of reading instruction (Guttentag & Haith, 1978), with American children at the end of first grade achieving a rate of oral reading fluency of about 60 (correct) words per minute for grade-level text (Below, Skinner, Fearrington, & Sorrell, 2010).

## 9.1.2 Learning to read and write

Learning to read involves forging connections between visual processes and linguistic processes to gain access to the meanings of written words and text. Similarly, learning to spell words, and to write words and sentences, involves linking meaning with graphical representations. In alphabetic writing systems, the child has to grasp the idea that graphemes correspond to speech sounds. Thus, brain circuits dedicated to visual and language processing need to be altered to support reading (Dehaene, 2010).

When learning alphabetic scripts, children typically start out by forming idiosyncratic associations between some part of the orthographic representation of a word and its corresponding name (Frith, 1985). For example, children may be able to differentiate *dog* and *cat* just based on the shape of the first letter, a strategy that will fail subsequently when trying to make finer distinctions, for example, between *dog* and *doll*. They may recognise other words (e.g. *pizza*) by a salient feature, such as the double *z*. As a consequence of the use of idiosyncratic cues, children will differ considerably in their sight vocabularies. Whatever visual cues children choose, given the vast number of words that they will encounter, this pictorial or associative approach will eventually tax their memory resources. As the associations between the images of words and their names become more differentiated, as well as in response to direct reading instruction, children will learn to recode individual letters into sounds. It is during this stage that the effortful sounding out of words typical for beginning readers can be observed. There is controversy with regards to how much reciting the alphabet and knowing the names for letters can help: Ehri (1980, 1991) has suggested that letter names can serve as cues for word identification; for example, the letter *j* ('*jay*') can serve as a cue for recognising the word *jail*. Others have argued that learning the names of letters like *b* or *f* is counterproductive because the letter names can interfere with the use of the letters as cues to phonemes (Snow, 2004). Although recognition of some words may benefit from letter names, for example, *bee, tepee,* or *I* (Treiman, Tincoff, & Richmond-Welty, 1996), letter names generally tend to obscure grapheme-to-phoneme relations, for example, when young children sound out a word like *cat* as *cee-ay-tee*, or when they attempt to spell *seat* as *ct* or *cake* as *kak*. Whereas parents and teachers in the United States tend to view the learning of letter names as an important foundation for literacy instruction, teachers in Britain emphasise sounds as opposed to letter names in early instruction. Interestingly, research suggests that British children initially show earlier learning of letter–sound correspondence rules than their American counterparts, although this advantage declines with age (Ellefson, Treiman, & Kessler, 2009).

In spelling, children's early grasp of the alphabetic principle is apparent when they use their knowledge of letter sounds to produce renditions of words like *sed* for *said* or *kr* for *car* (Treiman & Cassar, 1997). In many alphabetic languages, sound-to-spelling mappings tend to be less consistent than spelling-to-sound mappings. For example, in German, the vowel /a:/ can be spelled *a* or *aa* or *ah*; similarly, in English, the sound of the word /ki:/ contains no cue that indicates whether to spell it *kea* or *kee* or (correctly) as *key*. Because of this, and also because spelling requires production rather than recognition of word forms, spelling abilities are not necessarily linked to reading abilities, even in shallow orthographies (Rayner et al., 2001).

As children practice reading, the process of recoding letters into sounds increasingly becomes automatic, enabling them rapidly to map orthographic representations onto the corresponding word names and meanings. Automatic recognition of familiar words by sight makes it possible for children to utilise the lexical route (i.e. bypassing explicit letter–sound recoding) to gain fluency. However, as discussed in the previous section, the phonological route remains crucial each time a new word is encountered. In addition, as children grow their vocabularies, they increasingly rely on morphological knowledge in identifying new words and their meanings. Children learn correspondence rules between letter sequences and morphemes, such as the past-tense inflection *-ed* and the derivational inflections *-ion* and *-ian* (Nunes & Bryant, 2009). Noticing recurrent word endings leads to morphological awareness – that letter sequences may convey the same meanings across different words (such as an event or action occurring in the past). The consistent spelling of the morpheme highlights a consistency of meaning in the face of considerable variation in its pronunciation across different words (as in the past tense forms of *talked*, *towed*, and *folded*). Likewise, the different spellings of the morphemes *-ion* and *-ian* increase the child's awareness that these suffixes convey different meanings despite their identical pronunciation.

It is important to note here that researchers differ in their theoretical approaches to whether these different components of reading acquisition – word–name associations, phonological recoding, morphological analysis, and direct lexical access – are distinct stages characterised by qualitative shifts in underlying abilities (Frith, 1985; Stuart & Coltheart, 1988; Ehri, 1991), or whether they emerge out of an incremental build-up of knowledge about the various elements that characterise the relationship between orthographic input and linguistic output (Perfetti, 1992). This controversy between stage theories and incremental theories of development has been theoretically important across various domains of cognitive development (Munakata, McClelland, Johnson, & Siegler, 1997; van der Maas & Raijmakers, 2009). With respect to spelling, a number of studies indicate that children as well as adults show variability in their spellings of words, and self-report use of a number of different spelling strategies involving phonology, morphology, and direct lexical access (Farrington-Flint, Stash, & Stiller, 2008; Holmes & Malone, 2004; Sénéchal, Basque, & Leclaire, 2006). When spelling performance is assessed for individual children, there is still a high degree of variability in word spellings. Such variability, observed in the context of gradual changes in spelling ability, and the adaptive use of different spelling strategies based on factors such as the speed and accuracy, appears to be incompatible with a stage account (Rittle-Johnson & Siegler, 1999).

Because of differences in spelling–sound consistency and syllable complexity across languages, the time it takes for children to learn to read varies considerably. A large-scale comparison of the reading abilities of learners of 13 European languages after one year of schooling showed that reading acquisition was considerably faster for languages with shallow orthographies and simple CV(C) syllable structure (Seymour, Aro, & Erskine, 2003) than for languages with deep orthographies and complex syllable structures. For example, Finnish children made errors in reading only 2 per cent of words after one year of schooling, compared to 21 per cent errors for French children and 66 per cent for Scottish children. It takes two to three years longer to attain the same level of reading competency in English compared to Finnish, Greek, or Italian. In addition to requiring more years of practice, some researchers have suggested that learning to read English may differ qualitatively from learning to read a language with a shallow orthography (Seymour et al., 2003; Ziegler & Goswami, 2005): inconsistency of spelling forces English-speaking children to utilise a variety of orthographic units of different sizes such as individual letters (*f*, *s*, *t*), digraphs (*th*, *ck*, *a_e*), prefixes and suffixes (*co-*, *-ive*, *-al*), rimes (*-oap*, *-one*, *-ight*), and whole words (*eye*, *eight*, *said*). Through statistical learning of co-occurrence patterns, children might implicitly learn that grapheme-to-phoneme correspondence rules are context dependent – for example, that the letter *c* tends to be pronounced differently when it precedes the letters *a, o,* or *u* (as in *cat, cot, cut*) than when it precedes the letters *e* or *i* (as in *cell, cite*). Although the digraph *ea* usually represents the phoneme /iː/, as in *cheap, dream,* and *neat*, it often represents the phoneme /e/ when followed by *d*, as in *thread, dead, head, spread,* and *bread*. Some letter combinations, such as the split digraph *e_e*, occur often in polysyllabic words like *athlete, serene,* and *extreme*, but rarely in monosyllabic words. As children accumulate words in their sight vocabularies, they are likely to pick up on co-occurrence patterns like these. As described in Chapters 4 and 5, noticing consistencies in word endings plays an important role in the acquisition of inflectional and derivational suffixes, and the consistent spellings of word endings provide additional cues to the underlying processes of word formation.

### 9.1.3    *Literacy instruction methods*

What is the best way to teach children to read and spell words? Unlike learning to talk, learning to read does not come naturally to many children, especially when faced with an inconsistent spelling system. In alphabetical writing systems, learners need to grasp the mapping between spelling, sound, and meaning. Only very few children learning to read English will discover the alphabetic principle and the spelling-to-sound conversion rules on their own, even with sufficient print exposure. Most children will require instruction and practice. Below we briefly review the major teaching approaches.

According to the whole-word approach, children are taught to recognise words based on their overall shape. Children are encouraged to focus on and even trace the contours of words and to associate word forms directly with meanings. As indicated earlier, trying to access meaning directly from form will leave readers clueless when it comes to deciphering unfamiliar words, regardless of script. A whole-word approach seems most appropriate for the acquisition of a logographic script, like Chinese, in which several thousand different morphemic signs need to be memorised. Interestingly, in the 20th century, China introduced a phonetically based script called Pinyin, which is used in the initial stages of literacy education to bootstrap children into reading using spelling–sound conversion.

**whole-word approach**
an approach to reading instruction that teaches children to recognise words based on their overall shape (i.e. by sight).

**whole-language approach**
an approach to reading instruction that encourages children to engage directly with texts and to guess the meanings of words based on context.

A related approach is the whole-language approach. The mistaken rationale behind this approach is that learning to read comes naturally if children are given sufficient access to text, and pleasurable opportunities to read. It was assumed that spelling–sound correspondences would be discovered incidentally and without effort. There is a strong ideological imperative behind this approach, which is to spare children the boredom of being drilled in letter–sound mappings and to focus on the goal of reading, which is to uncover

**Figure 9.3**    *Children benefit from the explicit teaching of phonics, especially when the mapping of spelling to sound is inconsistent.*

*Source:* © zulufoto. Used under licence from Shutterstock.

meaning. So great was the intuitive appeal of the whole-language approach and the associated freedom of teachers to devise their own curricula that it became the mandated teaching standard in California in 1987. In a matter of years, children's reading abilities in California declined measurably (Ehri, Nunes, Stahl, & Willows, 2001).

Finally, the phonics approach teaches children in direct and systematic ways how to map letters onto sounds so that the pronunciation of any word can be uncovered. Phonics methods differ in the activities endorsed – for example, sounding out and blending sounds (synthetic phonics) vs. inferring sound–letter relationships (analytic phonics) – as well as in the size of the units for which letter–sound correspondences are taught (single letters vs. rimes, as in *beak–peak* [Goswami, 1986]). For example, activities such as instructing children to spell words as best they can (i.e. to invent spellings) have been used to encourage an analytic approach (Ouellette & Sénéchal, 2008). Phonological decoding has been shown to be the most successful principle underlying the acquisition of reading (Share & Stanovich, 1995). Recent meta-analyses of

**phonics approach**
an approach to reading instruction that teaches children to link speech sounds with letters and letter combinations.

**synthetic phonics**
literacy instruction method that emphasises the sounding out and blending of sounds.

**analytic phonics** literacy instruction method that encourages learners to link letters with corresponding sounds.

the relatively small number of existing randomised controlled trials that compared the effects of different teaching methods on reading accuracy revealed benefits of phonics instruction over whole-word and whole-language approaches, but no reliable differences between the different versions of phonics instruction (Ehri et al., 2001; Torgerson, Brooks, & Hall, 2006); see Figure 9.3. It is important to keep in mind that these findings were obtained for English; in more consistent orthographies, teaching methods do not seem to matter as much. The advantage for children learning consistent orthographies like Finnish or Greek persists even if the whole-language approach is used (Ziegler & Goswami, 2005). That is, when acquiring a transparent orthography, children are more likely to discover the consistent spelling-sound correspondences on their own.

**phonological decoding** also called **phonological recoding**; the use of grapheme-to-phoneme conversion rules in reading to convert printed symbols into the sound patterns of words.

The educational advantages of the phonics approach for English may seem paradoxical at first, in light of the finding that when flashed briefly, skilled readers recognise words faster than letters (Cattell, 1886). But careful experimentation has shown that even skilled readers briefly access the pronunciations of words. For example, if asked questions about an upcoming word, like *Is it a flower?*, skilled readers not only respond positively to words like *rose* but occasionally also to homophones, that is, words with the same pronunciation, like *rows* (Van Orden, Johnston, & Hale, 1988). This is clear evidence for some involvement of the phonological route even in highly skilled reading, and underscores the importance of using phonics. Without grasp of the principles underlying the recoding of letters into sounds, readers will have difficulty processing rare and new words.

**homophones** words that have the same pronunciation as other words but a different meaning, for example *bank* (of a river) vs. *bank* (financial institution).

Phonics instruction, while beneficial for reading instruction, is not sufficient to ensure that children will become accurate spellers. One consequence of associating letter names with vowels and consonants is that many English-speaking children come to have the misconception that the English vowels are *a, e, i, o,* and *u,* and often have little meta-cognitive awareness of the 21 different vowel sounds of British English (or the 15 or so different vowel sounds of American English). This leads children to consider the *e* in a split digraph (e.g. *o_e* as in *hope*) as a silent letter, as opposed to considering how its presence impacts the pronunciation of the preceding vowel (Nunes & Bryant, 2009). Similarly, they tend to see doublets such as *ff* or *tt* as alternative spellings of consonants, without considering how a doublet impacts the pronunciation of its preceding vowel. Interestingly, children learn about the distribution of doublets in words well before they pick up on their function: Treiman (1993) observed that, by the end of their first year of schooling, children appreciate that a doublet may occur in the middle or at the end of a word (e.g. *bottle* or *fuss*) but not at its beginning (*bbotle* or *ffus*), and they recognise that certain consonants often surface as doublets (e.g. *f, l, m, p, r, s, t*) whereas others do not (e.g. *h, j, k, v, x, y*). Young children's awareness of orthographic restrictions suggests

**doublets** reduplicated letters (e.g. *ss* in *dress*).

that they learn permissible letter sequences as they build their sight vocabularies, presumably through the process of statistical learning.

In contrast to their rapid learning of orthographic regularities, children have very little awareness that doublets affect the pronunciation of the preceding vowel prior to about 11 years of age (Cassar & Treiman, 1997). For children to learn conditional spelling rules that are context dependent may require explicit teaching: for instance, the child might be taught inflectional patterns, such as *hop → hopping, hope → hoping*, and asked to predict the distribution of double consonants in other verb forms, such as *begging, sitting*, and *riding*. Children greatly benefit from the explicit teaching of morphology (Bower et al., 2010; Deacon, Kirby, & Casselman-Bell, 2009; Nunes & Bryant, 2006), which increases their awareness of how prefixes and suffixes affect word spellings, pronunciations, and meanings, and improves their spelling performance over and above the effects of other variables such as phonological awareness, vocabulary size, and non-verbal intelligence. Children develop morphological awareness through structured activities that draw their attention to the contrasting semantic effects of different suffixes (e.g. *vegetable → vegetation, vegetarian*), and teach them conditional spelling rules (e.g.

**morphological awareness** explicit awareness or knowledge about the morphology of a language (i.e. awareness of how prefixes and suffixes are used to modify and create new word forms).

change *y* to *i* when adding a suffix, as in *silly → silliness, silliest*; drop the *e* only when the suffix begins with a vowel, as in *excite → exciting, excitable, excitement*).

# 9.2 HOW DOES LITERACY AFFECT LANGUAGE DEVELOPMENT?

## 9.2.1 *Literacy and phonemic awareness*

Since children are still learning language at the time they are learning to read, reading itself has the potential to shape language development. One area in which language development and reading influence each other is phonology. In Chapter 2, we described how infants discover the phonological distinctions of their native language. Subsequently, as children's vocabularies expand, they learn to make more and more subtle discriminations between the sound patterns of words (Jusczyk, 1992). As a result, children develop phonological awareness. Phonological awareness can be tested by asking children to clap or tap their fingers to the syllabic structure of a word

**phonological awareness** explicit awareness or knowledge that words are made up of smaller units of sound.

(Liberman, Shankweiler, Fischer, & Carter, 1974), or by presenting three words like *doll, hop, pop* and asking children which one is the odd one out (Bradley & Bryant, 1983). Children first show awareness of differences among larger units of sound, for example, syllables and their constituent parts like onsets and rimes or, as in the case of Japanese, morae (see Chapter 2). Only later do children show awareness of individual phonemes, although some researchers have suggested otherwise (Duncan, Seymour, & Hill, 1997). Which units of sound will dominate a child's phonological awareness largely depends on the structure of their language.

At 5 or 6 years of age, most children do not yet have **phonemic awareness**. Phonemic awareness can be tested by asking children to delete, for example, the fourth sound in words like *lapsed* or *faxed* (*s* in both cases) or by asking how many sounds words like *rich* or *pitch* contain (3 in each case). The fact that infants can discriminate

> **phonemic awareness**
> explicit awareness or knowledge of the smallest units of sound that carry meaning.

phonemes such as /ba/ and /pa/ (Eimas, Siqueland, Jusczyk, & Vigorito, 1971) does not mean that they have awareness of individual phonemes. Rather, phonemic awareness emerges only as a consequence of learning to read, as suggested by the fact that illiterate individuals typically fail in phonemic awareness tasks like sound deletion (Castro-Caldas, Miranda, Carmo, Reis, Leote, Ribeiro, et al., 1999; Lukatela, Carello, Shankweiler, & Liberman, 1995; Morais, Cary, Alegria, & Bertelson, 1979). Phonological awareness and reading acquisition are thus related in a reciprocal fashion: whereas some phonological awareness is necessary to grasp the alphabetic principle, reading acquisition increases awareness of the units of sound, especially of phonemes (Scribner & Cole, 1981). Because of this reciprocal relationship, phonological awareness prior to the onset of reading instruction is a reliable predictor of reading success (e.g. Bradley & Bryant, 1983; Stuart & Masterson, 1992). Phonemic awareness develops rapidly in children learning to read a language with a consistent, shallow orthography, like Finnish or Greek (Goswami, 2002). As a consequence, phonemic awareness prior to reading instruction turns out to be a much stronger predictor of reading speed and accuracy for children learning inconsistent, deep orthographies like English (Ziegler, Bertrand, Tóth, Csépe, Reis, Faísca, et al., 2010a), and has even been shown to predict reading success for the Chinese logographic script (McBride-Chang & Kail, 2002). In sum, reading relies on and further develops awareness of the sound patterns of one's language.

### 9.2.2   Literacy and grammatical development

Written language differs considerably from spoken language, in that it contains richer vocabulary (i.e. greater numbers of low-frequency words) and more complex grammatical **constructions** (Cunningham & Stanovich, 1998). Consequently, exposure to written texts is beneficial to grammatical development. Even in children's storybooks, sentences tend to be longer than in spoken language, with more embedded clauses and rare construction types, such as full passives (e.g. *His arms and legs were jointed and joined by wire so that his china elbows and china knees could be bent, giving him much freedom of movement* [DiCamillo, 2006: 1]). In recent studies with adults, it has been shown that individuals with higher educational attainment have better comprehension of rare construction types than individuals with lower educational attainment (Dabrowska & Street, 2006; Street & Dabrowska, 2010). Importantly, this research found that a self-report measure of the amount of time spent reading for pleasure was highly correlated with comprehension of so-called reversible passive sentences (e.g. *The girl was hugged by the boy*) and sentences containing universal quantifiers (e.g. *Every dog is in a basket*); see also Chapter 5. These benefits extend to morphology: in richly inflected languages like Polish, Russian, or Lithuanian, written text also contains more varied inflections than oral language; thus, Polish-speaking adults with higher educational attainment and larger vocabularies are more accurate in generalising inflectional patterns to novel nouns than their less educated peers (Dabrowska, 2008). These results suggest that life-long reading habits contribute to substantive individual differences among adults in their native language attainment (see also Chipere, 2003). Such individual differences in grammatical knowledge emerge in childhood and are predictive of children's writing abilities (Beers & Nagy, 2011).

### 9.2.3   Literacy and vocabulary development

At the time an American child starts school, he or she will have a vocabulary of about 5000 words (Table 9.1) (Anglin, 1993; Beck & McKeown, 1991). At the end of schooling this number will have increased to 40,000 to 100,000 words (Nagy & Anderson, 1984), an increase that is mainly due to reading (see Methodology Box 9.1 for a technique used to assess individual differences in vocabulary knowledge). To achieve this vocabulary size at 18 years of age, children must acquire an astonishing 8 to 22 new words per day during the school years! How can children possibly learn 22 or even just 8 new words per day through reading? Anglin (1993) has suggested that children's vocabularies grow as they learn more about the morphological patterns of word formation in their native language (e.g. *swim* → *swimmer* or *mind* → *mindful*; see Chapter 4 for further discussion). Acquisition of morphology helps children to infer the meanings of morphologically complex words (e.g. *instructive, lengthened, unbearable*) the first time they are encountered in text, and thereby improves the fluency of children's reading as well as their reading comprehension while building their vocabulary (Deacon & Kirby, 2004; Nagy, Berninger, & Abbott, 2006). It is important to note that, while phonological awareness and knowledge of orthographic regularities facilitate the development of reading early on, morphological awareness of inflectional and derivational patterns becomes an increasingly important factor in middle childhood and into adolescence, over and above the effects of these other factors (Berninger, Abbott, Nagy, & Carlisle, 2010; Nagy et al., 2006; Roman, Kirby, Parrila, Wade-Woolley, & Deacon, 2009). Morphological awareness directly contributes to improving children's spelling (Deacon et al., 2009; Nagy et al., 2006) by providing a strategy for spelling poly-morphemic words such as *walked* and *magician* that flout grapheme-to-phoneme correspondence rules. Knowledge of spelling patterns, in turn, increases vocabulary through mnemonic effects: remembering how to spell a word enhances memory for its meaning and pronunciation (Ehri & Rosenthal, 2007; Rosenthal & Ehri, 2008).

Often when encountering a word for the first time while reading, children will not immediately grasp its meaning. Rather, their understanding of the word may develop

## METHODOLOGY BOX 9.1    ASSESSING VOCABULARY KNOWLEDGE IN ADULTS

Beyond the early years, it is impossible to determine a person's vocabulary size accurately. However, estimates can be obtained by selecting a representative sample of words from unabridged, non-historical dictionaries, testing individuals on this sample, and then multiplying the proportion of known words by the total number of words in the dictionary. This is how the estimates of 40,000 to 100,000 words mentioned in this chapter were arrived at. However, such estimates are very much dependent on the definition of what counts as a word. In addition, the testing results may be affected by biases:

participants may be prone to exaggerating which words they know or they may be overly conservative.

To overcome this problem, some researchers provide participants with lists of words and invented non-words, and ask them to identify which words they know. This method provides an estimate of the relative (rather than absolute) vocabulary sizes of different people. An example is given in the list below (taken from West, Stanovich, & Mitchell, 1993). Go through the list and check the words you think you know (the solution is given at the end of this box).

| | | |
|---|---|---|
| 1. inflect | 15. optimise | 29. arrate |
| 2. eventuate | 16. purview | 30. metenetion |
| 3. audible | 17. gustation | 31. reportage |
| 4. concurrent | 18. sheal | 32. disconcert |
| 5. litany | 19. nuance | 33. neotatin |
| 6. ceiloplaty | 20. fusigenic | 34. epicurean |
| 7. suffuse | 21. comectial | 35. nitrous |
| 8. waterfowl | 22. asinine | 36. substratum |
| 9. connote | 23. reverent | 37. confluence |
| 10. sparkhouse | 24. tradured | 38. denotation |
| 11. ubiquitous | 25. rochead | 39. unction |
| 12. absolution | 26. nonquasity | 40. wanderlust |
| 13. ineffity | 27. irksome | |
| 14. polarity | 28. hyplexion | |

Because a simple proportion of correctly identified words may be subject to bias (i.e. if you are very conservative you may only check words for which you are able to provide a full definition despite the fact that you would be able to use the word appropriately), it is best to also take into account the number of false alarms, and to compute a sensitivity measure such as discriminability index (d') or the non-parametric

analog (A') (detailed explanations of these measures can be found in any description of Signal Detection Theory) to get an unbiased measure of your word knowledge. This, of course, will not be an estimate of the size of your vocabulary, but will allow for a comparison of your vocabulary knowledge with that of other people. And yes, the non-words are 6, 10, 13, 18, 20, 21, 24, 25, 26, 28, 29, 30, and 33.

**Table 9.1**  *Reading builds vocabulary through exposure to rare words. A comparison of written texts and speech shows that written texts contain a substantially more diverse vocabulary.*

| | Percentage of rare words (outside of a list of the 10,000 most common English word types) | Percentage of common words (contained in a list of the 5000 most common English word types) |
|---|---|---|
| **Written texts:** | | |
| Scientific abstracts | 12.8 | 70.3 |
| Newspapers | 6.8 | 84.3 |
| Popular magazines | 6.6 | 85.0 |
| Adult books | 5.3 | 88.4 |
| Comic books | 5.4 | 88.6 |
| Children's books | 3.1 | 92.3 |
| Preschool books | 1.6 | 94.1 |
| **Television** | | |
| Prime-time adult programs | 2.3 | 94.0 |
| Prime-time children's programs | 2.0 | 93.3 |
| **Adult speech** | | |
| Expert-witness testimony | 2.8 | 89.9 |
| Conversations of college graduates with friends/family | 1.7 | 93.9 |

*Source:* Adapted from Hayes, D. P. & Ahrens, M. G. (1988). Vocabulary simplification for children: A special case of 'motherese'? *Journal of Child Language,* 15, 395–410, with permission from Cambridge University Press.

**latent semantic analysis (LSA)** a mathematical model used to explain how a statistical learning mechanism operating over large amounts of text learns vocabulary; the underlying assumption is that words with closely related meanings will occur close together in text.

gradually as the child encounters the word on multiple occasions in various contexts of use; this is the process of **slow mapping** described in Chapter 4. Several researchers have attempted to model the process by which new words and their meanings are learned implicitly through the detection of co-occurrence patterns of words in text (Landauer & Dumais, 1997; Lund & Burgess, 1996). Landauer and Dumais (1997) introduced a mathematical model called **latent semantic analysis (LSA)** to explain how a statistical learning mechanism operating over large amounts of input from print could expand a reader's vocabulary. In LSA, a matrix is constructed with columns representing contexts (i.e. passages of text) and rows representing individual words. Each cell in the matrix contains information about the frequency of occurrence of a particular word in a particular text passage, which is accumulated over time. How can such information be useful for inferring word meaning? The idea is that the frequency with which words occur in the same text passages is a reflection of their relatedness in meaning. For example, close meaning associates like *salt* and *pepper* are likely to occur in the same sentence (e.g. in a cookbook), whereas words that are truly unrelated in meaning (e.g. *theorem* and *butter*) or near-synonyms (e.g. *couch* and *sofa*) will not. To arrive at good estimates of the similarities in meaning across all words, the dimensional space in which the words are represented in the original matrix (number of words × number of passages) has to be reduced. The specific mathematical method used for dimension reduction is not relevant to the present argument; what is important is that, as a result of this procedure, words are represented by vectors in *k*-dimensional space, and the similarity between these vectors can be computed. Representing all words in the same dimensional space allows LSA to infer the overall semantic relatedness of words from local co-occurrence information. Crucially, unlike theories that postulate *a priori* (i.e. innate) sets of semantic features for meaning representation (e.g. Collins & Quillian, 1969), in LSA the dimensions on which words are represented emerge as the result of statistical learning.

The implicit learning process that underlies the acquisition of word meanings from co-occurrences in text can be facilitated by explicit instruction. Clarke, Snowling, Truelove, and Hulme (2010) conducted a controlled randomised trial which showed that reading comprehension of poor readers improved when new words were taught explicitly, especially if the words were introduced and practised in multiple contexts. This corroborates other research indicating that explicit instruction benefits poor readers in the areas of phonics, morphology, vocabulary, and reading comprehension (e.g. Coyne, Simmons, Kame'enui, & Stoolmiller, 2004; Foorman, Francis, Fletcher, Schatschneider, & Mehta, 1998; Tsesmeli & Seymour, 2009). Explicit teaching may be crucial for the majority of children who do not read independently, and thus, have fewer opportunities to acquire new vocabulary and build literacy skills on their own.

## 9.2.4   Amplification of individual differences in literacy

For children taught to read English, dramatic individual differences in reading ability emerge during the first year of school. For example, after only two months of reading instruction, children with the highest reading abilities read an average of 12 words per reading session, whereas children with the lowest reading abilities read no words at all. After eight months of reading instruction, the high-ability group reads an average of 81 words per session, whereas the low-ability group read only 32 words (Biemiller, 1977/1978). Individual differences in reading fluency lead to enormous differences in the amount of running text children are exposed to in school: Nagy and Anderson (1984) estimated that an average reader in the middle grades might encounter 500,000 to 1,000,000 words of running text over the 100 days of school, whereas an avid reader might cover 10,000,000 words. Consequently, there are considerable individual differences in reading volume. To measure reading volume in children, many studies have used the Title Recognition Test (Cunningham & Stanovich, 1990), in which children are asked to pick out the names of children's books from a list of titles that includes an equal number of foils (made-up titles). This measure allows researchers to estimate the relative amount of print exposure for a given child (i.e. relative to other children), but does not provide an estimate of actual amount of reading.

Initial reading success clearly affects motivation to read: if reading is slow and laborious, children will be less inclined to read for meaning and for pleasure which, in turn, restricts their exposure to print. Moreover, individuals who spend more time reading for pleasure grow larger vocabularies than those who do not (West, Stanovich, & Mitchell, 1993), and acquire greater amounts of encyclopaedic or factual knowledge (Stanovich & Cunningham, 1993). Unfortunately, estimates of the actual amount of time children spend reading outside school are rather grim (Dreher & Baker, 2003), with many children rarely if ever reading outside school, for example over the summer holidays. Thus, the reciprocal relationships between fluency of reading, vocabulary size, and motivation to read can lead to rewarding gains of knowledge and expertise for some children, or, alternatively, can spiral into academic achievement problems for others (Reschly, 2010; Stanovich, 1986; Walberg & Tsai, 1983).

Over time, small ability differences at the outset of reading instruction tend to become amplified: this can be described as a 'Rich-Get-Richer' effect (Stanovich, 1986). This Rich-Get-Richer effect comes about because of the reciprocal relationships between vocabulary knowledge, phonological awareness, and reading skill. Starting at preschool, children with larger vocabularies have a larger database from which to extract phonological information at various levels. For example, knowing many words that end in -at, such as cat, fat, mat, bat, rat, sat, hat, that, flat, and gnat, makes it easier to discover their underlying onset-rime structure. Thus, at the outset of reading, vocabulary size affects reading skill by facilitating phonological awareness. In turn, skill at deciphering words leads to an increase in vocabulary size. Increased vocabulary knowledge exerts a further effect on reading: the larger a child's vocabulary, the more successful the child will be at guessing partially decoded words and at using context to infer the meanings of words in challenging texts (Nagy, 1988; Stanovich, 1986). This effect is even larger in inconsistent orthographies like English, where acquiring the principles underlying grapheme-to-phoneme recoding takes several years (Hanley, Masterson, Spencer, & Evans, 2004). Moreover, as reading becomes more fluent, vocabulary knowledge becomes even more essential: after all, accessing meaning directly via the lexical route works only for words that are familiar.

There is now a large body of evidence that individual differences in reading volume have pervasive consequences across cognitive and academic domains: a recent meta-analysis of 99 studies (Mol & Bus, 2011) found moderate to strong effects of print exposure (which included parent–child storybook reading as well as independent leisure time reading) on reading comprehension, technical reading and spelling, and academic achievement. Interestingly, among American first-graders, general intelligence is only weakly linked with reading abilities, which suggests that intelligence is not a good predictor of how fast children will learn to read. However, 5 years later at sixth grade, the correlation between reading ability and intelligence is much stronger, which suggests that during middle childhood reading shapes other cognitive abilities (Stanovich, Cunningham, & Feeman, 1984).

# 9.3 WHY IS LEARNING TO READ DIFFICULT FOR SOME CHILDREN?

## 9.3.1 Developmental dyslexia

In industrial societies, differences in reading ability have significant repercussions for educational attainment, yet individual differences at the outset of literacy acquisition tend to become amplified, with repercussions for cognitive development and academic achievement, as discussed in the previous section. This is especially devastating for those children who have persistent problems in learning to read, despite appropriate instruction and intelligence scores within the normal range. This condition is called developmental dyslexia, and differs from acquired dyslexia, which is typically due to brain injury. The International Dyslexia Association defines dyslexia as a specific language-based learning disability that is neurobiological in origin and contrasts with more general learning disabilities. It is characterised by difficulties with accurate and/or fluent word recognition (reading), and by poor spelling and decoding abilities. These deficits are

> **developmental dyslexia** a condition marked by persistent problems in learning to read and spell, despite appropriate instruction and intelligence scores within the normal range.

unexpected in relation to other cognitive abilities, the provision of effective classroom instruction, and motivation. Secondary consequences include difficulties in reading comprehension and reduced reading experience that may impede growth of vocabulary development and background knowledge (Lyons, Shaywitz, & Shaywitz, 2003). Developmental dyslexia runs in families (Raskind, Hus, Berniger, Thomson, & Wijsman, 2000; Scarborough, 1990b), and genetic linkage studies have begun to identify specific regions of the genome involved in the disorder (Grigorenko, 2001). Estimates of the prevalence of dyslexia among English speakers vary considerably from 6–9 per cent (Shaywitz, Shaywitz, Fletcher, & Escobar, 1990) up to 10–15 per cent of children (Vellutino, Fletcher, Snowling, & Scanlong, 2004). As will be described in Chapter 10, about 7 per cent of children show clinically significant impairments in language development, and receive a diagnosis of Specific Language Impairment (SLI) in cases where there is no evidence of

> **genetic linkage** the tendency for genes located near one another on the same chromosome to be inherited together; identification of linked sets of genes is often a critical step in locating the individual genes associated with specific developmental disabilities and diseases.

mental retardation, brain injury, or disease. SLI and dyslexia show similar patterns of familial aggregation, with about 50 per cent of children with SLI also having dyslexia (McArthur, Hogben, Edwards, Heath, & Mengler, 2000; Tomblin, Zhang, Buckwalter, & Catts, 2000). Given that reading requires both decoding skills and linguistic comprehension, children with SLI may have reading comprehension difficulties even if their decoding skills are intact (Hulme & Snowling, 2011). Recent studies suggest that 35 per cent of children with poor reading comprehension may have underlying language impairments (Nation, Clark, Marshall, & Durand, 2004; Nation, Cocksey, Taylor, & Bishop, 2010).

## 9.3.2   Possible causes of developmental dyslexia

In his pioneering work on reading disability, Samuel Orton (1925) suggested that the cause of dyslexia was a lack of hemispheric dominance – that is, a failure of the left hemisphere to become dominant in processing language (see Chapter 12 for further discussion of the neural basis of language processing, and Chapter 10 for a discussion of the neural basis of SLI). Abnormal neural organisation was thought to lead dyslexic readers to confuse symmetrical letters like *b* and *d* and to transpose the order of letters in words. Another hypothesis was that dyslexics had difficulty in processing auditory stimuli of brief duration, within or even outside the context of language processing (Tallal, 1980): thus, a child with dyslexia might fail to respond to the rapidly changing auditory cues embedded in the speech signal, which would negatively impact their development of phonological representations. More recently, Goswami and colleagues (Goswami, Thomson, Richardson, Stainthorp, Hughes, Rosen, et al., 2002) found evidence that children with dyslexia exhibit difficulties in the detection of rapid amplitude modulations – modulations of how quickly a sound changes in loudness – which are important for detecting rhythm and syllable onsets in speech. In early recognition of the overlapping symptoms of children with dyslexia and more general language impairments, Tallal and Piercy (1973a, 1973b, 1974, 1975) also proposed underlying deficits in auditory processing as a cause of 'developmental aphasia' (as SLI was called in the 1970s); see Chapter 10 for a more detailed discussion of this view.

Today the most widely held view is that dyslexia involves a deficit in phonological processing (Grigorenko, 2001; Mody, Studdert-Kennedy, & Brady, 1997; Shaywitz & Shaywitz, 2005; Vellutino et al., 2004; Ziegler, Pech-Georgel, Defau, & Grainger, 2010b) – an impairment in the ability to segment words into their component sounds, and in mapping graphemes to phonemes. Deficits in phonological processing are especially detrimental for children learning to read a language with a deep orthography, where the lack of a consistent mapping between graphemes and phonemes obscures the discovery of the underlying units of sound. Not surprisingly, the prevalence of dyslexia varies markedly across languages, and is rarely reported in children learning a language with a shallow, transparent orthography, like Finnish, Greek, or Italian. This has led many scholars and educators to wonder whether dyslexia is unique to writing systems, like English, with inconsistent spelling–sound correspondences, and whether dyslexia is just a medical label for the subset of children who struggle to cope with the complexities of such writing systems. However, when a large sample of Italian adults was tested, it emerged that there was a small subgroup whose reading abilities, although not as impaired as those of French or English dyslexics, differed markedly from normal Italian readers (Paulesu, Demonet, Fazio, McCrory, Chanoine, Brunswick, et al., 2001). In addition, fMRI scans of these individuals showed a pattern of reduced activity in their left temporal lobe similar to French and English dyslexics. These results suggest that the neuro-physiological basis of dyslexia may be the same across cultures and writing systems, but the manifestation of the deficit may be more severe in languages with inconsistent orthographies. It is important to point out that dyslexia, like SLI (see Chapter 10), is a heterogeneous condition (Reid, Szczerbinski, Iskierka-Kasperek, & Hansen, 2007; Ramus, Rosen, Dakin, Day, Castellote, White, et al., 2003): some individuals with dyslexia manifest deficits in visual processing (Eden, Van Meter, Rumsey, Maisog, Woods, & Zeffiro, 1996), while others have deficits in motor skill learning and balance (Brookes, Tinkler, Nicolsort, & Fawcett, 2010; Stoodley, Harrison, & Stein, 2006) in addition to their deficits in phonological processing. Future research will no doubt bring further insights into the various causes at the heart of this condition and how they may interact with the features of different writing systems.

## SUMMARY

- In literate societies, full participation in community life requires an ability to read and write. Caregivers vary in the extent to which they provide a home literacy environment that supports literacy acquisition.

- The speed of reading acquisition depends on how consistently the spelling patterns of a language map onto the sound patterns of the language. Literacy acquisition is faster in shallow orthographies with transparent grapheme-to-phoneme correspondences, like Italian, and slower in deep orthographies with a non-transparent relationship between spelling and sound, like English.

- Learning to read involves learning to recode letters into sounds to access meaning via the phonological route; as this process becomes automatised, meaning of words can often be accessed directly via the lexical route. Learning the morphological structure of words helps children to read and spell, especially in languages like English where inflected and derived forms often flout grapheme-to-phoneme correspondence rules.

- Teaching methods that make the relationships between spelling and sound explicit (e.g. phonics) have been shown to be more successful than other teaching methods, especially for languages with inconsistent orthographies like English. Children also benefit greatly from the explicit teaching of morphology.

- Vocabulary size and phonological awareness in preschoolers are strong predictors of reading success, and individual differences at the outset of reading tend to be amplified over time because they impact on how much a child will be motivated to read. Reading success, in turn, is related to vocabulary size, grammatical skills, and phonemic awareness in a reciprocal way, thereby affecting cognitive development and academic achievement.

- Developmental dyslexia involves persistent problems with reading in the absence of general cognitive deficits. Its prevalence is higher in individuals

**faced with inconsistent, deep orthographies. The likely cause is a deficit in phonological processing – a difficulty isolating phonemes and associating them with graphemes. Some dyslexics may also be affected by problems with visual processing and/or motor skill learning and balance.**

# FURTHER READING

## Key studies

Ziegler, J. C., Bertrand, D., Tóth, D., Csépe, V., Reis, A., Faísca, L., Saine, N., Lyytinen, H., Vaessen, A. & Blomert, L. (2010). Orthographic depth and its impact on universal predictors of reading: A cross-language investigation. *Psychological Science, 21*, 551–559.

## Overview articles

For a thorough overview of reading acquisition research, read Rayner, K., Foorman, B. R., Perfetti, C. A., Pesetsky, D. & Seidenberg, M. S. (2001). How psychological science informs the teaching of reading. *Psychological Science in the Public Interest, 2*, 31–74.

For the classical explanation of the Rich-Get-Richer effect in reading, read Stanovich, K. E. (1986). Matthew effects in reading: Some consequences of individual differences in the acquisition of literacy. *Reading Research Quarterly, 21*, 360–407.

## Books

For a detailed explanation of how English-speaking children learn to read and write, read Nunes, T. & Bryant, P. (2009). *Children's reading and spelling: Beyond the first steps.* Chichester: Wiley-Blackwell.

For an accessible introduction to the neuroscience of reading, read Dehaene, S. (2010). *Reading in the brain.* New York: Viking.

# 10 What Causes Language Impairments?

## KEY TERMS

agreement • anaphoric co-reference • artificial grammar • artificial language • autism spectrum disorder (ASD) • AXB design • basal ganglia • caudate nucleus • cerebellum • child language impairment • concordance rates • construction • developmental aphasia • discourse pressure • dyspraxia • event-related potentials (ERPs) • fast mapping • finite-state grammar • frontal lobe • genetic linkage • Index of Productive Syntax (IPSyn) • joint attention • late bloomers • late talkers • lexical bootstrapping • lexicon • magnetic resonance imaging (MRI) • mean length of utterances (MLU) • morphemes • non-word repetition task • perisylvian region • phonemic awareness • phonological awareness • phonological short-term memory • phonotactic probability • planum temporale • pragmatics • primary language impairment • procedural learning • procedural memory • semantic features • semantics • Specific Language Impairment (SLI) • statistical learning • syntactic bootstrapping • temporal lobe • Theory of Mind • tip-of-the-tongue • twin studies • verbal dyspraxia • verbal working memory • visual world paradigm

# CHAPTER OUTLINE

Approximately 7 per cent of children fail to develop language normally, despite normal hearing, non-verbal intelligence, and language input; these children receive the diagnosis of **Specific Language Impairment (SLI)** in cases where there is no evidence of brain injury or disease (e.g. cerebral infarction or haemorrhage, epilepsy), mental retardation, or developmental syndrome or disorder (e.g. **autism spectrum disorder (ASD)**, Down syndrome, Fragile X syndrome, Williams syndrome) (Tomblin, Records, Buckwalter, Zhang, Smith, & O'Brien, 1997). Most individuals with SLI have restricted listening and speaking skills throughout life, and roughly 50 per cent have difficulties acquiring literacy (see Chapter 9 on dyslexia) (McArthur, Hogben, Edwards, Heath, & Mengler, 2000; Tomblin, Zhang, Buckwalter, & Catts, 2000). In this chapter, we examine the range of symptoms that children with SLI exhibit and the probable causes of their language impairments. As we survey research findings, we will consider the possibility that, despite its label, SLI is not specific to language. Rather, much recent research suggests that the underlying cause of SLI may be a fairly general one, impacting other aspects of development such as motor control, working memory, and inhibitory control over attention, in addition to language. Although the term SLI is misleading in this regard, it is still the most widely used term in the field. However, other designations such as **primary language impairment** or **child language impairment** are gaining popularity as alternative ways of referring to these children, and may eventually come to replace the term SLI.

**primary language impairment, child language impairment** alternative names for Specific Language Impairment (SLI); impairment or delay in normal language development.

# 10.1 WHAT ARE THE SYMPTOMS OF SPECIFIC LANGUAGE IMPAIRMENT?

Children with SLI are a clinically diverse group who show impairments in auditory, phonological, lexical, and grammatical domains (Bishop, 1997; Leonard, 1998; Schwartz, 2009). There have been various efforts to sub-classify children with SLI, for example by contrasting children with receptive–expressive SLI with children with expressive-only SLI. However, such sub-groupings tend to reflect the degree of severity of the language impairment, as opposed to differences in its neurobiological or genetic basis. At this point there is no consensus on how to sub-classify the heterogeneous population of children with SLI (McArthur & Bishop, 2004). As we describe the language-processing deficits of these children, one needs to bear in mind that individual children may show various deficits to a greater or lesser extent, and some deficits may subside with age (Conti-Ramsden & Botting, 1999). Indeed, individual differences between children at the lower end of the distribution of language abilities tend to be greater than between children in the typical range.

## 10.1.1  Deficits in auditory processing

Tallal and Piercy (1973a, 1973b, 1974, 1975) were the first to document abnormalities in auditory processing in children with **developmental aphasia**, as SLI was called back in the 1970s. When presented with pairs of tones, varying in features such as frequency and duration, children (6- to 9-year-olds) with SLI were worse than control children in judging whether the second tone was longer or higher than the first (Tallal & Piercy, 1973a). When auditory and visual modalities were compared, the deficits were restricted to the auditory domain (Tallal & Piercy, 1973b) and to stimulus components that were brief in duration (Tallal & Piercy, 1974, 1975). Acknowledging the link between SLI and difficulties with literacy acquisition, these auditory processing deficits were also assumed to underlie developmental dyslexia (see Chapter 9). Tallal (1980) compared dyslexic children on auditory discrimination and temporal order tasks, and found that children with reading impairments also performed worse than their peers when the auditory stimuli were rapidly presented, but not when they occurred at a slower rate. Furthermore, their performance on a non-word reading test, which required them to decode unfamiliar word forms, was strongly correlated with their ability to respond accurately to the rapidly presented stimuli in the auditory tasks. Recent studies by Goswami (2002) have confirmed the role of detecting rapid changes in loudness for detecting rhythm and syllable onsets in speech (see Chapter 9). These various findings

> **developmental aphasia**  a term for Specific Language Impairment (SLI) that was used in the 1970s; refers to a delay in first-language acquisition in cases where there is no apparent brain damage, mental retardation or developmental syndrome.

suggest that children with SLI and dyslexia might have a common non-linguistic impairment in processing auditory information of brief duration. The idea that children with SLI and dyslexia cannot adequately perceive speech at its normal rate led Tallal to develop educational software called *Fast ForWord Language* (Scientific Learning Corporation, 1998) that selectively alters the rate of change of specific temporal characteristics of speech sounds with the purpose of enhancing children's speech perception. Unfortunately, the evidence to date that Fast ForWord Language improves language outcomes for children with SLI has been mixed (Cohen, Hodson, O'Hare, Boyle, Durrani, McCartney, et al., 2005; Gillam, Loeb, Hoffman, Bohman, Champlin, Thibodeau, et al., 2008; Merzenich, Jenkins, Johnston, Schreiner, Miller, & Tallal, 1996; Tallal, Miller, Bedi, Wang, & Nagarajan, 1996).

Bishop and colleagues have revisited the issue of auditory processing deficits, and suggested that pitch perception is impaired in many children with SLI and dyslexia, over and above any difficulties they may have in processing brief acoustic information (Bishop & McArthur, 2004; McArthur & Bishop, 2004; Mengler, Hogben, Michie, & Bishop, 2005). Mengler and colleagues presented children with an auditory discrimination task in which they had to decide whether the tone in the middle of a three-tone sequence was the same as the tone that preceded or followed it (i.e. the so-called AXB design). To determine the pitch discrimination threshold, tone frequencies were gradually moved closer together until the child performed at chance. Unlike intensity (loudness) judgements, which showed comparable thresholds for children with SLI and their typical peers, pitch thresholds were significantly higher for children with SLI – they required greater differences in pitch to distinguish tones. Furthermore, language ability, as measured using the Clinical Evaluation of Language Fundamentals test (see Methodology Box 10.1), was significantly correlated with pitch discrimination within the group of children with SLI. Other studies have shown that older individuals with SLI often score in the normal range on pitch discrimination tasks, but still show abnormal cortical responses when processing tone sequences (Bishop & McArthur, 2004; McArthur & Bishop, 2004). In McArthur and Bishop (2004), cortical activity, as measured through electrical event-related potentials (ERPs) (see Methodology Box 12.1), failed to differentiate individuals with SLI with poor performance on behavioural tasks from those with normal performance; both SLI sub-groups showed abnormal ERPs when compared to their age-matched controls. Indeed, the patterns of cortical activity of individuals with SLI tend to resemble those of younger typical children, which suggests that maturation of auditory processing networks may be delayed in SLI (Bishop & McArthur, 2004).

**AXB design** auditory discrimination task in which participants have to decide whether a tone in the middle of a three-tone sequence is the same as the tone that precedes or follows it.

# METHODOLOGY BOX 10.1   STANDARDISED ASSESSMENT TESTS OF LANGUAGE ABILITY

## *Articulation*

GFTA-2
Assesses articulation of the consonant sounds of Standard American English; both spontaneous and imitative sound production; norms for 2–21 years.

Goldman, R. & Fristoe, M. (2000). *Goldman–Fristoe test of articulation*, 2nd edn. Circle Pines, MN: American Guidance Service.

## *Auditory processing skills*

TAPS-3
Measures phonological segmentation and blending, auditory comprehension and reasoning; norms for 4–18 years.

Martin, N. & Brownell, R. (2005). *Test of auditory processing skills.* Novato, CA: Academic Therapy Publications.

## *Comprehensive language assessment*

RDLS III
Comprehension Scale (10 sections) and Expressive Scale (7 sections); 62 items focus on structural aspects of language; UK norms for 1;3–7;6.

Edwards, S., Fletcher, P., Garman, M., Hughes, A., Letts, C. & Sinka, I. (1997). *Reynell developmental language scales*, 3rd edn. London: Nelson.

CELF-4
Core subtests assess syntax, **semantics**, morphology, metalinguistics; additional subtests assess working memory, phonological awareness, preliteracy, pragmatics, social interaction; norms for 5–21 years.

Semel, E., Wiig, E. H. & Secord, W. (2003). *Clinical evaluation of language fundamentals*, 4th edn. San Antonio, TX: Pearson.

**semantics** the subfield of linguistics concerned with meaning; focuses on the relationship between linguistic units and what they represent.

CELF Preschool-2
Measures a broad range of language skills; norms for 3–6 years.

Wiig, E. H., Secord, W. & Semel, E. (2005). *Clinical evaluation of language fundamentals: Preschool-2.* San Antonio, TX: Pearson.

Renfrew Language Scales
Action picture test assesses information content and grammatical usage, bus story test assesses narrative ability, word finding test assesses expressive vocabulary; norms for 3–8 years.

Renfrew, C. (2004). *Renfrew language scales.* Milton Keynes: Speechmark Publishing Ltd.

TELD-3
Assesses receptive and expressive language skills; norms for 2;0–7;11.

Hresko, W. P., Reid, K. & Hammill, D. D. (1999). *Test of early language development*, 3rd edn. Austin, TX: PRO-ED.

Comprehensive language assessment (*Continued*)

**TOLD-P4**

Provides nine subtests that measure different components of spoken language (picture vocabulary, relational vocabulary, oral vocabulary, syntactic understanding, sentence imitation, morphological completion, word discrimination, word analysis, word articulation); norms for 4;0–8;11.

Hammill, D. D. & Newcomer, P. L. (1997). *Test of language development – primary*, 4th edn. Austin, TX: PRO-ED.

**TOLD-I4**

Provides six subtests that measure different components of spoken language (sentence combining, picture vocabulary, word ordering, relational vocabulary, morphological comprehension, multiple meanings); norms for 8;0–17;11.

Hammill, D. D. & Newcomer, P. L. (1997). *Test of language development – intermediate*. Austin, TX: PRO-ED.

**TOAL-4**

Provides six subtests that assess spoken and written language abilities of adolescents and young adults (word opposites, word derivations, spoken analogies, word similarities, sentence combining, orthographic usage); norms for 12;0–24;11.

Hammill, D. D., Brown, V. L., Larsen, S. C. & Wiederholt, J. L. (2007). *Test of adolescent and adult language*. Austin, TX: PRO-ED.

### Early language assessment

CDI-I: Words and Gestures (8–16 months).
CDI-II: Words and Sentences (16–30 months).
CDI-III: Extension (30–37 months).
Parental checklist for early vocabulary development: what infant comprehends, what infant says, what toddler says; norms for English and Spanish. Adaptations of the CDI are available for about 50 other languages.

Fenson, L., Marchman, V. A., Thal, D., Dale, P. S., Bates, E. & Reznick, J. S. (2007). *The MacArthur–Bates Communicative Development Inventories: User's guide and technical manual*. Baltimore, MD: Paul H. Brookes.

Rossetti Infant–Toddler Language Scale. Assesses preverbal and verbal areas of communication and interaction from birth through 3 years of age; uses direct observation and caregiver report to assess interaction-attachment, pragmatics, gestures, play, language comprehension, and expression; no norms available.

Rossetti, L. (1990). *Rossetti Infant–Toddler Language Scale: A measure of communication and interaction*. East Moline: IL: LinguiSystems.

| **Grammar** | |
|---|---|
| TROG-2<br>Measures understanding of grammatical contrasts; 4-alternative multiple choice test with lexical and grammatical foils; UK norms for 4–16 years. | Bishop, D. V. M. (2003). *Test for reception of grammar (TROG-2)*. Oxford: Pearson. |
| Rice/Wexler Test of Early Grammatical Impairment<br>Focuses on specific rules of grammar and misuse of certain verb forms; criterion referenced test for ages 3–8 years. | Rice, M. L. & Wexler, K. (2001). *Rice/Wexler Test of Early Grammatical Impairment*. San Antonio, TX: Pearson. |
| **Phonological short-term memory** | |
| CN REP<br>A reliable indicator of short-term memory, uses unfamiliar spoken items which the child must attempt to repeat; UK norms for 4–8 years. | Gathercole, S. E. & Baddeley, A. D. (1996). *The Children's test of non-word repetition*. London: Psychology Corporation. |
| **Reading** | |
| WRMT-III<br>Comprehensive assessment of reading readiness, basic reading skills and comprehension; norms for 5 to 75+ years. | Woodcock, R. N. (2011). *Woodcock reading mastery tests*, 3rd edn. San Antonio, TX: Pearson. |
| Martin and Pratt Non-word Reading Test<br>Tests phonological recoding with 52 non-words ranging in difficulty; norms for 6–16 years. | Martin, F. & Pratt, C. (2001). *Martin and Pratt Non-word Reading Test*. Melbourne: ACER Press. |
| Qualitative Reading Inventory-5<br>Assesses reading ability at emergent through high school levels with narrative and expository passages, comprehension questions and word lists; no norms available. | Leslie, L. & Caldwell, J. (2010). *Qualitative reading inventory*, 5th edn. London: Pearson Education. |
| Graded Non-word Reading Test<br>Allows assessment of discrepancies between word and non-word reading; UK norms for 5–11 years. | Snowling, M., Stothard, S. & McLean, J. (1996). *The Graded Non-word Reading Test*. Bury St. Edmunds: Thames Valley Test Publishers. |
| **Semantics** | |
| TOWK<br>Evaluates knowledge of figurative language, multiple meanings, conjunctions, receptive and expressive vocabulary; norms for 5–17 years. | Wiig, E. H. & Secord, W. (1992). *Test of word knowledge*. San Antonio, TX: Psychological Corporation. |

| Vocabulary: Expressive | |
|---|---|
| **EVT**<br>Measure of expressive vocabulary for Standard American English with 38 labelling items and 152 synonym items; norms for same population as PPVT-4 at ages 2;6 to 90+ years. | Williams, K. T. (2007). *Expressive vocabulary test.* San Antonio, TX: Pearson. |
| **TWF-2**<br>Assesses word finding skills: picture naming of nouns, verbs, and categories, sentence completion; norms for 4;0–12;11. | German, D. J. (2000). *Test of word finding*, 2nd edn. Austin, TX: PRO-ED. |
| **TAWF**<br>Assesses word finding skills: picture naming of nouns, verbs, and categories, sentence completion, description naming; norms for 12–80 years. | German, D. J. (1990). *Test of adolescent/adult word finding.* Austin, TX: PRO-ED. |
| Vocabulary: Receptive | |
| **PPVT-4**<br>A measure of receptive vocabulary for Standard American English with norms for ages 2;6 to 90+ years; 4-alternative forced choice picture selection task with 228 items (nouns, verbs, adjectives) at varying levels of difficulty. | Dunn, L. M. & Dunn, D. M. (2007). *Peabody picture vocabulary test*, 4th edn. San Antonio, TX: Pearson. |
| **BPVS3**<br>A measure of receptive vocabulary for British English with norms for 3–16 years; 4-alternative forced choice picture selection task similar to the PPVT. | Dunn, L. M., Dunn, L. M., Styles, B. & Sewell, J. (2009). *The British picture vocabulary scale*, 3rd edn. London: GL Assessments. |

## 10.1.2  Deficits in phonological processing

As previously discussed, SLI and dyslexia often occur in the same children and may have the same underlying genetic basis (Bishop, 2001). Both of these conditions are characterised by deficits in phonological processing (Kamhi & Catts, 1986). Young children with SLI often produce immature speech sounds, mispronounce words, and confuse words with similar sound patterns. A frequently used measure of phonological processing is the non-word repetition task (Gathercole, Willis, Baddeley, & Emslie, 1994). Many studies have shown that children with SLI demonstrate very poor non-word repetition, especially if non-words are three syllables in length or longer (Botting & Conti-Ramsden, 2001; Dollaghan & Campbell, 1998). Phonotactic probability impacts non-word repetition to a greater extent in children with SLI than in typical children (Munson et al., 2005b), and, interestingly, it affects their ability to inflect familiar verbs for past tense as well (Leonard, Davis, & Deevy, 2007). These findings suggest that children with SLI have greater difficulty reproducing sequences of speech sounds that are relatively rare in their language.

The non-word repetition task is widely considered to be a measure of phonological short-term memory. Because a new word form might decay before a new lexical entry can be established, deficits in phonological short-term memory are thought to have a direct impact on vocabulary acquisition (Baddeley, Gathercole, & Papagno, 1998). Unfortunately, the non-word repetition task is not a pure measure of phonological short-term memory – rather, the size and phonological diversity of a child's existing vocabulary affect task performance, as non-words resembling known words are easier to repeat (Snowling, Chiat, & Hulme, 1991). Although non-word repetition reflects both the capacity of phonological short-term memory and vocabulary knowledge, it remains useful as a clinical marker of SLI (Montgomery, 2002), along with sentence repetition (Conti-Ramsden, Botting, & Faragher, 2001). Non-word repetition accuracy is highly predictive of both lexical and grammatical processing (Montgomery, 1995; Munson, Edwards, & Beckman, 2005a; Rispens & Been, 2007), and recently has been linked to specific genetic markers (Newbury, Bishop & Monaco, 2005).

Another clinically relevant aspect of phonological processing concerns how readily children can select a target word from their vocabulary in the context of other words with similar sound patterns. Several recent studies suggest that children with SLI experience greater competition between words with overlapping sounds (Mainela-Arnold, Evans, & Coady, 2008; Seiger-Gardner & Brooks, 2008). Using a gating task, Mainela-Arnold and colleagues compared how large an acoustic chunk is necessary for spoken word recognition in children with SLI (8- to 12-year-olds) relative to their typical peers. In the gating task, children hear incrementally longer chunks as measured from the onset of the word; after each chunk is heard they guess the identity of the word until the end of the word is reached. Surprisingly, the children with SLI did not require significantly longer chunks for successful word recognition, but they were more likely to vacillate between correct and incorrect responses (phonologically related words). That is, from the point at which the word was first identified, the typical children tended to respond correctly on all successively longer chunks, whereas the children with SLI often produced incorrect responses after having previously made a correct response. This suggests that phonologically related alternatives remained in competition with the target word for a longer period for the children with SLI.

**non-word repetition task** a measure of phonological short-term memory; individuals are instructed to repeat meaningless sequences of syllables such as *amberillock* or *frovilankus* that vary in length (numbers of syllables).

**phonotactic probability** refers to the probability of different sequences of phonemes occurring in a given language.

**phonological short-term memory** the capacity to hold a sequence of speech sounds briefly in mind for a short amount of time.

A similar conclusion was drawn from results of a cross-modal picture–word interference study with 7- to 11-year-old children (Seiger-Gardner & Brooks, 2008). Children named a series of pictures, each paired with an auditory distractor presented over headphones. On the critical trials, the distractor either shared the onset with the name of the picture (e.g. the word *bed* paired with a picture of a bell, see Figure 10.1) or was unrelated (e.g. the word *sock* paired with a bell). Whereas the typical children showed phonological priming – faster naming of pictures paired with onset-related distractors – the children with SLI showed a different pattern. They experienced phonological interference – slower naming of pictures paired with onset-related distractors – when the distractor preceded its picture, and phonological priming when the picture came first. The phonological interference effect is suggestive of competition between words with overlapping sound patterns; this competition has the potential to disrupt lexical access in children who are less capable of suppressing contextually inappropriate words.

Another indicator of phonological difficulties in SLI is children's poor perform-ance on measures of **phonological awareness** (Catts, Adlof, Hogan, & Weismer, 2005); such tasks require children to manipulate the sounds that make up words, for exam-ple by counting the numbers of syllables in a word, coming up with words that rhyme with a target word, or segmenting a word into its constituent sounds. Phonological awareness and its development were discussed at greater length in Chapter 9 in the context of literacy acquisition. Poor phonological awareness in children with SLI is likely to contribute to the difficulties many of these children experience in learning to read and write. This effect, however, is bidirectional, as **phonemic awareness** of the smallest units of sound that carry meaning has been shown to emerge through lit-eracy acquisition (Wagner, Torgesen, & Rashotte, 1994).

**Figure 10.1**   *Stimuli from the picture–word interference paradigm used in Seiger-Gardner and Brooks (2008). Participants were asked to name a picture while at the same time hearing another word which could be either phonologically related (left panel) or unrelated (right panel) to the target picture.*

## 10.1.3 Deficits in lexical processing

Children with SLI have less diverse receptive and expressive vocabularies than their peers (Leonard, 1998; Oetting, Rice, & Swank, 1995; Rice, Buhr, & Nemeth, 1990; Stokes & Fletcher, 2000; Watkins, Kelly, Harbers, & Hollis, 1995). They exhibit a slower rate of word learning and more rapid forgetting of newly acquired words (Riches, Tomasello, & Conti-Ramsden, 2005). In **fast mapping** tasks, in which a child is briefly introduced to a novel word paired with its referent, children with SLI perform comparably to their peers on comprehension probes, but much worse than their peers when later asked to say the word (Dollaghan, 1987; Rice et al., 1990). This suggests that children with SLI require a higher frequency of exposure to a word for it to be successfully added to their expressive vocabularies (Windfuhr, Faragher, & Conti-Ramsden, 2002). With respect to retrieving words from their vocabularies, many children with SLI experience chronic word-finding difficulties, both in spontaneous conversation and in single-word naming tasks, such as picture naming (German, 1984; German & Simon, 1991; Leonard, Nippold, Kail, & Hale, 1983). They more frequently experience **tip-of-the-tongue** states in which they fail to retrieve the target word, but have an imminent sense of knowing it (Faust, Dimitrovsky, & Davidi, 1997). Their language is characterised by repetitions, substitutions, reformulations, pauses, and over-reliance on non-specific words (e.g. *stuff, thing*) (German, 1987; McGregor & Leonard, 1989).

Children with SLI name pictures more slowly than their peers with typical language development (Lahey & Edwards, 1996; Seiger-Gardner & Brooks, 2008; Seiger-Gardner & Schwartz, 2008), and they produce errors that are semantically related to the target (e.g. saying *table* when asked to name a picture of a desk) (Lahey & Edwards, 1999; McGregor, 1997). Such errors may be a consequence of gaps in the child's **lexicon** (i.e. they simply do not know the target word), sparse lexical representations lacking conceptual detail, or retrieval failures (McGregor, 1997; McGregor, Newman, Reilly, & Capone, 2002; Messer & Dockrell, 2006). McGregor and Waxman (1998) prompted children with word-finding difficulties to retrieve nouns at superordinate, basic, and subordinate levels. Children were shown a picture (e.g. a rose) and asked, for example, *Is this a dandelion?* The language-impaired children tended to answer questions appropriately (e.g. *No, it's a flower that's red and thorny*), but were much less successful in retrieving the correct noun than their peers with typical development. When asked to define words, children with language impairments produce fewer and less accurate definitions than typical children (Dockrell, Messer, George, & Ralli, 2003). McGregor and colleagues (2002), using a drawing and definition task, found a close relationship between children's ability to correctly name objects and their ability to provide appropriate **semantic features**. That is, for objects they could not name, the children were less able to provide appropriate semantic features, such as the object's function, physical attributes, or superordinate category. Hence, McGregor and colleagues concluded that children's limited semantic knowledge directly contributes to their word-finding difficulties.

Three recent studies (Brooks, Seiger-Gardner, & Sailor, under review; Hennessey, Leitão, & Mucciarone, 2010; Velez & Schwartz, 2010) explored semantic priming effects in children with SLI, and reported that children with SLI fail to benefit from semantic context to the same extent as their typically developing peers. Brooks and colleagues (under review) used the cross-modal picture–word interference task (see task description under Section 10.1.2). On some trials, the auditory distractor was semantically associated with the name of the target picture (e.g. the word *princess* paired with a picture of a castle), and on other trials it was unrelated (e.g. *milk* paired with a castle). Although picture naming was generally faster when the distractor was semantically related to the picture, the semantic priming effect was very weak in the children with SLI and correlated significantly with language ability. Hennessey and colleagues (2010) presented prime–target pairs such as *medicine–cure* and *quiet–whisper* in a primed word repetition task. They found that children with SLI, unlike their peers, were no faster in repeating the target words when they were primed. Velez and Schwartz (2010) used associated prime–target word pairs (e.g. *cat–dog, moon–sun*) in a word-recognition task, which required children to make an animacy judgement about each word. Like Hennessey and colleagues, they obtained significant semantic priming in typical children, and no effect in children with SLI. Together, these results suggest that children with SLI have weaker semantic connections within their lexical system.

Children with SLI have greater difficulty in acquiring verbs than nouns (Windfuhr et al., 2002), and they are less accurate in labelling events than even language-matched younger children (Loeb, Pye, Redmond, & Richardson, 1996). One factor contributing to their verb-learning difficulties is their inability to use syntactic bootstrapping as a word-learning strategy (Shulman & Guberman, 2007; van der Lely, 1994). Children with SLI are less capable of using syntactic cues in sentences to make inferences about the possible meanings of novel verbs. In one study, 6-year-old children with SLI were much less successful than their typically developing peers in acting out the meaning of a novel verb on the basis of the syntactic construction in which it was introduced (van der Lely, 1994). In another study, children were shown two scenes, one depicting an actor performing an action on another individual, and the other depicting both individuals performing a repetitive action in parallel. Typically developing preschool children were strongly biased to associate a novel verb in a transitive construction (e.g. *Look the rabbit is gorping the duck*) with the causative action, and a novel verb introduced in an intransitive construction (e.g. *Look the rabbit and duck are gorping*) with the repetitive motion, whereas language-matched 5-year-old children with SLI performed at chance (Shulman & Guberman, 2007).

## *10.1.4   Deficits in grammatical processing*

Children with SLI have profound difficulties in the acquisition and processing of syntax. In children with SLI of ages 9 years and older, syntactic difficulties are extremely persistent, and are resistant to treatment (van der Lely, 2005). These children have difficulties working out the precise functions of grammatical elements, and are delayed in generalizing syntactic patterns to new words (Conti-Ramsden & Windfuhr, 2002; Fletcher, Stokes, & Wong, 2005; Riches, Faracher, & Conti-Ramsden, 2006;

Shulman & Guberman, 2007; van der Lely, 1994). In their spontaneous speech, they produce functional morphemes, such as determiners (e.g. *a*, *the*), auxiliary verbs (e.g. *is*, *are*), complementisers (e.g. *that*, *which*), and inflections (e.g. *-ed*, *-s*, *-'s*), with lesser frequency and consistency than younger typical children matched on mean length of utterances (MLU) (Leonard, 1995; Miller & Leonard, 1998). They appear to have greater difficulties processing low-phonetic-substance inflections, such as the past tense *-ed* inflection, in comparison to a high-phonetic-substance inflection, such as the present progressive *-ing* (Montgomery & Leonard, 1998). Perhaps surprisingly, English-speaking children with SLI only rarely make agreement errors, for example, *The dogs barks at the girl* (Rice, Wexler, & Cleave, 1995). Indeed, their predominant error is to omit obligatory function words and grammatical morphemes. In contrast, children with SLI who speak more richly inflected languages (e.g. Spanish or Italian) make fewer errors with grammatical inflections. Moreover, as they rarely produce uninflected or infinitive forms of verbs, their errors tend to involve substitutions rather than omissions of inflections (Bedore & Leonard, 2001; Bortolini, Caselli, & Leonard, 1997). However, like English-speaking children with SLI, these children are more likely than their typical peers to omit function words (e.g. determiners, auxiliaries, complimentisers) in obligatory contexts (Leonard, 2009).

Children with SLI are conservative learners of syntax who do not flexibly use verbs in different constructions. One study specifically looked at how children with SLI respond to different types of elicitation questions (Loeb, Pye, Richardson, & Redmond, 1998). The experimenter first acted out an event and then asked the child a leading question – for example, after putting a baby to sleep, she asked *What did I do to the baby?*, or after throwing a ball, she asked *What did the ball do?* Loeb and colleagues reported that 5- to 6-year-old children with SLI produced less sophisticated responses than younger language-matched typical children. In particular, the children with SLI were less likely to use the periphrastic causative construction (e.g. *You made the baby sleep*) or the passive construction (e.g. *It was thrown*) – that is, they were less capable of varying the constructions in which they used English verbs in response to the discourse pressure of the elicitation questions.

With respect to comprehension, Evans and MacWhinney (1999) reported that English-speaking children with SLI were much less likely than their typical peers to use word order as a cue to sentence interpretation. When presented with sentences such as *Chair chases horse*, 7-year-old children with SLI tended to base their interpretations on noun animacy, selecting the horse as the one doing the chasing. Reliance on word order as a cue to sentence interpretation was strongly correlated with other measures of receptive language ability. Other studies have similarly shown that children with SLI over-rely on lexical and thematic information when interpreting complex constructions (Marinis & van der Lely, 2007; van der Lely & Harris, 1990; van der Lely & Stollwerck, 1997). For example, sentences involving anaphoric co-reference require a detailed syntactic analysis to constrain co-reference relationships. In the sentence *Elmo says Oscar was tickling himself*, the reflexive pronoun *himself* must refer to Oscar, whereas in

**discourse pressure**
the tendency for preceding utterances to constrain the form of subsequent utterances within a dialogue.

**anaphoric co-reference**
also called pronominal co-reference; the use of an anaphoric device (usually a pronoun) to refer back to an entity previously mentioned in the discourse.

*Elmo says Oscar is tickling him*, the pronoun *him* can refer either to Elmo or to some other entity not mentioned in the sentence, but *him* cannot refer to Oscar. Children with SLI performed at chance when sentence interpretation depended on syntactic information, but were adept at utilising semantic cues, such as the gender of the pronoun (herself = female) to constrain sentence interpretation (van der Lely & Stollwerck, 1997).

Due to their heavy reliance on semantic and contextual cues in sentence interpretation, children with SLI make errors with reversible sentences (van der Lely & Harris, 1990). In a reversible sentence, semantic information (e.g. noun animacy) fails to provide any information regarding who did what to whom; for example, in the sentence *The boy pushed the girl*, either the boy or the girl is capable of pushing the other. For a non-reversible sentence like *The boy pushed the chair*, only the boy is animate, which suggests that he is the one doing the pushing. Reversible sentences are difficult for children with SLI because they have to rely on word order to construct an accurate interpretation. Children with SLI have difficulties processing a variety of complex sentence structures: passives, as in *The boy was chased by the dog* (Leonard, Wong, Deevy, Stokes, & Fletcher, 2006; van der Lely, 1996); wh- questions, as in *Who did the dog chase down the street?* (Deevy & Leonard, 2004; Marinis & van der Lely, 2007; van der Lely & Battell, 2003); relative clauses, as in *The boy who is sitting behind the girl is very tall* (Friedmann & Novogrodsky, 2004; Hestvik, Schwartz, & Tornyova, 2010); finite and non-finite complement clauses, as in *Big Bird knew that Elmo fed the dog* or *Big Bird knew to feed the dog* (Owen & Leonard, 2006). Even sentences with lots of words but relatively simple syntax, as in *The little old blue car is going to hit the great big fast speeding train* can lead to processing difficulties.

### 10.1.5  Wider repercussions

In many cases, the language deficits of children with SLI affect their ability to sustain dialogue, and fully participate in conversational interactions – that is, these children show difficulties in the area of pragmatics (Conti-Ramsden & Friel-Patti, 1984; Craig & Evans, 1993). Children with SLI often have difficulties initiating social interactions with their peers, and joining into established peer-group interactions (Craig & Washington, 1993; Rice, Sell, & Hadley, 1991). They often fail to respond to the communicative bids of other children, and subsequently are often ignored by their peers (Hadley & Rice, 1991). From preschool age, children prefer to be friends with children who have higher levels of communicative competence (Gertner, Rice, & Hadley, 1994). Thus, the difficulties children with SLI experience in initiating and sustaining conversations with their peers translate into social difficulties and isolation for many of these children. One study found children with SLI to score higher than their typical peers on measures of social withdrawal, and to score lower on measures of sociability (Hart, Fujiki, Brinton, & Hart, 2004); another study found their poor social competence put them at greater risk of being bullied at school (Conti-Ramsden & Botting, 2004). By pre-adolescence, children with SLI have lower self-esteem than their peers; they have more negative views of their academic abilities, social skills, and behaviour (Jerome, Fujiki, Brinton, & James, 2002), and are at increased risk for depression and anxiety (Conti-Ramsden & Botting, 2008).

Although, by adolescence, many individuals with SLI have learned to manage their disability fairly well in their everyday interactions, they may still show deficits in more verbally demanding situations. For example, in one recent study (Wetherell, Botting, & Conti-Ramsden, 2007), adolescents with SLI were found to be much more impaired in telling a story than in having a conversation. The narratives of children with SLI have been shown to be less structurally complex and less coherent than those of their typical peers; their narratives are characterised by poor sequencing of information, grammatical errors, and omission of plot details (Liles, 1985; Norbury & Bishop, 2003). As described in Chapter 7, narrative development impacts various aspects of cognitive development, including the development of emotion under-standing and Theory of Mind; the limited evidence to date suggests that children with language impairments may be delayed in each of these areas (Dimitrovsky, Spector, Levy-Shiff, & Vakil, 1998; Farrant, Fletcher, & Maybery, 2006; Farrar, Johnson, Tompkins, Easters, Zelisis-Medus, & Benigno, 2009; Ford & Milosky, 2008; Trauner, Ballantyne, Chase, & Tallal, 1993).

# 10.2 WHICH CHILDREN ARE AT RISK FOR SPECIFIC LANGUAGE IMPAIRMENT?

## 10.2.1 Genetic basis of language impairment

Language impairments run in families (Ingram, 1959; Stromswold, 1998; Tallal, Hirsch, Realpe-Bonilla, Brzustowicz, Bartlett, & Flax, 2001; Tomblin, 1989). Having a first-degree relative with SLI increases one's chance of having SLI by a factor of four (Tomblin, 2009). The high rate of familial aggregation of SLI is thought to be largely due to genetic factors, which lead to abnormalities in how the cerebral cortex develops (Tropper & Schwartz, 2009). Evidence of genetic involvement in SLI comes from twin studies (Bishop, North, & Donlan, 1995; Lewis & Thompson, 1992; Tomblin & Buckwalter, 1998) and genetic linkage studies (Marcus & Fisher, 2003; Newbury, Bishop, & Monaco, 2005). The twin studies have documented significantly higher concordance rates (the proportion of twins having the same trait, i.e. both having SLI) for monozy-gotic (identical) twins, who share all their genes, than for dizygotic (fraternal) twins, who share only 50 per cent of their genes. Across studies, concordance ranges from .70 to .96 for monozygotic twins

**twin studies** research methodology used to determine the influence of genes and environment on traits and behaviour; involves a comparison of the concordance rates for identical and fraternal twins for a given trait.

**concordance rates** the proportion of twins hav-ing the same trait; com-parison of concordance rates for identical and fraternal twins can help geneticists to determine whether the trait has a genetic basis.

**verbal dyspraxia** also called verbal apraxia or apraxia of speech; a speech–motor disorder characterised by difficulties in planning and articulating speech sounds.

in comparison to .46 to .69 for dizygotic twins (Tomblin, 2009). Considerable progress in the search for genetic markers associated with SLI has been made in recent years. Mutations in one candidate gene, FOXP2 (see Chapter 12) have been linked to language impairment in an extended family in the UK (Vargha-Khadem, Watkins, Price, Ashburner, Alcock, Connelly, et al., 1998) as well as several other families (Feuk, Kalervo, Lipsanen-Nyman, Skaug, Nakabayashi, Finucane, et al., 2006; MacDermot, Bonora, Sykes, Coupe, Lai, Vernes, et al., 2004; Tomblin, Shriberg, Murray, Patil, & Williams, 2004); these mutations are strongly predictive of speech-motor problems (also called verbal dyspraxia). However, studies of other individuals and families with SLI have failed to find a FOXP2 mutation (Meaburn, Dale, Craig, & Plomin, 2002; O'Brien, Zhang, Nishimura, Tomblin, & Murray, 2003), which indicates that it is not the only genetic cause of language impairments and most likely not the cause of SLI. As researchers in the field search for other genetic markers associated with SLI, advances are being made at a rapid pace. In recent years, several regions on chromosomes 13q, 16q, and 19q have been linked to deficits in phonological short-term memory that are characteristic of many individuals with SLI (Newbury et al., 2005). It is also worth noting that, while SLI is widely considered to have a genetic basis, there are other pre- and perinatal factors that put infants at risk for language impairments; in particular, preterm babies tend to have poorer language-learning outcomes than full-term babies, even in cases where there is no discernible brain damage or general cognitive delay (Guarini, Sansavini, Fabbri, Alessandroni, Faldella, & Karmiloff-Smith, 2009).

## 10.2.2 Neural markers of language impairment

SLI is associated with abnormal development in how the brain processes language, but it is, by its diagnostic criteria, not associated with any focal lesion or injury to a specific area of the brain. Chapter 12 will provide a summary of the neural basis of language development; here we provide only a brief description of the neurobiology of SLI. Several distinct neuroanatomical regions on either side of the Sylvian fissure (a deep groove separating the frontal lobe and temporal lobe of the brain) play an important role in language processing and appear to develop atypically in individuals with SLI (see Figure 10.2). In individuals with typical language development, a region of the temporal lobe called the planum temporale tends to be larger in the left cerebral hemisphere than in the right (Geschwind & Levitsky, 1968), which correlates with the left hemisphere playing a dominant role in speech processing. This asymmetry in the length of the planum temporale is evident from the third trimester of gestation (Chi, Dooling, & Gilles, 1977; Wada, Clark, & Hamm, 1975; Witelson & Pallie, 1973; Witelson, 1977), and suggests that the left hemisphere already shows specialisation for language processing at birth. Interestingly, several post-mortem studies of individuals with dyslexia and/or

**frontal lobe** a region of the human brain located at the front of each cerebral hemisphere.

**temporal lobe** a region of the human brain located beneath the Sylvian fissure of each cerebral hemisphere.

**planum temporale** a region of the cortex located near the Sylvian fissure in the temporal lobe adjacent to the auditory cortex; the left planum temporale is involved in the higher-order integration of the sound patterns of speech.

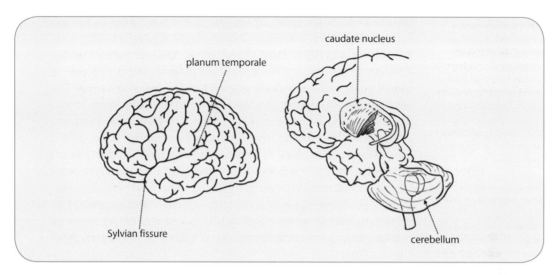

**Figure 10.2** *Cortical (left) and subcortical (right) brain areas for which abnormal development has been found in individuals with SLI.*

*Source:* Image by Michael Almodovar.

SLI found a lack of asymmetry in the length of the planum temporale (Cohen, Campbell, & Yaghmai, 1989; Galaburda, Sherman, Rosen, Aboitiz, & Geschwind, 1985; Humphreys, Kaufmann, & Galaburda, 1990). Each of these studies also found various cellular abnormalities in the perisylvian region (i.e. on both sides of the Sylvian fissure) in both hemispheres. Structural magnetic resonance imaging (MRI) has provided further evidence linking SLI with abnormal patterns of cortical growth (De Fossé, Hodge, Makris, Kennedy, Caviness, McGrath, et al., 2004; Jernigan, Hesselink, Sowell, & Tallal, 1991; Plante, Swisher, & Vance, 1989; Plante, Swisher, Vance, & Rapesak, 1991), with most individuals with SLI failing to show the typical pattern of leftward asymmetry in regions linked to language functioning – that is, in the inferior frontal region associated with the processing of grammar – and in the perisylvian region (encompassing the planum temporale) associated with integration of the sound patterns of speech. There is also evidence of structural abnormalities, including the presence of an extra sulcus or groove in the inferior frontal lobe (Jackson & Plante, 1997), a region involved in the processing of grammar.

In addition to these cortical regions, several subcortical structures involved in language processing show abnormal development in individuals with SLI. These include the cerebellum and the

**perisylvian region** areas of the cerebral cortex on both sides of the Sylvian fissure, the deep groove that separates the frontal and parietal lobes (above) from the temporal lobe (below).

**magnetic resonance imaging (MRI)** a medical imaging technique that uses magnetic fields to produce detailed images of soft tissue, such as the human brain.

**cerebellum** one of several subcortical structures involved in language processing that shows abnormal development in individuals with SLI; located at the base of the brain, it plays an important role in motor coordination.

**caudate nucleus** one of several subcortical structures involved in language processing that shows abnormal development in individuals with SLI; the caudate nucleus is located within the basal ganglia and plays a role in the control of voluntary movement.

**basal ganglia** in concert with the inferior frontal lobe forms a functional network supporting skill acquisition; becomes activated when simple and higher-level grammatical structures are processed.

**procedural memory** one of two types of long-term memory (the other being declarative memory); involved in sequence learning and the coordination of sequences of actions.

caudate nucleus, the latter being part of the basal ganglia (Hodge, Makris, Kennedy, Caviness, Howard, McGrath, et al., 2010; Jernigan et al., 1991; Tallal, Jernigan, & Trauner, 1994; Vargha-Khadem et al., 1998). The cerebellum plays an important role in motor coordination, including speech-motor programming. The basal ganglia, in concert with the inferior frontal lobe, form a functional network supporting skill acquisition (Ullman & Pierpont, 2005). More specifically, these structures comprise a procedural memory system involved in the learning of coordinated sequences of actions, and the control of their execution. Procedural memory plays a critical role in the learning of the sequential patterns – that is, how the elements in a series are ordered – and thus plays an important role in grammar acquisition and the emergent automaticity of grammatical operations (Packard & Knowlton, 2002; Ullman, 2001).

In several studies, structural and functional abnormalities have been observed in family members (parents and siblings) without language impairments, as well as in the affected children (Jackson & Plante, 1997; Plante et al., 1989, 1991). These findings suggest that, in addition to neurobiological development, other factors in the environment may contribute to SLI. It remains to be determined why neuroanatomical abnormalities result in language impairments in some individuals but not in others.

## 10.2.3   Diagnosing language impairment

Toddlers at 24 months of age who have fewer than 50 words in their expressive vocabularies and do not yet produce any word combinations (i.e. multi-word utterances) are considered to be late talkers (Desmarais, Sylvestre, Meyer, Bairati, & Rouleau, 2008; Rescorla, 1989). These children, who are somewhat more likely to be boys than girls, fail to show the burst in vocabulary growth during the second year of life that is characteristic of most typical children (see Chapter 4 on vocabulary spurt). Some late talkers catch up to their peers with typical development over the preschool years – these children are sometimes referred to as late bloomers. Unfortunately, some late talkers have continuing difficulties with language processing and are later diagnosed with SLI.

**late bloomers** late-talking toddlers who apparently catch up to their peers during the preschool years.

Language delay during the toddler years can be assessed through vocabulary checklists, such as the widely used MacArthur–Bates Child Development Inventory (see Methodology Box 4.1), and through spontaneous speech sampling. Using the MacArthur–Bates CDI, late talkers have been identified as children below the 10th percentile in expressive vocabulary for their age (Dale, Price, Bishop, & Plomin, 2003; Thal & Tobias, 1994; Weismer & Evans, 2002). Spontaneous speech sampling has been widely used to assess the lexical diversity and grammatical complexity of young children's productive speech. Lexical diversity may be measured by computing the number of different words produced in a sample of fixed size (Watkins et al., 1995). Two commonly used measures of grammatical development are the child's mean length of utterances (a measure of the number of morphemes within an utterance [Brown, 1973]) and the Index of Productive Syntax (IPSyn) (Scarborough, 1990a). The IPSyn requires a sample of 100 spontaneous utterances, and uses a checklist for 56 syntactic and morphological forms, grouped into categories: noun phrases, verb phrases, questions and negations, and sentence structures. The IPSyn may provide a more sensitive measure of grammatical development in preschool children than MLU (Sagae, Lavie, & MacWhinney, 2005). Calculations of both MLU and IPSyn can be done automatically using the CLAN programs provided through the Child Language Data Exchange System (CHILDES); see Methodology Box 6.1.

> **Index of Productive Syntax (IPSyn)**
> a measure of grammatical development based on a sample of 100 spontaneous utterances, and using a checklist for 56 syntactic and morphological forms.

An obvious limitation of spontaneous speech sampling is that it requires considerable time and effort to produce accurate transcriptions for analysis. Fortunately, a wide variety of diagnostic tests have been developed to assess different aspects of language development in children, with some measures focusing on phonological processing, and others focusing on lexical development (receptive vocabulary, expressive vocabulary), grammatical development (morphology and syntax), and reading (word recognition and non-word decoding). A representative sample of such measures is described in Methodology Box 10.1.

## 10.2.4   Predicting outcomes for late talkers

Individual differences in language abilities tend to be fairly stable throughout childhood (but see Ukoumunne, Wake, Carlin, Bavin, Lum, Skeat, et al. [2011] for evidence that language development may be uneven in some children). In one longitudinal study, toddlers who were identified as late talkers between the ages of 2;0 and 2;7 continued to lag behind their peers on MLU and IPSyn measures at ages 3;0 and 4;0 (Rescorla, Dahlsgaard, & Roberts, 2000). Among the late talkers, recovery was more rapid for vocabulary growth than for syntactic and morphological development (Rescorla, Roberts, & Dahlsgaard, 1997). When the children were re-evaluated at 9, 13, and 17 years of age (Rescorla, 2002, 2005, 2009), the late talkers tended to perform in the normal range across measures of vocabulary, grammar, reading, and writing, but still remained significantly below their control group matched on socio-economic status and non-verbal intelligence. Importantly, expressive vocabulary size at age 2 years still predicted 17 per cent of the variance in vocabulary/grammar, and verbal memory scores at age 17, providing strong evidence of continuity in language development. Another longitudinal study similarly reported that late talkers show long-term weaknesses in processing language when compared with their typical peers (Stothard, Snowling, Bishop, Chipchase, & Kaplan, 1998).

Like other children, late talkers show a high degree of continuity in lexical and grammatical development. Moyle, Weismer, Evans, and Lindstrom followed 30 late talkers and 30 typical children from ages 2;0 to 5;6, measuring growth in vocabulary and grammar at 6-month intervals. At each time point, vocabulary and grammar measures showed strong concurrent correlations (i.e. vocabulary measures at age 2;0 correlated with grammar measures at age 2;0; vocabulary measures at age 2;6 correlated with grammar measures at age 2;6; etc.). However, when using cross-lagged statistics (i.e. correlating vocabulary at age 2;0 with grammar at age 2;6; correlating grammar at age 2;0 with vocabulary at age 2;6; etc.), grammatical abilities were less predictive of future vocabulary growth in the late talkers than in their typical peers. This finding suggests that morphological and syntactic cues (e.g. past tense and plural markers, English word order) played less of a role in constraining the meanings of novel words for the late talkers. In other words, the late talkers seemed less capable than their peers of utilising syntactic bootstrapping to build their vocabulary (Gleitman, 1990; see Chapter 4). In contrast, in both groups, vocabulary size was strongly predictive of future grammatical abilities, which supports the lexical bootstrapping hypothesis that grammar results from the accumulated lexical knowledge of how individual words are used (Bates & Goodman, 1997; see Chapter 4). Interestingly, the significant cross-lagged statistics relating vocabulary to later grammatical abilities were observed at younger ages in typical children in comparison to late talkers, which suggests that a critical mass of vocabulary needs to be acquired before it impacts grammar. Thus, slow vocabulary growth delays the onset of its beneficial effect on grammatical development.

Among late talkers two related factors might distinguish which children fully recover (the late bloomers) from those with more persistent problems: their language comprehension and the extent of their gesture usage (Thal, Tobias, & Morrison, 1991; Thal & Tobias, 1992). As described in Chapter 3, breadth of gesture usage in children tends to be correlated with their grasp of spoken language (e.g. O'Reilly, Painter, & Bornstein, 1997). Capone and McGregor (2004) have suggested that use of gestures by late talkers serves as a compensatory mechanism to facilitate social engagement with others, and is prognostic of more positive long-term outcomes. Although little research has specifically looked at late talkers, other studies of infants with developmental delays indicate that gesture use in pretend play, and the amount of gesturing used to initiate social interaction and to respond to the communicative bids of others, are predictive of future language abilities (Calandrella & Wilcox, 2000; Kennedy, Sheridan, Radlinski, & Beeghly, 1991). More generally, the failure to use eye gaze, prelinguistic vocalisation (e.g. grunts), and pointing gestures to direct the attention of others, and to initiate joint attention, may be of clinical value in distinguishing children with autism spectrum disorder (ASD) from other children with language delays (Crais, Watson, & Baranek, 2009). Such information is important for diagnosis, as there is considerable overlap in the social and communicative impairments (Layfer, Tager-Flusberg, Dowd, Tomblin, & Folstein, 2008; Tager-Flusberg, 2004), and the associated neurobiological abnormalities (De Fossé et al., 2004; Hodge et al., 2010), of children with SLI and ASD.

# 10.3 WHAT MIGHT EXPLAIN SPECIFIC LANGUAGE IMPAIRMENT?

An important question is whether specific aspects of syntax and morphology are absent or impaired in children with SLI, or whether SLI simply represents the tail end of a normal distribution of language abilities among children (Weismer, 2007). In this section we survey proposals that a representational deficit in a specialised syntax module is the cause of SLI (e.g. Rice & Wexler, 1996; van der Lely, 1994, 1998, 2005) or, alternatively, whether more general processing mechanisms can account for SLI (e.g. Joanisse & Seidenberg, 2003; Leonard, Weismer, Miller, Francis, Tomblin, & Kail, 2007; Ullman & Pierpont, 2005). An emerging view is that SLI is linked to a number of different cognitive deficits, including weaknesses in auditory processing, working-memory capacity, and procedural learning. What remains unclear is whether non-linguistic and language-related deficits in SLI stem from a common neurological deficit, or whether subtle cognitive weaknesses lead to a cascade of detrimental effects on language development (Kohnert, Windsor, & Danahy Ebert, 2009).

> **procedural learning**
> implicit learning of sequences via the procedural memory system; such learning is often assumed to occur without awareness.

## 10.3.1 Deficits in grammatical representation

Representational theories of SLI posit that children with SLI have specific deficits in linguistic knowledge. One of the first representational accounts of SLI was the Extended Optional Infinitive (EOI) hypothesis (Rice & Wexler, 1996; Rice, Wexler, & Cleave, 1995), which proposed that a central deficit in SLI involves the part of grammar responsible for tense marking. Children with SLI treat tense marking as optional, although, in English, it is obligatory. Rice and Wexler proposed that typical children go through an optional infinitive stage as well, but this stage of normal development extends over a longer period of time in children with SLI. The EOI account proposed that children with SLI know the rules for tense marking but lack the knowledge that tense marking is obligatory in certain linguistic contexts. A limitation of the EOI account is that it fails to explain the broad range of difficulties experienced by children with SLI.

According to the Representational Deficit for Dependent Relations (RDDR) account, the deficit lies in the computational syntactic system (van der Lely, 1994; van der Lely & Stollwerck, 1997). Central to the RDDR account was the identification of a subgroup of children with Grammatical SLI (G-SLI), characterised by persistent receptive and expressive language impairments restricted to core grammatical operations (but see Bishop, Bright, James, Bishop, & van der Lely, 2000). The grammatical representations of these children have been viewed as 'underspecified' due to incomplete syntactic analysis (van der Lely, 1996; van der Lely & Stollwerck, 1997). In addition to their deficits in the domains of morphology and syntax, children with G-SLI often have difficulties processing phonology, especially with more complex linguistic stimuli (van der Lely, 2005). A more recent formulation of the RRDR account, called the Computational Grammatical Complexity (CGC) hypothesis, proposes that children with SLI are impaired in the computations underlying hierarchical, structurally complex forms across one or more components of grammar (van der Lely, 1998, 2005). Whereas the RDDR account emphasises difficulties with the application of grammatical rules, the CGC account emphasises difficulties in the construction of hierarchical linguistic representations (see Chapter 5).

## 10.3.2   Processing deficits

Because children with SLI tend to experience difficulties with basic auditory processing, as discussed earlier (Tallal & Piercy, 1973a, 1973b, 1974, 1975), it has been suggested that these deficits may lie at the core of SLI. Using a computational model of the language-processing system, Joanisse and Seidenberg (2003) showed that low-level deficits in speech perception can have cascading effects on higher levels of linguistic processing. An earlier proposal along the same lines was the Surface Account (Leonard, 1989). Leonard proposed that children with SLI have low-level auditory processing deficits that affect their perception of grammatical morphemes with brief duration, such as tense-marking inflections (e.g. past tense -ed, third person singular -s). Inflections with low perceptual salience will be more difficult for children with SLI to learn and process.

McMurray, Samelson, Lee, and Tomblin (2010) have suggested that individuals with SLI have a fast rate of decay of information in phonological short-term memory. They used the **visual world paradigm** in which an array of objects is shown to participants on a computer along with a set of spoken instructions to mouse-click on specific objects (e.g. *Click on the candle;* see Figure 10.3). McMurray and colleagues monitored eye movements to the various objects in the array as the participants processed the spoken instructions. Crucially, on some of the trials, one of the alternative pictures in the array was phonologically related to the target (e.g. a can; see left panel of Figure 10.3), whereas on other trials all the alternatives were unrelated (see right panel of Figure 10.3). Adolescents with SLI experienced a greater degree of competition from the phonological competitor over a longer interval than their peers; that is, they looked more often at the can, and continued to make eye movements to the can even after the point of disambiguation of the target (i.e. the offset of the word *candle* in the instructions). The extended time course of interference from the phonologically related competitor in adolescents with SLI resembles a pattern observed in 5- to 6-year-old typical children (Sekerina & Brooks, 2007). Like the finding from the picture–word interference study by Seiger-Gardner and Brooks (2008) described earlier, these data suggest that SLI children suffer longer from phonological competition than typical children. McMurray et al. (2010) used these data to evaluate computational models varying in parameters such as processing speed, vocabulary size, quality of sensory and phonological representations, and found that increasing the decay rate for the auditory trace led to the best fitting model of their data. That is, the representations of the spoken words seemed to decay more rapidly in short-term memory, leaving individuals with SLI more susceptible to interference from words with similar sound patterns.

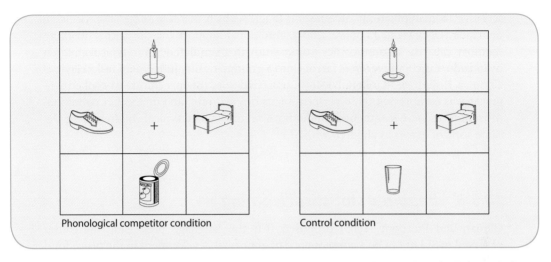

**Figure 10.3**  *Examples of visual stimuli used in the visual world paradigm. Children with SLI display more looks to a phonological competitor, for example,* can *(see left panel) when asked to click on the* candle.

Children with SLI are much slower to process spoken language than their typically developing peers (Miller, Kail, Leonard, & Tomblin, 2001). Montgomery (2005, 2006) has argued that children with SLI are less efficient in allocating attention to multiple sources of information. They are less capable of executing the various operations required for retrieving, evaluating, and integrating the semantic–syntactic properties of incoming words to construct sentence interpretations. Montgomery suggests that the slow processing speed of children with SLI is a consequence of their limited verbal working memory capacity – an interpretation that fits well with the literature linking individual differences in adult sentence processing to differences in verbal working memory capacity (Carpenter, Miyake, & Just, 1995). Verbal working memory capacity can be assessed by having children recall lists of words while performing a secondary task to increase information processing load. For example, in Montgomery (2000), children were asked to recall a list of words (e.g. *truck, cow, thumb, shirt, leaf* ), but had to reorder the list in accordance with the size of the objects before saying them. Verbal working memory tasks differ from phonological short-term memory tasks (such as non-word repetition) by requiring one to actively process and manipulate linguistic information at the same time as one attempts to remember a list of words. Such measures indicate that children with SLI have less verbal working memory capacity than their typically developing peers (Montgomery, 2000; Weismer, Evans, & Hesketh, 1999).

> **verbal working memory**  the capacity to actively hold verbal information (words, sentences) in mind while processing other, additional information.

The detrimental effects of a limited verbal working memory capacity should be greater for longer and more structurally complex sentences. In support of this hypothesis, Grela and Leonard (2000) have observed that children with SLI make more agreement errors with auxiliaries (e.g. *is, are*) as sentences increase in length and complexity. Similarly, in processing questions, children with SLI are highly sensitive to manipulations of question length, which increase sentence-processing demands (Deevy and Leonard, 2004). Additional support for the verbal working memory capacity account comes from a study that simulated SLI in typical children by introducing cognitive stress factors into a grammaticality judgement task (Hayiou-Thomas, Bishop, & Plunkett, 2004). In one condition, the speech rate of spoken sentences was compressed to 50 per cent of its original rate, and in another condition, the sentences were lengthened. Under both circumstances, typical children made the same sorts of errors as children with SLI.

### 10.3.3   Impaired statistical learning

Ullman and Pierpont (2005) proposed that the language processing difficulties observed in SLI might be a consequence of abnormal development in the procedural memory system which supports motor skill learning and statistical learning of patterns and sequences. This hypothesis is supported by neurobiological evidence of abnormalities in the basal ganglia and cerebellum in children with SLI – structures known to play a role in the learning, coordination, and timing of motor and cognitive skills. Under this hypothesis, associative learning of sequences should correlate with children's language abilities. Several studies have tested whether individuals with SLI show deficits in the statistical learning of grammatical patterns and sequential dependencies (Evans, Saffran, & Robe-Torres, 2009; Lum, Gelgic, & Conti-Ramsden, 2010; Plante, Gómez, & Gerken, 2002; Tomblin, Mainela-Arnold, & Zhang, 2007); see Methodology Box 11.1 for further description of sequence learning tasks. Plante and

**finite-state grammar**
an artificial grammar characterised by a finite set of elements (e.g. letters, syllables, tones) and a finite set of links between the elements (i.e. permissible sequences).

colleagues (2002) used a finite-state grammar to generate sentences in an artificial language consisting of CVC nonce words (an example sentence is *fim sag tup dak sag tup*), and tested whether young adults with a learning disability or dyslexia would show impaired learning of the word order rules of the artificial grammar. Consistent with the proposed deficit in procedural learning, after exposure to a representative set of sentences, the adults with language/learning disability showed impaired performance in judging whether new sentences obeyed the rules of the artificial grammar, relative to a non-learning disabled group. In a study with school-aged children, Evans and colleagues (2009) similarly found poor learning of the statistical patterns of an artificial language in the group with SLI. In their first study, after 21 minutes of listening time, children with SLI failed to learn the patterns embedded in the artificial language, whereas their typical peers succeeded. After doubling the amount of listening time in a second study, the children with SLI now performed above chance with non-word sequences, but not with tone sequences. In support of the procedural learning hypothesis, performance on the statistical learning task correlated with children's vocabulary knowledge.

Tomblin and colleagues (2007) tested teenagers with SLI on a serial reaction time (SRT) task in which they were instructed to press a series of buttons corresponding to the spatial locations of a series of visual stimuli. In the 'random' blocks, the spatial locations of the stimuli varied pseudo-randomly across trials, whereas in the 'patterned' blocks, the order of the varying spatial locations was generated by a

10-element sequence, which was repeated 10 times to produce 100 trials. In support of the procedural learning hypothesis, teenagers with SLI showed a slower learning rate during the patterned blocks in comparison to their peers, but did not differ on the random blocks (see also Lum et al. [2010] for similar results with 7- to 8-year-olds). The difference in learning rate for the patterned blocks was observed when groups were defined by grammatical abilities, but not when they were defined by vocabulary size, which suggests that performance on the SRT task was more strongly related to grammar learning.

The procedural learning deficit hypothesis gains further support from a broad literature documenting motor development and coordination abnormalities in children with SLI (Hill, 2001). Some children with SLI have symptoms of **dyspraxia**, a motor-learning difficulty that is associated with impaired planning of movement (Dewey & Wall, 1997); these children show delays both in walking and in talking (Trauner, Wulfeck, Tallal, & Hesselink, 2000). Motor impairments have been documented both for gross motor and fine motor coordination. For example, Bishop and Edmundson (1987) reported that performance on a manual dexterity task (peg movement) was predictive of language outcomes for late talkers. Research on speech-motor activity (e.g. lip movements) during non-word production found children with SLI to have more variable articulation than their typical peers, which suggests that speech-motor control is less mature in SLI (Goffman, 2004). Marton (2009) reported that children with SLI have difficulties imitating hand movements; in this study, gross motor coordination was predictive of imitation skills in children with SLI, but not in typical controls. The gross motor difficulties of many children with SLI resemble those of children described as clumsy who may or may not have concomitant language impairments (Hill, 1998; Powell & Bishop, 1992). These findings confirm a general link between aspects of motor development (e.g. measured through having children repeat sequences of finger taps or bounce back a ball) and aspects of language development such as verbal fluency (e.g. measured by asking a child to name as many animals as they can within one minute) which suggests that children with SLI may lie on the lower end of a continuum of general procedural and motor abilities (Wassenberg, Feron, Kessels, Hendriksen, Kalff, Kroes, et al., 2006).

> **dyspraxia** a motor-learning difficulty associated with impaired planning of movement and coordination.

## SUMMARY

- A consistent proportion of children show deficits in language development in the absence of cognitive deficits in other domains, a condition that has been termed Specific Language Impairment (SLI) and appears to have a genetic component.

- Deficits in children with SLI differ widely in severity and domain of impairment, making classification difficult. Children with SLI can show deficits in one or several of the following areas: auditory processing, phonological processing, lexical development, and syntactic development.

- Neuroimaging studies suggest that children with SLI show abnormalities related to reduced hemispheric asymmetry in cortical and subcortical areas that are involved in language processing.

- While some children diagnosed as 'late talkers' around 2 years of age catch up in their language development, children with SLI show persistent impairments later on which can often be predicted by reduced vocabulary size at an earlier age.

- A number of explanations for SLI have been suggested which mainly differ in whether the assumed core deficit is strictly language-related or whether it encompasses more general cognitive abilities.

  - Language-specific explanations suggest that SLI is the result of deficient grammatical representations such as a lack of representations of obligatory morphological marking or difficulties with representation and processing of hierarchical syntactic representations.

  - General cognitive explanations suggest that deficits in non-linguistic abilities such as general auditory processing or working memory capacity can have cascading effects for language development. It has also been suggested that SLI may be the result of a procedural deficit which underlies motor skill learning and motor coordination of articulation, as well as statistical learning of sequences.

# FURTHER READING

## Key studies

For evidence on deficits in statistical learning in children with SLI, read Evans, J. L., Saffran, J. R. & Robe-Torres, K. (2009). Statistical learning in children with specific language impairment. *Journal of Speech, Language, and Hearing Research, 52*, 321–335.

## Overview articles

For overviews of potential causes of SLI, read Ullman, M. T. & Pierpont, E. I. (2005). Specific Language Impairment is not specific to language: The procedural deficit hypothesis. *Cortex, 41*, 399–433 and Bishop, D. V. M. (2006). What causes specific language impairment in children? *Current Directions in Psychological Science, 15*, 217–221.

## Books

For a comprehensive resource on SLI and other disorders affecting language development, such as autism, read Schwartz, R. G. (ed.) (2009). *Handbook of child language disorders*. New York: Psychology Press.

# 11 How do Deaf Children Acquire Language?

## KEY TERMS

- artificial grammar • auditory nerve • Auditory Scaffolding Hypothesis • babbling • cheremes • cochlea • cochlear implants • constructions • critical period • derivational morphology • discourse • executive functioning • finite-state grammar • gesture sentences • home sign • lexicon • manually coded English • morphemes • morphology • numerical cognition • open-set test • phonemes • primary auditory cortex • prosody • serial reaction time (SRT) task • sign languages • symbolic gestures • syntax • temporal lobes • Theory of Mind • word-specific formulae

# CHAPTER OUTLINE

In the United Kingdom roughly 1 in 1000 infants is born with a hearing impairment (Fortnum, Summerfield, Marshall, Davis, & Bamford, 2001). Children with varying degrees of hearing impairment are often encouraged to lip-read and to acquire the spoken language of the surrounding hearing community. Learning a spoken language like English is not an easy task for a profoundly deaf child, and it is often unsuccessful. Under ideal circumstances, deaf children are raised and educated alongside other deaf individuals and are exposed to one of the world's **sign languages**, such as British Sign Language or American Sign Language, from a young age. Sign languages are complex human languages that use manual gestures and facial expressions as the mode of communication; they are not equivalent to the languages spoken in the same communities, but rather have their own grammatical features. In the first part of this chapter, we will explore whether the acquisition of a sign language differs from the acquisition of a spoken language in its general features and time course.

As more than 90–95 per cent of deaf children are born to hearing parents (Mitchell & Karchmer, 2004), many of these children are not exposed to a sign language until they enter school. This may delay their exposure to language due to their inability to process the spoken language of their community. However, in recent years it has become increasingly common for deaf individuals to receive **cochlear implants**. These are devices that convert sound waves into neural impulses, thereby enabling deaf individuals to gain a partial sense of hearing. The timing of implantation of these devices also affects at what age deaf children may be exposed to language. Deafness therefore provides a natural

**cochlear implants**
implanted electrical devices that convert sound waves into neural impulses, thereby providing deaf individuals with a partial sense of hearing.

experiment that allows researchers to investigate how delays in language input impact language development. We will review some of the evidence in this chapter and expand on the issue of a critical period further in Chapter 12. We will also examine the consequences of deafness on other aspects of social and cognitive development.

Not all deaf children, however, are exposed to a language. Some deaf children invent their own gestural communication systems called home sign that they use within their families. In the final part of the chapter, we explore the characteristics of home sign systems and their similarities to human languages. We also explore the social circumstances under which the home sign of a community of deaf individuals might evolve into a fully formed human language.

> **critical period**
> a time period in early development during which the organism displays heightened sensitivity to a particular type of stimulus (e.g. visual input or language).

# 11.1   ARE SIGN LANGUAGES ACQUIRED DIFFERENTLY FROM SPOKEN LANGUAGES?

## 11.1.1   *Structure and processing of sign languages*

Until the pioneering studies of American Sign Language (ASL) demonstrated it to be a bona fide language with a complex grammar (Klima & Bellugi, 1979; Stokoe, Casterline, & Croneberg, 1965), the sign languages of the world had been thought to be gestural communication systems without genuine linguistic structure. We now know that sign languages are natural languages with prosodic, phonological, morphological, and syntactic structure (Emmorey, 2002; Liddell, 2003; Sandler & Lillo-Martin, 2006). Sign languages are structurally unrelated to the languages spoken in the same communities: even though the United States and the United Kingdom share English as a common language, ASL and British Sign Language (BSL) are historically independent, and mutually unintelligible. Due to their use of the visual/gestural modality, as opposed to the auditory/vocal modality, sign languages have grammars that are distinct from spoken languages. Individual signs are made up of five elements that can be remembered using the acronym HOLME: Hand shape, (palm) Orientation, Location (place of articulation), Movement, and (facial) Expression: see Figure 11.1. Each of these elements may be articulated in multiple ways to distinguish one sign from another. Stokoe and colleagues, in a *Dictionary of American Sign Language* (Stokoe, Casterline, & Croneberg, 1965), referred to the different possible values for each element as cheremes, but this term is no longer widely used; instead, the sets of formational

> **cheremes** out-of-use term for basic units of gesture in sign languages; the distinct hand shapes, orientations, locations, movements, and facial expressions that make up individual signs are now referred to as phonemes in analogy to spoken language.

**Figure 11.1**    *All sign languages are articulated in the visual/gestural modality using combinations of hand shapes, orientations, locations, and movements, accompanied by facial expressions.*
*Source:* © Vladimir Mucibabic. Used under licence from Shutterstock.

elements are referred to as phonemes, because they are functionally equivalent to the phonemes of spoken languages (see Chapter 2). The manual gestures of a sign language are combined with different facial expressions and upper-body positions, which constitute the prosody of a sign language. In addition, mouthing (including movements of the tongue), head movements, patterns of eye gaze, and eyebrow height all serve to further modify signs.

The different elements of HOLME constitute a complex combinatorial system in which different elements are associated with different components of meaning. This combinatorial system constitutes the morphology of a sign language. Comparison of spoken and sign languages reveals striking differences in how information is packaged; more specifically, the visual–spatial modality permits multiple components of meaning to be packaged within a single sign. Whereas spoken languages impose a linear arrangement of words, sign languages allow different morphemes to be expressed simultaneously – for example, the motion element of a sign might express a verb while the hand shape and orientation elements simultaneously express a noun. Furthermore, the affixes (prefixes and suffixes) of spoken languages, marking features such as number (*dog* → *dogs*) or tense (*walk* → *walked*), are generally absent in sign languages. ASL has very rich derivational morphology (e.g. aspects of an event such as its frequency, intensity, duration or repetition are marked with specific morphemes), but lacks inflectional morphemes for marking number or tense. The syntax of sign languages like ASL and BSL uses a topic–comment structure in which background information (the topic) is often mentioned prior to the main clause of the sentence (the comment). Although nouns are frequently omitted in the main clauses of sentences, the order of the nouns in relation to the verb determines the meaning of the sentence: ASL uses Subject–Verb–Object word order (like English) whereas BSL uses Object–Subject–Verb word order.

In spoken languages, it is generally assumed that word meanings show an arbitrary relationship to form – for instance, the word for 'book' is *libro* in Spanish, *llyfr* in Welsh, *knjiga* in Croatian, and *kitap* in Turkish. In contrast, the lexicon of a sign language tends to exhibit a higher degree of iconicity: while spoken languages do contain onomatopoetic expressions (e.g. *crash*, *boom*) and sound symbolism (e.g. the [sl] sound in *slip*, *slide*, *slick*, and *slobber*) (see Chapter 4), the HOLME elements of signs are much more likely to resemble what they represent due to the affordances of gesture to symbolically render 'through pantomime' entities in the real world (Taub, 2001). Figure 11.2 shows the BSL signs for *camera* and *chocolate*, which differ in their degree of iconicity – no doubt, many individuals with no prior exposure to BSL could guess the meaning of the *camera* sign, but few would guess the meaning of *chocolate*. Iconicity seems to be beneficial for linguistic processing, because the meanings of iconic signs may be accessed more rapidly than the meanings of non-iconic signs (Thompson, Vinson, & Vigliocco, 2009, 2010). This suggests that the arbitrariness of form–meaning pairings in spoken languages is not a universal design feature of all languages, but rather reflects constraints imposed by the auditory/vocal modality. It is easier to produce a larger number of forms that bear resemblance to their referents in the visual/gestural modality.

**Figure 11.2**   *BSL signs for* camera *(left) and* chocolate *(right), which show differing degrees of iconicity/arbitrariness.*

*Source:* Photographs taken from supplementary videos to accompany: Vinson, D.P., Cormier, K., Denmark, T., Schembri, A. & Vigliocco, G. (2008). The British Sign Language (BSL) norms for age of acquisition, familiarity, and iconicity. *Behavior Research Methods*, 40, 1079–1087. Reprinted with kind permission of the authors.

Given these structural differences between spoken and sign languages, one might ask to what extent the neural mechanisms underlying language processing are affected by language modality. As described in Chapters 10 and 12, left-hemispheric regions on either side of the Sylvian fissure (the groove separating the frontal and temporal lobes of the brain) play an important role in processing spoken language. There is now overwhelming evidence that sign language processing engages the very same structures (see MacSweeney, Capek, Campbell, & Woll [2008] for a review), which lends support to the view that these regions are specialised for processing abstract linguistic structures and not just auditory stimuli. Native ASL signers show similar patterns of activation in temporal regions when producing names of things as is found in native speakers of a language like English (Emmorey, Grabowski, McCullough, Damasio, Ponto, Hichwa, et al., 2003); furthermore, there is no evidence that the production of iconic versus non-iconic signs invokes differential processing in naming tasks (Emmorey, Grabowski, McCullough, Damasio, Ponto, Hichwa, et al., 2004). However, ASL signers show greater activation of right-hemispheric regions when recognising high imagery signs than is evident for English speakers recognising high imagery words (Emmorey & Corina, 1993), even though signers and English speakers show similar patterns of left-hemispheric dominance for abstract signs and words. Moreover, in sentence comprehension, sign language processing results in greater bilateral activation than spoken language processing (Atkinson, Marshall, Woll, & Thacker, 2005; Bavelier, Corina, Jezzard, Clark, Karni, Lalwani et al., 1998; Neville, Bavelier, Corina, Rauschecker, Karni, Lalwani, et al., 1998). Taken together, the evidence suggests that the use of visual/gestural imagery in sign languages engages additional neural networks that are not required for spoken languages.

## 11.1.2   Acquisition of sign languages

Infants (hearing or deaf) born to deaf parents who are exposed to a sign language from birth show the normal progression of linguistic milestones – first babbling, then producing first words, followed by word combinations and increasingly complex combinatorial signing. Language development appears to proceed in essentially the same fashion regardless of the modality of the input (Bonvillian, 2000; Meier & Newport, 1990). Babies exposed to sign language babble in the manual modality (Petitto & Marentette, 1991). Such babbling is distinguishable from other hand movements made by infants by its rate (frequency) and its position relative to the body (Petitto et al., 2001, 2004). Petitto and her colleagues (2001, 2004) attached light-emitting diodes to the infants' hands, which allowed them to precisely track hand location and trajectory. Using this motion-tracking system, the researchers compared the rhythmic characteristics and spatial distribution of hand movements of three hearing infants born to deaf parents, who were exposed exclusively to one or two distinct sign languages (ASL and/or Langue des Signes Québécoise), with those of three hearing infants born to hearing parents, who were exposed to a spoken language (English or French) at ages 6, 10, and 12 months. Whereas all infants produced high-frequency hand movements positioned away from the body that are typical for infants of those ages, only sign-exposed babies additionally produced low-frequency hand movements in the area in front of the body (i.e. the space used for signing). The rhythm of these low-frequency hand movements corresponded to the rhythm in which sign syllables are typically produced. Although the rhythmic patterns of signed and spoken languages are quite different (Dolata, Davies, & McNeilage, 2008), the hand movements observed in sign-exposed infants demonstrate a general sensitivity to the rhythmic structure of the specific communication system infants are exposed to. This result confirmed Petitto and Marentette's (1991) earlier observations that sign-exposed deaf infants are able to extract the rhythmic patterns of the ambient language and reproduce them in the form of silent manual babble.

Longitudinal studies of hearing and deaf infants exposed to a sign language from birth indicate that first signs tend to appear at somewhat younger ages than first words appear in infants exposed to spoken languages (Bonvillian, Orlansky, & Novack, 1983; Folven & Bonvillian, 1991; Prinz & Prinz, 1979). For example, Bonvillian (2000) reported a mean age of 8.5 months for first signs in comparison to 11 to 14 months for first words. These findings suggest that the motor prerequisites for sign production are achieved at earlier ages than those required for speech, perhaps because the motor requirements for signing are somewhat less complex than those required for articulation. Still, like hearing infants producing their first spoken words, sign-exposed infants make 'articulation' errors. When signs were examined for the elements of hand shape, location, and movement ('HLM' of HOLME), 5- to 18-month-old infants were most accurate in producing signs in the correct locations, and were least accurate in producing the correct hand shapes (Bonvillian & Siedlecki, 2000). Interestingly, a similar pattern has been observed for hearing infants' perception of ASL signs, with 6- and 10-month-olds showing accurate discrimination of sign locations and the signer's facial expressions, while failing to discriminate hand shapes and movements (Wilbourn & Casasola, 2007). Thus, despite their early production of signs, infants require considerable time to master the various elements that distinguish one sign from another and produce many forms that are not fully accurate. Furthermore, when Folven and Bonvillian (1991) focused on signs that were referential (i.e., names for things), they no longer found an advantage for sign-exposed babies relative to their peers; this suggests that the conceptual prerequisites for naming do not vary as a function of language modality (see Chapter 3). Examination of later milestones (production of sign combinations and more complex grammatical constructions) also fails to uncover any substantive difference in the time course of sign language and spoken language development (Meier & Newport, 1990).

### 11.1.3   Age of exposure to sign language and language acquisition

Because the overwhelming majority of deaf infants are born to hearing parents who may have little or no knowledge about sign languages, there is a great deal of variation in the age at which deaf individuals are first exposed to a sign language. This provides a unique opportunity to study the effect of age of exposure on language learning and processing. Researchers have compared native signers (exposed to a sign language from birth) with late signers (typically exposed at age 10 years or later). The main conclusion across many studies is that fluency in production and comprehension of a sign language depends on the age of exposure to the language, rather than the number of years of its use as a primary means of communication. In other words, the processing differences between native and late signers persist even if the late signers have used a sign language daily for decades, and are not fluent in a spoken language (Mayberry, 2007; Newport, 1990). Age of exposure impacts sign language acquisition and processing at all levels: prosodic, phonological, lexical, morphological, and syntactic. Here we briefly summarise some of the relevant findings.

With respect to prosody, the utterances produced by native signers are often judged to be more rhythmic than those of late signers, with late signers failing to produce some of the rhythmic patterns that mark units of discourse (Braem, 1999). At the phonemic level, early and late signers differ in their sensitivity to the minimal contrasts (e.g. in the amount of finger spreading) that distinguish signs (Best, Mathur, Miranda, & Lillo-Martin, 2010). However, not all aspects of sign perception are affected by age of exposure – for example, facial expressions distinguishing speech acts, such as questions, are perceived similarly by early and late signers (Campbell, Woll, Benson, & Wallace, 1999). With respect to vocabulary, late signers are slower to identify signs than their native-signing peers (Emmorey & Corina, 1990). Like children with language impairments (see Chapter 10), late signers are more likely to substitute a word with a general meaning under circumstances where a word with a more specific meaning is desired. Late signers are also more likely to make slips-of-the-hand errors, where they erroneously produce a sign that is visually similar to the intended target (Mayberry & Fischer, 1989; Mayberry & Eichen, 1991).

More striking effects of age of exposure have been observed for grammatical processing. Several studies have used a grammaticality judgement paradigm to assess morphological and syntactic proficiency in signers as a function of their age of exposure to sign (e.g. Boudreault & Mayberry, 2006; Emmorey, Bellugi, Friederici, & Horn, 1995; Newport, 1990): these studies have documented near chance levels of performance for late signers for some of the more complex constructions of American Sign Language (ASL). For example, some ASL verbs (e.g. GIVE, ASK) require that signs be produced with hand movements from one spatial position to another – this movement is necessary to indicate who did what to whom. When verbs were shown with incorrect morphology (e.g. use of hand orientation, rather than movement to indicate who performed the action), native signers were able to detect the errors, whereas late signers were not (Emmorey et al., 1995).

Importantly, early exposure to a sign language confers an advantage for children in learning a spoken language: native signers surpass their late-signing peers in learning the vocabulary and grammar of the spoken language, and they are more sensitive to grammatical errors (Brasel & Quigley, 1977; Mayberry & Lock, 2003). They also show greater facility in learning to read and write (Padden & Ramsey, 2000; Singleton, Morgan, DiGello, Wiles, & Rivers, 2004; Strong & Prinz, 1997, 2000). Indeed, proficiency in ASL has been shown to predict English reading skills even after effects of print exposure, non-verbal intelligence, and comprehension of manually coded English are removed (Chamberlain & Mayberry, 2008). (Manually coded English refers to ways of rendering the English language through a variety of manual gestures, or through finger-spelling or hand signs that code English phonemes.) In this study, the deaf adults with high ASL proficiency obtained English reading skills at a post secondary-school level, whereas the deaf adults with low ASL proficiency read at about the level of an average 9-year-old.

> **manually coded English** a system for rendering English through manual gestures; manually coded English approximates the grammar of English, and is structurally unrelated to any sign language (e.g. American Sign Language, British Sign Language).

These results are perhaps surprising, given that most deaf children born to hearing parents are strongly encouraged from birth to learn a spoken language (e.g. through lip-reading), whereas native-signing deaf children born to deaf parents are exposed to a spoken language only later, at the time they enter school. The advantage for native signers in acquiring a spoken language is very strong evidence against the common misconception that sign language exposure impedes a deaf child's acquisition of a spoken language. Native-signing deaf children often become fluent bilinguals in both a sign language and a spoken language, whereas late-signing deaf children fail to achieve high levels of proficiency in either language (Mayberry, 2007; Newport, 1990). Because most deaf children born to hearing parents are unable to learn a spoken language as a first language, they are apt to suffer the negative consequences of prolonged linguistic isolation. Failure to acquire a first language in childhood profoundly affects all subsequent language learning, irrespective of the modality of language input (Mayberry, Lock, & Kazmi, 2002). Indeed, even adults who lose their hearing later in life (i.e. after having acquired a spoken language as children) are more successful in acquiring a sign language than late signers who are born deaf and are not exposed to any language input during childhood (Mayberry, 1993). This suggests that the neural plasticity required for effective language learning and processing diminishes when language input is absent during infancy and early childhood – that is, exposure to some form of natural language input must be provided during a critical period for the neural systems supporting language to properly develop (see Chapter 12 for further discussion). Thus, a necessary goal of public health education is to inform parents of deaf infants of the great importance of very early access to a sign language for their child's social, emotional, and cognitive well being.

## 11.1.4    Age of exposure to sign language and cognitive development

Early exposure to a sign language in deaf children is not just important for the acquisition of language, but for cognitive development in general. The most compelling evidence for the importance of early exposure to language in cognitive development comes from studies of the development of a Theory of Mind. From the toddler years through middle childhood, children come to understand the role of mental states (e.g. beliefs, desires, attitudes, emotions, and intentions) in human behaviour. Children are thought to achieve understanding of the mental lives of people by participating in conversational exchanges of thoughts, feelings, and points of view (Carpendale & Lewis, 2004; Nelson, 1996, 2007); see Chapter 8 for a description of the relationship between Theory of Mind development and various measures of language development such as children's vocabulary size, syntactic complexity, and conversational skills. Not surprisingly, children with Specific Language Impairment (SLI) show poor performance on Theory of Mind tasks relative to their typical peers (Farrant, Fletcher, & Mayberry, 2006; Farrar, Johnson, Tompkins, Easters, Zelisis-Medus, & Benigno, 2009); the observed delays in Theory of Mind development in Specific Language Impairment appear to be reflective of more general deficits in the area of pragmatics (see Chapter 10).

It is now well established that late-signing deaf children are severely delayed in the development of Theory of Mind relative to native-signing deaf children, as well as hearing children (e.g. Jackson, 2001; Peterson & Siegal, 1995, 1998, 1999; Peterson & Slaughter, 2006; Russell, Hosie, Gray, Scott, Hunter, Banks, et al., 1998). Deaf children exposed to a sign language from birth show apparently normal development of Theory of Mind, and might even outperform hearing children on some tasks (Courtin, 2000; Courtin & Melot, 2005). Late signers' poor performance across a wide range of Theory of Mind, tasks appears to be due to their late exposure to language, rather than to deficits in vocabulary or syntax, or in other, more general, aspects of cognition (Meristo, Falkman, Hjelmquist, Tedoldi, Surian, & Siegal, 2007; Meristo & Hjelmquist, 2009). Thus, even when older late-signing deaf children were matched with younger native signers on their comprehension of (British) Sign Language, the younger native signers still outperformed the late signers on Theory of Mind tasks (Woolfe, Want, & Siegal, 2002). Nevertheless, in this study, Theory of Mind task performance remained correlated with language proficiency for the late-signing children. Interestingly, in a recent study of adult users of Nicaraguan Sign Language, significant improvements were observed in Theory of Mind task performance over a 2-year period as users acquired the signs for various mental states (Pyers & Senghas, 2009). Additional evidence that early language exposure is critical to Theory of Mind development comes from cochlear implant users: given the observed variability in language-learning outcomes for children with cochlear implants (see Section 11.3.1), we would expect that Theory of Mind development would also be variable. Indeed, across cochlear implant users, Theory of Mind performance is strongly correlated with general language measures such as the rate of language development, syntactic proficiency, and knowledge of mental state terms (Macaulay & Ford, 2006; Peterson, 2004; Remmel & Peters, 2009). In cochlear implant users with good spoken language skills, performance on Theory of Mind tasks tends to be comparable to children with normal hearing.

Late-signing deaf children have been reported to show other cognitive effects of linguistic deprivation relative to their peers, such as greater impulsivity and lesser control of attention (Harris, 1978; O'Brien, 1987; Parasnis, Samar, & Berent, 2003), reduced working memory capacity (Krakow & Hanson, 1985; Logan, Maybery, & Fletcher, 1996), and poor academic skills and achievement (Antia, Jones, Reed, & Kreimeyer, 2009; Marschark, 2003; Traxler, 2000; Vernon & Koh, 1971). Deaf children are reported to have deficits in executive functioning – in their capacity to control, monitor, and self-regulate behaviour during problem-solving activities (Figueras,

Edwards, & Langdon, 2008; Remine, Care, & Brown, 2008); these deficits correlate with the extent of their language impairment. Lack of early exposure to a language also impacts the development of numerical cognition: deaf children tend to lag behind their peers in acquiring numerical concepts (e.g. fractions), arithmetic, and measurement skills (Bull, 2008); as adults they often show deficits in numerical estimation and mathematical reasoning tasks (Bull, Marschark, Sapere, Davidson, Murphy, & Nordmann, 2011) and are slower in making numerical judgements than hearing adults (Bull, Marschark, & Blatto-Vallee, 2005). These findings complement the cross-linguistic research described in Chapter 8, which suggests that language plays a formative role in the construction of certain numerical concepts, such as the use of number words for the exact enumeration of large quantities.

# 11.2  HOW DOES PARTIAL RESTORATION OF HEARING AFFECT LANGUAGE DEVELOPMENT?

For many hearing parents, the practical challenges of providing a deaf infant with a language-rich environment have led them to explore cochlear implants as an alternative solution. With advances in medical technology, cochlear implants offer the promise of a cure for deafness – at the present time, there is mounting evidence that cochlear implants provided in the first year of life can successfully restore a partial sense of hearing. Here we briefly describe the functioning of these devices, and the factors that are predictive of their success in the treatment of deafness.

## 11.2.1  The mechanics of cochlear implants

Over the past several decades, major technological advances have been made in the manufacture of cochlear implant (CI) devices that provide a partial sense of hearing to deaf individuals who have a functioning auditory nerve. Figure 11.3 illustrates a CI device and

> **auditory nerve** nerve that connects the cochlea with the brain.

its major components; it should be noted that the various external components have become much smaller in recent years due to advances in micro-technology. In modern CI devices, the external parts fit into a small hearing-aid-sized unit worn behind the ear, and development is underway for devices that have no external parts.

As shown in the figure, CI devices have an external part that consists of a microphone, a sound processor, and a transmitter. The external components collect the sound waves and convert them into a series of radio-frequency digital signals that are transmitted through intact skin to the internal components of the device.

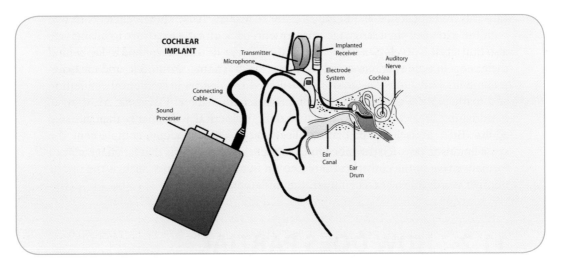

**Figure 11.3**   *External and internal components of a cochlear implant device.*

*Source:* Original artwork by Michael Almodovar.

**cochlea** a spiral-shaped structure in the inner ear containing hair cells that convert sound waves into neural impulses to be transmitted to the brain.

The internal receiver further processes the signals and conveys the information through a multi-channel electrode system that is inserted into the cochlea at a depth of 22 to 30 mm; this electrode array electrically stimulates the spiral ganglion cells of the auditory nerve. As in typical hearing individuals, these neural impulses are relayed via the thalamus to the primary auditory cortex, located in the temporal lobes of the brain, and are perceived as sound (see Chapter 12). Although the sound processors of CI devices have been specifically designed to convey the frequencies (pitches) of sound most important for speech to be intelligible, the speech input to CI users remains acoustically degraded relative to normal speech. Thus, despite the fact that the auditory system appears to be well adapted to cope with temporally and spectrally degraded speech (Loizou, Dorman, & Tu, 1999), CIs tend to perform best under quiet listening conditions (Friesen, Shannon, Baskent, & Wang, 2001). Fortunately, as even smaller devices using nano-technology offer enormous potential to increase the numbers of different frequencies of sound that can be transmit-

**primary auditory cortex** comprises Heschl's gyrus, which makes up the posterior part of the superior temporal gyrus in the temporal lobe; this area is involved in processing the basic features of sound including pitch, volume, and timing.

ted simultaneously (Clark, 2009), the capabilities of CI devices to restore hearing are likely to improve markedly in the years to come.

Starting in the 1980s, physicians began to use CIs to restore hearing in adults. These early devices were successfully used with adults who had become deaf later in life, that is, after they had already acquired language, but they were less successful in supporting speech perception in congenitally deaf adults (Eddington, 1980; Wilson, Finley, Lawson, Wolford, Eddington, & Rabinowitz, 1991; Teoh, Pisoni, & Miyamoto, 2004). Starting in the 1990s, surgeons began implanting CIs in young congenitally deaf children. The overwhelming majority of child CI users were able to successfully learn a spoken language based on auditory input (Svirsky, Robbins, Kirk, Pisoni, &

Miyamoto, 2000). Thus, the limited success of CIs in providing adequate hearing in older recipients appears to be due to the closure of a critical period for auditory learning; during the critical period, auditory stimulation must be present for the central auditory processing pathways to develop normally (Sharma, Nash, & Dorman, 2009). It is now becoming increasingly common for CIs to be implanted in infants during the first year of life, usually when the infant is between 7 and 12 months old. Also, because they provide better sound localisation, bilateral CIs are gaining in popularity.

Many CI users are able to communicate using a spoken language without the aid of sign language or lip-reading. A commonly used measure of how well CI users perceive speech is the open-set test. This type of test requires the CI user to recognise speech in the absence of any visual cues (i.e. similarly to what is required to perceive speech over the telephone or radio). Open-set word recognition can be tested by embedding words in sentences, or by presenting lists of unrelated words. Even with the demanding task of identifying unrelated words without visual cues, CI users implanted during early childhood show high rates of success (Waltzman, Cohen, Gomolin, Green, Shapiro, Hoffman, et al., 1997). A growing body of research has examined individual differences in speech perception and production outcomes for children as a function of pre-implantation hearing ability, length of CI use, mode of communication post-surgery, and age of implantation (Peterson, Pisoni, & Miyamoto, 2010). Children who have some residual hearing at the time of surgery have better outcomes than children with lesser hearing ability, and speech processing abilities tend to improve substantially over the initial months of CI use. Children who exclusively use oral communication during rehabilitation also tend to fare better than children using both oral communication and sign language.

> **open-set test** a test used to assess spoken word recognition in the absence of contextual cues.

However, the most important variable related to language-learning outcomes is the age of implantation, which is probably due to the limited potential for the auditory cortex to reorganise in response to auditory stimulation in older individuals (for a more detailed discussion of changes in brain plasticity, see Chapter 12). Early implantation thus allows for more normal neural development of the auditory processing pathways (Schauwers, Govaerts, & Gillis, 2005). Children who receive their implants before 3 years of age have significantly better speech recognition than children with later implantation, and infants implanted before 12 months of age typically fare even better (Colletti, Carner, Miorelli, Guida, Colletti, & Fiorino, 2005; Miyamoto, Houston, & Bergeson, 2005; Van Deun, van Wieringen, Scherf, Deggouj, Desloovere, Offeciers, et al., 2010). Infants implanted between 6 and 12 months of age show spoken word recognition abilities similar to infants with normal hearing (Miyamoto et al., 2005); however, other research suggests that young CI users may process spoken words at a slower rate than their peers (Grieco-Colub, Saffran, & Litowsky, 2009). With bilateral cochlear implants, most children are able to achieve above-chance accuracy in sound localisation, but fare better if their first implant occurred prior to 2 year of age (Van Deun et al., 2010). Like adults, children implanted at 12 years of age or older tend to have very limited success with their implants (Teoh et al., 2004).

With respect to learning to speak, young CI users may require as little as a month of auditory experience before they begin to babble (Schauwers, Gillis, Daemers, De Beukelaer, De Ceulaer, Yperman, et al., 2004); their babble shows normal characteristics, but with somewhat less syllable variation than in typical children (Schauwers, Gillis, & Govaerts, 2008). With respect to speech intonation (speech melody), results again show a normal developmental progression in young CI users, with better outcomes for those implanted at younger ages (Snow & Ertmer, 2009). In another study (Ertmer & Inniger, 2009), two young CI users (implanted before age 2) were observed to progress from babbling to spoken word production to combining words with fewer intervening months than (younger) hearing children. Such findings of rapid gains in speech production indicate that young children with CIs might have the potential to fully catch up with their peers once their hearing is restored.

Taken together, the findings presented so far suggest that for deaf people to acquire a fully functioning communication system, they must be exposed to language early in life. Regardless of whether a family opts for or against a cochlear implant for a deaf child, the consensus in the field is that intervention should begin in infancy for the child to have the most positive language-learning outcome. This can mean either early exposure to signs through a signing community, or early implantation of a cochlear device. Delays in exposure to a first language impact not only language development, but other aspects of social and cognitive development as well. These pervasive negative effects associated with delays in exposure to language among the deaf highlight the importance of early detection of deafness (preferably at birth) and the necessity of prompt treatment – in the form of adequate exposure to a sign language from infancy, and early cochlear implantation if so desired.

## 11.2.2    The importance of sound

**Auditory Scaffolding Hypothesis** hypothesis that exposure to sound (i.e. through spoken language) supports the ability to learn sequential information.

It has been suggested recently that exposure to a spoken language may be important for the ability to fully and efficiently process temporal sequences. Conway, Pisoni, and Kronenberger (2009) proposed the Auditory Scaffolding Hypothesis. This hypothesis is based on two lines of evidence: an auditory modality advantage for processing temporal sequences among hearing adults and a disadvantage in sequencing tasks for congenitally deaf individuals who experience delays in exposure to auditory stimulation (see Methodology Box 11.1).

Among hearing adults, sequential patterns of sounds are learned more accurately than sequences of images or tactile sensations. Conway and Christiansen (2005) created simple sequences using an artificial grammar, the elements of which could be presented either in the auditory modality (as a series of sounds), in the visual modality (as a series of images), or in the tactile modality (as a series of pulses presented to one's fingertips). After a learning phase, adult participants were given a grammaticality judgement task asking them to decide which sequences were permissible ones and which sequences were not. Accuracy in making grammaticality judgements was highest in the group that had learned the grammar from sequences of sounds. Moreover, learning of auditory sequences was less affected when the stimuli were presented at a faster rate (Conway & Christiansen, 2009). Thus, sequences seem to be learned and processed most reliably when presented in the auditory modality. This

# METHODOLOGY BOX 11.1    ASSESSING SEQUENCE LEARNING ABILITIES

From studies of word segmentation in infants to studies of grammatical processing in children with Specific Language Impairment, researchers have found that implicit learning of sequences plays a crucial role in language development. We will describe two paradigms that are frequently used to examine statistical learning of sequences of elements: the artificial grammar learning (AGL) task and the serial reaction time (SRT) task. It is important to note here that the elements may be presented in any modality: for example, they can be letters or coloured squares (visual modality), spoken syllables or tones (auditory modality), or finger-tip pulses (tactile modality).

In the AGL task, participants are exposed to strings of elements that were generated by a set of rules. In classical studies (e.g. Reber, 1967, 1989), participants viewed strings of letters generated by a finite-state grammar (see Figure 11.4). After the exposure phase, they were given a grammaticity judgement task in which novel sequences of letters were presented, some of which followed the rules of the finite state grammar, and some of which did not. The main finding, which has been replicated numerous times, was that most adults could distinguish between the grammatically correct and incorrect sequences at rates significantly above chance, although they rarely if ever could explicitly state the underlying rules.

**serial reaction time (SRT) task** a reaction time measure of implicit, procedural learning; participants are asked to respond as quickly as possible to a non-random sequence of spatial stimuli by button press; the reaction time decrease over blocks of trials is used as a measure of learning.

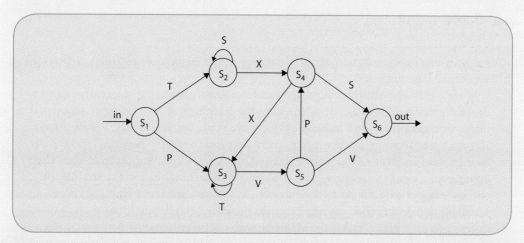

**Figure 11.4**  *Schematic diagram of a finite-state grammar used to generate letter strings by following any path from the initial state $S_1$ to the final state $S_6$. For example, this grammar could create strings like TSSXS or PTTTVPXVV, etc.*

*Source:* Redrawn from Reber, A.S. (1989). *Journal of Experimental Psychology: General, 118(3)*, 219–235, with permission from APA.

*(Continued)*

The basic structure of the AGL task (exposure phase followed by presentation of novel grammatical and ungrammatical test sequences) has been adapted for use with children, including infants; this paradigm has been used with syllable and tone stimuli in many studies utilising a variety of grammatical rules – for example, Saffran et al. (1996) discussed in Chapter 2; Gómez (2000), Gómez and Gerken (1999) discussed in Chapter 5; Evans, Saffran, and Robe-Torres (2009), Plante, Gómez, and Gerken (2002) discussed in Chapter 10.

In the SRT task, participants are exposed to a series of elements (typically on a computer screen) and are asked to touch each element as it appears; for example, the stimuli might be coloured squares that appear at different locations on a touch screen. Unbeknownst to the participant, the sequence of elements is generated by an underlying set of rules. To test learning, reaction times (RTs) are measured over blocks of trials. As participants implicitly learn the rules, their RTs to respond to each element in the series decrease. Overall learning is assessed by comparing RTs for blocks of trials following the trained rules with RTs for blocks of trials in random order. The SRT task has been used with visual stimuli (e.g. coloured squares) to document modality-general deficits in sequence learning in individuals with SLI – for example, Lum, Gelgic, and Conti-Ramsden (2010), Tomblin, Mainela-Arnold, and Zhang (2007) discussed in Chapter 10. Recently, the SRT task has been adapted to present language stimuli (written syllables) generated by an artificial grammar (Misyak, Christiansen, & Tomblin, 2010), but this task version has yet to be tested with children. In this task variant, participants hear sequences of syllables generated by an artificial grammar and must touch the corresponding written words on the touch screen as quickly as possible. As in other SRT tasks, learning is calculated as the RT difference for syllable strings that followed the grammatical rules, versus syllable strings that were randomly generated.

suggests that experience with spoken language might facilitate one's ability to process sequential information.

If exposure to spoken language facilitates sequential processing, then early auditory deprivation should result in impairment in the learning and processing of sequential information. Conway and colleagues (Conway et al., 2009; Conway, Pisoni, Anaya, Karpicke, & Henning, 2010) tested 5- to 10-year-old children who were congenitally deaf but had received CIs to restore hearing between 10 and 39 months of age. They completed a motor sequencing task (successively touching their index, middle, ring, and little finger with the tip of their thumb) as well as a sequence-learning task using visual input (sequences of coloured squares presented at different locations on a computer screen). In both tasks, the children with cochlear implants performed worse than age-matched children with normal hearing. This suggests that early auditory deprivation due to deafness can hinder the development of non-linguistic temporal processing and sequencing skills.

The relationship between sound processing and general sequencing skills may come about for two reasons. First, sound may be more likely to carry higher-order information about sequential patterns than other modalities. In other words, in our environment, relevant patterns of temporal change may occur more frequently in sound than in visual scenes or tactile stimuli. If exposure to sound is diminished then opportunities for learning about temporal sequence are lost. Second, listening to and producing spoken language may provide opportunities for vocally rehearsing temporal sequences. Vocal rehearsal, in turn, may strengthen the ability to learn and process temporal sequences. Both of these factors probably play a role in how exposure to the sound patterns of language strengthens cognitive processes involved in encoding, learning, and manipulating information inherent in temporal sequences. However, it remains unclear whether it is early exposure to language per se or early exposure to spoken language that is responsible for bootstrapping sequence learning. To date, no studies have been conducted to examine the role of language modality in sequence learning. Thus, we do not know whether children exposed to a sign language from birth are superior to late-signing children in their temporal processing, nor do we know whether native-signing children differ from native-speaking children in non-linguistic temporal processing and sequence learning. Such studies are crucial for ascertaining what aspects of language acquisition impact on how people process temporal sequences.

# 11.3 CAN DEAF CHILDREN CREATE THEIR OWN COMMUNICATION SYSTEMS?

Deaf children born to hearing parents are no less motivated to communicate with their caregivers and to participate in family life than hearing children. In this section we explore how deaf children cope with the challenges of communicating with others in the absence of an accessible language. In Chapter 3 we described how hearing infants use **symbolic gestures** at the time they start producing their first words, and how such gestures play a supportive role as toddlers make the transition to multi-word speech. Here we explore how gesture use becomes more elaborate and systematic in deaf children who rely on their gestures to carry the full burden of conveying their communicative intentions.

## 11.3.1 *Gestural communication in isolated deaf children*

Explorations of how isolated deaf children communicate with others have provided important insights into the inherent abilities of children to create systems of communication in the absence of linguistic input. It is often assumed that the linguistic structures produced by young children are largely copied from others; that children rapidly converge on the linguistic patterns in the ambient language and reproduce them in their own attempts at communication. For isolated deaf children, there is no ambient language from which to extract and reproduce patterns – under such circumstances, do children create utterances that are linguistically complex and systematic?

The answer to this question is yes. Isolated children interact socially with their caregivers and family members, and communicate with them through a system of manual gestures called home sign (Goldin-Meadow, 2003). In home sign, everyday activity-related movements become the basis for communicative signs – for example, the hand-shape gesture associated with a specific object (e.g. a cup, a toothbrush) comes to stand for the object or an associated action. Additionally, other gestures such as pointing are recruited to pick out specific entities relevant to the communicated message – for example, to request a drink, the child might make a 'cup' hand shape accompanied by a tilting motion towards the mouth to indicate drinking, with a pointing gesture to self to make the request. These symbolic gestures – just like the ones used by hearing children (see Chapter 3) – are used to refer to things in the world; they comprise the basic lexical building blocks of home sign. The gesture combinations of home sign are similar to those that hearing individuals produce when required to convey a message without using language – for example, travellers will use similar gestures to make simple requests (e.g. to order a coffee and a pastry) when they do not speak the language of the community they are visiting. Importantly, such discrete sequences of gestures do not normally accompany speech, which tends to be accompanied by emphatic movements that are more continuous in nature. Because hearing parents of deaf children usually speak to their children (indeed, they usually want their children to learn to lip-read), their gesturing tends to have a different quality to that of their children. The mismatch between the gestural input and the home sign produced by isolated deaf children suggests that the gestural input need not be language-like in order to engage some of the child's language acquisition mechanisms, even if they will not lead to full linguistic competence.

Research on the home sign systems created by isolated deaf children and adults in the United States, China, and Nicaragua (e.g. Coppola & Newport, 2005; Goldin-Meadow & Mylander, 1998; Goldin-Meadow, Mylander, & Franklin, 2007) has uncovered some striking similarities amongst the home sign systems of children, regardless of culture, and some striking dissimilarities to the spoken languages of the respective communities (English, Mandarin Chinese, and Spanish). In each home sign system, researchers have observed consistency in the ordering of gestures used in gesture combinations; these word-order biases are reminiscent of the consistent word-order patterns observed in the **word-specific formulae** of young hearing children who are producing their very first word combinations (see Chapter 5). There is evidence that deaf children construct grammatical categories of gestures – making a broad distinction between predicates (properties, actions, relationships) and their arguments (the entities having those properties, actions, relationships). This suggests that home sign systems contain gestures that function as verbs and other gestures that function as nouns (Goldin-Meadow, Butcher, Mylander, & Dodge, 1994). Home signers systematically vary the order of gestures in accordance with their grammatical roles. For example, Goldin-Meadow and Mylander (1998) observed the gesture combinations of eight isolated deaf children and their mothers (four American, four Chinese) and found the dyads in both cultures to convey messages in gesture sentences rather than single gestures. They reported that, in sentences containing nouns and verbs, all the children were biased to order their gestures in a consistent way. For an intransitive sentence (e.g. to express the meaning 'the mouse goes in the hole'), children usually produced the gesture for the noun ('mouse') before the verb ('go'). For a transitive sentence (e.g. to express the meaning 'the mouse eats the cheese'), children usually produced the direct object ('cheese') before the verb ('eats'), and often omitted the subject ('mouse'), thus producing Object–Verb word order that contrasts with the Subject–Verb–Object word order of English. In contrast to their children, the mothers did not order their gestures in a consistent way, which confirms that the children were not merely imitating their mothers. Unfortunately, we cannot determine whether mothers failed to mark grammatical distinctions in their gesture combinations due to their reliance on a spoken language as a primary means of communication, or due to maturational factors that prevented them from using gestures as flexibly as their young children. Ideally, one should examine the home sign produced by the younger siblings of isolated deaf children for grammatical patterns, which would support the maturational account.

> **gesture sentences** sequences of gestures in the home sign produced by isolated deaf children; these convey meanings similar to the early word combinations of hearing children.

Another study (Coppola & Newport, 2005) examined the gesture combinations of isolated deaf adults in Nicaragua; these adults had used home sign their entire lives, as they had never been exposed to a sign language and were unable to learn the Spanish spoken in their communities. Coppola and Newport asked the deaf adults to describe in home sign a large number of video clips depicting different sorts of events (e.g. running, kissing, seeing, being happy). To encourage the adults to produce complete utterances, the researchers had a family member fluent in the home sign (i.e. the conversational partner) select from an array of four pictures for each event the one corresponding to the gestured description. Across their gesture sentences, each deaf adult was consistent in their grammatical marking of the sentence subject. That is, in describing the videos for 'a man is happy', 'a woman is running', and 'a rug is flapping', deaf adults consistently produced the gesture for 'man', 'woman', or 'rug' before producing the gesture for the verb. Similar results were obtained for transitive sentences and for larger units of discourse (i.e. multiple sentence sets), which suggest that the deaf adults' grammatical categories were quite abstract.

Home sign systems display morphological complexity as well as grammatical patterns. Goldin-Meadow and her colleagues (Goldin-Meadow, Mylander, & Butcher, 1995; Goldin-Meadow et al., 2007) examined the individual gestures of the American and Chinese mother–child dyads for evidence of morphological structure. Each gesture was classified in accordance with the use of specific hand shapes and types of movement. For each feature coded (e.g. placement of thumb relative to fingers, palm shape, hand breadth), both the children and their mothers were observed to produce parametric variations in home signs that were associated with specific components of meaning (e.g. the length, diameter, and shape of the handled object). By combining different hand shapes with different types of movement, the children created a generative system of gestures that allowed them to flexibly create new meanings as needed. The distinctions between morphemes observed in the individual children were not traceable to their mothers' gestures, which suggests that isolated deaf children go beyond the input to create combinatorial systems. Other studies indicate that isolated deaf children use home sign to refer to objects that are not physically present (Butcher, Mylander, & Goldin-Meadow, 1991), and they produce gesture sentences that refer to generic categories and their properties – for example, to express meanings such as 'birds fly' (Goldin-Meadow, Gelman, & Mylander, 2005). These findings suggest that isolated deaf children retain an ability to communicate about events beyond the immediate here-and-now, and to make inductive generalisations about events in the world. Although home sign systems never have the structural complexity or large vocabularies of natural languages, these systems are clearly language-like. It seems that internal standards of well-formedness, basic grammatical categories, and conceptual distinctions emerge spontaneously in self-generated communication systems when children have sufficient time to create them (Singleton, Morford, & Goldin-Meadow, 1993).

## 11.3.2   Creation of sign language

Over the past half century, researchers have had the opportunity to study the emergence of two new sign languages: Nicaraguan Sign Language, which arose in the late 1970s in Nicaragua (Senghas, 2003; Senghas, Senghas, & Pyers, 2005), and Al-Sayyid Bedouin Sign Language, which arose in the 1930s in the Negev region of present-day Israel (Sandler, Meir, Padden, & Aronoff, 2005; Senghas, 2005). These two new languages provide important information regarding what sorts of factors promote the growth of a lexicon and the creation of more systematic ways of marking grammatical relationships in utterances – in effect, how lexical, morphological, and syntactic complexity is constructed over the span of a few generations. The study of these indigenous sign languages suggests that language structures emerge spontaneously from self-organising negotiations of meaning within communities of speakers. The fact that the home sign used by individual deaf children within their families never obtains the complexity of a natural language supports the view that there must be extensive intergeneration exchanges of information for home signs to be taken up as the words of a new language and for them to be used in systematic ways to build an open-ended set of possible utterances. Thus, for a sign language to emerge, there must be a sufficient number of individuals within a generation using gesture as a primary means of communication. In Nicaragua, this occurred when the government created an elementary school for deaf children and a vocational school for deaf adolescents, where sizeable cohorts of deaf individuals congregated outside school hours and communicated using their respective home signs. Even though the Nicaraguan schools were not conducting classes in a sign language (i.e. they were using oralist methods to teach children to lip-read and to read and write in Spanish), the social nexus was sufficiently robust for the various home signs used by individuals to become widely used – to become the conventional ways of referring to things in the world within the community of users of Nicaraguan Sign Language. Importantly, from the 1990s the elementary school began to employ deaf adults as teaching assistants and translators within the classrooms; these assistants provided Nicaraguan Sign Language: input to young children, who then acquired it as their first language: see Senghas et al. (2005) for further details.

In the Negev, hereditary deafness within a close-knit community created a situation in which many families had deaf family members, deaf individuals fully participated in community life, and deaf and hearing members of the community frequently married one another (Sandler et al., 2005). These factors created sufficient opportunities for the home signs created by individuals to spread through contact within extended families. Interestingly, recent experimental studies of the evolution of human communication systems also indicates that horizontal transactions within a generation are crucial for the convergence of forms and meanings – in effect, for a group of users to obtain agreement that a particular form is to be used to convey a particular meaning across various communicative situations (Fay, Garrod, Roberts, & Swoboda, 2010). In the experimental studies, individuals who were required to communicate over successive turns with different individuals within the group rapidly converged on more formal systems that enabled all members of the group to communicate with one another. In contrast, isolated pairs of individuals who were required to communicate only with each other communicated in idiosyncratic ways – that is, they created communication systems analogous to home sign. This suggests that linguistic conventions result from a social collaborative process involving multiple speakers interacting with multiple partners on multiple occasions.

The second factor that appears to be critical for language genesis is for new generations (or cohorts) to adopt the communication system as children and to streamline and systematise its features over successive generations (McWhorter, 1997). Young children's capacity to systematise noisy input to construct linguistic generalisations has been demonstrated both in naturalistic studies and experimentally. An important case study (Singleton & Newport, 2004) examined the sign language development of a deaf child (Simon) exposed to ASL from birth by his deaf parents, who had both acquired ASL after childhood. Despite the fact that both his parents were late signers who inconsistently produced morphological forms and made grammatical errors, Simon's production of ASL was superior to his parents and was equivalent to that of children exposed to input from native signers. That is, Simon seemed to construct abstract grammatical rules that guided his production of ASL despite the inaccuracies and noisy input he received from his parents. Children's ability to regularise inconsistent patterns (i.e. to maximise central tendencies) in linguistic input has been confirmed in experimental studies using artificial language stimuli (Hudson Kam & Newport, 2005; see Chapter 1), and in observations of the signing produced by successive cohorts of children learning Nicaraguan Sign Language (Senghas & Coppola, 2001; Senghas, Kita, & Ozyurek, 2004). In Nicaragua, each successive generation modified the current usage and linguistic practices they encountered in the community to make them more systematic – for example, by segmenting holistic gestures into component morphemes that are recombined in systematic ways, and by creating new devices for indicating co-reference (Senghas & Coppola, 2001; Senghas et al., 2004). Whereas the signing of the initial cohorts of students was characterised by redundant expressions and frequent clarifications of meaning, over time this redundancy was drastically reduced (Senghas et al., 2005). Thus, over successive generations, younger users of Nicaraguan Sign Language enriched the grammar in ways that supported more precise, efficient, and flexible communication, and made the language more systematic. Although older learners continued to add words to their vocabularies after adolescence, their grammatical systems tended to become entrenched, and they usually failed to adopt the modifications created by their younger peers. These observations suggest that the young learners were responsible for the structural reorganisation of Nicaraguan Sign Language over time, whereas the older generations have played the crucial role of creating a stable social order that provides children with the necessary language input.

If we treat the emergence of sign languages as a test case that may provide a glimpse on how languages in general may have evolved, then these findings suggest that the cognitive constraints and requirements of child learners may play an important role in the emergence of language.

## SUMMARY

- **Many congenitally deaf individuals acquire a sign language used by the surrounding deaf community. Sign languages have developed naturally in generations of deaf individuals and bear all the hallmarks of natural languages. Sign languages recruit the same neural substrate in the brain as spoken languages, but also make use of additional neural circuits related to visual and spatial processing.**

- **Children who are exposed to sign language from birth exhibit the same milestones of language acquisition as children acquiring spoken languages. The onset of signing may be slightly earlier than the onset of speech in hearing children, due to somewhat reduced motor complexity of signs. However, onset of referential use of sign language parallels that found in the acquisition of spoken languages because it relies on similar cognitive prerequisites.**

- **Congenitally deaf children tend to acquire sign language at different ages depending on when this input becomes available. If exposure to sign language is delayed, individuals will exhibit reduced fluency and proficiency. Acquiring sign language early in life also confers an advantage for the later acquisition of literacy in a spoken language and prevents cognitive deficits associated with Theory of Mind, executive functioning, and numerical cognition.**

- **Recently, technological advances in the development of cochlear implants have led to the possibility of partially restoring hearing in deaf individuals. While acquisition of a spoken language remains difficult for individuals who receive cochlear implants later in life, especially after 12 years of age, toddlers who receive cochlear implants before 2 years of age tend to be very successful in acquiring spoken language.**

- Deaf individuals show subtle deficits in processing of temporal sequences in any modality. According to the Auditory Scaffolding Hypothesis, this deficit comes about because deaf individuals are not exposed to the full richness of temporal information that is carried by the sound patterns of spoken language.

- When deaf children are not exposed to language they will spontaneously create their own system of communication called home sign. In doing so, they will often go beyond the limited gestural input they receive by creating more sophisticated ways of combining gestures. Still, home sign does not exhibit the structural complexity and the combinatorial potential of natural languages.

- Home sign can develop into a *bona fide* sign language when communities of deaf individuals start negotiating conventionalised uses of signs as their primary system of communication. Crucially, structural complexity and grammar emerge when these sign systems are passed on to new generations of learners who acquire them as their first language early in life.

# FURTHER READING

## Key studies

For evidence of silent babbling in children exposed to sign language, read Petitto, L. A., Holowka, S., Sergio, L. E. & Ostry, D. (2001). Language rhythms in baby hand movements. *Nature, 413*, 35–36.

## Overview Articles

For a compelling argument why language input early in life matters, read Mayberry, R. I. (2007). When timing is everything: Age of first-language acquisition effects on second-language learning. *Applied Psycholinguistics, 28*, 537–549.

## Books

For more information on how sign languages are processed in the brain, read Emmorey, K. (2002). *Language, cognition, and the brain: Insights from sign language research*. Mahwah, NJ: Lawrence Erlbaum Associates.

For an overview of research on home sign, read Goldin-Meadow, S. (2003). *The resilience of language: What gesture creation in deaf children can tell us about how all children learn language*. New York: Psychology Press.

## KEY TERMS

● angular gyrus ● anterior ● aphasia ● basal ganglia ● Broca's area ● Brodmann areas ● constructions ● diffusion tensor imaging (DTI) ● discourse ● electro-encephalogram (EEG) ● event-related potentials (ERPs) ● fissure ● focal lesions ● FOXP2 ● frontal lobe ● functional magnetic resonance imaging (fMRI) ● fusiform gyrus ● gyrus ● hemodynamic responses ● imprinting ● inferior ● inferior frontal gyrus ● inferior temporal gyrus ● inflectional morphology ● middle temporal gyrus ● myelinisation ● near-infrared optical topography ● near-infrared spectroscopy (NIRS) ● occipital lobe ● parietal lobe ● planum temporale ● positron emission tomography (PET) ● posterior ● pre-central gyrus ● primary auditory cortex ● semantic ● sulcus ● superior ● superior temporal gyrus ● superior temporal sulcus ● Sylvian fissure ● temporal lobe ● verbal dyspraxia ● Wernicke's area

## CHAPTER OUTLINE

This chapter is not intended to provide a comprehensive overview of the neural basis of language (for such an overview, see Denes [2011] or Stemmer and Whitaker [2008], listed in Further Reading at the end of this chapter). Instead, we will focus on a number of specific questions related to how the neural pathways dedicated to processing language develop. We will ask to what extent the functional capacity for language is localised in specific brain areas from birth. To this end, we will review recent neuroimaging work examining the ontogenesis of functional specialisation for language in the brain. We will take a brief look at research exploring the genetic underpinnings of neural specialisation for language. We will also explore how the brain adapts to linguistic skills that are not ubiquitous and are acquired later in life, such as reading. Furthermore, we will consider to what extent functional plasticity of the brain diminishes over the lifespan, and ask whether there is a critical period for language development.

# 12.1    WHICH AREAS OF THE BRAIN PROCESS LANGUAGE?

**parietal lobe** a region of the human brain located behind the frontal lobe of each cerebral hemisphere.

**occipital lobe** a region of the human brain located at the rear of each cerebral hemisphere.

In exploring how the developing brain processes language, we will start by providing a very general summary of how language is processed in the adult brain. However, before we begin locating functional neural networks or modules, it is necessary for us to introduce some of the terms used to label different brain regions. The neocortex is broadly divided into four areas called lobes (i.e. **frontal lobe**, **temporal lobe**, **parietal lobe**, and **occipital lobe**; see Figure 12.1). Within the neocortex, it is possible to identify specific anatomical structures, such as a groove (called a **sulcus** or **fissure**, depending on how deep it is)

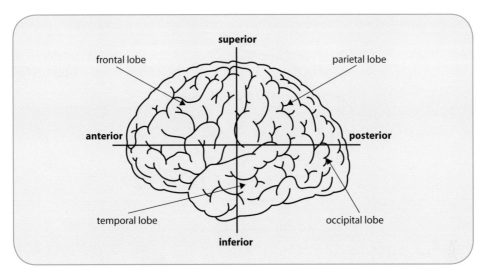

**Figure 12.1** *Directional terms and lobes of the neocortex.*

*Source:* Image by Michael Almodovar.

or a bump (called a **gyrus**). To describe the locations of such structures in the brain, the directional terms **anterior** (front), **posterior** (back), **superior** (top), and **inferior** (bottom) are commonly used (e.g. 'left inferior frontal gyrus' refers to a bump located towards the bottom of the left frontal lobe). A more specific system for labelling cortical areas was developed over a century ago by the German neuroscientist, Korbinian Brodmann. Brodmann (1909) identified functionally differentiated areas by distinctive cell types and patterns of neural connectivity – these are the so-called **Brodmann areas**, numbered from 1 to 52.

In addition, **Broca's area** and **Wernicke's area** are regions of the left hemisphere that were named after scholars who identified their functional involvement in language processing through autopsies. These regions are primarily of historical importance, as there is considerable disagreement about the actual locations and boundaries of Broca's and Wernicke's areas. We will not use the terms Broca's area and Wernicke's area as primary labels of the brain structures involved in language processing. Instead, we will use the alternative classification systems, described above, with the approximate locations of the relevant structures in the left hemisphere shown in Figure 12.2.

### 12.1.1 Processing speech sounds in the brain

Auditory information is initially processed in the primary auditory cortices situated in the left and right temporal lobes. The **primary auditory cortex** comprises Heschl's gyrus, which makes up the posterior part of the

**sulcus** a groove or furrow within the brain.

**fissure** a groove or deep furrow within the brain.

**gyrus** a ridge in the cerebral cortex.

**anterior** towards the front, in front of (refers to locations in the brain).

**posterior** behind (refers to locations in the brain).

**superior** on top of (refers to locations in the brain).

**inferior** below (refers to locations in the brain).

**Brodmann areas** numbered from 1 to 52; brain areas functionally differentiated by distinctive cell types and patterns of neural connectivity.

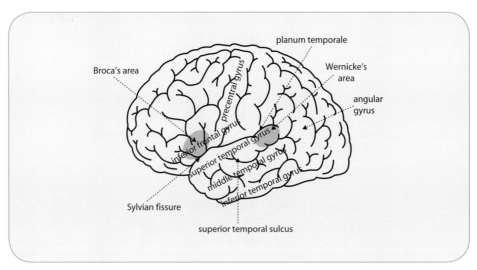

Figure 12.2    *Anatomical structures associated with language processing in the neocortex.*
*Source:* Image by Michael Almodovar.

**Broca's area**
region of the left inferior frontal gyrus; it is named after Pierre Paul Broca, a physician who identified its functional involvement in language processing.

**Wernicke's area**
region of the left superior temporal gyrus; named after Carl Wernicke, a neurologist who identified its functional involvement in language processing.

**superior temporal gyrus**  a ridge located in the temporal lobe, adjacent to the Sylvian fissure, containing the primary auditory cortex.

superior temporal gyrus. Activation of this area is associated with the temporal processing of auditory sequences. With respect to the language-specific aspects of auditory perception, the posterior part of the left superior temporal sulcus is involved in processing the phonetic features of speech, and the right superior temporal gyrus is involved in processing speech prosody. The anterior part of the left superior temporal sulcus becomes activated as sequences of speech sounds are meaningfully interpreted. The left planum temporale is responsible for the higher-order integration of the sound patterns of speech. This structure is in the posterior part of the superior temporal gyrus close to the Sylvian fissure, and provides an interface between speech perception and adjacent speech-motor areas, located in the frontal lobes. Interestingly, already at birth the left planum temporale is larger than its right hemispheric counterpart (Wada, Clark, & Hamm, 1975; Witelson, 1977). Thus, it appears that from infancy speech perception involves a dedicated network located primarily in the left temporal lobe.

## 12.1.2   Processing grammar in the brain

Grammatical information is processed primarily in the left prefrontal cortex, in a region corresponding roughly to Broca's area. In particular, various sub-parts of the left inferior frontal gyrus (located in front of the Sylvian fissure) and the inferior part of the pre-central gyrus (part of the pre-motor cortex), as well as sub-cortical structures called the basal ganglia (not depicted), become activated when simple and higher-level grammatical structures are processed. Such activity can be identified, for example, by studying the origin of event-related potentials (ERPs) in response to grammatical errors in sentences like *The lion in the roars* (cf. Oberecker, Friedrich, & Friederici, 2005). In addition, the anterior part of the left superior temporal gyrus seems to be involved in processing grammatical information. Thus, a dedicated network for processing grammatical structures appears to reside in the left frontal lobe and in the anterior part of the left temporal lobe.

## 12.1.3   Processing meaning in the brain

The processing of meaning seems to be distributed across a wide network of interconnected sites located in both anterior and posterior cortical regions. Historically, the locus of semantic processing, especially for comprehending words, was assumed to be in the posterior part of the superior temporal gyrus, in a region also known as Wernicke's area. However, more recent data from ERP and fMRI studies (see Methodology Box 12.1) suggest that the processing of word meaning (semantic processing) and of text content (discourse processing) is distributed across a range of interconnected areas. For example, regions of the inferior temporal gyrus, close to visual processing areas in the occipital lobe, are activated when processing imageable words (e.g. *dragon*, *castle*), whereas words denoting graspable objects (e.g. *doorknob*, *pencil*) activate anterior areas in the pre-motor and motor cortex, located near the inferior part of the pre-central gyrus. Furthermore, semantic relationships between words activate part of the left inferior frontal gyrus. As mentioned earlier, part of the left superior temporal sulcus is involved in mapping speech sounds onto meaning. The homologous right hemispheric region is involved in discourse processing, understanding metaphor, integrating information from larger chunks of speech or text, and interpreting emotional tone of voice. This suggests that the left hemispheric regions involved in the processing of meaning are predominantly specialised in the processing of smaller units of meaning (e.g. individual words) while the right-hemisphere areas control processing of larger units of discourse. Finally, sustained activity in parts of the inferior frontal gyrus during comprehension tasks suggests that these more anterior areas are involved in executive control over language processing (Shafer & Garrido-Nag, 2008), for example in inhibiting contextually inappropriate meanings of words.

**inferior frontal gyrus**  a ridge located towards the bottom of the frontal lobe of the brain; the left inferior frontal gyrus roughly corresponds to Broca's area, a region implicated in language processing, especially grammatical processing and speech production.

**superior temporal sulcus**  a groove that separates the superior temporal gyrus from the middle temporal gyrus.

**Sylvian fissure**  also called the lateral sulcus; the deep groove that separates the frontal and parietal lobes from the temporal lobe.

**pre-central gyrus**  part of the pre-motor cortex in the frontal lobe; becomes activated when simple and higher-level grammatical structures are processed.

**inferior temporal gyrus**  a ridge located below the middle temporal sulcus; parts of it are activated when high-imagery words are processed.

## 12.1.4   Connecting the different circuits

For language processing to occur it is not sufficient for the cortical areas described above to be activated in isolation; rather, information needs to be exchanged between them. This information exchange is accomplished via white-matter fibre bundles that

# METHODOLOGY BOX 12.1   STUDYING LANGUAGE PROCESSING IN THE BRAIN

## A. METHODS OF FUNCTIONAL BRAIN IMAGING

Functional imaging methods provide information about which brain areas are activated during various language-processing tasks, thus allowing researchers to pinpoint which brain areas are responsible for processing various aspects of language. The methods most commonly used are positron emission tomography (PET), functional magnetic resonance imaging (fMRI), and near-infrared spectroscopy (NIRS); the latter is sometimes also called near-infrared optical topography. These methods are based on detecting changes in blood flow and blood oxygenation (the hemodynamic response), which follows 1–5 seconds after an increase in neural activity.

**functional magnetic resonance imaging (fMRI)** a brain-imaging technique that allows researchers to study the level of neural activity (i.e., blood-oxygen level changes) in various brain areas associated with the processing of specific stimuli; see also hemodynamic responses.

**near-infrared spectroscopy (NIRS)** also called near-infrared optical topography; functional brain-imaging technique used to identify substances through the light spectrum emitted or absorbed by them.

**hemodynamic responses** changes in blood flow and blood oxygenation associated with neural activity; measurement of dynamic changes in blood flow in response to specific stimuli is the basis of functional magnetic resonance imaging (fMRI) technology.

### POSITRON EMISSION TOMOGRAPHY (PET):

During PET, a radioactive compound is injected. Once the compound has been deposited in tissues of interest, the positrons emitted during radioactive decay are annihilated upon interaction with an electron. This creates a pair of gamma-ray photons, which can be detected when the participant has been placed inside the scanner. To map neural activity in the brain, PET exploits the fact that areas of increased blood flow are associated with higher radioactivity.

PET has been used to investigate brain areas involved in language processing in adults. It has excellent spatial resolution but limited temporal resolution. In other words, it gives a fairly accurate picture of which brain areas are involved in processing. However, it does not provide information regarding how long different areas are activated, or information about the progression of activation across different areas. Additionally, because the injection of a compound makes PET an invasive procedure, it is unsuitable for use with non-clinical populations of children.

**positron emission tomography (PET)** functional brain-imaging technique that uses an injection of a radioactive compound (an analogue of glucose) to map neural activity in the brain; exploits the fact that areas of increased blood flow during task processing will have higher radioactivity.

### FUNCTIONAL MAGNETIC RESONANCE IMAGING (fMRI):

Level of blood oxygenation changes the magnetic resonance signal of blood, which can be detected inside a powerful magnetic field. For fMRI, individuals are placed inside a long narrow tube surrounded by a large magnet, and are presented with various stimuli and tasks through visual and auditory projections. This allows researchers to study the level of neural activity in various brain areas that are associated with processing the presented stimuli. Unfortunately, fMRI does not tolerate movement from participants and can be perceived as threatening due to the necessity to lie motionless within the restricted confines of the scanner and the noise generated during the scans. These reasons make fMRI difficult to use with children in a state of wakefulness. However, recently some laboratories have been successful in using fMRI with infants who were awake by managing to distract them by projecting interesting and engaging images inside the scanner. Still, the difficulty of using this method with children limits the efficiency of this method.

Like PET, fMRI has also limited temporal resolution. This is because the hemodynamic response peaks around 5 seconds after the increase in neural activity, making it difficult to associate neural responses with specific events. In order to gain information about the temporal characteristics of the involvement of different brain areas in different aspects of language processing, researchers use electrophysiological methods.

### NEAR-INFRARED SPECTROSCOPY (NIRS):

Spectroscopy is used to identify substances through the light spectrum emitted or absorbed by them. In its use for functional brain imaging, this method exploits the fact that concentrations of chemicals associated with changes in blood oxygenation and blood volume can be detected by their different specific spectra in the near-infrared range. It is a relatively non-invasive technique because sensors are portable and can be attached to the participant's head. NIRS has good temporal resolution but is limited to imaging the cortex and has reduced spatial resolution compared to PET and fMRI. Still, the non-invasive nature of NIRS has recently increased its popularity as a method

for studying brain activation during language processing in infants.

### B. ELECTROPHYSIOLOGICAL METHODS

Electrophysiological methods detect changes in the postsynaptic electrical potentials of neurons which propagate to the scalp where they can be measured using a voltmeter (see Figure 12.3). When neurons in a circuit fire in synchrony in response to a specific stimulus, they act like a dipole with a positive and a negative end, through which electrical impulses are propagated. These impulses that occur in response to specific neural events are too small to be detected in the overall electro-encephalogram (EEG). However, when multiple electrical responses time-locked to a specific event are averaged, characteristic patterns of changes in voltage can be observed, because the averaging process decreases the contribution of random fluctuations in electric potential. These averaged time-locked patterns are called event-related potentials (ERPs). The characteristic ERP voltage change patterns (also called ERP components) are referred to by a letter (P for positive or N for negative) indicating polarity and a number indicating the latency, that is, how many milliseconds after stimulus onset the voltage deflection occurred. In Chapter 2, we already mentioned one such component, the N200, a mismatch negativity that typically occurs in response to detection of an oddball in a series of stimuli, which indicates the automatic perception of novelty. Other components are the P300, typically an indicator of attentional processes, the N400, which is sensitive to difficulties in finding words and integrating meaning

> **electroencephalo-gram (EEG)** a recording of electrical activity over the scalp using a multiple electrode cap; this electrophysiological method is called electroencephalography.

*(Continued)*

**Figure 12.3** *Electrophysiological measures from the scalp that are time-locked to the presentation of a specific auditory stimulus can provide detailed information about language processing.*
*Source:* © Jon Wilson. Courtesy of Science Photo Library.

(e.g. as in the semantically anomalous sentence *The pizza was too hot to drink*), or the P600, which is sensitive to grammatically ill-formed sentences.

ERP has excellent temporal resolution and is relatively tolerant to movement, making it a more suitable method for studying brain responses in infants and young children. When multi-channel measurements across the scalp are obtained, ERPs also provide some indication about the localisation of the source of the electrical activity. This information can then be compared with fMRI data to obtain a more detailed picture of the specific brain activity in different regions associated with different tasks.

**diffusion tensor imaging (DTI)** a magnetic resonance imaging (MRI) technique that allows researchers to produce images of neural fibre tracts consisting of bundles of axons.

connect the temporal–parietal lobe circuits with the frontal lobe circuits involved in language processing. In older models, the role of information exchange was attributed to the arcuate fasciculus, a bundle of fibres connecting superior temporal regions (Wernicke's area) to inferior frontal regions (Broca's area). Recent studies using diffusion tensor imaging (DTI) suggest that the connectivity between the main cortical language areas is more complex and consists of at least two pathways. One pathway, which possibly consists of two sub-pathways, extends from inferior frontal regions to superior temporal regions and is involved in phonological and lexical–semantic processing. The other pathway, also possibly consisting of two sub-parts, extends from inferior frontal regions to anterior parts of the superior temporal gyrus and to Heschl's gyrus. These pathways are thought to be involved in syntactic processing and in comprehension (Friederici, 2009).

# 12.2   WHEN DOES NEURAL SPECIALISATION FOR LANGUAGE DEVELOP?

In 95–98 per cent of neurologically intact individuals, specialisation for language is found in the left hemisphere. This suggests that, at birth, the cerebral hemispheres are not equipotential for language. However, the fact that children can recover language after trauma to the left cerebral hemisphere indicates that language abilities are not irreversibly localised in the left hemisphere. (This topic will be described in more detail in Section 12.3.1.) In this section, we will discuss when and how left-hemispheric specialisation emerges during development.

## 12.2.1   Early specialisation of cortical areas for speech processing

If there were no early specialisation for speech processing one would expect that activation in response to human speech should be widely distributed across cortical areas in infants. One way of studying infants' sensitivity to features specific to human speech is to compare cortical activation elicited by forward and backward speech. Backward speech, while still providing rapidly changing acoustic stimulation, sounds highly unnatural and violates prosodic and phonotactic constraints on language. In 3-month-old infants exposed to forward and backward speech, fMRI scans have shown that activation is concentrated in the same regions of the left hemisphere that are involved in language processing in adults (Dehaene-Lambertz, Dehaene, & Hertz-Pannier, 2002). Moreover, at this early age, there already appears to be some functional differentiation within this network, such that some language regions, such as the angular gyrus, are sensitive to language-specific features differentiating forward from backward speech, whereas other areas within the temporal lobes are not, and thus appear to be involved in more general aspects of auditory processing. This evidence suggests that, by three months of age, functional specialisation for language can be detected in the developing brain.

**angular gyrus**
a ridge located in the parietal lobe, near the edge of the temporal lobe; it is involved in language processing.

Subsequent research has demonstrated that increased left-hemispheric sensitivity to forward speech (compared to backward speech) can be observed even in neonates (Peña et al., 2003). However, as the interaction between hemisphere and type of speech was not significant in this study, it remained unclear whether this advantage reflects a specific left-hemispheric bias for processing linguistic information or a general bias for processing rapid transitions of sounds. This difference can be tested by comparing infants' brain activation while listening to speech versus musical stimuli which are characterised by slower sound transitions. Dehaene-Lambertz and colleagues (2009) scanned 2-month-old infants who were listening to sentences read by their mothers, equivalent sentences read by unfamiliar women, and passages from a piano sonata by Mozart. In response to both sets of sentences, but not in response to the musical passages, activation was more pronounced in the left as compared to the right planum temporale, an area that in adults is responsible for processing speech-specific characteristics of sound. This confirms that some left-hemispheric areas are already specialised for certain aspects of language at two months of age. It seems plausible that the aspects of language that are preferentially processed in the left hemisphere at this early age involve the rapidly changing acoustic transitions that differentiate speech from music.

One question that arises is how to reconcile an early left-hemispheric specialisation for language with the observation described in Chapter 2 that very young infants are able to make distinctions between familiar and unfamiliar languages based on prosodic information (Mehler et al., 1988). In adults, speech prosody is processed in the right hemisphere (Allen, 1983). Thus, along with an explanation for the emergence of a left-hemispheric specialisation for temporally fine-grained aspects of language, it is also necessary to trace the emergence of a right-hemispheric specialisation for processing speech prosody. To explore this issue, Homae and colleagues (Homae, Watanabe, Nakano, Asakawa, & Taga, 2006) presented normal and prosodically flattened speech to 3-month-old sleeping infants. Hemodynamic responses (see Methodology Box 12.1) were obtained using near-infrared optical topography, which is portable and less expensive than MRI, but has reduced spatial resolution. This method provides a very approximate localisation of activation, thus making it difficult to pinpoint the exact anatomical structures involved in specific cognitive processes. Nonetheless, compared to flattened speech, prosodically normal speech elicited greater activation in the temporal–parietal regions of the right hemisphere, that is, in the region surrounding the posterior part of the superior temporal gyrus. Thus, right-hemispheric specialisation for speech prosody appears to be in place already shortly after birth.

In sum, the neuroimaging data obtained with young infants indicate that functional hemispheric specialisation for language can be detected at birth or shortly thereafter. This does not mean, of course, that the various areas involved in language processing are fully dedicated to specific linguistic functions at birth. As we have discussed in Chapter 2, and as we will illustrate below, neural commitment to features of the ambient language occurs gradually over the first year of life and beyond. What then drives the early hemispheric specialisation for speech? Most likely, genetic predispositions are responsible for an early proclivity of the left hemisphere to process rapid acoustic transitions; this early proclivity would, in turn, facilitate processing of speech segments with brief duration, such as phonemes, words, and grammatical morphemes, as opposed to longer units such as prosodic contours, which are processed in the right hemisphere. Thus, functional specialisation is viewed as developing in response to infants' increasing exposure to and mastery of language. There is now direct evidence that brain activation in response to specific aspects of language is directly linked to children's language proficiency. For example, pairing pictures with non-words (e.g. *moop*) elicits an N400, a specific ERP component associated with detection of violations in meaning (see Methodology Box 12.1). When toddlers at one year of age were exposed to combinations of pictures with either words or non-words, the N400 was observed only in children with high word production skills, as measured by a parental questionnaire (Friedrich & Friederici, 2010). This shows that further functional specialisation in the brain develops in tight conjunction with emerging language skills.

It is also important to note that the anatomical structures that connect the inferior frontal and superior temporal regions mature fairly late in development; full myelinisation may not be completed until seven years of age. Late maturation of the pathways involved in information exchange between cortical language regions is in line with data showing that children have difficulties in processing complex grammatical constructions during and even beyond the preschool years (see Chapter 5). Thus, while early functional specialisation of cortical areas for aspects of language forms the basis of language processing in infancy, development of full connectivity between the cortical language areas takes considerably longer.

> **myelinisation** the production of myelin, a white fatty matter that forms an insulating layer around the axons of neurons and is essential for neuronal conductivity and proper neuronal functioning.

## 12.2.2  Genetic underpinnings of neural specialisation

In the previous section we discussed evidence that functional specialisation of various brain areas for language emerges rather early in development. We will now explore what is known about the genetic underpinnings of the functional specialisation for language.

In the early 1990s, the case of a British family with inherited language deficits, known as the KE family, was first described in the literature (Hurst, Baraitser, Auger, Graham, & Norrell, 1990). Over four generations, about half the members of this family exhibited profound speech and language difficulties. Most strikingly, the affected members of the KE family had specific difficulties with inflectional morphology, that is, with producing inflections such as past tense -*ed*, which lead some researchers to propose that the KE family suffered from an inherited grammar-specific disorder (Gopnik, 1990; Gopnik & Crago, 1991). However, subsequent research revealed that the affected individuals had difficulties controlling finely coordinated movement sequences of the mouth, tongue, lips and soft palate, a condition referred to as verbal dyspraxia. The affected individuals also displayed more general deficits with movements involving the lower part of the face (Vargha-Khadem, Watkins, Alcock, Fletcher, & Passingham, 1995). Furthermore, their language deficits were not restricted to inflectional morphology, as originally described, but involved non-word identification, phoneme manipulation, and comprehension of complex sentence structures as well (Marcus & Fisher, 2003). Some affected individuals also showed minor to moderate intellectual deficits (Vargha-Khadem et al., 1995).

Functional imaging studies which compared the affected with unaffected members of the KE family revealed abnormal patterns of activation in a number of language areas such as the left middle temporal gyrus and Broca's area (Liégeois, Connelly, Baldeweg, Connelly, Gadian, Mishkin, et al., 2003; Vargha-Khadem et al., 1998). The pattern of inheritance in the KE family pointed to a single-gene disorder, suggesting that the problems were the result of damage to just one gene. Finding this gene could potentially shed light on the genetic determinants of functional specialisation for language in the brain. Subsequent genetic analyses identified a locus on chromosome 7, specifically, a mutation in a gene called FOXP2 (Forkhead bOX P2) belonging to a family of forkhead transcription factors, for which the resulting regulatory proteins are involved in a variety of control functions affecting cellular differentiation and proliferation.

**middle temporal gyrus** a ridge located in the temporal lobe that is involved in language processing.

**FOXP2** Forkhead bOX protein P2 gene located on the 7th chromosome; encodes the FOXP2 protein that belongs to a family of forkhead transcription factors.

Is FOXP2 the gene that controls the development of functional specialisation for language in the brain? Despite some hyperbole in the popular press in the 1990s touting FOXP2 as the 'gene for language' or even the 'gene for grammar', there is no evidence that FOXP2 is specifically responsible for language development. Three arguments suggest that the role of FOXP2 is considerably more complex. First, while FOXP2 is expressed in various parts of the brain, including the cortex, the basal ganglia, the thalamus, and the cerebellum, it is also expressed in other tissues such as the lung, the gut, and the heart. This suggests that FOXP2 is involved in a variety of functions and is not unique to language. The fact that the KE family displayed a combination of oro-facial motor and language deficits, but not other deficits, may be related to the fact that their disruption in FOXP2 is heterozygous – that is, it involves only one copy of the gene. Perhaps having one intact copy of FOXP2 is enough to perform control functions for some tissue types, but it may not be enough to control all functions related to the brain (Marcus & Fisher, 2003). Secondly, despite the complex motor and linguistic deficits associated with FOXP2, there is no genetic evidence that FOXP2 mutations are involved in the majority of cases of Specific Language Impairment, which also runs in families (see Chapter 10). This makes it clear that a multitude of genes are likely to be involved in controlling the neural organisation of language.

Finally, FOXP2 exists in many vertebrates, where it performs roughly similar functions. Mice, for example, have a similar version of the gene, as do monkeys, songbirds, crocodiles or zebra fish, among others. Genetic studies on FOXP2-knockout mice suggest that FOXP2 is involved in modulating synaptic plasticity, particularly in neural circuits involved in motor-skill learning (Groszer, Keays, Deacon, de Bono,

Prasad-Mulcare, Gaub, et al., 2008). This leaves open the possibility that the contribution of FOXP2 to human language is based on plasticity in neural circuits involved in motor-skill acquisition, rather than in circuits involved in language and communication *per se* (Fisher & Scharff, 2009). After all, speech requires extraordinarily complex and fine-grained motor coordination. Perhaps FOXP2 disruptions manifest themselves disproportionally in speech and language-related disorders because language relies on complex, fine-motor skills to a greater extent than other human behaviours. It is also conceivable that language itself is based primarily on evolutionarily older motor-skill learning circuits, which over time could have been co-opted for language processing (Lieberman, 2000). This fits well with the finding that there has been selection for FOXP2 during evolution of our hominin ancestors over the last 200,000 years (Enard, Przeworski, Fisher, Lai, Wiebe, Kitano, et al., 2002).

The role of FOXP2 in songbirds is particularly revealing with respect to understanding its role in human language: knockdown (i.e. reduction or silencing) of FOXP2 expression in the brain areas responsible for song learning in zebra finches has been shown to result in incomplete copying of the tutor song and increased variability in song production (Haesler, Rochefort, Georgi, Licznerski, Oster, & Scharff, 2007). These findings are intriguing when compared to the incomplete and inaccurate production of words and the highly variable pronunciation observed in members of the KE family. Further analyses suggest that the deficits in bird song most likely involve sensory–motor integration rather than pure motor difficulties, which suggests that FOXP2 is involved with neural plasticity during times of sensorimotor learning. Thus, while FOXP2 is certainly not a gene that uniquely controls language, it most likely is involved in the control of some of the functions that language builds upon. At present, it seems that FOXP2 is involved in regulating the plasticity of neural circuits relevant for language development. The extent to which the observed effects of FOXP2 disruption – language disorders in humans, impairment of sensorimotor song learning in birds, and abnormal motor-skill learning in mice – rely on the same molecular mechanisms remains to be determined by future research.

### 12.2.3   Adapting the brain to literacy

The evidence presented so far shows that language capitalises on specific propensities of various neural circuits in the human brain, with the result that some specialisation for language emerges quite early in development. But how does the brain handle language-related skills that are acquired relatively late, such as reading (see Chapter 9)? The emergence of writing systems, dating back only several thousand years, is, in evolutionary terms, too recent an event for specially dedicated neural pathways to have evolved. Thus, unlike spoken or signed languages, reading cannot rely on functionally pre-specified areas of the brain. Yet not only can the human brain handle this task with exquisite speed and mastery, but the same cortical area, located in the middle part of the left **fusiform gyrus** (adjacent to the inferior

**fusiform gyrus** a ridge on the interior side of the temporal lobe; it appears to be involved in word recognition (reading).

temporal gyrus on the inner side of the temporal lobe; not visible in Figure 12.2), appears to be involved in word recognition across the different writing systems of the world's languages (Cohen, Dehaene, Naccache, Lehéricy, Dehaene-Lambertz, Hénaff, et al., 2000). How is this possible? Dehaene (2010) has proposed that learning to read involves 'neuronal recycling': during literacy acquisition, the various processes involved in reading come to 'piggyback' on already existing mental capacities, specifically those involved in processing visual information.

The human visual system operates in a hierarchical fashion: the primary visual area, located in the occipital lobe, is responsible for the detection of lines and object contours as well as the presence and intensity of different wavelengths of light. Neurons in the secondary visual area respond to specific curves and simple combinations of lines. Further up the hierarchy of visual processing, neurons respond to even more complex constellations of lines and curves as well as to the full spectrum of hues. This hierarchical nature of visual processing is what ultimately allows neurons at the next stage to respond to complex visual configurations such as objects and faces while preserving shape invariance and colour constancy regardless of angle of viewing or illumination.

A careful comparison of the different writing systems of the world's languages suggests that these seemingly diverse systems share a set of underlying commonalities that appear to fit well with the propensities of the human visual system. First, writing systems mirror the hierarchical structure of vision: most characters consist of two, three or four strokes which, in turn, contain two, three or four basic line segments. At the next level, two, three or four characters tend to form word roots or affixes in alphabetic languages, or complex characters in logographic scripts (Changizi & Shimojo, 2005). Second, combinations of individual strokes mirror frequent configurations of basic features found in natural visual scenes. For example, if an object partially occludes another object, like a cube partially occluding the edge of the surface it stands on (see Figure 12.4), the contours of these objects form specific feature configurations at the points of juncture in non-arbitrary ways. In human writing systems, the frequency of particular stroke combinations such as T or L or X corresponds to the frequency of occurrence of such basic feature configurations in the environment (Changizi & Shimojo, 2005), thereby utilising an input that the human visual system is well adapted to handle.

Thus, writing systems capitalise on the evolved ability of the visual system to respond to certain configurations of lines and curves found in natural scenes. Over the course of learning to read, neural networks that evolved for object recognition adapt to grapheme recognition. As a result, part of the brain areas that are specialised in detection of complex feature constellations become re-dedicated to visual word processing. This explains why roughly the same left occipital–temporal region of the neocortex handles grapheme processing regardless of one's language and writing system. It also emphasises that the success of human cultural inventions depends, among other things, on how well they are adapted to existing functional capabilities of the brain.

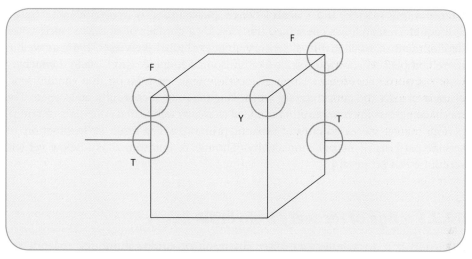

**Figure 12.4** *Junctions of contours typically occurring in natural visual scenes.*
*Source:* Adapted from Dehaene, S. (2010). *Reading in the brain.* New York: Viking.

## 12.3 IS THERE A CRITICAL PERIOD FOR LANGUAGE DEVELOPMENT?

During development, functional dedication of brain areas to various aspects of language emerges as a result of both genetically predetermined processing predispositions, as described in Section 12.2.1, and subsequent input-based specialisation of neural pathways. Does this process of neural specialisation require language input to be available within a critical window of time, or is the brain sufficiently malleable to allow for functional specialisation to occur throughout life? In other words, can humans master a language only when it is encountered during a critical period early in life, or is successful language learning possible throughout the lifespan? Two lines of evidence can shed light on this question. First, we can examine the degree of recovery following brain injury (i.e. lesions due to disease or trauma) as a function of the age at which the injury occurred. Second, we can examine language attainment as a function of the age at which the language input was first encountered. Within the latter line of evidence, a distinction needs to be made as to whether it is exposure to a first or a second language that varies by age.

The idea of a critical period can be traced back to Konrad Lorenz's description of the phenomenon of **imprinting**. The period

**imprinting** a phenomenon whereby many animals form a lifelong attachment to a specific stimulus (e.g. a gosling to its mother) if that stimulus is encountered during a critical period early in life.

of imprinting is short and sharply defined and learning is irreversible afterwards. Subsequent research has confirmed this idea for a number of domains, such as the development of basic low-level sensory abilities (Hubel & Wiesel, 1963) as well as more complex sensorimotor skills like birdsong (Doupe & Kuhl, 2008). Lenneberg (1967) applied this idea to language development, postulating that maturational changes restrict the period during which language can successfully be learned. The mechanisms by which maturation can lead to clearly delineated endpoints of critical periods involve increased rates of synaptic pruning, which result in 'fossilisation' of specific patterns of neural connectivity (Thomas & Johnson, 2008). Below we will scrutinise this proposal.

## 12.3.1    Age of recovery from brain injury

**focal lesions** brain damage in a restricted, circumscribed area of tissue; often the result of strokes, tumours, epileptic seizures or trauma.

**aphasia** condition caused by damage to the language-processing areas in the left cerebral hemisphere; characterised by various patterns of language impairment depending on the extent of damage and the neural circuits involved.

Focal lesions are often the result of strokes, tumours, epileptic seizures, or trauma. There is a large body of evidence showing that children with focal lesions in the left hemisphere display normal or near-normal language abilities (Bates, 1999). Moreover, even after removal of the entire left hemisphere (e.g. due to disease), language abilities will recover if the surgery is performed during childhood (Vargha-Khadem, Carr, Isaacs, Brett, Adams, & Mishkin, 1997). In contrast, adults with damage to the language-processing areas in the left hemisphere develop a condition called aphasia.

When left-hemispheric lesions are sustained early in life, that is, before five years of age, individuals subsequently tend to display right-hemispheric language lateralisation and their language abilities develop according to a normal trajectory (Booth, MacWhinney, Thulborn, Sacco, Voyvodic, & Feldman, 1999; Helmstaedter, Kurthen, Linke, & Elger, 1997), albeit at a somewhat slower rate (Dick, Wulfeck, Krupa-Kwiatkowski, & Bates, 2004). However, when lesions occur later in life, the right hemisphere is less likely to take over language processing and language tends to remain localised in the damaged left hemisphere (Benson, FitzGerald, LeSueur, Kennedy, Kwong, Buchbinder, et al., 1999). This age-dependent pattern of recovery from left-hemispheric lesions has been interpreted as evidence for a loss of brain plasticity, which is necessary for cortical networks to functionally reorganise to take on language-processing requirements.

A closer look at the neuroimaging data, however, reveals that the picture is not so simple: while age of trauma is a good predictor of the likelihood of hemispheric reorganisation at the group level, it is a poor predictor on an individual level (Liégeois, Connelly, Cross, Boyd, Gadian, & Vargha-Khadem, 2004). Thus, some individuals with early left-hemispheric damage retain left-hemispheric specialisation. This occurs because shifting language functions to the right hemisphere is not the only way in which the brain can reorganise after early damage. In some patients, early lesions close to dedicated language areas, such as Broca's area, will result in intra-hemispheric reorganisation and will not lead to right-hemispheric language specialisation.

Intra-hemispheric reorganisation has also been observed in some adults with left-hemispheric damage who showed good recovery of language (Liégeois et al., 2004). This pattern of findings suggests that, while there is age-related decline in the brain plasticity required for functional reorganisation, there is also considerable variability in the way the brain can reorganise itself after trauma. Thus, the strong view of a critical period after which a general loss of plasticity precludes reorganisation of the neural circuits supporting language needs to be modified to take into account the complexity of individual differences, as well as evidence of cortical reorganisation in adulthood.

## 12.3.2   Age of exposure to a second language

To examine effects of age of language exposure on language attainment, one would ideally vary the age at which language input is first encountered by the developing child, an approach that is neither practically feasible nor ethically justifiable. Very few naturally occurring cases of severe language deprivation in early childhood have been documented (Curtiss, 1977). In these cases, the learning outcome after exposure to language is difficult to interpret in light of potential neurological abnormalities in these children, and their prolonged exposure to abuse. Considerably more information can be gleaned from congenitally deaf children who were first exposed to a sign language at a later age due to unavailability of sign language input early in life (see Chapter 11 on deaf children born to hearing parents). The body of evidence discussed in Chapter 11 suggests that, while delays in language exposure do not preclude the ability to learn a sign language, early exposure is essential for subsequent language use to be highly fluent and grammatically correct.

It may in this context be instructive to consult findings on the acquisition of other complex sensory and motor skills, like the acquisition of musical expertise, for which age of first exposure tends to vary to a much larger extent than for language (Trainor, 2005). For example, there is evidence that in keyboard players, the age of onset of musical lessons is positively related to the enlargement of the area of the motor cortex representing the fingers (Amunts, Schlaug, Jaencke, Steinmetz, Schleicher, Dabringhaus, et al., 1997). Similarly, size of electrophysiological responses to sound also correlates with age of onset of music lessons (Pantev, Roberts, Schulz, Engelien, & Ross, 2001; Trainor, Desjardins, & Rockel, 1999). It is unlikely that these correlations are the result of a self-selection bias such that individuals with a genetic advantage in motor abilities or pitch perception are more likely to opt for early music lessons; instead, the observation that trumpet players show increased sensitivity to trumpet sounds and violin players show increased sensitivity to violin sounds (Pantev et al., 2001) supports the idea that earlier sustained exposure to specific musical inputs leads to a greater neural commitment for processing those inputs. This suggests that there is unlikely to be a clearly delineated critical period for the acquisition of complex abilities; rather, the degree of neural commitment and ultimate skill attainment continuously decline with later exposure to relevant inputs.

Another important line of evidence comes from the study of second language acquisition. What are the effects of age of first exposure to a second language on attained proficiency and the neural organisation of each language? In a widely cited study, Johnson and Newport (1989) used a grammaticality judgement task to test English proficiency in native speakers of Korean and Chinese who had arrived in the United States between the ages of 3 and 39 years. Age of arrival was used as an index of when individuals were first exposed to the second language in an immersion context. Note that duration of immersion was roughly the same for all participants: the early arrivals were younger and had spent roughly the same number of years in the USA as the late arrivals. In line with the findings on early and late signers, the early arrivals outperformed the late arrivals in judging the grammaticality of sentences, with individuals with an age of arrival before seven years of age showing native-like performance. It should be noted, however, that while behavioural measures of language proficiency might fail to detect differences between monolingual native speakers of a language and second-language learners with an early age of arrival, electrophysiological methods may reveal subtle differences. For example, Shafer and Garrido-Nag (2008) reported weaker ERPs to an English phonological contrast in Spanish–English bilinguals who had learned English before five years of age in comparison to English monolinguals.

Further results of the Johnson and Newport (1989) study showed a continuous decline in performance on the grammaticality judgement task for individuals with arrival ages between seven years and puberty. Performance for individuals with an age of arrival after puberty was characterised by large individual differences. Johnson and Newport (1989) concluded that the observed age effects were due to maturational processes, and that once maturation is complete, other factors such as motivation and general cognitive abilities account for the variability in learning outcomes. Thus, according to this interpretation, the critical period for language learning ends around puberty. However, when Birdsong and Molis (2001) attempted to replicate the findings of Johnson and Newport (1989), with native speakers of Spanish differing in age of arrival in the United States, they found continuous decline of performance in the grammaticality judgement task even after puberty. The lack of a discontinuity in the relationship between age of arrival and proficiency in a second language was confirmed in an analysis of the US census data for over 2 million native speakers of Spanish and over 300,000 native speakers of Chinese who provided data on their age of arrival in the USA and on their proficiency in English (Hakuta, Bialystok, & Whiley, 2003). This large-scale survey, like the study by Birdsong and Molis (2001), showed continuous decline of language proficiency as a function of age of arrival throughout the lifespan, which counters the view that puberty marks the end point of a critical period for language development.

Interestingly, Birdsong and Molis (2001) also found that more than 10 per cent of their late arrivals (age of arrival > 17 years) scored above 95 per cent correct on the grammaticality judgement task. Such native-like proficiency in some late learners has been demonstrated in several other studies, not just for the domain of grammar (e.g. Juffs & Harrington, 1995; White & Genesee, 1996) but for phonology as well (Bongaerts, 1999). This is striking in light of the commonly held belief that adults who learn a new language will at least retain an accent, even if they reach a high level of proficiency in grammar and vocabulary. However, Flege, Munro, and MacKay (1995) found that the degree of perceived foreign accent, while undeniably determined by when in life individuals started learning their second language, was also affected by language dominance and by how often these individuals used the second language in their daily lives. Thus, individuals who arrived in a new country and learned a new language later in life tended to use their first language more, while individuals who arrived early tended to use their first language to a lesser extent. Language dominance has a measurable effect on accent in both languages: native speakers of Korean who arrived in the USA early in life had little or no foreign accent in English, but displayed noticeable accents in their Korean pronunciation. The opposite was true for native speakers of Korean who had entered the USA later in life (Yeni-Komshian, Flege, & Liu, 2000). These studies do not support the idea of a sharply delineated critical period for second language learning, but rather suggest that the relationship between age of exposure and ultimate level of attainment in a second language may be explained by how often individuals use each of their languages and the degree of interference between languages.

### 12.3.3   *Neural representation of a second language*

When an individual acquires a second language, which cortical areas are recruited for processing this new language? Research using fMRI suggests that if both languages are acquired early in life they will involve the same left-hemispheric brain regions (Perani & Abutalebi, 2005) – but what happens when one language is acquired later in life? Does the later learned language recruit a different cortical network from the first language? Recent fMRI evidence is not conclusive: while some studies show activation in the same cortical areas for first- and second-language processing (Perani, Paulesu, Sebastián-Gallés, Dupoux, Dehaene, Bettinardi, et al., 1998; Pu, Liu, Spinks, Mahankali, Xiong, Feng, et al., 2001), others suggest that first and second languages recruit different areas (Dehaene, Dupoux, Mehler, Cohen, Paulesu, Perani, et al., 1997; Kim, Relkin, Lee, & Hirsch, 1997). A recent study suggests that additional resources are needed for processing a late second language, but the additional neuronal activity is found predominantly in areas that are already specialised for language, such as Broca's area (Wartenburger, Heekeren, Abutalebi, Cappa, Villringer, & Perani, 2003). Thus, languages acquired later in life tend to share many of the neural circuits used by one's first language.

Perhaps second languages require additional neural resources not because they are acquired later in life, but because individuals are less proficient in them? To explore this issue, Briellmann, Saling, Connell, Waites, Abbott, and Jackson (2004) scanned polyglot speakers of four languages as they were asked to silently generate verbs (e.g. *swim*) in response to a series of nouns (e.g. *fish*). Irrespective of when the second language was acquired, lesser proficiency in the language resulted in greater cerebral activation of the language circuits during word generation. This suggests that the amount of activation was linked to the degree of effort required to generate words in the second language. However, in another study (Perani, Abutalebi, Paulesu, Brambati, Scifo, Cappa, et al., 2003), when proficiency in first and second languages was identical, individuals showed measurably larger activation for their second language during a word-generation task, even when there was only a small difference in the age of acquisition of the two languages (e.g. when the second language was acquired at three years of age). This finding suggests that additional cortical resources are needed to generate words in a second language – even for a second language acquired early in life. Conversely, when it comes to comprehension, lesser proficiency in a second language has been linked to lesser activation of the neural substrate (Perani et al., 1998); one interpretation of this finding is that individuals activate a smaller associative network when comprehending the language in which they are less proficient. In addition to age of acquisition and proficiency, frequency of use is another factor that impacts the amount of activation of language circuits. Indeed, greater cortical activation has been observed when processing a lesser-used second language, even if the individual's proficiency in the second language is as high as in their first language (Perani et al., 2003).

Recently, foreign adoption has provided an interesting context for exploring the neural substrate of first- and second-language acquisition (see Figure 12.5). In many instances, the children involved in international adoptions stop using their first

Figure 12.5   *International adoptions allow scientists to explore how the brain adapts to the replacement of a first language by a new language after the adoption.*
*Source:* © Thomas M Perkins.  Used under licence from Shutterstock.

language and develop native levels of proficiency in their second language. In this situation, the second language appears to take over the cortical areas that previously were dedicated to processing the first language. Evidence for this comes from a study of Korean adoptees to France who reported not to have any recollection of their first language (Pallier, Dehaene, Poline, LeBihan, Argenti, Dupoux, et al., 2003). These individuals had been adopted into French families between three and eight years of age, and had not had any further exposure to Korean since the time of their adoption. Importantly, at the time of testing, the Korean adoptees, like native French controls, were unable to distinguish Korean from a number of other, unknown foreign languages. Crucially, fMRI data obtained while the adoptees were listening to sentences in the different languages also showed no difference between Korean and the other unfamiliar languages. Moreover, exposure to French activated the same brain areas in the Korean adoptees as in French native speakers. This suggests that during early childhood, the involved brain circuits are plastic enough to accommodate cortical representation of another language. Even though neural commitment to the ambient language starts during the first year of life, it apparently takes many years of further consolidation for a language to become stably represented in the brain, and a change in linguistic environment can reverse the initial neural commitment. However, the fMRI data also showed that the extent of cortical activation in response to the French stimuli was somewhat smaller in the Korean adoptees. This is in line with the aforementioned findings (Perani et al., 1998) that lesser proficiency in a language is associated with less extensive activation during comprehension tasks. It might also suggest that the replacement of Korean by French was not quite complete.

Even though the adoptees in the Pallier et al. (2003) study appeared not to recognise Korean, one might wonder whether a first language can ever be truly forgotten. Recently, Bowers, Mattys, and Gage (2009) explored this issue in adults who had early childhood exposure to Zulu or Hindi, but no further exposure to these languages as adults. Bowers and colleagues trained the adults to discriminate a Zulu and a Hindi phonological contrast over a set of 30 training sessions. Although no learning occurred during the initial training sessions, from around the 15th session participants who had encountered Zulu as children showed improvement in performance with the Zulu, but not with the Hindi contrast. Similarly, participants exposed to Hindi as children started to show improved performance with the Hindi, but not with the Zulu contrast. This improvement in discrimination ability for the 'forgotten' language was only evident when participants were younger than 40 years of age. This suggests that when too much time has elapsed since the time of exposure to a language in childhood, any residual implicit knowledge of the language may indeed decay completely, making relearning less likely. These findings invite the speculation that the Korean adoptees tested by Pallier and colleagues (2003), who were all below 32 years of age, might indeed have shown some residual implicit knowledge of Korean had they been given the task of relearning Korean phonology.

In sum, over the course of development, certain brain areas become optimised for processing language and are engaged as individuals gain proficiency in a second language. The available evidence argues against a strictly delineated critical period for language development; rather, neural plasticity is reduced gradually as a consequence of learning, with new abilities competing for access to functionally specified neural networks. This competition may be amplified by entrenchment of representations learned early, which makes it necessary to reconfigure an already committed system, a process that takes time and makes learning of new abilities slower (Thomas & Johnson, 2008). The same logic can also explain effects of early language deprivation: if early neural commitment to language does not take place, the relevant areas may become committed to processing other types of information, which reduces the capacity for those areas to re-dedicate themselves to processing language at a later point during development. Thus, it may be more accurate to view age-related decline in the ability to learn language as the result of diminishing neural resources due to the neural commitment that takes place during development, rather than as the result of a biologically predetermined process of maturation that concludes within a critical period.

## SUMMARY

- **In the majority of people the neural circuits dedicated to language processing are located in the left hemisphere, which suggests that there is a genetic predisposition for the two hemispheres to process different aspects of the auditory environment.**

- **From as early as two months of age, functional specialisation for language can be detected using functional neuroimaging techniques. Brain activation at this early age is specific to language and can be differentiated from other auditory sequences like music.**

- **At the same time, the right hemisphere shows early specialisation for processing speech prosody. Thus, from infancy, children show similar patterns of brain activation during language processing as adults, across both hemispheres.**

- **There is evidence that some mechanisms relevant for language, such as sensorimotor coordination and motor skill learning, are regulated by FOXP2, a gene that serves as a transcription factor controlling the expression of other genes. Disruption of FOXP2 in humans leads to language disorders.**

- **The brain has the capacity to adapt to complex language-related tasks such as reading later in life. Writing systems tend to use sets of features that the visual system is adapted to process, which explains why orthographic word forms are processed in the same brain area regardless of writing system.**

- **While functional specialisation for language in the brain emerges in infancy, plasticity allows for later reorganisation in case of brain injury. Although this plasticity generally declines after childhood, there is considerable variability in the patterns of reorganisation.**

- The earlier the exposure to a certain set of stimuli, be it language or music, the greater the neural commitment. If language input is present early in life, the dedicated neural circuits will further consolidate beyond the biases found shortly after birth.

- The ability to learn a second language also declines with age of first exposure, but this may be due in part to insufficient input and practice with the second language. In general, bilingual individuals utilise the same neural substrate in processing their first and second languages.

- Children adopted into foreign families may forget their first language. In such cases, the second language appears to take over the neural circuits previously dedicated to processing the first language. Still, some implicit knowledge of 'forgotten' languages can be recovered after a period of relearning.

# FURTHER READING

## *Key studies*

For information on early functional specialisation for language in the brain, read Dehaene-Lambertz, G., Montavont, A., Jobert, A., Allirol, L., Dubois, J., Hertz-Pannier, L. et al. (2009). Language or music, mother or Mozart? Structural and environmental influences on infants' language networks. *Brain and Language, 114,* 53–65.

To learn about the effect of age of acquisition of a second language, read Pallier, C., Dehaene, S., Poline. J. B., LeBihan, D., Argenti, A. M., Dupoux, E. & Mehler, J. (2003). Brain imaging of language plasticity in adopted adults: Can a second language replace the first? *Cerebral Cortex, 13,* 155–161.

## *Overview Articles*

For an accessible review of the role of FOXP2 in human language, read Marcus, G. F. & Fisher, S. E. (2003). FOXP2 in focus: What can genes tell us about speech and language? *Trends in Cognitive Sciences, 7,* 257–262.

For a recent overview of the neural basis of first and second language, read Perani, D. & Abutalebi, J. (2005). The neural basis of first and second language processing. *Current Opinion in Neurobiology, 15,* 202–206.

## *Books*

For a better understanding of how language is processed in the brain, read Denes, G. (2011). *Talking heads: The neuroscience of language.* New York: Psychology Press or Stemmer, B. & Whitaker, H. A. (2008). *Handbook of the neuroscience of language.* London: Academic Press.

# Glossary

**abjads**   writing systems in which symbols (graphemes) encode consonants but not vowels.

**affiliative speech**   use of language as a means of establishing and maintaining connectedness to others, through collaborative or obliging speech acts that support, elaborate or affirm the remarks of others.

**agreement**   grammatical phenomenon in which a grammatical feature of one word is aligned with a grammatical feature of another word (e.g. a noun might agree with a verb, adjective or pronoun in person, number or gender).

**alloparents**   individuals besides the parents who engage in the care and provisioning of offspring.

**allophones**   pronunciation variants of individual speech sounds that do not mark distinctions in meaning.

**alphabets**   writing systems that code both consonants and vowels.

**analytic phonics**   literacy instruction method that encourages learners to link letters with corresponding sounds.

**analytic strategy**   style of early language production whereby children heavily use individual words and a high proportion of object names to convey meanings; compare with holistic strategy.

**anaphoric co-reference**   also called pronominal co-reference; the use of an anaphoric device (usually a pronoun) to refer back to an entity previously mentioned in the discourse.

**angular gyrus**   a ridge located in the parietal lobe, near the edge of the temporal lobe; it is involved in language processing.

**anterior**   towards the front, in front of (refers to locations in the brain).

**aphasia**   condition caused by damage to the language-processing areas in the left cerebral hemisphere; characterised by various patterns of language impairment depending on the extent of damage and the neural circuits involved.

**arguments**   linguistic expressions that indicate what a predicate is about; usually a noun phrase, but other grammatical constituents are possible arguments (e.g. 'how to drive his tractor' in *John taught me how to drive his tractor*).

**argument structure**   also called valence; verb-specific expectations regarding the number and placement of noun phrases and other obligatory grammatical constituents.

**artificial grammar**   experimental methodology which examines implicit learning of grammatical patterns; participants are exposed to sequences of stimuli (e.g. syllables, tones, letters) generated by a set of rules and are subsequently tested on their ability to distinguish sequences that follow the rules from those that do not.

**artificial language**   experimental methodology which teaches participants aspects of an artificially created miniature language to control for prior knowledge and to reduce the complexity associated with natural languages; some variants are referred to as the artificial grammar learning task.

**assertive speech**   use of language to influence others and to assert one's independence.

**auditory nerve**   nerve that connects the cochlea with the brain.

**Auditory Scaffolding Hypothesis**   hypothesis that exposure to sound (i.e. through spoken language) supports the ability to learn sequential information.

**autism spectrum disorder (ASD)**   developmental disability characterised by social and communicative deficits, restriction of interests, repetitive behaviour.

**autobiographical memory**   assemblage of memories of personally experienced events.

**AXB design**   auditory discrimination task in which participants have to decide whether a tone in the middle of a three-tone sequence is the same as the tone that precedes or follows it.

**babbling**   obligatory vocalisations of pre-verbal infants; includes canonical and variegated babbling stages.

**babbling drift**   infants' production of more accurate approximations of ambient speech sounds as language-specific information about phonemes in memory gradually consolidates.

**baby sign programmes**   parenting movement that advocates the teaching of symbolic gestures to pre-verbal infants.

**basal ganglia**   in concert with the inferior frontal lobe forms a functional network supporting skill acquisition; becomes activated when simple and higher-level grammatical structures are processed.

**bilingualism**   acquisition and use of two languages.

**Broca's area**   region of the left inferior frontal gyrus; it is named after Pierre Paul Broca, a physician who identified its functional involvement in language processing.

**Brodmann areas**   numbered from 1 to 52; brain areas functionally differentiated by distinctive cell types and patterns of neural connectivity.

**canonical babbling**   pre-verbal vocalisations consisting of repetition of syllables such as *dadada* or *bababa*.

**cardinal word principle**   the underlying principle of counting which implies that the last number reached as items are counted indicates the number of items in the whole set.

**case markers**   inflections that mark the thematic roles of nouns (i.e. who did what to whom).

**caudate nucleus**   one of several subcortical structures involved in language processing that shows abnormal development in individuals with SLI; the caudate nucleus is located within the basal ganglia and plays a role in the control of voluntary movement.

**cerebellum**   one of several subcortical structures involved in language processing that shows abnormal development in individuals with SLI; the cerebellum is located at the base of the brain and plays an important role in motor coordination, including speech–motor programming.

**cheremes**   out-of-use term for basic units of gesture in sign languages; the distinct hand shapes, orientations, locations, movements, and facial expressions that make up individual signs are now referred to as phonemes in analogy to spoken language.

**Child Language Data Exchange System (CHILDES)**   an online, publicly available archive of child language data with transcripts, audio, and video of children acquiring their first language(s).

**child language impairment**   alternative name for Specific Language Impairment (SLI); impairment or delay in normal language development.

**child-directed speech**   also called infant-directed speech; the typical speech register used when talking to infants and small children.

**childhood amnesia**   inability of adults to recall personally experienced events from infancy and early childhood.

**closed syllables**   type of syllable ending in a consonant, as in *mop* or *pad*.

**co-articulation**   how the pronunciation of a speech sound is influenced by the articulation of the preceding and following speech sounds.

**cochlea**   a spiral-shaped structure in the inner ear containing hair cells that convert sound waves into neural impulses to be transmitted to the brain.

**cochlear implants**   implanted electrical devices that convert sound waves into neural impulses, thereby providing deaf individuals with a partial sense of hearing.

**Codes for the Human Analysis of Transcripts (CHAT)**   a system for transcribing and coding speech samples; this common format allows users to conduct searches and analyse transcripts using CLAN software (all transcripts in the CHILDES archive are in CHAT format).

**collective breeders**   certain species of animals (including humans) that pool the resources of group members to care for their offspring.

**communicative intentions**   a speaker's goals that motivate an act of communication in a specific context.

**compound words**   a word consisting of more than one stem; the result of a word-formation process by which a new word is created by combining other words.

**Computerised Language Analysis (CLAN)**   a set of computerised analytical tools (software) that allow users to conduct searches and analyse CHAT-formatted transcripts; users may analyse any of the transcripts in the CHILDES archive using the CLAN programs.

**concordance rates**   the proportion of twins having the same trait; comparison of concordance rates for identical and fraternal twins can help geneticists to determine whether the trait has a genetic basis.

**consonants**   phonemes like /p/, /t/, or /s/ that are produced by constricting the airflow in different parts of the oral cavity in different ways.

**conspecifics**   members of one's own species.

**constructions**   also called syntactic structures; the structural configurations of words in a sentence.

**Construction Grammar**   a theoretical framework for the study of syntax that views linguistic constructions as the basic building blocks of grammar; this framework contrasts with Generative Grammar, with its abstract syntactic constituents and very general combinatorial operations.

**content words**   nouns, verbs, adjectives, and adverbs (i.e. the words that convey content or meaning); content words contrast with function words, which have grammatical functions.

**conventional gestures**   culture-specific hand and body movements used to convey specific meanings (e.g. nodding one's head indicates 'yes', shaking one's head indicates 'no' in Western Europe but not in Greece, Turkey, or Bulgaria).

**conversational implicatures**   utterances where a speaker intentionally violates one of the Gricean maxims to make a specific communicative point (i.e. to express a non-literal meaning).

**cooing**   'gooing' sounds that begin around 2 months of age, involving tongue articulations at the back of the mouth.

**coordinated interpersonal timing**   changes in the temporal patterning of one person's behaviour in response to another person's behaviour.

**critical period**   a time period in early development during which the organism displays heightened sensitivity to a particular type of stimulus (e.g. visual input or language); if learners are not exposed to the relevant stimuli during the critical period, they may lack functional skills in the relevant domain throughout life.

**declarative memory**   one of two types of long-term memory (the other being procedural memory); comprises memory for facts and knowledge that can be consciously recalled.

**deep orthography**   a writing system in which there is no simple one-to-one correspondence between the letters of the alphabet and the phonemes of the language (e.g. English).

**deferred imitation**   imitation of another person's behaviour without cueing; requires a delay between the child observing the action-to-be-imitated and the child's imitation of it.

**deictic gestures**   hand and body movements, such as pointing, that can only be interpreted in context, because their meaning varies depending on their circumstances of use.

**derivational affixes**   word-form modifications that change the meaning of a word to fit a new semantic context and/or to change its part of speech; for example, adding the suffix *-ment* to a verb creates a noun, as in *govern → government*; adding the prefix *un-* to the verb *do*, as in *do → undo*, changes its meaning.

**derivational morphology**   the subfield of linguistics concerned with the processes by which word-form modifications create new words with distinct meanings; relies on changes in derivational affixes.

**developmental aphasia**   a term for Specific Language Impairment (SLI) that was used in the 1970s; refers to a delay in first-language acquisition in cases where there is no apparent brain damage, mental retardation, or developmental syndrome.

**developmental dyslexia**   a condition marked by persistent problems in learning to read and spell, despite appropriate instruction and intelligence scores within the normal range.

**diffusion tensor imaging (DTI)**   a magnetic resonance imaging (MRI) technique that allows researchers to produce images of neural fibre tracts consisting of bundles of axons.

**digit span**   the length of the longest list of numbers that an individual can repeat back in the correct order immediately after presentation of the last number.

**digraphs**   letter combinations such as *ng, th, sh,* or *ch*, as in *thing, chair,* and *shingle*, used to represent phonemes.

**dimensional change card sorting (DCCS) task**   a widely used measure of the executive control of attention in preschool-aged children (3- to 5-year-olds); children must sort cards first by one dimension (e.g. shape) and then switch rules to sort the same cards by a different dimension (e.g. colour).

**diminutives**   derivational affixes used to modify word forms to express smallness, intimacy, and endearment; diminutives are frequent in the child-directed speech registers of many languages.

**discourse**   conversational aspects of language use, which may be applicable to specific social contexts.

**discourse novelty**   any aspect of an event (e.g. a novel object or action) that is new information within the context of an ongoing conversation.

**discourse pressure**   the tendency for preceding utterances to constrain the form of subsequent utterances within a dialogue.

**ditransitive verbs**   verbs that require three arguments (subject, direct object, indirect object), for example the verb *give* in the sentence *John gave Mary a book*.

**doublets**   reduplicated letters (e.g. *ss* in *dress*).

**Down syndrome**   a developmental disability caused by all or part of an extra 21st chromosome; Down syndrome is associated with abnormalities in physical growth and facial characteristics, and with mental retardation.

**Duchenne smiles**   smiles that express genuine enjoyment; can be identified by a raising of the corners of the lips, accompanied by a cheek raise that creates crow's feet around the eyes.

**dyadic interaction**   a communicative interaction between two individuals; here mainly used to describe the face-to-face communicative interactions of infants and their caregivers.

**dyspraxia**   a motor-learning difficulty associated with impaired planning of movement and coordination.

**electroencephalogram (EEG)**   a recording of electrical activity over the scalp using a multiple electrode cap; this electrophysiological method is called electroencephalography.

**emotive gestures**   hand and body movements that express emotion, such as jumping up and down, or stamping one's feet.

**emphatic gestures**   hand and body movements that punctuate a speaker's message (i.e. are used to emphasise a point).

**encephalisation**   increased cranial volume relative to body size (i.e. the amount of brain mass that exceeds what is expected given the animal's body mass).

**epistemic triangle**   refers to the social context of referential communication (i.e. word learning); for shared meanings to be established, both the child and another person must be attentive to some aspect of the external world, and must be mutually aware that they are attending to the same thing.

**etymology**   the historical origins of words.

**event-related potentials (ERPs)**   electrophysiological response to an external stimulus; ERPs are measured using electroencephalography (EEG) by averaging the multiple electrical responses that are time-locked to a specific event.

**executive functioning**   a control system, mainly situated in the frontal lobe of the neocortex, that manages other cognitive functions; involved in the deliberate control of attention, planning, selection of task-relevant responses, suppression of task-irrelevant responses, and task switching.

**fast mapping**   a process supporting rapid word learning in toddlers; an ability to link a new word to a concept after only a few exposures to the word in an informative context.

**finite-state grammar**   an artificial grammar characterised by a finite set of elements (e.g. letters, syllables, tones) and a finite set of links between the elements (i.e. permissible sequences); grammatical sequences are generated from a starting position, adding elements by following the possible links until an end state is reached.

**fissure**   a groove or deep furrow within the brain.

**focal lesions**   brain damage in a restricted, circumscribed area of tissue; often the result of strokes, tumours, epileptic seizures, or trauma.

**formants**   the most prominent frequencies, in terms of amplitude, in the sound spectrum of the voice.

**FOXP2**   Forkhead bOX protein P2 gene located on the 7th chromosome; encodes the FOXP2 protein that belongs to a family of forkhead transcription factors for which the resulting regulatory proteins are involved in a variety of control functions affecting cellular differentiation and proliferation.

**frequency**   how often a morpheme occurs in the language; for affixes, frequency is largely determined by how essential they are to the generation of well-formed utterances.

**frontal lobe**   a region of the human brain located at the front of each cerebral hemisphere

**function words**   determiners, pronouns, auxiliary verbs, conjunctions, prepositions, and particles (i.e. words that indicate the grammatical relationships between other words in the sentence); function words contrast with content words that carry the meaning of the sentence.

**functional magnetic resonance imaging (fMRI)**   a brain-imaging technique that allows researchers to study the level of neural activity (i.e. blood-oxygen level changes) in various brain areas associated with the processing of specific stimuli; see also hemodynamic responses.

**fundamental frequency**   the lowest of the formants, abbreviated $F_0$; what is perceived as the voice pitch of different speakers.

**fusiform gyrus**   a ridge on the interior side of the temporal lobe; it appears to be involved in word recognition (reading).

**gaze following**   the ability to visually track where another individual is looking.

**generalised imitation**   the ability to imitate a modelled action using a new set of objects.

**Generative Grammar**   a theoretical framework for the study of syntax, first proposed by Noam Chomsky, that involves a set of abstract rules to generate all possible sentences of a language; contrasts with Construction Grammar.

**generativity**   the unlimited productivity of human languages (i.e. property of a self-contained system that generates an infinite number of possible sentences).

**genetic linkage**   the tendency for genes located near one another on the same chromosome to be inherited together; identification of linked sets of genes is often a critical step in locating the individual genes associated with specific developmental disabilities and diseases.

**gesture sentences**   sequences of gestures in the home sign produced by isolated deaf children; these convey meanings similar to the early word combinations of hearing children.

**glottis**   the part of the vocal tract that contains the vocal folds.

**graphemes**   visual symbols (e.g. letters) used in writing systems that encode aspects of sound or meaning.

**grapheme-to-phoneme conversion rules**   probabilistic rules that associate printed symbols (e.g. individual letters and letter combinations) with speech sounds, potentially allowing any newly encountered word to be pronounced irrespective of its meaning.

**Gricean maxims**   a set of principles that govern cooperative verbal exchanges of information.

**gyrus**   a ridge in the cerebral cortex.

**hemodynamic responses**   changes in blood flow and blood oxygenation associated with neural activity; measurement of dynamic changes in blood flow in response to specific stimuli is the basis of functional magnetic resonance imaging (fMRI) technology.

**hierarchical Bayesian inference**   a process of inference that allows a rational learner to evaluate a hypothesis (e.g. a set of grammatical rules) about how certain data (e.g. the specific language input encountered) may have been generated; can operate on multiple levels (e.g. sentences → specific grammar → general type of grammar) and involves maximising the trade-off between simplicity of hypothesis and goodness of fit to the data.

**hierarchical Bayesian modelling**   a mathematical framework used to model hierarchical Bayesian inference.

**high-amplitude sucking procedure**   a habituation procedure that allows researchers to study how neonates and very young infants (up to 5 or 6 months of age) discriminate stimuli by measuring their rate of sucking on a pacifier; when a particular stimulus is repeated, infants will lose interest and their sucking rate will decline – therefore, an increase in sucking rate following a change in stimulus is evidence that the change was detected.

**hints**   speech acts that require the listener to infer that an utterance was not meant as a statement, but as an indirect request.

**holistic strategy**   a style of early speech production whereby the infant uses a high proportion of unanalysed holistic phrases as single-word utterances (e.g. *here-you-are* or *what's-dat?*); compare with analytic strategy.

**home literacy environment**   the extent to which the home environment supports children's literacy development; this includes factors such as the number of books and other written materials in the home as well as how often and for how long the child reads with caregivers.

**home sign**   the gestural communication systems created by isolated deaf children who are not exposed to a sign language.

**hominin**   refers to humans and their ancestors, and includes all the Homo species, all the Australopithecines, and others such as Ardipithecus; this term is more specific and replaces the previous term 'hominid'.

**homophones**   words that have the same pronunciation as other words but a different meaning, for example *bank* (of a river) vs. *bank* (financial institution).

**hyper-articulation**   exaggerated articulation that maximises the acoustic differences between phonemes (e.g. between different vowels).

**hyperbole**   non-literal language use consisting of an exaggerated statement or claim.

**iambic**   a weak–strong stress pattern, as in *guitar* or *surprise*.

**iconic gestures**   hand and body movements that physically resemble their referents.

**idioms**   types of non-literal expression, in which a word or phrase has a conventional meaning that differs from its literal meaning.

**imprinting**   a phenomenon whereby many animals form a lifelong attachment to a specific stimulus (e.g. a gosling to its mother) if that stimulus is encountered during a critical period early in life.

**inattentional blindness**   a failure to perceive something in plain sight.

**Index of Productive Syntax (IPSyn)**   a measure of grammatical development based on a sample of 100 spontaneous utterances, and utilising a checklist for 56 syntactic and morphological forms.

**indirect negative evidence**   information available in the input that potentially indicates which child-produced forms are ungrammatical; for example when a caregiver repeats what their child has said, but recasts the utterance using the correct grammatical construction.

**inductive generalisation**   process by which children generalise properties of an exemplar to other members of the category.

**infant-directed speech**   also called child-directed speech; the typical speech register used when talking to infants and small children.

**inferior**   below (refers to locations in the brain).

**inferior frontal gyrus**   a ridge located towards the bottom of the frontal lobe of the brain; the left inferior frontal gyrus roughly corresponds to Broca's area, a region implicated in language processing, especially grammatical processing and speech production.

**inferior temporal gyrus**   a ridge located below the middle temporal sulcus; parts of it are activated when high-imagery words are processed.

**inflectional affixes**   word-form modifications that change the meaning of a word to fit its grammatical context; for example, adding the suffix *-s* to indicate plural number, as in *bottle* → *bottles*.

**inflectional morphology**   the subfield of linguistics concerned with the processes by which word-form modifications mark changes in grammatical features, such as number, gender, and tense; relies on inflectional affixes.

**International Phonetic Alphabet (IPA)**   a standardised system of phonetic transcription that uses an inventory of signs (letters and diacritics) to represent the sounds used in spoken languages.

**intersubjectivity**   mutual awareness between two or more people that they are experiencing something together and have a shared understanding of the situation.

**intonation**   variation in pitch while speaking; used for emphasis as well as for other communicative purposes, such as asking a question, stating a point of fact, or conveying sarcasm; can also convey emotion.

**intransitive verbs**   verbs that require only one argument (the subject), for example the verb *sleep* in the sentence *The baby is sleeping.*

**irony**   a non-literal expression intended to mean the exact opposite of what the speaker has said.

**item-based**   the view that children learn on an item-by-item basis the combinatorial properties of each word they encounter.

**joint attention**   the coordination of the infant's attention with that of another person to some aspect of the world.

**late bloomers**   late-talking toddlers who apparently catch up to their peers during the preschool years.

**late talkers**   toddlers at 24 months of age who have fewer than 50 words in their expressive vocabularies and do not yet produce any multi-word utterances.

**latent semantic analysis (LSA)**   a mathematical model used to explain how a statistical learning mechanism operating over large amounts of text learns vocabulary; the underlying assumption is that words with closely related meanings will occur close together in text.

**Less-Is-More**   a proposal that the limited working memory capacity of infants aids language learning by restricting the size of the units they can process.

**lexical bootstrapping**   hypothesis proposing that knowledge of grammar is the product of accumulated item-specific knowledge of how individual words are used.

**lexical entry**   the listing of an individual word in one's mental vocabulary; contains information about the word's meaning, pronunciation, part of speech, grammatical features, spelling.

**lexical route**   one of two processing routes involved in reading; the reader accesses a word's meaning and pronunciation directly from its spelling, using whole-word recognition as opposed to phonological decoding.

**lexicon**   a person's vocabulary knowledge, which includes word meanings, pronunciations, spellings, and grammatical information.

**linguistic relativism**   the conjecture that the diverse features of the world's languages might promote different ways of perceiving and thinking about the world.

**logical problem of language acquisition**   the view that languages are too complicated to be learned from the input; that children must have innate knowledge of language because the input is too impoverished to provide sufficient information regarding the structure of the ambient language.

**logographic scripts**   writing systems whereby symbols (graphemes) encode entire morphemes.

**longitudinal studies**   a research design whereby individual development is tracked over a period of time.

**low-pass filtered**   natural speech that has passed through a filter to block sound wave frequencies above a specific cut-off point.

**MacArthur–Bates Communicative Development Inventory (CDI)**   a parental checklist that measures vocabulary development in infants and toddlers.

**magnetic resonance imaging (MRI)**   a medical imaging technique that uses magnetic fields to produce detailed images of soft tissue, such as the human brain.

**magnetoencephalography (MEG)**   a brain-imaging technique that records the magnetic fields generated by the brain's electrical activity.

**manner of articulation**   how the airflow during speech production is manipulated by the movements of articulators, such as the tongue, lips, and jaws.

**manually coded English**   a system for rendering English through manual gestures; manually coded English approximates the grammar of English, and is structurally unrelated to any sign language (e.g. American Sign Language, British Sign Language).

**mean length of utterances (MLU)**   a commonly used measure of grammatical development; a measure of the average number of morphemes per utterance.

**merge** a single combinatory operation that combines words into syntactic units, whereby the merged unit retains the grammatical features of one of its constituents.

**meta-analysis** a statistical technique used to examine overall trends across studies and to identify possible moderators of effect sizes across studies.

**metalinguistic awareness** explicit awareness or knowledge about the structure and properties of a language.

**metaphor** non-literal language use involving an implied comparison of two unlike things that happen to share one or more important characteristics.

**metrical stress** phenomenon where one syllable tends to be more prominent than the others when multiple syllables are combined to form words.

**middle temporal gyrus** a ridge located in the temporal lobe that is involved in language processing.

**mismatch negativity** a specific electrical signature (event-related potential) elicited by the brain's detection of an oddball in a series of auditory stimuli.

**mora** a unit of syllable weight; consonant–vowel syllables with short vowels, (e.g. *the*) have one mora, whereas consonant–vowel syllables with long vowels (e.g. *pie*) have two morae.

**mora-timed** a type of stress pattern in languages where the rhythmical structure is based on a unit smaller than the syllable (i.e. the mora).

**morpheme** the basic building block of word meaning; the smallest linguistic unit with distinct conceptual meaning.

**morphological awareness** explicit awareness or knowledge about the morphology of a language (i.e. awareness of how prefixes and suffixes are used to modify and create new word forms).

**morphological paradigm** a set of words with the same stem but with different inflections (e.g. the case-marking paradigm of the Russian noun *stol* [table]: *stol, stola, stolu, stolom, stole, stoly, stolov, stolam, stolami, stolakh*).

**morphology** the subfield of linguistics concerned with the processes by which word forms are modified, using derivational and inflectional affixes to create new words.

**motionese** a mode of action displayed by mothers when demonstrating the properties of novel objects to their children; characterised by gestures and movements in close proximity to the child, which are enthusiastic, repetitive, and relatively large in scale.

**mutual exclusivity bias** a word-learning heuristic whereby children assume that the meanings of different words are distinct from one another without any overlap in the range of their referents.

**myelinisation** the production of myelin, a white fatty matter that forms an insulating layer around the axons of neurons and is essential for neuronal conductivity and proper neuronal functioning.

**natural pedagogy** the use of ostensive signals to indicate that cultural knowledge is being taught within a communicative interaction.

**near-infrared optical topography** also called near-infrared spectroscopy; functional brain-imaging technique used to identify substances through the light spectrum emitted or absorbed by them; this method exploits the fact that concentrations of chemicals associated with changes in blood oxygenation and blood volume can be detected by their different specific spectra in the near-infrared range.

**near-infrared spectroscopy (NIRS)** also called near-infrared optical topography; functional brain-imaging technique used to identify substances through the light spectrum emitted or absorbed by them; this method exploits the fact that concentrations of chemicals associated with changes in blood oxygenation and blood volume can be detected by their different specific spectra in the near-infrared range.

**negative evidence**   evidence in the input provided to children that potentially tells them what forms are incorrect; for example, caregivers might correct children's pronunciation, vocabulary or grammar each time they produce an incorrect form; negative evidence in the form of grammar lessons or explicit teaching seems to be rare in child-directed speech.

**non-word repetition task**   a measure of phonological short-term memory; individuals are instructed to repeat meaningless sequences of syllables such as *amberillock* or *frovilankus* that vary in length (numbers of syllables).

**noun bias**   a word-learning bias marked by a disproportionate number of count nouns in toddlers' early vocabularies.

**noun phrase**   a grammatical phrase based on a noun or a pronoun.

**novel name, nameless category (N3C) principle**   a word-learning heuristic whereby children will search for a yet-to-be-named category whenever they hear a novel word.

**numerical cognition**   the cognitive underpinnings of number concepts and mathematics.

**object (direct object, indirect object)**   grammatical roles that occur with transitive and ditransitive verbs; for example, in the sentence *Mary baked John a cake*, the direct object is *a cake* and the indirect object is *John*.

**occipital lobe**   a region of the human brain located at the rear of each cerebral hemisphere.

**oddball detection paradigm**   an event-related potential (ERP) paradigm used to measure a specific electrophysical response to a novel auditory stimulus (i.e. a mismatch negativity); this task involves presentation of a series of identical auditory stimuli occasionally interspersed with a different stimulus.

**open syllables**   type of syllable structure in which syllables lack a syllable coda, for example as in the words *cyc, pay, spy*.

**open-set test**   a test used to assess spoken word recognition in the absence of contextual cues.

**orthography**   the writing system of a language.

**over-extension**   word-learning errors that occur when a child uses a word to refer to items outside its category.

**over-generalisation errors**   speech production errors that occur when a child uses an affix or a grammatical construction with a word for which the affix or construction does not normally apply; this results in the production of unconventional forms such as *goed* (went) or *broom it* (sweep it).

**over-imitation**   faithful reproduction of a modelled action, to include wasteful or unnecessary details that are irrelevant to the goal of the action.

**parameters**   within the Generative Grammar framework, all languages are thought to have the same underlying principles and to vary only with respect to specific features (parameters).

**parietal lobe**   a region of the human brain located behind the frontal lobe of each cerebral hemisphere.

**parsing**   the ability to analyse and interpret the syntactic structure of a sentence.

**parts of speech**   also called word classes; grammatical categories of words (e.g. noun, verb, adjective, etc.) determined by the range of syntactic contexts in which the word appears, and its morphological forms.

**perisylvian region**   areas of the cerebral cortex on both sides of the Sylvian fissure, the deep groove that separates the frontal and parietal lobes (above) from the temporal lobe (below).

**phonemes**   phones that carry distinctions in meaning.

**phonemic awareness**   explicit awareness or knowledge of the smallest units of sound that carry meaning.

**phones**   the various speech sounds that humans are able to produce.

**phonetics**   the subfield of linguistics concerned with the articulatory and acoustic properties of speech.

**phonics approach**   an approach to reading instruction that teaches children to link speech sounds with letters and letter combinations.

**phonological awareness**   explicit awareness or knowledge that words are made up of smaller units of sound.

**phonological bootstrapping**   a proposal that children use phonological and prosodic cues to identify grammatical structures.

**phonological decoding**   also called phonological recoding; the use of grapheme-to-phoneme conversion rules in reading to convert printed symbols into the sound patterns of words.

**phonological neighbours**   words that differ in pronunciation only with respect to a single phoneme (e.g. *bet* has the neighbours *set, bat, beg*).

**phonological recoding**   also called phonological decoding; the use of grapheme-to-phoneme conversion rules in reading to convert printed symbols into the sound patterns of words.

**phonological route**   one of two processing routes involved in reading; the reader accesses the meaning of words by converting letters and letter combinations into speech sounds.

**phonological short-term memory**   the capacity to hold a sequence of speech sounds briefly in mind for a short amount of time.

**phonology**   the subfield of linguistics concerned with the sound patterns of languages (i.e. how speech sounds encode meaning).

**phonotactic constraints**   language-specific restrictions on what sequences of phonemes are permissible.

**phonotactic probability**   refers to the probability of different sequences of phonemes occurring in a given language.

**place of articulation**   specifies where in the oral cavity the airflow is constricted during speech sound production.

**planum temporale**   a region of the cortex located near the Sylvian fissure in the temporal lobe adjacent to the auditory cortex; the left planum temporale is involved in the higher-order integration of the sound patterns of speech.

**polyadic interactions**   communicative interactions involving more than two individuals.

**positron emission tomography (PET)**   functional brain-imaging technique that uses an injection of a radioactive compound (an analogue of glucose) to map neural activity in the brain; exploits the fact that areas of increased blood flow during task processing will have higher radioactivity due to increased glucose metabolism.

**posterior**   behind (refers to locations in the brain).

**poverty of the stimulus**   assertion put forth by Noam Chomsky that the grammars of human languages are too complex to be learned, given the limited amount of language input that children receive; that language acquisition must be supported by innate knowledge of grammar.

**pragmatics**   the subfield of linguistics concerned with the use of language in social context.

**pre-central gyrus**   part of the pre-motor cortex in the frontal lobe; becomes activated when simple and higher-level grammatical structures are processed.

**predicate–argument structure**   the propositional content of an utterance, comprising a set of entities (i.e. arguments) and their relationships and/or properties (i.e. predicates).

**predicates**   linguistic expressions that describe a property or relationship of their argument(s); predicates are typically verb phrases.

**pre-emption**   when a linguistic expression blocks production of another form; for example the irregular past-tense form *went* blocks production of *goed*.

**pretend play**   in an act of pretence, the child creates an imaginary scenario in which an object or person (or an imaginary object or person) takes on the properties and/or roles of another object or person.

**primary auditory cortex**   comprises Heschl's gyrus, which makes up the posterior part of the superior temporal gyrus in the temporal lobe; this area is involved in processing the basic features of sound, including pitch, volume, and timing.

**primary language impairment**   alternative name for Specific Language Impairment (SLI); impairment or delay in normal language development.

**principle of contrast**   a word-learning heuristic whereby children resist synonyms; the notion that all the words in one's vocabulary have different meanings and contexts of use.

**principles**   within the Generative Grammar framework, all languages are thought to have the same underlying abstract rules (principles) and to vary only with respect to specific parameters.

**procedural learning**   implicit learning of sequences via the procedural memory system; such learning is often assumed to occur without awareness.

**procedural memory**   one of two types of long-term memory (the other being declarative memory); involved in sequence learning and the coordination of sequences of actions; procedural memory seems to play an important role in grammar acquisition, and the emergent automaticity of grammatical operations.

**productivity**   the extent to which a prefix or suffix may be applied to a variety of different word types.

**prosodic boundaries**   end of a prosodic unit (i.e. a stretch of speech with a distinct prosodic contour); boundaries are often marked by a lowering of pitch and a lengthening of the preceding speech sounds.

**prosody**   the sound structure of speech at the level of the entire utterance; encompasses changes in voice quality, rhythm, speech rate, and intonation.

**quantifier spreading errors**   comprehension errors involving sentences containing a universal quantifier, such as *every* or *each*; the child incorrectly infers that a sentence like *Every car is in a garage* entails its converse – that every garage has a car in it.

**quasi-vowel**   a sound that infants begin to make at around 2 months of age; involves a short uninterrupted vowel-like sound.

**recognitory gestures**   also called nominal gestures, gestural labels, or gesture names; realistic play actions on objects, such as holding an empty cup to one's lips or using a spoon to pretend eat.

**recursion**   feature of grammar whereby syntactic rules (e.g. merge) can be applied to their own output to build increasingly complex syntactic units.

**reduplicative babbling**   the first stage of babbling, consisting of repetitions of consonant–vowel syllables such as *dadada* or *bababa*.

**referential communication task**   a perspective-taking task involving two participants who must communicate with each other about a complex object display; the critical feature of the task is that the participants are seated on opposite sides of the display, with part of the display occluded from one side.

**rime**    part of a syllable, consisting of the syllable nucleus and optional syllable coda (e.g. the *at* in words like *cat, mat, hat,* and *bat*).

**ritualisation**    a learning mechanism by which an abbreviated portion of an action sequence comes to elicit a specific response; for example, the infant may use an extended arm gesture to request an out-of-reach object.

**role-reversal imitation**    an act of imitation in which the infant assumes the role of the caregiver; for example, the mother performs an action on her son (e.g. touches his nose) and the child subsequently performs the same action back on his mother; alternatively, the mother performs an action on herself, and her son subsequently performs the same action on himself.

**Sapir–Whorf hypothesis**    a conjecture that the diverse features of the world's languages might promote different ways of perceiving and thinking about the world.

**sarcasm**    an expression intended to mean the opposite of what the speaker has said; a cutting remark produced with the intention of taunting or ridiculing another person.

**scaffolding**    caregiver behaviour that supports a child's joint activity with others, by taking into consideration the child's developmental status.

**scalar implicature**    a form of conversational implicature, involving a quantifier (e.g. *all, some, many*); when a weak term is used, the listener assumes that the speaker had a reason for not using a stronger term (e.g. *some* leads to the inference *not all*).

**schemas**    patterns or representations that are an abstraction over learned exemplars and support generalisation.

**semantic**    pertaining to the meanings of linguistic units.

**semantic associations**    links between words that are based on meaning and co-occurrence of use within a semantic field, such as *salt* and *pepper.*

**semantic features**    the specific components of meaning associated with a linguistic unit.

**semantic fields**    sets of words that are related in meaning, which are used in reference to particular domains of experience.

**semantic representations**    mental representations of the meanings of linguistic units.

**semantic role**    the relationship of a participant in an event (i.e. an argument) to the main verb (i.e. a predicate); also called a thematic role.

**semantics**    the subfield of linguistics concerned with meaning; focuses on the relationship between linguistic units and what they represent.

**serial reaction time (SRT) task**    a reaction time measure of implicit, procedural learning; participants are asked to respond as quickly as possible to a non-random sequence of spatial stimuli by button press; the reaction time decrease over blocks of trials is used as a measure of learning.

**shallow orthography**    a transparent writing system in which each letter corresponds to a single phoneme and each phoneme is usually expressed with a single letter, for example Finnish.

**shape bias**    a word-learning heuristic marked by toddlers' selective attention to the shapes of objects as the main feature that distinguishes object names (e.g. the important feature that distinguishes *cup* from *plate* is shape and not colour or material).

**sign languages**    types of language used by communities of deaf individuals; rely on manual gestures and facial expressions.

**slow mapping**    a process of gradual learning whereby a word's lexical entry becomes more detailed as the child is exposed to its varied contexts of use.

**social referencing**    the tendency to look at a significant other (e.g. a caregiver) when faced with an ambiguous situation or stimulus to gain information from the caregiver's reaction about that situation or stimulus.

**social shaping**   the process whereby a caregiver responds contingently and positively to an infant's communicative bids, and thereby increases the quantity and quality of the infant's speech and gesture.

**Specific Language Impairment (SLI)**   a developmental disability characterised by clinically significant delays in language development in the absence of mental retardation, brain injury, or disease.

**speech act**   the functional aspect of an utterance, for example whether the utterance asks a question, makes a promise or affirms someone's point of view.

**speech register**   a speech style used in a specific social situation and/or with specific people; it may involve variation in the prosodic, phonological, grammatical, and lexical characteristics of speech.

**statistical learning**   implicit, procedural learning of probabilistic co-occurrence patterns (e.g. between adjacent and non-adjacent morphemes, speech sounds, letter combinations).

**still-face effect**   infants exhibit distress when an adult suddenly freezes movement of her face in dyadic interaction; an indicator that young infants have social expectations that people will engage responsively and provide contingent feedback during face-to-face interaction.

**stress-timed languages**   type of stress pattern in languages where the metrical stress tends to occur at regular intervals.

**structural alignment**   the detection of an invariant relational pattern over different lexical items; a mechanism that underlies the use of analogy to support generalisation or metaphor comprehension.

**subject**   the most prominent grammatical role in a sentence; what the predicate is about.

**sulcus**   a groove or furrow within the brain.

**superior**   on top of (refers to locations in the brain).

**superior temporal gyrus**   a ridge located in the temporal lobe, adjacent to the Sylvian fissure, containing the primary auditory cortex; the left superior temporal gyrus roughly corresponds to Wernicke's area, a region implicated in language processing, especially comprehension; the right superior temporal gyrus is involved in the processing of speech prosody.

**superior temporal sulcus**   a groove that separates the superior temporal gyrus from the middle temporal gyrus; the left superior temporal sulcus is involved in processing the phonetic features of speech; the anterior portion of the left superior temporal sulcus is involved in mapping speech sounds onto meaning.

**syllabic script**   a type of writing system whereby symbols (graphemes) encode syllables.

**syllables**   units of organisation of sequences of phonemes within words; contains a syllable nucleus and an optional syllable onset and/or syllable coda.

**syllable coda**   refers to one or several consonants at the end of a syllable.

**syllable nucleus**   the syllable peak, usually the vowel, but occasionally a syllabic consonant, as in the final syllable of *button or butter.*

**syllable onset**   refers to one or several consonants at the beginning of a syllable.

**syllable-timed languages**   type of stress pattern in languages where the metrical stress tends to be placed on a certain syllable in the word (e.g. the next-to-last syllable) and syllables are otherwise of roughly equivalent length.

**Sylvian fissure**   also called the lateral sulcus; the deep groove that separates the frontal and parietal lobes from the temporal lobe.

**symbolic gestures**   communicative hand and body movements associated with specific meanings; encompasses iconic, conventional, and deictic gestures.

**symbolic reference**   the notion that words and gestures are used to refer to things (i.e. to point out something about the world).

**syntactic bootstrapping**   a proposal that children can use syntactic information to infer properties of a novel word, such as its part of speech.

**syntactic priming**   the tendency to use the same grammatical construction over successive utterances; for example, after hearing a sentence in the passive voice, as in *The boy is being chased by the girl*, producing a sentence like *The baby is being carried by the woman* rather than *The woman is carrying the baby*.

**syntax**   the subfield of linguistics concerned with how words are arranged to form sentences.

**synthetic phonics**   literacy instruction method that emphasises the sounding out and blending of sounds.

**talkativeness**   a general index of verbal ability, often measured as the amount of speech produced per unit of time.

**taxonomic bias**   a word-learning heuristic whereby children follow a principle of extendibility, and assume that words label categories of things as opposed to specific individuals.

**temporal lobe**   a region of the human brain located beneath the Sylvian fissure of each cerebral hemisphere.

**terrestrial bipedalism**   two-footed walking on the ground.

**Theory of Mind**   awareness that people have mental states (such as knowledge, beliefs, desires, and intentions) which may differ from one's own.

**thinking for speaking**   the idea that each language requires its own language-specific modes of thinking; that speakers of a language must attend to aspects of the world that are obligatorily encoded in the grammar of their language.

**tip-of-the-tongue**   a phenomenon involving a failure to retrieve a word; it is accompanied by a strong feeling of imminent retrieval – the person knows the word but cannot bring it to mind.

**token frequency**   how often a given construction or schema is used in general, regardless of how many different words it occurs with.

**tonal languages**   languages that use pitch to distinguish word meanings (e.g. Mandarin Chinese).

**transitive verbs**   verbs that require two arguments (subject, direct object), for example the verb *carry* in the sentence *Jill is carrying the baby*.

**transparency**   the extent to which a word stem is recognisable when it occurs in the context of an affix.

**triadic interactions**   communicative interactions between two individuals involving joint attention to entities (object, events) in the world.

**trochaic**   a strong–weak stress pattern, as in *daddy* or *candle*.

**twin studies**   research methodology used to determine the influence of genes and environment on traits and behaviour; involves a comparison of the concordance rates for identical and fraternal twins for a given trait.

**type frequency**   how often a given construction or schema is used with different words.

**under-extension**   word-learning errors that occur when a child uses a word in one context yet fails to use the same word in other appropriate contexts.

**understatement**   non-literal language which uses restraint when describing a situation, for example, by conveying a situation as less important or serious than it actually is.

**Universal Grammar**   a component of the theoretical framework proposed by Noam Chomsky; the innate language faculty that constrains children's hypotheses about the grammar of their language.

**valence**   also called argument structure; verb-specific expectations regarding the number and placement of noun phrases and other obligatory grammatical constituents; not to be confused with emotional valence.

**variegated babbling**   the second stage of babbling that incorporates different combinations of syllables, such as in the sequence *badabu*.

**verb phrase**   a grammatical phrase based on a verb.

**verbal dyspraxia**   also called verbal apraxia or apraxia of speech; a speech–motor disorder characterised by difficulties in planning and articulating speech sounds; affected individuals have difficulty controlling finely coordinated movement sequences of the mouth, tongue, lips, and soft palate.

**verbal working memory**   the capacity to actively hold verbal information (words, sentences) in mind while processing other, additional information.

**visual world paradigm**   an experimental task used with an eye-tracking device; monitors a participant's attention to objects in a visual array as they process a set of spoken instructions to manipulate specific objects.

**vocabulary spurt**   an increase in the rate of word learning occurring in the second year of life.

**voice onset time (VOT)**   the amount of time that elapses between the release of air and the onset of vocal fold vibration in consonant production.

**voicing**   refers to an aspect of articulation (i.e. whether the vocal folds are vibrating or not while the airflow is manipulated during speech sound production).

**vowels**   phonemes like /a/, /i/, or /u/ that are produced with an open vocal tract (i.e. the airflow above the glottis is not constricted); vowel articulation differs in tongue position and lip rounding; acoustically, vowels differ in first and second formant.

**Wernicke's area**   region of the left superior temporal gyrus; named after Carl Wernicke, a neurologist who identified its functional involvement in language processing.

**whole-language approach**   an approach to reading instruction that encourages children to engage directly with texts and to guess the meanings of words based on context.

**whole-object bias**   word-learning bias marked by toddlers' tendency to assume that words label whole objects as opposed to salient parts.

**whole-word approach**   an approach to reading instruction that teaches children to recognise words based on their overall shape (i.e. by sight).

**word classes**   also called parts of speech; grammatical categories of words (e.g. noun, verb, adjective, etc.), determined by the range of syntactic contexts in which the word appears, and its morphological forms.

**word combinations**   sequences of words; some word combinations are idioms (e.g. *give up* 'quit').

**word-specific formulae**   the child's first syntactic templates or schemas used to produce word combinations; these consist of a relational term and a slot (e.g. *all gone* _____ used to produce utterances such as *all gone milk* or *all gone cookies*).

**word-to-world mapping**   the process of associating words with their referents in the world.

**wug test**   an experimental task designed by Jean Berko to test children's productive use of grammatical morphemes, such as plural and past-tense inflections.

Abdel Rahman, R. & Melinger, A. (2009). Semantic context effects in language production: A swinging lexical network proposal and a review. *Language and Cognitive Processes, 24*, 713–734.

Abitbol, M. M. (1987). Obstretrics and posture in pelvic anatomy. *Journal of Human Evolution, 16*, 243–255.

Acredolo, L. & Goodwyn, S. (1988). Symbolic gesturing in normal infants. *Child Development, 59*, 450–466.

Acredolo, L. & Goodwyn, S. (1996). *Baby signs: How to talk with your baby before your baby can talk.* Chicago, IL: Contemporary Books.

Adams, A.-M. & Gathercole, S. E. (1996). Phonological working memory and spoken language development in young children. *The Quarterly Journal of Experimental Psychology A: Human Experimental Psychology, 49A*, 216–233.

Adamson, L. B. (1995). *Communication development during infancy.* Madison, WI: Brown & Benchmark Publishers.

Adamson, L. B. & Bakeman, R. (1984). Mothers' communicative acts: Changes during infancy. *Infant Behavior and Development, 7*, 467–478.

Adamson, L. B., Bakeman, R., Deckner, D. F. & Romski, M. (2009). Joint engagement and the emergence of language in children with autism and Down syndrome. *Journal of Autism and Developmental Disorders, 39*, 84–96.

Adamson, L. B. & Frick, J. E. (2003). The still face: A history of a shared experimental paradigm. *Infancy, 4*, 451–473.

Agnetta, B. & Rochat, P. (2004). Imitative games by 9-, 14-, and 18-month-old infants. *Infancy, 6*, 1–36.

Agnoli, F. & Zhu, J. J. (1989). One, due, san: Learning to count in English, Italian, and Chinese. Paper presented at the meeting of the Society of Research in Child Development, Kansas City, MO.

Akhtar, N. (2005). The robustness of learning through overhearing. *Developmental Science, 8*, 199–209.

Akhtar, N., Dunham, F. & Dunham, P. J. (1991). Directive interactions and early vocabulary development: The role of joint attentional focus. *Journal of Child Language, 18*, 41–50.

Akhtar, N., Jipson, J. & Callanan, M. (2001). Learning words through overhearing. *Child Development, 72*, 416–430.

Akhtar, N. & Tomasello, M. (1996). Two-year-olds learn words for absent objects and actions. *British Journal of Developmental Psychology, 14*, 79–93.

Akhtar, N. & Tomasello, M. (1997). Young children's productivity with word order and verb morphology. *Developmental Psychology, 33*, 952–965.

Aksu-Koç, A. (1998). The role of input versus universal predispositions in the emergence of tense–aspect morphology: Evidence from Turkish. *First Language, 18*, 255–280.

Albareda-Castellot, B., Pons, F. & Sebastián-Gallés, N. (2010). The acquisition of phonetic categories in bilingual infants: New data from an anticipatory eye movement paradigm. *Developmental Science, 14*, 395–401.

Albright, A. & Hayes, B. (2003). Rules vs. analogy in English past tenses: A computational/experimental study. *Cognition, 90*, 119–161.

Aldrich, N. J., Tenenbaum, H. R., Brooks, P. J., Harrison, K. & Sines, J. (2011). Perspective-taking in children's narratives about jealousy. *British Journal of Developmental Psychology, 29*, 86–109.

Allen, M. (1983). Models of hemisphere specialization. *Psychological Bulletin, 93*, 73–104.

Ambridge, B. & Lieven, E. V. M. (2011). *Child language acquisition: Contrasting theoretical approaches.* Cambridge: Cambridge University Press.

Ambridge, B., Pine, J. M., Rowland, C. F. & Young, C. R. (2008). The effect of verb semantic class and verb frequency (entrenchment) on children's and adults' graded judgements of argument structure. *Cognition, 106*, 87–129.

Ambridge, B., Rowland, C. F., Theakston, A. L. & Tomasello, M. (2006). Comparing different accounts of inversion errors in children's non-subject wh-questions: 'What experiment data can tell us?' *Journal of Child Language, 33*, 519–557.

Amunts, K., Schlaug, G., Jaencke, L., Steinmetz, H., Schleicher, A., Dabringhaus, A. & Zilles, K. (1997). Motor cortex and hand motor skills: Structural compliance in the human brain. *Human Brain Mapping, 5*, 206–215.

Anderson, K. J. & Leaper, C. (1998). Meta-analyses of gender effects on conversational interruption: Who, what, when, where, and how. *Sex Rosles, 39*, 225–252.

Anglin, J. (1993). Vocabulary development: A morphological analysis. *Monographs of the Society for Research in Child Development, 58*, Serial No. 238.

Antia, S. D., Jones, P. B., Reed, S. & Kreimeyer, K. H. (2009). Academic status and progress of deaf and hard-of-hearing students in general education classrooms. *Journal of Deaf Studies and Deaf Education, 14*, 293–311.

Aslin, R. N. (1993). Segmentation of fluent speech into words: Learning models and the role of maternal input. In B. de Boysson-Bardies, S. de Shonen, P. W. Jusczyk, P. MacNeilage & J. Morton (eds), *Developmental neurocognition: Speech and face processing in the first year of life* (pp. 305–315). The Netherlands: Kluwer Academic Publishers.

Aslin, R. N., Woodward, J. Z., LaMendola, N. P. & Bever, T. G. (1996). Models of word segmentation in fluent maternal speech to infants. In J. L. Morgan & K. Demuth (eds), *Signal to syntax: Bootstrapping from speech to grammar in early acquisition* (pp. 117–134). Mahwah, NJ: Erlbaum.

Astington, J. W. & Baird, J. A. (eds) (2005). *Why language matters for Theory of Mind.* New York: Oxford University Press.

Atkinson, J., Marshall, J., Woll, B. & Thacker, A. (2005). Testing comprehension abilities in users of British Sign Language following CVA. *Brain and Language, 94*, 233–248.

Austin, J. L. (1992). *How to do things with words.* Oxford: Oxford University Press.

Baddeley, A., Gathercole, S. & Papagno, C. (1998). The phonological loop as a language learning device. *Psychological Review, 105*, 158–173.

Bakeman, R. & Adamson, L. B. (1984). Coordinating attention to people and objects in mother–infant and peer–infant interaction. *Child Development, 55*, 1278–1289.

Baldwin, D. (1993). Infants' ability to consult the speaker for clues to word reference. *Journal of Child Language, 20*, 395–418.

Baldwin, D. A., Baird, J. A., Saylor, M. M. & Clark, M. A. (2001). Infants parse dynamic action. *Child Development, 72*, 708–717.

Bamberg, M. & Damrad-Frye, R. (1991). On the ability to provide evaluative comments: Further explorations of children's narrative competencies. *Journal of Child Language, 18*, 689–710.

Bannard, C. & Matthews, D. E. (2008). Stored word sequences in language learning: The effect of familiarity of children's repetition of four-word combinations. *Psychological Science, 19*, 241–248.

Bannard, C., Lieven, E. V. & Tomasello, M. (2009). Modeling children's early grammatical knowledge. *Proceedings of the National Academy of Sciences, 106*, 17284–17289.

Bar Shalom, E. (2002). Tense and aspect in early child Russian. *Language Acquisition: A Journal of Developmental Linguistics, 10*, 321–337.

Bard, E. G. & Anderson, A. H. (1983). The unintelligibility of speech to children. *Journal of Child Language, 10*, 265–292.

Barner, D., Brooks, N. & Bale, A. (2011). Accessing the unsaid: The role of scalar alternatives in children's pragmatic inference. *Cognition, 118*, 87–96.

Barnett, M. A., Burns, S. R., Sanborn, F. W., Bartel, J. S. & Wilds, S. J. (2004). Antisocial and prosocial teasing: Perceptions and individual differences. *Social Development, 12*, 292–310.

Barrett, M. (1982). The holophrastic hypothesis: Conceptual and empirical issues. *Cognition, 11*, 47–76.

Barrett, M. (1983). The course of early lexical development: A review and an interpretation. *Early Child Development and Care, 11*, 19–32.

Barrett, M., Harris, M. & Chasin, J. (1991). Early lexical development and maternal speech: A comparison of children's initial and subsequent uses of words. *Journal of Child Language, 18*, 21–40.

Bartels, A. & Zeki, S. (2004). The neural correlates of maternal and romantic love. *NeuroImage, 21*, 1155–1166.

Bartsch, K. & Wellman, H. M. (1995). *Children talk about the mind.* Oxford: Oxford University Press.

Batchelder, E. O. (2002). Bootstrapping the lexicon: A computational model of infant speech segmentation. *Cognition, 83*, 167–206.

Bates, E. (1999). Plasticity, localization and language development. In S. Broman & J. M. Fletcher (eds), *The changing nervous system: Neurobehavioral consequences of early brain disorders* (pp. 214–253). New York: Oxford University Press.

Bates, E., Benigni, L., Bretherton, I., Camaioni, L., Volterra, V., Carlson, V., Carpen, K. & Rosser, M. (1979). *The emergence of symbols: Cognition and communication in infancy.* New York: Academic Press.

Bates, E., Bretherton, I., Snyder, L., Shore, C. & Volterra, V. (1980). Vocal and gestural symbols at 13 months. *Merrill-Palmer Quarterly, 26*, 407–423.

Bates, E. & Dick, F. (2002). Language, gesture, and the developing brain. *Developmental Psychobiology, 40*, 293–310.

Bates, E. & Goodman, J. (1997). On the inseparability of grammar and the lexicon: Evidence from acquisition, aphasia, and real-time processing. *Language and Cognitive Processes, 12*, 507–584.

Bates, E. & MacWhinney, B. (1979). A functionalist approach to the acquisition of grammar. In E. Ochs & B. Schieffelin (eds), *Developmental pragmatics.* New York: Academic Press.

Bates, E., MacWhinney, B., Caselli, C., Devescovi, A., Natale, F. & Venza, V. (1984). A crosslinguistic study of the development of sentence interpretation strategies. *Child Development, 55*, 341–354.

Bauer, P. J. (2006). *Remembering the times of our lives: Memory in infancy and beyond.* Mahwah, NJ: Lawrence Erlbaum Associates.

Bauer, D. J., Goldfield, B. A. & Reznick, J. S. (2002). Alternative approaches to analyzing individual differences in the rate of early vocabulary development. *Applied Psycholinguistics, 23*, 313–336.

Bavelier, D., Corina, D., Jezzard, P., Clark, V., Karni, A., Lalwani, A., Rauschecker, J. P., Braun, A., Turner, R. & Neville, H. J. (1998). Hemispheric specialization for English and ASL: Left invariance–right variability. *Neuroreport, 9*, 1537–1542.

Bavin, E. L. (1992). The acquisition of Walpiri. In D. I. Slobin (ed.), *The crosslinguistic study of language acquisition* (Vol. 3, pp. 309–371). Hillsdale, NJ: Lawrence Erlbaum Associates.

Beck, I. & McKeown, M. (1991). Conditions of vocabulary acquisition. In R. Barr, M. L. Kamil, P. Mosenthal & P. D. Pearson (eds), *Handbook of reading research* (Vol. 2, pp. 789–814). New York: Longman.

Becker, J. A. (1994a). Pragmatic socialization: Parental input to preschoolers. *Discourse Processes*, *17*, 131–148.

Becker, J. (1994b). 'Sneak-shoes', 'sworders', and 'nose-beards': A case study of lexical innovations. *First Language*, *14*, 195–211.

Bedore, L. & Leonard, L. (2001). Grammatical morphology deficits in Spanish-speaking children with specific language impairment. *Journal of Speech, Language, and Hearing Research*, *44*, 905–924.

Beers, S. F. & Nagy, W. E. (2011). Writing development in four genres from grades three to seven: Syntactic complexity and genre differentiation. *Reading and Writing*, *24*, 183–202.

Behne, T., Carpenter, M., Call, J. & Tomasello, M. (2005). Unwilling versus unable: Infants' understanding of intentional action. *Developmental Psychology*, *41*, 328–337.

Below, J. L., Skinner, C. H., Fearrington, J. Y. & Sorrell, C. A. (2010). Gender differences in early literacy: Analysis of kindergarten through fifth-grade dynamic indicators of basic early literacy probes. *School Psychology Review*, *39*, 240–257.

Bencini, G. M. & Valian, V. V. (2008). Abstract sentence representations in 3-year-olds: Evidence from language production and comprehension. *Journal of Memory and Language*, *59*, 97–113.

Benson, R. R., FitzGerald, D. B., LeSueur, L. L., Kennedy, D. N., Kwong, K., Buchbinder, B. R. et al. (1999). Language dominance determined by whole brain functional MRI in patients with brain lesions. *Neurology*, *52*, 798–809.

Berko, J. (1958). The child's learning of English morphology. *Word*, *14*, 150–177.

Berko, J. & Brown, R. (1960). Psycholinguistic research methods. In P. H. Mussen (ed.), *Handbook of research methods in child development* (pp. 517–557). New York: John Wiley & Sons.

Berko Gleason, J., Perlmann, R. Y., Ely, R. & Evans, D. W. (1994). *The babytalk register: Parents' use of diminutives*. In J. L. Sokolov & C. A. Snow (eds), *Handbook of research in language development using CHILDES* (pp. 50–76). Hillsdale, NJ: Lawrence Erlbaum Associates.

Berman, R. A. & Slobin, D. I. (1994). *Relating events in narrative: A crosslinguistic developmental study*. Hillsdale, NJ: Lawrence Erlbaum Associates.

Bernardis, P., Bello, A., Pettenati, P., Stefanini, S. & Gentilucci, M. (2008). Manual actions affect vocalizations of infants. *Experimental Brain Research*, *184*, 599–603.

Bernicot, J., Laval, V. & Chaminaud, S. (2007). Nonliteral language forms in children: In what order are they acquired in pragmatics and metapragmatics? *Journal of Pragmatics*, *39*, 2115–2132.

Berninger, V. W., Abbott, R. D., Nagy, W. & Carlisle, J. (2010). Growth in phonological, orthographic, and morphological awareness in grades 1 to 6. *Journal of Psycholinguistic Research*, *39*, 141–163.

Bertenthal, B. I., Proffitt, D. R. & Kramer, S. J. (1987). The perception of biomechanical motions by infants: Implementation of various processing constraints. *Journal of Experimental Psychology: Human Perception and Performance*, *13*, 577–585.

Bertin, E. & Striano, T. (2006). The still-face response in newborn, 1.5-, and 3-month-old infants. *Infant Behavior and Development*, *29*, 294–297.

Bertoncini, J., Bijeljac-Babic, R., Blumstein, S. & Mehler, J. (1987). Discrimination in neonates of very short CVs. *Journal of the Acoustical Society of America*, *82*, 31–37.

Best, C. T., Mathur, G., Miranda, K. A. & Lillo-Martin, D. (2010). Effects of sign language experience on categorical perception of dynamic ASL pseudosigns. *Attention, Perception, & Psychophysics*, *72*, 747–762.

Best, C. T. & McRoberts, G. W. (2003). Infant perception of nonnative contrasts that adults assimilate in different ways. *Language and Speech*, *46*, 183–216.

Bettes, B. A. (1988). Maternal depression and motherese: Temporal and intonational features. *Child Development, 59*, 1098–1096

Bialystok, E. (1986). Factors in the growth of linguistic awareness. *Child Development, 57*, 498–510.

Bialystok, E. (1988). Levels of bilingualism and levels of linguistic awareness. *Developmental Psychology, 24*, 560–567.

Bialystok, E. (1999). Cognitive complexity and attentional control in the bilingual mind. *Child Development, 70*(3), 636–644.

Bialystok, E. (2007). Cognitive effects of bilingualism: How linguistic experience leads to cognitive change. *International Journal of Bilingual Education and Bilingualism, 10*, 210–223.

Bialystok, E. & Codd, J. (1997). Cardinal limits: Evidence from language awareness and bilingualism for developing concepts of number. *Cognitive Development, 12*, 85–106.

Bialystok, E. & Martin, M. M. (2004). Attention and inhibition in bilingual children: Evidence from the dimensional change card sort task. *Developmental Science, 7*, 325–339.

Bialystok, E., Martin, M. M. & Viswanathan, M. (2005). Bilingualism across the lifespan: The rise and fall of inhibitory control. *International Journal of Bilingualism, 9*, 103–119.

Bialystok, E. & Shapero, D. (2005). Ambiguous benefits: The effect of bilingualism on reversing ambiguous figures. *Developmental Science, 8*, 595–604.

Biemiller, A. (1977/1978). Relationships between oral reading rates for letters, words, and simple text in the development of reading achievement. *Reading Research Quarterly, 13*, 223–253.

Birch, S. A. J. & Bloom, P. (2007). The curse of knowledge in reasoning about false beliefs. *Psychological Science, 18*, 382–386.

Birdsong, D. & Molis, M. (2001). On the evidence for maturational constraints in second language acquisition. *Journal of Memory and Language, 44*, 235–249.

Bishop, D. V. M. (1997). *Uncommon understanding: Development and disorders of language comprehension in children.* Hove, UK: Psychology Press.

Bishop, D. V. M. (2001). Genetic influences on language impairment and literacy problems in children: Same or different? *Journal of Child Psychology and Psychiatry, 42*, 189–198.

Bishop, D. V. M., Bright, P., James, C., Bishop, S. J. & van der Lely, H. K. J. (2000). Grammatical SLI: A distinct subtype of developmental language impairment? *Applied Psycholinguistics, 21*, 159–181.

Bishop, D. V. M. & Edmundson, A. (1987). Specific language impairment as a maturational lag: Evidence from longitudinal data on language and motor development. *Developmental Medicine and Child Neurology, 29*, 442–459.

Bishop, D. V. M. & McArthur, G. M. (2004). Immature cortical responses to auditory stimuli in specific language impairment. Evidence from ERPs to rapid tone sequences. *Developmental Science, 7*, F11–F18.

Bishop, D. V., North, T. & Donlan, C. (1995). Genetic basis of specific language impairment: Evidence from a twin study. *Developmental Medicine and Child Neurology, 37*, 56–71.

Blake, J., Vitale, G., Osborne, P. & Olshansky, E. (2005). A cross-cultural comparison of communicative gestures in human infants during the transition to language. *Gesture, 5*(1/2), 201–217.

Bloom, K. & Lo, E. (1990). Adult perceptions of vocalizing infants. *Infant Behavior and Development, 13*, 209–219.

Bloom, L. (1991). *Language development from two to three.* New York: Cambridge University Press.

Bloom, L. (1993). *The transition from infancy to language: Acquiring the power of expression.* New York: Cambridge University Press.

Bloom, L. & Tinker, E. (2001). The intentionality model and language acquistion. *Monographs of the Society for Research in Child Development, 66* (No. 4), Serial No. 267.

Bloom, P. (2002). *How children learn the meanings of words*. Cambridge, MA: MIT Press.

Bock, J. K. (1986). Syntactic persistence in language production. *Cognitive Psychology, 18*, 355–387.

Bogin, B. (1998). From caveman cultivate to fast food: The evolution of human nutrition. *Growth Hormone and IGF Research, 8*, 79–86.

Bohannon, J. N. & Stanowicz, L. (1988). The issue of negative evidence: Adult responses to children's language errors. *Developmental Psychology, 24*, 684–689.

Bongaerts, T. (1999). Ultimate attainment in foreign language pronunciation: The case of very advanced late foreign language learners. In D. Birdsong (ed.), *Second language acquisition and the Critical Period Hypothesis* (pp. 133–159). Mahwah, NJ: Lawrence Erlbaum Associates.

Bonifacci, P., Giombini, L., Bellocchi, S. & Contento, S. (2010). Speed of processing, anticipation, inhibition and working memory in bilinguals. *Developmental Science, 14*, 256–269.

Bono, M. A., Daley, T. & Sigman, M. (2004). Relations among joint attention, amount of intervention and language gain in autism. *Journal of Autism and Developmental Disorders, 34*, 495–505.

Bonvillian, J. D. (2000). Sign language development. In M. Barrett (ed.), *The development of language* (pp. 277–310). East Sussex, UK: Psychology Press.

Bonvillian, J. D. & Siedlecki, T. (2000). Young children's acquisition of the formational aspects of American Sign Language: Parental report findings. *Sign Language Studies, 1*, 45–64.

Bonvillian, J. D., Orlansky, M. D. & Novack, L. L. (1983). Developmental milestones: Sign language acquisition and motor development. *Child Development, 54*, 1435–1445.

Booth, J. R., MacWhinney, B., Thulborn, K. R., Sacco, K., Voyvodic, J. & Feldman, H. (1999). Functional organization of activation patterns in children: Whole brain fMRI imaging during three different cognitive tasks. *Progress in Neuropsychopharmocology and Biological Psychiatry, 23*, 669–682.

Bornstein, M. H. (ed.) (1989). *Maternal responsiveness: Characteristics and consequences*. San Francisco: Jossey-Bass.

Bornstein, M. H., Hahn, C.-S. & Haynes, O. M. (2004). Specific and general language performance across early childhood: Stability and gender considerations. *First Language, 24*, 267–304.

Bornstein, M. H. & Haynes, O. M. (1998). Vocabulary competence in early childhood: Measurement, latent construct, and predictive validity. *Child Development, 69*, 654–671.

Bornstein, M. H., Tamis-LeMonda, C. S., Hahn, C.-H. & Haynes, O. M. (2008). Maternal responsiveness to children at three ages: Longitudinal analysis of a multidimensional, modular, and specific parenting construct. *Developmental Psychology, 44*, 867–874.

Bortfeld, H., Morgan, J., Golinkoff, R. & Rathbun, K. (2005). Mommy and me: Familiar names help launch babies into speech stream segmentation. *Psychological Science, 16*, 298–304.

Bortolini, U., Caselli, M. C. & Leonard, L. (1997). Grammatical deficits in Italian-speaking children with specific language impairment. *Journal of Speech, Language, and Hearing Research, 40*, 809–820.

Bosch, L. & Sebastián-Gallés, N. (2001). Evidence of early language discrimination abilities in infants from bilingual environments. *Infancy, 2*, 29–49.

Botting, N. & Conti-Ramsden, G. (2001). Non-word repetition and language development in children with specific language impairment (SLI). *International Journal of Language and Communication Disorders, 36*(4), 421–432.

Boudreault, P. & Mayberry, R. I. (2006). Grammatical processing in American Sign Language: Age of first-language acquisition effects in relation to syntactic structure. *Language and Cognitive Processes, 21*, 608–635.

Bower, P. N., Kirby, J. R. & Deacon, S. H. (2010). The effects of morphological instruction on literacy skills: A systematic review of the literature. *Review of Educational Research, 80*, 144–179.

Bowerman, M. (1988). The 'no-negative evidence' problem: How do children avoid constructing an overly general grammar? In J. Hawkins (ed.), *Explaining language universals* (pp. 73–101). Oxford: Blackwell.

Bowerman, M. (1996). Learning how to structure space for language: A crosslinguistic perspective. In P. Bloom, M. Peterson, L. Nadel & M. Garrett (eds), *Language and space* (pp. 385–486). Cambridge, MA: MIT Press.

Bowerman, M. & Croft, W. (2007). The acquisition of the English causative alternation. In M. Bowerman & P. Brown (eds), *Crosslinguistic perspectives on argument structure: Implications for learnability* (pp. 279–308). Hillsdale, NJ: Lawrence Erlbaum Associates.

Bowers, J. S., Mattys, S. L. & Gage, S. H. (2009). Preserved implicit knowledge of a forgotten childhood language. *Psychological Science*, *20*, 1064–1069.

Bowlby, J. (1982). *Attachment*, 2nd edn. *Attachment and loss* (Vol. 1). New York: Basic/Harper Collins.

Boyatzis, C. J. & Watson, M. W. (1993). Preschool children's symbolic representation of objects through gestures. *Child Development*, *64*, 729–735.

Boyd, J. K. & Goldberg, A. E. (2011). Learning what *not* to say: The role of statistical preemption and categorization in *a*-adjective production. *Language*, *87*(1), 1–29.

Bradley, L. & Bryant, P. E. (1983). Categorizing sounds and learning to read – A causal connection. *Nature*, *301*, 419–421.

Bradley, R. H., Caldwell, B. M., Rock, S. L., Ramey, C. T., Barnard, K. E., Gray, C., Hammond, M. A., Mitchell, S., Gottfried, A. W., Siegel, L. & Johnson, D. L. (1989). Home environment and cognitive development in the first 3 years of life: A collaborative study involving six sites and three ethnic groups in North America. *Developmental Psychology*, *25*, 217–235.

Braem, P. B. (1999). Rhythmic temporal patterns in the signing of deaf early and late learners of Swiss German Sign Language. *Language and Speech*, *42*(2/3), 177–208.

Braine, M. D. S. (1971). On two types of models of the internalization of grammars. In D. I. Slobin (ed.), *The ontogenesis of grammar* (pp. 153–186). New York: Academic Press.

Braine, M. D. S. (1976). Children's first word combinations. *Monographs of the Society for Research in Child Development*, *1* (No. 1), Serial No. 164.

Braine, M. D. S. (1992). What sort of innate structure is needed to 'bootstrap' into syntax? *Cognition*, *45*, 77–100.

Braine, M. D. S., Brody, R. E., Fisch, S. M., Weisberger, M. J. & Blum, M. (1990). Can children use a verb without exposure to its argument structure? *Journal of Child Language*, *17*, 313–342.

Braine, M. D. S. & Brooks, P. J. (1995). Verb argument structure and the problem of avoiding an overgeneral grammar. In M. Tomasello & W. E. Merriman (eds), *Beyond names for things: Young children's acquisition of verbs* (pp. 352–376). Hillsdale, NJ: Lawrence Erlbaum Associates.

Brand, R. J., Baldwin, D. A. & Ashburn, L. A. (2002). Evidence for 'motionese': Modifications in mothers' infant-directed action. *Developmental Science*, *5*, 72–83.

Brasel, K. & Quigley, S. P. (1977). The influence of certain language and communication environments on the development of language in deaf individuals. *Journal of Speech and Hearing Research*, *20*, 95–107.

Brent, M. R. & Cartwright, T. A. (1996). Distributional regularity and phonotactic constraints are useful for segmentation. *Cognition*, *61*, 93–125.

Bretherton, I., McNew, S., Snyder, L. & Bates, E. (1983). Individual differences at 20 months: Analytical versus holistic strategies in language acquisition. *Journal of Child Language*, *10*, 293–320.

Briellmann, R. S., Saling, M. M., Connell, A. B., Waites, A. B., Abbott, D. F. & Jackson, G. D. (2004). A high-field functional MRI study of quadrilingual subjects. *Brain and Language*, *89*, 531–542.

Brodmann, K. (1909). *Vergleichende Lokalisationslehre der Grosshirnrinde in ihren Prinzipien dargestellt auf Grund des Zellenbaues*. Leipzig: Johann Ambosius Barth Verlag.

Bronfenbrenner, U. (1986). Ecology of the family as a context for human development: Research perspectives. *Developmental Psychology, 22*, 723–742.

Brookes, R. L., Tinkler, S., Nicolsort, R. I. & Fawcett, A. J. (2010). Striking the right balance: Motor difficulties in children and adults with dyslexia. *Dyslexia: An International Journal of Research and Practice, 16*, 358–373.

Brooks, P. J. & Braine, M. D. S. (1996). What do children know about the universal quantifiers *all* and *each? Cognition, 60*, 235–268.

Brooks, P. J., Kempe, V. & Sionov, A. (2006). The role of learner and input variables in learning inflectional morphology. *Applied Psycholinguistics, 27*, 185–209.

Brooks, P. J. & MacWhinney, B. (2000). Phonological priming in children's picture naming. *Journal of Child Language, 27*, 335–366.

Brooks, P. J., Seiger-Gardner, L. & Sailor, K. (under review). Contrasting effects of associates and coordinates in children with and without specific language impairment: A picture-word interference study.

Brooks, P. J. & Sekerina, I. A. (2005/2006). Shortcuts to quantifier interpretation in children and adults. *Language Acquisition, 13*, 177–206.

Brooks, P. J. & Tomasello, M. (1999a). How children constrain their argument structure constructions. *Language, 75*, 720–738.

Brooks, P. J. & Tomasello, M. (1999b). Young children learn to produce passives with novel verbs. *Developmental Psychology, 35*, 29–44.

Brooks, P. J., Tomasello, M., Dodson, K. & Lewis, L. (1999). Young children's overgeneralizations with fixed transitivity verbs. *Child Development, 70*, 1325–1337.

Brooks, P. J. & Zizak, O. (2002). Does preemption help children learn verb transitivity? *Journal of Child Language, 29*, 759–781.

Brooks, R. & Meltzoff, A. N. (2005). The development of gaze following and its relation to language. *Developmental Science, 8*, 535–543.

Broomfield, J. & Dodd, B. (2004). Children with speech and language disability: Caseload characteristics. *International Journal of Language and Communication Disorders, 39*, 303–324.

Brown, P. & Levinson, S. C. (2000). Frames of spatial reference and their acquisition in Tenejapan Tzeltal. In L. Nucci, G. B. Saxe & E. Turiel (eds), *Culture, thought and development* (pp. 167–197). Hillsdale, NJ: Lawrence Erlbaum Associates.

Brown, R. (1957). Linguistic determinism and part of speech. *Journal of Abnormal and Social Psychology, 55*, 1–5.

Brown, R. (1959). *Words and things*. Glencoe, IL: The Free Press.

Brown, R. (1973). *A first language: The early stages*. Cambridge, MA: Harvard University Press.

Brown, R. & Hanlon, C. (1970). Derivational complexity and order of acquisition in child speech. In J. R. Hayes (ed.), *Cognition and the development of language* (pp. 11–53). New York: John Wiley & Sons.

Bruner, J. (1972). The nature and uses of immaturity. *American Psychologist, 27*, 687–708.

Bruner, J. (1983). *Child's talk: Learning to use language*. New York: Norton.

Bryant, G. A. & Barrett, H. C. (2007). Recognizing intentions in infant-directed speech: Evidence for universals. *Psychological Science, 18*, 746–751.

Bull, R. (2008). Deafness, numerical cognition, and mathematics. In M. Marschark & P. Hauser (eds), *Deaf cognition: Foundations and outcomes* (pp. 170–200). New York: Oxford University Press.

Bull, R., Marschark, M. & Blatto-Vallee, G. (2005). SNARC hunting: Examining number representation in deaf students. *Learning and Individual Differences, 15,* 223–236.

Bull, R., Marschark, M., Sapere, P., Davidson, W. A., Murphy, D. & Nordmann, E. (2011). Numerical estimation in deaf and hearing adults. *Learning and Individual Differences, 21,* 453–457.

Burgess, S. R., Hecht, S. A. & Lonigan, C. J. (2002). Relations of the home literacy environment (HLE) to the development of reading-related abilities: A one-year longitudinal study. *Reading Research Quarterly, 37,* 408–426.

Burnham, D., Kitamura, C. & Vollmer-Conna, U. (2002). What's new pussycat? On talking to babies and animals. *Science, 296,* 1435.

Bushnell, I. W. R., Sai, F. & Mullin, J. T. (1989). Neonatal recognition of the mother's face. *British Journal of Developmental Psychology, 7,* 3–15.

Butcher, C., Mylander, C. & Goldin-Meadow, S. (1991). Displaced communication in a self-styled gesture system: Pointing at the nonpresent. *Cognitive Development, 6,* 315–342.

Butterworth, B., Reeve, R., Reynolds, F. & Lloyd, D. (2008). Numerical thought with and without words: Evidence from indigenous Australian children. *Proceedings of the National Academy of Sciences of the USA, 105,* 13179–13184.

Bybee, J. (1985). *Morphology: A study of the relation between meaning and form.* Amsterdam: John Benjamins.

Bybee, J. (1995). Regular morphology and the lexicon. *Language and Cognitive Processes, 10,* 425–455.

Calandrella, A. & Wilcox, J. (2000). Predicting language outcomes for young prelinguistic children with developmental delay. *Journal of Speech, Language, and Hearing Research, 43,* 1061–1071.

Campbell, A. L., Brooks, P. & Tomasello, M. (2000). Factors affecting young children's use of pronouns as referring expressions. *Journal of Speech, Language, and Hearing Research, 43,* 1337–1347.

Campbell, R., Woll, B., Benson, P. J. & Wallace, S. B. (1999). Categorical perception of face actions: Their role in Sign Language and in communicative facial displays. *The Quarterly Journal of Experimental Psychology, 52A,* 67–95.

Campos, J. & Sternberg, C. (1981). Perception, appraisal, and emotion: The onset of social referencing. In M. Lamb & L. Sherrod (eds), *Infant social cognition: Empirical and theoretical considerations* (pp. 273–314). Hillsdale, NJ: Lawrence Erlbaum Associates.

Capelli, C. A., Nakagawa, N. & Madden, C. M. (1990). How children understand sarcasm: The role of context and intonation. *Child Development, 61,* 1824–1841.

Capirci, O., Iverson, J., Pizzuto, E. & Volterra, V. (1996). Gestures and words during the transition to two-word speech. *Journal of Child Language, 23,* 645–673.

Capone, N. C. & McGregor, K. K. (2004). Gesture development: A review for clinical and research practices. *Journal of Speech, Language, and Hearing Research, 47,* 173–186.

Caprin, C. & Guasti, M. T. (2009). Acquisition of morphosyntax in Italian: A cross-sectional study. *Applied Psycholinguistics, 30,* 23–52.

Carey, S. (1978). The child as word learner. In J. Bresnan, G. Miller & M. Halle (eds), *Linguistic theory and psychological reality* (pp. 264–269). Cambridge, MA: MIT Press.

Carey, S. (2010). Beyond fast mapping. *Language Learning and Development, 6,* 184–205.

Carey, S. & Bartlett, E. (1978). Acquiring a single new word. *Papers and Reports on Child Language Development, 15,* 17–29.

Carlson, S. M. & Meltzoff, A. N. (2008). Bilingual experience and executive functioning in young children. *Developmental Science, 11,* 282–328.

Carpendale, J. I. M. & Carpendale, A. B. (2010). The development of pointing: From personal directedness to interpersonal direction. *Human Development, 53,* 110–126.

Carpendale, J. I. M. & Lewis, C. (2004). Constructing an understanding of mind: The development of children's social understanding within social interaction. *Behavioral and Brain Sciences*, *27*, 79–151.

Carpenter, M., Nagell, K. & Tomasello, M. (1998). Social cognition, joint attention, and communicative competence from 9 to 15 months of age. *Monographs of the Society for Research in Child Development*, *63*, Serial No. 255.

Carpenter, P. A., Miyake, A. & Just, M. A. (1995). Language comprehension: Sentence and discourse processing. *Annual Review of Psychology*, *46*, 91–100.

Carver, R. P. (1990). *Reading rate: A review of research and theory*. New York: Academic Press.

Cassar, M. & Treiman, R. (1997). The beginnings of orthographic knowledge: Children's knowledge of double letters in words. *Journal of Educational Psychology*, *89*, 631–644.

Cassidy, K. W. & Kelly, M. H. (2001). Children's use of phonology to infer grammatical class in vocabulary learning. *Psychonomic Bulletin and Review*, *8*, 519–523.

Castro-Caldas, A., Miranda, P. C., Carmo, I., Reis, A., Leote, F., Ribeiro, C. & Ducla-Soares, E. (1999). Influence of learning to read and write on the morphology of the corpus callosum. *European Journal of Neurology*, *6*, 23–28.

Cattell, J. M. (1886). The time it takes to see and name objects. *Mind*, *11*, 63–65.

Catts, H. W., Adlof, S. M., Hogan, T. P. & Weismer, S. E. (2005). Are specific language impairment and dyslexia distinct disorders? *Journal of Speech, Language, and Hearing Research*, *48*(6), 1378–1396.

Chamberlain, C. & Mayberry, R. I. (2008). American Sign Language syntactic and narrative comprehension in skilled and less skilled readers: Bilingual and bimodal evidence for the linguistic basic of reading. *Applied Psycholinguistics*, *29*, 367–388.

Changizi, M. A. & Shimojo, S. (2005). Character complexity and redundancy in writing systems over human history. *Proceedings of the Royal Society B: Biological Sciences*, *272*, 267–275.

Chapman, M. (1991). The epistemic triangle: Operative and communicative components of cognitive development. In M. Chandler & M. Chapman (eds), *Criteria for competence: Controversies in the conceptualization and assessment of children's abilities* (pp. 209–228). Mahwah, NJ: Lawrence Erlbaum Associates.

Charman, T., Baron-Cohen, S., Swettenham, J., Baird, G., Drew, A. & Cox, A. (2003). Predicting language outcome in infants with autism and pervasive developmental disability. *International Journal of Language and Communication Disorders*, *38*, 265–285.

Chater, N. & Christiansen, M. H. (2010). Language acquisition meets language evolution. *Cognitive Science*, *34*, 1131–1157.

Chen, X., Striano, T. & Rakoczy, H. (2004). Auditory–oral matching behavior in newborns. *Developmental Science*, *7*, 42–47.

Chen, Z.-Y., Cowell, P. E., Varley, R. & Wang, Y.-C. (2009). A cross-language study of verbal and visuospatial working memory span. *Journal of Clinical and Experimental Neuropsychology*, *31*, 385–391.

Cheour-Luhtanen, M., Alho, K., Kujala, T., Sainio, K., Reinikainen, K., Renlund, M., Aaltonen, O., Eerola, O. & Näätänen, R. (1995). Mismatch negativity indicates vowel discrimination in newborns. *Hearing Research*, *82*, 53–58.

Chi, J. G., Dooling, E. C. & Gilles, F. H. (1977). Gyral development of the human brain. *Annals of Neurology*, *1*, 86–93.

Childers, J. B., Vaughan, J. & Burquest, D. A. (2007). Joint attention and word learning in Ngas-speaking toddlers in Nigeria. *Journal of Child Language*, *34*, 199–225.

Chipere, N. (2003). *Understanding complex sentences: Native speaker variations in syntactic competence*. Basingstoke: Palgrave.

Choi, H., Won, Y. & Lee, K. (2003). Comparison of selective attention between Chinese monolinguals and Korean–Chinese bilinguals. *Bilingualism*, *23*, 113–135.

Choi, S. (1997). Language-specific input and early semantic development: Evidence from children learning Korean. In D. I. Slobin (ed.), *The crosslinguistic study of language acquisition: Vol. 5 Expanding the contexts* (pp. 41–133). Hillsdale, NJ: Lawrence Erlbaum Associates.

Choi, S. (2000). Caregiver input in English and Korean: Use of nouns and verbs in book-reading and toy-play contexts. *Journal of Child Language*, *27*, 69–96.

Choi, S. & Bowerman, M. (1991). Learning to express motion events in English and Korean: The influence of language-specific lexicalization patterns. *Cognition*, *41*(1–3), 83–121.

Choi, S. & Gopnik, A. (1995). Early acquisition of verbs in Korean: A cross-linguistic study. *Journal of Child Language*, *22*, 497–529.

Choi, S., McDonough, L., Bowerman, M. & Mandler, J. M. (1999). Early sensitivity to language-specific spatial categories in English and Korean. *Cognitive Development*, *14*, 241–268.

Chomsky, N. (1957). *Syntactic structures.* The Hague: Mouton.

Chomsky, N. (1965). *Aspects of the theory of syntax.* Cambridge, MA: MIT Press.

Chomsky, N. (1995). *The minimalist program.* Cambridge, MA: MIT Press.

Chouinard, M. M. & Clark, E. V. (2003). Adult reformulations of child errors as negative evidence. *Journal of Child Language*, *30*, 637–669.

Christiansen, M. H., Allen, J. & Seidenberg, M. S. (1998). Learning to segment speech using multiple cues: A connectionist model. *Language and Cognitive Processes*, *13*, 221–268.

Christiansen, M. H. & Chater, N. (2008). Language as shaped by the brain. *Behavioral & Brain Sciences*, *31*, 489–558.

Christophe, A., Dupoux, E., Bertoncini, J. & Mehler, J. (1994). Do infants perceive word boundaries? An empirical study of the bootstrapping of lexical acquisition. *Journal of the Acoustical Society of America*, *95*, 1570–1580.

Christophe, A. & Morton, J. (1998). Is Dutch native English? Linguistic analysis by 2-month-olds. *Developmental Science*, *1*, 215–219.

Chrysikou, E. G., Novick, J. M., Trueswell, J. C. & Thompson-Schill, S. L. (2011). The other side of cognitive control: Can a lack of cognitive control benefit language and cognition? *Topics in Cognitive Science*, *3*, 253–256.

Clahsen, H. & Felser, C. (2006). Grammatical processing in language learners. *Applied Psycholinguistics*, *27*, 3–42.

Clark, E. V. (1982). The young word maker: A case study of innovations in the child's lexicon. In E. Wanner & L. R. Gleitman (eds), *Language acquisition: The state of the art* (pp. 390–425). Cambridge: Cambridge University Press.

Clark, E. V. (1993). *The lexicon in acquisition.* Cambridge: Cambridge University Press.

Clark, E. V. (1997). Conceptual perspective and lexical choice in acquisition. *Cognition*, *64*, 1–37.

Clark, G. (2009). The multi-channel cochlear implant: Past present and future perspectives. *Cochlear Implants International*, *10*(Suppl. 1), 2–13.

Clark, H. H. (1996). *Using language.* Cambridge: Cambridge University Press.

Clarke, P. J., Snowling, M. J., Truelove, E. & Hulme, Ch. (2010). Children's reading comprehension difficulties: A randomized controlled trial. *Psychological Science*, *21*, 1106–1116.

Cohen, L., Dehaene, S., Naccache, L., Lehéricy, S., Dehaene-Lambertz, G., Hénaff, M. & Michel, M. (2000). The visual word form area: spatial and temporal characterization of an initial stage of reading in normal subjects and posterior split-brain patients. *Brain*, *123*, 291–307.

Cohen, M., Campbell, R. & Yaghmai, F. (1989). Neuropathological abnormalities in developmental dysphasia. *Annals of Neurology*, *25*, 567–570.

Cohen, W., Hodson, A., O'Hare, A., Boyle, J., Durrani, T., McCartney, E. et al. (2005). Effects of computer-based intervention through acoustically modified speech (Fast ForWord) in severe mixed receptive–expressive language impairment: Outcomes from a randomized controlled trial. *Journal of Speech, Language and Hearing Research, 48*(3), 715–729.

Colletti, V., Carner, M., Miorelli, V., Guida, M., Colletti, L. & Fiorino, F. G. (2005). Cochlear implantation at under 12 months: Reports on 10 patients. *The Laryngoscope, 115*(3), 445–449.

Collins, A. M. & Quillian, M. R. (1969). Retrieval time from semantic memory. *Journal of Verbal Behavior and Verbal Learning, 8*, 240–247.

Colomé, À., Laka, I. & Sebastián-Gallés, N. (2010). Language effects in addition: How you say it counts. *The Quarterly Journal of Experimental Psychology, 63*, 965–983.Coltheart, M., Rastle, K., Perry, C., Langdon, R. & Ziegler, J. C. (2001). DRC: A Dual Route Cascaded model of visual word recognition and reading aloud. *Psychological Review, 108*, 204–256.

Connellan, J., Baron-Cohen, S., Wheelwright, S., Bataki, A. & Ahluwalia, J. (2000). Sex differences in human neonatal social perception. *Infant Behavior and Development, 23*, 113–118.

Conti-Ramsden, G. & Botting, N. (1999). Classification of children with specific language impairment: Longitudinal considerations. *Journal of Speech, Language, and Hearing Research, 42*, 1195–1204.

Conti-Ramsden, G. & Botting, N. (2004). Social difficulties and victimization in children with SLI at 11 years of age. *Journal of Speech, Language, and Hearing Research, 47*, 145–161.

Conti-Ramsden, G. & Botting, N. (2008). Emotional health in adolescents with and without a history of specific language impairment (SLI). *Journal of Child Psychology and Psychiatry, 49*, 516–525.

Conti-Ramsden, G., Botting, N. & Faragher, B. (2001). Psycholinguistic markers for specific language impairment (SLI). *Journal of Child Psychology and Psychiatry, 42*, 741–748.

Conti-Ramsden, G. & Friel-Patti, S. (1984). Mother–child dialogues: A comparison of normal and language impaired children. *Journal of Communication Disorders, 17*, 19–35.

Conti-Ramsden, G. & Windfuhr, K. (2002). Productivity with word-order and morphology: A comparative look at children with SLI and children with normal language abilities. *International Journal of Language and Communication Disorders, 37*, 17–30.

Conway, C. M. & Christiansen, M. H. (2005). Modality-constrained statistical learning of tactile, visual, and auditory sequences. *Journal of Experimental Psychology, 31*, 24–39.

Conway, C. M. & Christiansen, M. H. (2009). Seeing and hearing in space and time: Effects of modality and presentation rate on implicit statistical learning. *European Journal of Cognitive Psychology, 21*, 561–580.

Conway, C. M., Bauernschmidt, A., Huang, S. S. & Pisoni, D. B. (2010). Implicit statistical learning in language processing: Word predictability is the key. *Cognition, 114*, 356–371.

Conway, C. M., Pisoni, D. B., Anaya, E. M., Karpicke, J. & Henning, S. C. (2010). Implicit sequence learning in deaf children with cochlear implants. *Developmental Science, 14*, 69–82.

Conway, C. M., Pisoni, D. B. & Kronenberger, W. G. (2009). The importance of sound for cognitive sequencing abilities: The auditory scaffolding hypothesis. *Current Directions in Psychological Science, 18*, 275–279.

Cooper, R. P. & Aslin, R. N. (1990). Preference for infant-directed speech in the first month after birth. *Child Development, 61*, 1584–1595.

Coppens, Y. (1994). The east side story: The origin of humankind. *Scientific American, 270*, 62–69.

Coppola, M. & Newport, E. L. (2005). Grammatical subjects in home sign: Abstract linguistic structure in adult primary gesture systems without linguistic input. *Proceedings of the National Academy of Sciences of the USA, 102*(52), 19249–19253.

Courtin, C. (2000). The impact of sign language on the cognitive development of deaf children: The case of theory of mind. *Journal of Deaf Studies and Deaf Education, 5*, 266–276.

Courtin, C. & Melot, A.-M. (2005). Metacognitive development of deaf children: Lessons from the appearance–reality and false belief tasks. *Developmental Science, 8*, 16–25.

Cowan, N. & Alloway, T. (2009). Development of working memory in childhood. In M. L. Courage and N. Cowan (eds), *The development of memory in infancy and childhood*, 2nd edn. (pp. 303–342). New York: Psychology Press.

Coyne, M. D., Simmons, D. C., Kame'enui, E. J. & Stoolmiller, M. (2004). Teaching vocabulary during shared storybook readings: An examination of differential effects. *Exceptionality, 12*, 145–162.

Craig, H. K. & Evans, J. L. (1993). Pragmatics and SLI: Within-group variations in discourse behaviors. *Journal of Speech and Hearing Research, 36*, 777–789.

Craig, H. K. & Washington, J. A. (1993). Access behaviors of children with specific language impairment. *Journal of Speech and Hearing Research, 36*, 322–337.

Crais, E. R., Watson, L. R. & Baranek, G. T. (2009). Use of gesture development in profiling children's prelinguistic communication skills. *American Journal of Speech-Language Pathology, 18*, 95–108.

Croft, W. A. (2001). *Radical construction grammar: Syntactic theory in typological perspective*. Oxford: Oxford University Press.

Crowley, K., Callanan, M. A., Tenenbaum, H. R. & Allen, E. (2001). Parents explain more often to boys than to girls during shared scientific thinking. *Psychological Science, 12*, 258–261.

Crown, C. L., Feldstein, S., Jasnow, M. D., Beebe, B. & Jaffe, J. (2002). The cross-modal coordination of interpersonal timing: Six-week-old infants' gaze with adults vocal behavior. *Journal of Psycholinguistic Research, 31*, 1–23.

Csibra, G. & Gergely, G. (2009). Natural pedagogy. *Trends in Cognitive Sciences, 13*, 148–153.

Csibra, G. & Gergely, G. (2011). Natural pedagogy as evolutionary adaptation. *Philosophical Transactions of the Royal Society B, 366*, 1149–1157.

Culp, A. M., Osofsky, J. D. & O'Brien, M. (1996). Language patterns of adolescent and older mothers and their one-year-old children: A comparison study. *First Language, 16*, 61–76.

Cunningham, A. E. & Stanovich, K. E. (1990). Assessing print exposure and orthographic processing skill in children: A quick measure of reading experience. *Journal of Educational Psychology, 82*, 733–740.

Cunningham, A. E. & Stanovich, K. E. (1998). What reading does for the mind. *Journal of Direct Instruction, 1*, 137–149.

Curtiss, S. R. (1977). *Genie: A linguistic study of a modern day 'wild child'*. New York: Academic Press.

Cutler, A. (1994). Segmentation problems, rhythmic solutions. *Lingua, 92*, 81–104.

Cutting, A. L. & Dunn, J. (1999). Theory of mind, emotion understanding, language, and family background: Individual differences and interrelations. *Child Development, 70*, 853–865.

Dąbrowska, E. (2006). Low-level schemas or general rules? The role of diminutives in the acquisition of Polish case inflections. *Language Sciences, 28*, 120–135.

Dąbrowska, E. (2008). The effects of frequency and neighborhood density of adult speakers' productivity with Polish case inflections: An empirical test of usage-based approaches to morphology. *Journal of Memory and Language, 58*, 931–951.

Dąbrowska, E. & Street, J. (2006). Individual differences in language attainment: Comprehension of passive sentences by native and non-native English speakers. *Language Sciences, 28*, 604–615.

Dale, P., Price, T. S., Bishop, D. V. & Plomin, R. (2003). Outcomes of early language delay: I. Predicting persistent and transient language difficulties at 3 and 4 years. *Journal of Speech, Language, and Hearing Research, 46*, 544–560.

de Boysson-Bardies, B., Hallé, P., Sagart, L. & Durand, C. (1989). A crosslinguistic investigation of vowel formants in babbling. *Journal of Child Language, 16*, 1–17.

de Boysson-Bardies, B., Sagart, L. & Durand, C. (1984). Discernible differences in the babbling of infants according to target language. *Journal of Child Language, 11*, 1–15.

de Boysson-Bardies, B. & Vihman, M. M. (1991). Adaptation to language: Evidence from babbling and first words in four languages. *Language, 67*, 297–319.

De Fossé, L., Hodge, S. M., Makris, N., Kennedy, D. N., Caviness, V. S. Jr., McGrath, L., Steele, H., Ziegler, D. A., Herbert, M. R., Frazier, J. A., Tager-Flusberg, H. & Harris, G. J. (2004). Language-association cortex asymmetry in autism and specific language impairment. *Annals of Neurology, 56*, 757–766.

De Léon, L. (1994). Exploration in the acquisition of geocentric location by Tzotzil children. *Linguistics, 32*, 857–884.

de Villiers, J. (2000). Language and theory of mind: What are the developmental relationships? In S. Baron-Cohen, H. Tager-Flusberg & D. Cohen (eds), *Understanding other minds: Perspectives from developmental cognitive neuroscience* (pp. 83–123). Oxford: Oxford University Press.

Deacon, S. H. & Kirby, J. R. (2004). Morphological awareness: Just 'more phonological'? The roles of morphological and phonological awareness in reading development. *Applied Psycholinguistics, 25*, 223–238.

Deacon, S. H., Kirby, J. R. & Casselman-Bell, M. (2009). How robust is the contribution of morphological awareness to general spelling outcomes? *Reading Psychology, 30*, 301–318.

Deacon, T. W. (1997). *The symbolic species: The co-evolution of language and the brain.* New York: Norton.

Deák, G. O. & Maratsos, M. (1998). On having complex representations of things: Preschoolers use multiple words for objects and people. *Developmental Psychology, 34*, 224–240.

DeCasper, A. J. & Fifer, W. P. (1980). Of human bonding: Newborns prefer their mothers' voices. *Science, 208*, 1174–1176.

DeCasper, A. J. & Spence, M. J. (1986). Prenatal maternal speech influences newborns' perception of speech sounds. *Infant Behavior and Development, 9*, 133–150.

Deckner, D. F., Adamson, L. B. & Bakeman, R. (2006). Child and maternal contributions to shared reading: Effects of language and literacy development. *Journal of Applied Developmental Psychology, 27*, 31–41.

Deevy, P. & Leonard, L. B. (2004). The comprehension of wh-questions in children with specific language impairment. *Journal of Speech, Language, and Hearing Research, 47*, 802–815.

Dehaene-Lambertz, G., Dehaene, S. & Hertz-Pannier, L. (2002). Functional neuroimaging of speech perception in infants. *Science, 298*, 2013–2015.

Dehaene-Lambertz, G., Montavont, A., Jobert, A., Allirol, L., Dubois, J., Hertz-Pannier, L. et al. (2009). Language or music, mother or Mozart? Structural and environmental influences on infants' language networks. *Brain and Language, 114*, 53–65.

Dehaene, S. (2010). *Reading in the brain.* New York: Viking.

Dehaene, S., Dupoux, E., Mehler, J., Cohen, L., Paulesu, E., Perani, D. et al. (1997). Anatomical variability in the cortical representation of first and second language. *NeuroReport, 8*, 3809–3815.

Dell, G. S. (1986). A spreading-activation theory of retrieval in sentence production. *Psychological Review, 93*, 283–321.

Dell, G. S. & Reich, P. A. (1981). Stages in sentence production: An analysis of speech error data. *Journal of Verbal Learning and Verbal Behaviour, 20*, 611–629.

DeLoache, J. S. (2004). Becoming symbol-minded. *Trends in Cognitive Sciences, 8*, 66–70.

Demorest, A., Silberman, L., Gardner, H. & Winner, E. (1983). Telling it as it isn't: Children's understanding of figurative language. *British Journal of Developmental Psychology, 1*, 121–134.

Desmarais, C., Sylvestre, A., Meyer, F., Bairati, I. & Rouleau, N. (2008). Systematic review of the literature on characteristics of late-talking toddlers. *International Journal of Communication Disorders*, *43*, 361–389.

Dewey, D. & Wall, K. (1997). Praxis and memory deficits in language-impaired children. *Developmental Neuropsychology*, *13*, 507–512.

Dews, S. & Winner, E. (1995). Muting the meaning: A social function of irony. *Metaphor and Symbolic Activity*, *10*, 3–19.

Dews, S., Winner, E., Kaplan, J., Rosenblatt, E., Hunt, M., Lim, K., McGovern, A., Qualter, A. & Smarsh, B. (1996). Children's understanding of the meaning and functions of verbal irony. *Child Development*, *67*, 3071–3085.

Di Sciullo, A. M. & Williams, E. (1987). *On the definition of word*. Cambridge, MA: MIT Press.

DiCamillo, K. (2006). *The miraculous journey of Edward Tulane*. Cambridge, MA: Candlewick Press.

Dick, F., Wulfeck, B., Krupa-Kwiatkowski, M. & Bates, E. (2004). The development of complex sentence interpretation in typically developing children compared with children with specific language impairments or early unilateral focal lesions. *Developmental Science*, *7*, 360–377.

Dimitrovsky, L., Spector, H., Levy-Shiff, R. & Vakil, E. (1998). Interpretation of facial expressions of affect in children with learning disabilities with verbal or nonverbal deficits. *Journal of Learning Disabilities*, *31*, 286–292.

Dockrell, J. E., Messer, D., George, R. & Ralli, A. (2003). Beyond naming patterns in children with WFDs – Definitions for nouns and verbs. *Journal of Neurolinguistics*, *16*(2/3), 191–211.

Dodd, B. (1975). Children's understanding of their own phonological forms. *Quarterly Journal of Experimental Psychology*, *27*, 165–172.

Doherty-Sneddon, G. (2008). The great baby signing debate. *The Psychologist*, *21*, 300–303.

Dolata, J. K., Davies, B. L. & McNeilage, P. F. (2008). Characteristics of the rhythmic organization of vocal babbling: Implications for an amodal linguistic rhythm. *Infant Behavior and Development*, *31*, 422–431.

Dollaghan, C. A. (1987). Fast mapping in normal and language-impaired children. *Journal of Speech and Hearing Disorders*, *52*(3), 218–222.

Dollaghan, C. & Campbell, T. F. (1998). Nonword repetition and child language impairment. *Journal of Speech, Language, and Hearing Research*, *41*(5), 1136–1146.

Donaldson, M. & McGarrigle, J. (1974). Some clues to the nature of semantic development. *Journal of Child Language*, *1*, 185–194.

Doupe, A. J. & Kuhl, P. K. (2008). Birdsong and human speech: Common themes and mechanisms. In H. P. Zeigler & P. Marler (eds), *Neuroscience of Birdsong* (pp. 5–31). Cambridge: Cambridge University Press.

Dreher, M. J. & Baker, L. (2003). Motivating struggling readers to succeed: Introduction to the theme. *Reading and Writing Quarterly*, *19*, 1–4.

Dromi, E. (1987). *Early lexical development*. Cambridge: Cambridge University Press.

Dunbar, R. I. M. (1993). The co-evolution of neocortical size, group size and language in humans. *Behavioral and Brain Sciences*, *16*, 681–735.

Dunbar, R. I. M. (1996). *Grooming, gossip and the evolution of language*. London: Faber and Faber.

Duncan, L. G., Seymour, P. H. K. & Hill, S. (1997). How important are rhyme and analogy in beginning reading? *Cognition*, *63*, 171–208.

Dunham, P. J., Dunham, F. & Curwin, A. (1993). Joint-attentional states and lexical acquisition at 18 months. *Developmental Psychology*, *29*, 827–831.

Dunn, J. & Munn, P. (1985). Becoming a family member: Family conflict and the development of social understanding in the second year. *Child Development, 56*, 480–492.

Eddington, D. K. (1980). Speech discrimination in deaf subjects with cochlear implants. *Journal of the Acoustical Society of America, 68*, 885–891.

Eden, G. F., Van Meter, J. W., Rumsey, J. M., Maisog, J. M., Woods, R. P. & Zeffiro, T. A. (1996). Abnormal processing of visual motion in dyslexia revealed by functional brain imaging. *Nature, 382*, 66–69.

Edwards, J., Beckman, M. E. & Munson, B. (2004). The interaction between vocabulary size and phonotactic probability effects on children's production accuracy and fluency in nonword repetition. *Journal of Speech, Language, and Hearing Research, 47*, 421–436.

Ehri, L. C. (1980). The role of orthography in printed word learning. In J. G. Kavanagh & R. L. Venezky (eds), *Orthography, reading, and dyslexia* (pp. 155–170). Baltimore, MD: University Park Press.

Ehri, L. C. (1991). Learning to read and spell words. In L. Rieben & C. A. Perfetti (eds), *Learning to read: Basic research and its implications* (pp. 57–73). Hillsdale, NJ: Lawrence Erlbaum Associates.

Ehri, L. C. (2005). Development of sight word reading: Phases and findings. In M. Snowling & C. Hulme (eds), *The science of reading: A handbook* (pp. 135–154). Malden, MA: Blackwell.

Ehri, L. C., Nunes, S. R., Stahl, S. A. & Willows, D. M. (2001). Systematic phonics instruction helps students learn to read: Evidence from the National Reading Panel's meta-analysis. *Review of Educational Research, 71*, 393–447.

Ehri, L. C. & Rosenthal, J. (2007). Spellings of words: A neglected facilitator of vocabulary learning. *Journal of Literacy Research, 39*, 389–409.

Ehri, L. C. & Soffer, A. G. (1999). Graphophonemic awareness: Development in elementary students. *Scientific Studies of Reading, 3*, 1–30.

Eilan, N., Hoerl, C., McCormack, T. & Roessler, J. (eds) (2005). *Joint attention: Communication and other minds.* Oxford: Oxford University Press.

Eimas, P. D. (1975). Auditory and phonetic coding of the cues for speech: Discrimination of the {r–l} distinction by young infants. *Perception and Psychophysics, 18*, 341–347.

Eimas, P. D., Siqueland, E. R., Jusczyk, P. & Vigorito, J. (1971). Speech perception in infants. *Science, 171*, 303–306.

Eisenberg, A. R. (1986). Verbal play in two Mexicano homes. In B. B. Schieffelin & E. Ochs (eds), *Language socialization across cultures: Studies in the social and cultural foundations of language* (pp. 182–198). New York: Cambridge University Press.

Ejiri, K. (1998). Relationship between rhythmic behavior and canonical babbling in infant vocal development. *Phonetica, 55*, 226–237.

Ejiri, K. & Masataka, N. (2001). Co-occurrence of preverbal vocal behavior and motor action in early infancy. *Developmental Science, 4*, 40–48.

Ekman, P. & Friesen, W.V. (1978). *Facial Action Coding System: A technique for the measurement of facial movement.* Palo Alto, CA: Consulting Psychologists Press.

Ellefson, M. R., Treiman, R. & Kessler, B. (2009). Learning to label letters by sounds or names: A comparison of England and the United States. *Journal of Experimental Child Psychology, 102*, 323–341.

Ellis, N. C. & Hennelly, R. A. (1980). A bilingual word-length effect: Implication for intelligence testing and the relative ease of mental calculations in Welsh and English. *British Journal of Psychology, 71*, 43–51.

Ellis, N. C. & Sinclair, S. G. (1996). Working memory in the acquisition of vocabulary and syntax: Putting language in good order. *The Quarterly Journal of Experimental Psychology A: Human Experimental Psychology*, 49A, 234–250.

Ely, R. & Gleason, J. B. (2006). *I'm sorry I said that:* Apologies in young children's discourse. *Journal of Child Language*, 33, 599–620.

Emmorey, K. (2002). *Language, cognition, and the brain: Insights from sign language research.* Mahwah, NJ: Lawrence Erlbaum Associates.

Emmorey, K., Bellugi, U., Friederici, A. & Horn, P. (1995). Effects of age of acquisition on grammatical sensitivity: Evidence from on-line and off-line tasks. *Applied Psycholinguistics*, 16, 1–23.

Emmorey, K. & Corina, D. (1990). Lexical recognition in sign language: Effects of phonetic structure and morphology. *Perceptual and Motor Skills*, 71, 1227–1252.

Emmorey, K. & Corina, D. (1993). Hemispheric specialization for ASL signs and English words: Differences between imageable and abstract forms. *Neuropsychologia*, 31, 645–653.

Emmorey, K., Grabowski, T., McCullough, S., Damasio, H., Ponto, L. L. B., Hichwa, R. D. & Bellugi, U. (2003). Neural systems underlying lexical retrieval for sign language. *Neuropsychologia*, 41, 85–95.

Emmorey, K., Grabowski, T., McCullough, S., Damasio, H., Ponto, L., Hichwa, R. & Bellugi, U. (2004). Motor-iconicity of sign language does not alter the neural systems underlying tool and action naming. *Brain and Language*, 89, 27–37.

Enard, W., Przeworski, M., Fisher, S. E., Lai, C. S. L., Wiebe, V., Kitano, T., Monaco, A. P. & Pääbo, S. (2002). Molecular evolution of FOXP2, a gene involved in speech and language. *Nature*, 418, 869–872.

Enfield, N. J. (2001). 'Lip pointing': With a discussion of form and function with reference to data from Laos. *Gesture*, 1, 185–212.

Epley, N., Morewedge, C. K. & Keysar, B. (2004). Perspective taking in children and adults: Equivalent egocentrism but differential correction. *Journal of Experimental Social Psychology*, 40, 760–768.

Ertmer, D. J. & Inniger, K. J. (2009). Characteristics of the transition to spoken words in two young cochlear implant recipients. *Journal of Speech, Language, and Hearing Research*, 52, 1579–1594.

Ervin-Tripp, S. (1974). Children's verbal turn-taking. In E. Ochs & B. Schieffelin (eds), *Developmental pragmatics* (pp. 391–414). New York: Academic Press.

Eskritt, M., Whalen, J. & Lee, K. (2008). Preschoolers can recognize violations of the Gricean maxims. *British Journal of Developmental Psychology*, 26, 435–443.

Evans, J. L. & MacWhinney, B. (1999). Sentence processing strategies in children with expressive and expressive-receptive specific language impairments. *International Journal of Language and Communication Disorders*, 34, 117–134.

Evans, J. L., Saffran, J. R. & Robe-Torres, K. (2009). Statistical learning in children with specific language impairment. *Journal of Speech, Language, and Hearing Research*, 52, 321–335.

Evans, N. & Levinson, S. C. (2009). The myth of language universals: Language diversity and its importance for cognitive science. *Behavioral and Brain Sciences*, 32, 429–492.

Everett, D. (2005). Cultural constraints on grammar and cognition in Pirahã: Another look at the design features of human language. *Current Anthropology*, 46, 621–634.

Fagan, M. K. & Iverson, J. M. (2007). The influence of mouthing on infant vocalization. *Infancy*, 11, 191–202.

Falk, D. (2004). Prelinguistic evolution in early hominins: Whence motherese? [Target article and commentaries]. *Behavioral and Brain Sciences*, 27, 491–541.

Farrant, B. M., Fletcher, J. & Maybery, M. T. (2006). Specific language impairment, theory of mind, and visual perspective taking: Evidence for simulation theory and the developmental role of language. *Child Development, 77*, 1842–1853.

Farrar, M. J., Johnson, B., Tompkins, V., Easters, M., Zilisi-Medus, A. & Benigno, J. P. (2009). Language and theory of mind in preschool children with specific language impairment. *Journal of Communication Disorders, 42*, 428–441.

Farrington-Flint, L., Stash, A. & Stiller, J. (2008). Monitoring variability and change in children's spelling strategies. *Educational Psychology, 28*, 133–149.

Farroni, T., Csibra, G., Simeon, F. & Johnson, M. H. (2002). Eye contact detection in humans from birth. *Proceedings of the National Academy of Sciences of the USA, 99*, 9602–9605.

Farroni, T., Johnson, M. H., Menon, E., Zulian, L., Faraguna, D. & Csibra, G. (2005). Newborns' preference for face-relevant stimuli: Effects of contrast polarity. *Proceedings of the National Academy of Sciences of the USA, 102*, 17245–17250.

Faust, M., Dimitrovsky, L. & Davidi, S. (1997). Naming difficulties in language-disabled children: Preliminary findings with the application of the Tip-of-the-Tongue paradigm. *Journal of Speech, Language, and Hearing Research, 40*, 1026–1036.

Fay, N., Garrod, S., Roberts, L. & Swoboda, N. (2010). The interactive evolution of human communication systems. *Cognitive Science, 34*, 351–386.

Feigenson, L., Dehaene, S. & Spelke, E. (2004). Core systems of number. *Trends in Cognitive Sciences, 8*, 307–314.

Feinman, S. & Lewis, M. (1983). Social referencing at 10 months: A second-order effect on infants' responses to strangers. *Child Development, 54*, 878–887.

Fennell, C.T., Byers-Heinlein, K. & Werker, J. F. (2007). Using speech sounds to guide word learning: The case of bilingual infants. *Child Development, 78*, 1510–1525.

Fenson, L., Dale, P. S., Reznick, J. S., Bates, E., Thal, D. J. & Pethick, S. J. (1994). Variability in early communicative development. *Monographs of the Society for Research in Child Development, 59*, Serial No. 242.

Ferguson, C. A. & Farwell, C. B. (1975). Words and sounds in early language acquisition: Initial consonants in the first fifty words. *Language, 51*, 419–439.

Ferguson, C. A. (1977). Babytalk as a simplified register. In C. A. Ferguson & C. Snow (eds), *Talking to children: Language input and acquisition* (pp. 219–236). New York: Cambridge University Press.

Fernald, A. (1992). Human vocalizations to infants as biologically relevant signals: An evolutionary perspective. In J. H. Barkow, L. Cosmides & J. Tooby (eds), *The Adapted Mind: Evolutionary psychology and the generation of culture* (pp. 391–428). New York: Oxford University Press.

Fernald, A. (2001). Hearing, listening, and understanding: Auditory development in infancy. In G. Bremner & A. Fogel (eds), *Blackwell handbook of infant development. Handbooks of developmental psychology* (pp. 35–70). Malden, MA: Blackwell.

Fernald, A. & Mazzie, C. (1991). Prosody and focus in speech to infants and adults. *Developmental Psychology, 27*, 209–221.

Fernald, A., Perfors, A. & Marchman, V. A. (2006). Picking up speed in understanding: Speech processing efficiency and vocabulary growth across the 2nd year. *Developmental Psychology, 42*, 98–116.

Fernald, A., Swingley, D. & Pinto, J. P. (2001). When half a word is enough: Infants can recognize spoken words using partial phonetic information. *Child Development, 72*, 1003–1015.

Fernald, A., Taeschner, T., Dunn, J., Papousek, M., de Boysson-Bardies, B. & Fukui, I. (1989). A cross-language study of prosodic modifications in mothers' and fathers' speech to preverbal infants. *Journal of Child Language, 16*, 477–501.

Fernandes, K. J., Marcus, G. F., Di Nubila, J. A. & Vouloumanos, A. (2006). From semantics to syntax and back again: Argument structure in the third year of life. *Cognition, 100*, B10–B20.

Ferry, A. L., Hespos, S. J. & Waxman, S. R. (2010). Categorization in 3- and 4-month-old infants: An advantage of words over tones. *Child Development, 81*, 472–479.

Feuk, L., Kalervo, A., Lipsanen-Nyman, M., Skaug, J., Nakabayashi, K., Finucane, B. et al. (2006). Absence of a paternally inherited *FOXP2* gene in developmental verbal dyspraxia. *American Journal of Human Genetics, 79*, 965–972.

Figueras, B., Edwards, L. & Langdon, D. (2008). Executive function and language in deaf children. *Journal of Deaf Studies and Deaf Education, 13*, 362–377.

Fillmore, C. J. (1968). The case for case. In E. Bach and R. T. Harms (eds), *Universals in linguistic theory* (pp. 1–88). New York: Holt, Rinehart & Winston.

Finlay, B. L., Darlington, R. B. & Nicastro, N. (2001). Developmental structure in brain evolution. *Behavioral and Brain Sciences, 24*, 263–308.

Fisher, A. V. & Sloutsky, V. M. (2005). When induction meets memory: Evidence for gradual transition from similarity-based to category-based induction. *Child Development, 76*, 583–597.

Fisher, C. & Tokura, H. (1996). Acoustic cues to grammatical structure in infant-directed speech: Cross-linguistic evidence. *Child Development, 67*, 3192–3218.

Fisher, S. E. & Scharff, C. (2009). FOXP2 as a molecular window into speech and language. *Trends in Genetics, 25*, 166–177.

Fivush, R. (1998). Gendered narratives: Elaboration, structure and emotion in parent–child reminiscing across the preschool years. In C. P. Thompson, D. J. Herrmann, D. Bruce, J. D. Read, D. G. Payne & M. P. Toglia (eds), *Autobiographical memory: Theoretical and applied perspectives* (pp. 79–104). Hillsdale, NJ: Lawrence Erlbaum Associates.

Flege, J. E., Munro, M. J. & MacKay, I. R. A. (1995). Factors affecting strength of perceived foreign accent in a second language. *Journal of the Acoustical Society of America, 97*, 3125–3134.

Flege, J. E., Takagi, N. & Mann, V. (1996). Lexical familiarity and English-language experience affect Japanese adults' perception of /ɹ/ and /l/. *Journal of the Acoustical Society of America, 99*, 1161–1173.

Fletcher, K. L. & Reese, E. (2005). Picture book reading with young children: A conceptual framework. *Developmental Review, 25*, 64–103.

Fletcher, P., Stokes, S. & Wong, A. (2005). Constructions and language development: Implications for language impairment. In P. Fletcher & J. F. Miller (eds), *Developmental theory and language disorders* (pp. 35–51). Amsterdam: John Benjamins.

Fogel, A. & Hannan, T. E. (1985). Manual actions of nine- to fifteen-week-old human infants during face-to-face interaction with their mothers. *Child Development, 56*, 1271–1279.

Folven, R. J. & Bonvillian, J. D. (1991). The transition from nonreferential to referential language in children acquiring American Sign Language. *Developmental Psychology, 27*, 806–816.

Foorman, B. R., Francis, D. J., Fletcher, J. M., Schatschneider, C. & Mehta, P. (1998). The role of instruction in learning to read: Preventing reading failure in at-risk children. *Journal of Educational Psychology, 90*, 37–55.

Ford, J. A. & Milosky, L. M. (2008). Inference generation during discourse and its relation to social competence: An online investigation of abilities of children with and without language impairment. *Journal of Speech, Language, and Hearing Research, 51*, 367–380.

Fortnum, H. M., Summerfield, A. Q., Marshall, D. H., Davis, A. C. & Bamford, J. M. (2001). Prevalence of permanent childhood hearing impairment in the United Kingdom and implications for universal neonatal hearing screening: Questionnaire-based ascertainment study. *British Medical Journal, 323*, 536.

Foulkes, P., Docherty, G. & Watt, D. (2005). Phonological variation in child-directed speech. *Language, 81*, 177–206.

Foy, J. G. & Mann, V. (2003). Home literacy environment and phonological awareness in preschool children: Differential effects for rhyme and phoneme awareness. *Applied Psycholinguistics, 24*, 59–88.

Franco, F. & Butterworth, G. E. (1996). Pointing and social awareness: Declaring and requesting in the second year of life. *Journal of Child Language, 23*, 307–336.

Franklin, A. & Davies, I. R. L. (2004). New evidence for infant colour categories. *British Journal of Developmental Psychology, 22*, 349–377.

Franklin, A., Drivonikou, G. V., Bevis, L., Davies, I. R. L., Kay, P. & Regier, T. (2008). Categorical perception of color is lateralized to the right hemisphere in infants, but to the left hemisphere in adults. *Proceedings of the National Academy of Sciences of the USA, 105*, 3221–3225.

Franklin, A., Drivonikou, G. V., Clifford, A., Kay, P., Regier, T. & Davies, I. R. L. (2008). Lateralization of categorical perception of color changes with color term acquisition. *Proceedings of the National Academy of Sciences of the USA, 105*, 18221–18225.

Freeman, N. H. (1985). Reasonable errors in basic reasoning. *Educational Psychology, 5*(3/4), 239–249.

Friederici, A. D. (2009). Pathways to language: Fiber tracts in the human brain. *Trends in Cognitive Sciences, 13*, 175–181.

Friedman, W. J. (2004). Time in autobiographical memory. *Social Cognition, 22*, 591–605.

Friedman, W. J. (2005). Developmental and cognitive perspectives on humans' sense of the times of past and future events. *Learning and Motivation, 36*, 145–158.

Friedmann, N. & Novogrodsky, R. (2004). Acquisition of relative clause comprehension in Hebrew: A study of SLI and normal development. *Journal of Child Language, 31*, 661–681.

Friedrich, M. & Friederici, A. D. (2010). Maturing brain mechanisms and developing behavioral language skills. *Brain and Language, 114*, 66–71.

Friesen, L. M., Shannon, R. V., Baskent, D. & Wang, X. (2001). Speech recognition as a function of the number of spectral channels: Comparison of acoustic hearing and cochlear implants. *Journal of the Acoustical Society of America, 110*, 1150–1163.

Frith, U. (1985). Beneath the surface of developmental dyslexia. In K. E. Patterson, J.C. Marshall & M. Coltheart (eds), *Surface dyslexia: Neuropsychological and cognitive studies of phonological reading* (pp. 301–330). London: Lawrence Erlbaum Associates.

Frost, R., Katz, L. & Bentin, S. (1987). Strategies for visual word recognition and orthographic depth: A multilingual comparison. *Journal of Experimental Psychology: Human Perception and Performance, 13*, 104–115.

Führ, M. (2002). Coping humor in early adolescence. *Humor, 15*, 283–304.

Fulkerson, A. L. & Waxman, S. R. (2007). Words (but not tones) facilitate object categorization: Evidence from 6- and 12-month-olds. *Cognition, 105*, 218–228.

Galaburda, A. M., Sherman, G. F., Rosen, G. D., Aboitiz, F. & Geschwind, N. (1985). Developmental dyslexia: Four consecutive patients with cortical anomalies. *Annals of Neurology, 18*, 222–233.

Ganger, J. & Brent, M. R. (2004). Reexamining the vocabulary spurt. *Developmental Psychology, 40*, 621–632.

Garbin, G., Sanjuan, A., Forn, C., Bustamante, J. C., Rodriguez-Pujadas, A., Belloch, V., Hernandez, M., Costa, A. & Ávila, C. (2010). Bridging language and attention: Brain basis of the impact of bilingualism on cognitive control. *NeuroImage, 53*, 1272–1278.

Garcia, J. (1999). *Sign with your baby: How to communicate with infants before they can speak*. Seattle, WA: Northlight Communications.

Gardner, M. F. (1990). *Expressive one-word picture vocabulary test – revised*. Novato, CA: Academic Therapy Publications.

Garrod, S. & Anderson, A. (1987). Saying what you mean in dialogue: A study in conceptual and semantic co-ordination. *Cognition*, *27*, 181–218.

Garrod, S. & Clark, A. (1993). The development of dialogue co-ordination skills in schoolchildren. *Language and Cognitive Processes*, *8*(1), 101–126.

Gathercole, S. E., Willis, C. S., Baddeley, A. D. & Emslie, H. (1994). The children's test of nonword repetition: A test of phonological working memory. *Memory*, *2*, 103–127.

Gathercole, S. E. & Baddeley, A. D. (1989). Evaluation of the role of phonological STM in the development of vocabulary in children: A longitudinal study. *Journal of Memory and Language*, *28*, 200–213.

Gathercole, S. E. & Baddeley, A. D. (1990). The role of phonological memory in vocabulary acquisition: A study of young children learning new names. *British Journal of Psychology*, *81*, 439–454.

Gathercole, S. E., Hitch, G. J., Service, E. & Martin, A. J. (1997). Phonological short-term memory and new word learning in children. *Developmental Psychology*, *33*, 966–979.

Gelman, S. A. & Markman, E. M. (1986). Categories and induction in young children. *Cognition*, *23*, 183–209.

Gelman, S. A. & Markman, E. M. (1987). Young children's inductions from natural kinds: The role of categories and appearances. *Child Development*, *58*, 1532–1541.

Gentilucci, M. & Dalla Volta, R. (2008). Spoken language and arm gestures are controlled by the same motor control system. *The Quarterly Journal of Experimental Psychology*, *61*, 944–957.

Gentner, D. (1982). Why nouns are learned before verbs: Linguistic relativity versus natural partitioning. In S. A. Kuczaj (ed.), *Language development: Vol. 2 Language, thought and culture* (pp. 301–334). Hillsdale, NJ: Lawrence Erlbaum Associates.

Gentner, D. & Namy, L. L. (2006). Analogical processes in language learning. *Current Directions in Psychological Science*, *15*, 297–301.

German, J. D. (1984). Diagnosis of word-finding disorders in children with learning disabilities. *Journal of Learning Disabilities*, *17*, 353–359.

German, J. D. (1987). Spontaneous language profiles of children with word-finding problems. *Language, Speech, and Hearing Services in Schools*, *8*, 217–230.

German, J. D. & Simon, E. (1991). Analysis of children's word-finding skills in discourse. *Journal of Speech and Hearing Research*, *34*, 309–316.

Gershkoff-Stowe, L. (2002). Object naming, vocabulary growth, and the development of word retrieval abilities. *Journal of Memory and Language*, *46*, 665–687.

Gershkoff-Stowe, L., Connell, B. & Smith, L. (2006). Priming overgeneralizations in two- and four-year-old children. *Journal of Child Language*, *33*, 461–486.

Gershkoff-Stowe, L. & Hahn, E. R. (2007). Fast mapping skills in the developing lexicon. *Journal of Speech, Language, and Hearing Research*, *50*, 682–697.

Gershkoff-Stowe, L. & Smith, L. B. (2004). Shape and the first hundred nouns. *Child Development*, *75*, 1098–1114.

Gertner, B. L., Rice, M. L. & Hadley, P. A. (1994). Influence of communicative competence on peer preferences in a preschool classroom. *Journal of Speech and Hearing Research*, *37*, 913–923.

Gertner, Y., Fisher, C. & Eisengart, J. (2006). Learning words and rules: Abstract knowledge of word order in early sentence comprehension. *Psychological Science*, *17*, 684–691.

Geschwind, N. & Levitsky, W. (1968). Left–right asymmetry in temporal speech region. *Science*, *161*(3837), 186–187.

Geurts, B. (2003). Quantifying kids. *Language Acquisition*, *11*, 197–218.

Gilbert, A. L., Regier, T., Kay, P. & Ivry, R. B. (2005). Whorf hypothesis is supported in the right visual field but not the left. *Proceedings of the National Academy of Sciences of the USA, 103,* 489–494.

Gillam, R. B., Loeb, D. F., Hoffman, L. M., Bohman, T., Champlin, C. A., Thibodeau, L. et al. (2008). The efficacy of Fast ForWord language intervention in school-age children with language impairment: A randomized controlled trial. *Journal of Speech, Language, and Hearing Research, 51*(1), 97–119.

Gillette, J., Gleitman, H., Gleitman, L. & Lederer, A. (1999). Human simulations of vocabulary learning. *Cognition, 73,* 135–176.

Gleason, J. B. & Ely, R. (2002). Gender differences in language development. In A. M. De Lisi and R. De Lisi (eds), *Biology, society, and behavior: The development of sex differences in cognition* (pp. 127–154). Westport, CT: Ablex.

Gleason, J. B., Perlmann, R. Y. & Greif, E. B. (1984). What's the magic word: Learning language through politeness routines. *Discourse Processes, 7,* 493–502.

Gleitman, L. (1990). The structural sources of verb meanings. *Language Acquisition, 1,* 3–35.

Gleitman, L. R., Cassidy, K., Nappa, R., Papafragou, A. & Trueswell, J. C. (2005). Hard words. *Language Learning and Development, 1,* 23–64.

Glucksberg, S., Krauss, R. M. & Weisberg, R. (1966). Referential communication in nursery school children: Method and some preliminary findings. *Journal of Experimental Child Psychology, 3*(4), 333–342.

Goffman, L. (2004). Kinematic differentiation of prosodic categories in normal and disordered language development. *Journal of Speech, Language, and Hearing Research, 47,* 1088–1102.

Gogate, L. J. (2010). Learning of syllable–object relations by preverbal infants: The role of temporal synchrony and syllable distinctiveness. *Journal of Experimental Child Psychology, 103,* 178–197.

Gogate, L. J., Bahrick, L. E. & Watson, J. D. (2000). A study of multimodal motherese: The role of temporal synchrony between verbal labels and gestures. *Child Development, 71,* 878–894.

Gogate, L. J., Bolzani, L. H. & Betancourt, E. (2006). Attention to maternal multimodal naming by 6- to 8-month-old infants and learning of word–object relations. *Infancy, 9,* 259–288.

Gogate, L. J. & Hollich, G. (2010). Invariance detection within an interactive system: A perceptual gateway to language development. *Psychological Review, 117,* 496–516.

Gogtay, N., Giedd, J., Lusk, L., Hayashi, K. M., Greenstein, D. K., Vaituzis, A. C., Nugent, T. F., Herman, D., Clasen, L. S., Toga, A. W., Rapoport, J. L. & Thompson, P. M. (2004). Dynamic mapping of human cortical development during childhood through early adulthood. *Proceedings of the National Academy of Sciences of the USA, 101,* 8174–8179.

Goldberg, A. E. (1995). *Constructions: A construction grammar approach to argument structure.* Chicago: University of Chicago Press.

Goldberg, A. E. (2006). *Constructions at work: The nature of generalization in language.* Oxford: Oxford University Press.

Goldberg, A. E. & Jackendoff, R. (2004). The English resultative as a family of constructions. *Language, 80,* 532–568.

Goldin-Meadow, S. (1999). The role of gesture in communication and thinking. *Trends in Cognitive Science, 3,* 419–429.

Goldin-Meadow, S. (2003). *The resilience of language: What gesture creation in deaf children can tell us about how all children learn language.* New York: Psychology Press.

Goldin-Meadow, S., Butcher, C., Mylander, C. & Dodge, M. (1994). Nouns and verbs in a self-styled gesture system: What's in a name? *Cognitive Psychology, 27,* 259–319.

Goldin-Meadow, S., Gelman, S. A. & Mylander, C. (2005). Expressing generic concepts with and without a language model. *Cognition, 96,* 109–126.

Goldin-Meadow, S. & Mylander, C. (1998). Spontaneous sign systems created by deaf children in two cultures. *Nature, 391*(6664), 279–281.

Goldin-Meadow, S., Mylander, C. & Butcher, C. (1995). The resilience of combinatorial structure at the word level: Morphology in self-styled gesture systems. *Cognition, 56,* 195–262.

Goldin-Meadow, S., Mylander, C. & Franklin, A. (2007). How children make language out of gesture: Morphological structure in the gesture systems developed by American and Chinese deaf children. *Cognitive Psychology, 55,* 87–135.

Goldstein, M. H., King, A. P. & West, M. J. (2003). Social interaction shapes babbling: Testing parallels between birdsong and speech. *Proceedings of the National Academy of Sciences of the USA, 100,* 8030–8035.

Goldstein, M. H. & Schwade, J. A. (2008). Social feedback to infants' babbling facilitates rapid phonological learning. *Psychological Science, 19*(5), 515–523.

Goldstein, M. H., Schwade, J. A. & Bornstein, M. H. (2009). The value of vocalizing: Five-month-old infants associate their own noncry vocalizations with responses from caregivers. *Child Development, 80,* 636–644.

Golestani, N. & Zatorre, R. J. (2008). Individual differences in the acquisition of second language phonology. *Brain and Language, 109,* 55–67.

Golinkoff, R. M. & Alioto, A. (1995). Infant-directed speech facilitates lexical learning in adults hearing Chinese: Implications for language acquisition. *Journal of Child Language, 22,* 703–726.

Golinkoff, R. M., Hirsh-Pasek, K., Bailey, L. M. & Wenger, N. R. (1992). Young children and adults use lexical principles to learn new nouns. *Developmental Psychology, 28,* 99–108.

Golinkoff, R. M., Mervis, C. & Hirsh-Pasek, K. (1994). Early object labels: The case for a developmental lexical principles framework. *Journal of Child Language, 21,* 125–155.

Gollan, T. H. & Acenas, L.-A. R. (2004). What is a TOT? Cognate and translation effects on tip-of-the-tongue states in Spanish–English and Tagalog–English bilinguals. *Journal of Experimental Psychology: Learning, Memory, and Cognition, 30,* 246–269.

Gollan, T. H., Montoya, R. I., Fennema-Notestine, C. & Morris, S. K. (2005). Bilingualism affects picture naming but not picture classification. *Memory and Cognition, 33,* 1220–1234.

Gollan, T. H., Montoya, R. I. & Werner, G. (2002). Semantic and letter fluency in Spanish–English bilinguals. *Neuropsychology, 16,* 562–576.

Gómez, R. L. (2002). Variability and the detection of invariant structure. *Psychological Science, 13,* 431–436.

Gómez, R. L. & Gerken, L. A. (1999). Artificial language learning by one-year-olds leads to specific and abstract knowledge. *Cognition, 70,* 109–135.

Gómez, R. L. & Lakusta, L. (2004). A first step in form-based category abstraction by 12-month-old infants. *Developmental Science, 7,* 567–580.

Goodwyn, S. W. & Acredolo, L. P. (1993). Symbolic gesture versus word: Is there a modality advantage for onset of symbol use? *Child Development, 64,* 688–701.

Goodwyn, S. W., Acredolo, L. P. & Brown, C. A. (2000). Impact of symbolic gesturing on early language development. *Journal of Nonverbal Behavior, 24,* 81–103.

Gopnik, M. (1990). Genetic basis of grammar defect. *Nature, 347,* 26.

Gopnik, M. & Crago, M. (1991). Familial aggregation of a developmental language disorder. *Cognition, 39,* 1–50.

Gordon, P. (2004). Numerical cognition without words: Evidence from Amazonia. *Science, 306,* 496–499.

Gordon, R. C. & Grimes, B. F. (eds) (2005). *Ethnologue: Languages of the world*, 15th edn. Dallas, TX: SIL International.

Goswami, U. (1986). Children's use of analogy in learning to read: A developmental study. *Journal of Experimental Child Psychology, 42*, 73–83.

Goswami, U. (2002). Phonology, learning to read and dyslexia: A crosslinguistic analysis. In V. Csépe (ed.), *Dyslexia: Different brain, different behaviour* (pp. 1–40). Amsterdam: Kluwer Academic.

Goswami, U., Thomson, J., Richardson, U., Stainthorp, R., Hughes, D., Rosen, S. & Scott, S. K. (2002). Amplitude envelope onsets and developmental dyslexia: A new hypothesis. *Proceedings of the National Academy of Sciences of the USA, 99*, 10911–10916.

Gould, S. J. (1977). *Ontogeny and phylogeny*. Cambridge, MA: Harvard University Press.

Gray, J. (1992). *Men are from Mars, women are from Venus: A practical guide for improving communication and getting what you want in your relationships*. New York: Harper Collins.

Greif, E. B. & Gleason, J. B. (1980). Hi, thanks, and goodbye: More routine information. *Language in Society, 9*, 159–166.

Grela, B. G. & Leonard, L. B. (2000). The influence of argument–structure complexity on the use of auxiliary verbs by children with SLI. *Journal of Speech, Language, and Hearing Research, 43*, 1115–1125.

Grieco-Colub, T. M., Saffran, J. R. & Litovsky, R. Y. (2009). Spoken word recognition in toddlers who use cochlear implants. *Journal of Speech, Language, and Hearing Research, 52*, 1390–1400.

Griffin, E. A. & Morrison, F. J. (1997). The unique contribution of home literacy environment to differences in early literacy skills. *Early Child Development and Care, 127/128*, 233–243.

Grigorenko, E. (2001). Developmental dyslexia: An update on genes, brains, and environments. *Journal of Child Psychology and Psychiatry, 42*, 91–125.

Groszer, M., Keays, D. A., Deacon, R. M. J., de Bono, J. P., Prasad-Mulcare, S., Gaub, S., Baum, M G., French, C. A., Nicod, J. et al. (2008). Impaired synaptic plasticity and motor learning in mice with a point mutation implicated in human speech deficits. *Current Biology, 18*, 354–362.

Guarini, A., Sansavini, A., Fabbri, S., Alessandroni, R., Faldella, G. & Karmiloff-Smith, A. (2009). Reconsidering the impact of preterm birth of language outcome. *Early Human Development, 85*, 639–645.

Guttentag, R. & Haith, M. (1978). Automatic processing as a function of age and reading ability. *Child Development, 49*, 707–716.

Gvozdev, A. N. (1961). *Voprosy izucheniya detskoy rechi* [The development of language in children]. Moscow: Akademiya Pedagogicheskikh Nauk RSFSR.

Haden, C. A. & Fivush, R. (1996). Contextual variation in maternal conversational styles. *Merrill-Palmer Quarterly, 42*, 200–227.

Haden, C. A., Ornstein, P. A., Eckerman, C. O. & Didow, S. M. (2001). Mother–child conversational interactions as events unfold: Linkages to subsequent remembering. *Child Development, 72*, 1016–1031.

Hadley, P. A. & Rice, M. L. (1991). Conversational responsiveness of speech- and language-impaired preschoolers. *Journal of Speech, Language, and Hearing Research, 34*, 1308–1317.

Haesler, S., Rochefort, C., Georgi, B., Licznerski, P., Oster, P. & Scharff, C. (2007). Incomplete and inaccurate vocal imitation after knockdown of FoxP2 in songbird basal ganglia nucleus Area X. *PLoS Biology, 5*, e321.

Haidle, M. N. (2010). Working-memory capacity and the evolution of modern cognitive potential: Implications from animal and early human tool use. *Current Anthropology, 51*(Suppl. 1), S149–S166.

Haith, M. M., Bergman, T. & Moore, M. J. (1977). Eye contact and face scanning in early infancy. *Science, 198*(4319), 853–855.

Hakuta, K., Bialystok, E. & Wiley, E. (2003). Critical evidence: A test of the critical period hypothesis for second language acquisition. *Psychological Science, 14,* 31–38.

Hanley, J. R., Masterson, J., Spencer, L. H. & Evans, D. (2004). How long do the advantages of learning a transparent orthography last? An investigation of the reading skills and incidence of dyslexia in Welsh children at 10 years of age. *Quarterly Journal of Experimental Psychology: Human Experimental Psychology, 57*(A), 1393–1410.

Hannan, T. E. & Fogel, A. (1987). A case-study assessment of 'pointing' during the first three months of life. *Perceptual and Motor Skills, 65,* 187–194.

Harley, K. & Reese, E. (1999). Origins of autobiographical memory. *Developmental Psychology, 35,* 1338–1348.

Harley, T. A. (1984). A critique of top-down independent levels models of speech production: Evidence from non-plan-internal speech errors. *Cognitive Science, 8,* 191–219.

Harrington, M. & Sawyer, M. (1992). L2 working memory capacity and L2 reading skill. *Studies in Second Language Acquisition, 14,* 25–38.

Harris, M., Barlow-Brown, F. & Chasin, J. (1995). The emergence of referential understanding: Pointing and the comprehension of object names. *First Language, 15,* 19–34.

Harris, M. & Pexman, P. M. (2003). Children's perception of the social functions of verbal irony. *Discourse Processes, 36,* 147–165.

Harris, R. I. (1978). The relationship of impulse control to parent hearing status, manual communication, an academic achievement in deaf children. *American Annals of the Deaf, 123,* 52–67.

Hart, B. & Risley, T. R. (1999). *The social world of children learning to talk.* Baltimore, MD: Paul H. Brookes Publishing.

Hart, K. I., Fujiki, M., Brinton, B. & Hart, C. H. (2004). The relationship between social behavior and severity of language impairment. *Journal of Speech, Language, and Hearing Research, 47,* 647–662.

Hart, S. A., Petrill, S. A., DeThorne, L. S., Deater-Deckard, K., Thompson, L. A., Schatschneider, C. & Cutting, L. E. (2009). Environmental influences on the longitudinal covariance of expressive vocabulary: Measuring the home literacy environment in a genetically sensitive design. *Journal of Child Psychology and Psychiatry, 50,* 911–919.

Haspelmath, M. (2007). Pre-established categories don't exist: Consequences for language description and typology. *Linguistic Typology, 11,* 119–132.

Hasson, U., Ghazanfar, A. A., Galantucci, B., Garrod, S. & Keysers, C. (2012). Brain-to-brain coupling: a mechanism for creating and sharing a social world. *Trends in Cognitive Sciences, 16,* 114–121.

Hauser, M. D., Chomsky, N. & Fitch, W. T. (2002). The faculty of language: What is it, who has it, and how did it evolve? *Science, 298,* 1569–1579.

Hayes, D. P. & Ahrens, M. G. (1988). Vocabulary simplification for children: A special case of 'motherese'? *Journal of Child Language, 15,* 395–410.

Hayiou-Thomas, M. E., Bishop, D. V. M. & Plunkett, K. (2004). Simulating SLI: General cognitive processing stressors can produce a specific linguistic profile. *Journal of Speech, Language, and Hearing Research, 47,* 1347–1362.

Hayne, H. (2004). Infant memory development: Implications for childhood amnesia. *Developmental Review, 24,* 33–73.

Heath, S. B. (1983). *Ways with words.* Cambridge: Cambridge University Press.

Heathcote, A., Brown, S. & Mewhort, D. J. K. (2000). The power law repealed: The case for an exponential law of practice. *Psychonomic Bulletin and Review, 7*(2), 185–207.

Helmstaedter, C., Kurthen, M., Linke, D. B. & Elger, C. E. (1997). Patterns of language dominance in focal left and right hemisphere epilepsies: Relation to MRI findings, EEG, sex, and age at onset of epilepsy. *Brain and Cognition, 33,* 135–150.

Hennessey, N. W., Leitão, S. & Mucciarone, K. (2010). Verbal repetition skill in language impaired children: Evidence of inefficient lexical processing? *International Journal of Speech-Language Pathology, 12,* 47–57.

Hestvik, A., Schwartz, R. G. & Tornyova, L. (2010). Relative clause gap-filling in children with specific language impairment. *Journal of Psycholinguistic Research, 39,* 443–456.

Hickmann, M. (2003). *Children's discourse: Person, space and time across languages.* Cambridge: Cambridge University Press.

Hill, E. L. (1998). A dispraxic deficit in specific language impairment and developmental coordination disorder: Evidence from hand and arm movements. *Developmental Medicine and Child Neurology, 40,* 388–395.

Hill, E. L. (2001). Non-specific nature of specific language impairment: A review of the literature with regard to concomitant motor impairments. *International Journal of Communication Disorders, 36,* 149–171.

Hilton, D. J. (1995). The social context of reasoning: Conversational inference and rational judgment. *Psychological Bulletin, 118,* 248–271.

Hirsh-Pasek, K. & Treiman, R. (1982). Doggerel: Motherese in a new context. *Journal of Child Language, 9,* 229–237.

Hirsh-Pasek, K., Kemler Nelson, D., Jusczyk, P., Cassidy, K.W., Druss, B. & Kennedy, L. (1987). Clauses are perceptual units for prelinguistic infants. *Cognition, 26,* 269–286.

Hodge, S. M., Makris, N., Kennedy, D. N., Caviness, V. S. Jr., Howard, J., McGrath, L., Steele, S., Frazier, J. A., Tager-Flusberg, H. & Harris, G. J. (2010). Cerebellum, language, and cognition in autism and specific language impairment. *Journal of Autism and Developmental Disabilities, 40,* 300–316.

Hoff-Ginsberg, E. (1991). Mother–child conversation in different social classes and communicative settings. *Child Development, 62,* 782–796.

Hoff-Ginsberg, E. (1998). The relation of birth order and socioeconomic status to children's language experience and language development. *Applied Psycholinguistics, 19,* 603–629.

Hoff-Ginsberg, E. & Krueger, W. (1991). Older siblings as conversational partners. *Merrill-Palmer Quarterly, 37,* 465–482.

Hoff, E. (2003). The specificity of environmental influence: Socioeconomic status affects early vocabulary development via maternal speech. *Child Development, 71,* 1368–1378.

Hoff, E. (2006). How social contexts support and shape language development. *Developmental Review, 26,* 55–88.

Hohne, E. A. & Jusczyk, P. W. (1994). Two-month-old infants' sensitivity to allophonic differences. *Perception and Psychophysics, 56,* 613–623.

Hoicka, E. & Gattis, M. (2008). Do the wrong thing: How toddlers tell a joke from a mistake. *Cognitive Development, 23,* 180–190.

Hoicka, E., Jutsum, S. & Gattis, M. (2008). Humor, abstraction, and disbelief. *Cognitive Science, 32,* 985–1002.

Hollich, G. J., Newman, R. S. & Jusczyk, P. W. (2005). Infants' use of synchronized visual information to separate streams of speech. *Child Development, 76,* 598–613.

Hollich, G., Golinkoff, R. M. & Hirsh-Pasek, K. (2007). Young children associate novel words with complex objects rather than salient parts. *Developmental Psychology, 43,* 1051–1061.

Holmes, V. M. & Malone, N. (2004). Adult spelling strategies. *Reading and Writing, 17,* 537–566.

Homae, F., Watanabe, H., Nakano, T., Asakawa, K. & Taga, G. (2006). The right hemisphere of sleeping infant perceives sentential prosody. *Neuroscience Research, 54,* 276–280.

Hood, M., Conlon, E. & Andrews, G. (2008). Preschool home literacy practices and children's literacy development: A longitudinal analysis. *Journal of Educational Psychology, 100*, 252–271.

Horner, V. & Whiten, A. (2005). Causal knowledge and imitation/emulation switching in chimpanzees (Pan troglodytes) and children (Homo sapiens). *Animal Cognition, 8*, 164–181.

Houston-Price, C., Plunkett, K. & Harris, P. (2005). 'Word-learning wizardry' at 1;6. *Journal of Child Language, 32*, 175–189.

Howe, C. (1976). The meaning of two-word utterances in the speech of young children. *Journal of Child Language, 3*, 29–48.

Hrdy, S. B. (1999). *Mother Nature: Natural selection and the female of the species.* London: Chatto and Windus.

Hrdy, S. B. (2005). Comes the child before man: How cooperative breeding and prolonged post-weaning dependence shaped human potential. In B. Hewlett & M. Lamb (eds), *Hunter gatherer childhoods: Evolutionary, developmental and cultural perspectives* (pp. 65–91). Piscataway, NJ: Transaction Publishers.

Hrdy, S. B. (2009). *Mothers and others: The evolutionary origins of mutual understanding.* Boston, MA: Harvard University Press.

Hubel, D. & Wiesel, T. (1963). Receptive fields of cells in striate cortex of very young, visually inexperienced kittens. *Journal of Neurophysiology, 26*, 994–1002.

Hudson Kam, C. L. & Newport, E. L. (2005). Regularizing unpredictable variation: The roles of adult and child learners. *Language Learning and Development, 1*, 151–195.

Hulme, C. & Snowling, M. J. (2011). Children's reading comprehension difficulties: Nature, causes and treatments. *Current Directions in Psychological Science, 20*, 139–142.

Humphreys, P., Kaufmann, W. E. & Galaburda, A. M. (1990). Developmental dyslexia in women: Neuropathological findings in three patients. *Annals of Neurology, 28*, 727–738.

Hurewitz, F., Brown-Schmidt, S., Thorpe, K., Gleitman, L. R. & Trueswell, J. C. (2000). One frog, two frog, red frog, blue frog: Factors affecting children's syntactic choices in production and comprehension. *Journal of Psycholinguistic Research, 29*, 597–626.

Hurst, J. A., Baraitser, M., Auger, E., Graham, F. & Norell, S. (1990). An extended family with a dominantly inherited speech disorder. *Developmental Medicine and Child Neurology, 32*(4), 352–355.

Huttenlocher, J., Haight, W., Bryk, A., Seltzer, M. & Lyons, T. (1991). Early vocabulary growth: Relation to language input and gender. *Developmental Psychology, 27*, 236–248.

Huttenlocher, J., Vasilyeva, M., Cymerman, E. & Levine, S. (2002). Language input at home and at school: Relation to child syntax. *Cognitive Psychology, 45*, 337–374.

Huttenlocher, J., Vasilyeva, M. & Shimpi, P. (2004). Syntactic priming in young children. *Journal of Memory and Language, 50*, 182–195.

Huttenlocher, J., Vasilyeva, M., Waterfall, H. R., Vevea, J. L. & Hedges, L. V. (2007). The varieties of speech to young children. *Developmental Psychology, 43*, 1062–1083

Hyde, J. S. & Linn, M. C. (1988). Gender differences in verbal ability: A meta-analysis. *Psychological Bulletin, 107*, 139–155.

Imai, M., Kita, S., Nagumo, M. & Okada, H. (2008). Sound symbolism facilitates early verb learning. *Cognition, 109*, 54–65.

Ingram, T. T. S. (1959). Specific developmental disorders of speech in childhood. *Brain, 82*, 450–454.

Inhelder, B. & Piaget, J. (1958). *The growth of logical thinking from childhood to adolescence.* New York: Basic Books.

Inhelder, B. & Piaget, J. (1964). *The early growth of logic in the child.* London: Routledge and Kegan Paul.

Iverson, J. M. (2010). Developing language in a developing body: The relationship between motor development and language development. *Journal of Child Language, 37,* 229–261.

Iverson, J. M., Capirci, O. & Caselli, M. C. (1994). From communication to language in two modalities. *Cognitive Development, 9,* 23–43.

Iverson, J. M., Capirci, O., Longobardi, E. & Caselli, M. C. (1999). Gesturing in mother–child interactions. *Cognitive Development, 14,* 57–75.

Iverson, J. M. & Fagan, M. K. (2004). Infant vocal–motor coordination: Precursor to the gesture–speech system? *Child Development, 75,* 1053–1066.

Iverson, J. M. & Goldin-Meadow, S. (2005). Gesture paves the way for language development. *Psychological Science, 16,* 367–371.

Iverson, J. M., Hall, A. J., Nickel, L. & Wozniak, R. H. (2007). The relationship between onset of reduplicated babble and laterality biases in infant rhythmic arm movements. *Brain and Language, 101,* 198–207.

Iverson, J. M. & Thelen, E. (1999). Hand, mouth, and brain: The dynamic emergence of speech and gesture. *Journal of Consciousness Studies, 6,* 19–40.

Jackson, A. L. (2001). Language facility and theory of mind development in deaf children. *Journal of Deaf Studies and Deaf Education, 6,* 161–176.

Jackson, T. & Plante, E. (1997). Gyral morphology in the posterior sylvian region in families affected by developmental language disorders. *Neuropsychology Review, 6,* 81–94.

Jacobson, J. L., Boersma, D. C., Fields, R. B. & Olson, K. L. (1983). Paralinguistic features of adult speech to infants and small children. *Child Development, 54,* 436–442.

Jaeger, J. J. (1992). 'Not by the chair of my hinny hin hin': Some general properties of slips of the tongue in young children. *Journal of Child Language, 19,* 335–366.

Jaeger, J. J. (2005). *Kids' slips: What young children's slips of the tongue reveal about language development.* Mahwah, NJ: Lawrence Erlbaum Associates.

Jaffe, J., Beebe, B., Feldstein, S., Crown, C. L. & Jasnow, M. D. (2001). Rhythms of dialogue in infancy: Coordinated timing in development. *Monographs of the Society for Research in Child Development, 66,* No. 2.

Jakobson, R. (1941). *Kindersprache, Aphasie und allgemeine Lautgesetze* [Child language, aphasia and phonological universals]. Uppsala, Sweden: Almqvist & Wiksell.

James, S. R. (1989). Hominid use of fire in the Lower and Middle Pleistocene: A review of the evidence. *Current Anthropology, 30,* 1–26.

Jernigan, T. L., Hesselink, J. R., Sowell, E. & Tallal, P. A. (1991). Cerebral structure on magnetic resonance imaging in language and learning-impaired children. *Archives of Neurology, 48,* 539–545.

Jerome, A. C., Fujiki, M., Brinton, B. & James, S. L. (2002). Self-esteem in children with specific language impairment. *Journal of Speech, Language, and Hearing Research, 45,* 700–714.

Jisa, H. (1985). French preschoolers' use of *et puis* (and then). *First Language, 5,* 169–184.

Joanisse, M. F. & Seidenberg, M. S. (2003). Phonology and syntax in specific language impairment: Evidence from a connectionist model. *Brain and Language, 86,* 40–56.

Johnson, J. S. & Newport, E. L. (1989). Critical period effects in second language learning: The influence of maturational state on the acquisition of English as a second language. *Cognitive Psychology, 21,* 60–99.

Johnston, J. R. (1988). Children's verbal representation of spatial location. In J. Stiles-Davis, M. Kritchevsky & U. Bellugi (eds), *Spatial cognition: Brain bases and development* (pp. 195–206). Hillsdale, NJ: Lawrence Erlbaum Associates.

Johnston, J. C., Durieux-Smith, A. & Bloom, K. (2005). Teaching gestural signs to infants to advance child development: A review of the evidence. *First Language, 25*(2), 235–251.

Jolly, H. R. & Plunkett, K. (2008). Inflectional boostrapping in two-year-olds. *Language and Speech*, *51*, 45–59.

Juffs, A. & Harrington, M. (1995). Parsing effects in second language sentence processing. *Studies in Second Language Acquisition*, *17*, 483–516.

Jusczyk, P. W. (1992). Developing phonological categories from the speech signal. In C. L. Ferguson, L. Meen & C. Stoel-Gammon (eds), *Phonological development: Models, research, implications* (pp. 17–64). Parkton, MD: York Press.

Jusczyk, P. W. & Hohne, E. A. (1997). Infants' memory for spoken words. *Science*, *277*(5334), 1984–1986.

Jusczyk, P. W., Hohne, E. A. & Bauman, A. (1999). Infants' sensitivity to allophonic cues to word segmentation. *Perception and Psychophysics*, *61*, 1465–1476.

Jusczyk, P. W., Houston, D. M. & Newsome, M. (1999). The beginnings of word segmentation in English-learning infants. *Cognitive Psychology*, *39*, 159–207.

Jusczyk, P. W., Rosner, B. S., Cutting, J. E., Foard, C. F. & Smith, L. B. (1977). Categorical perception of nonspeech sounds by 2-months-old infants. *Perception and Psychophysics*, *21*, 50–54.

Kamhi, A. G. & Catts, H. W. (1986). Toward an understanding of developmental language and reading disorders. *Journal of Speech and Hearing Disorders*, *51*, 337–347.

Kaminski, J., Call, J. & Fischer, J. (2004). Word learning in a domestic dog: Evidence for 'fast mapping'. *Science*, *304*(5677), 1682–1683.

Kang, H.-K. (2001). Quantifier spreading: Linguistic and pragmatic considerations. *Lingua*, *111*, 591–627.

Kaplan, P. S., Bachorowski, J.-A. & Zarlengo-Strauss, P. (1999). Child-directed speech produced by mothers with symptoms of depression fails to promote associative learning in 4-month-old infants. *Child Development*, *70*, 560–570.

Karmiloff-Smith, A. (1992). *Beyond modularity: A developmental perspective on cognitive science*. Cambridge, MA: MIT Press.

Katsos, N. & Bishop, D. V. M. (2011). Pragmatic tolerance: Implications for the acquisition of informativeness and implicature. *Cognition*, *120*, 67–81.

Kaushanskaya, M. & Marian, V. (2009). The bilingual advantage in novel word learning. *Psychonomic Bulletin and Review*, *16*, 705–710.

Kay, P. & Regier, T. (2003). Resolving the question of colour naming universals. *Proceedings of the National Academy of Sciences of the USA*, *100*, 9085–9089.

Kay, P. & Regier, T. (2006). Language, thought, and color: Recent developments. *Trends in Cognitive Sciences*, *10*, 51–54.

Kaye, K. (1977). Towards the origin of dialogue. In H. R. Schaffer (ed.), *Studies in mother–infant interaction* (pp. 89–117). New York: Academic Press.

Kehoe, M. & Stoel-Gammon, C. (1997). Truncation patterns in English-speaking children's word productions. *Journal of Speech, Language, and Hearing Research*, *40*, 526–541.

Kelly, M. H. (1992). Using sound to solve syntactic problems: The role of phonology in grammatical category assignments. *Psychological Review*, *99*, 349–364.

Kelly, M. H. & Bock, J. K. (1988). Stress in time. *Journal of Experimental Psychology: Human Perception and Performance*, *14*, 389–403.

Keltner, D., Capps, L., Kring, A. M., Young, R. C. & Heerey, E. A. (2001). Just teasing: A conceptual analysis and empirical review. *Psychological Bulletin*, *127*, 229–248.

Kempe, V. (2009). Child-directed speech prosody in adolescents: Relationship to 2D:4D, empathy, and attitudes towards children. *Personality and Individual Differences*, *47*, 610–615.

Kempe, V. & Brooks, P. J. (2008). Second language learning of complex inflectional systems. *Language Learning*, *58*, 703–746.

Kempe, V., Brooks, P. J. & Gillis, S. (2005). Diminutives in child-directed speech supplement metric with distributional word segmentation cues. *Psychonomic Bulletin and Review, 12*(1), 145–151.

Kempe, V., Brooks, P. J., Mironova, N. & Fedorova, O. (2003). Diminutivization supports gender acquisition in Russian children. *Journal of Child Language, 30,* 471–485.

Kempe, V., Brooks, P. J., Mironova, N., Pershukova, A. & Fedorova, O. (2007). Playing with word endings: Morphological variation in the learning of Russian noun inflections. *British Journal of Developmental Psychology, 25, 55–77.*

Kempe, V., Brooks, P. J. & Pirott, L. (2001). How can child-directed speech facilitate the acquisition of morphology? In M. Almgren, A. Barrena, M.-J. Ezeizabarrena, I. Idiazabal & B. MacWhinney (eds), *Research on Child Language Acquisition: Proceedings of the 8th Conference of the International Association for the Study of Child Language* (pp. 1237–1247). Medford, MA: Cascadilla Press.

Kempe, V., Schaeffler, S. & Thoresen, J. C. (2010). Prosodic disambiguation in child-directed speech. *Journal of Memory and Language, 62,* 204–225.

Kempe, V., Ševa, N., Brooks, P. J., Mironova, N., Pershukova, A. & Fedorova, O. (2009). Elicited production of case-marking in Russian and Serbian children: Are diminutive nouns easier to inflect? *First Language, 29,* 147–165.

Kemper, S. (1994). Elderspeak: Speech accommodations to older adults. *Aging, Neuropsychology, and Cognition, 1,* 17–28.

Kendon, A. (2004). *Gesture: Visible action as utterance.* Cambridge: Cambridge University Press.

Kennedy, M., Sheridan, M., Radlinski, S. & Beeghly, M. (1991). Play–language relationships in young children with developmental delays: Implications for assessment. *Journal of Speech and Hearing Research, 34,* 112–122.

Kent, R. D. (1992). The biology of phonological development. In C. A. Ferguson, L. Menn & C. Stoel-Gammon (eds), *Phonological development: models, research, and implications* (pp. 65–90). Timonium, MD: York Press.

Kenward, B., Karlsson, M. & Persson, J. (2011). Over-imitation is better explained by norm learning than by distorted causal learning. *Proceedings of the Royal Society B, 278,* 1239–1246.

Khetarpal, N., Majid, A. & Regier, T. (2009). Spatial terms reflect near-optimal spatial categories. *Proceedings of the 31st Annual Conference of the Cognitive Science Society,* pp. 2396–2401.

Kidd, E., Stewart, A. J. & Serratrice, L. (2011). Children do not overcome lexical biases where adults do: The role of the referential scene in garden-path recovery. *Journal of Child Language, 38,* 222–234.

Kim, K. H. S., Relkin, N. R., Lee, K.-M. & Hirsch, J. (1997). Distinct cortical areas associated with native and second languages. *Nature, 388,* 171–174.

King, K. & Melzi, G. (2004). Intimacy, imitation and language learning: Spanish diminutives in mother–child conversation. *First Language, 24*(2), 241–261.

Kirby, S., Christiansen, M. H. & Chater, N. (2009). Syntax as an adaptation to the learner. In D. Bickerton & E. Szathmary (eds), *Biological foundations and the evolution of syntax* (pp. 325–343). Cambridge, MA: MIT Press.

Kirkham, N. Z., Slemmer, J. A. & Johnson, S. P. (2002). Visual statistical learning in infancy: Evidence for a domain general learning mechanism. *Cognition, 83,* B35–B42.

Kita, S. (2009). Cross-cultural variation of speech-accompanying gesture: A review. *Language and Cognitive Processes, 24,* 145–167.

Kita, S. (ed.) (2003). *Pointing: Where language, culture, and cognition meet.* Mahwah, NJ: Lawrence Erlbaum Associates.

Kita, S., Danziger, E. & Stolz, C. (2001). Cultural specificity of spatial schemas, as manifested in spontaneous gestures. In M. Gattis (ed.), *Spatial schemas and abstract thought* (pp. 115–146). Cambridge, MA: MIT Press.

Kitamura, C., Thanavishuth, C., Burnham, D. & Luksaneeyanawin, S. (2002). Universality and specificity in infant-directed speech: Pitch modifications as a function of infant age and sex in a tonal and non-tonal language. *Infant Behavior and Development*, *24*, 372–392.

Klein, D. N. & Kuiper, N. A. (2006). Humor styles, peer relationships, and bullying in middle childhood. *Humor*, *19*, 383–404.

Kleinknecht, E. E. & Beike, D. R. (2004). How knowing and doing inform an autobiography: Relations among preschoolers' theory of mind, narrative, and event memory skills. *Applied Cognitive Psychology*, *18*, 245–264.

Klima, E. & Bellugi, U. (1979). *The signs of language.* Cambridge, MA: Harvard University Press.

Knoll, M. & Uther, M. (2004). Motherese and Chinese: Evidence of acoustic changes in speech directed at infants and foreigners. *Journal of the Acoustical Society of America*, *116*, 2522–2522.

Kobayashi, H. & Koshima, D. (2001). Unique morphology of the human eye and its adaptive meaning: Comparative studies on external morphology of the primate eye. *Journal of Human Evolution*, *40*, 419–435.

Kohnert, K., Windsor, J. & Danahy Ebert, K. (2009). Primary or 'specific' language impairment and children learning a second language. *Brain and Language*, *109*, 101–111.

Konner, M. (2010). *The evolution of childhood: Relationships, emotion, mind.* Cambridge, MA: Harvard University Press.

Kovács, A. M. & Mehler, J. (2009). Cognitive gains in 7-month-old bilingual infants. *Proceedings of the National Academy of Sciences of the USA*, *106*, 6556–6560.

Krakow, R. A. & Hanson, V. L. (1985). Deaf signers and serial recall in the visual modality: Memory for signs, fingerspelling, and print. *Memory and Cognition*, *13*, 265–272.

Krauss, R. M. & Glucksberg, S. (1969). The development of communication: Competence as a function of age. *Child Development*, *40*(1), 255–266.

Krentz, U. C. & Corina, D. C. (2008). Preference for language in early infancy: The human language bias is not speech specific. *Developmental Science*, *11*, 1–9.

Kuczaj, S. & Daly, M. (1979). The development of hypothetical reference in the speech of young children. *Journal of Child Language*, *8*, 35–50.

Kuhl, P. K., Andruski, J. E., Christovich, I. A., Christovich, L. A., Kozhevnikova, E. V., Ryskina, V. L., Stolyarova, E. I., Sundberg, U. & Lacerda, F. (1997). Cross-language analysis of phonetic units in language addressed to infants. *Science*, *277*, 684–686.

Kuhl, P. K., Conboy, B. T., Coffey-Corina, S., Padden, D., Rivera-Gaxiola, M. & Nelson, T. (2008). Phonetic learning as a pathway to language: new data and native language magnet theory expanded (NLM-e). *Philosophical Transactions of the Royal Society B*, *363*, 979–1000.

Kuhl, P. K. & Meltzoff, A. N. (1982). The bimodal perception of speech in infancy. *Science*, *218*, 1138–1141.

Kuhl, P. K. & Meltzoff, A. N. (1984). The intermodal representation of speech in infants. *Infant Behavior and Development*, *7*, 361–381.

Kuhl, P. K. & Meltzoff, A. N. (1988). Speech as an intermodal object of perception. In A. Yonas (ed), *Perceptual development in infancy: The Minnesota Symposia on Child Psychology*, Vol. 20 (pp. 235–266). Hillsdale, NJ: Lawrence Erlbaum Associates.

Kuhl, P. K. & Meltzoff, A. N. (1996). Infant vocalizations in response to speech: Vocal imitation and developmental change. *Journal of the Acoustical Society of America*, *100*, 2425–2438.

Kuhl, P. K. & Miller, J. D. (1975). Speech perception by the chinchilla: Voiced–voiceless distinction in alveolar plosive consonants. *Science*, *190*, 69–72.

Kuhl, P. K., Stevens, E., Hayashi, A., Deguchi, T., Kiritani, S. & Iverson, P. (2006). Infants show a facilitation effect for native language phonetic perception between 6 and 12 months. *Developmental Science, 9*, F13–F21.

Kuhl, P. K., Tsao, F. M. & Liu, H. M. (2003). Foreign language experience in infancy: Effects of short-term exposure and social interaction on phonetic learning. *Proceedings of the National Academy of Sciences of the USA, 100*, 9096–9101.

Kyratzis, A., Ross, T. S. & Koymen, S. B. (2010). Validating justifications in preschool girls' and boys' friendship group talk: Implications for linguistic and socio-cognitive development. *Journal of Child Language, 37*, 115–144.

Ladefoged, P. (2001). *Vowels and consonants: An introduction to the sounds of language.* Oxford: Blackwell.

Lahey, M. & Edwards, J. (1996). Why do children with specific language impairment name pictures more slowly than their peers? *Journal of Speech and Hearing Research, 39*, 1081–1098.

Lahey, M. & Edwards, J. (1999). Naming errors of children with specific language impairment. *Journal of Speech, Language, and Hearing Research, 42*, 195–205.

Lakusta, L., Wagner, L., O'Hearn, K. & Landau, B. (2007). Conceptual foundations of spatial language: Evidence for a goal bias in infants. *Language Learning and Development, 3*, 179–197.

Lancy, D. (2009). *The anthropology of childhood: Cherubs, chattel and changlings.* Cambridge: Cambridge University Press.

Landau, B., Smith, L. B. & Jones, S. S. (1988). The importance of shape in early lexical learning. *Cognitive Development, 3*, 299–321.

Landau, B., Smith, L. B. & Jones, S. S. (1992). Syntactic context and the shape bias in children's and adults' lexical learning. *Journal of Memory and Language, 31*, 807–825.

Landauer, T. K. & Dumais, S. T. (1997). A solution to Plato's problem: The Latent Semantic Analysis theory of the acquisition, induction, and representation of knowledge. *Psychological Review, 104*, 211–240.

Lavelli, M. & Fogel, A. (2005). Developmental changes in the relationship between the infant's attention and emotion during early face-to-face communication: The 2-month transition. *Developmental Psychology, 41*, 265–280.

Layfer, O. T., Tager-Flusberg, H., Dowd, M., Tomblin, J. B. & Folstein, S. E. (2008). Overlap between autism and specific language impairment: Comparison of autism diagnostic interview and autism diagnostic observation schedule scores. *Autism Research, 1*, 284–296.

Leaper, C. (1991). Influence and involvement in children's discourse: Age, gender and partner effects. *Child Development, 62*, 797–811.

Leaper, C. (2000). Gender, affiliation, assertion, and the interactive context of parent–child play. *Developmental Psychology, 36*, 381–393.

Leaper, C., Anderson, K. J. & Sanders, P. (1998). Moderators of gender effects on parents' talk to their children: A meta-analysis. *Developmental Psychology, 34*, 3–27.

Leaper, C. & Ayers, M. M. (2007). A meta-analytic review of gender variations in adults' language use: Talkativeness, affiliative speech, and assertive speech. *Personality and Social Psychology Review, 11*, 328–363.

Leaper, C. & Smith, T. E. (2004). A meta-analytic review of gender variations in children's language use: Talkativeness, affiliative speech, and assertive speech. *Developmental Psychology, 40*, 993–1027.

Lee, S. A. S., Davis, B. & MacNeilage, P. (2010). Universal production patterns and ambient language in babbling: A cross-linguistic study of Korean- and English-learning infants. *Journal of Child Language, 37*, 293–318.

Leichtman, M., Wang, Q. & Pillemer, D. B. (2003). Cultural variations in interdependence and autobiographical memory: Lessons from Korea, China, India, and the United States. In R. Fivush & C. Haden (eds), *Autobiographical memory and the construction of a narrative self: Developmental and cultural perspectives* (pp. 73–98). Hillsdale, NJ: Lawrence Erlbaum Associates.

Leman, P. J., Ahmed, S. & Ozarow, L. (2005). Gender, gender relations, and the social dynamics of children's conversations. *Developmental Psychology, 41,* 64–74.

Lenneberg, E. H. (1967). *Biological foundations of language.* New York: John Wiley & Sons.

Leonard, L. B. (1989). Language learnability and specific language impairment in children. *Applied Psycholinguistics, 10,* 179–202.

Leonard, L. B. (1995). Functional categories in the grammars of children with specific language impairment. *Journal of Speech and Hearing Research, 38,* 1270–1283.

Leonard, L. B. (1998). *Children with specific language impairment.* Cambridge, MA: MIT Press.

Leonard, L. B. (2009). Cross-linguistic studies of child-language disorders. In R. G. Schwartz (ed.), *Handbook of child language disorders* (pp. 308–324). New York: Psychology Press.

Leonard, L. B., Davis, J. & Deevy, P. (2007). Phonotactic probability and past tense use by children with specific language impairment and their typically developing peers. *Clinical Linguistics and Phonetics, 21*(10), 747–758.

Leonard, L. B., Nippold, M. A., Kail, R. & Hale, C. A. (1983). Picture naming in language-impaired children. *Journal of Speech and Hearing Research, 26,* 609–615.

Leonard, L. B., Weismer, S. E., Miller, C. A., Francis, D. J., Tomblin, J. B. & Kail, R. V. (2007). Speed of processing, working memory, and language impairment in children. *Journal of Speech, Language, and Hearing Research, 50*(2), 408–428.

Leonard, L. B., Wong, A. M.-Y., Deevy, P., Stokes, S. F. & Fletcher, P. (2006). The production of passives by children with specific language impairment: Acquiring English or Cantonese. *Applied Psycholinguistics, 27,* 267–299.

Leopold, W. F. (1947). *Speech development of a bilingual child, Vol. II. Sound-learning in the first two years* (Vol. 6). Evanston, IL: Northwestern University.

Levelt, W. J. M., Roelofs, A. & Meyer, A. S. (1999). A theory of lexical access in speech production. *Behavioral and Brain Sciences, 22,* 1–75.

Levin, B. (1993). *English verb classes and alternations.* Chicago, IL: Chicago University Press.

Levinson, S. C. (2003). *Space in language and cognition: Explorations in cognitive diversity.* Cambridge: Cambridge University Press.

Levinson, S. C. & Evans, N. (2010). Time for a sea-change in linguistics: Response to comments on 'The Myth of Language Universals'. *Lingua, 120,* 2733–2758.

Lewis, B. A. & Thompson, L. A. (1992). A study of developmental speech and language disorders in twins. *Journal of Speech and Hearing Research, 35,* 1086–1094.

Lewis, M. P. (2009). *Ethnologue: Languages of the world,* 16th edn. Dallas, TX: SIL International.

Liberman, I. Y., Shankweiler, D., Fischer, F. W. & Carter, B. (1974). Explicit syllable and phoneme segmentation in the young child. *Journal of Experimental Child Psychology, 18,* 201–212.

Liddell, S. K. (2003). *Grammar, gesture, and meaning in American Sign Language.* Cambridge: Cambridge University Press.

Liebal, K., Behne, T., Carpenter, M. & Tomasello, M. (2009). Infants use shared experience to interpret pointing gestures. *Developmental Science, 12,* 264–271.

Lieberman, P. (2000). *Human language and our reptilian brain.* Cambridge, MA: Harvard University Press.

Liégeois, F., Connelly, A., Baldeweg, T., Connelly, A., Gadian, D. G., Mishkin, M. & Vargha-Khadem, F. (2003). Language fMRI abnormalities associated with FOXP2 gene mutation. *Nature Neuroscience, 6,* 1230–1237.

Liégeois, F., Connelly, A., Cross, J. H., Boyd, S. G., Gadian, D. G. & Vargha-Khadem, F. (2004). Language reorganization in children with early onset lesions of the left hemisphere: An fMRI study. *Brain, 127,* 1229–1236.

Lieven, E. V. M. (1994). Crosslinguistic and cross cultural aspects of language addressed to children. In C. Galloway and B. J. Richards (eds), *Input and interaction in language acquisition* (pp. 56–73). Cambridge: Cambridge University Press.

Lieven, E., Behrens, H., Speares, J. & Tomasello, M. (2003). Early syntactic creativity: A usage-based approach. *Journal of Child Language, 30,* 333–367.

Liles, B. Z. (1985). Cohesion in the narratives of normal and language-disordered children. *Journal of Speech and Hearing Research, 28,* 123–133.

Lisker, L. & Abramson, A. S. (1971). Distinctive features and laryngeal control. *Language, 47,* 767–785.

Liu, H.-M., Kuhl, P. K. & Tsao, F.-M. (2003). An association between mothers' speech clarity and infant speech discrimination skills. *Developmental Science, 6,* F1–F10.

Lock, A. (1978). The emergence of language. In A. Lock (ed.), *Action, gesture, and symbol: The emergence of language* (pp. 3–18). New York: Academic Press.

Lock, A. J. (1991). Early language development from a personal perspective. *Anales de Psicología, 7,* 137–149.

Locke, J. L. (1993). *The child's path to spoken language.* Cambridge, MA: Harvard University Press.

Locke, J. L. (2001). First communion: The emergence of vocal relationships. *Social Development, 10,* 294–308.

Locke, J. L. (2006). Parental selection of vocal behavior: Crying, cooing, babbling, and the evolution of language. *Human Nature, 17,* 155–168.

Locke, J. L. (2007). Bimodal signaling in infancy: motor behavior, referencing, and the evolution of spoken language. *Interaction Studies, 8,* 159–175.

Locke, J. L. & Bogin, B. (2006). Language and life history: A new perspective on the development and evolution of human language. *Behavioral and Brain Sciences, 29,* 259–280.

Loeb, D. F., Pye, C., Redmond, S. & Richardson, L. Z. (1996). Eliciting verbs from children with specific language impairment. *American Journal of Speech-Language Pathology, 5,* 17–30.

Loeb, D. F., Pye, C., Richardson, L. Z. & Redmond, S. (1998). Causative alternations of children with specific language impairment. *Journal of Speech, Language, and Hearing Research, 41,* 1103–1114.

Logan, K., Maybery, M. & Fletcher, J. (1996). The short-term memory of profoundly deaf people for words, signs, and abstract spatial stimuli. *Applied Cognitive Psychology, 10,* 105–119.

Loizou, E. (2005). Infant humor: The theory of the absurd and the empowerment theory. *International Journal of Early Years Education, 13,* 43–53.

Loizou, E. (2006). Young children's explanation of pictoral humor. *Early Childhood Education Journal, 33,* 425–431.

Loizou, P., Dorman, M. & Tu, Z. (1999). On the number of channels needed to understand speech. *Journal of the Acoustical Society of America, 106,* 2097–2103.

Lukatela, K., Carello, C., Shankweiler, D. & Liberman, I. Y. (1995). Phonological awareness in illiterates: Observations from Serbo-Croatian. *Applied Psycholinguistics, 16,* 463–487.

Lum, J. A. G., Gelgic, C. & Conti-Ramsden, G. (2010). Procedural and declarative memory in children with and without specific language impairment. *International Journal of Language and Communication Disorders, 45*(1), 96–107.

Lund, K. & Burgess, C. (1996). Producing high-dimensional semantic spaces from lexical co-occurrence. *Behavior Research Methods, Instrumentation, and Computers, 28,* 203–208.

Luo, Y. & Baillargeon, R. (2005). Can a self-propelled box have a goal? Psychological reasoning in 5-month-old infants. *Psychological Science, 16,* 601–608.

Lupyan, G. (2008). From chair to 'chair': A representational shift account of object labelling effects on memory. *Journal of Experimental Psychology: General, 137,* 348–369.

Lupyan, G. & Dale, R. (2010). Language structure is partly determined by social structure. *PLoS ONE, 5,* e8559.

Lupyan, G., Rakison, D. H. & McClelland, J. L. (2007). Language is not just for talking: Redundant labels facilitate learning of novel categories. *Psychological Science, 18*(12), 1077–1083.

Lyons, D. E., Young, A. G. & Keil, F. C. (2007). The hidden structure of overimitation. *Proceedings of the National Academy of Sciences of the USA, 104,* 19751–19756.

Lyons, G. R., Shaywitz, S. E. & Shaywitz, B. A. (2003). A definition of dyslexia. *Annals of Dyslexia, 53,* 1–14.

Lyytinen, P., Laakso, M., Poikkeus, A. & Rita, N. (1999). The development and predictive relations of play and language across the second year. *Scandinavian Journal of Psychology, 40,* 177–186.

Macaulay, C. E. & Ford, R. M. (2006). Language and theory of mind development in prelingually deafened children with cochlear implants: A preliminary investigation. *Cochlear Implants International, 7,* 1–14.

Maccoby, E. E. & Jacklin, C. N. (1989). Gender segregation in children. In H. W. Reese (ed.), *Advances in child development and behavior,* Vol. 20 (pp. 239–287). New York: Academic Press.

MacDermot, K. D., Bonora, E., Sykes, N., Coupe, A. M., Lai, C. S. L., Vernes, S. C. et al. (2005). Identification of FOXP2 truncation as a novel cause of developmental speech and language deficits. *American Journal of Human Genetics, 76,* 1074–1080.

Mack, A. & Rock, I. (1998). *Inattentional blindness.* Cambridge, MA: MIT Press.

MacKay, D. G. (1970). Spoonerisms: The structure of errors in the serial order of speech. *Neuropsychologia, 8,* 323–350

Macnamara, J. (1972). Cognitive basis of language learning in young infants. *Psychological Review, 79*(1), 1–13.

MacNeilage, P. F. & Davis, B. L. (2000). On the origin of internal structure of word forms. *Science, 288,* 527–530.

MacSweeney, M., Capek, C. M., Campbell, R. & Woll, B. (2008). The signing brain: The neurobiology of sign language. *Trends in Cognitive Sciences, 12*(11), 432–440.

MacWhinney, B. (1977). Starting points. *Language, 53,* 152–187.

MacWhinney, B. (2004). A multiple process solution to the logical problem of language acquisition. *Journal of Child Language, 31,* 883–914.

MacWhinney, B. & Snow, C. E. (1985). The Child Language Data Exchange System. *Journal of Child Language, 12,* 271–296.

Mahon, M. & Crutchley, A. (2006). Performance of typically-developing school-age children with English as an additional language (EAL) on the British Picture Vocabulary Scales II (BPVS II). *Child Language Teaching and Therapy, 22,* 333–353.

Mainela-Arnold, E., Evans, J. L. & Coady, J. A. (2008). Lexical representations in children with SLI: Evidence from a frequency-manipulated gating task. *Journal of Speech, Language, and Hearing Research, 51*(2), 381–393.

Majid, A., Bowerman, M., Kita, S., Haun, D. & Levinson, S. (2004). Can language restructure cognition? The case for space. *Trends in Cognitive Sciences, 8,* 108–114.

Mampe, B., Friederici, A. D., Christophe, A. & Wemke, K. (2009). Newborns' cry melody is shaped by their native language. *Current Biology*, *19*, 1–4.

Mandel, D. R., Jusczyk, P. W. & Pisoni, D. B. (1995). Infants' recognition of the sound patterns of their own names. *Psychological Science*, *6*, 315–318.

Mandler, J. M. (2004). Thought before language. *Trends in Cognitive Sciences*, *8*, 508–513.

Mandler, J. M. & McDonough, L. (1993). Concept formation in infancy. *Cognitive Development*, *8*, 291–318.

Mandler, J. M. & McDonough, L. (1998). Studies in inductive inference in infancy. *Cognitive Psychology*, *37*, 60–96.

Mani, N. & Plunkett, K. (2010). In the infant's mind's ear: Evidence for implicit naming in 18-month-olds. *Psychological Science*, *21*, 908–913.

Mani, N. & Plunkett, K. (2011) Phonological priming and cohort effects in toddlers. *Cognition*, *121*, 196–206.

Maratsos, M. (1990). Are actions to verbs as objects are to nouns? On the differential semantic bases of form, class, category. *Linguistics*, *28*, 1351–1379.

Marchman, V. & Bates, E. (1994). Continuity in lexical and morphological development: A test of the critical mass hypothesis. *Journal of Child Language*, *21*, 339–366.

Marcus, G. F. & Fisher, S. E. (2003). FOXP2 in focus: What can genes tell us about speech and language? *Trends in Cognitive Sciences*, *7*, 257–262.

Marcus, G. F., Pinker, S., Ullman, M., Hollander, M., Rosen, J. T. & Xu, F. (1992). Overregularization in language acquisition. *Monographs of the Society for Research in Child Development*, *57*(4), 1–165.

Marcus, G. F., Vijayan, S., Bandi Rao, S. & Vishton, P. M. (1999). Rule learning by seven-month-old infants. *Science*, *283*, 77–80.

Mareschal, D. & Quinn, P. C. (2001). Categorization in infancy. *Trends in Cognitive Sciences*, *5*, 443–450.

Marinis, T. & van der Lely, H. K. J. (2007). On-line processing of wh-questions in children with G-SLI and typical children. *International Journal of Language and Communication Disorders*, *42*, 557–582.

Marinkovic, K., Dhond, R. P., Dale, A. M., Glessner, M., Carr, C. & Halgren, F. (2003). Spatiotemporal dynamics of modality-specific and supramodal word processing. *Neuron*, *38*, 487–497.

Markman, E. M. (1989). *Categorization and naming in children: Problems of induction*. Cambridge, MA: MIT Press.

Markman, E. M. (1990). Constraints children place on word meanings. *Cognitive Science*, *14*, 57–77.

Markman, E. M., Wasow, J. L. & Hansen, M. B. (2003). Use of the mutual exclusivity assumption by young word learners. *Cognitive Psychology*, *37*, 241–275.

Marschark, M. (2003). Interactions of language and cognition in deaf learners: From research to practice. *International Journal of Audiology*, *42*, S41–S48.

Marton, K. (2009). Imitation of body posture and hand movement in children with specific language impairment. *Journal of Experimental Child Psychology*, *102*, 1–13.

Marton, K. & Schwartz, R. G. (2003). Working memory capacity and language processes in children with specific language impairment. *Journal of Speech, Language, and Hearing Research*, *46*, 1138–1153.

Masataka, N. (1996). Perception of motherese in a signed language by 6-month-old deaf infants. *Developmental Psychology*, *32*, 874–879.

Masataka, N. (1998). Perception of motherese in Japanese Sign Language by 6-month-old hearing infants. *Developmental Psychology*, *34*, 241–246.

Masataka, N., Koda, H., Urasopon, N. & Watanabe, K. (2009). Free-ranging macaque mothers exaggerate tool-using behavior when observed by offspring. *PLoS ONE, 4*, e4768.

Matthews, D. & Bannard, C. (2010). Children's production of unfamiliar word sequences is predicted by positional variability and latent classes in a large sample of child-directed speech. *Cognitive Science, 34*, 465–488.

Matthews, D., Lieven, E., Theakston, A. & Tomasello, M. (2006). The effect of perceptual availability and prior discourse on young children's use of referring expressions. *Applied Psycholinguistics, 27*, 403–422.

Mattys, S. L. & Jusczyk, P. W. (2001). Phonotactic cues for segmentation of fluent speech by infants. *Cognition, 78*, 91–121.

Mattys, S. L., Jusczyk, P. W., Luce, P. A. & Morgan, J. L. (1999). Phonotactic and prosodic effects on word segmentation in infants. *Cognitive Psychology, 38*, 465–494.

Maurer, D., Pathman, T. & Mondloch, C. J. (2006). The shape of boubas: sound-shape correspondences in toddlers and adults. *Developmental Science, 9*, 316–322.

Mayberry, R. I. & Lock, E. (2003). Age constraints on first versus second language acquisition: Evidence for linguistic plasticity and epigenesis. *Brain and Language, 87*, 369–384.

Mayberry, R. I. (1993). First-language acquisition after childhood differs from second-language acquisition: The case of American Sign Language. *Journal of Speech and Hearing Research, 36*, 1258–1270.

Mayberry, R. I. (2007). When timing is everything: Age of first-language acquisition effects on second-language learning. *Applied Psycholinguistics, 28*, 537–549.

Mayberry, R. I. & Eichen, E. (1991). The long-lasting advantage of learning sign language in childhood: Another look at the critical period for language acquisition. *Journal of Memory and Language, 30*, 486–512.

Mayberry, R. I. & Fischer, S. D. (1989). Looking through phonological shape to lexical meaning: The bottleneck of non-native sign language processing. *Memory and Cognition, 17*, 740–754.

Mayberry, R. I., Lock, E. & Kazmi, H. (2002). Linguistic ability and early language exposure. *Nature, 417*(6884), 38.

Mayer, M. (1969). *Frog, where are you?* New York: Dial Press.

Mayer, M. & Mayer, M. (1975). *One frog too many.* New York: Dial Books.

Mayor, J. & Plunkett, K. (2010). A neurocomputational account of taxonomic responding and fast mapping in early word learning. *Psychological Review, 117*, 1–31.

Mayor, J. & Plunkett, K. (2011). A statistical estimate of infant and toddler vocabulary size from CDI analysis. *Developmental Science, 14*, 769–785.

McArthur, G. M. & Bishop, D. V. M. (2004). Which people with specific language impairment have auditory processing deficits? *Cognitive Neuropsychology, 21*, 79–94.

McArthur, G. M., Hogben, J. H., Edwards, V. T., Heath, S. M. & Mengler, E. D. (2000). On the 'specifics' of specific reading disability and specific language impairment. *Journal of Child Psychology and Psychiatry, 41*, 869–874.

McBrearty, S. & Brooks, A. S. (2000). The revolution that wasn't: A new interpretation of the origin of modern human behavior. *Journal of Human Evolution, 39*, 453–563.

McBride-Chang, C. & Kail, R. V. (2002). Cross-cultural similarities in the predictors of reading acquisition. *Child Development, 73*, 1392–1407.

McClelland, J. L. & Patterson, K. (2002). Rules of connections in past-tense inflections: What does the evidence rule out? *Trends in Cognitive Sciences, 6*(11), 465–472.

McCloskey, L. A. (1996). Gender and the expression of status in children's mixed-age conversations. *Journal of Applied Developmental Psychology, 17*, 117–133.

McCune-Nicolich, L. (1981). Toward symbolic functioning: Structure of early pretend games and the potential parallels with language. *Child Development, 52,* 785–797.

McCune, L. & Vihman, M. M. (2001). Early phonetic and lexical development: A productivity approach. *Journal of Speech, Language, and Hearing Research, 44,* 670–684.

McCune, L., Vihman, M. M., Roug-Hellichius, L., Delery, D. B. & Gogate, L. (1996). Grunt communication in human infants (*Homo sapiens*). *Journal of Comparative Psychology, 110,* 27–37.

McDonough, L., Choi, S. & Mandler, J. (2003). Understanding spatial relations: Flexible infants, lexical adults. *Cognitive Psychology, 46,* 229–259.

McGregor, K. K. (1997). The nature of word-finding errors of preschoolers with and without word-finding deficits. *Journal of Speech, Language, and Hearing Research, 40,* 1232–1244.

McGregor, K. K., Friedman, R. M., Reilly, R. M. & Newman, R. M. (2002). Semantic representation and naming in children. *Journal of Speech, Language, and Hearing Research, 45,* 332–346.

McGregor, K. K. & Leonard, L. B. (1989). Facilitating word-finding skills of language-impaired children. *Journal of Speech and Hearing Disorders, 54,* 141–147.

McGregor, K. K., Newman, R. M., Reilly, R. M. & Capone, N. C. (2002). Semantic representation and naming in children with Specific Language Impairment. *Journal of Speech, Language, and Hearing Research, 45,* 998–1014.

McGregor, K. K. & Waxman, S. R. (1998). Object naming at multiple hierarchical levels: A comparison of preschoolers with and without word-finding deficits. *Journal of Child Language, 25,* 419–430.

McGuigan, N., Makinson, J. & Whiten, A. (2011). From over-imitation to super-copying: Adults imitate causally irrelevant aspects of tool use with higher fidelity than young children. *British Journal of Psychology, 102,* 1–18.

McKnight, C. C., Crosswhite, F. J., Dossey, J. A., Kifer, E., Swafford, J. O., Travers, K. J. & Cooney, T. J. (1987). *The under-achieving curriculum: Assessing U.S. school mathematics from an international perspective.* Champaign, IL: Stipes.

McMurray, B. (2007). Defusing the childhood vocabulary explosion. *Science, 317,* 631.

McMurray, B., Samelson, V. M., Lee, S. H. & Tomblin, J. B. (2010). Individual differences in online spoken word recognition: Implications for SLI. *Cognitive Psychology, 60,* 1–39.

McNeill, D. (1992). *Hand and mind: What gestures reveal about thought.* Chicago, IL: University of Chicago Press.

McPherron, S. P., Alemseged, Z., Marean, C. W., Wynn, J. G., Reed, D., Gerads, D., Bobe, R. & Béarat, H. A. (2010). Evidence for stone-tool-assisted consumption of animal tissues before 3.39 million years ago at Dikika, Ethiopia. *Nature, 466,* 857–860.

McWhorter, J. H. (1997). *Towards a new model of Creole genesis.* New York: Peter Lang.

Meaburn, E., Dale, P. S., Craig, I. W. & Plomin, R. (2002). Language-impaired children: No sign of the FOXP2 mutation. *NeuroReport, 13,* 1075–1077.

Mehler, J. & Christophe, A. (1995). Maturation and learning of language in the first year of life. In M. S. Gazzaniga (ed.), *The cognitive neurosciences* (pp. 943–954). Cambridge, MA: MIT Press.

Mehler, J., Jusczyk, P. W., Lambertz, G., Halsted, N., Bertoncini, J. & Amiel-Tison, C. (1988). A precursor of language acquisition in young infants. *Cognition, 29,* 143–178.

Meier, R. P. & Newport, E. L. (1990). Out of the hands of babes: On a possible sign advantage in language acquisition. *Language, 66,* 1–23.

Melinder, A., Forbes, D., Tronick, E., Fikke, L. & Gredebäck, G. (2010). The development of the still-face effect: Mothers do matter. *Infant Behavior and Development, 33,* 472–481.

Meltzoff, A. N. (1988a). Infant imitation and memory: Nine-month-olds in immediate and deferred tests. *Child Development, 59,* 217–225.

Meltzoff, A. N. (1988b). Infant imitation after a 1-week delay: Long-term memory for novel acts and multiple stimuli. *Developmental Psychology, 24,* 470–476.

Meltzoff, A. N. (1995). Understanding the intentions of others: Re-enactment of intended acts by 18-month-old children. *Developmental Psychology, 31,* 838–850.

Meltzoff, A. N. & Moore, M. K. (1977). Imitation of facial and manual gestures by human neonates. *Science, 198,* 75–78.

Melzi, G. & King, K. (2003). Spanish diminutives in mother-child conversations. *Journal of Child Language, 30,* 281–304.

Mengler, E. D., Hogben, J. H., Michie, P. & Bishop, D. V. M. (2005). Poor frequency discrimination is related to oral language disorder in children: A psychoacoustic study. *Dyslexia, 11,* 155–173.

Meristo, M., Falkman, K. W., Hjelmquist, E., Tedoldi, M., Surian, L. & Siegal, M. (2007). Language access and theory of mind reasoning: Evidence from deaf children in bilingual and oralist environments. *Developmental Psychology, 43,* 1156–1169.

Meristo, M. & Hjelmquist, E. (2009). Executive functions and theory-of-mind among deaf children: Different routes to understanding other minds? *Journal of Cognition and Development, 10*(1/2), 67–91.

Merriman, W. E. & Bowman, L. L. (1989). The mutual exclusivity bias in children's word learning. *Monographs of the Society for Research in Child Development, 54,* Serial No. 220.

Mervis, C. B. & Bertrand, J. (1994). Acquisition of the novel name-nameless category (N3C) principle. *Child Development, 65,* 1646–1663.

Mervis, C. B., Golinkoff, R. M. & Bertrand, J. (1994). Two-year-olds readily learn multiple labels for the same basic-level category. *Child Development, 65,* 1163–1177.

Merzenich, M. M., Jenkins, W. M., Johnston, P., Schreiner, C., Miller, S. L. & Tallal, P. (1996). Temporal processing deficits of language-learning impaired children ameliorated by training. *Science, 271*(5245), 77–81.

Messer, D. (1978). The integration of mothers' referential speech with joint play. *Child Development, 49,* 781–787.

Messer, D. & Dockrell, J. E. (2006). Children's naming and word-finding difficulties: Descriptions and explanations. *Journal of Speech, Language, and Hearing Research, 49,* 309–324.

Messinger, D., Ekas, N., Ruvolo, P. & Fogel, A. (2012). 'Are you interested, baby?' Young infants exhibit stable patterns of attention during interaction. *Infancy, 17*(2), 233–244.

Messinger, D., Fogel, A. & Dickson, K. L. (1999). What's in a smile? *Developmental Psychology, 35,* 701–708.

Meyer, D. E. & Schvaneveldt, R. W. (1971). Facilitation in recognizing pairs of words: Evidence of a dependence between retrieval operations. *Journal of Experimental Psychology, 90,* 227–234.

Miller, C. A. & Leonard, L. B. (1998). Deficits in finite verb morphology: Some assumptions in recent accounts of specific language impairment. *Journal of Speech, Language, and Hearing Research, 41,* 701–707.

Miller, C. A., Kail, R., Leonard, L. B. & Tomblin, J. B. (2001). Speed of processing in children with specific language impairment. *Journal of Speech, Language, and Hearing Research, 44,* 416–433.

Miller, K. F. & Stigler, J. W. (1987). Computing in Chinese: Cultural variation in a basic cognitive skill. *Cognitive Development, 2,* 279–305.

Miller, K. F., Smith, C. M., Zhu, J. & Zhang, H. (1995). Preschool origins of cross-national differences in mathematical competence: The role of number-naming systems. *Psychological Science, 6,* 56–60.

Miller, P. (1986). Teasing as language socialization and verbal play in a white working class community. In B. B. Schieffelin & E. Ochs (eds), *Language socialization across cultures: Studies in the social and cultural foundations of language* (pp. 199–212). New York: Cambridge University Press.

Miller, P. M., Danaher, D. L. & Forbes, D. (1986). Sex-related strategies for coping with interpersonal conflict in children aged five and seven. *Developmental Psychology, 22,* 543–548.

Minami, M. & McCabe, A. (1995). Rice balls and bear hunts: Japanese and North American family narrative patterns. *Journal of Child Language, 22,* 423–445.

Mintz, T. H., Newport, E. L. & Bever, T. G. (2002). The distributional structure of grammatical categories in speech to young children. *Cognitive Science, 26,* 393–424.

Misyak, J. B., Christiansen, M. H. & Tomblin, J. B. (2010). Sequential expectations: The role of prediction-based learning in language. *Topics in Cognitive Science, 2,* 138–153.

Mitchell, R. E. & Karchmer, M. A. (2004). Chasing the mythical ten percent: Parental hearing status of deaf and hard of hearing students in the United States. *Sign Language Studies, 4,* 138–163.

Miura, I. T., Okamoto, Y., Kim, C. C., Chang, C.-M., Steere, M. & Fayol, M. (1994). Comparisons of children's cognitive representation of number: China, France, Japan, Korea, Sweden and the United States. *International Journal of Behavioral Development, 17,* 401–411.

Miura, I. T., Okamoto, Y., Kim, C. C., Steere, M. & Fayol, M. (1993). First graders' cognitive representation of number and understanding of place value: cross-national comparisons – France, Japan, Korea, Sweden, and the United States. *Journal of Educational Psychology, 85,* 24–30.

Miyake, A. & Friedman, N. P. (1998). Individual differences in second language proficiency: Working memory as language aptitude. In A. F. Healy & L. E. Bourne, Jr. (eds), *Foreign language learning: Psycholinguistic studies on training and retention* (pp. 339–364). Mahwah, NJ: Lawrence Erlbaum Associates.

Miyamoto, R. T., Houston, D. M. & Bergeson, T. (2005). Cochlear implantation in deaf infants. *The Laryngoscope, 115,* 1376–1380.

Mody, M., Studdert-Kennedy, M. & Brady, S. (1997). Speech perception deficits in poor readers: Auditory processing or phonological coding? *Journal of Experimental Child Psychology, 64,* 199–231.

Moerk, E. (1991). Positive evidence for negative evidence. *First Language, 11*(32), 219–251.

Moerk, E. (1994). Corrections in first language acquisition: Theoretical controversies and factual evidence. *International Journal of Psycholinguistics, 10,* 33–58.

Mol, S. E. & Bus, A. G. (2011). To read or not to read: A meta-analysis of print exposure from infancy to early adulthood. *Psychological Bulletin, 137,* 267–296.

Monaghan, P., Chater, N. & Christiansen, M. H. (2005). The differential role of phonological and distributional cues in grammatical categorisation. *Cognition, 96,* 143–182.

Montgomery, J. W. (1995). Sentence comprehension in children with specific language impairment: The role of phonological working memory. *Journal of Speech and Hearing Research, 38,* 187–199.

Montgomery, J. W. (2000). Verbal working memory and sentence comprehension in children with specific language impairment. *Journal of Speech, Language, and Hearing Research, 43,* 293–308.

Montgomery, J. W. (2002). Understanding the language difficulties of children with specific language impairments: Does verbal working memory matter? *American Journal of Speech-Language Pathology, 11,* 77–91.

Montgomery, J. W. (2005). Effects of input rate and age on the real-time language processing of children with specific language impairment. *International Journal of Language and Communication Disorders, 40,* 171–188.

Montgomery, J. W. (2006). Real-time language processing in school-age children with specific language impairment. *International Journal of Language and Communication Disorders, 41,* 275–291.

Montgomery, J. W. & Evans, J. L. (2009). Complex sentence comprehension and working memory in children with specific language impairment. *Journal of Speech, Language, and Hearing Research, 52,* 269–288.

Montgomery, J. W. & Leonard, L. B. (1998). Real-time inflectional processing by children with specific language impairment: Effects of phonetic substance. *Journal of Speech, Language, and Hearing Research*, 41, 1432–1443.

Montgomery, J. W., Magimairaj, B. M. & Finney, M. C. (2010). Working memory and specific language impairment: An update on the relation and perspectives on assessment and treatment. *American Journal of Speech-Language Pathology*, 19, 78–94.

Moore, C. & Dunham, P. J. (eds) (1995). *Joint attention: Its origins and role in development*. Hillsdale, NJ: Lawrence Erlbaum Associates.

Morais, J., Cary, L., Alegria, J. & Bertelson, P. (1979). Does awareness of speech as a sequence of phones arise spontaneously? *Cognition*, 7, 323–331.

Morford, M. & Goldin-Meadow, S. (1992). Comprehension and production of gesture in combination with speech in one-word speakers. *Journal of Child Language*, 19, 559–580.

Morgan, J. & Demuth, C. (1996). *Signal to syntax: Bootstrapping from speech to grammar in early acquisition*. Hillsdale, NJ: Lawrence Erlbaum Associates.

Morton, J. B. & Harper, S. N. (2007). What did Simon say? Revisiting the bilingual advantage. *Developmental Science*, 10, 719–726.

Moyle, M. J., Weismer, S. E., Evans, J. L. & Lindstrom, M. J. (2007). Longitudinal relationships between lexical and grammatical development in typical and late-talking children. *Journal of Speech, Language, and Hearing Research*, 50, 508–528.

Mullen, M. K. & Yi, S. (1995). The cultural context of talk about the past: Implications for the development of autobiographical memory. *Cognitive Development*, 10, 407–419.

Munakata, Y., McClelland, J. L., Johnson, M. H. & Siegler, R. S. (1997). Rethinking infant knowledge: Toward an adaptive process account of successes and failures in object permanence tasks. *Psychological Review*, 104, 686–713.

Munson, B. (2001). Phonological pattern frequency and speech production in adults and children. *Journal of Speech, Language, and Hearing Research*, 44, 778–792.

Munson, B., Edwards, J. & Beckman, M. E. (2005a). Relationships between nonword repetition accuracy and other measures of linguistic development in children with phonological disorders. *Journal of Speech, Language, and Hearing Research*, 48, 61–78.

Munson, B., Kurtz, B. A. & Windsor, J. (2005b). The influence of vocabulary size, phonotactic probability, and wordlikeness on nonword repetitions of children with and without Specific Language Impairment. *Journal of Speech, Language, and Hearing Research*, 48, 1033–1047.

Näätänen, R., Lehtokoski, A., Lennes, M., Cheour, M., Huotilainen, M., Iivonen, A., Vainio, M., Alku, P., Ilmoniemi, R. J., Luuk, A., Allik, J., Sinkkonen, J. & Alho, K. (1997). Language-specific phoneme representations revealed by electric and magnetic brain responses. *Nature*, 385, 432–434.

Nadig, A. S. & Sedivy, J. C. (2002). Evidence of perspective-taking constraints in children's on-line reference resolution. *Psychological Science*, 13(4), 329–336.

Nagy, E. (2008). Innate intersubjectivity: Newborns' sensitivity to communication disturbance. *Developmental Psychology*, 44, 1779–1784.

Nagy, W. E. (1988). *Teaching vocabulary to improve reading comprehension*. Newark, DE: International Reading Association.

Nagy, W. E. & Anderson, R. (1984). The number of words in printed school English. *Reading Research Quarterly*, 19, 304–330.

Nagy, W., Berninger, V. W. & Abbott, R. D. (2006). Contributions of morphology beyond phonology to literacy outcomes of upper elementary and middle-school students. *Journal of Educational Psychology*, 98, 134–147.

Naigles, L. R. (1990). Children learn syntax to learn verb meanings. *Journal of Child Language, 17*, 357–374.

Namy, L. L., Acredolo, L. & Goodwyn, S. (2000). Verbal labels and gestural routines in parental communication with young children. *Journal of Nonverbal Behavior, 24*, 63–79.

Nation, K., Clarke, P., Marshall, C. M. & Durand, M. (2004). Hidden language impairments in children: Parallels between poor reading comprehension and specific language impairment? *Journal of Speech, Language, and Hearing Research, 47*, 199–211.

Nation, K., Cocksey, J., Taylor, J. S. H. & Bishop, D. V. M. (2010). A longitudinal investigation of early reading and language skills in children with poor reading comprehension. *Journal of Child Psychology and Psychiatry, 51*, 1031–1039.

Nazzi, T., Bertoncini, J. & Mehler, J. (1998). Language discrimination by newborns: Toward an understanding of the role of rhythm. *Journal of Experimental Psychology: Human Perception and Performance, 24*, 756–766.

Nazzi, T., Jusczyk, P. W. & Johnson, E. K. (2000). Language discrimination by English-learning 5-month-olds: Effects of rhythm and familiarity. *Journal of Memory and Language, 43*, 1–19.

Nelson, K. (1978). Early speech in its communicative context. In F. D. Minifie & L. L. Lloyd (eds), *Communicative and cognitive abilities: Early behavioral assessment* (pp. 443–473). Baltimore, MD: University Park Press.

Nelson, K. (1985). *Making sense: The acquisition of shared meaning*. Orlando, FL: Academic Press.

Nelson, K. (1986). Event knowledge and cognitive development. In K. Nelson (ed.), *Event knowledge: Structure and function in development* (pp. 1–19). Hillsdale, NJ: Lawrence Erlbaum Associates.

Nelson, K. (1996). *Language in cognitive development: Emergence of the mediated mind*. New York: Cambridge University Press.

Nelson, K. (2007). *Young minds in social worlds: Experience, meaning, and memory*. Cambridge, MA: Harvard University Press.

Nelson, K. (ed.) (1989). *Narratives from the crib*. Cambridge, MA: Harvard University Press.

Nelson, K. & Fivush, R. (2004). The emergence of autobiographical memory: A social cultural developmental theory. *Psychological Review, 111*, 486–511.

Nelson, K. & Gruendel, J. (1986). Children's scripts. In K. Nelson (ed.), *Event knowledge: Structure and function in development* (pp. 21–46). Hillsdale, NJ: Lawrence Erlbaum Associates.

Nelson, K., Plesa, D. & Henseler, S. (1998). Children's theory of mind: An experiential interpretation. *Human Development, 41*, 7–29.

Nelson, K., Plesa Skwerer, D., Goldman, S., Henseler, S., Presler, N. & Walkenfeld, F. F. (2003). Entering a community of minds: An experiential approach to 'theory of mind'. *Human Development, 46*, 24–46.

Nelson, K. E., Welsh, J. A., Vance Trup, E. M. & Greenberg, M. T. (2011). Language delays of impoverished preschool children in relation to early academic and emotion recognition skills. *First Language, 31*, 164–194.

Nettle, D. (2007). Language and genes: A new perspective on the origins of human cultural diversity. *Proceedings of the National Academy of Sciences of the USA, 104*, 10755–10756.

Neville, H. J., Bavelier, D., Corina, D., Rauschecker, J., Karni, A., Lalwani, A., Braun, A., Clark, V., Jezzard, P. & Turner, R. (1998). Cerebral organization or language in deaf and hearing subjects: Biological constraints and effects of experience. *Proceedings of the National Academy of Sciences of the USA, 95*, 922–929.

Newbury, D. F., Bishop, D. V. M. & Monaco, A. P. (2005). Genetic influences on language impairment and phonological short term memory. *Trends in Cognitive Sciences, 9*(11), 528–534.

Newport, E. L. (1990). Maturational constraints on language learning. *Cognitive Science, 14*, 11–28.

Nicely, P., Tamis-LeMonda, C. S. and Bornstein, M. H. (1999). Mothers' attuned responses to infant affect expressivity promote earlier achievement of language milestones. *Infant Behavior and Development, 22*, 557–568.

Nielsen, M. (2006). Copying actions and copying outcomes: social learning through the second year. *Developmental Psychology, 42*, 555–565.

Ninio, A. (1980). Picture-book reading in mother–infant dyads belonging to two sub-groups in Israel. *Child Development, 51*, 587–590.

Ninio, A. (1992). The relation of children's single word utterances to single word utterances in the input. *Journal of Child Language, 19*, 87–110.

Ninio, A. (1999). Pathbreaking verbs in syntactic development and the question of prototypical transitivity. *Journal of Child Language, 26*, 619–653.

Ninio, A. (2005). Testing the role of semantic similarity in syntactic development. *Journal of Child Language, 32*, 35–61.

Ninio, A. (2006). *Language and the learning curve: A new theory of syntactic development.* Oxford: Oxford University Press.

Ninio, A. (2011). *Syntactic development, its input and output.* Oxford: Oxford University Press.

Ninio, A. & Bruner, J. (1978). The achievement and antecedents of labeling. *Journal of Child Language, 5*, 1–15.

Ninio, A. & Snow, E. C. (1996). *Pragmatic development.* Boulder, CO: Westview Press.

Nitschke, J., Nelson, E., Rusch, B., Fox, A., Oakes, T. & Davidson, R. (2004). Orbitofrontal cortex tracks positive mood in mothers viewing pictures of their newborn infants. *NeuroImage, 21*, 583–592.

Norbury, C. F. & Bishop, D. V. M. (2003). Narrative skills of children with communication impairments. *International Journal of Language and Communication Disorders, 38*(3), 287–313.

Noveck, I. A. (2001). When children are more logical adults: Experimental investigations of scalar implicature. *Cognition, 78*(2), 165–188.

Novick, J. M., Trueswell, J. C. & Thompson-Schill, S. L. (2005). Cognitive control and parsing: Reexamining the role of Broca's area in sentence comprehension. *Cognitive, Affective, and Behavioral Neuroscience, 5*, 263–281.

Nuckolls, J. B. (1999). The case for sound symbolism. *Annual Review of Anthropology, 28*, 225–252.

Nunes, T. & Bryant, P. (2006). *Improving literacy by teaching morphemes.* Oxford: Routledge.

Nunes, T. & Bryant, P. (2009). *Children's reading and spelling: Beyond the first steps.* West Sussex: Wiley-Blackwell.

Nwokah, E. E. (1987). Maidese versus motherese: Is the language input of child and adult caregivers similar? *Language and Speech, 30*, 213–237.

Nygaard, L. C., Cook, A. E. & Namy, L. L. (2009). Sound to meaning correspondences facilitate word learning. *Cognition, 112*, 181–186.

O'Brien, D. H. (1987). Reflection–impulsivity in total communication and oral deaf and hearing children: A developmental study. *American Annals of the Deaf, 132*, 213–217.

O'Brien, E. K., Zhang, X. Y., Nishimura, C., Tomblin, J. B. & Murray, J. C. (2003). Association of specific language impairment (SLI) to the region of 7q31. *American Journal of Human Genetics, 72*, 1536–1543.

O'Connor, J. D. (1982). *Phonetics.* Harmondsworth, UK: Penguin Books.

O'Grady, W. (1997). *Syntactic development.* Chicago, IL: University of Chicago Press.

O'Grady, W. (2005). *Syntactic carpentry: An emergentist approach to syntax.* Mahwah, NJ: Lawrence Erlbaum Associates.

O'Reilly, A. W., Painter, K. M. & Bornstein, M. H. (1997). Relations between language and symbolic gesture development in early childhood. *Cognitive Development, 12*, 185–197.

Oberecker, R., Friedrich, M. & Friederici, A. D. (2005). Neural correlates of syntactic processing in two-year-olds. *Journal of Cognitive Neuroscience, 17*, 1667–1678.

Oetting, J. B., Rice, M. L. & Swank, L. K. (1995). Quick incidental learning (QUIL) of words by school-age children with and without SLI. *Journal of Speech and Hearing Research, 38*, 434–445.

Olguin, R. & Tomasello, M. (1993). Two-year-olds do not have a grammatical category of verb. *Cognitive Development, 8*, 245–272.

Oller, D. K. (2000). *The emergence of the speech capacity.* Mahwah, NJ: Lawrence Erlbaum Associates.

Oller, D. K. & Eilers, R. E. (eds) (2002). *Language and literacy in bilingual children.* Clevedon, UK: Multilingual Matters.

Oller, D. K., Eilers, E. E., Urbano, R. & Cobo-Lewis, A. B. (1997). Development of precursors to speech in infants exposed to two languages. *Journal of Child Language, 24*, 407–425.

Oller, D. K., Wieman, L. A., Doyle, W. J. & Ross, C. (1976). Infant babbling and speech. *Journal of Child Language, 3*, 1–11.

Olofson, E. L. & Baldwin, D. (2011). Infants recognize similar goals across dissimilar actions involving object manipulation. *Cognition, 118*, 258–264.

Olson, D. R. (1994). *The world on paper: The conceptual and cognitive implications of writing and reading.* New York: Cambridge University Press.

Olson, D. R. (1996). Towards a psychology of literacy: On the relations between speech and writing. *Cognition, 60*, 83–104.

Olson, D. R. (2002). What writing does to the mind. In E. Amsel & J. P. Byrnes (eds), *Language, literacy, and cognitive development: The development and consequences of symbolic communication* (pp. 153–165). Mahwah, NJ: Lawrence Erlbaum Associates.

Orton, S. T. (1925). 'Word blindness' in school children. *Archives of Neurology and Psychiatry, 14*, 581–615.

Oshima-Takane, Y. (1988). Children learn from speech not addressed to them: The case of personal pronouns. *Journal of Child Language, 15*, 95–108.

Oshima-Takane, Y., Goodz, E. & Deverensky, J. L. (1996). Birth order effects on early language development: Do secondborn children learn from overheard speech? *Child Development, 67*, 621–634.

Ouellette, G. & Sénéchal, M. (2008). Pathways to literacy: A study of invented spelling and its role in learning to read. *Child Development, 79*, 899–913.

Owen, A. J. & Leonard, L. B. (2006). The production of finite and nonfinite complement clauses by children with specific language impairment and their typically developing peers. *Journal of Speech, Language, and Hearing Research, 29*, 548–571.

Özçalişkan, Ş. & Goldin-Meadow, S. (2005). Gesture is at the cutting edge of early language development. *Cognition, 96*, B101–B113.

Özçalişkan, Ş. & Goldin-Meadow, S. (2009). When gesture–speech combinations do and do not index linguistic change. *Language and Cognitive Processes, 24*, 190–217.

Packard, M. & Knowlton, B. (2002). Learning and memory functions of the basal ganglia. *Annual Review of Neuroscience, 25*, 563–593.

Padden, C. & Ramsey, C. (2000). American Sign Language and reading ability in deaf children. In C. Chamberlain, J. P. Morford & R. I. Mayberry (eds), *Language acquisition by eye* (pp. 165–189). Hillsdale, NJ: Lawrence Erlbaum Associates.

Pallier, C., Dehaene, S., Poline. J. B., LeBihan, D., Argenti, A. M., Dupoux, E. & Mehler, J. (2003). Brain imaging of language plasticity in adopted adults: can a second language replace the first? *Cerebral Cortex, 13*, 155–161.

Pan, B. A. & Snow, C. E. (1999). The development of conversational and discourse skills. In M. Barrett (ed.), *The development of language* (pp. 229–249). Hove, UK: Psychology Press.

Pantev, C., Roberts, L. E., Schulz, M., Engelien, A. & Ross, B. (2001). Timbre-specific enhancement of auditory cortical representations in musicians. *NeuroReport, 12*, 1–6.

Papaeliou, C. F. & Trevarthen, C. (2006). Prelinguistic pitch patterns expressing communication and apprehension. *Journal of Child Language, 33*, 163–178.

Papoušek, H. & Papoušek, M. (1989). Forms and functions of vocal matching in interactions between mothers and their precanonical infants. *First Language, 9*, 137–158.

Parasnis, I., Samar, V. J. & Berent, G. P. (2003). Deaf adults without attention deficit hyperactivity disorder display reduced perceptual sensitivity and elevated impulsivity on the test of variables of attention (T.O.V.A). *Journal of Speech, Language, and Hearing Research, 46*, 1166–1183.

Patterson, M. & Werker, J. F. (2003). Two-month-old infants match phonetic information in lips and voice. *Developmental Science, 6*, 191–196.

Paulesu, E., Demonet, J. F., Fazio, F., McCrory, E., Chanoine, V., Brunswick, N., Cappa, S. F., Cossu, G., Habib, M., Frith, C. D. & Frith, U. (2001). Dyslexia, cultural diversity and biological unity. *Science, 291*, 2165–2167.

Payne, A. C., Whitehurst, G. J. & Angell, A. L. (1994). The role of home literacy environment in the development of language ability in preschool children from low-income families. *Early Childhood Research Quarterly, 9*(3/4), 427–440.

Pearson, B. Z., Fernández, S. C. & Oller, D. K. (1993). Lexical development in bilingual infants and toddlers: Comparison to monolingual norms. *Language Learning, 43*, 93–120.

Peña, M., Maki, A., Kovacic, D., Dehaene-Lambertz, G., Koizumi, H., Bouquet, F. et al. (2003). Sounds and silence: An optical topography study of language recognition at birth. *Proceedings of the National Academy of Sciences of the USA, 100*, 11702–11705.

Penton-Voak, I. S., Cahill, S., Pound, N., Kempe, V., Schaeffler, S. & Schaeffler, F. (2007). Male facial attractiveness, perceived personality, and child-directed speech. *Evolution and Human Behavior, 28*, 253–259.

Perani, D. & Abutalebi, J. (2005). The neural basis of first and second language processing. *Current Opinion in Neurobiology, 15*, 202–206.

Perani, D., Abutalebi, J., Paulesu, E., Brambati, S., Scifo, P., Cappa, S. F. & Fazio, F. (2003). The role of age of acquisition and language usage in early, high-proficient bilinguals: a fMRI study during verbal fluency. *Human Brain Mapping, 19*, 170–182.

Perani, D., Paulesu, E., Sebastián-Gallés, N., Dupoux, E., Dehaene, S., Bettinardi, V. et al. (1998). The bilingual brain proficiency and age of acquisition of the second language. *Brain, 121*, 1841–1852.

Perfetti, C. A. (1992). The representation problem in reading acquisition. In P. B. Gough, L.C. Ehri & R. Treiman (eds), *Reading acquisition* (pp. 145–174). Hillsdale, NJ: Lawrence Erlbaum Associates.

Perfetti, C. A. & Zhang, S. (1995). Very early phonological activation in Chinese reading. *Journal of Experimental Psychology: Learning, Memory and Cognition, 21*, 24–33.

Perfors, A., Tenenbaum, J. B., Griffiths, T. L. & Xu, F. (2011). A tutorial introduction to Bayesian models of cognitive development. *Cognition, 120*, 302–321.

Perfors, A., Tenenbaum, J. B. & Regier, T. (2011). The learnability of abstract syntactic principles. *Cognition, 118*, 306–338.

Peters, A. (1983). *The units of language acquisition.* Cambridge: Cambridge University Press.

Peters, A. & Menn, L. (1993). False starts and filler syllables: Ways to learn grammatical morphemes. *Language, 69*, 742–777.

Peterson, C. & McCabe, A. (1988). The connective *and*. *First Language, 8,* 19–28.

Peterson, C. C. (2004). Theory-of-mind development in oral deaf children with cochlear implants or conventional hearing aids. *Journal of Child Psychology and Psychiatry, 45,* 1096–1106.

Peterson, C. C. & Siegal, M. (1999). Representing inner worlds: Theory of mind in autistic, deaf, and normal hearing children. *Psychological Science, 10,* 126–129.

Peterson, C. C. & Siegal, M. (1995). Deafness, conversation and theory of mind. *Journal of Child Psychology and Psychiatry, 36,* 459–474.

Peterson, C. C. & Siegal, M. (1998). Changing focus on the representational mind: Deaf, autistic and normal children's concepts of false photos, false drawings and false beliefs. *British Journal of Developmental Psychology, 16,* 301–320.

Peterson, C. C. & Slaughter, V. P. (2006). Telling the story of theory of mind: Deaf and hearing children's narratives and mental state understanding. *British Journal of Developmental Psychology, 24,* 151–179.

Peterson, E., Danziger, E., Wilkins, D., Levinson, S. C., Kita, S. & Senft, G. (1998). Semantic typology and spatial conceptualization. *Language, 74,* 557–589.

Peterson, G. R. & Barney, H. L. (1952). Control methods used in the study of vowels. *Journal of the Acoustical Society of America, 24,* 175–184.

Peterson, N. R., Pisoni, D. B. & Miyamoto, R. T. (2010). Cochlear implants and spoken language processing abilities: Review and assessment of the literature. *Restorative Neurology and Neuroscience, 28,* 237–250.

Petitto, L. A. & Marentette, P. F. (1991). Babbling in the manual mode: Evidence for the ontogeny of language. *Science, 251,* 1483–1496.

Petitto, L. A., Holowka, S., Sergio, L. E. & Ostry, D. (2001). Language rhythms in baby hand movements. *Nature, 413,* 35–36.

Petitto, L. A., Holowka, S., Sergio, L. E., Levy, B. & Ostry, D. J. (2004). Baby hands that move to the rhythm of language: Hearing babies acquiring sign languages babble silently on the hands. *Cognition, 93,* 43–73.

Pexman, P. M., Glenwright, M., Krol, A. & James, T. (2005). An acquired taste: Children's perceptions of humor and teasing in verbal irony. *Discourse Processes, 40,* 259–288.

Piaget, J. (1952). *The origins of intelligence in the child.* Madison, CT: International Universities Press.

Pica, P., Lemer, C., Izard, V. & Dehaene, S. (2004). Exact and approximate arithmetic in an Amazonian indigene group. *Science, 306,* 499–503.

Piccin, T. B. & Waxman, S. R. (2007). Why nouns trump verbs in word learning: New evidence from children and adults in the human simulation paradigm. *Language Learning and Development, 3,* 295–323.

Pickering, M. J. & Branigan, H. P. (1998). The representation of verbs: Evidence from syntactic priming in language production. *Journal of Memory and Language, 39,* 633–651.

Pillemer, D. (1998). *Momentous events, vivid memories.* Cambridge, MA: Harvard University Press.

Pilley, J. W. & Reid, A. K. (2011). Border collie comprehends object names as verbal referents. *Behavioural Processes, 86,* 184–195.

Pine, J. M. and Lieven, E. V. M. (1997). Slot and frame patterns in the development of the determiner category. *Appied Psycholinguistics, 18,* 123–138.

Pine, J. M., Lieven, E. V. M. & Rowland, C. F. (1994). Stylistic variation at the 'single-word' stage: Relations between maternal speech characteristics and children's vocabulary composition and usage. *Child Development, 68,* 807–891.

Pinker, S. (1989). *Learnability and cognition: The acquisition of argument structure.* Cambridge, MA: MIT Press.

Pinker, S. (1999). *Words and rules: The ingredients of language.* New York: Basic Books.

Pinker, S. & Bloom, P. (1990). Natural language and natural selection. *Behavioral and Brain Sciences, 13*, 707–784.

Pixner, S., Moeller, K., Hermanova, V., Nuerk, H. C. & Kaufmann, L. (2011). Whorf reloaded: Language effects on nonverbal number processing in first grade – A trilingual study. *Journal of Experimental Child Psychology, 108*, 371–382.

Pizer, G., Walters, K. & Meier, R. P. (2007). Bringing up baby with baby signs: Language ideologies and socialization in hearing families. *Sign Language Studies, 7*, 387–430.

Plante, E., Gómez, R. L. & Gerken, L. A. (2002). Sensitivity to word order cues by normal and language/learning disabled adults. *Journal of Communication Disorders, 35*, 453–462.

Plante, E., Swisher, L. & Vance, R. (1989). Anatomical correlates of normal and impaired language in a set of dizygotic twins. *Brain and Language, 37*, 643–655.

Plante, E., Swisher, L., Vance, R. & Rapcsak, S. (1991). MRI findings in boys with specific language impairment. *Brain and Language, 41*, 52–66.

Portocarrero, J. S., Burright, R. G. & Donovick, P. J. (2007). Vocabulary and verbal fluency of bilingual and monolingual college students. *Archives of Clinical Neuropsychology, 22*, 415–422.

Powell, R. P. & Bishop, D. V. M. (1992). Clumsiness and perceptual problems in children with specific language impairment. *Developmental Medicine and Child Neurology, 34*, 755–765.

Prasada, S. (1993). Learning names for solid substances: Quantifying solid entities in terms of proportions. *Cognitive Development, 8*, 83–104.

Preston, J. L., Frost, S. J., Mencl, W. E., Fulbright, R. K., Landi, N., Grigorenko, E., Jacobsen, L. & Pugh, K. R. (2010). Early and late talkers: School-age language, literacy, and neurolinguistic differences. *Brain, 133*, 2185–2195.

Prinz, P. M. & Prinz, E. A. (1979). Simultaneous acquisition of ASL and spoken English (in a hearing child of a deaf mother and hearing father). Phase 1: Early lexical development. *Sign Language Studies, 25*, 283–296.

Pu, Y., Liu, H. L., Spinks, J. A., Mahankali, S., Xiong, J., Feng, C. M. et al. (2001). Cerebral hemodynamic response in Chinese (first) and English (second) language processing revealed by event-related functional MRI. *Magnetic Resonance Imaging, 19*, 643–647.

Pye, C. (1986). Quiche Mayan speech to children. *Journal of Child Language, 13*, 85–100.

Pyers, J. & Senghas, A. (2009). Language promotes false-belief understanding: Evidence from learners of a new sign language. *Psychological Science, 20*, 805–812.

Quinn, P. C. & Eimas, P. D. (1996). Perceptual cues that permit categorical differentiation of animal species by infants. *Journal of Experimental Child Psychology, 63*, 189–211.

Quinn, P. C., Eimas, P. D. & Rosenkrantz, S. L. (1993). Evidence for representations of perceptually similar natural categories by 3-month-old and 4-month-old infants. *Perception, 22*, 463–475.

Quinn, P. C., Eimas, P. D. & Tarr, M. J. (2001). Perceptual categorization of cat and dog silhouettes by 3- to 4-month-old infants. *Journal of Experimental Psychology, 79*, 78–94.

Racine, T. P. & Carpendale, J. I. M. (2007). The role of shared practice in joint attention. *British Journal of Developmental Psychology, 25*, 3–25.

Rack, J., Hulme, C., Snowling, M. & Wightman, J. (1994). The role of phonology in young children's learning to read words: The direct-mapping hypothesis. *Journal of Experimental Child Psychology, 57*, 42–71.

Ragir, S. (1985). Retarded development: The evolutionary mechanism underlying the emergence of the human capacity for language. *The Journal of Mind and Behavior, 6*, 451–468.

Ragir, S. (2000). How is a stone tool like a sentence? In B. Bichakjian, T. Chernigovskaya, A. Kendon & A. Moller (eds), *Becoming Loquens: More Studies in Language Origins* (pp. 49–74). Frankfurt am Main: Peter Lang.

Ragir, S. (2001). Changes in perinatal conditions selected for neonatal immaturity. *Behavioral and Brain Science, 24,* 291–292.

Ramscar, M. & Yarlett, D. (2007). Linguistic self-correction in the absence of feedback: A new approach to the logical problem of language acquisition. *Cognitive Science, 31,* 927–960.

Ramscar, M. (2002). The role of meaning in inflection: why the past tense does not require a rule. *Cognitive Psychology, 45,* 45–94.

Ramscar, M. & Gitcho, N. (2007). Developmental change and the nature of learning in childhood. *Trends in Cognitive Sciences, 11,* 274–279.

Ramus, F. & Mehler, J. (1999). Language identification with suprasegmental cues: A study based on speech resynthesis. *Journal of the Acoustical Society of America, 105,* 512–521.

Ramus, F., Rosen, S., Dakin, S. C., Day, B. L., Castellote, J. M., White, S. & Frith, U. (2003). Theories of developmental dyslexia: Insights from a multiple case study of dyslexic adults. *Brain: A Journal of Neurology, 126,* 841–865.

Raskind, W. H., Hsu, L., Berninger, V. W., Thomson, J. B. & Wijsman, E. M. (2000). Familial aggregation of dyslexia phenotypes. *Behavior Genetics, 30,* 385–396.

Rayner, K., Foorman, B. R., Perfetti, C. A., Pesetsky, D. & Seidenberg, M. S. (2001). How psychological science informs the teaching of reading. *Psychological Science in the Public Interest, 2,* 31–74.

Reber, A. S. (1967). Implicit learning of artificial grammars. *Journal of Verbal Learning and Verbal Behavior, 77,* 317–327.

Reber, A. S. (1989). Implicit learning and tacit knowledge. *Journal of Experimental Psychology: General, 118*(3), 219–235.

Reddy, V. (2001). Infant clowns: The interpersonal creation of humor in infancy. *Enfance, 3,* 247–256.

Redford, M. A., Davis, B. L. & Miikkulainen, R. (2004). Phonetic variability, and prosodic structure in mothers. *Infant Behavior and Development, 27,* 477–498.

Reese, E., Haden, C. A. & Fivush, R. (1993). Mother–child conversations about the past: Relationships of style and memory over time. *Cognitive Development, 8,* 403–430.

Regier, T. (2003). Emergent constraints on word-learning: A computational review. *Trends in Cognitive Science, 7,* 263–268.

Regier, T. (2005). The emergence of words: Attentional learning in form and meaning. *Cognitive Science, 29,* 819–865.

Regier, T. & Kay, P. (2009). Language, thought and color: Whorf was half right. *Trends in Cognitive Sciences, 13,* 439–446.

Regier, T., Kay, P. & Khetarpal, N. (2007). Color naming reflects optimal partitions of color space. *Proceedings of the National Academy of Sciences of the USA, 104,* 1436–1441.

Reid, A. A., Szczerbinski, M., Iskierka-Kasperek, E. & Hansen, P. (2007). Cognitive profiles of adult developmental dyslexics: Theoretical implications. *Dyslexia: An International Journal of Research and Practice, 13,* 1–24.

Reid, V. M. & Striano, T. (2007). The directed attention model of infant social cognition. *European Journal of Developmental Psychology, 4,* 100–110.

Reid, V. M. & Striano, T. (2009). The directed attention model of infant social cognition: Further evidence. In T. Striano & V. M. Reid (eds), *Social cognition: Development, neuroscience and autism* (pp. 157–166). West Sussex: Wiley-Blackwell.

Reid, V. M., Striano, T., Kaufman, J. & Johnson, M. (2004). Eye gaze cuing facilitates neural processing of objects in 4-month-old infants. *Neuroreport, 15,* 2553–2556.

Reilly, J. S. & Bellugi, U. (1996). Competition on the face: Affect and language in ASL motherese. *Journal of Child Language, 23,* 219–239.

Remine, M. D., Care, E. & Brown, P. M. (2008). Language ability and verbal and nonverbal executive functioning in deaf students communicating in spoken English. *Journal of Deaf Studies and Deaf Education, 13,* 531–545.

Remmel, E. & Peters, K. (2009). Theory of mind and language in children with cochlear implants. *Journal of Deaf Studies and Deaf Education, 14,* 218–236.

Reschly, A. L. (2010). Reading and school completion: Critical connections and Matthew effects. *Reading and Writing Quarterly, 26,* 67–90.

Rescorla, L. (1989). The language development survey: A screening tool for delayed language in toddlers. *Journal of Speech and Hearing Disorders, 54*(4), 587–599.

Rescorla, L. (2002). Language and reading outcomes to age 9 in late-talking toddlers. *Journal of Speech, Language, and Hearing Research, 45,* 360–371.

Rescorla, L. (2005). Age 13 language and reading outcomes in late-talking toddlers. *Journal of Speech, Language, and Hearing Research, 48,* 459–472.

Rescorla, L. (2009). Age 17 language and reading outcomes in late-talking toddlers: Support for a dimensional perspective on language delay. *Journal of Speech, Language, and Hearing Research, 52,* 16–30.

Rescorla, L., Dahlsgaard, K. & Roberts, J. (2000). Late-talking toddlers: MLU and IPSyn outcomes at 3;0 and 4;0. *Journal of Child Language, 27,* 643–664.

Rescorla, L., Roberts, J. & Dahlsgaard, K. (1997). Late talkers at 2: Outcome at age 3. *Journal of Speech and Hearing Research, 40,* 556–566.

Rice, M. L. & Wexler, K. (1996). Toward tense as a clinical marker of specific language impairment in English-speaking children. *Journal of Speech and Hearing Research, 39,* 1239–1257.

Rice, M. L., Buhr, J. C. & Nemeth, M. (1990). Fast mapping word-learning abilities of language delayed preschoolers. *Journal of Speech and Hearing Disorders, 55*(1), 33–42.

Rice, M. L., Sell, M. A. & Hadley, P. A. (1991). Social interactions of speech- and language-impaired children. *Journal of Speech and Hearing Research, 34,* 1299–1307.

Rice, M. L., Wexler, K. & Cleave, P. L. (1995). Specific language impairment as a period of extended optional infinitive. *Journal of Speech and Hearing Research, 38,* 850–863.

Richerson, P. J. & Boyd, R. (2004). *Not by genes alone: How culture transformed human evolution.* Chicago, IL: University of Chicago Press.

Richerson, P. J. & Boyd, R. (2010). Why possibly language evolved. *Biolinguistics, 4,* 289–306.

Riches, N. G., Faracher, B. & Conti-Ramsden, G. (2006). Verb schema use and input dependence in 5-year-old children with specific language impairment (SLI). *International Journal of Language and Communication Disorders, 41,* 117–135.

Riches, N. G., Tomasello, M. & Conti-Ramsden, G. (2005). Verb learning in children with SLI: Frequency and spacing effects. *Journal of Speech, Language, and Hearing Research, 48,* 1397–1411.

Rispens, J. & Been, P. (2007). Subject–verb agreement and phonological processing in developmental dyslexia and specific language impairment: A closer look. *International Journal of Language and Communication Disorders, 42,* 293–305.

Rittle-Johnson, B. & Siegler, R. S. (1999). Learning to spell: Variability, choice, and change in children's strategy use. *Child Development, 70,* 332–348.

Roberson, D., Davidoff, J., Davies, I. R. L. & Shapiro, L. R. (2004). The development of color categories in two languages: A longitudinal study. *Journal of Experimental Psychology: General, 133,* 554–571.

Roberson, D., Davies, I. R. L. & Davidoff, J. (2000). Color categories are not universal: Replications and new evidence from a stone-age culture. *Journal of Experimental Psychology: General, 129,* 369–398.

Roberts, P. M., Garcia, L. J., Desrochers, A. & Hernandez, D. (2002). English performance of proficient bilingual adults on the Boston Naming Test. *Aphasiology, 16,* 635–645.

Rochat, P. (2007). Intentional action arises from early reciprocal exchanges. *Acta Psychologica, 124,* 8–25.

Rochat, P., Querido, J. G. & Striano, T. (1999). Emerging sensitivity to the timing and structure of protoconversation in early infancy. *Developmental Psychology, 35,* 950–957.

Rodriguez, E. T., Tamis-LeMonda, C. S., Spellman, M. E., Pan, B. A., Raikes, H., Lugo-Gil, J. & Luze, G. (2009). The formative role of home literacy experiences across the first three years of life in children from low-income families. *Journal of Applied Developmental Psychology, 30,* 677–694.

Roeper, T. (2007). *The prism of grammar.* Cambridge, MA: MIT Press.

Roeper, T. & Williams, E. (eds) (1987). *Parameter setting.* Dordrecht: Reidel.

Rogoff, B. (1990). *Apprenticeship in thinking: Cognitive development in social context.* New York: Oxford University Press.

Rogoff, B. (2003). *The cultural nature of human development.* Oxford: Oxford University Press.

Rolland, N. (2004). Was the emergence of home-bases and domestic fire a punctuated event? A review of the Middle Pleistocene record in Eurasia. *Asian Perspectives, 43,* 248–280.

Roman, A. A., Kirby, J. R., Parrila, R. K., Wade-Woolley, L. & Deacon, S. H. (2009). Toward a comprehensive view of the skills involved in word reading in grades 4, 6, and 8. *Journal of Experimental Child Psychology, 102,* 96–113.

Rosenberg, K. & Trevarthan, W. (1996). Bipedalism and human birth: The obstetrical dilemma revisited. *Evolutionary Anthropology, 4,* 161–168.

Rosenberg, K. & Trevarthan, W. (2002). Birth, obstetrics, and human evolution. *BJOG: An International Journal of Obstetrics and Gynaecology, 109,* 1199–1206.

Rosenthal, J. & Ehri, L. C. (2008). The mnemonic value of orthography for vocabulary learning. *Journal of Educational Psychology, 100,* 175–191.

Rovee-Collier, C. & Giles, A. (2010). Why a neuromaturational model of memory fails: exuberant learning in early infancy. *Behavioural Processes, 83,* 197–206.

Rowland, C. F. (2007). Explaining errors in children's questions. *Cognition, 104,* 106–134.

Roy, B. C., Frank, M. C. & Roy, D. (2009). Exploring word learning in a high-density longitudinal corpus. In N. A. Taatgen & H. van Rijn (eds), *Proceedings of the 31st Annual Conference of the Cognitive Science Society.* Austin, TX: Cognitive Science Society.

Rozendaal, M. & Baker, A. (2010). The acquisition of reference: Pragmatic aspects and the influence of language input. *Journal of Pragmatics, 42,* 1866–1879.

Ruff, C. B. (1995). Biomechanics of the hip and birth in early Homo. *American Journal of Physical Anthropology, 98,* 527–574.

Rumelhart, D. E. & McClelland, J. L. (1986). On learning the past tenses of English verbs. In J. L. McClelland, D. E. Rumelhart & the PDP Research Group (eds), *Parallel distributed processing: Explorations in the microstructure of cognition: Vol. 2. Psychological and biological models.* Cambridge, MA: Bradford Books/MIT Press.

Russell, P. A., Hosie, J. A., Gray, C. D., Scott, C., Hunter, N., Banks, J. S. & Macaulay, M. C. (1998). The development of theory of mind in deaf children. *Journal of Child Psychology and Psychiatry, 39,* 903–910.

Sabbagh, M. A., Xu, F., Carlson, S. M., Moses, L. J. & Lee, K. (2006). The development of executive functioning and theory of mind: A comparison of Chinese and US preschoolers. *Psychological Science, 17,* 74–81.

Saffran, J. R. (2002). Constraints on statistical language learning. *Journal of Memory and Language*, *47*, 172–196.

Saffran, J. R., Aslin, R. N. & Newport, E. L. (1996). Statistical learning by 8-month-old infants. *Science, 274*, 1926–1928.

Saffran, J. R., Johnson, E. K., Aslin, R. N. & Newport, E. L. (1999). Statistical learning of tone sequences by human infants and adults. *Cognition, 70*, 27–52.

Saffran, J. R., Werker, J. F. & Werner, L. A. (2006). The infant's auditory world: Hearing, speech, and the beginnings of language. In D. Kuhn & M. Siegler (eds), *Handbook of child psychology*, 6th edn. (pp. 58–108). New York: John Wiley & Sons.

Saffran, J. R. & Wilson, D. P. (2003). From syllables to syntax: Multi-level statistical learning by 12-month-old infants. *Infancy, 4*, 273–284.

Sagae, K., Lavie, A. & MacWhinney, B. (2005). Automatic measurement of syntactic development. *Proceedings of the 43rd Annual Meeting of the Association for Computational Linguistics* (pp. 197–204).

Sambeth, A., Ruohio, K., Alku, P., Fellman, V. & Huotilainen, M. (2008). Sleeping newborns extract prosody from continuous speech. *Clinical Neurophysiology, 119*, 332–341.

Samuelson, L. K. & Smith, L. B. (2005). They call it like they see it: Spontaneous naming and attention to shape. *Developmental Science, 8*, 182–198.

Sandler, W. & Lillo-Martin, D. (2006). *Sign language and linguistic universals.* Cambridge: Cambridge University Press.

Sandler, W., Meir, I., Padden, C. & Aronoff, M. (2005). The emergence of grammar: Systematic structure in a new language. *Proceedings of the National Academy of Sciences of the USA, 102*, 2661–2665.

Santelmann, L. & Jusczyk, P. (1998). Sensitivity to discontinuous dependencies in language learners: Evidence for processing limitations. *Cognition, 69*, 105–134.

Santelmann, L., Berk, S., Austin, J. Somashekar, S. & Lust, B. (2002). Continuity and development in the acquisition of inversion in yes/no questions: Dissociating movement and inflection. *Journal of Child Language, 29*, 813–842.

Sapir, E. (1921). *Language.* New York: Harcourt, Brace & Co.

Saracho, O. N. & Spodek, B. (2010). Parents and children engaging in storybook reading. *Early Child Development and Care, 180*, 1379–1389.

Savage, C., Lieven, E., Theakston, A. & Tomasello, M. (2006). Structural priming as implicit learning in language acquisition: The persistence of lexical and structural priming in 4-year-olds. *Language Learning and Development, 2*, 27–49.

Savickienė, I. & Dressler, W. U. (eds) (2007). *Acquisition of diminutives: A cross-linguistic perspective.* Amsterdam: John Benjamins.

Saxton, M. (2000). Negative evidence and negative feedback: immediate effects on the grammaticality of child speech. *First Language, 20*, 221–252.

Saxton, M., Houston-Price, C. & Dawson, N. (2005). The prompt hypothesis: Clarification requests as corrective input for grammatical errors. *Applied Psycholinguistics, 26*, 393–414.

Scarborough, H. S. (1990a). Index of productive syntax. *Applied Psycholinguistics, 11*, 1–12.

Scarborough, H. S. (1990b). Very early language deficits in dyslexic children. *Child Development, 61*, 1728–1743.

Schafer, G. & Plunkett, K. (1998). Rapid word learning by fifteen-month-olds under tightly controlled conditions. *Child Development, 69*, 309–320.

Schauwers, K., Gillis, S., Daemers, K., De Beukelaer, C., De Ceulaer, G., Yperman, M. & Govaerts, P. (2004). Normal hearing and language development in a deaf-born child. *Otology and Neurotology, 25*, 924–929.

Schauwers, K., Gillis, S. & Govaerts, P. (2008). The characteristics of prelexical babbling after cochlear implantation between 5 and 20 months of age. *Ear and Hearing, 29*, 627–637.

Schauwers, K., Govaerts, P. & Gillis, S. (2005). Language acquisition in deaf children with a cochlear implant. In P. Fletcher & J. Miller (eds), *Developmental theory and language disorders* (pp. 95–119). Amsterdam: John Benjamins.

Schieffelin, B. B. (1985). The acquisition of Kaluli. In D. I. Slobin (ed.), *The crosslinguistic study of language acquisition: Vol. 1: The data* (pp. 525–594). Hillsdale, NJ: Lawrence Erlbaum Associates.

Schieffelin, B. B. (1986). Teasing and shaming in Kaluli children's interactions. In B. B. Schieffelin & E. Ochs (eds), *Language socialization across cultures: Studies in the social and cultural foundations of language* (pp. 165–181). New York: Cambridge University Press.

Schwartz, R. G. (ed.) (2009). *Handbook of child language disorders*. New York: Psychology Press.

Schwartz, R. G. & Leonard, L. B. (1982). Do children pick and choose? An examination of phonological selection and avoidance in early lexical acquisition. *Journal of Child Language, 9*, 319–336.

Schwartz, R. G., Leonard, L. B., Frome Loeb, D. M. & Swanson, L. A. (1987). Attempted sounds are sometimes not: An expanded view of phonological selection and avoidance. *Journal of Child Language, 14*, 411–418.

Schwier, C., van Maanen, C., Carpenter, M. & Tomasello, M. (2006). Rational imitation in 12-month-old infants. *Infancy, 10*, 303–311.

Scientific Learning Corporation. (1998). Fast ForWord Language [Computer software]. Berkeley, CA: Author.

Scribner, S. & Cole, M. (1981). *The psychology of literacy*. Cambridge, MA: MIT Press.

Sear, R., Steel, F., McGregor, I. & Mace, R. (2002). The effects of kin on child mortality in rural Gambia. *Demography, 39*, 43–63.

Searle, J. (1969) *Speech acts*. Cambridge: Cambridge University Press.

Sebastián-Gallés, N. & Bosch, L. (2002). Building phonotactic knowledge in bilinguals: role of early exposure. *Journal of Experimental Psychology: Human Perception and Performance, 28*, 974–989.

Sehley, S. & Snow, C. E. (1992). The conversational skills of school-aged children. *Social Development, 1*, 18–35.

Seidl, A. (2007). Infants' use and weighting of prosodic cues in clause segmentation. *Journal of Memory and Language, 57*, 24–48.

Seiger-Gardner, L. & Brooks, P. J. (2008). Effects of onset- and rhyme-related distractors on phonological processing in children with specific language impairment. *Journal of Speech, Language, and Hearing Research, 51*, 1263–1281.

Seiger-Gardner, L. & Schwartz, R. G. (2008). Lexical access in children with and without specific language impairment: A cross-modal picture-word interference study. *International Journal of Communication Disorders, 43*, 528–551.

Sekerina, I. A. & Brooks, P. J. (2007). Eye movements during spoken word recognition in Russian children. *Journal of Experimental Child Psychology, 98*, 20–45.

Sénéchal, M. (2006). Testing the home literacy model: Parental involvement in kindergarten is differentially related to grade 4 reading comprehension, fluency, spelling, and reading for pleasure. *Scientific Studies of Reading, 10*, 59–87.

Sénéchal, M., Basque, M. T. & Leclaire, T. (2006). Morphological knowledge as revealed in children's spelling accuracy and reports of spelling strategies. *Journal of Experimental Child Psychology, 95*, 231–254.

Sénéchal, M. & LeFevre, J.-A. (2002). Parental involvement in the development of children's reading skill: A five-year longitudinal study. *Child Development, 73*, 445–460.

Sénéchal, M., Pagan, S., Lever, R. & Ouellette, G. P. (2008). Relations among the frequency of shared reading and 4-year-old children's vocabulary, morphological and syntactic comprehension, and narrative skills. *Early Education and Language Development, 19*, 27–44.

Senghas, A. (2003). Intergenerational influence and ontogenetic development in the emergence of spatial grammar in Nicaraguan Sign Language. *Cognitive Development, 18*, 511–531.

Senghas, A. (2005). Language emergence: Clues from a new Bedouin sign language. *Current Biology, 15*(12), 463–465.

Senghas, A. & Coppola, M. (2001). Children creating language: How Nicaraguan Sign Language acquired a spatial grammar. *Psychological Science, 12*, 323–328.

Senghas, A., Kita, S. & Ozyurek, A. (2004). Children creating core properties of language: Evidence from an emerging sign language in Nicaragua. *Science, 305*(5691), 1779–1782.

Senghas, R. J., Senghas, A. & Pyers, J. E. (2005). The emergence of Nicaraguan Sign Language: Questions of development, acquisition, and evolution. In J. Langer, S. T. Parker & C. Milbrath, *Biology and knowledge revisited: From neurogenesis to psychogenesis* (pp. 287–306). Mahwah, NJ: Lawrence Erlbaum Associates.

Seymour, P. H. K., Aro, M. & Erskine, J. M. (2003). Foundation literacy acquisition in European orthographies. *British Journal of Psychology, 94*, 143–174.

Shafer, V. L. & Garrido-Nag, K. (2008). The neurodevelopmental bases of language. In E. Hoff & M. Shatz (eds), *Blackwell handbook of language development* (pp. 21–45). Oxford: Blackwell.

Share, D. L. & Stanovich, K. E. (1995). Cognitive processes in early reading development: Accommodating individual differences into a model of acquisition. *Issues in Education, 1*, 1–57.

Sharma, A., Nash, A. A. & Dorman, M. (2009). Cortical development, plasticity, and re-organization in children with cochlear implants. *Journal of Communication Disorders, 42*, 272–279.

Shaywitz, S. E. & Shaywitz, B. A. (2005). Dyslexia (specific reading disability). *Biological Psychiatry, 57*, 1301–1309.

Shaywitz, S. E., Shaywitz, B. A., Fletcher, J. M. & Escobar, M. D. (1990). Prevalence of reading disability in boys and girls. *Journal of the American Medical Association, 264*, 998–1002.

Sheldon, A. (1990). Pickle fights: Gendered talk in preschool disputes. *Discourse Processes, 13*, 5–31.

Sherzer, J. (1972). Verbal and nonverbal deixis: The pointed lip gesture among the San Blas Cuna. *Language in Society, 2*, 117–131.

Shi, R., Werker, J. & Morgan, J. (1999). Newborn infants' sensitivity to perceptual cues to lexical and grammatical words. *Cognition, 72*, B11–B21.

Shockey, L. & Bond, Z. S. (1980). Phonological processes in speech addressed to children. *Phonetica, 37*, 267–274.

Shriberg, L. D., Tomblin, J. B. & McSweeny, J. L. (1999). Prevalence of speech delay in 6-year-old children and comorbidity with language impairment. *Journal of Speech, Language, and Hearing Research, 42*, 1461–1481.

Shukla, M., White, K. S. & Aslin, R. N. (2011). Prosody guides the rapid mapping of auditory word forms onto visual objects in 6-mo-old infants. *Proceedings of the National Academy of Sciences of the USA, 108*, 6038–6043.

Shulman, C. & Guberman, A. (2007). Acquisition of verb meaning through syntactic cues: A comparison of children with autism, children with specific language impairment (SLI) and children with typical language development (TLD). *Journal of Child Language, 34*, 411–423.

Shultz, T. R. (1974). Development of the appreciation of riddles. *Child Development, 45*, 100–105.

Shultz, T. R. & Pilon, R. (1973). Development of the ability to detect linguistic ambiguity. *Child Development, 44*, 728–733.

Shute, B. & Wheldall, K. (2001). How do grandmothers speak to their grandchildren? Fundamental frequency and temporal modifications in the speech of British grandmothers to their grandchildren. *Educational Psychology, 21*, 493–503.

Siegal, M., Iozzi, L. & Surian, L. (2009). Bilingualism and conversational understanding in young children. *Cognition, 110*, 115–122.

Siller, M. & Sigman, M. (2002). The behaviors of parents of children with autism predict the subsequent development of their children's communication. *Journal of Autism and Developmental Disorders, 32*, 77–89.

Siller, M. & Sigman, M. (2008). Modeling longitudinal change in the language abilities of children with autism: Parent behaviors and child characters as predictors of change. *Developmental Psychology, 44*, 1691–1704.

Simcock, G. & Hayne, H. (2002). Breaking the barrier? Children fail to translate their preverbal memories into language. *Psychological Science, 13*, 225–231.

Singh, L., Morgan, J. & Best, C. (2002). Infants' listening preferences: Baby talk or happy talk? *Infancy, 3*, 365–394.

Singleton, J. L. & Newport, E. L. (2004). When learners surpass their models: The acquisition of American Sign Language from inconsistent input. *Cognitive Psychology, 49*, 370–407.

Singleton, J. L., Morford, J. P. & Goldin-Meadow, S. (1993). Once is not enough: Standards of well-formedness in manual communication created over three different timespans. *Language, 69*, 683–715.

Singleton, J. L., Morgan, D., DiGello, E., Wiles, J. & Rivers, R. (2004). Vocabulary use by low, moderate, and high ASL-proficient writers compared to hearing ESL and monolingual speakers. *Journal of Deaf Studies and Deaf Education, 9*, 86–103.

Slade, L. & Ruffman, T. (2005). How language does (and does not) relate to theory of mind: A longitudinal study of syntax, semantics, working memory, and false belief. *British Journal of Developmental Psychology, 23*, 117–141.

Slobin, D. I. (1996). From 'thought and language' to 'thinking for speaking'. In J. Gumperz & S. Levinson (eds), *Rethinking linguistic relativity* (pp. 70–96). Cambridge: Cambridge University Press.

Slobin, D. I. & Bever, T. G. (1982). Children use canonical sentence schemas: A crosslinguistic study of word order and inflection. *Cognition, 12*, 229–265.

Sloutsky, V. M. (2003). The role of similarity in the development of categorization. *Trends in Cognitive Sciences, 7*, 246–251.

Smith, L. B. & Chen, Y. (2008). Infants rapidly learn word-referent mappings via cross-situational statistics. *Cognition, 106*, 1558–1568.

Smith, L. B., Jones, S. S. & Landau, B. (1992). Count nouns, adjectives, and perceptual properties in children's novel word interpretations. *Developmental Psychology, 28*, 273–286.

Smith, L. B., Jones, S. S., Landau, B., Gershkoff-Stowe, L. & Samuelson, L. (2002). Object name learning provides on-the-job training for attention. *Psychological Science, 13*, 13–19.

Snedeker, J. & Trueswell, J. C. (2004). The developing constraints on parsing decisions: The role of lexical-biases and referential scenes in child and adult sentence processing. *Cognitive Psychology, 49*, 238–299.

Snedeker, J. & Yuan, S. (2008). Effects of prosodic and lexical constraints on parsing in young children (and adults). *Journal of Memory and Language, 58*, 574–608.

Snedeker, J., Li, P. & Yuan, S. (2003). Cross-cultural differences in the input to early word learning. In *Proceedings of the 25th Annual Conference of the Cognitive Science Society* (pp. 1094–1100). Mahwah, NJ: Lawrence Erlbaum Associates.

Snow, C. E. & Ferguson, C. (1977). *Talking to children.* Cambridge: Cambridge University Press.

Snow, C. (1977). The development of conversation between mothers and babies. *Journal of Child Language, 4,* 1–22.

Snow, C. E. (2004). What counts as literacy in early childhood? In K. McCartney & D. Phillips (eds), *Handbook of early child development.* Oxford: Blackwell.

Snow, C. E. & Ninio, A. (1985). The contracts of literacy: Learning how to learn from reading books. In W. Teale (ed.), *Emergent literacy: Writing and reading* (pp. 116–138). Norwood, NJ: Ablex.

Snow, C. E., Perlmann, R. Y., Gleason, J. B. & Hooshyar, N. (1990). Developmental perspectives on politeness: Sources of children's knowledge. *Journal of Pragmatics, 14,* 289–305.

Snow, D. & Ertmer, D. (2009). The development of intonation in young children with cochlear implants: A preliminary study of the influence of age at implantation and length of implant experience. *Child Linguistics and Phonetics, 23,* 665–679.

Snowling, M. J., Chiat, S. & Hulme, C. (1991). Words, nonwords, and phonological processes: Some comments on Gathercole, Willis, Emslie and Baddeley. *Applied Psycholinguistics, 12,* 369–373.

Soderstrom, M. (2007). Beyond babytalk: Re-evaluating the nature and content of speech input to preverbal infants. *Developmental Review, 27,* 501–532.

Soderstrom, M., Blossom, M., Foygel, R. & Morgan, J. L. (2008). Acoustical cues and grammatical units in speech to two preverbal infants. *Journal of Child Language, 35,* 869–902.

Soja, N. (1992). Inferences about the meanings of nouns: The relationship between perception and syntax. *Cognitive Development, 7,* 29–46.

Southgate, V., Chevallier, C. & Csibra, G. (2009). Sensitivity to communicative relevance tells young children what to imitate. *Developmental Science, 12,* 1013–1019.

Spaepen, E., Coppola, M., Spelke, E. S., Carey, S. E. & Goldin-Meadow, S. (2010). Language without a number model. *Proceedings of the National Academy of Sciences of the USA, 108,* 3163–3168.

Spelke, E. S. & Kinzler, K. D. (2007). Core knowledge. *Developmental Science, 10,* 89–96.

Spence, M. J. & Moore, D. S. (2002). Categorization of infant-directed speech: Development from 4 to 6 months. *Developmental Psychobiology, 42,* 97–109.

St. Clair, M. C., Monaghan, P. & Christiansen, M. H. (2010). Learning grammatical categories from distributional cues: Flexible frames for language acquisition. *Cognition, 116,* 341–360.

Stanovich, K. E. (1986). Matthew effects in reading: Some consequences of individual differences in the acquisition of literacy. *Reading Research Quarterly, 21,* 360–407.

Stanovich, K. E. & Cunningham, A. E. (1993). Where does knowledge come from? Specific associations between print exposure and information acquisition. *Journal of Educational Psychology, 85,* 211–229.

Stanovich, K. E., Cunningham, A. E. & Feeman, D. J. (1984). Intelligence, cognitive skills, and early reading progress. *Reading Research Quarterly, 19,* 278–303.

Stern, D. N. (1985). *The interpersonal world of the infant.* New York: Basic Books.

Stoel-Gammon, C. (2011). Relationships between lexical and phonological development in young children. *Journal of Child Language, 38,* 1–34.

Stoel-Gammon, C. & Cooper, J. A. (1984). Patterns of early lexical and phonological development. *Journal of Child Language, 11,* 247–271.

Stokes, S. F. & Fletcher, P. (2000). Lexical diversity and productivity in Cantonese-speaking children with specific language impairment. *International Journal of Language and Communication Disorders, 35,* 527–541.

Stokes, S. F. & Klee, T. (2009). Factors that influence vocabulary development in two-year-old children. *Journal of Child Psychology and Psychiatry, 50,* 498–505.

Stokoe, W. C., Casterline, D. & Croneberg, C. (1965). *A dictionary of American Sign Language on linguistic principles.* Washington, DC: Gallaudet College Press.

Stoodley, C. J., Harrison, E. P. D. & Stein, J. F. (2006). Implicit motor learning deficits in dyslexic adults. *Neuropsychologia*, *44*, 795–798.

Storkel, H. (2004). Do children acquire dense neighborhoods? An investigation of similarity neighborhoods in lexical acquisition. *Applied Psycholinguistics*, *25*, 201–221.

Storkel, H. (2009). Developmental differences in the effects of phonological, lexical, and semantic variables on word learning by infants. *Journal of Child Language*, *36*, 291–321.

Stothard, S. E., Snowling, M. J., Bishop, D. V. M., Chipchase, B. B. & Kaplan, C. A. (1998). Language impaired preschoolers: A follow-up into adolescence. *Journal of Speech, Language, and Hearing Research*, *41*, 407–418.

Street, J. A. & Dąbrowska, E. (2010). More individual differences in language attainment: How much to adult native speakers of English know about passives and quantifiers? *Lingua*, *120*, 2080–2094.

Striano, T., Henning, A. & Stahl, D. (2005). Sensitivity to social contingencies between 1 and 3 months of age. *Developmental Science*, *8*, 509–519.

Striano, T., Reid, V. M. & Hoehl, S. (2006). Neural mechanisms of joint attention in infancy. *European Journal of Neuroscience*, *23*, 2819–2823.

Striano, T. & Rochat, P. (2000). Emergence of selective social referencing in infancy. *Infancy*, *1*, 253–264.

Stromswold, K. (1998). Genetics of spoken language disorders. *Human Biology*, *70*, 297–324.

Strong, M. & Prinz, P. (1997). A study of the relationship between American Sign Language and English literacy. *Journal of Deaf Studies and Deaf Education*, *2*, 37–46.

Strong, M. & Prinz, P. (2000). Is American Sign Language skill related to English literacy? In C. Chamberlain, J. P. Morford & R. I. Mayberry (eds), *Language acquisition by eye* (pp. 131–141). Hillsdale, NJ: Lawrence Erlbaum Associates.

Stuart, M. & Coltheart, M. (1988). Does reading develop in a sequence of stages? *Cognition*, *30*, 139–181.

Stuart, M. & Masterson, J. (1992). Patterns of reading and spelling in 10-year-old children related to prereading phonological abilities. *Journal of Experimental Child Psychology*, *54*, 168–187.

Svirsky, M. A., Robbins, A. M., Kirk, K. I., Pisoni, D. B. & Miyamoto, R. T. (2000). Language development in profoundly deaf children with cochlear implants. *Psychological Science*, *11*, 153–158.

Swan, D. W. (2000). How to build a lexicon: A case study of lexical errors and innovations. *First Language*, *20*, 187–204.

Swingley, D. (2005). 11-month-olds' knowledge of how familiar words sound. *Developmental Science*, *8*, 432–443.

Tager-Flusberg, H. (2004). Do autism and specific language impairment represent overlapping language disorders? In M. L. Rice & S. F. Warren (eds), *Developmental language disorders: From phenotypes to etiologies* (pp. 31–52). Mahwah, NJ: Lawrence Erlbaum Associates.

Tallal, P. (1980). Auditory temporal perception, phonics, and reading disabilities in children. *Brain and Language*, *9*, 182–198.

Tallal, P. & Piercy, M. (1973a). Defects of nonverbal auditory perception in children with developmental aphasia. *Nature*, *241*, 468–469.

Tallal, P. & Piercy, M. (1973b). Developmental aphasia: Impaired rate of non-verbal processing as a function of sensory modality. *Neuropsychologia*, *11*, 389–398.

Tallal, P. & Piercy, M. (1974). Developmental aphasia: Rate of auditory processing and selective impairment of consonant processing. *Neuropsychologia*, *12*, 83–94.

Tallal, P. & Piercy, M. (1975). Developmental aphasia: The perception of brief vowels and extended stop consonants. *Neuropsychologia*, *13*, 69–74.

Tallal, P., Hirsch, L. S., Realpe-Bonilla, T., Brzustowicz, L. M., Bartlett, C. & Flax, J. F. (2001). Familial aggregation in specific language impairment. *Journal of Speech, Language, and Hearing Research*, 44, 1172–1182.

Tallal, P., Jernigan, T. & Trauner, D. (1994). Developmental bilateral damage to the head of the caudate nuclei: Implications for speech–language pathology. *Journal of Medical Speech Language Pathology*, 2, 23–28.

Tallal, P., Miller, S. L., Bedi, G., Wang, X. & Nagarajan, S. S. (1996). Language comprehension in language-learning impaired children improved with acoustically modified speech. *Science*, 271(5245), 81–84.

Tamis-LeMonda, C. S., Bornstein, M. H. & Baumwell, L. (2001). Maternal responsiveness and children's achievement of language milestones. *Child Development*, 72, 748–767.

Tannen, D. (1990). *You just don't understand: Women and men in conversation*. New York: Harper Collins.

Tardif, T. (1996). Nouns are not always learned before verbs: Evidence from Mandarin speakers' early vocabularies. *Developmental Psychology*, 32, 492–504.

Tardif, T., Fletcher, P., Liang, W., Zhang, Z., Kaciroti, N. & Marchman, V. A. (2008). Baby's first 10 words. *Developmental Psychology*, 44, 929–938.

Tardif, T., Gelman, S. & Xu, F. (1999). Putting the 'noun bias' in context: A comparison of English and Mandarin. *Child Development*, 70, 620–635.

Taub, S. F. (2001). *Language from the body: Iconicity and metaphor in American Sign Language*. Cambridge: Cambridge University Press.

Tenenbaum, H. R. (2009). 'You'd be good at that': Gender patterns in parent–child talk about courses. *Social Development*, 18, 447–463.

Tenenbaum, H. R. & Leaper, C. (2003). Parent–child conversations about science: The socialization of gender inequities? *Developmental Psychology*, 39, 34–47.

Teoh, S. W., Pisoni, D. B. & Miyamoto, R. T. (2004). Cochlear implantation in adults with prelingual deafness. Part 1. Clinical results. *The Larngoscope*, 114, 1536–1540.

Thal, D. & Tobias, S. (1992). Communicative gestures in children with delayed onset of oral expressive vocabulary. *Journal of Speech and Hearing Research*, 35, 1281–1289.

Thal, D. & Tobias, S. (1994). Relationships between language and gesture in normally developing and late-talking toddlers. *Journal of Speech and Hearing Research*, 37, 157–170.

Thal, D., Tobias, S. & Morrison, D. (1991). Language and gesture in late talkers: a 1-year follow-up. *Journal of Speech and Hearing Research*, 34, 604–612.

Theakston, A. L. (2004). A role of entrenchment in children's and adults' performance on grammaticality judgement tasks. *Cognitive Development*, 19, 15–34.

Theakston, A. L., Lieven, E. V. M., Pine, J. M. & Rowland, C. F. (2002). Going, going, gone: The acquisition of the verb 'go'. *Journal of Child Language*, 29, 783–811.

Thelen, E. (1991). Motor aspects of emergent speech: A dynamic approach. In N. A. Krasnegor, D. M. Rumbaugh, R. L. Schiefelbusch & M. Studdert-Kennedy (eds), *Biological and behavioral determinants of language development* (pp. 339–362). Hillsdale, NJ: Erlbaum.

Thiessen, E. D., Hill, E. A. & Saffran, J. R. (2005). Infant-directed speech facilitates word segmentation. *Infancy*, 7, 53–71.

Thomas, M. S. C. & Johnson, M. H. (2008). New advances in understanding sensitive periods in brain development. *Current Directions in Psychological Science*, 17, 1–5.

Thompson-Schill, S., Ramscar, M. & Chrysikou, E. (2009). Cognition without control: When a little frontal lobe goes a long way. *Current Directions in Psychological Science*, 18, 259–263.

Thompson, R. B. (1999). Gender differences in preschoolers' help-eliciting communication. *Journal of Genetic Psychology*, 160, 357–368.

Thompson, R. L., Vinson, D. P. & Vigliocco, G. (2009). The link between form and meaning in American Sign Language: Lexical processing effects. *Journal of Experimental Psychology: Learning Memory and Cognition, 35,* 550–557.

Thompson, R. L., Vinson, D. P. & Vigliocco, G. (2010). The link between form and meaning in British Sign Language: Effects of iconicity for phonological decisions. *Journal of Experimental Psychology: Learning Memory and Cognition, 36,* 1017–1027.

Tincoff, R. & Jusczyk, P. W. (1999). Some beginnings of word comprehension in 6-month-olds. *Psychological Science, 10,* 172–175.

Tipper, S. (1992). Selection for actions: The role of inhibitory mechanisms. *Current Directions in Psychological Science, 1,* 105–112.

Tomasello, M. (1992). *First verbs: A case study of early grammatical development.* Cambridge: Cambridge University Press.

Tomasello, M. (1999). *The cultural origins of human cognition.* Cambridge, MA: Harvard University Press.

Tomasello, M. (2000). The item-based nature of children's early syntactic development. *Trends in Cognitive Sciences, 4,* 156–163.

Tomasello, M. (2003). *Constructing a language: A usage-based theory of language acquisition.* Cambridge, MA: Harvard University Press.

Tomasello, M. (2008). *Origins of human communication.* Cambridge, MA: MIT Press.

Tomasello, M. & Akhtar, N. (1995). Two-year-olds use pragmatic cues to differentiate reference to objects and actions. *Cognitive Development, 10,* 201–224.

Tomasello, M., Akhtar, N., Dodson, K. & Rekau, L. (1997). Differential productivity in young children's use of nouns and verbs. *Journal of Child Language, 24,* 373–387.

Tomasello, M. & Brooks, P. J. (1998). Young children's earliest transitive and intransitive constructions. *Cognitive Linguistics, 9,* 379–395.

Tomasello, M., Carpenter, M. & Liszkowski, U. (2007). A new look at infant pointing. *Child Development, 78,* 705–722.

Tomasello, M. & Haberl, K. (2003). Understanding attention: 12- and 18-month-olds know what is new for other persons. *Developmental Psychology, 39,* 906–912.

Tomasello, M., Strosberg, R. & Akhtar, N. (1996). Eighteen-month-old children learn words in non-ostensive contexts. *Journal of Child Language, 23,* 157–176.

Tomblin, J. B. (1989). Familial concentration of developmental language impairment. *Journal of Speech and Hearing Disorders, 54,* 287–295.

Tomblin, J. B. (2009). Genetics of child language disorders. In R. G. Schwartz (ed.), *Handbook of child language disorders* (pp. 232–256). New York: Psychology Press.

Tomblin, J. B. & Buckwalter, P. (1998). The heritability of poor language achievement among twins. *Journal of Speech and Hearing Research, 41,* 188–199.

Tomblin, J. B., Mainela-Arnold, E. & Zhang, X. (2007). Procedural learning in adolescents with and without specific language impairment. *Language Learning and Development, 3,* 269–293.

Tomblin, J. B., Records, N. L., Buckwalter, P., Zhang, X., Smith, E. & O'Brien, M. (1997). Prevalence of specific language impairment in kindergarten children. *Journal of Speech and Hearing Research, 40,* 1245–1260.

Tomblin, J. B., Shriberg, L., Murray, J., Patil, S. & Williams, C. (2004). Speech and language characteristics associated with a 7/13 translocation involving *FOXP2. American Journal of Medical Genetics. Part B, Neuropsychiatric Genetics, 130B,* 97.

Tomblin, J. B., Zhang, X., Buckwalter, P. & Catts, H. (2000). The association of reading disability, behavioral disorders, and language impairment among second-grade children. *Journal of Child Psychology and Psychiatry, 41,* 473–482.

Torgerson, C. J., Brooks, G. & Hall, J. (2006). *A systematic review of the research literature on the use of phonics in the teaching of reading and spelling*. London: Department for Education and Skills (DfES).

Torkildsen, J. V. K., Syversen, G., Simonsen, H. G., Moen, I., Smith, L. & Lindgren, M. (2007). Electrophysiological correlates of auditory semantic priming in 24-month-olds. *Journal of Neurolinguistics, 20,* 332–351.

Trainor, L. J. (2005). Are there critical periods for musical development? *Developmental Psychobiology, 46,* 262–278.

Trainor, L. J., Austin, C. & Desjardins, R. (2000). Is infant-directed speech prosody a result of the vocal expression of emotion? *Psychological Science, 11,* 180–195.

Trainor, L. J. & Desjardins, R. N. (2002). Pitch characteristics of infant-directed speech affect infants' ability to discriminate vowels. *Psychonomic Bulletin and Review, 9,* 335–340.

Trainor, L. J., Desjardins, R. N. & Rockel, C. (1999). A comparison of contour and interval processing in musicians and non-musicians using event-related potentials. *Australian Journal of Psychology, 51,* 147–153.

Trauner, D. A., Ballantyne, A., Chase, C. & Tallal, P. (1993). Comprehension and expression of affect in language-impaired children. *Journal of Psycholinguistic Research, 22,* 445–452.

Trauner, D. A., Wulfeck, B., Tallal, P. & Hesselink, J. (2000). Neurological and MRI profiles of children with developmental language impairment. *Developmental Medicine and Child Neurology, 42,* 470–475.

Traxler, C. B. (2000). Measuring up to performance standards in reading and mathematics: Achievement of selected deaf and hard-of-hearing students in the national norming of the 9th Edition Stanford Achievement Test. *Journal of Deaf Studies and Deaf Education, 5,* 337–348.

Trehub, S. E. (1973). Infants' sensitivity to vowel and tonal contrasts. *Developmental Psychology, 9,* 91–96.

Treiman, R. (1993). *Beginning to spell: A study of first-grade children.* New York: Oxford University Press.

Treiman, R. & Cassar, M. (1997). Spelling acquisition in English. In C. A. Perfetti, L. Rieben & M. Fayol (eds), *Learning to spell: Research, theory, and practice across languages* (pp. 61–80). Mahwah, NJ: Lawrence Erlbaum Associates.

Treiman, R., Tincoff, R. & Richmond-Welty, D. (1996). Letter names help children to connect print and speech. *Developmental Psychology, 32,* 505–514.

Trevarthen, C. (2001). Intrinsic motives for companionship in understanding. Their origin, development, and significance for infant mental health. *Infant Mental Health Journal, 22*(1/2), 95–131.

Trevarthen, C. & Hubley, P. (1978). Secondary intersubjectivity: Confidence, confiding and acts of meaning in the first year. In A. Lock (ed.), *Action, gesture and symbol: The emergence of language* (pp. 183–229). New York: Academic Press.

Tronick, E. Z., Als, H., Adamson, L. B., Wise, S. & Brazelton, T. B. (1978). The infant's response to entrapment between contradictory messages in face-to-face interaction. *Journal of American Academy of Child Psychiatry, 17,* 1–13.

Tropper, B. & Schwartz, R. G. (2009). Neurobiology of child language disorders. In R. G. Schwartz (ed.), *Handbook of child language disorders* (pp. 174–200). New York: Psychology Press.

Trueswell, J. C., Sekerina, I. A., Hill, N. M. & Logrip, M. L. (1999). The kindergarten-path effect: Studying on-line sentence processing in young children. *Cognition, 73,* 89–134.

Tsesmeli, S. N. & Seymour, P. H. K. (2009). The effects of training of morphological strucure on spelling derived words by dyslexic adults. *British Journal of Psychology, 100,* 565–592.

Tucker, G. R. (2003). A global perspective on bilingualism and bilingual education. In C. B. Paulston & G. R. Tucker (eds), *Sociolinguistics: The essential readings.* Malden, MA: Blackwell.

Tulving, E. (1985). How many memory systems are there? *American Psychologist, 40*, 385–398.

Tulving, E. (2002). Episodic memory: From mind to brain. *Annual Review of Psychology, 53*, 1–25.

Ukoumunne, O. C., Wake, M., Carlin, J., Bavin, E. L., Lum, J., Skeat, J., Williams, J., Conway, L., Cini, E. & Reilly, S. (2011). Profiles of language development in pre-school children: A longitudinal latent class analysis of data from the Early Language in Victoria study. *Child: Care, Health and Development*. First published online: 24 Mar 2011, DOI: 10.1111/j.1365-2214.2011.01234.x.

Ullman, M. T. (2001). A neurocognitive perspective on language: The declarative/ procedural model. *Nature Reviews Neuroscience, 2*, 717–726.

Ullman, M. T. & Pierpont, E. I. (2005). Specific language impairment is not specific to language. *Cortex, 41*, 399–433.

Užgiris, I. (1981). Two functions of imitation during infancy. *International Journal of Behavioral Development, 4*, 1–12.

van de Weijer, J. (2002). How much does an infant hear in a day? Paper presented at the GALA 2001 Conference on Language Acquisition, Lisboa.

van der Lely, H. K. J. (1994). Canonical linking rules: Forward vs. reverse linking in normally developing and specifically language impaired children. *Cognition, 51*, 29–72.

van der Lely, H. K. J. (1996). Specifically language impaired and normally developing children: Verbal passive vs. adjectival passive sentence interpretation. *Lingua, 98*, 243–272.

van der Lely, H. K. J. (1998). SLI in children: Movement, economy, and deficits in the computational–syntactic system. *Language Acquisition, 7*, 161–192.

van der Lely, H. K. J. (2005). Domain-specific cognitive systems: Insight from Grammatical SLI. *Trends in Cognitive Sciences, 9*, 53–57.

van der Lely, H. K. J. & Battell, J. (2003). Wh-movement in children with grammatical SLI: A test of the RDDR hypothesis. *Language, 79*, 153–181.

van der Lely, H. K. J. & Harris, M. (1990). Comprehension of reversible sentences in specifically language-impaired children. *Journal of Speech and Hearing Disorders, 55*, 101–117.

van der Lely, H. K. J. & Stollwerck, L. (1997). Binding theory and specifically language impaired children. *Cognition, 62*, 245–290.

van der Maas, H. L. & Raijmakers, M. E. J. (2009). Transitions in cognitive development: Prospects and limitations of a neural dynamic approach. In J. Spencer, M. S. C. Thomas & J. L. McClelland (eds), *Toward a new grand theory of development: Connectionism and dynamical systems theory reconsidered*. Oxford: Oxford University Press.

Van Deun, L., van Wieringen, A., Scherf, F., Deggouj, N., Desloovere, C., Offeciers, F. E., Van de Heyning, P. H., Dhooge, I. J. & Wouters, J. (2010). Earlier intervention leads to better sound localization in children with bilateral cochlear implants. *Audiology and Neurotology, 15*, 7–17.

Van Orden, G. C., Johnston, J. C. & Hale, B. L. (1988). Word identification in reading proceeds from spelling to sound to meaning. *Journal of Experimental Psychology: Learning, Memory, and Cognition, 14*, 371–386.

Vargha-Khadem, F., Carr, L. J., Isaacs, E., Brett, E., Adams, C. & Mishkin, M. (1997). Onset of speech after left hemispherectomy in a nine-year-old boy. *Brain, 120*, 159–182.

Vargha-Khadem, F., Watkins, K., Alcock, K., Fletcher, P. & Passingham, R. (1995). Praxic and nonverbal cognitive deficits in a large family with a genetically transmitted speech and language disorder. *Proceedings of the National Academy of Sciences of the USA, 92*, 930–933.

Vargha-Khadem, F., Watkins, K. E., Price, C. J., Ashburner, J., Alcock, K. J., Connelly, A., Frackowiak, R. S., Friston, K. J., Pembrey, M. E., Mishkin, M. et al. (1998). Neural basis of an inherited speech and language disorder. *Proceedings of the National Academy of Sciences of the USA, 95*, 12695–12700.

Velez, M. & Schwartz, R. (2010). Spoken word recognition in school-age children with SLI: Semantic, phonological and repetition priming. *Journal of Speech, Language, and Hearing Research*, *53*, 1616–1628.

Vellutino, F. R., Fletcher, J. M., Snowling, M. J. & Scanlong, D. M. (2004). Specific reading disability (dyslexia): What have we learned in the past four decades? *Journal of Child Psychology and Psychiatry*, *45*, 2–40.

Verhoeven, L. & Perfetti, C. A. (2003). Introduction to this special issue: The role of morphology in learning to read. *Scientific Studies of Reading*, *7*, 209–217.

Vernon, M. & Koh, S. D. (1971). Effects of oral preschool compared to early manual communication on education and communication in deaf children. *American Annals of the Deaf*, *116*, 569–574.

Vihman, M. M. (1996). *Phonological development: The origins of language in the child*. Cambridge, MA: Blackwell.

Vihman, M. M., Ferguson, C. A. & Elbert, M. (1986). Phonological development from babbling to speech: Common tendencies and individual differences. *Applied Psycholinguistics*, *7*, 3–40.

Vihman, M. M., Macken, M. A., Miller, R., Simmons, J. & Miller, J. (1985). From babbling to speech: A re-assessment of the continuity issue. *Language*, *61*, 397–445.

Voland, E., Chasiotis, A. & Schiefenhoevel, W. (eds) (2004). *Grandmotherhood: The evolutionary significance of the second half of female life*. Piscataway, NJ: Rutgers University Press.

Vouloumanos, A. & Werker, J. F. (2004). Tuned to the signal: The privileged status of speech for young infants. *Developmental Science*, *7*, 270–276.

Vouloumanos, A. & Werker, J. F. (2007). Listening to language at birth: Evidence for a bias for speech in neonates. *Developmental Science*, *10*, 159–171.

Vousden, J. I. & Maylor, E. A. (2006). Speech errors across the lifespan. *Language and Cognitive Processes*, *21*, 48–77.

Vygotsky, L. S. (1978). *Mind in society: The development of higher psychological processes*. Cambridge, MA: Harvard University Press.

Vygotsky, L. S. (1986). *Thought and language*. Cambridge, MA: MIT Press.

Vygotsky, L. S. (1987). Thinking and speech. In R. W Rieber & A. S. Carton (eds), *The collected works of L. S. Vygotsky, Vol. 1: Problems of general psychology*. New York: Plenum Press (original published 1934).

Wada, J. A., Clarke, R. & Hamm, A. (1975). Cerebral hemispheric asymmetry in humans. *Archives of Neurology*, *32*, 239–246.

Wagner, R. K., Torgesen, J. K. & Rashotte, C. A. (1994). Development of reading-related phonological processing abilities: New evidence of bi-directional causality from a latent variable longitudinal study. *Developmental Psychology*, *30*, 73–87.

Walberg, H. J. & Tsai, S. (1983). Matthew effects in education. *American Educational Research Journal*, *20*, 359–373.

Waltzman, S. B., Cohen, N. J., Gomolin, R. H., Green, J. E., Shapiro, W. H., Hoffman, R. A. & Roland, J. T. Jr. (1997). Open-set speech perception in congenitally deaf children using cochlear implants. *American Journal of Otology*, *18*, 342–349.

Wang, Q., Leichtman, M. D. & Davies, K. (2000). Sharing memories and telling stories: American and Chinese mothers and their 3-year-olds. *Memory*, *8*, 159–177.

Warren-Leubecker, A. & Bohannon, J. (1984). Intonation patterns in child-directed speech: Mother–father differences. *Child Development*, *55*, 1541–1548.

Wartenburger, I., Heekeren, H. R., Abutalebi, J., Cappa, S. F., Villringer, A. & Perani, D. (2003). Early setting of grammatical processing in the bilingual brain. *Neuron*, *37*, 159–170.

Wassenberg, R., Feron, F. J., Kessels, A. G., Hendriksen, J. G. M., Kalff, A. C., Kroes, M., Hurks, P. P. M., Beeren, M., Jolles, J. & Vles, J. S. H. (2006). Relation between cognitive and motor performance in 5- to 6-year-old children: Results from a large-scale cross-sectional study. *Child Development, 76*, 1092–1103.

Wassmann, J. & Dasen, P. R. (1998). Balinese spatial orientation: Some empirical evidence of moderate linguistic relativity. *Journal of the Royal Anthropological Institute, 4*, 689–711.

Watkins, R. V., Kelly, D. J., Harbers, H. M. & Hollis, W. (1995). Measuring children's lexical diversity: Differentiating typical and impaired language learners. *Journal of Speech and Hearing Research, 38*, 1349–1355.

Watson, J. S. (1972). Smiling, cooing, and 'the game'. *Merrill-Palmer Quarterly, 18*, 323–339.

Waxman, S. R. & Braun, I. (2005). Consistent (but not variable) names as invitations to form object categories: New evidence from 12-month-old infants. *Cognition, 95*, B59–B68.

Waxman, S. R. & Markow, D. B. (1995). Words as invitations to form categories: Evidence from 12- to 13-month-old infants. *Cognitive Psychology, 29*, 257–302.

Weigel, D. J., Martin, S. S. & Bennett, K. K. (2006). Contributions of the home literacy environment to preschool-age children's emerging literacy and language skills. *Early Child Development and Care, 176*(3/4), 357–378.

Weikum, W.M., Vouloumanos, A., Navarro, J., Soto-Faraco, S., Sebastián-Gallés, N. & Werker, J. F. (2007). Visual language discrimination in infancy. *Science, 316*, 1159.

Weismer, S. E. (2007). Typical talkers, late talkers, and children with specific language impairment: A language endowment spectrum? In R. Paul (ed.), *Language disorders from a developmental perspective: Essays in honor of Robin S. Chapman* (pp. 83–101). Mahwah, NJ: Lawrence Erlbaum Associates.

Weismer, S. E. & Evans, J. L. (2002). The role of processing limitations in early identification of specific language impairment. *Topics in Language Disorders, 22*, 15–29.

Weismer, S. E., Evans, J. L. & Hesketh, L. J. (1999). An evaluation of verbal working memory capacity in children with specific language impairment. *Journal of Speech, Language, and Hearing Research, 42*, 1249–1260.

Weizman, Z. O. & Snow, C. E. (2001). Lexical input as related to children's vocabulary acquisition: Effects of sophisticated exposure and support for meaning. *Developmental Psychology, 37*, 265–279.

Wellman, H. M. & Cross, D. (2001). Meta-analysis of theory-of-mind development: The truth about false belief. *Child Development, 72*, 655–684.

Weppelman, T. L., Bostow, A., Schiffer, R., Elbert-Perez, E. & Newman, R. S. (2003). Children's use of the prosodic characteristics of infant-directed speech. *Language and Communication, 23*, 63–80.

Werker, J. F. & Byers-Heinlein, K. (2008). Bilingualism in infancy: First steps in perception and comprehension. *Trends in Cognitive Sciences, 12*, 144–151.

Werker, J. F., Cohen, L. B., Lloyd, V. L., Casasola, M. & Stager, C. L. (1998). Acquisition of word-object associations by 14-month-old infants. *Developmental Psychology, 34*, 1289–1309.

Werker, J. F. & Pegg, J. E. (1992). Infant speech perception and phonological acquisition. In C. A. Ferguson, L. Menn & C. Stoel-Gammon (eds), *Phonological development: models, research, and implications* (pp. 285–311). Timonium, MD: York Press.

Werker, J. F. & Tees, R. C. (1984). Cross-language speech perception: Evidence for perceptual reorganization during the first year of life. *Infant Behavior and Development, 7*, 49–63.

Werner, H. & Kaplan, B. (1963). *Symbol formation*. New York: John Wiley & Sons.

West, R. F., Stanovich, K. E. & Mitchell, H. R. (1993). Reading in the real world and its correlates. *Reading Research Quarterly, 28*, 34–50.

Wetherell, D., Botting, N. & Conti-Ramsden, G. (2007). Narrative in adolescent specific language impairment (SLI): A comparison with peers across two different narrative genres. *International Journal of Language and Communication Disorders, 42*, 583–605.

White, L. & Genesee, F. (1996). How native is near-native? The issue of ultimate attainment in adult second language acquisition. *Second Language Research, 12*, 238–265.

White, S. H. & Pillemer, D. B. (1979). Childhood amnesia and the development of a socially accessible memory system. In J. F. Kihlstrom & F. J. Evans (eds), *Functional disorders of memory* (pp. 29–74). Hillsdale, NJ: Lawrence Erlbaum Associates.

Whorf, B. (1956). *Language, thought and reality.* Cambridge, MA: MIT Press.

Wilbourn, M. P. & Casasola, M. (2007). Discriminating signs: Perceptual precursors to acquiring a visual–gestural language. *Infant Behavior and Development, 30*, 153–160.

Williams, J. N. & Lovatt, P. (2005). Phonological memory and rule learning. *Language Learning, 55*(Suppl. 1), 177–233.

Wilson, B. S., Finley, C. C., Lawson, D. T., Wolford, R. D., Eddington, D. K. & Rabinowitz, W. M. (1991). Better speech recognition with cochlear implants. *Nature, 352*, 236–238.

Wilson, D. & Sperber, D. (2004). Relevance theory. In L. Horn & G. Ward (eds), *Handbook of pragmatics* (pp. 607–632). Oxford: Blackwell.

Wimmer, H. & Perner, J. (1983). Beliefs about beliefs: Representation and constraining function of wrong beliefs in young children's understanding of deception. *Cognition, 13*, 103–128.

Windfuhr, K., Faragher, B. & Conti-Ramsden, G. (2002). Lexical learning skills in young children with specific language impairment (SLI). *International Journal of Language and Communication Disorders, 37*, 415–432.

Witelson, S. F. (1977). Anatomic asymmetry in the temporal lobes: Its documentation, phylogenesis, and relationship to functional asymmetry. *Annals of the New York Academy of Sciences, 299*, 328–354.

Witelson, S. F. & Pallie, W. (1973). Left hemisphere specialization for language in the newborn. Neuroanatomic evidence of asymmetry. *Brain, 96*, 641–643.

Wittgenstein, L. (1953). *Philosophical investigations.* Oxford, UK: Blackwell.

Woodward, A. L., Markman, E. M. & Fitzsimmons, C. M. (1994). Rapid word learning in 13- and 18-month-olds. *Developmental Psychology, 30*, 553–566.

Woolfe, T., Want, S. C. & Siegal, M. (2002). Signposts to development: Theory of mind in deaf children. *Child Development, 73*, 3–21.

Wrangham, R. W., Cheney, D., Seyfarth, R. & Sarmiento, E. (2010). Shallow-water habitats as sources of fallback foods for hominins. *American Journal of Physical Anthropology, 140*, 630–642.

Wrangham, R. W., Jones, J. H., Laden, G., Pilbeam, D. & Conklin-Brittain, N. (1999). The raw and the stolen. *Current Anthropology, 40*, 567–594.

Wynn, K. (1992). Children's acquisition of the number words and the counting system. *Cognitive Psychology, 24*, 220–251.

Xu, F. (2002). The role of language in acquiring object kind concepts in infancy. *Cognition, 85*, 223–250.

Yeni-Komshian, G. H., Flege, J. E. & Liu, S. (2000). Pronunciation proficiency in the first and second languages of Korean–English bilinguals. *Bilingualism: Language and Cognition, 3*, 131–141.

Zeifman, D., Delaney, S. & Blass, E. M. (1996). Sweet taste, looking, and calm in 2- and 4-week-old infants: The eyes have it. *Developmental Psychology, 32*, 1090–1099.

Zelazo, P. D., Frye, D. & Rapus, T. (1996). An age-related dissociation between knowing rules and using them. *Cognitive Development, 11*, 37–63.

Zentella, A. C. (1997). *Growing up bilingual: Puerto Rican children in New York.* Malden, MA: Blackwell.

Ziegler, J. C., Bertrand, D., Tóth, D., Csépe, V., Reis, A., Faísca, L., Saine, N., Lyytinen, H., Vaessen, A. & Blomert, L. (2010a). Orthographic depth and its impact on universal predictors of reading: A cross-language investigation. *Psychological Science, 21*, 551–559.

Ziegler, J. C. & Goswami, U. (2005). Reading acquisition, developmental dyslexia, and skilled reading across languages: A psycholinguistic grain size theory. *Psychological Bulletin, 131*, 3–29.

Ziegler, J. C., Pech-Georgel, C., Dufau, S. & Grainger, J. (2010b). Rapid processing of letters, digits, and symbols: What purely visual–attentional deficit in developmental dyslexia? *Developmental Science, 13*, F8–F14.

Zukow-Goldring, R. (1997). A social ecological realist approach to the emergence of the lexicon: Educating attention to amodal invariants in gesture and speech. In C. Dent-Read & P. Zukow-Goldring (eds), *Evolving explanations of development: Ecological approaches to organism–environment systems* (pp. 199–252). Washington, DC: American Psychological Association.

# Name Index

# Subject Index

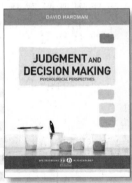

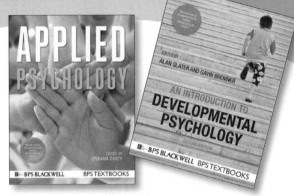

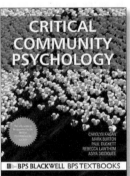

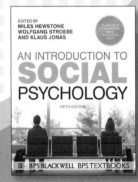

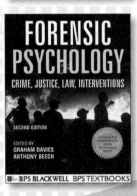